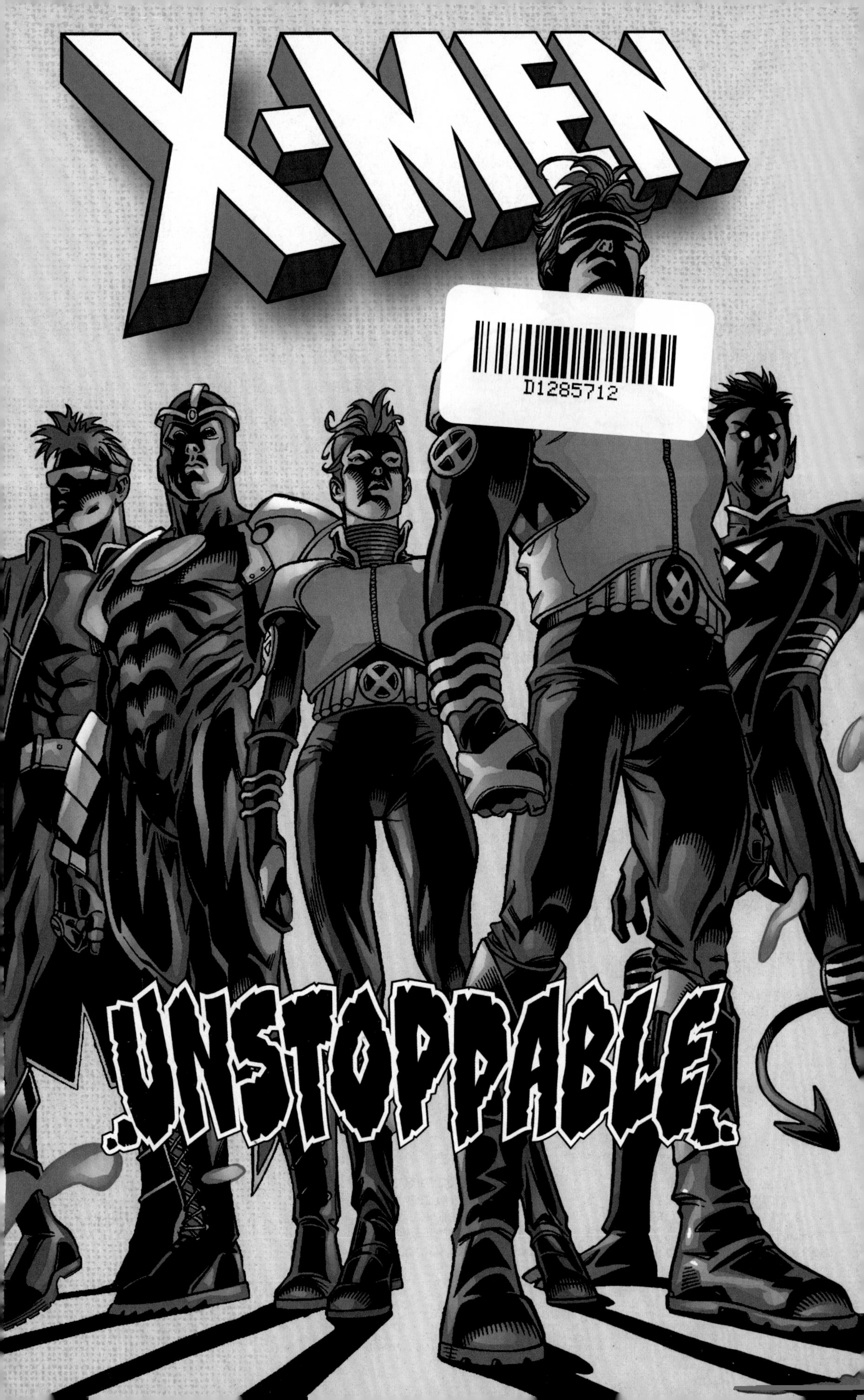
X-MEN
.UNSTOPPABLE.

X-MEN UNSTOPPABLE

WRITER
CHUCK AUSTEN

UNCANNY X-MEN #410-412

PENCILER **RON GARNEY**
INKER **MARK MORALES**
COLORIST **HI-FI DESIGN**
LETTERER **RICHARD STARKINGS & COMICRAFT's SAIDA TEMOFONTE**

UNCANNY X-MEN #413-415

ARTIST **SEAN PHILLIPS**
COLORIST **HI-FI DESIGN**
LETTERERS **RICHARD STARKINGS & COMICRAFT'S JIMMY BETANCOURT** (#413) **& SAIDA TEMOFONTE** (#414-415)

X-MEN UNLIMITED #44

PENCILER **ROMANO MOLENAAR**
INKER **DANNY MIKI**
COLORIST **DEAN WHITE**
LETTERER **RANDY GENTILE**

UNCANNY X-MEN #416-420

ARTIST **KIA ASAMIYA**
COLORIST **J.D. SMITH**
LETTERER **PAUL TUTRONE**

SPECIAL THANKS TO C.B. CEBULSKI & AKI YANAGI

X-MEN UNLIMITED #45

PENCILER **POP MHAN**
INKER **DEREK FRIDOLFS**
COLORIST **SOTOCOLOR'S J. BROWN**
LETTERER **RANDY GENTILE**

UNCANNY X-MEN #421-424

PENCILER **RON GARNEY**
INKERS **MARK MORALES** WITH **NELSON & DAN GREEN** (#423-424)
COLORIST **J.D. SMITH**
LETTERER **CHRIS ELIOPOULOS**

ASSISTANT EDITORS **MIKE RAICHT, NOVA REN SUMA & STEPHANIE MOORE**
CONSULTING EDITOR **RALPH MACCHIO**
ASSOCIATE EDITORS **C.B. CEBULSKI & MIKE RAICHT**
EDITORS **MIKE MARTS, BRIAN SMITH & C.B. CEBULSKI**

X-MEN CREATED BY **STAN LEE & JACK KIRBY**

COVER ART **RON GARNEY** (UNCANNY X-MEN #410-411)
STEVE UY (UNCANNY X-MEN #412-415 & #419)
KIA ASAMIYA & STUDIO TRON (UNCANNY X-MEN #416-418 & #420)
MIZUKI SAKAKIBARA (X-MEN UNLIMITED #44)
PHIL NOTO (X-MEN UNLIMITED #45)
CHRIS BACHALO (UNCANNY X-MEN #421)
PHILIP TAN & BRIAN HABERLIN (UNCANNY X-MEN #422-424)

COLLECTION EDITOR **MARK D. BEAZLEY**
ASSISTANT EDITOR **CAITLIN O'CONNELL**
ASSOCIATE MANAGING EDITOR **KATERI WOODY**
ASSOCIATE MANAGER, DIGITAL ASSETS **JOE HOCHSTEIN**
SENIOR EDITOR, SPECIAL PROJECTS **JENNIFER GRÜNWALD**

VP PRODUCTION & SPECIAL PROJECTS **JEFF YOUNGQUIST**
RESEARCH & LAYOUT **JEPH YORK**
BOOK DESIGNER **JAY BOWEN**
PRODUCTION **DEB WEINSTEIN**
SVP PRINT, SALES & MARKETING **DAVID GABRIEL**

EDITOR IN CHIEF **C.B. CEBULSKI**
CHIEF CREATIVE OFFICER **JOE QUESADA**
PRESIDENT **DAN BUCKLEY**
EXECUTIVE PRODUCER **ALAN FINE**

X-MEN: UNSTOPPABLE. Contains material originally published in magazine form as UNCANNY X-MEN #410-424 and X-MEN UNLIMITED #44-45. First printing 2018. ISBN 978-1-302-91612-1. Published by MARVEL WORLDWIDE, INC., a subsidiary of MARVEL ENTERTAINMENT, LLC. OFFICE OF PUBLICATION: 135 West 50th Street, New York, NY 10020. Copyright © 2018 MARVEL No similarity between any of the names, characters, persons, and/or institutions in this magazine with those of any living or dead person or institution is intended, and any such similarity which may exist is purely coincidental. **Printed in Canada.** DAN BUCKLEY, President, Marvel Entertainment; JOHN NEE, Publisher; JOE QUESADA, Chief Creative Officer; TOM BREVOORT, SVP of Publishing; DAVID BOGART, SVP of Business Affairs & Operations, Publishing & Partnership; DAVID GABRIEL, SVP of Sales & Marketing, Publishing; JEFF YOUNGQUIST, VP of Production & Special Projects; DAN CARR, Executive Director of Publishing Technology; ALEX MORALES, Director of Publishing Operations; DAN EDINGTON, Managing Editor; SUSAN CRESPI, Production Manager; STAN LEE, Chairman Emeritus. For information regarding advertising in Marvel Comics or on Marvel.com, please contact Vit DeBellis, Custom Solutions & Integrated Advertising Manager, at vdebellis@marvel.com. For Marvel subscription inquiries, please call 888-511-5480. **Manufactured between 12/6/2018 and 1/7/2019 by SOLISCO PRINTERS, SCOTT, QC, CANADA.**

10 9 8 7 6 5 4 3 2 1

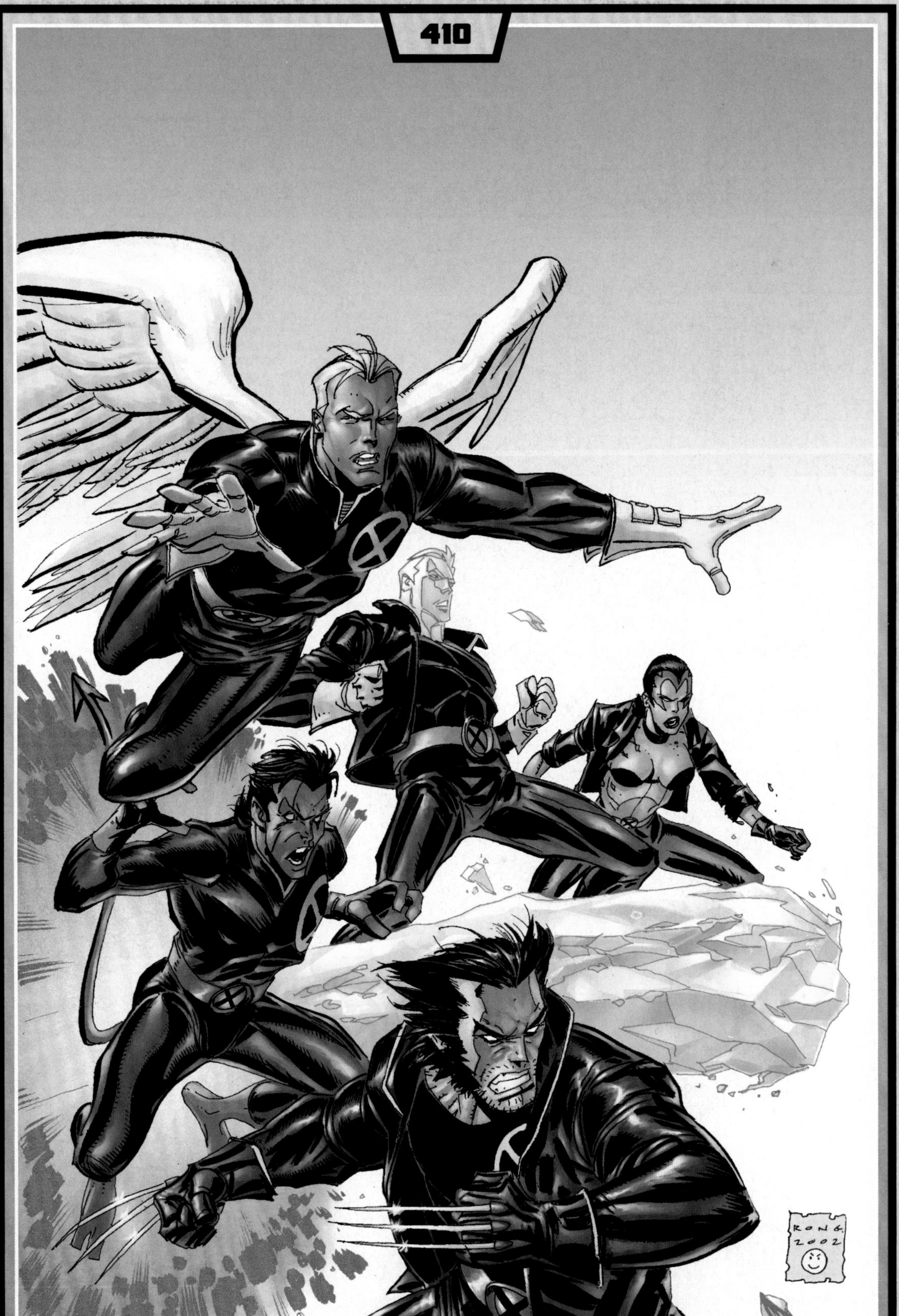
410
RONG
2002

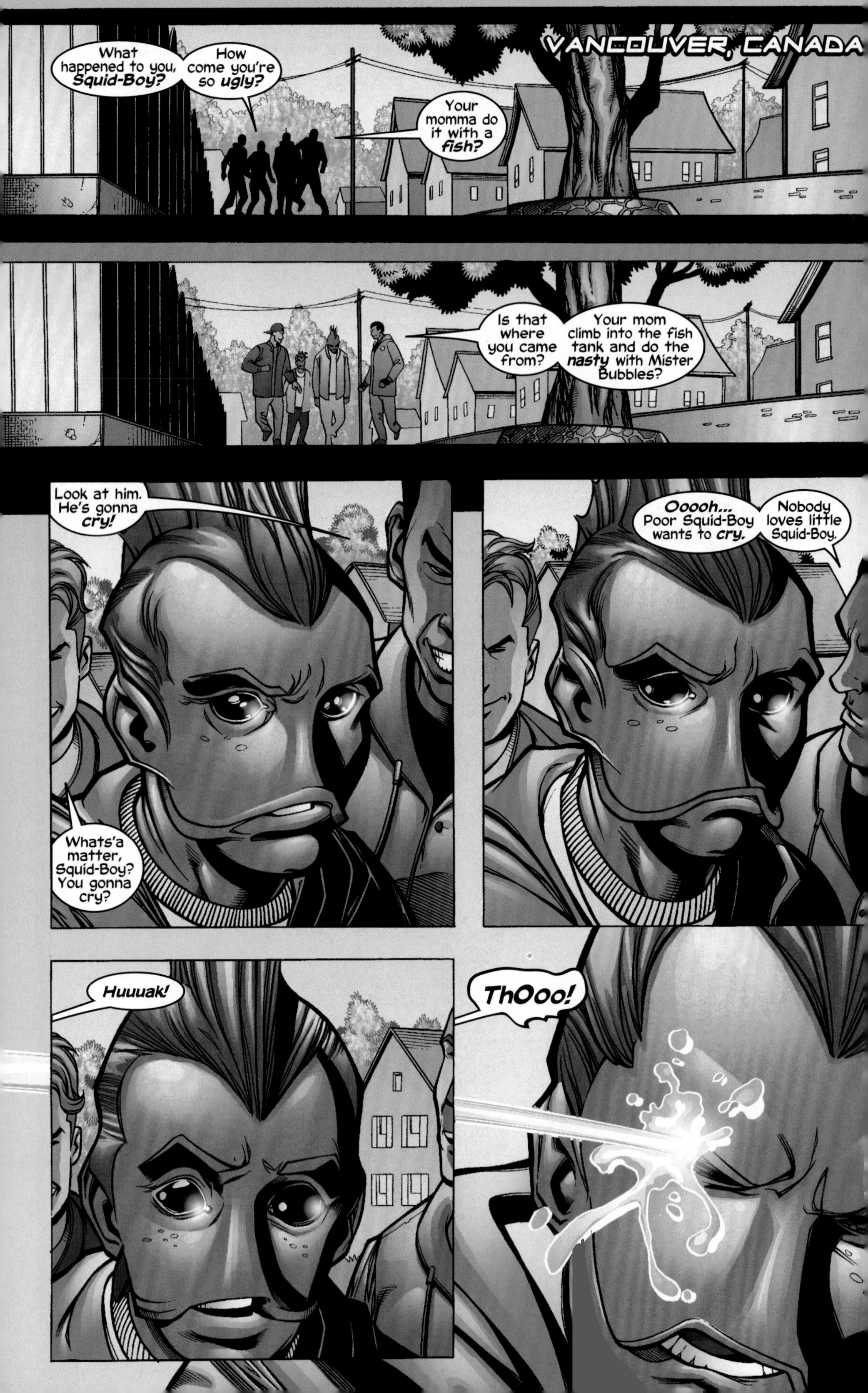
VANCOUVER, CANADA
What happened to you, Squid-Boy?
How come you're so ugly?
Your momma do it with a fish?
Is that where you came from?
Your mom climb into the fish tank and do the nasty with Mister Bubbles?
Look at him. He's gonna cry!
Whats'a matter, Squid-Boy? You gonna cry?
Ooooh... Poor Squid-Boy wants to cry.
Nobody loves little Squid-Boy.
Huuuak!
ThOoo!

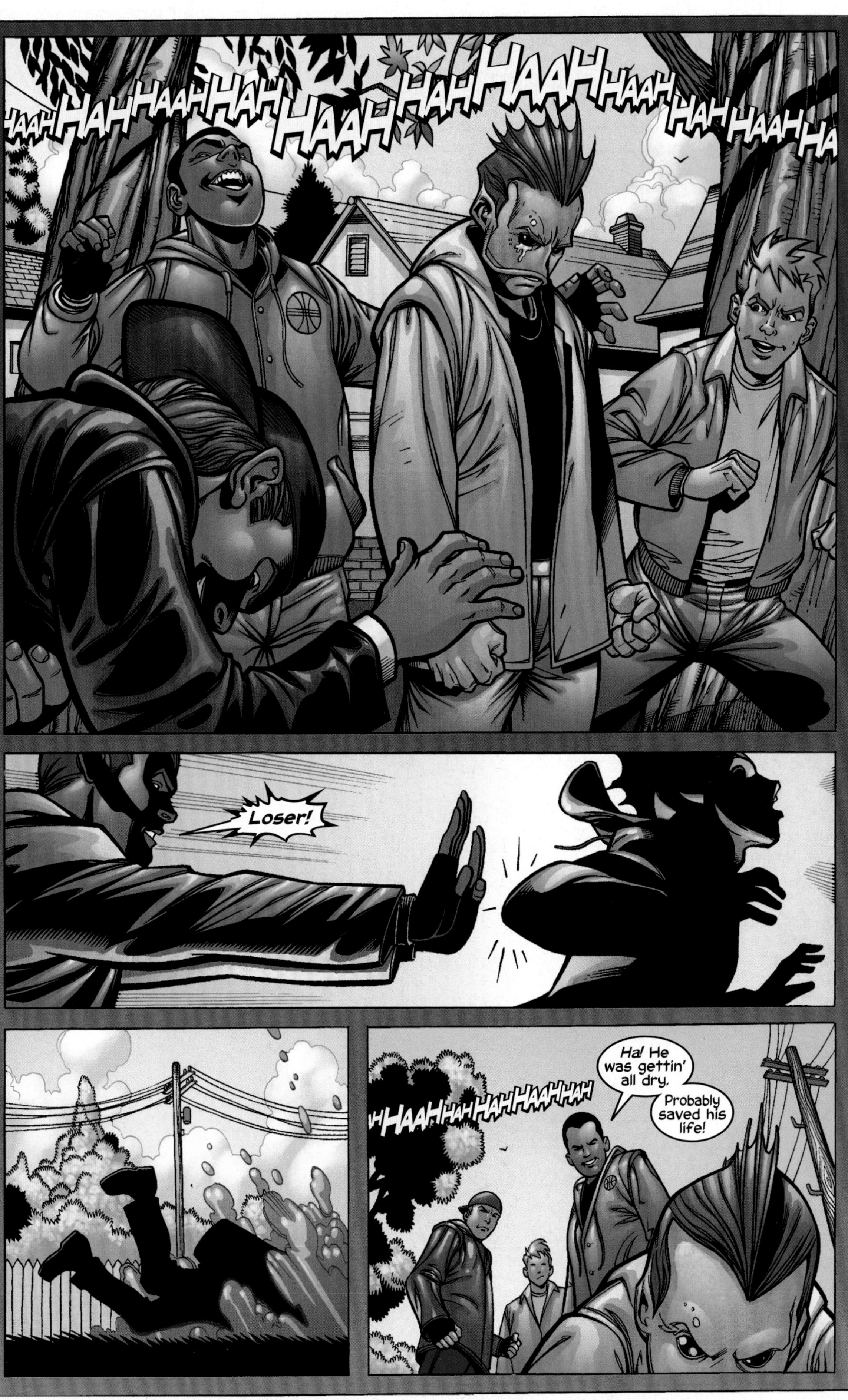

HAAH HAH HAAH HAH HAAH HAH HAAH HAAH HAH HAAH HA
Loser!
HAAH HAH HAH HAAH HAH
Ha! He was gettin' all dry.
Probably saved his life!

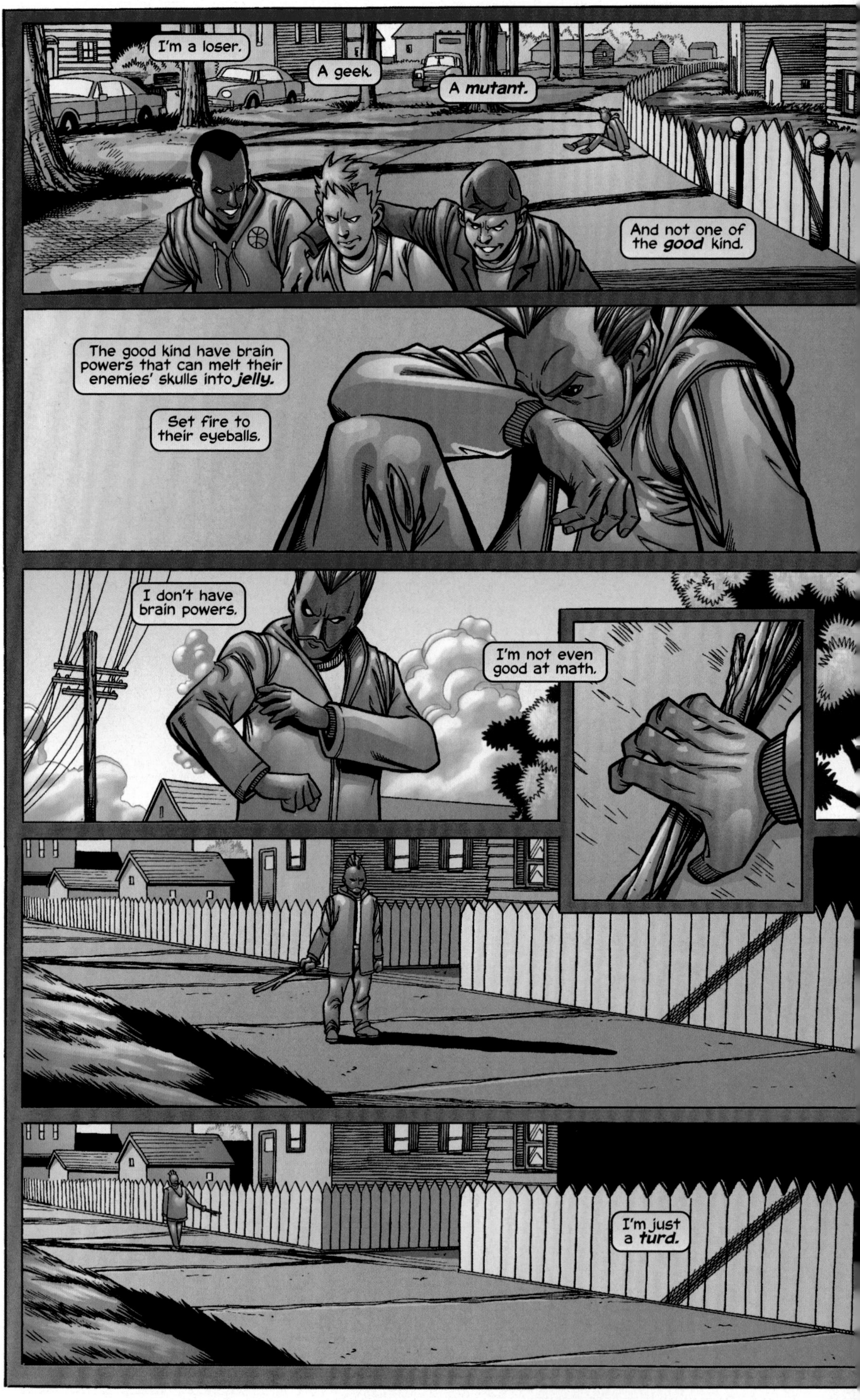
I'm a loser.
A geek.
A *mutant.*
And not one of the *good* kind.
The good kind have brain powers that can melt their enemies' skulls into *jelly.*
Set fire to their eyeballs.
I don't have brain powers.
I'm not even good at math.
I'm just a *turd.*

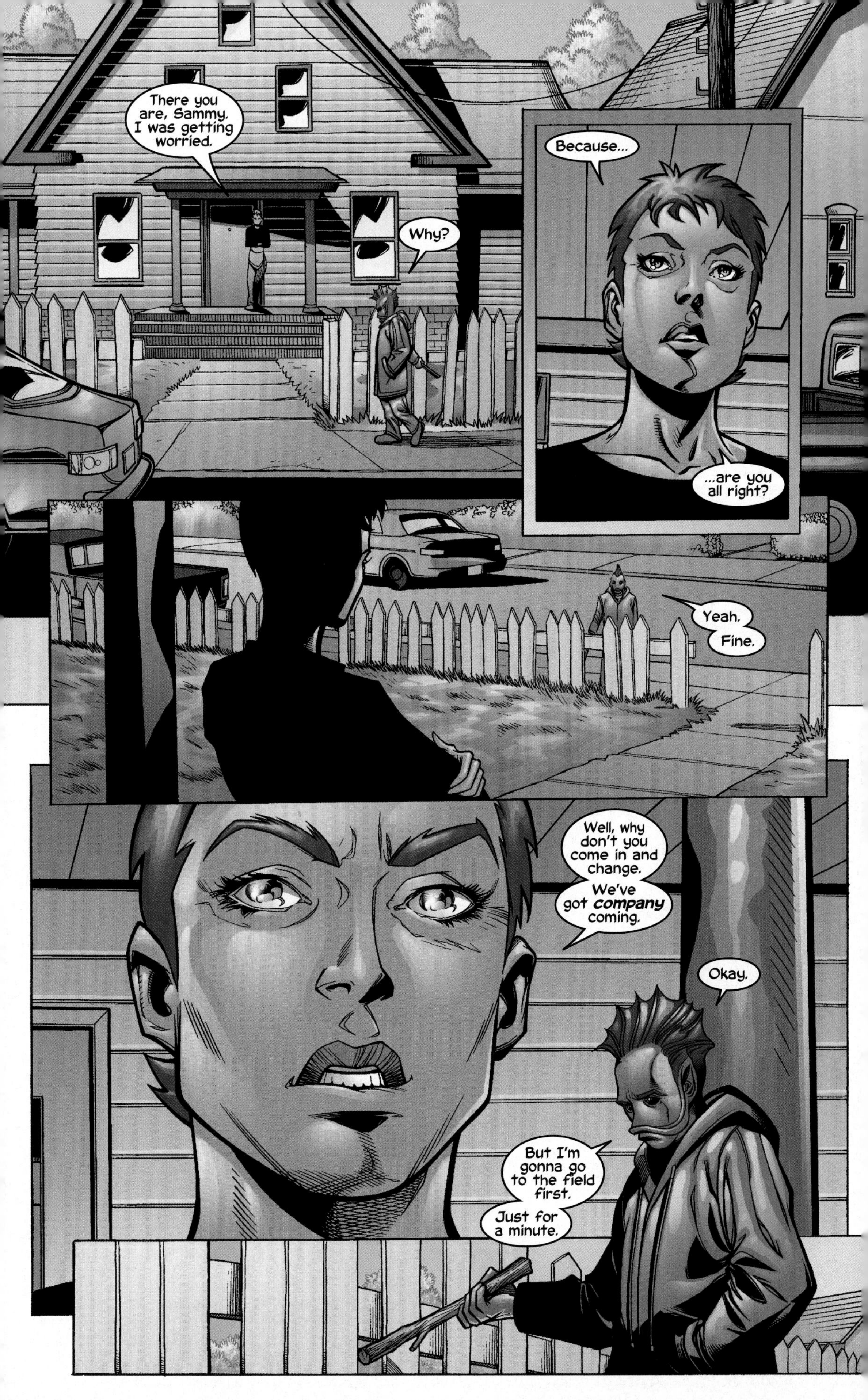
There you are, Sammy. I was getting worried.
Why?
Because...
...are you all right?
Yeah.
Fine.
Well, why don't you come in and change.
We've got *company* coming.
Okay.
But I'm gonna go to the field first.
Just for a minute.

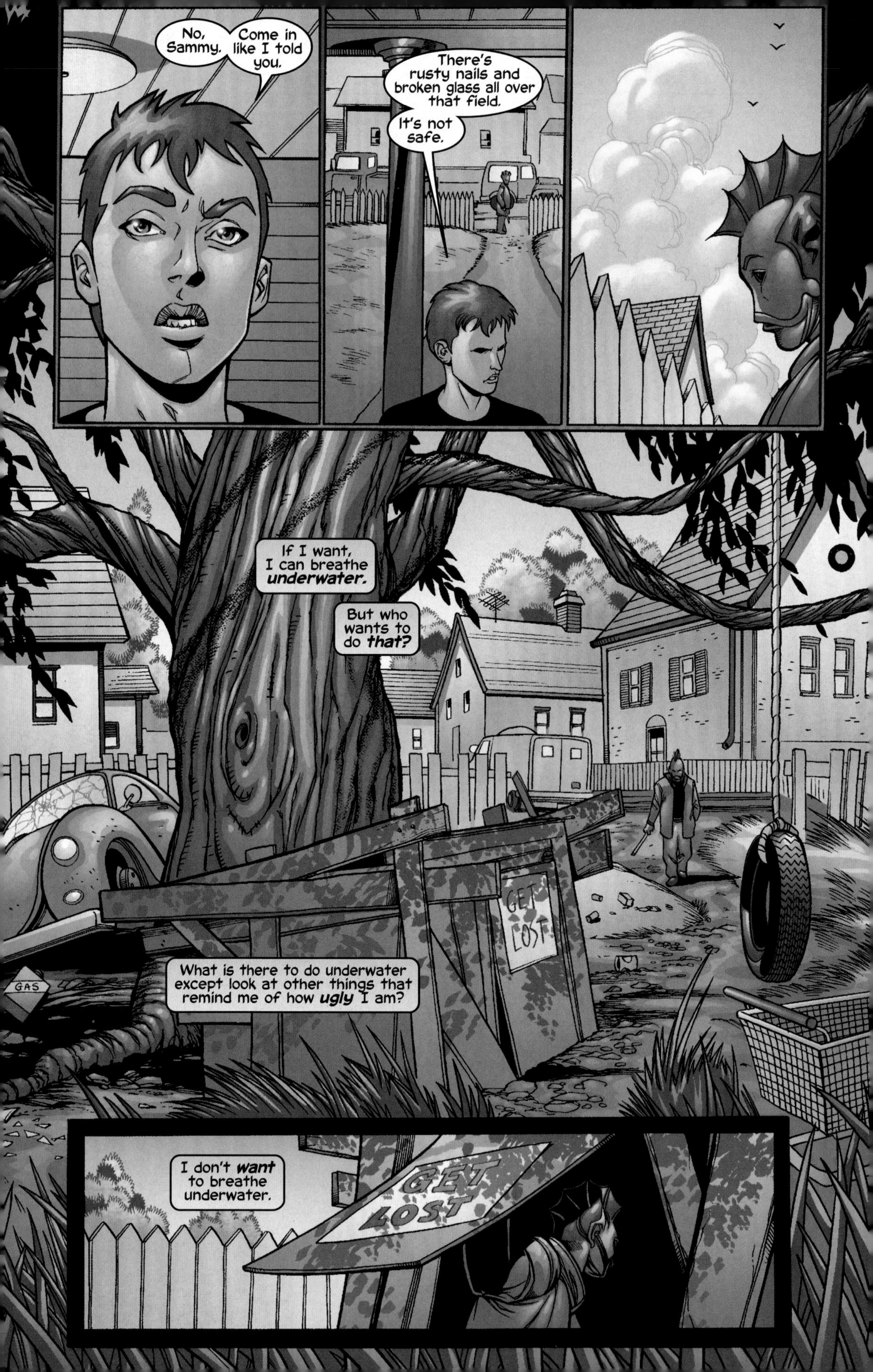
No, Sammy.
Come in like I told you.
There's rusty nails and broken glass all over that field.
It's not safe.
If I want, I can breathe *underwater.*
But who wants to do *that?*
GAS
GET LOST
What is there to do underwater except look at other things that remind me of how *ugly* I am?
I don't *want* to breathe underwater.
GET LOST

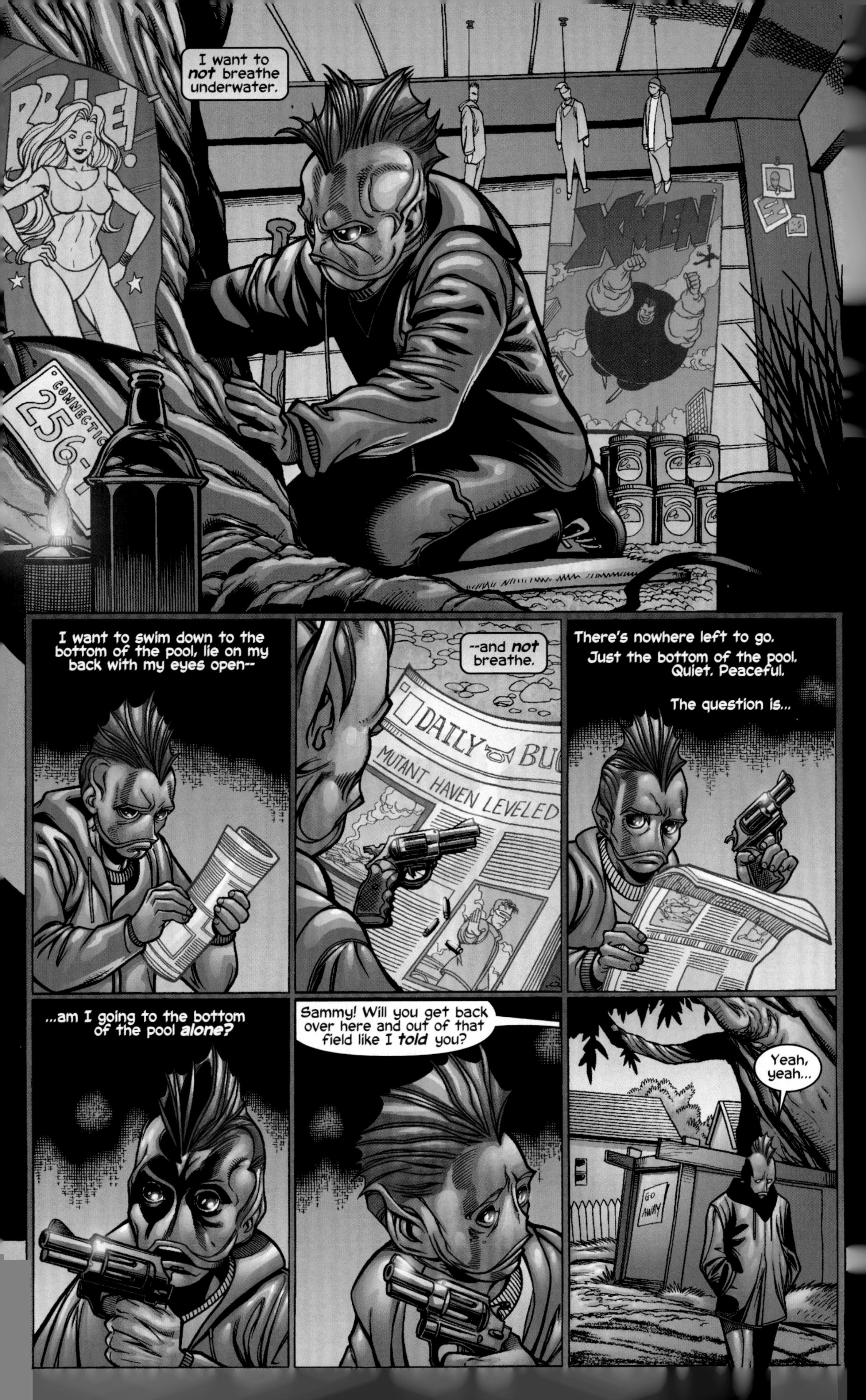
I want to *not* breathe underwater.
X-MEN
I want to swim down to the bottom of the pool, lie on my back with my eyes open--
--and *not* breathe.
DAILY BU
MUTANT HAVEN LEVELED
There's nowhere left to go.
Just the bottom of the pool. Quiet. Peaceful.
The question is...
...am I going to the bottom of the pool *alone?*
Sammy! Will you get back over here and out of that field like I *told* you?
Yeah, yeah...
GO AWAY

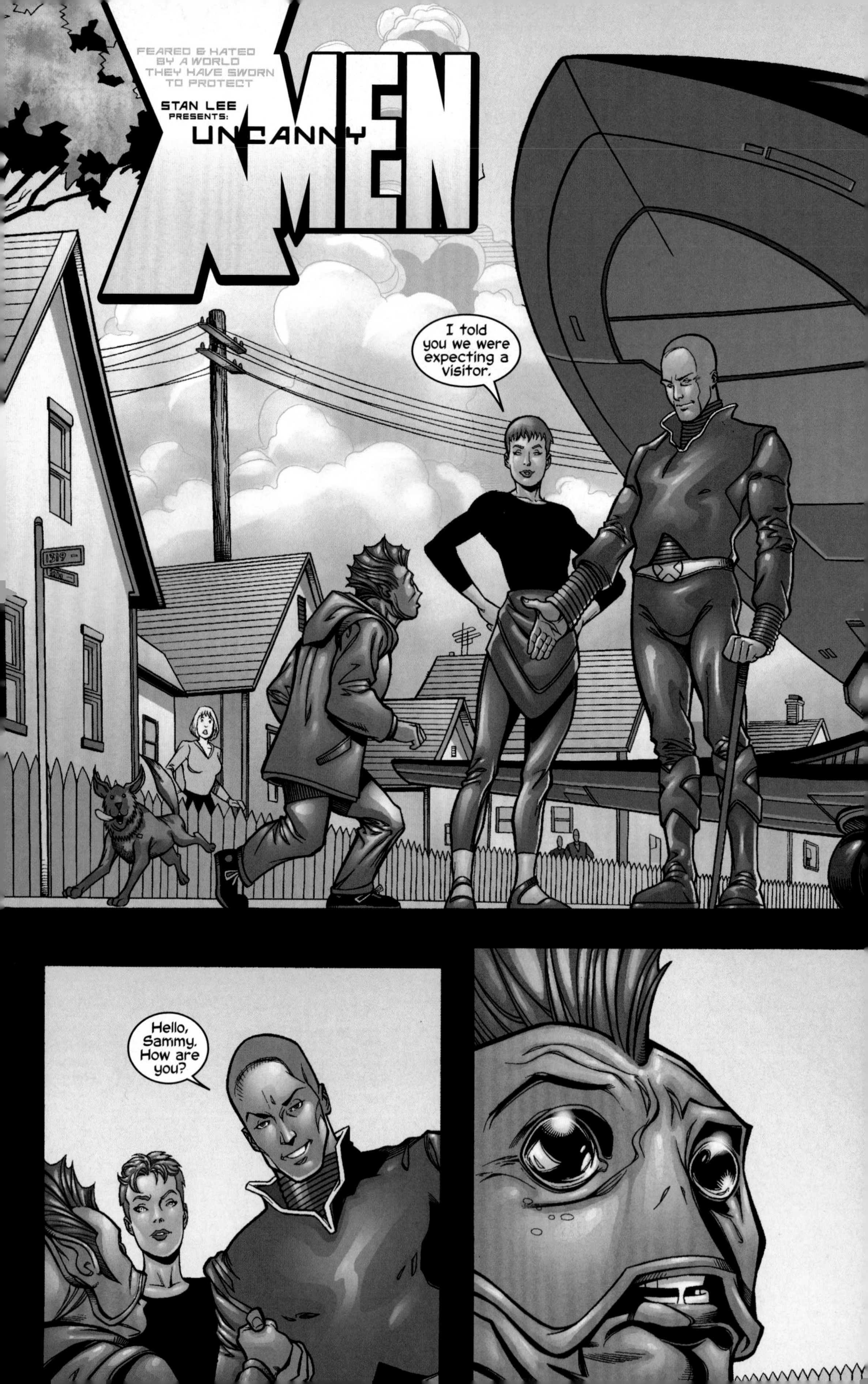
FEARED & HATED BY A WORLD THEY HAVE SWORN TO PROTECT
STAN LEE PRESENTS:
UNCANNY X-MEN
I told you we were expecting a visitor.
Hello, Sammy. How are you?

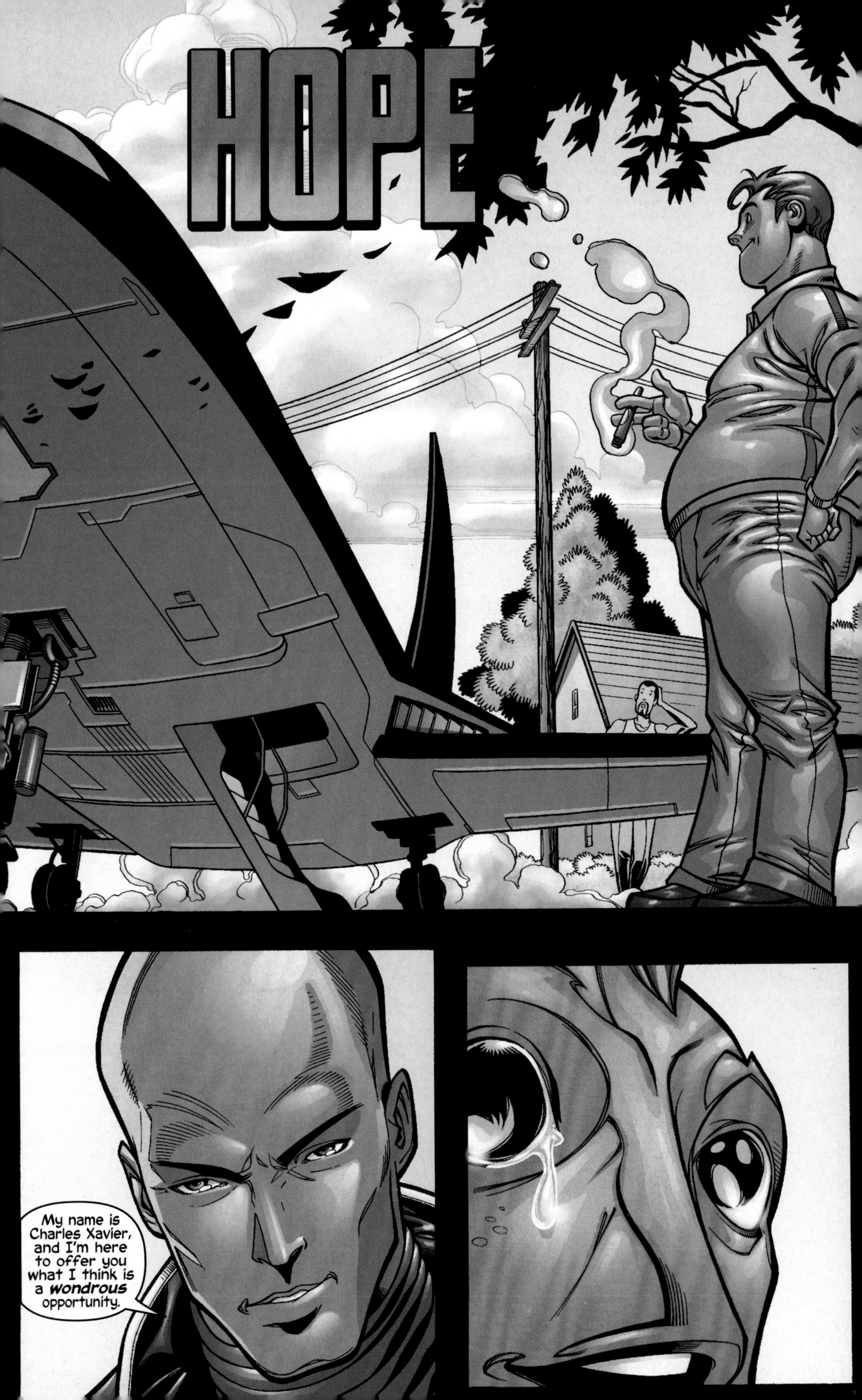
HOPE
My name is Charles Xavier, and I'm here to offer you what I think is a ***wondrous*** opportunity.

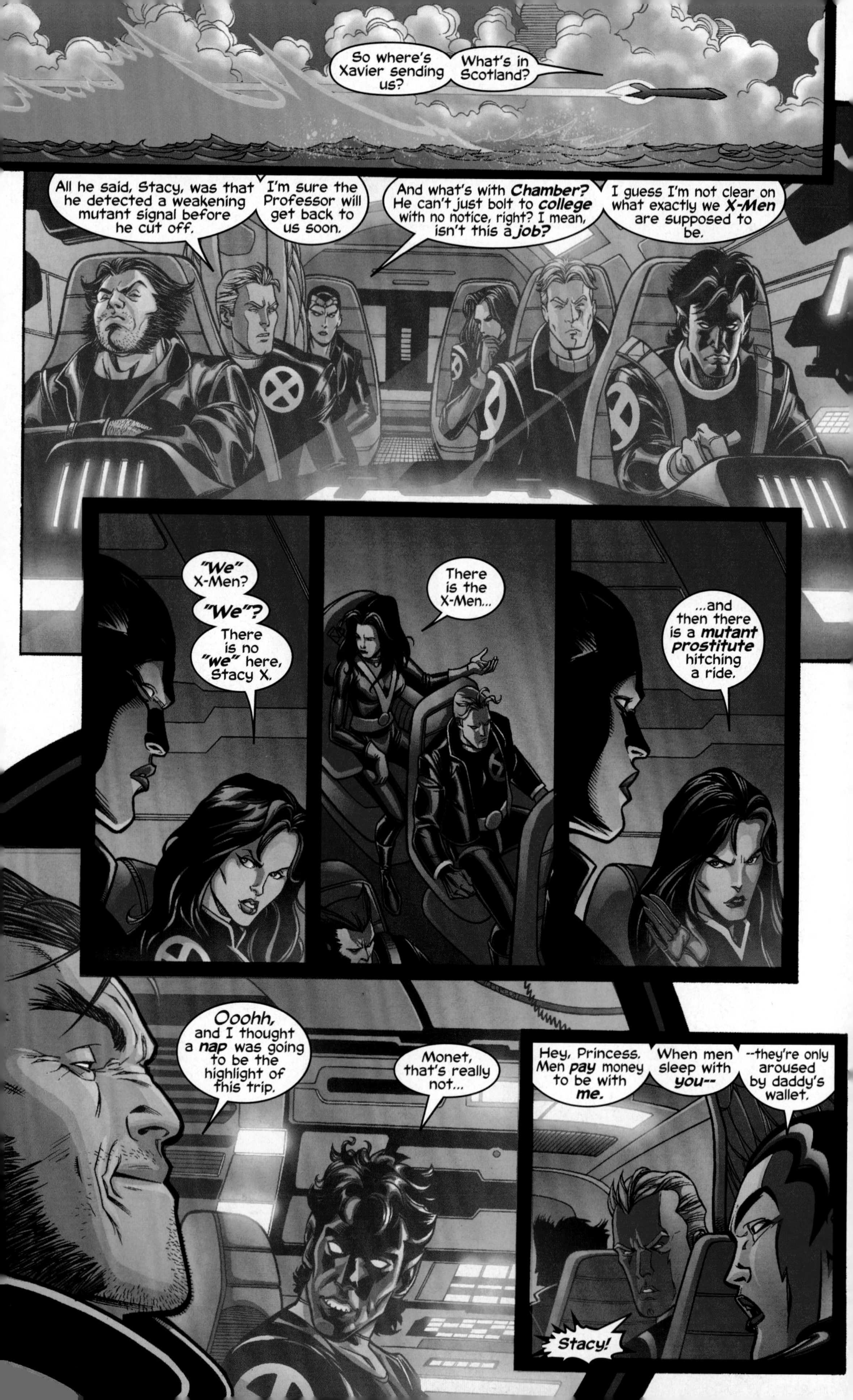
So where's Xavier sending us?
What's in Scotland?
All he said, Stacy, was that he detected a weakening mutant signal before he cut off.
I'm sure the Professor will get back to us soon.
And what's with Chamber? He can't just bolt to college with no notice, right? I mean, isn't this a job?
I guess I'm not clear on what exactly we X-Men are supposed to be.
"We" X-Men?
"We"?
There is no "we" here, Stacy X.
There is the X-Men...
...and then there is a mutant prostitute hitching a ride.
Ooohh, and I thought a nap was going to be the highlight of this trip.
Monet, that's really not...
Hey, Princess. Men pay money to be with me.
When men sleep with you--
--they're only aroused by daddy's wallet.
Stacy!

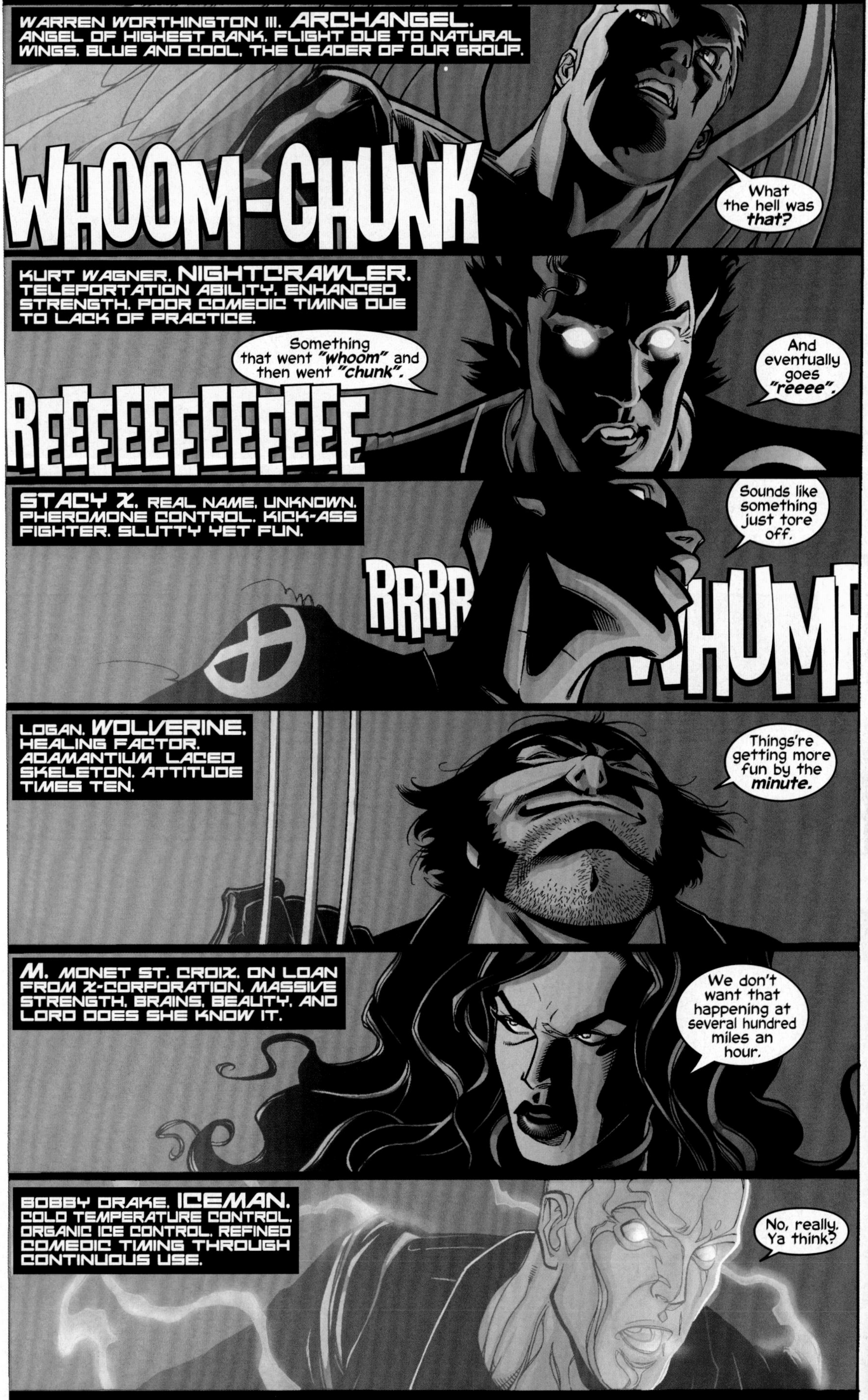
WARREN WORTHINGTON III. ARCHANGEL. ANGEL OF HIGHEST RANK. FLIGHT DUE TO NATURAL WINGS. BLUE AND COOL. THE LEADER OF OUR GROUP.
WHOOM-CHUNK
What the hell was that?
KURT WAGNER. NIGHTCRAWLER. TELEPORTATION ABILITY. ENHANCED STRENGTH. POOR COMEDIC TIMING DUE TO LACK OF PRACTICE.
Something that went "whoom" and then went "chunk".
REEEEEEEEEEEE
And eventually goes "reeee".
STACY X. REAL NAME, UNKNOWN. PHEROMONE CONTROL. KICK-ASS FIGHTER. SLUTTY YET FUN.
Sounds like something just tore off.
RRRR
WHUMP
LOGAN. WOLVERINE. HEALING FACTOR. ADAMANTIUM LACED SKELETON. ATTITUDE TIMES TEN.
Things're getting more fun by the minute.
M. MONET ST. CROIX. ON LOAN FROM X-CORPORATION. MASSIVE STRENGTH, BRAINS, BEAUTY, AND LORD DOES SHE KNOW IT.
We don't want that happening at several hundred miles an hour.
BOBBY DRAKE. ICEMAN. COLD TEMPERATURE CONTROL. ORGANIC ICE CONTROL. REFINED COMEDIC TIMING THROUGH CONTINUOUS USE.
No, really. Ya think?

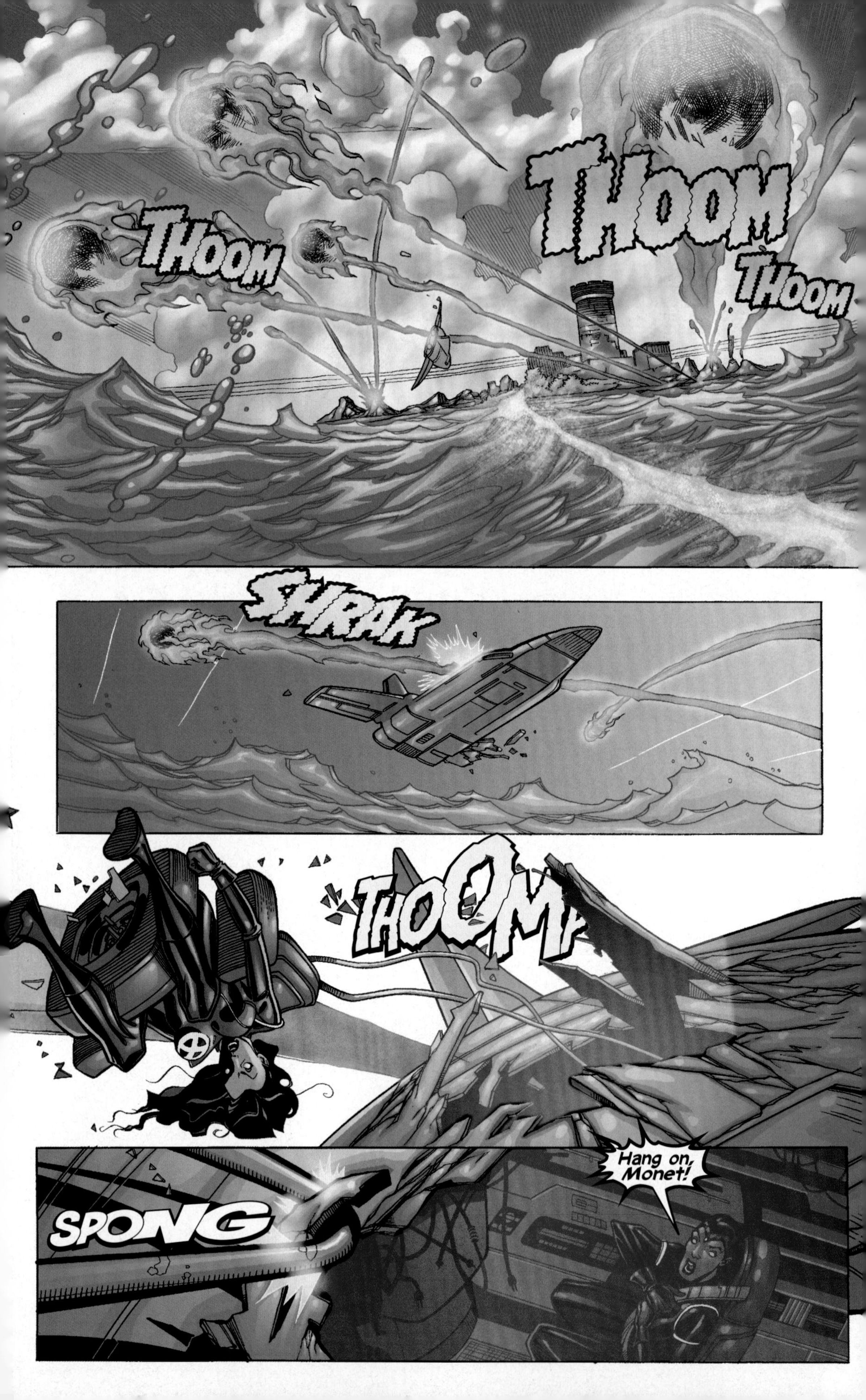
THOOM
THOOM
THOOM
SHRAK
THOOM
SPONG
Hang on, Monet!

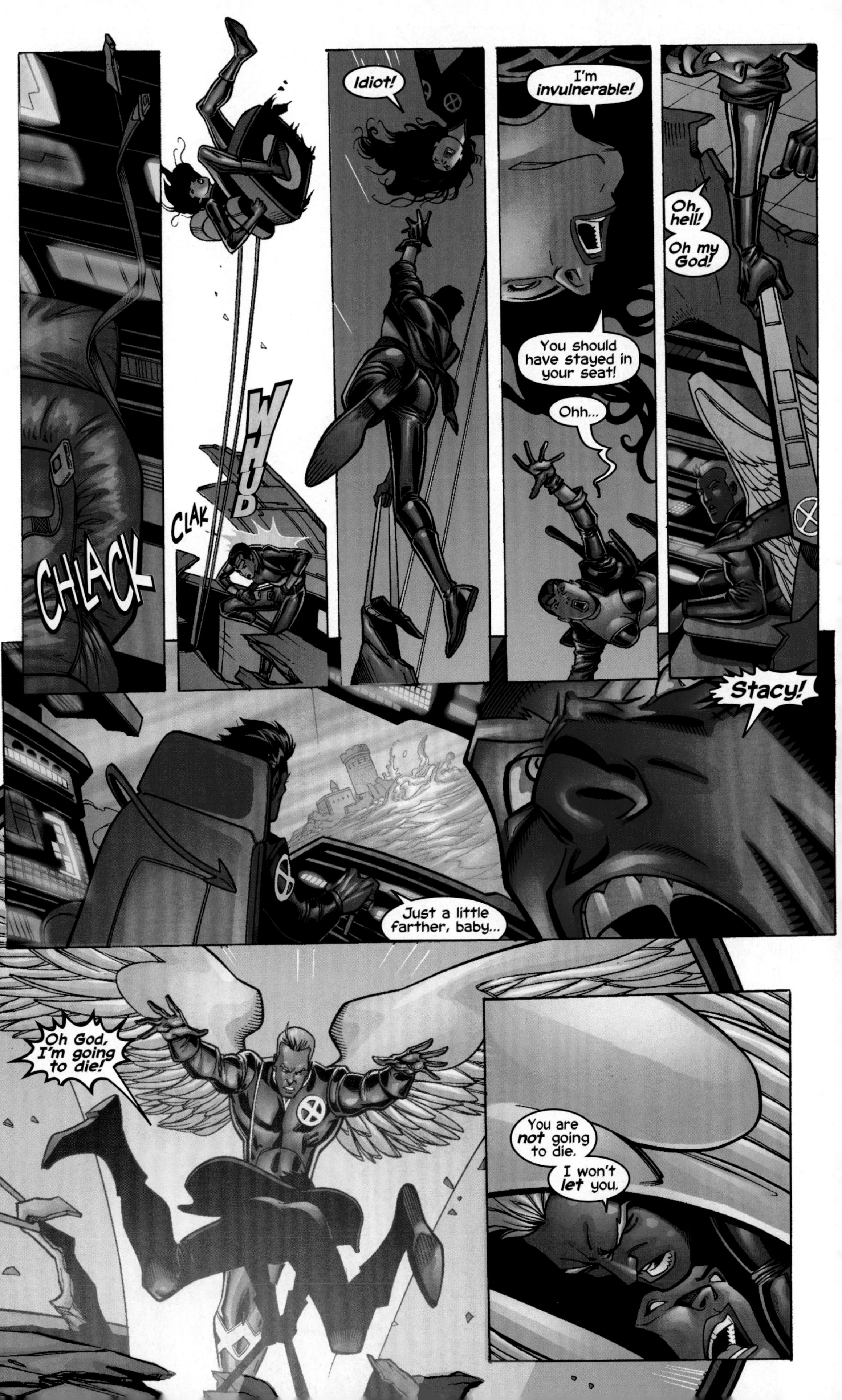

CHLACK
CLAK
WHUD
Idiot!
I'm invulnerable!
You should have stayed in your seat!
Ohh...
Oh, hell!
Oh my God!
Stacy!
Just a little farther, baby...
Oh God, I'm going to die!
You are not going to die.
I won't let you.

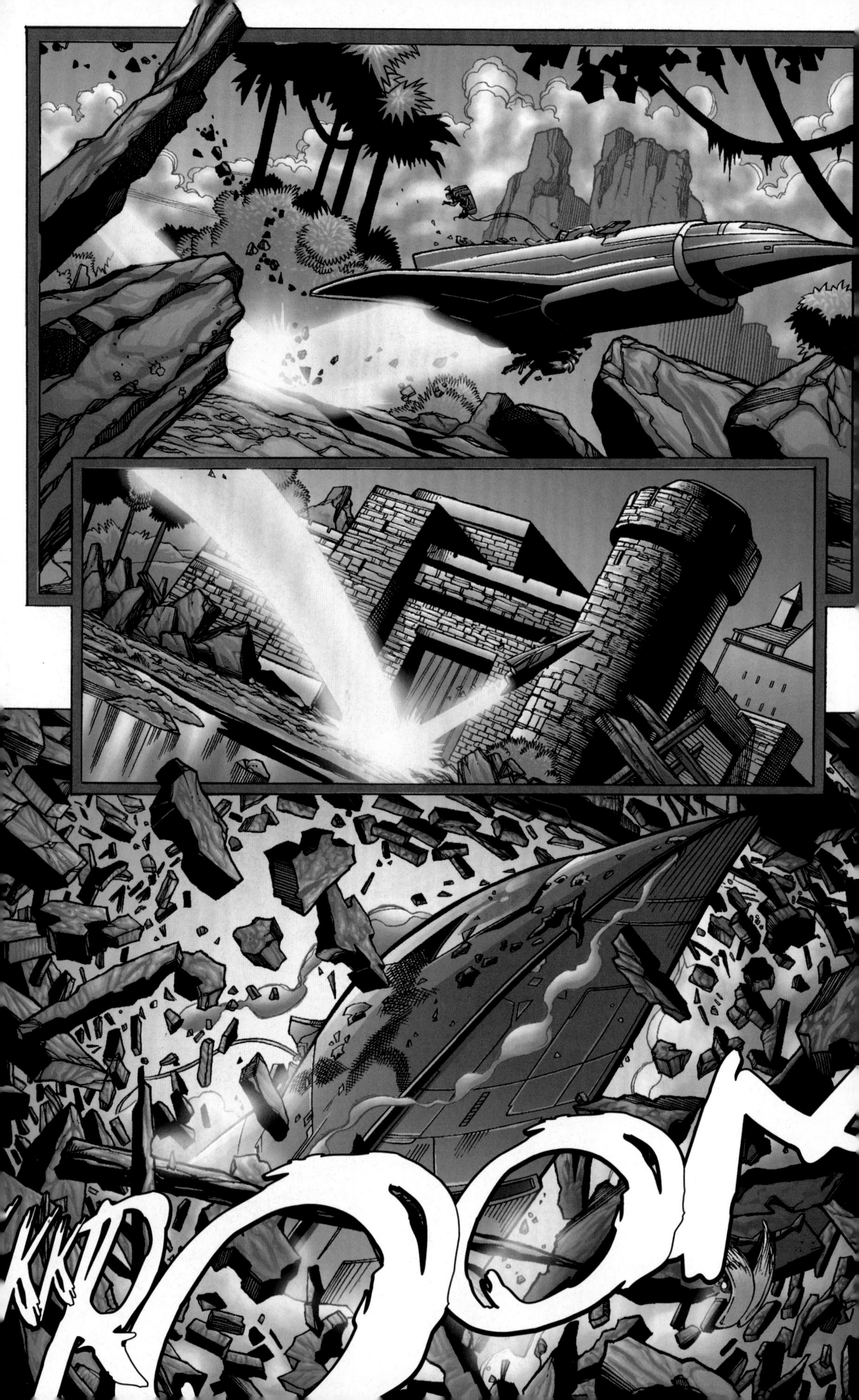
KKTD
KROOOM

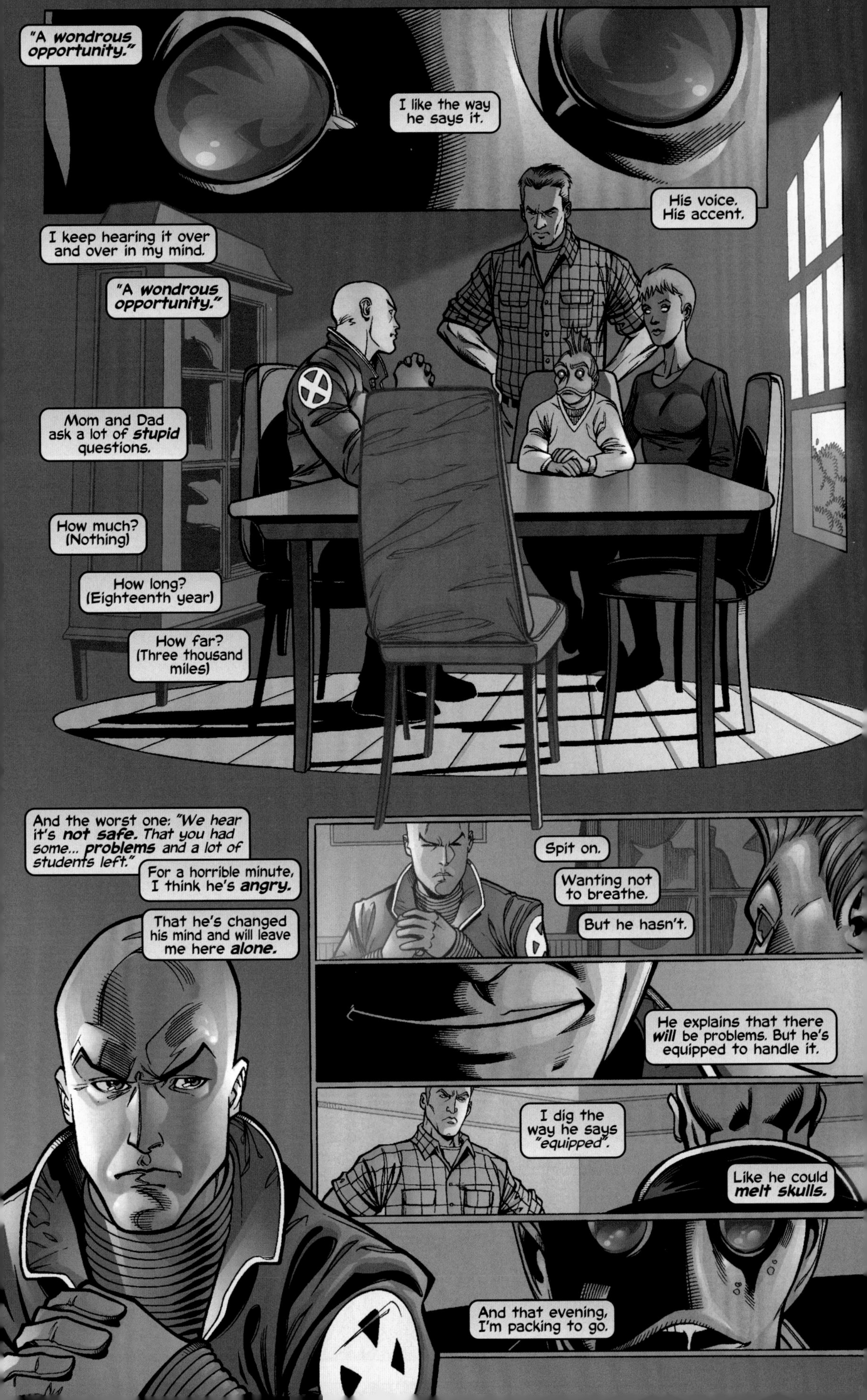
"A wondrous opportunity."
I like the way he says it.
His voice. His accent.
I keep hearing it over and over in my mind.
"A wondrous opportunity."
Mom and Dad ask a lot of stupid questions.
How much? (Nothing)
How long? (Eighteenth year)
How far? (Three thousand miles)
And the worst one: "We hear it's not safe. That you had some... problems and a lot of students left."
For a horrible minute, I think he's angry.
That he's changed his mind and will leave me here alone.
Spit on.
Wanting not to breathe.
But he hasn't.
He explains that there will be problems. But he's equipped to handle it.
I dig the way he says "equipped".
Like he could melt skulls.
And that evening, I'm packing to go.

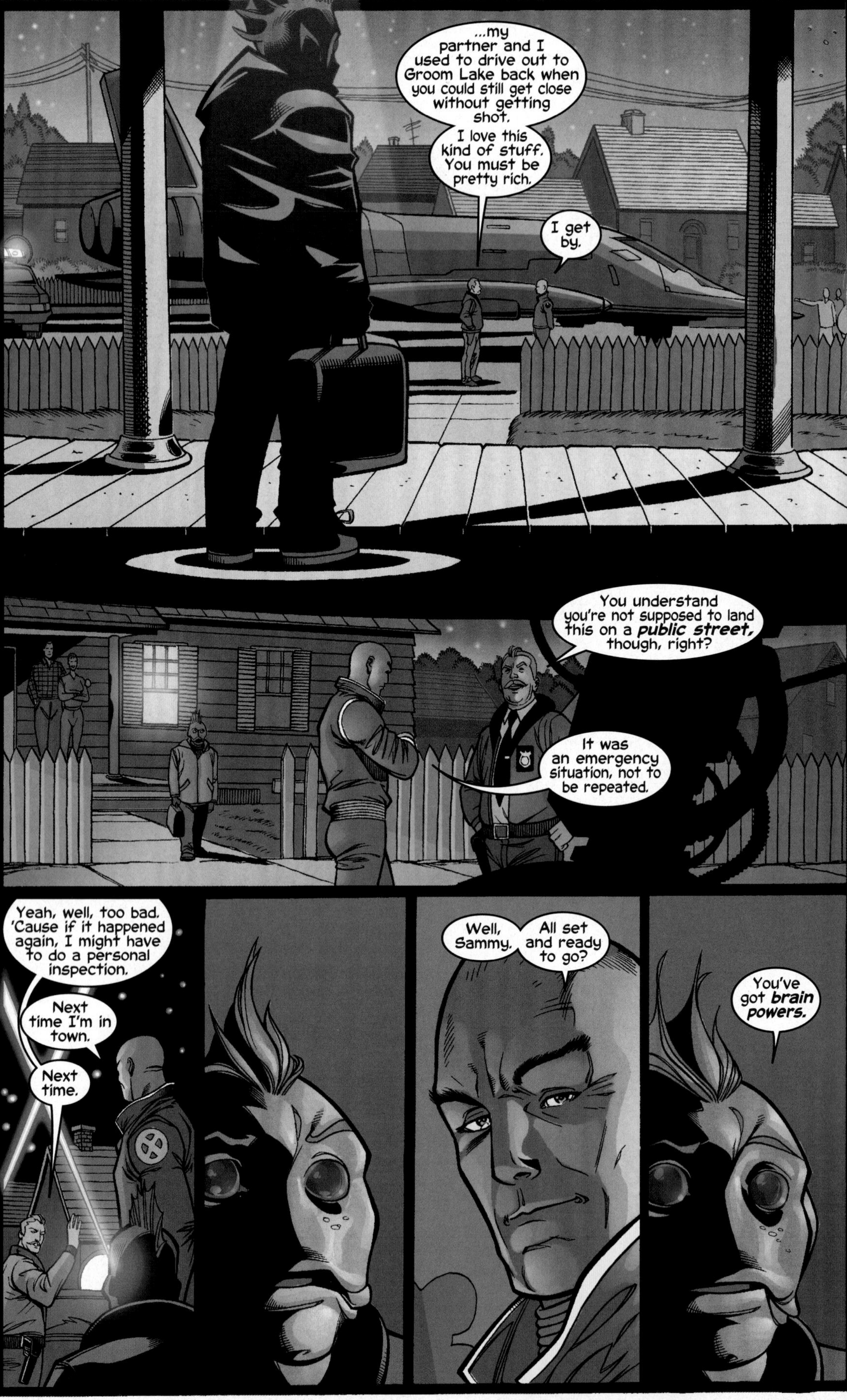
...my partner and I used to drive out to Groom Lake back when you could still get close without getting shot.
I love this kind of stuff. You must be pretty rich.
I get by.
You understand you're not supposed to land this on a *public street,* though, right?
It was an emergency situation, not to be repeated.
Yeah, well, too bad. 'Cause if it happened again, I might have to do a personal inspection.
Next time I'm in town.
Next time.
Well, Sammy.
All set and ready to go?
You've got *brain powers.*

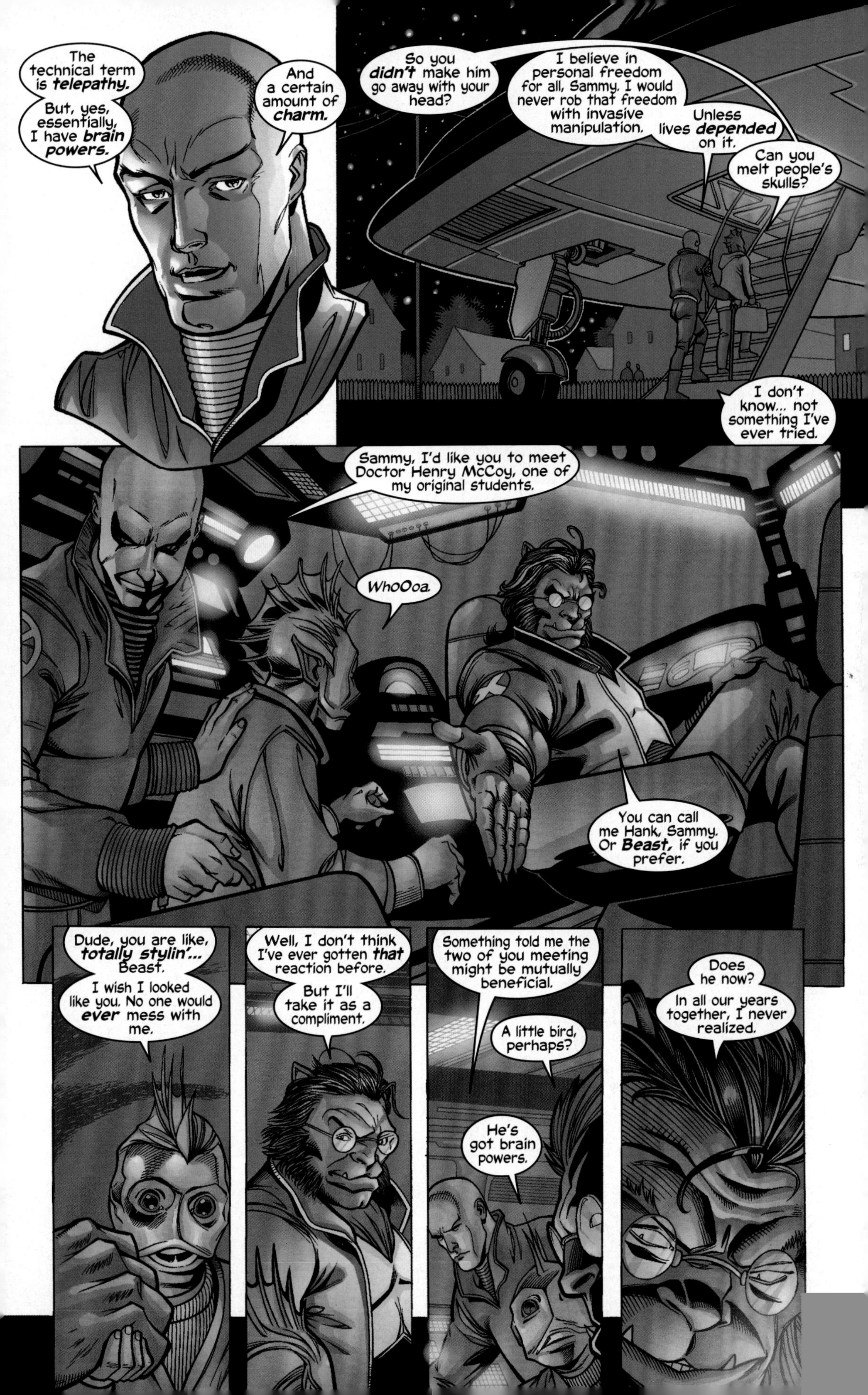

The technical term is telepathy.
But, yes, essentially, I have brain powers.
And a certain amount of charm.
So you didn't make him go away with your head?
I believe in personal freedom for all, Sammy. I would never rob that freedom with invasive manipulation.
Unless lives depended on it.
Can you melt people's skulls?
I don't know... not something I've ever tried.
Sammy, I'd like you to meet Doctor Henry McCoy, one of my original students.
WhoOoa.
You can call me Hank, Sammy. Or Beast, if you prefer.
Dude, you are like, totally stylin'... Beast.
I wish I looked like you. No one would ever mess with me.
Well, I don't think I've ever gotten that reaction before.
But I'll take it as a compliment.
Something told me the two of you meeting might be mutually beneficial.
A little bird, perhaps?
He's got brain powers.
Does he now?
In all our years together, I never realized.

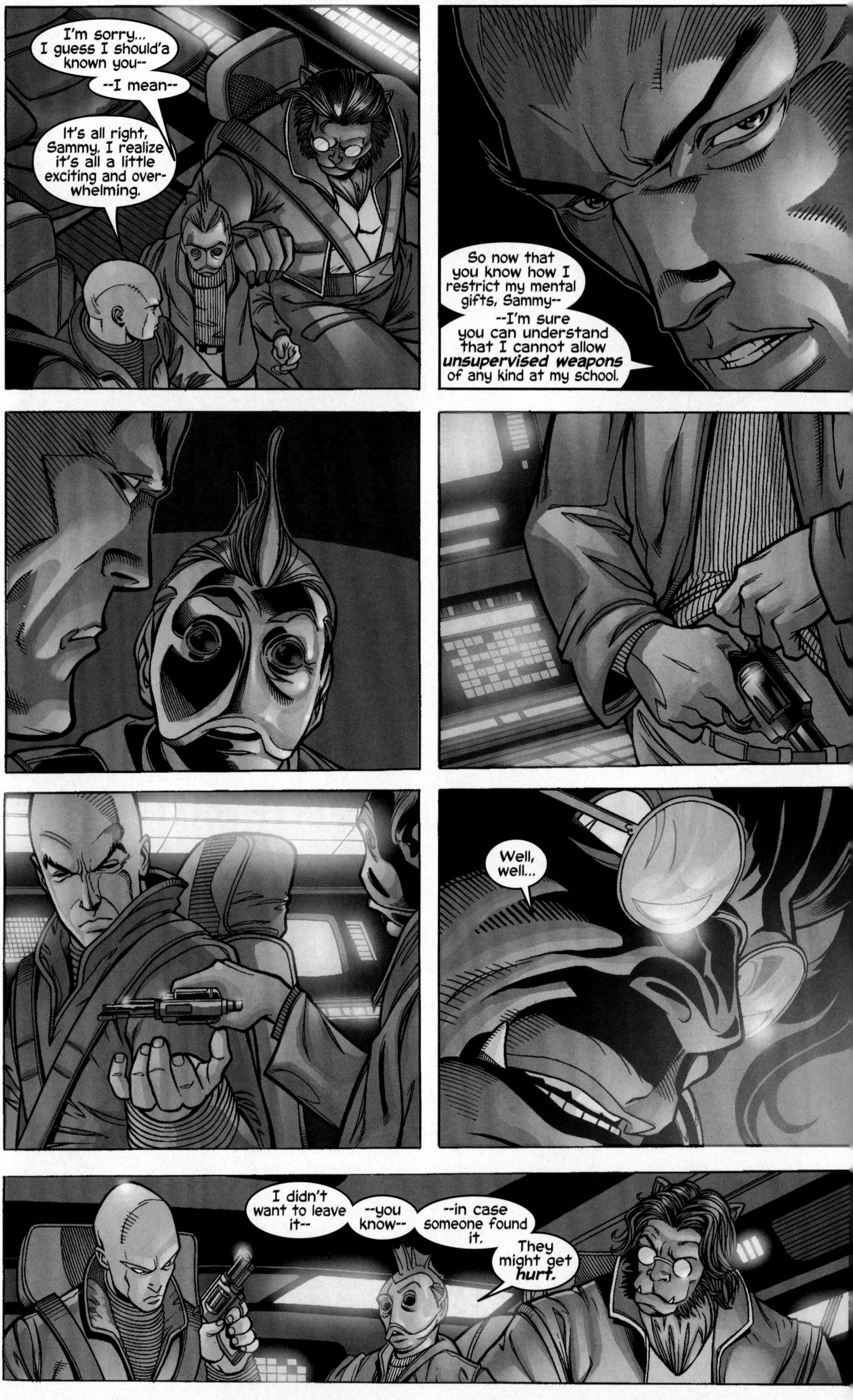
I'm sorry... I guess I should'a known you--
--I mean--
It's all right, Sammy. I realize it's all a little exciting and overwhelming.
So now that you know how I restrict my mental gifts, Sammy--
--I'm sure you can understand that I cannot allow unsupervised weapons of any kind at my school.
Well, well...
I didn't want to leave it--
--you know--
--in case someone found it.
They might get hurt.

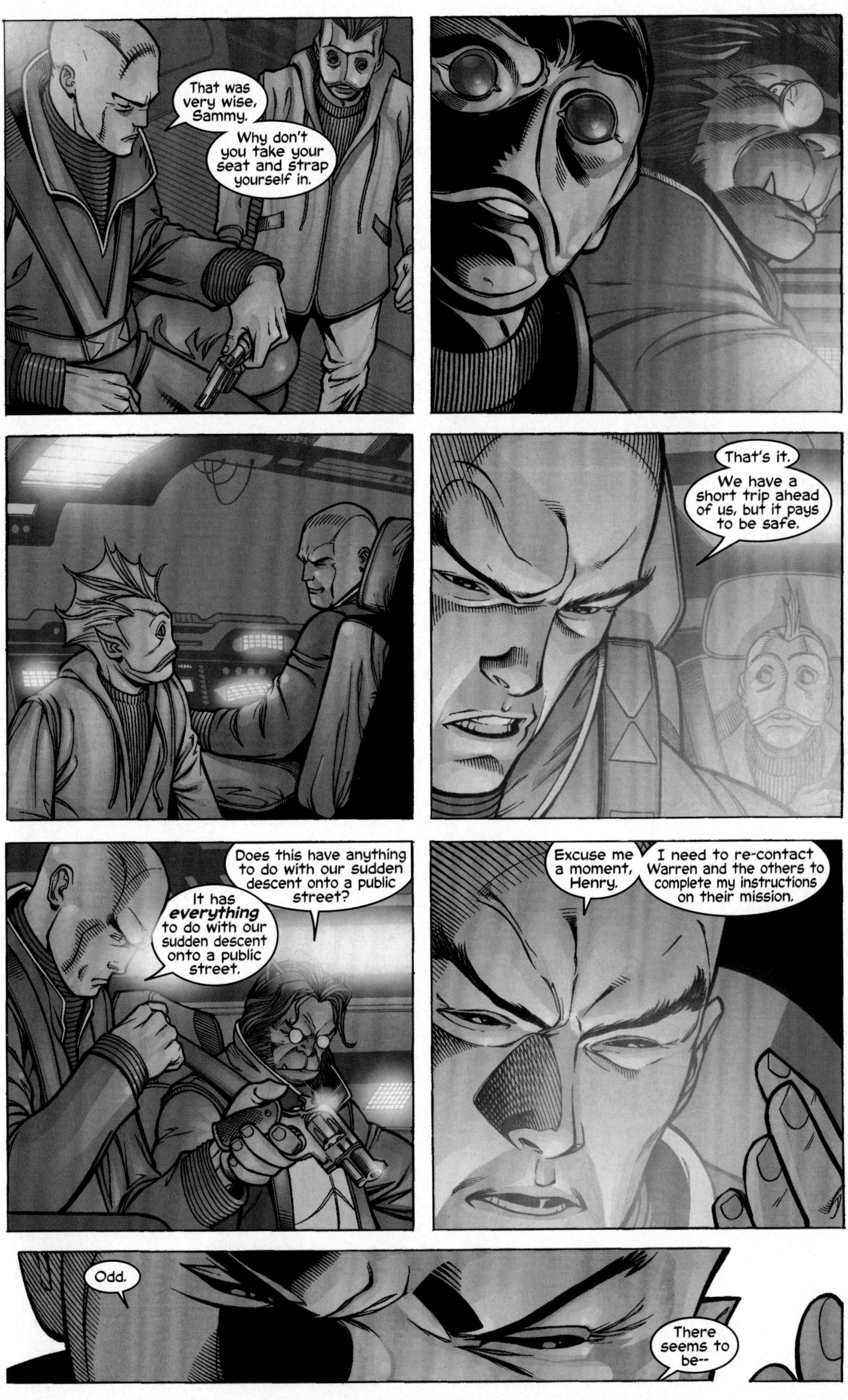
That was very wise, Sammy.
Why don't you take your seat and strap yourself in.
That's it.
We have a short trip ahead of us, but it pays to be safe.
Does this have anything to do with our sudden descent onto a public street?
It has *everything* to do with our sudden descent onto a public street.
Excuse me a moment, Henry.
I need to re-contact Warren and the others to complete my instructions on their mission.
Odd.
There seems to be--

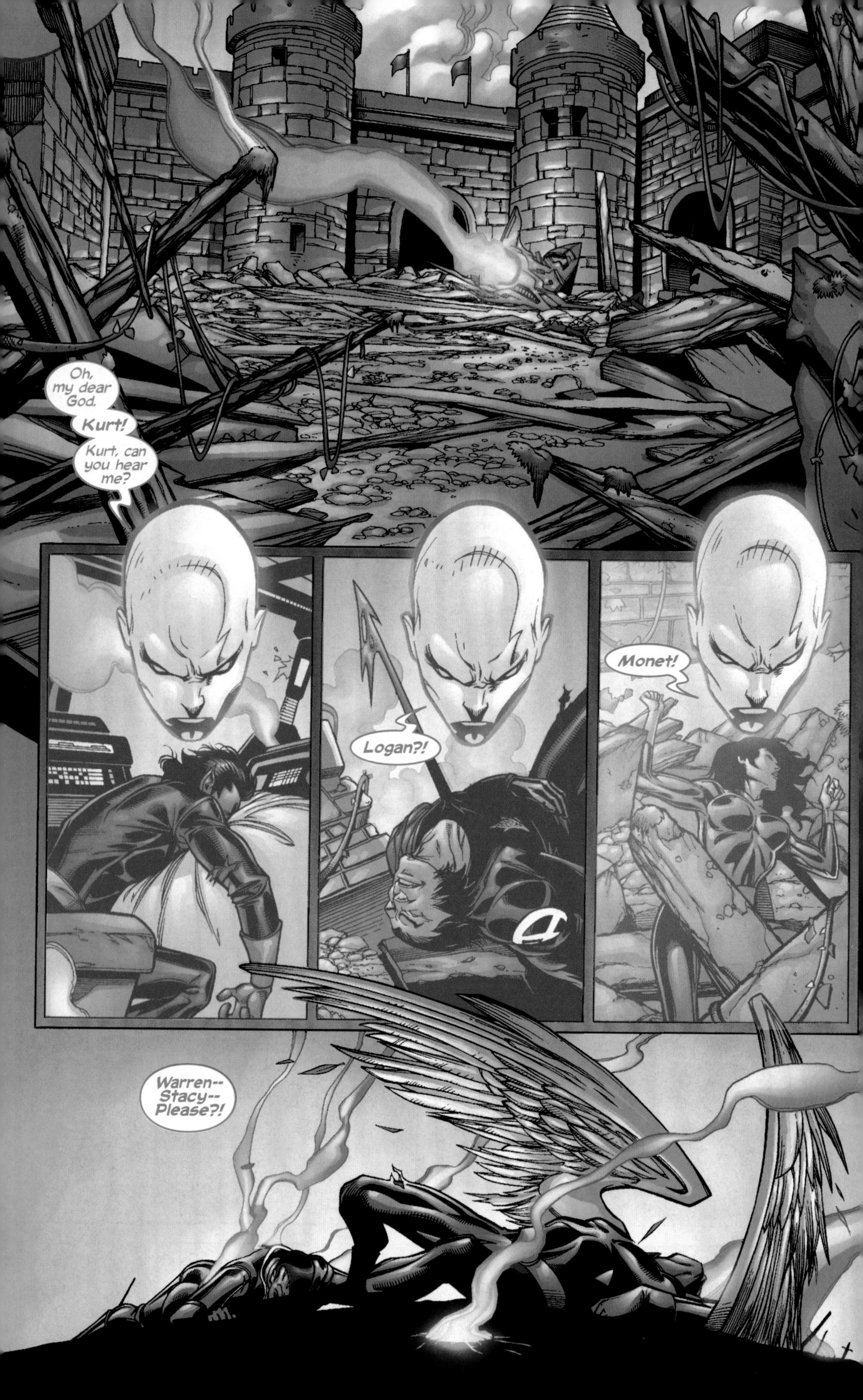
Oh, my dear God.
Kurt!
Kurt, can you hear me?
Logan?!
Monet!
Warren-- Stacy-- Please?!

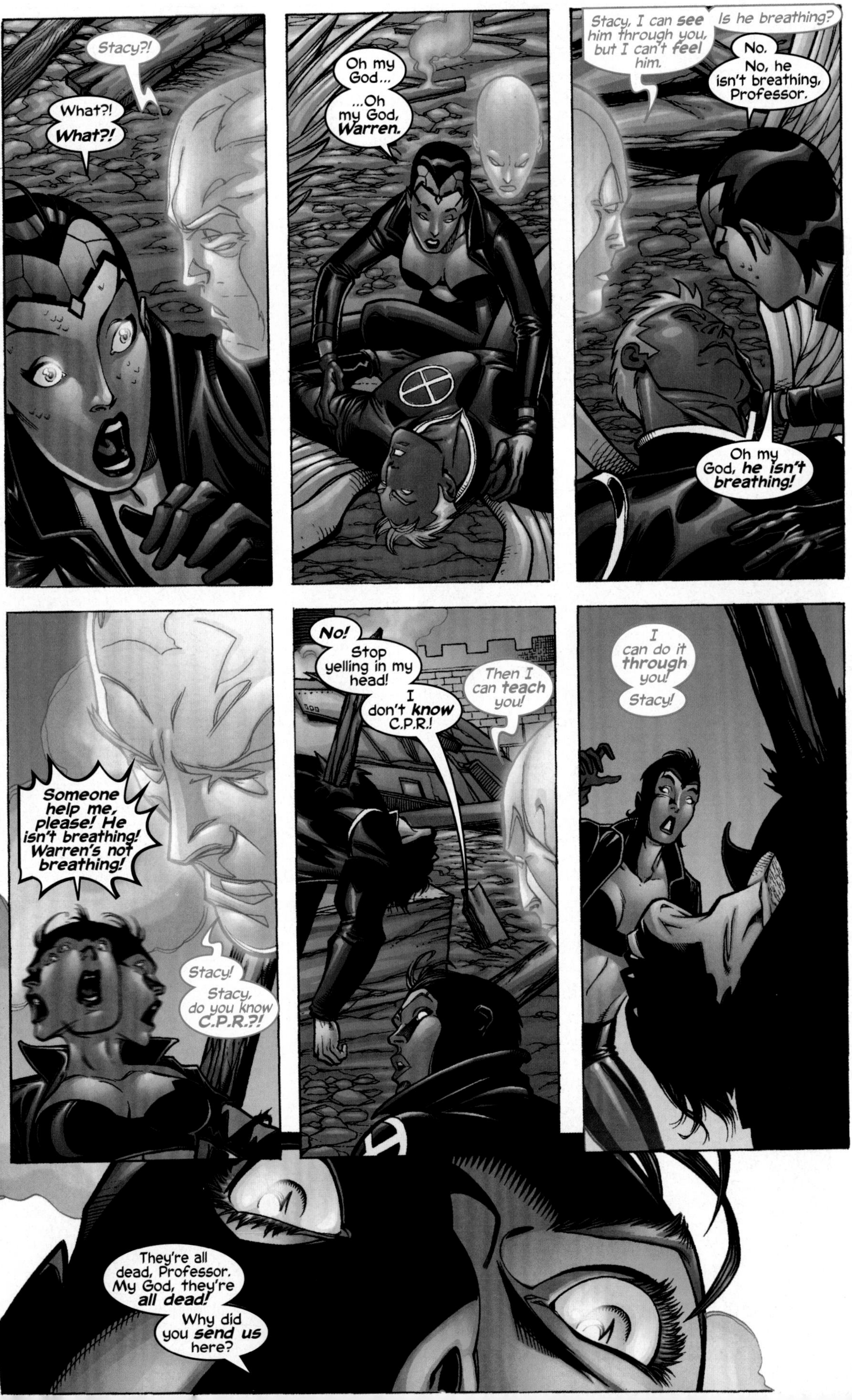
Stacy?!
What?! What?!
Oh my God...
...Oh my God, Warren.
Stacy, I can see him through you, but I can't feel him.
Is he breathing?
No.
No, he isn't breathing, Professor.
Oh my God, he isn't breathing!
Someone help me, please! He isn't breathing! Warren's not breathing!
Stacy!
Stacy, do you know C.P.R.?!
No!
Stop yelling in my head!
I don't know C.P.R.!
Then I can teach you!
I can do it through you!
Stacy!
They're all dead, Professor. My God, they're all dead!
Why did you send us here?

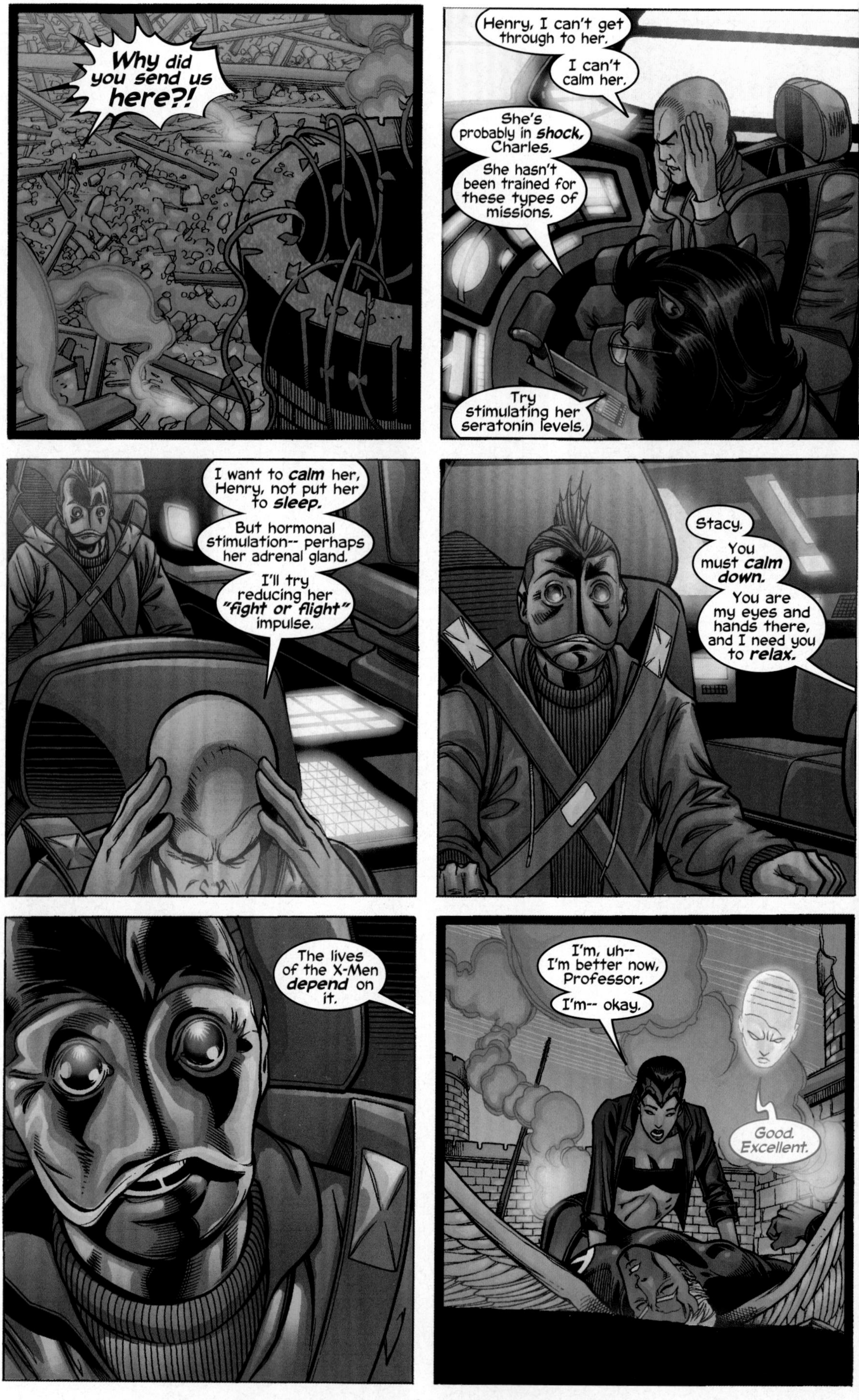
Why did you send us here?!
Henry, I can't get through to her.
I can't calm her.
She's probably in shock, Charles.
She hasn't been trained for these types of missions.
Try stimulating her seratonin levels.
I want to calm her, Henry, not put her to sleep.
But hormonal stimulation-- perhaps her adrenal gland.
I'll try reducing her "fight or flight" impulse.
Stacy.
You must calm down.
You are my eyes and hands there, and I need you to relax.
The lives of the X-Men depend on it.
I'm, uh-- I'm better now, Professor.
I'm-- okay.
Good. Excellent.

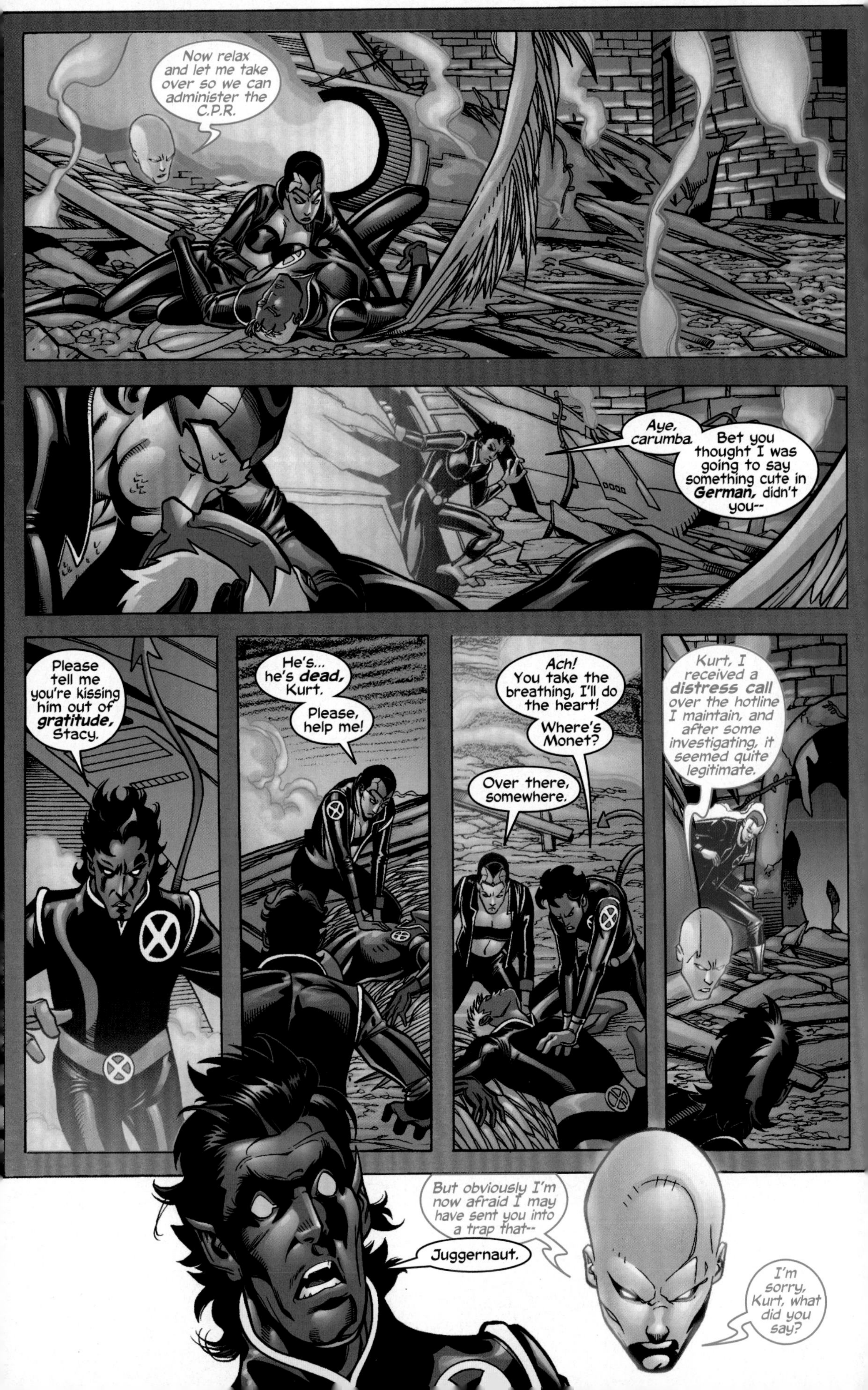
Now relax and let me take over so we can administer the C.P.R.
Aye, carumba.
Bet you thought I was going to say something cute in German, didn't you--
Please tell me you're kissing him out of gratitude, Stacy.
He's... he's dead, Kurt.
Please, help me!
Ach! You take the breathing, I'll do the heart!
Where's Monet?
Over there, somewhere.
Kurt, I received a distress call over the hotline I maintain, and after some investigating, it seemed quite legitimate.
But obviously I'm now afraid I may have sent you into a trap that--
Juggernaut.
I'm sorry, Kurt, what did you say?

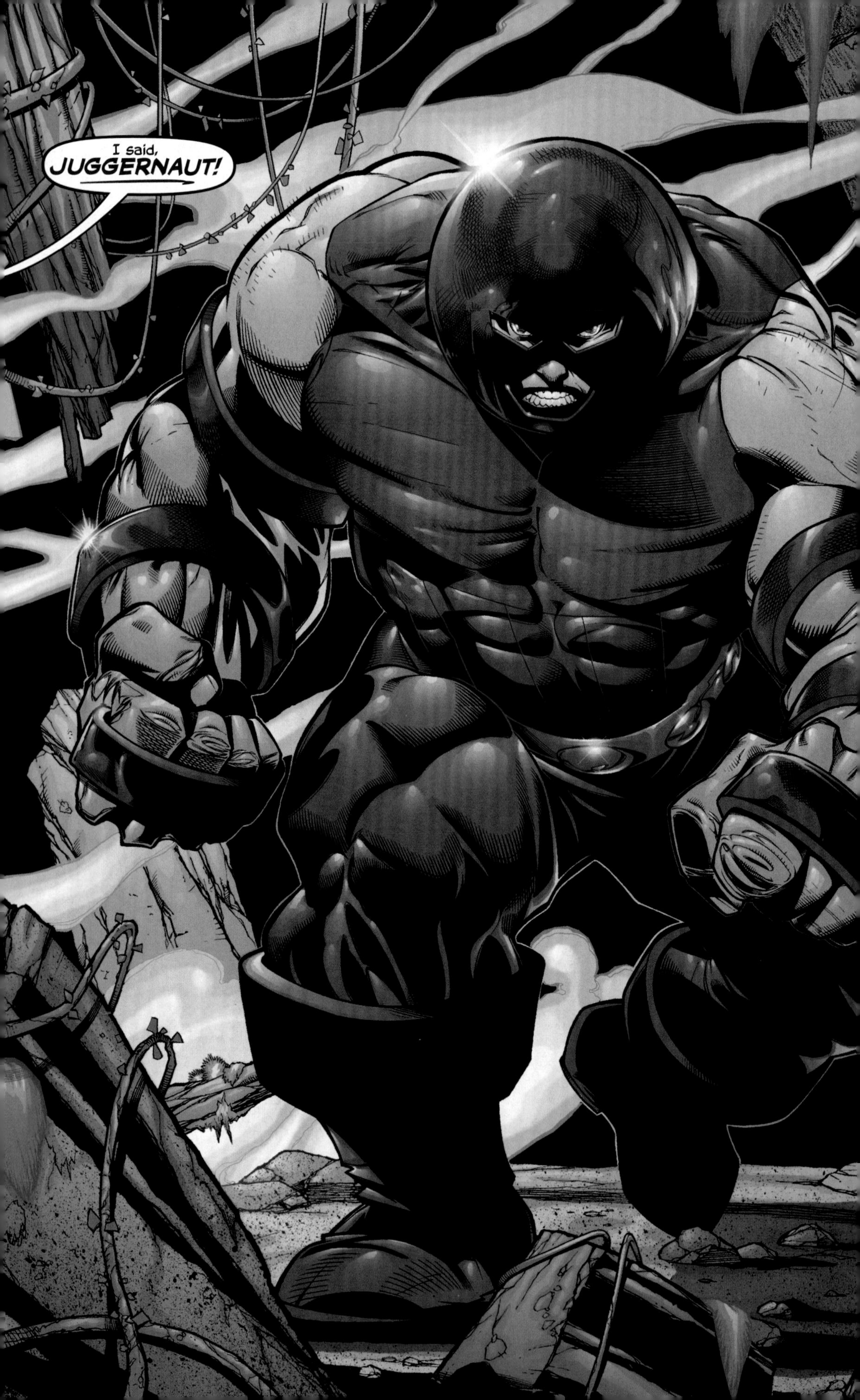
I said, JUGGERNAUT!

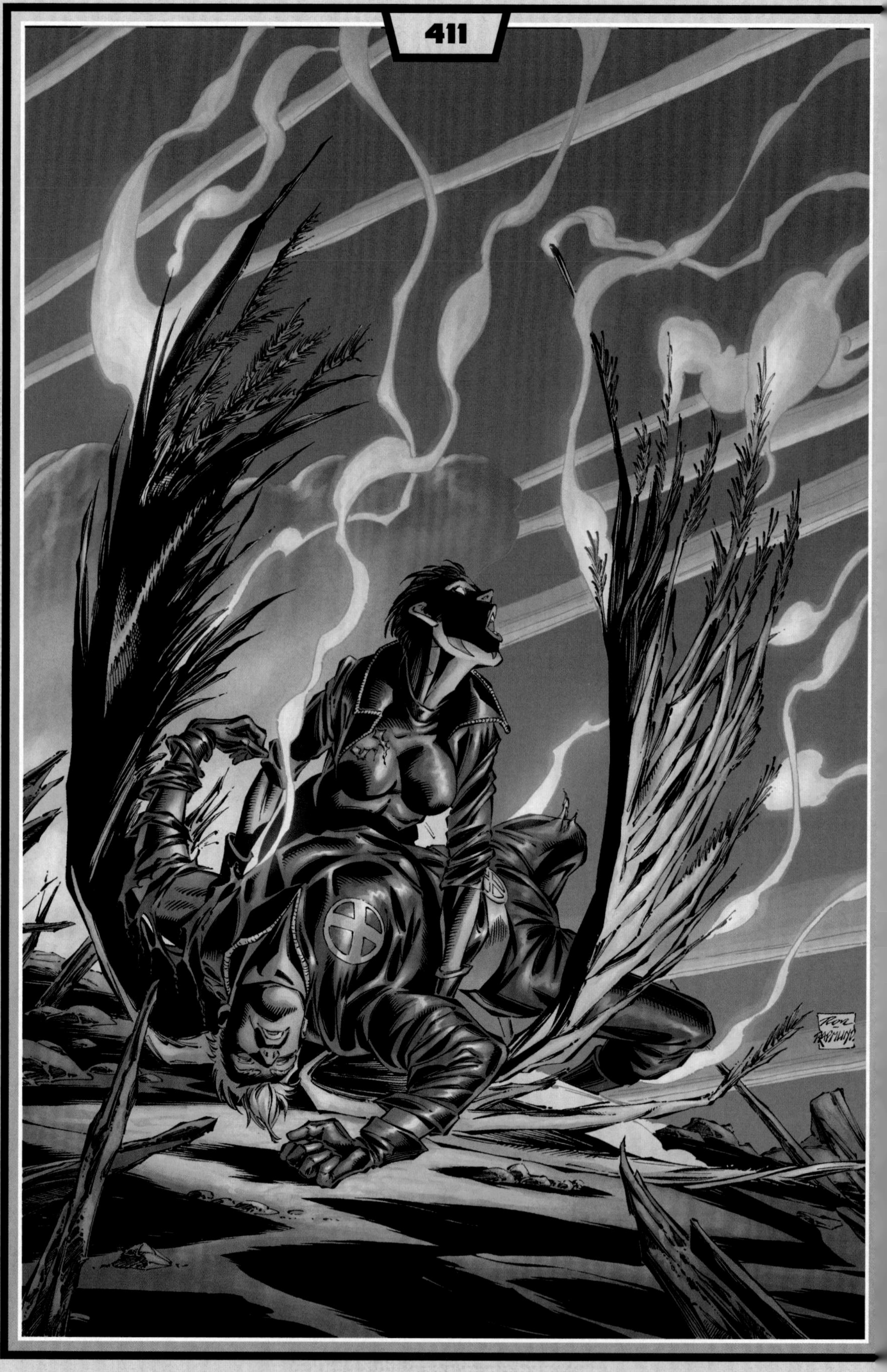
411

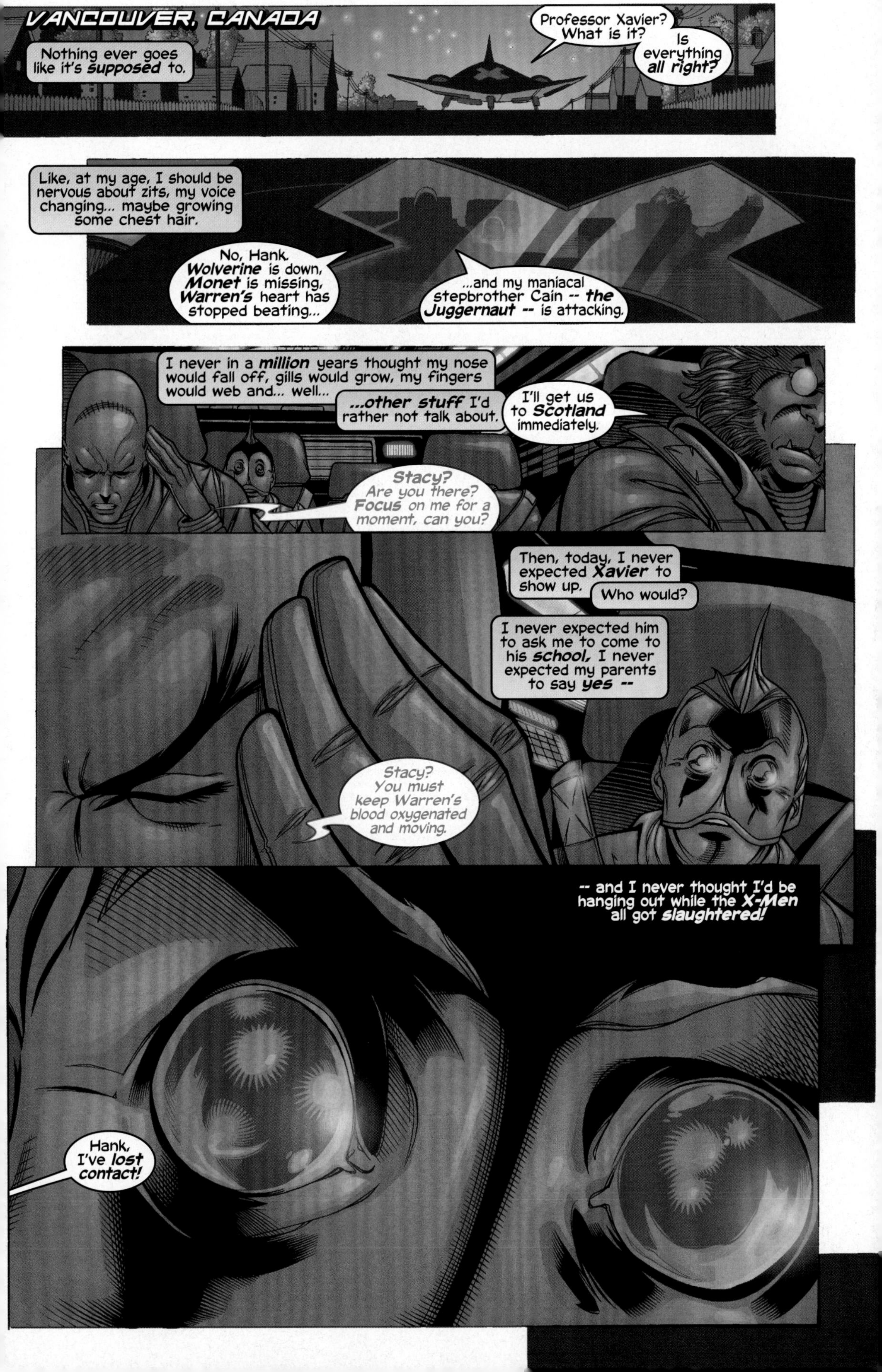
VANCOUVER, CANADA
Nothing ever goes like it's supposed to.
Professor Xavier? What is it?
Is everything all right?
Like, at my age, I should be nervous about zits, my voice changing... maybe growing some chest hair.
No, Hank. Wolverine is down, Monet is missing, Warren's heart has stopped beating...
...and my maniacal stepbrother Cain -- the Juggernaut -- is attacking.
I never in a million years thought my nose would fall off, gills would grow, my fingers would web and... well...
...other stuff I'd rather not talk about.
I'll get us to Scotland immediately.
Stacy? Are you there? Focus on me for a moment, can you?
Then, today, I never expected Xavier to show up.
Who would?
I never expected him to ask me to come to his school, I never expected my parents to say yes --
Stacy? You must keep Warren's blood oxygenated and moving.
-- and I never thought I'd be hanging out while the X-Men all got slaughtered!
Hank, I've lost contact!

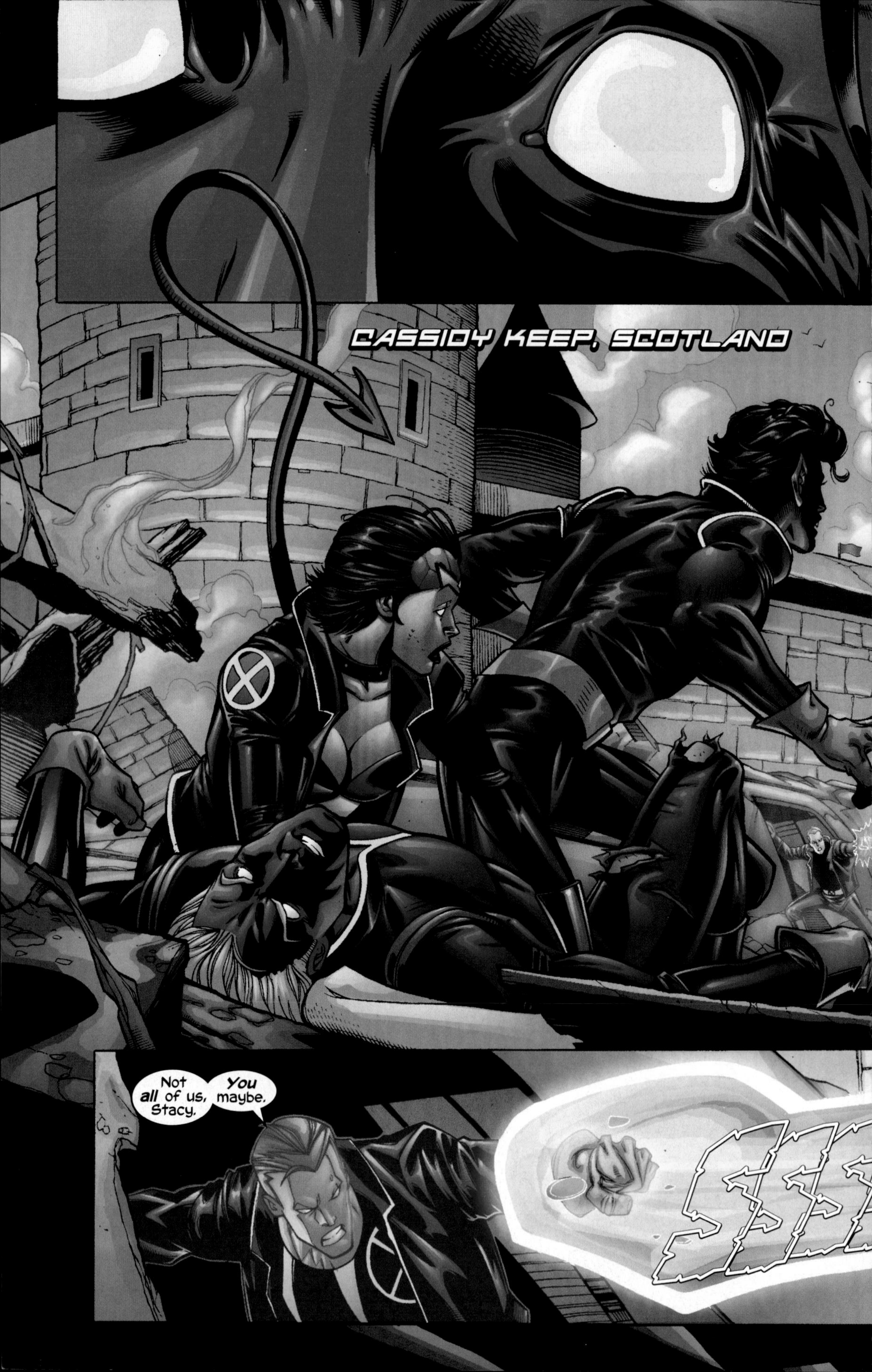
CASSIDY KEEP, SCOTLAND
Not all of us, Stacy.
You maybe.

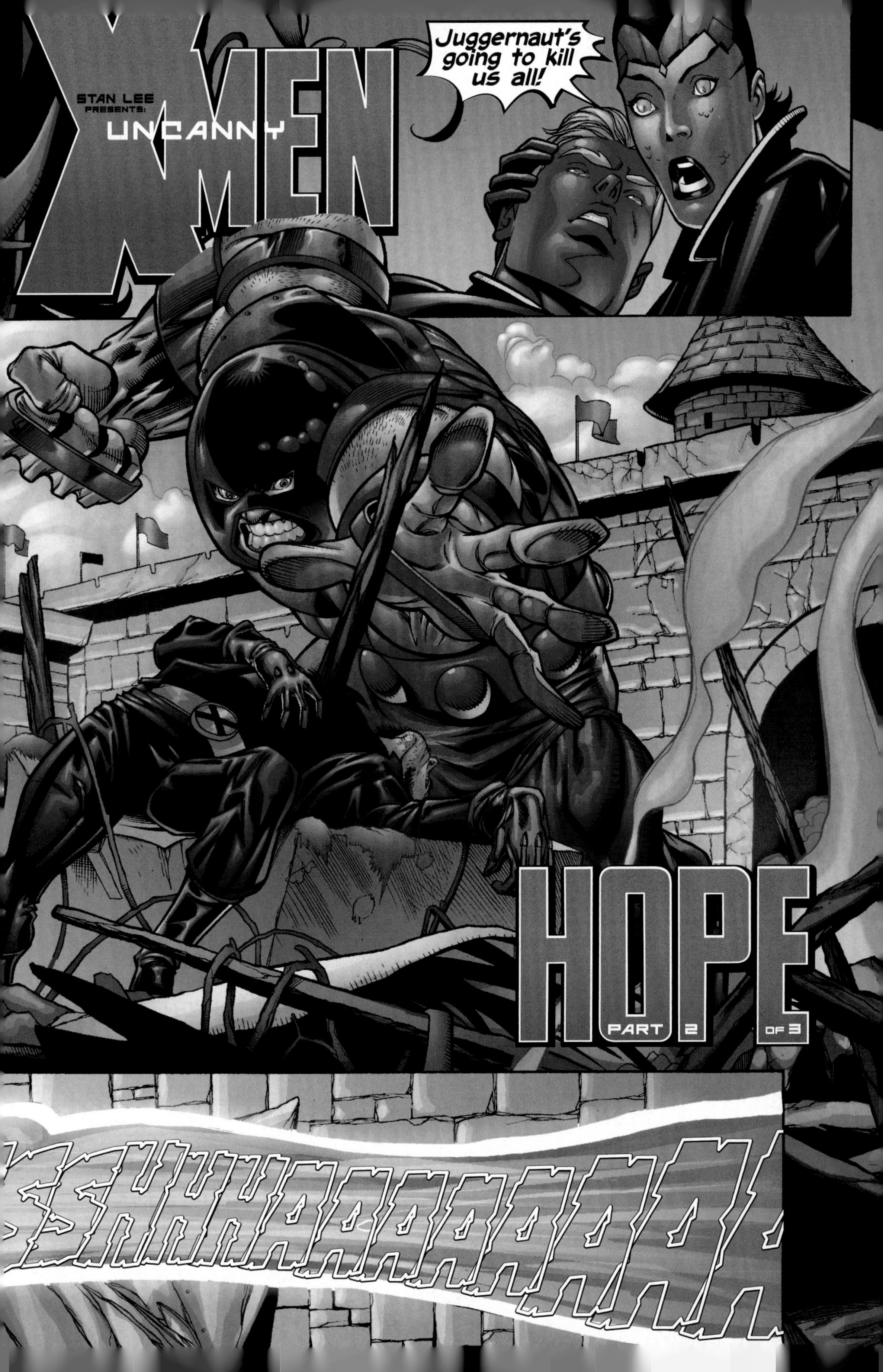
STAN LEE PRESENTS:
UNCANNY X-MEN
Juggernaut's going to kill us all!
HOPE
PART 2 OF 3
SHHHAAAAAAAA

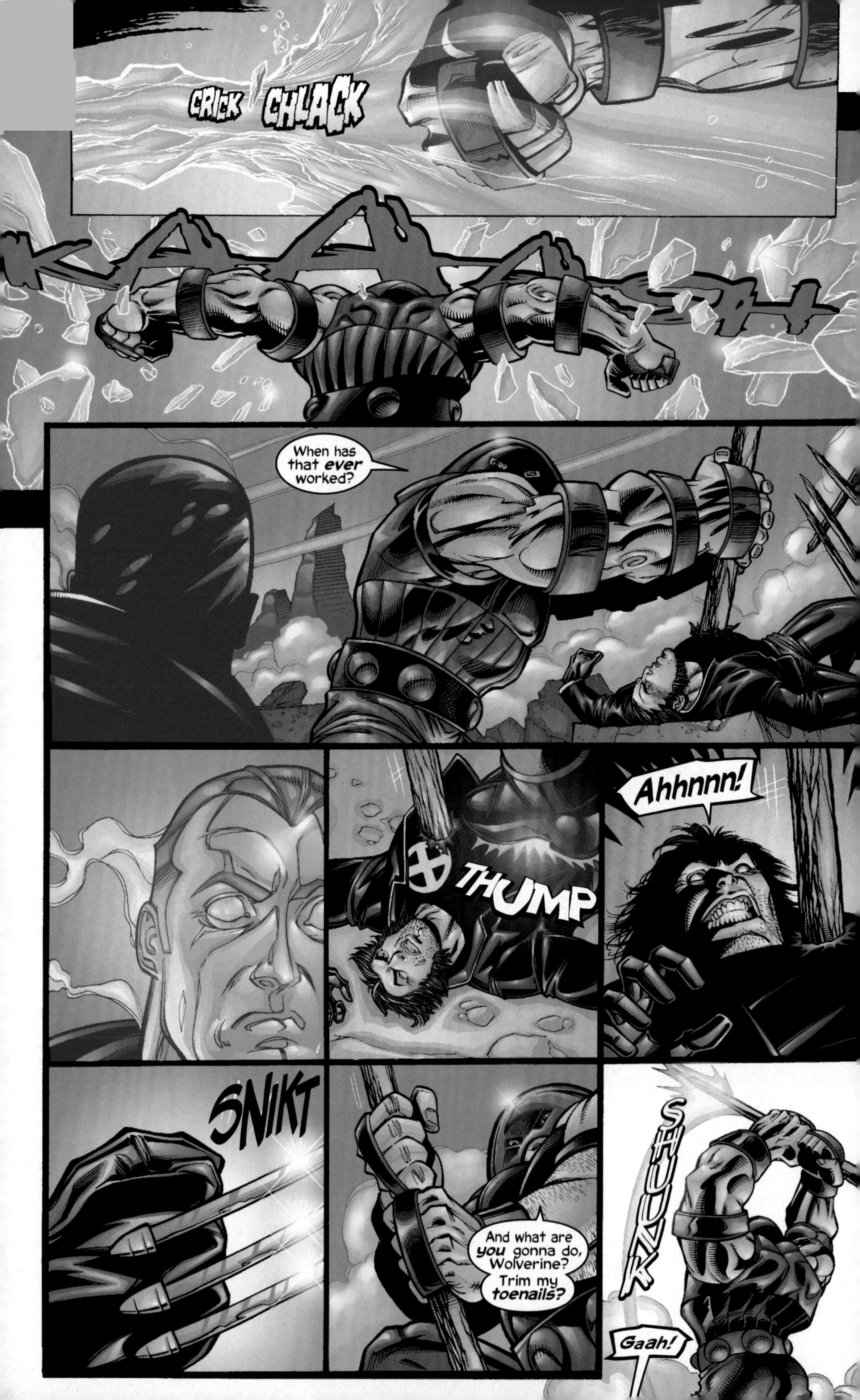
CRICK
CHLACK
KAAASHH
When has that ever worked?
THUMP
Ahhnnn!
SNIKT
And what are you gonna do, Wolverine? Trim my toenails?
SHUNK
Gaah!

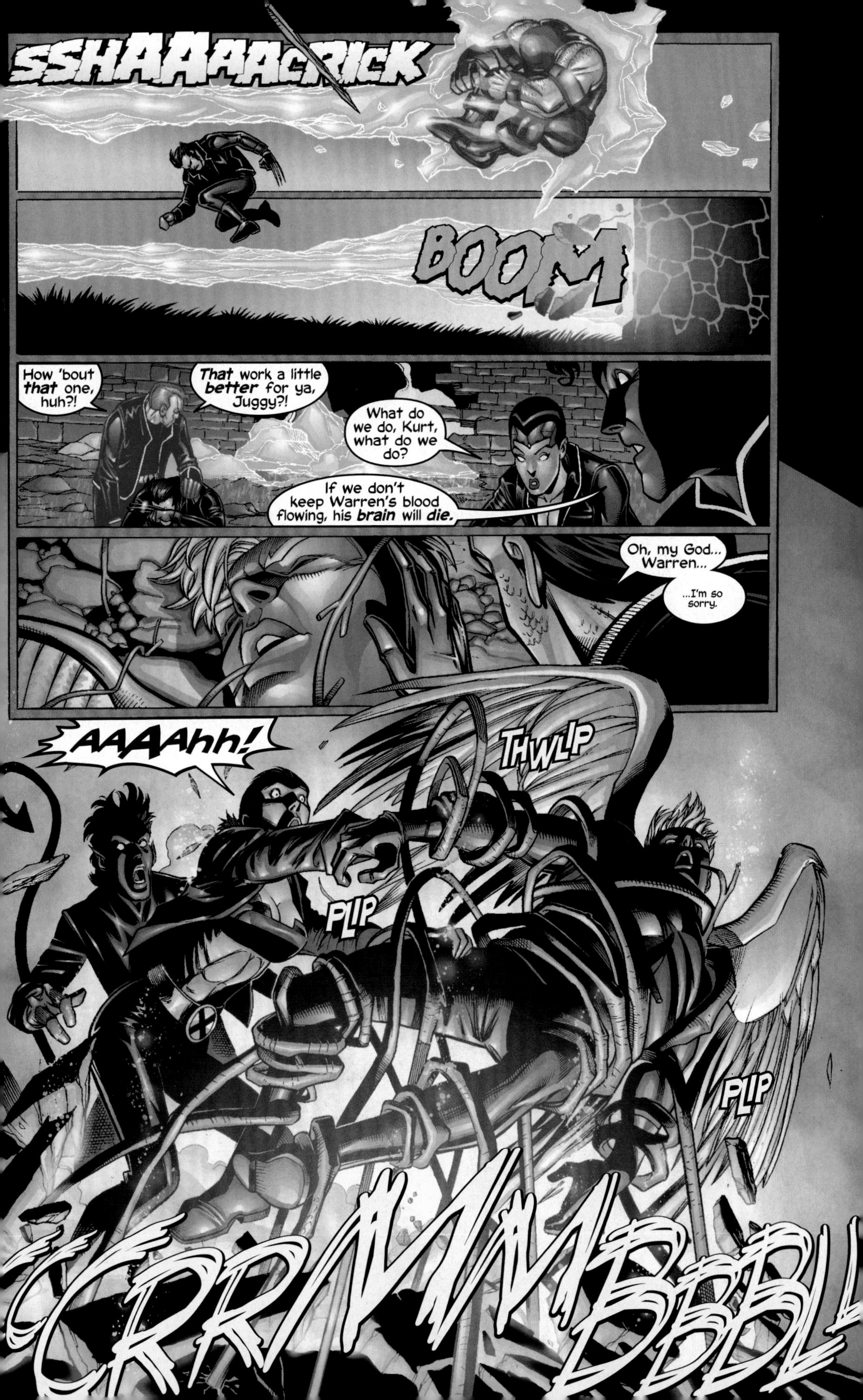
SSHAAAACRICK
BOOM
How 'bout that one, huh?!
That work a little better for ya, Juggy?!
What do we do, Kurt, what do we do?
If we don't keep Warren's blood flowing, his brain will die.
Oh, my God... Warren...
...I'm so sorry.
AAAAhh!
THWLIP
PLIP
PLIP
CRRMMBBBL

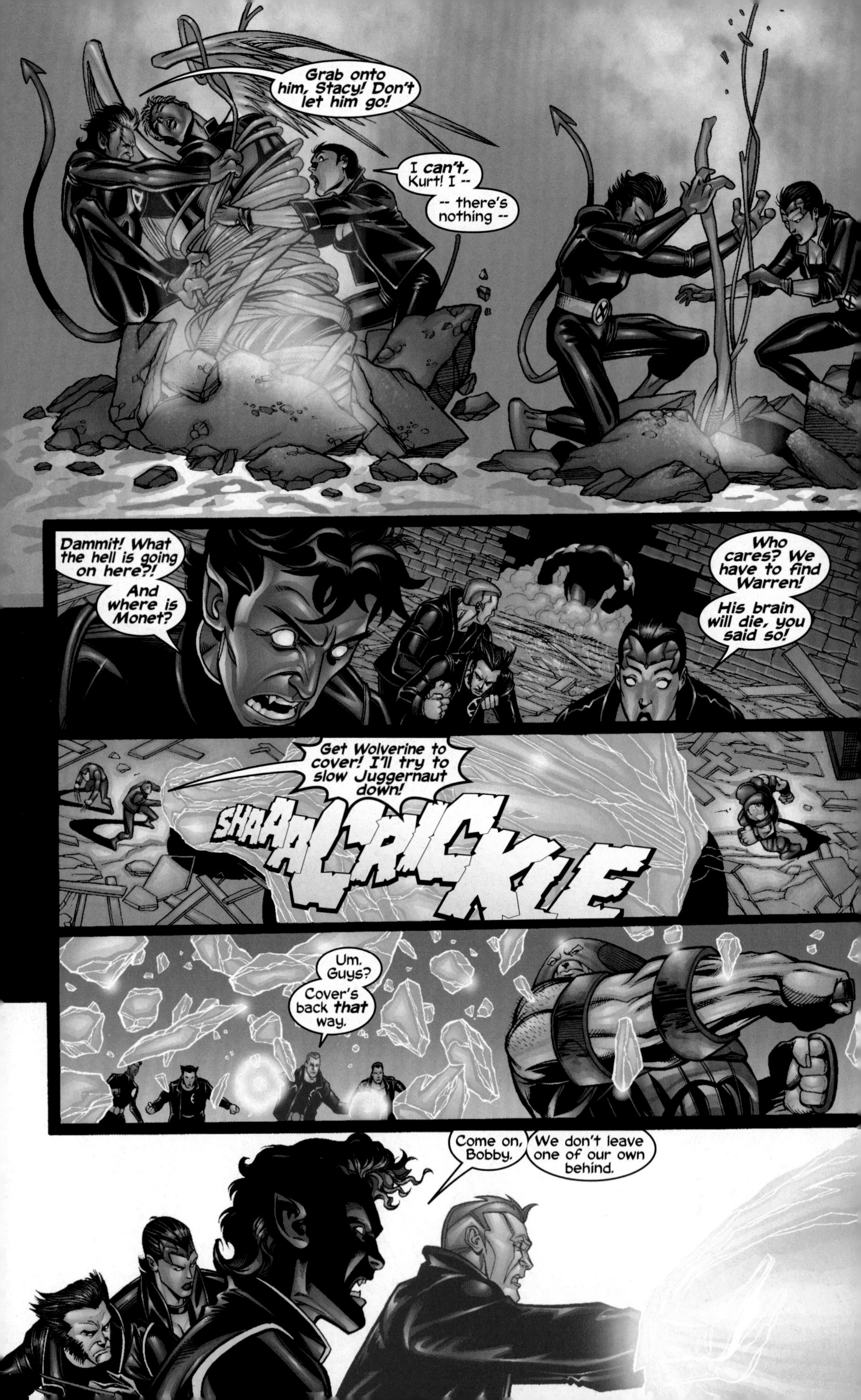
Grab onto him, Stacy! Don't let him go!
I can't, Kurt! I --
-- there's nothing --
Dammit! What the hell is going on here?!
And where is Monet?
Who cares? We have to find Warren!
His brain will die, you said so!
Get Wolverine to cover! I'll try to slow Juggernaut down!
SHAAALRICKLE
Um. Guys?
Cover's back that way.
Come on, Bobby.
We don't leave one of our own behind.

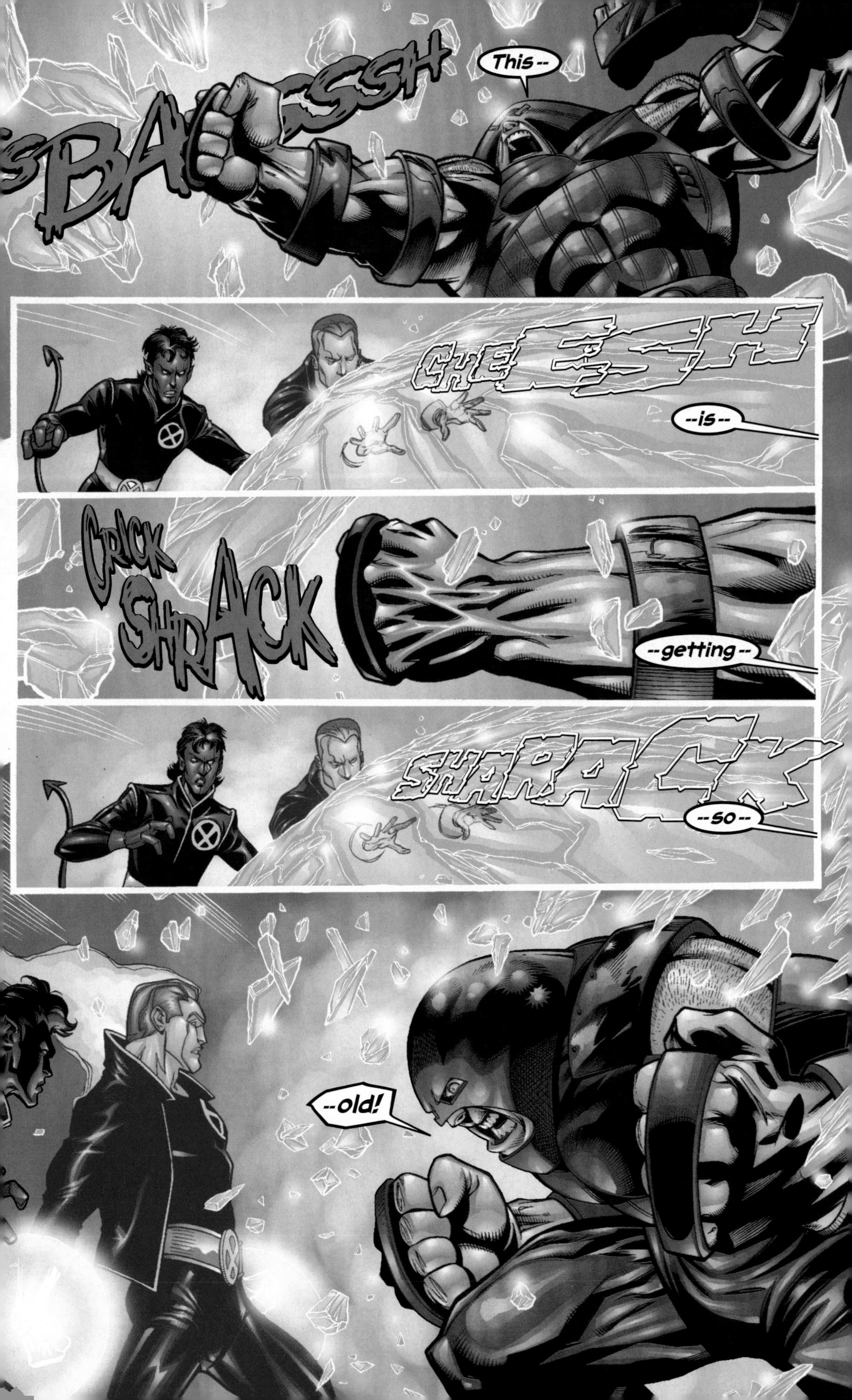
SBASSH
This--
CHESH
--is--
CRICK SHRACK
--getting--
SHRACK
--so--
--old!

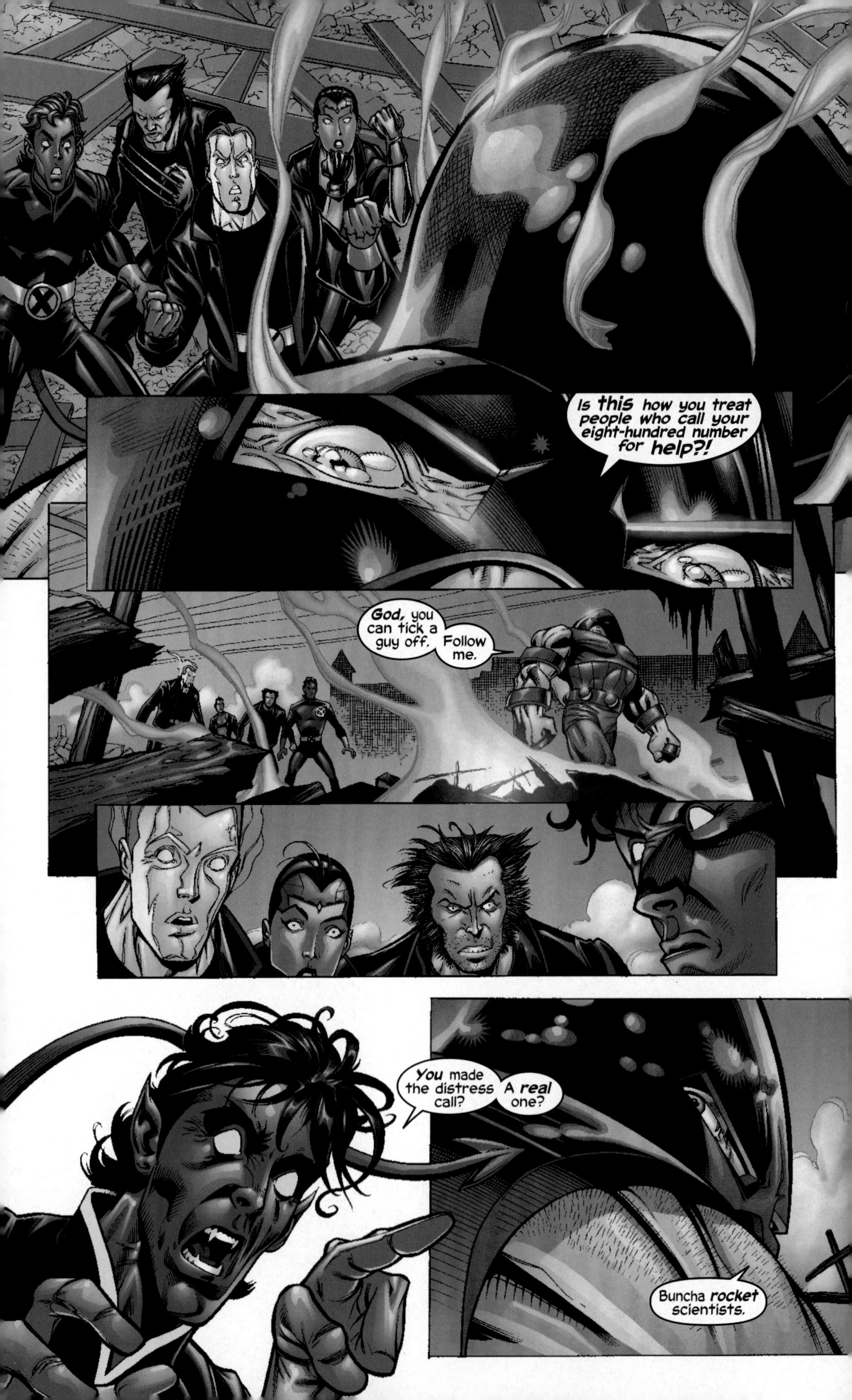
Is this how you treat people who call your eight-hundred number for help?!
God, you can tick a guy off.
Follow me.
You made the distress call?
A real one?
Buncha rocket scientists.

Who **else** do you **see** here?

But, you mean a *genuine* distress call?

You're asking for our **help** with something?

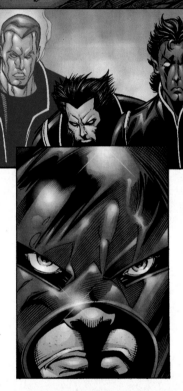

Then why didn't you just come out and **say that?**

What's with the "clip my toenails" and yanking out the stake, and--?!

Oh, I'm sorry, Wolverine. How *awful* of me. You didn't like that wooden spike jammed through your lung?

Sure. *Loved* it.

Then I'll be sure to put it *back* when we're all done.

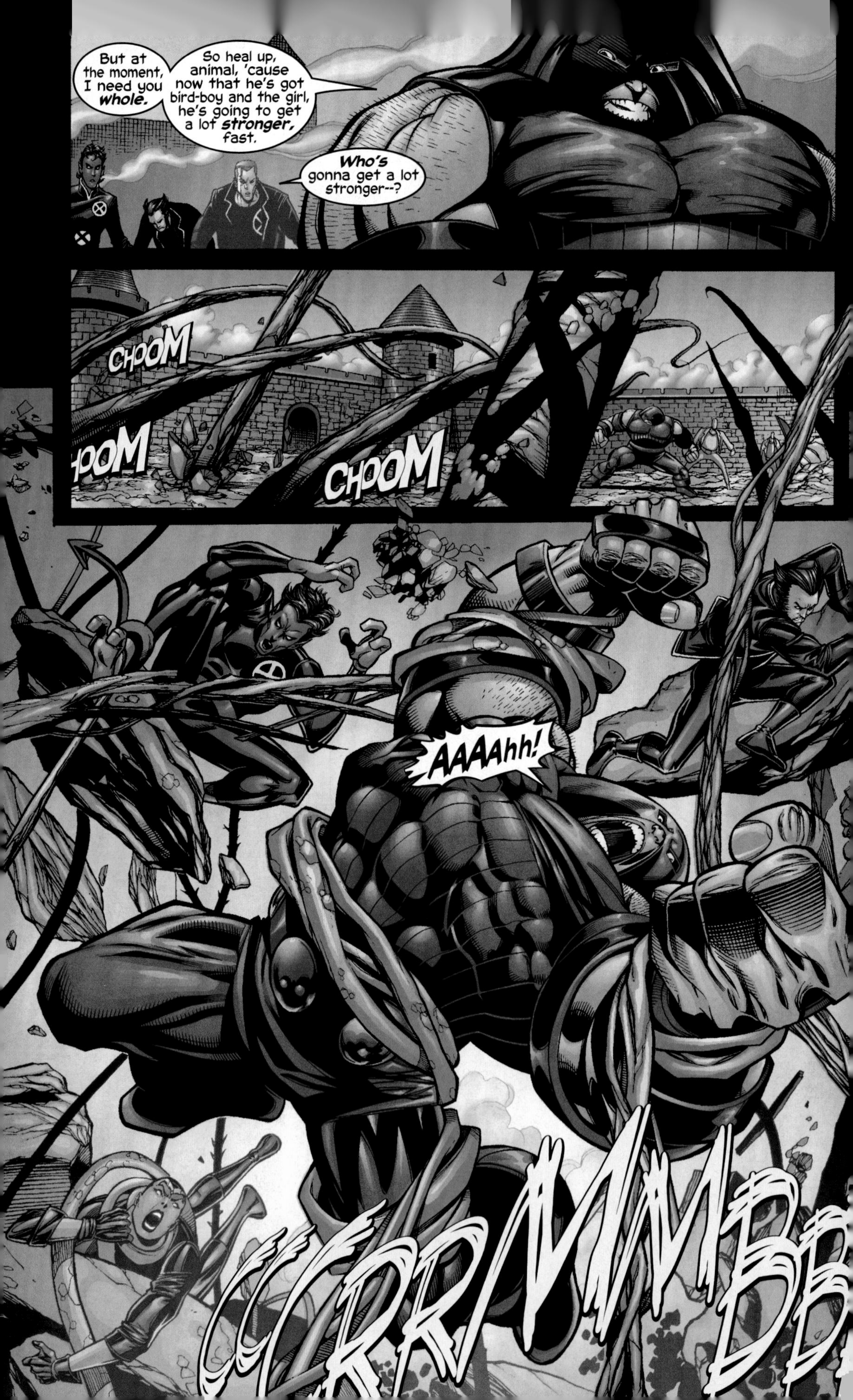

But at the moment, I need you *whole.*
So heal up, animal, 'cause now that he's got bird-boy and the girl, he's going to get a lot *stronger,* fast.
Who's gonna get a lot stronger--?
CHOOM
CHOOM
CHOOM
AAAAhh!

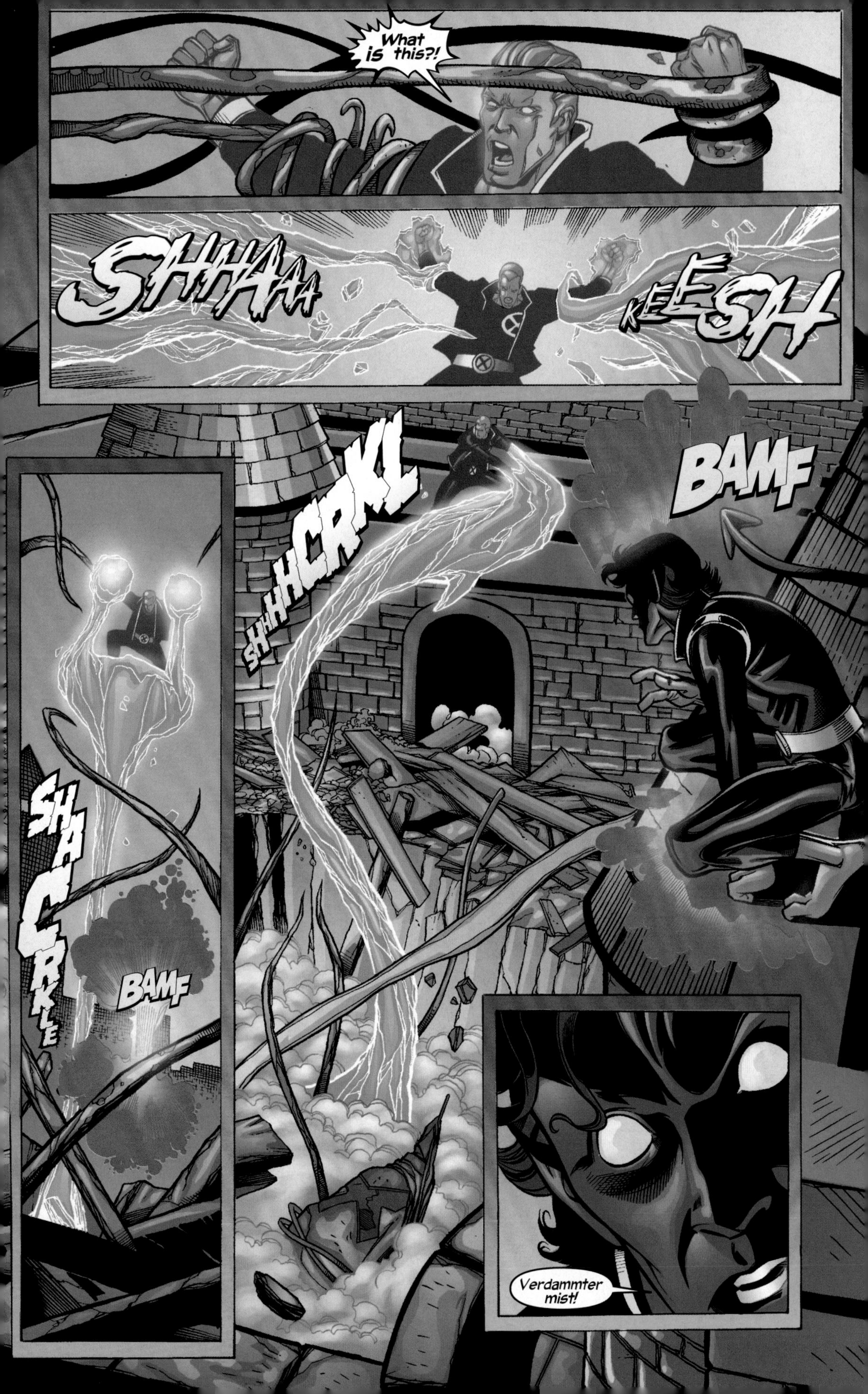
What is this?!
SHHAAA
KEESH
SHHHCRKL
BAMF
SHACRKLE
BAMF
Verdammter mist!

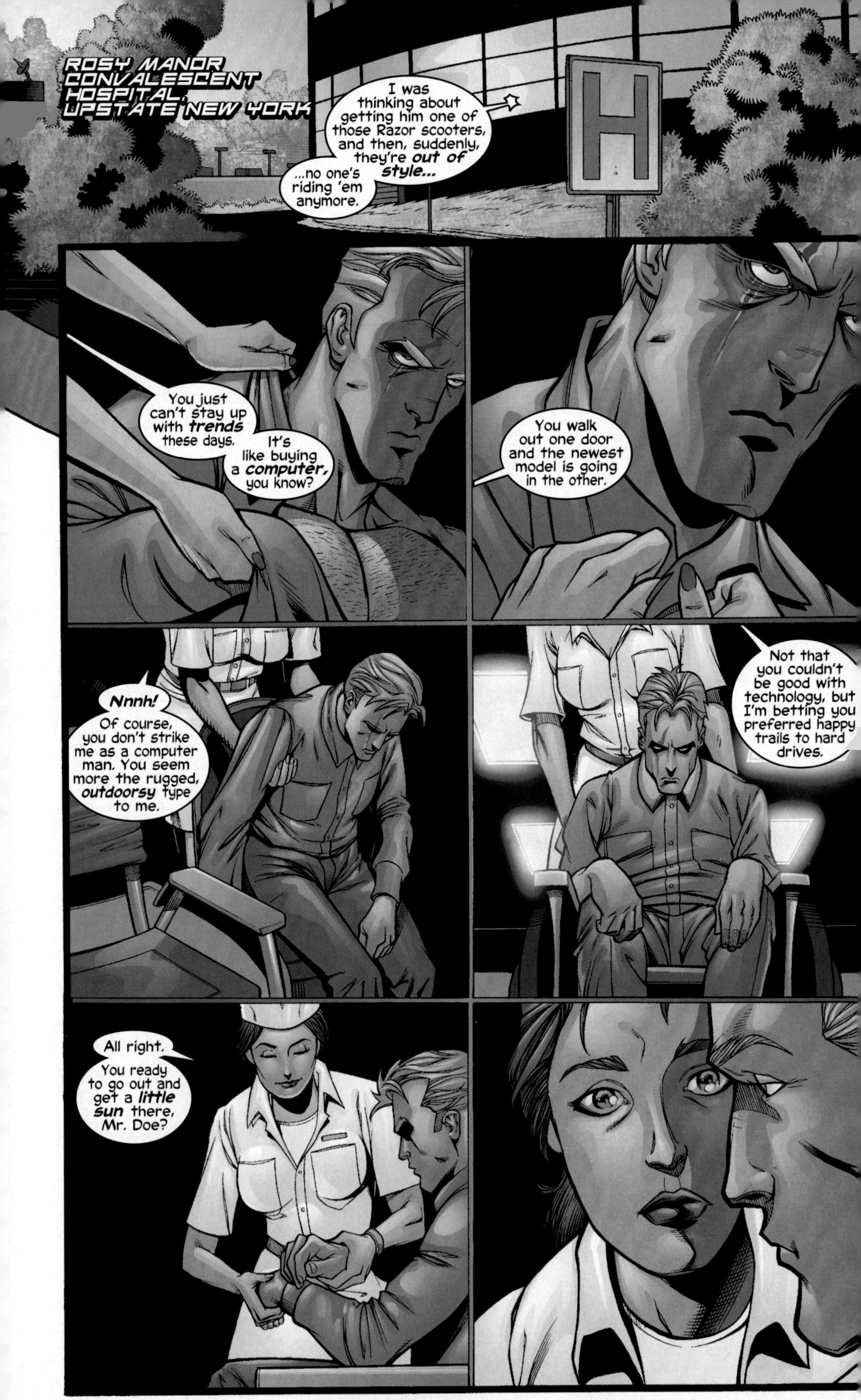
ROSY MANOR CONVALESCENT HOSPITAL, UPSTATE NEW YORK
I was thinking about getting him one of those Razor scooters, and then, suddenly, they're out of style...
...no one's riding 'em anymore.
You just can't stay up with trends these days.
It's like buying a computer, you know?
You walk out one door and the newest model is going in the other.
Nnnh!
Of course, you don't strike me as a computer man. You seem more the rugged, outdoorsy type to me.
Not that you couldn't be good with technology, but I'm betting you preferred happy trails to hard drives.
All right.
You ready to go out and get a little sun there, Mr. Doe?

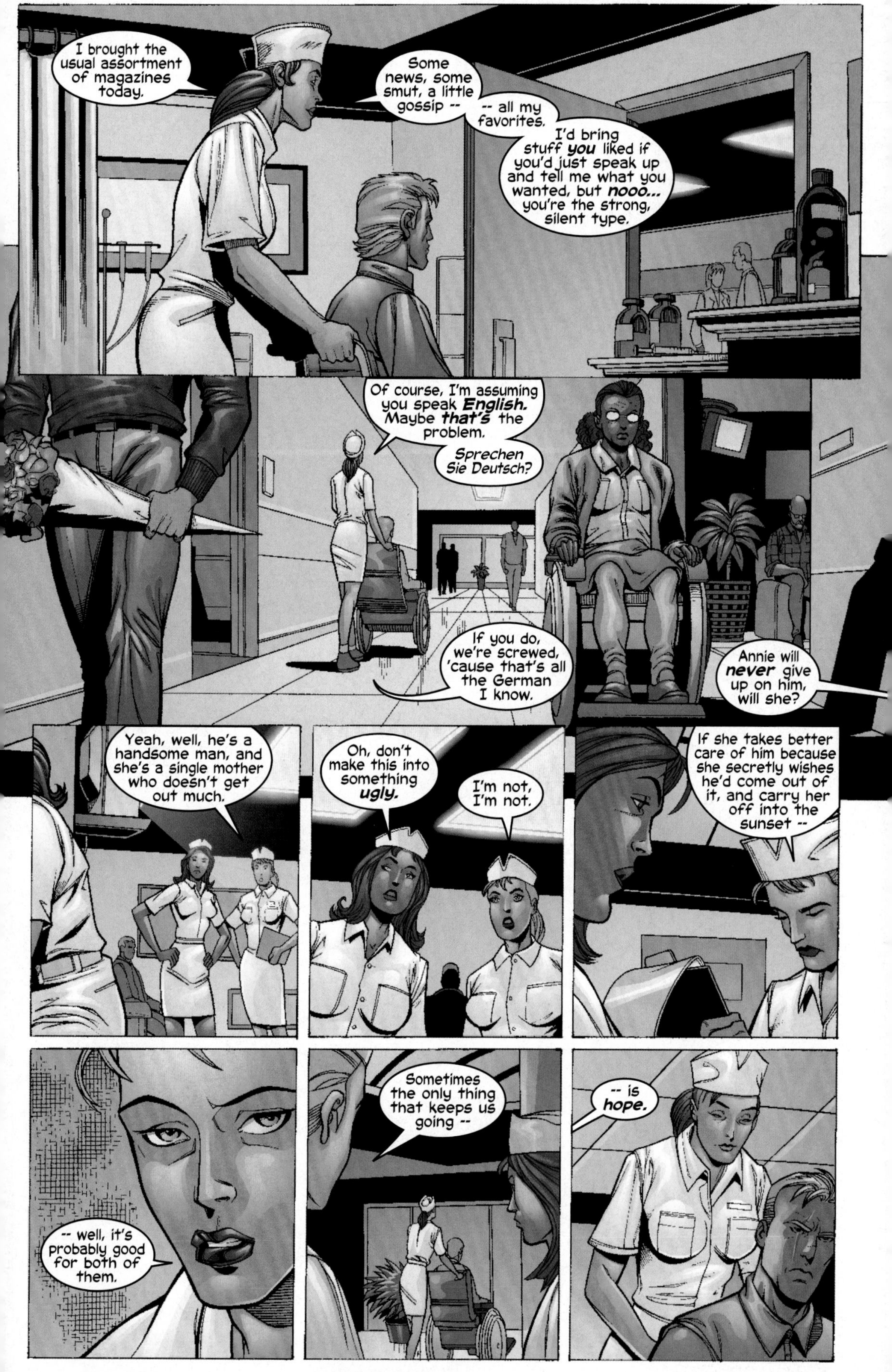
I brought the usual assortment of magazines today.
Some news, some smut, a little gossip --
-- all my favorites.
I'd bring stuff you liked if you'd just speak up and tell me what you wanted, but nooo... you're the strong, silent type.
Of course, I'm assuming you speak English. Maybe that's the problem.
Sprechen Sie Deutsch?
If you do, we're screwed, 'cause that's all the German I know.
Annie will never give up on him, will she?
Yeah, well, he's a handsome man, and she's a single mother who doesn't get out much.
Oh, don't make this into something ugly.
I'm not, I'm not.
If she takes better care of him because she secretly wishes he'd come out of it, and carry her off into the sunset --
-- well, it's probably good for both of them.
Sometimes the only thing that keeps us going --
-- is hope.

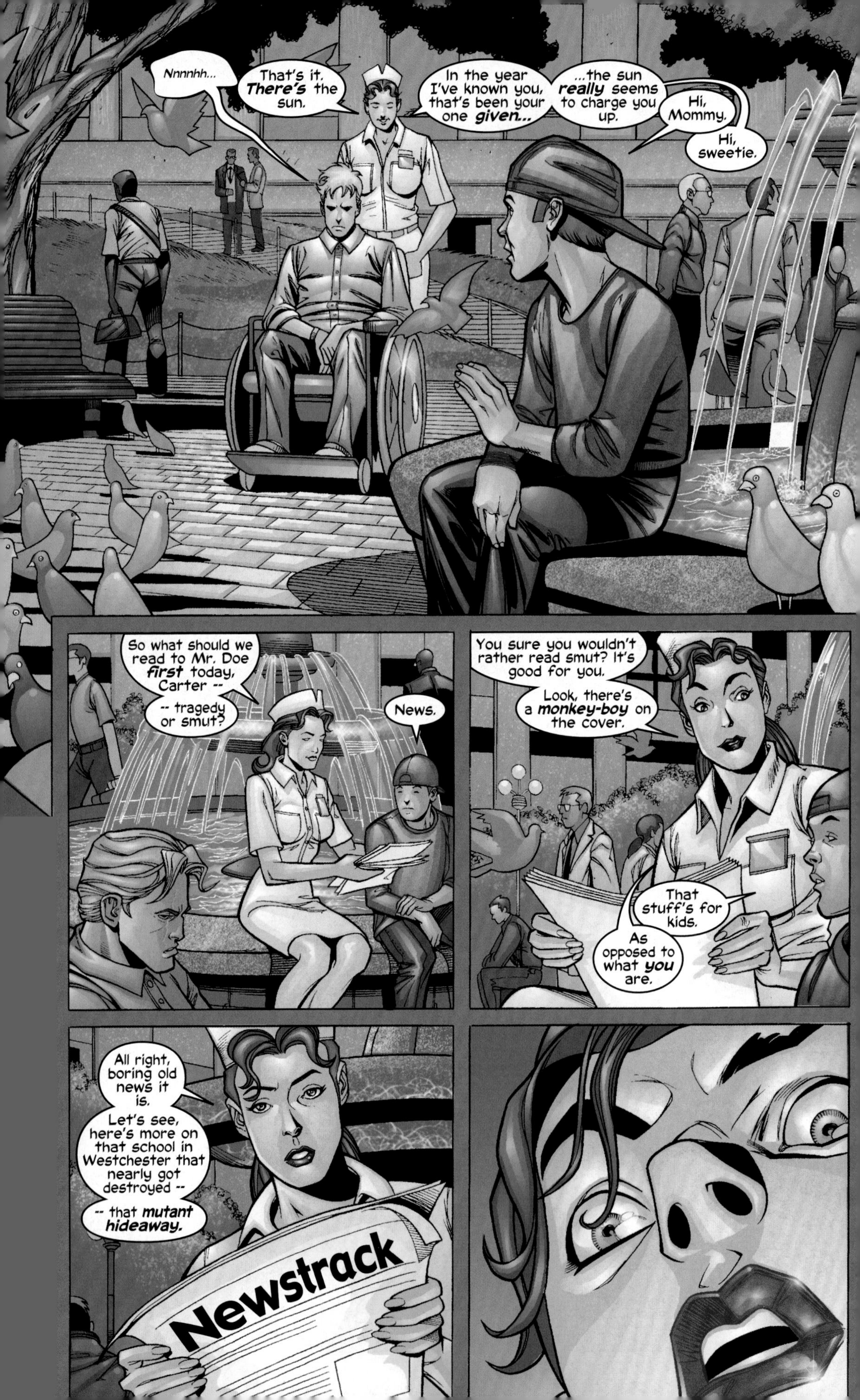

Nnnnhh...
That's it. **There's** the sun.
In the year I've known you, that's been your one **given...**
...the sun **really** seems to charge you up.
Hi, Mommy.
Hi, sweetie.
So what should we read to Mr. Doe **first** today, Carter --
-- tragedy or smut?
News.
You sure you wouldn't rather read smut? It's good for you.
Look, there's a **monkey-boy** on the cover.
That stuff's for kids.
As opposed to what **you** are.
All right, boring old news it is.
Let's see, here's more on that school in Westchester that nearly got destroyed --
-- that **mutant hideaway.**
Newstrack

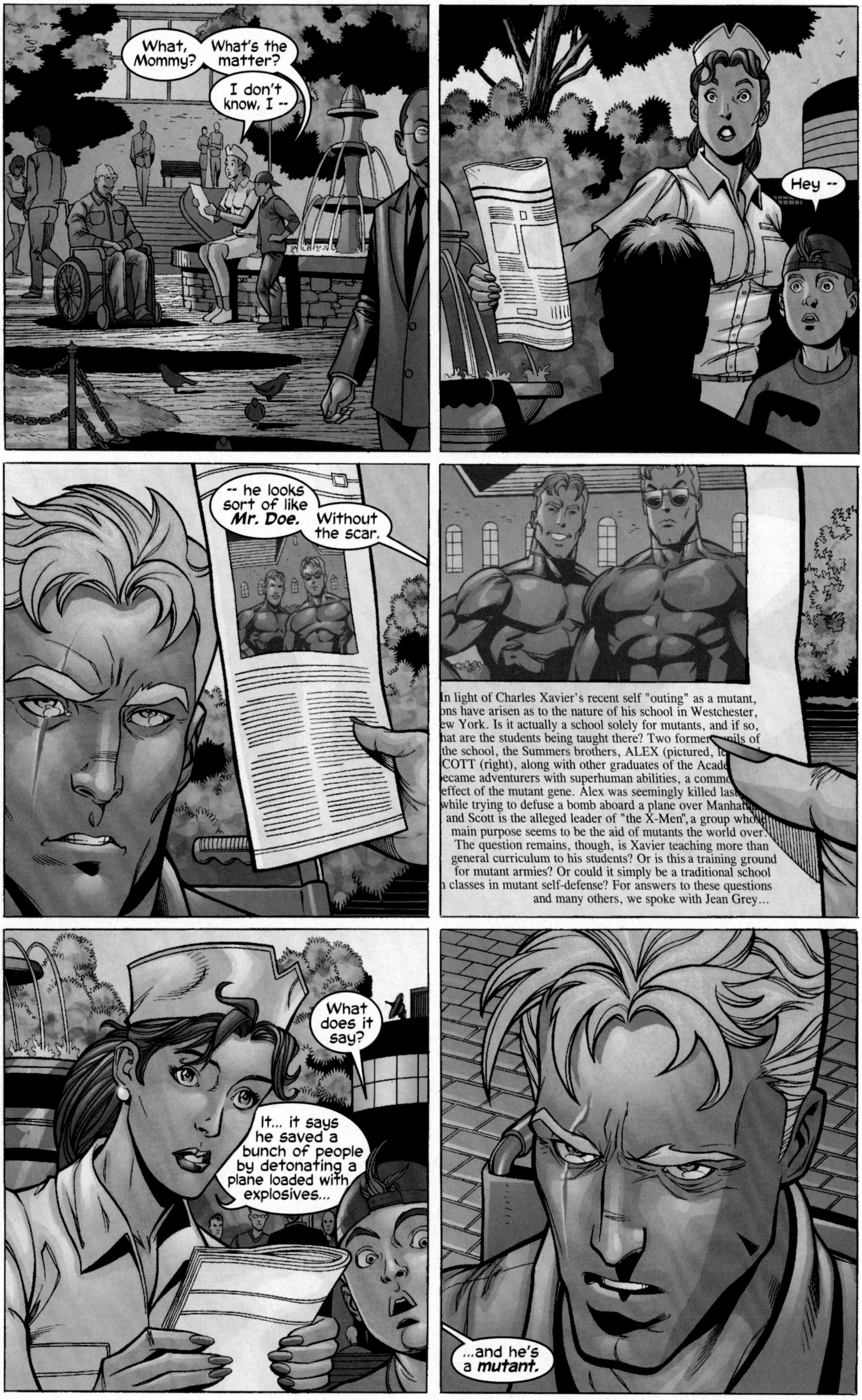
What, Mommy?
What's the matter?
I don't know, I --
Hey --
-- he looks sort of like **Mr. Doe.**
Without the scar.
In light of Charles Xavier's recent self "outing" as a mutant,
ons have arisen as to the nature of his school in Westchester,
ew York. Is it actually a school solely for mutants, and if so,
hat are the students being taught there? Two former pupils of
the school, the Summers brothers, ALEX (pictured, le
COTT (right), along with other graduates of the Acade
became adventurers with superhuman abilities, a commo
effect of the mutant gene. Alex was seemingly killed las
while trying to defuse a bomb aboard a plane over Manhat
and Scott is the alleged leader of "the X-Men", a group whose
main purpose seems to be the aid of mutants the world over.
The question remains, though, is Xavier teaching more than
general curriculum to his students? Or is this a training ground
for mutant armies? Or could it simply be a traditional school
h classes in mutant self-defense? For answers to these questions
and many others, we spoke with Jean Grey...
What does it say?
It... it says he saved a bunch of people by detonating a plane loaded with explosives...
...and he's a *mutant.*

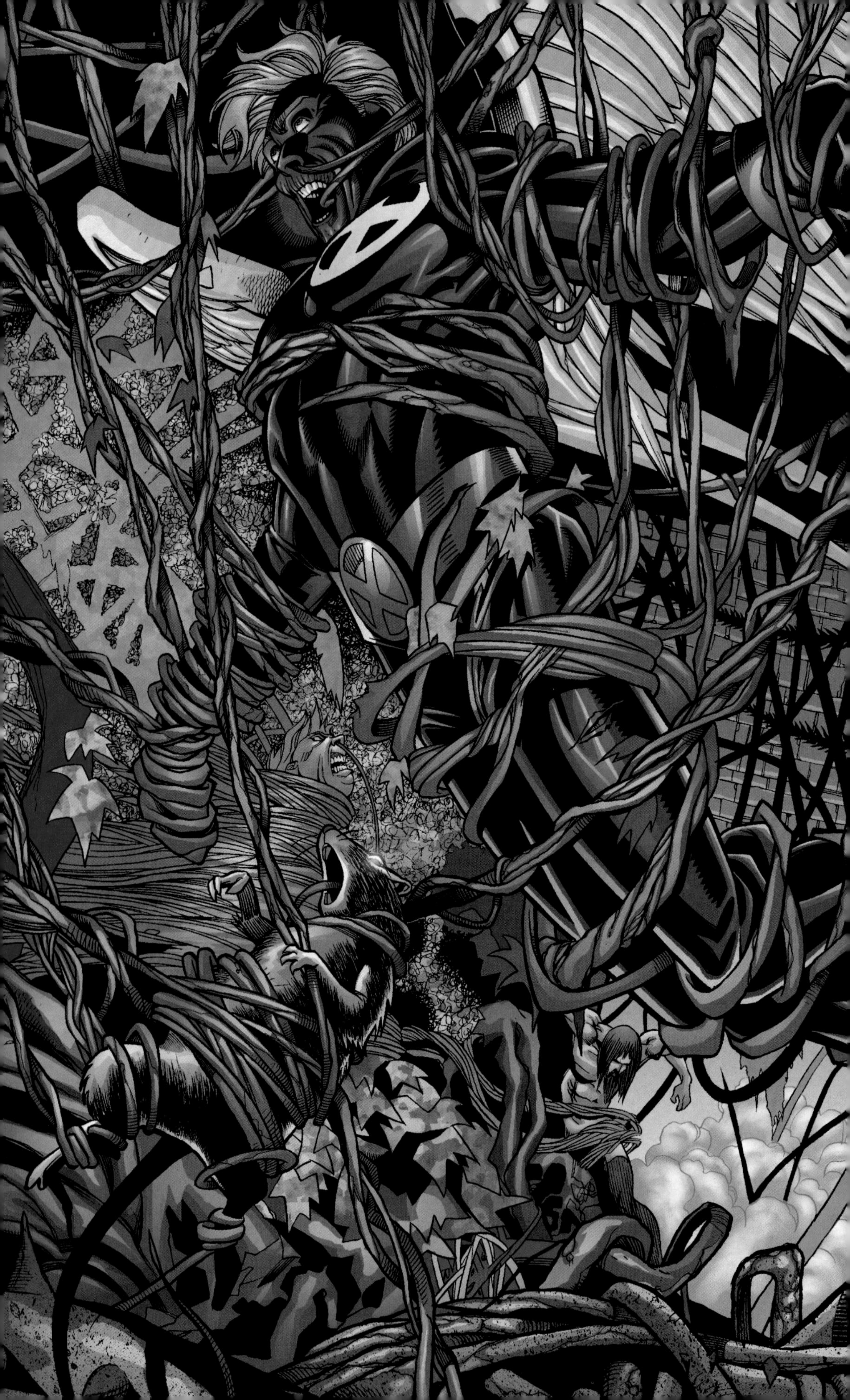

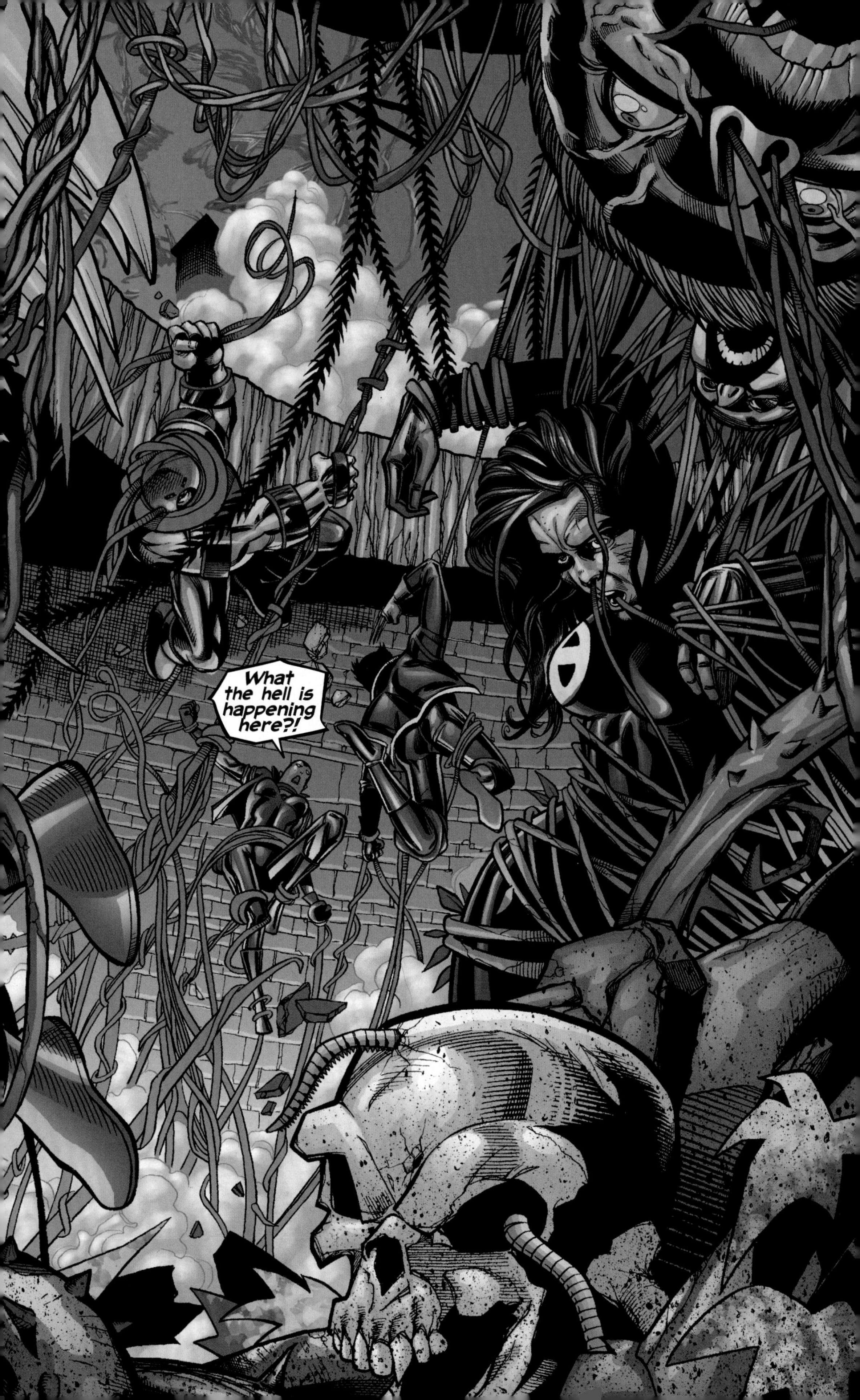
What the hell is happening here?!

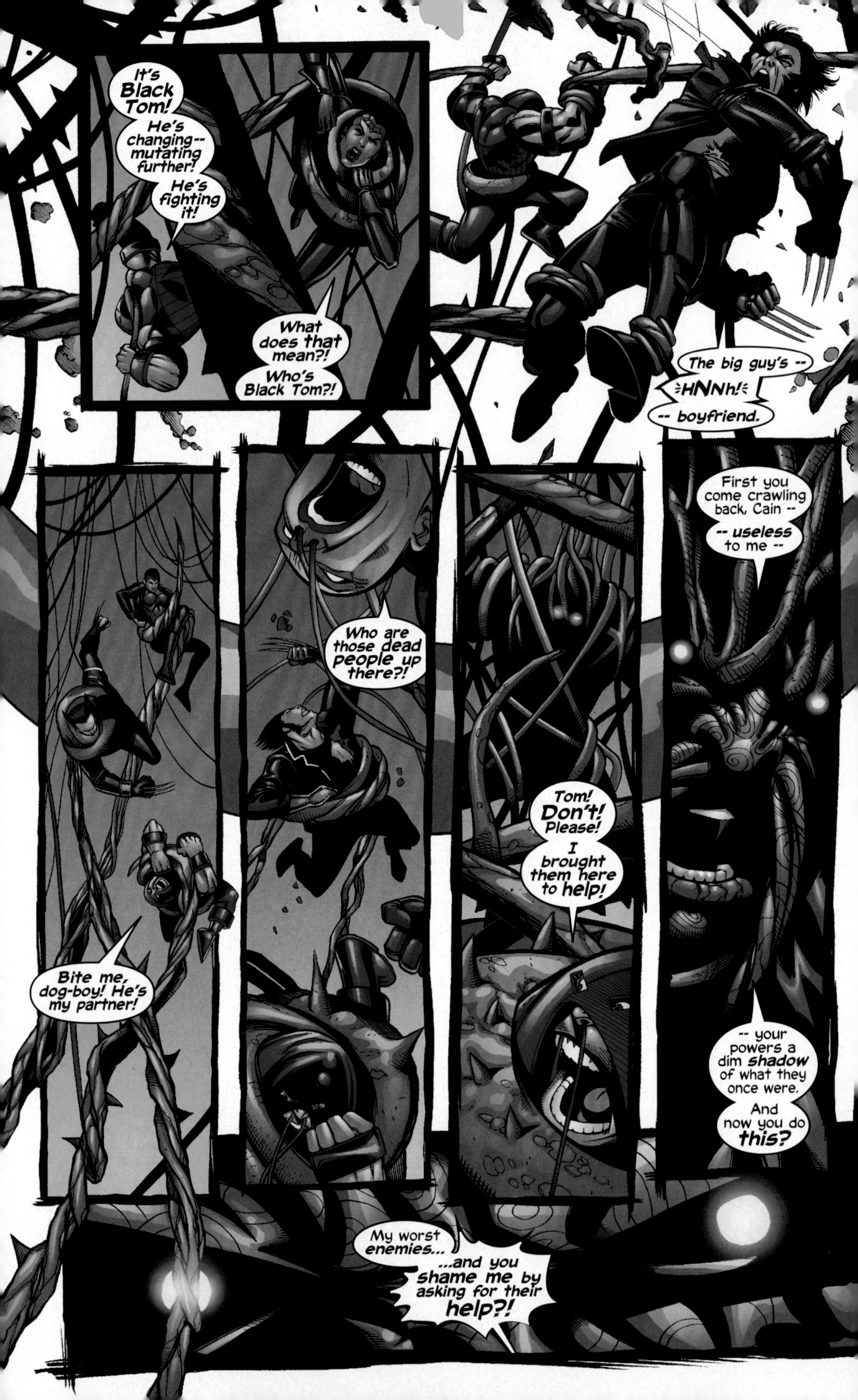
It's Black Tom!
He's changing-- mutating further!
He's fighting it!
What does that mean?!
Who's Black Tom?!
The big guy's --
HNNh!
-- boyfriend.
Bite me, dog-boy! He's my partner!
Who are those dead people up there?!
Tom! Don't! Please!
I brought them here to help!
First you come crawling back, Cain --
-- useless to me --
-- your powers a dim shadow of what they once were.
And now you do this?
My worst enemies...
...and you shame me by asking for their help?!

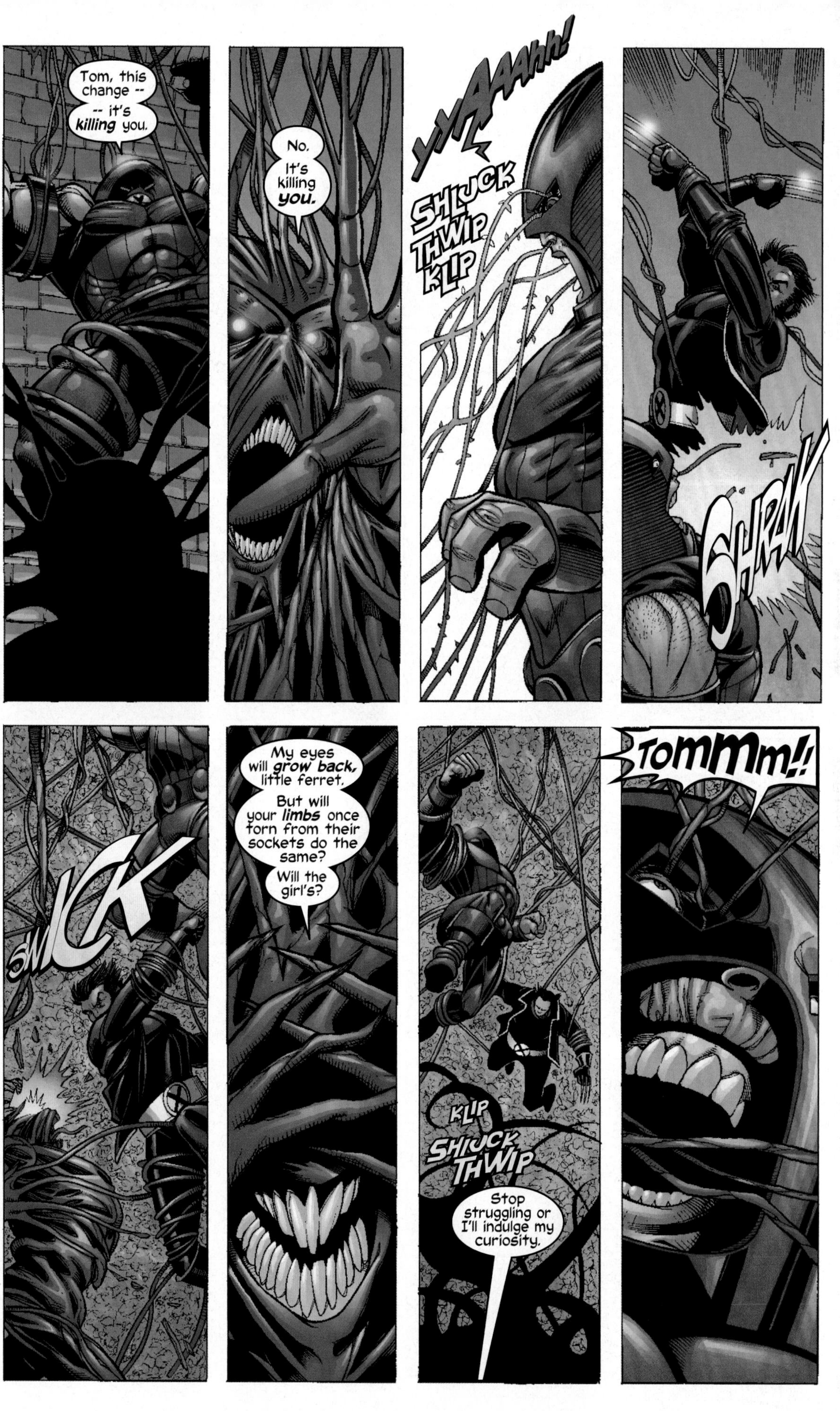
Tom, this change --
-- it's *killing* you.
No. It's killing *you.*
YYAAAAhh!
SHLUCK THWIP KLIP
SHRAK
SWICK
My eyes will *grow back,* little ferret.
But will your *limbs* once torn from their sockets do the same?
Will the girl's?
KLIP SHLUCK THWIP
Stop struggling or I'll indulge my curiosity.
TOMMm!!

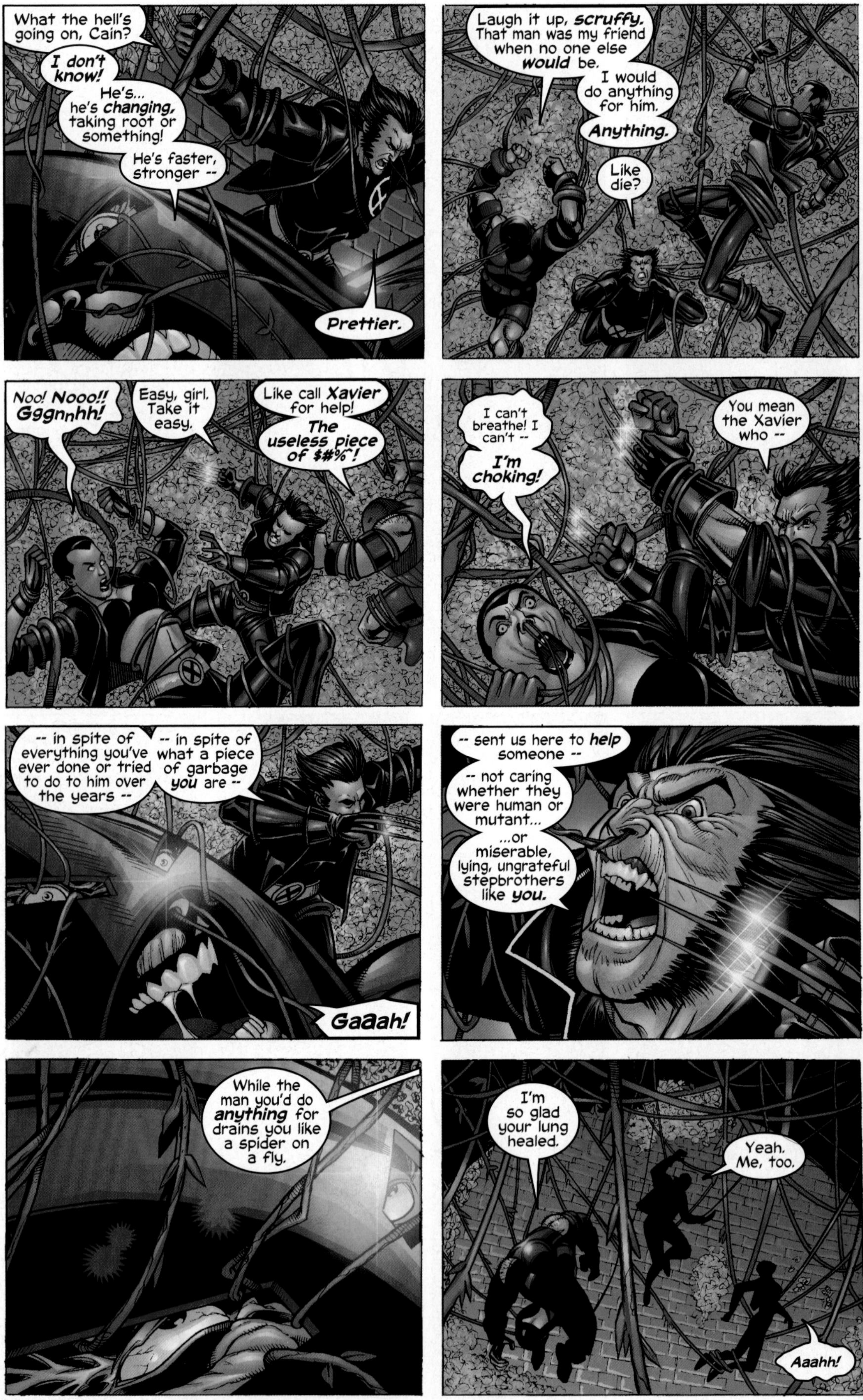

What the hell's going on, Cain?
I don't know!
He's... he's changing, taking root or something!
He's faster, stronger --
Prettier.
Laugh it up, scruffy. That man was my friend when no one else would be.
I would do anything for him.
Anything.
Like die?
Noo! Nooo!! Gggnnhh!
Easy, girl. Take it easy.
Like call Xavier for help!
The useless piece of $#%^!
I can't breathe! I can't --
I'm choking!
You mean the Xavier who --
-- in spite of everything you've ever done or tried to do to him over the years --
-- in spite of what a piece of garbage you are --
Gaaah!
-- sent us here to help someone --
-- not caring whether they were human or mutant...
...or miserable, lying, ungrateful stepbrothers like you.
While the man you'd do anything for drains you like a spider on a fly.
I'm so glad your lung healed.
Yeah. Me, too.
Aaahh!

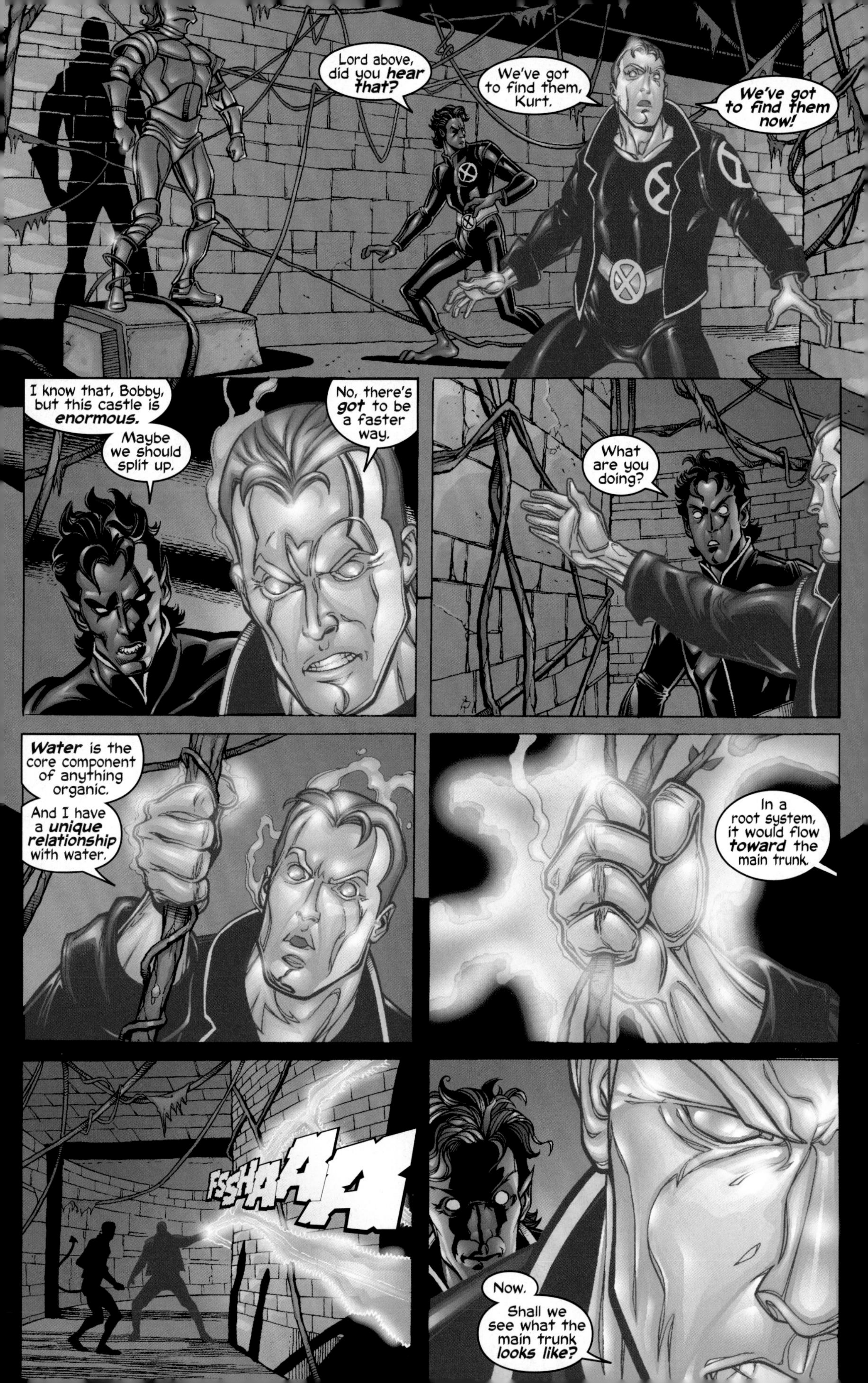

Lord above, did you **hear that?**
We've got to find them, Kurt.
We've got to find them now!
I know that, Bobby, but this castle is **enormous.**
Maybe we should split up.
No, there's **got** to be a faster way.
What are you doing?
Water is the core component of anything organic.
And I have a **unique relationship** with water.
In a root system, it would flow **toward** the main trunk.
FSSHAAAK
Now.
Shall we see what the main trunk **looks like?**

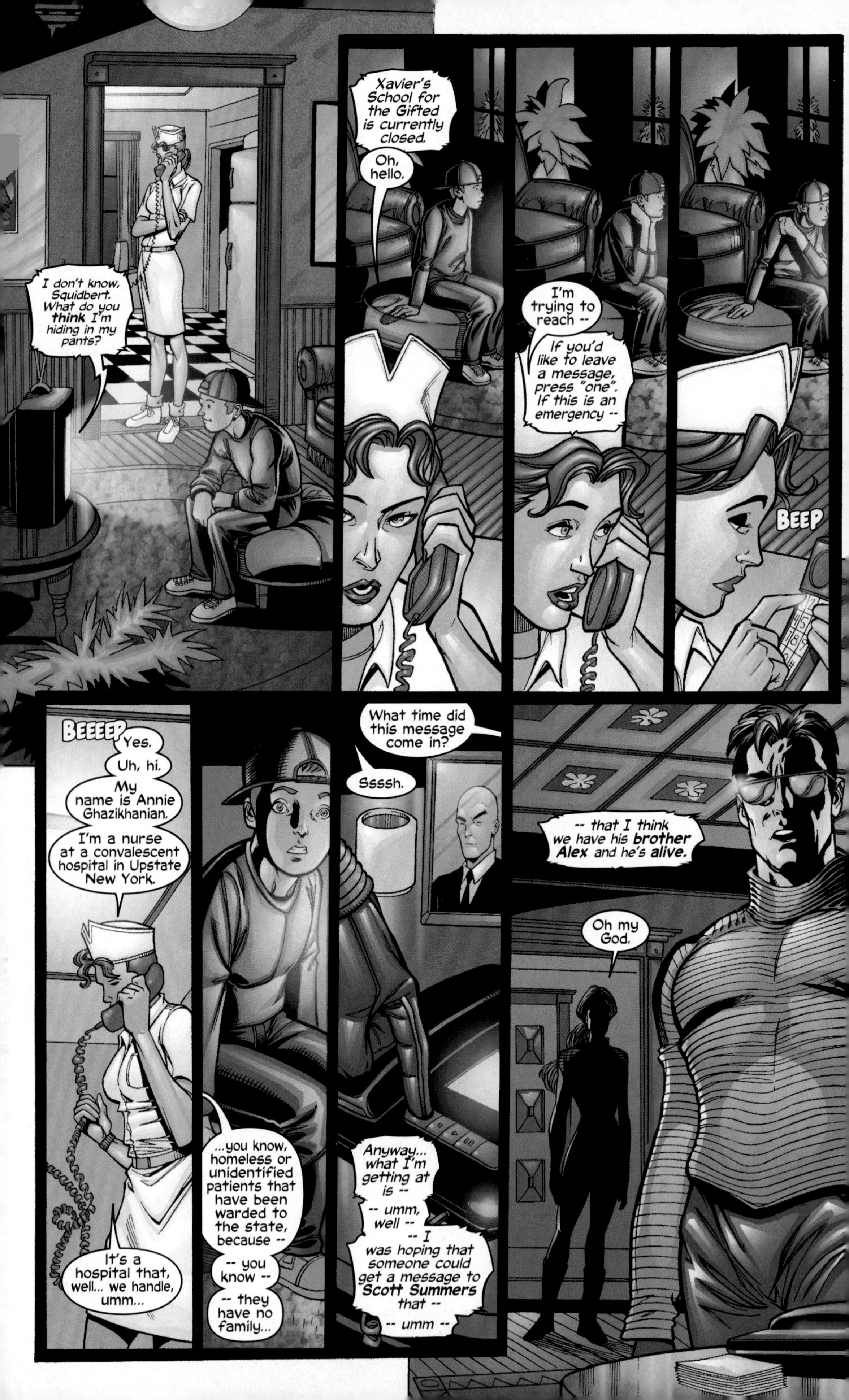

I don't know, Squidbert. What do you think I'm hiding in my pants?
Xavier's School for the Gifted is currently closed.
Oh, hello.
I'm trying to reach --
If you'd like to leave a message, press "one". If this is an emergency --
BEEP
BEEEEP
Yes.
Uh, hi.
My name is Annie Ghazikhanian.
I'm a nurse at a convalescent hospital in Upstate New York.
It's a hospital that, well... we handle, umm...
...you know, homeless or unidentified patients that have been warded to the state, because --
-- you know --
-- they have no family...
What time did this message come in?
Ssssh.
Anyway... what I'm getting at is --
-- umm, well --
-- I was hoping that someone could get a message to Scott Summers that --
-- umm --
-- that I think we have his brother Alex and he's alive.
Oh my God.

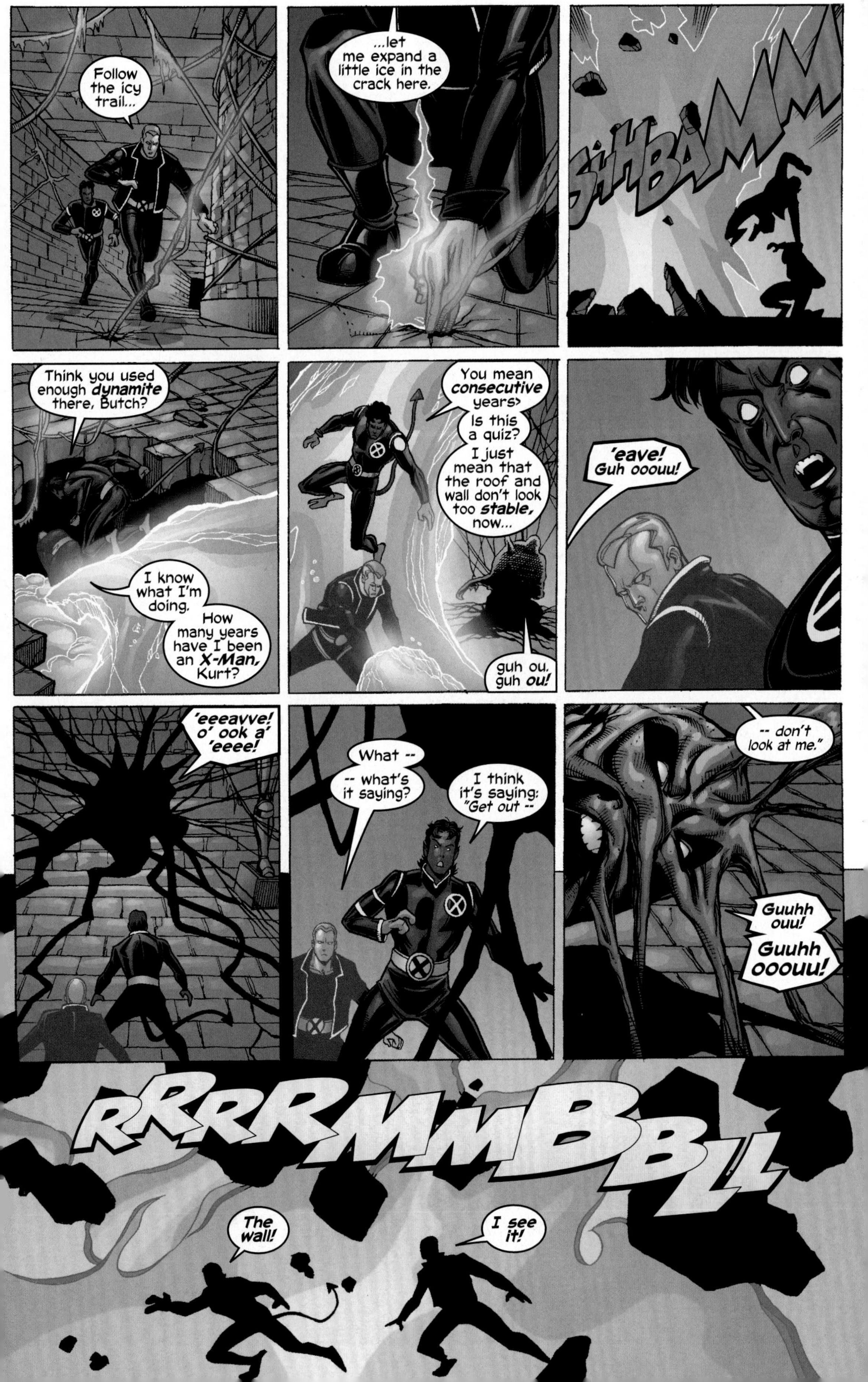
Follow the icy trail...
...let me expand a little ice in the crack here.
SHBAMM
Think you used enough dynamite there, Butch?
I know what I'm doing.
How many years have I been an X-Man, Kurt?
You mean consecutive years?
Is this a quiz?
I just mean that the roof and wall don't look too stable, now...
guh ou, guh ou!
'eave! Guh ooouu!
'eeeavve! o' ook a' 'eeee!
What --
-- what's it saying?
I think it's saying: "Get out --
-- don't look at me."
Guuhh ouu!
Guuhh ooouu!
RRRRMMMBBLL
The wall!
I see it!

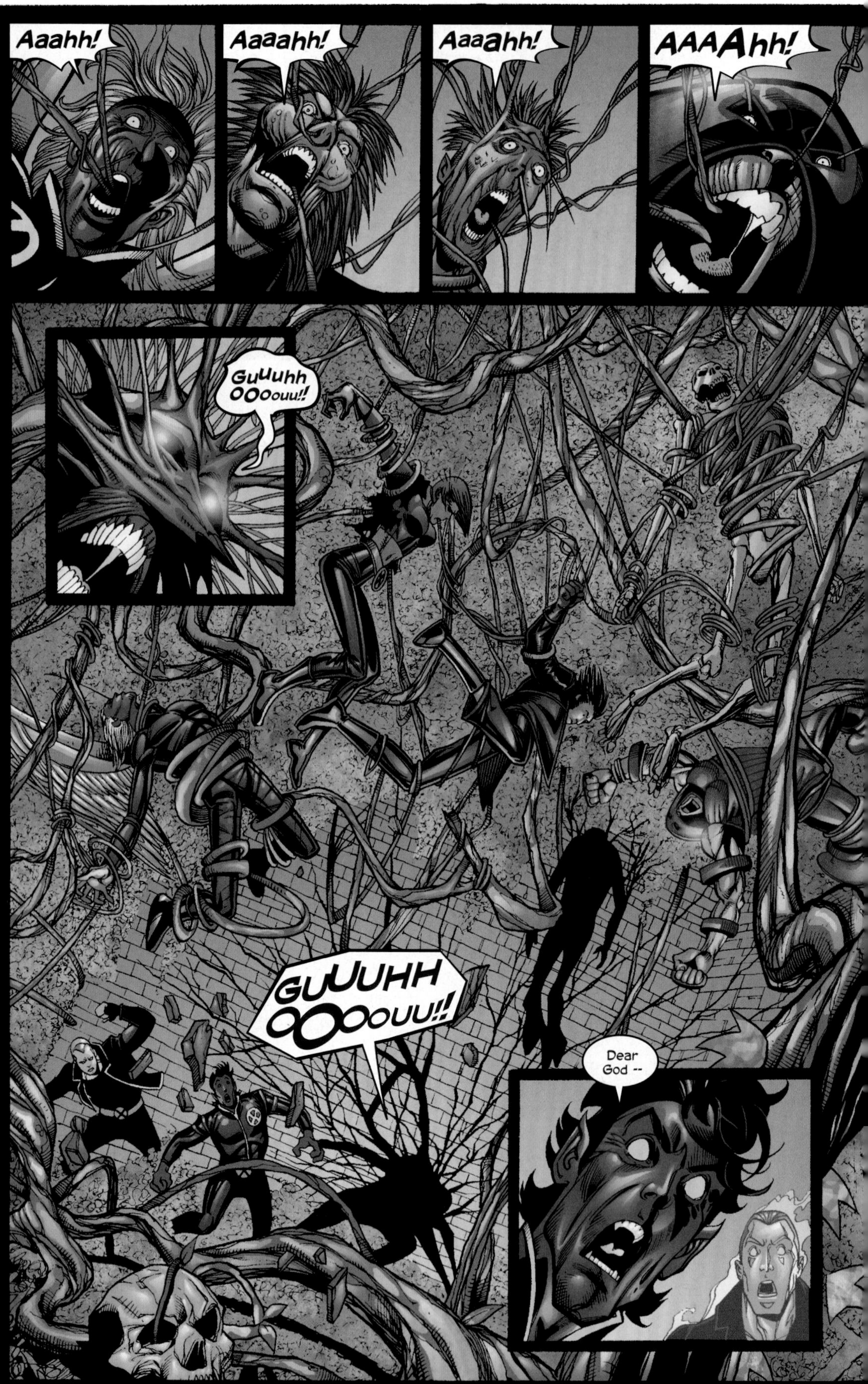
Aaahh!
Aaaahh!
Aaaahh!
AAAAhh!
Guuuhh
OOOouu!!
GUUUHH
OOOOOUU!!
Dear
God --

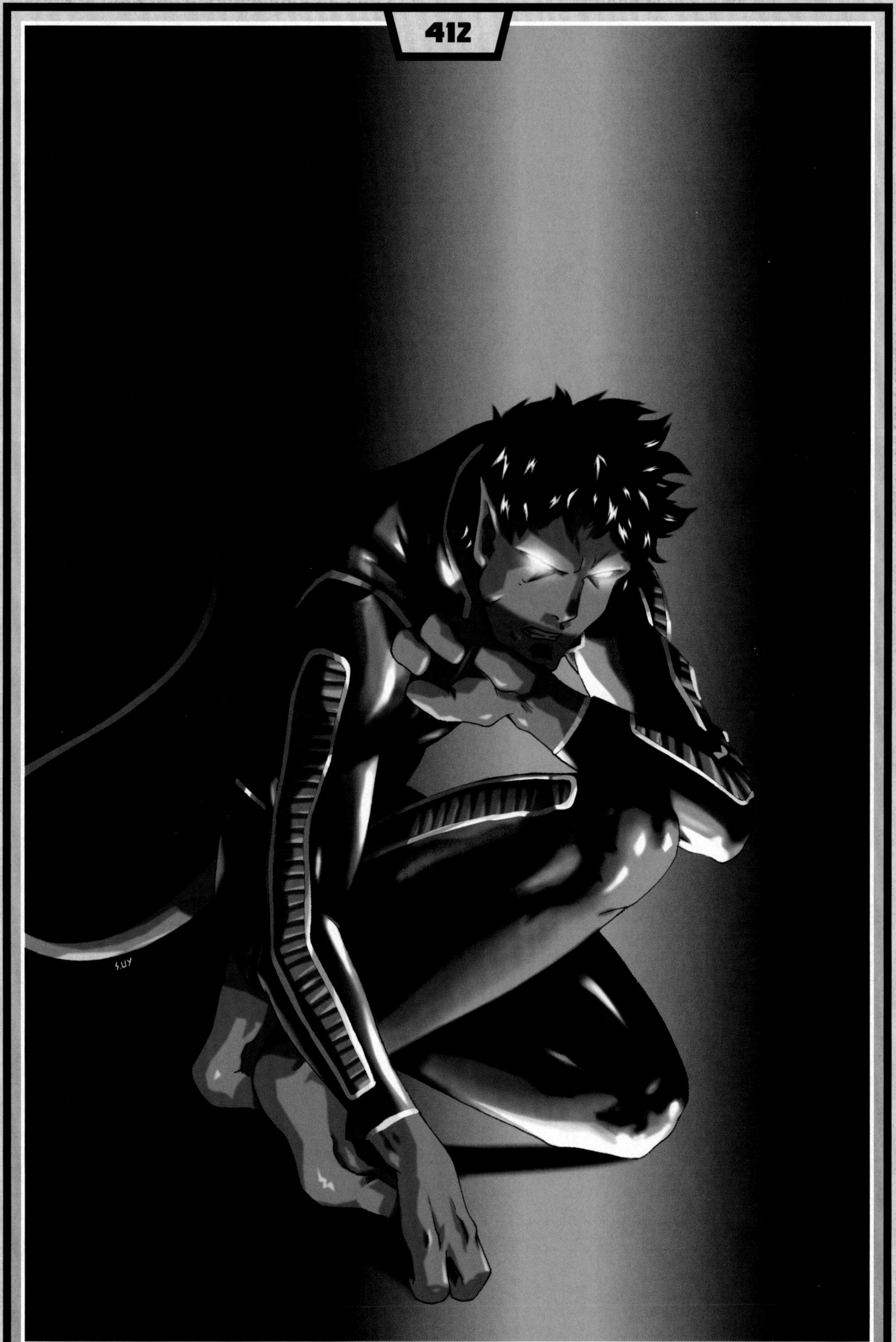
412

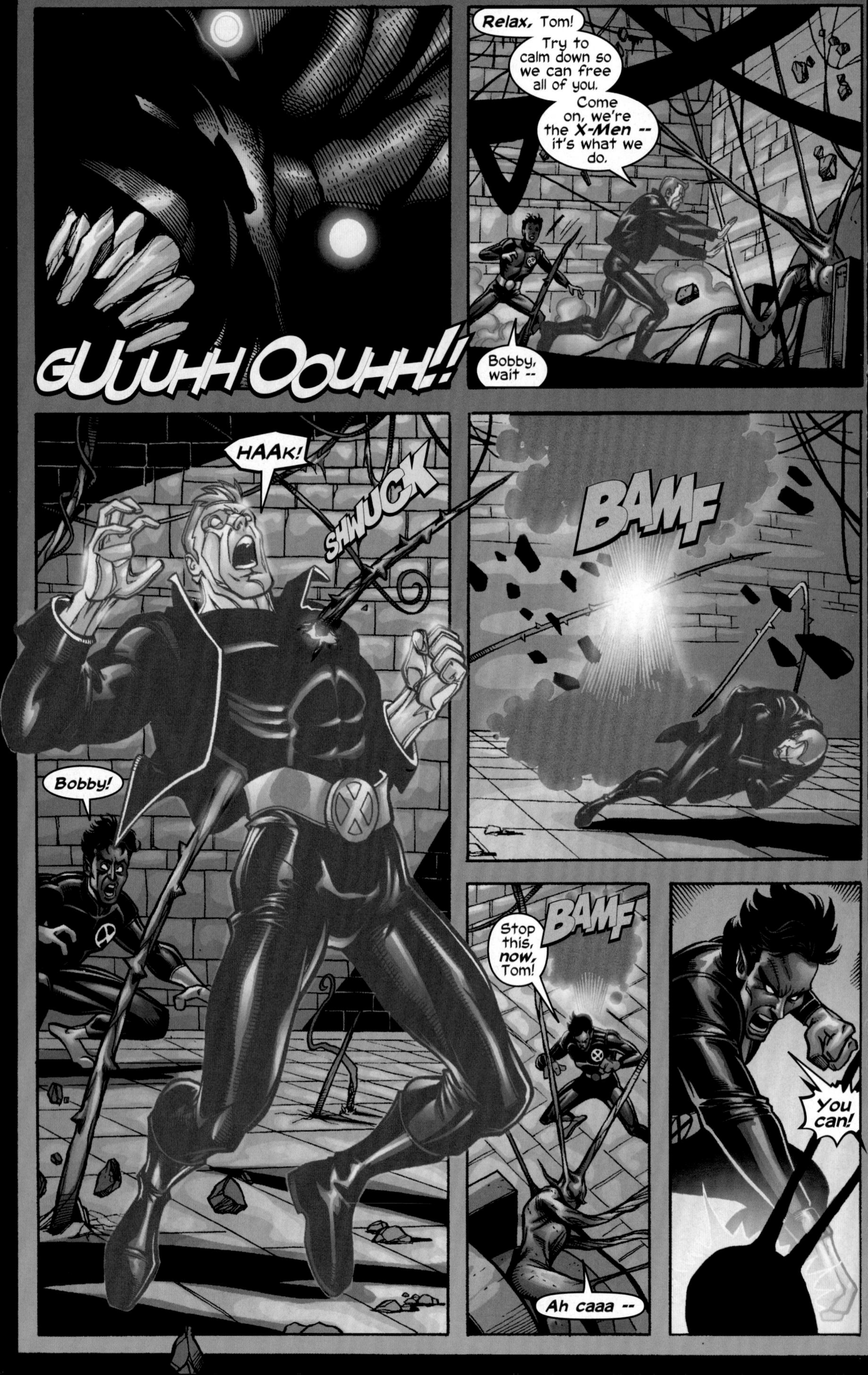
GUUUHH OOUHH!!
Relax, Tom!
Try to calm down so we can free all of you.
Come on, we're the X-Men -- it's what we do.
Bobby, wait --
HAAK!
SHWUCK
Bobby!
BAMF
BAMF
Stop this, now, Tom!
Ah caaa --
You can!

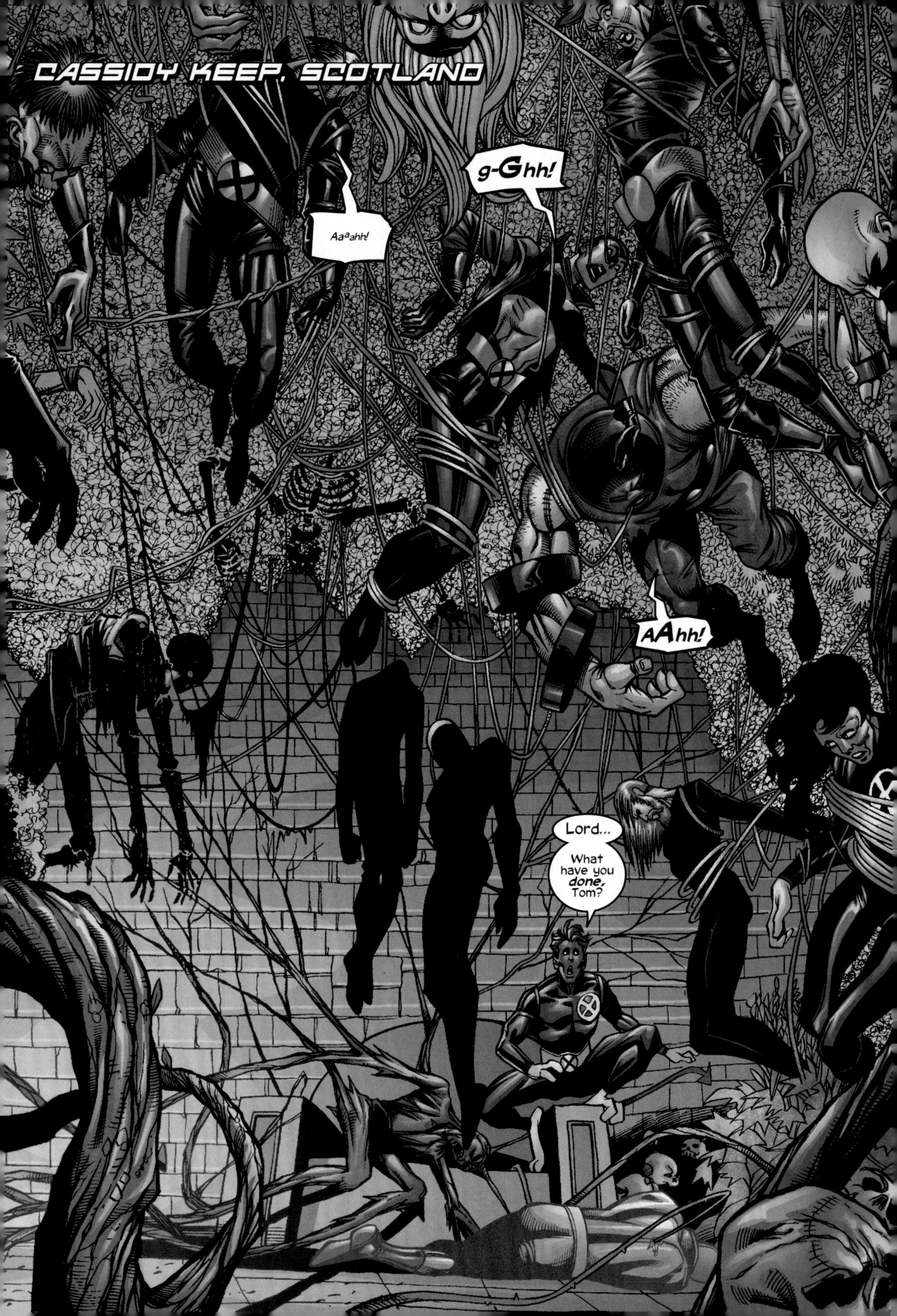
CASSIDY KEEP, SCOTLAND
Aaaahh!
g-Ghh!
AAhh!
Lord...
What have you done, Tom?

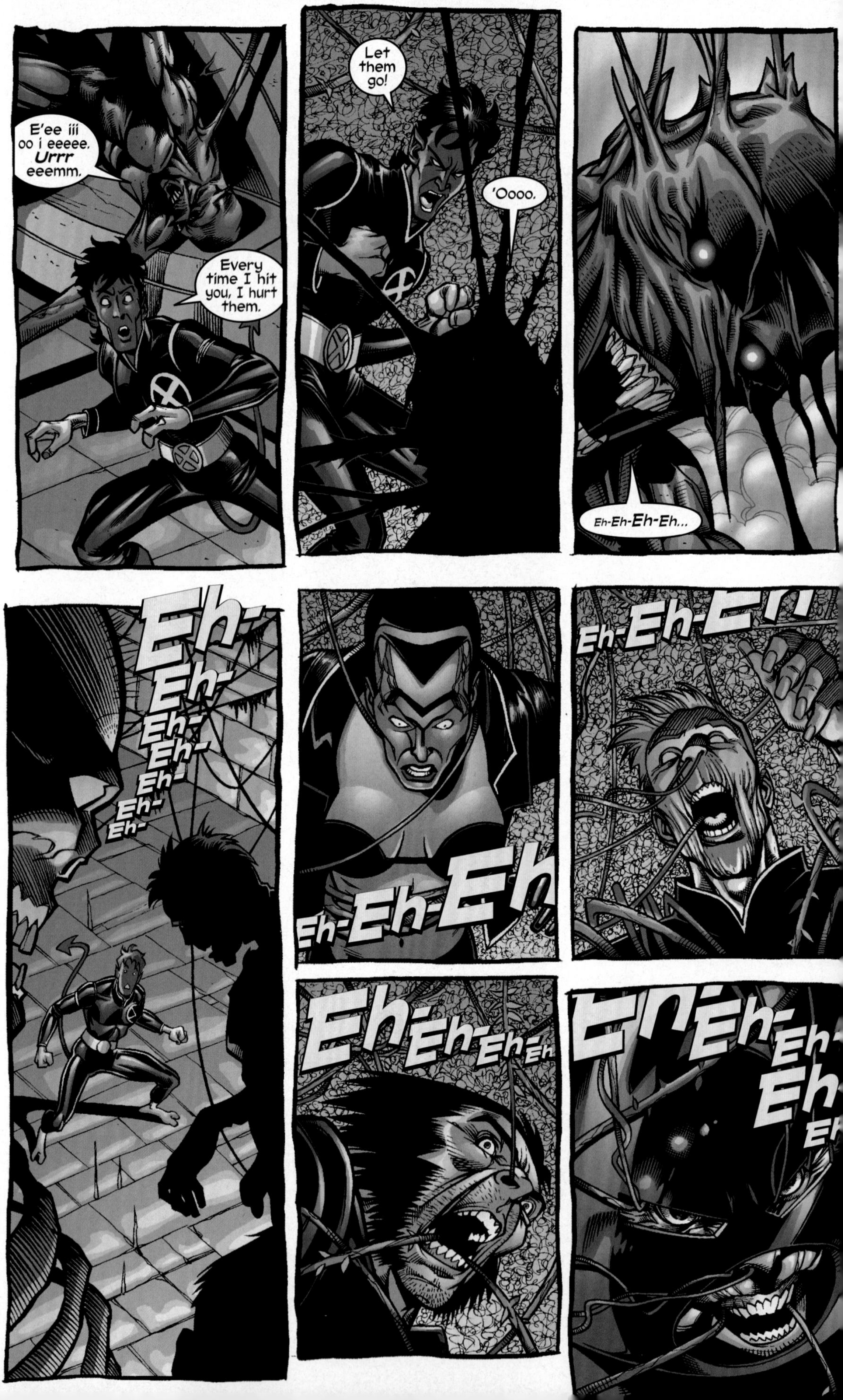

E'ee iii oo i eeeee. Urrr eeemm.
Every time I hit you, I hurt them.
Let them go!
'Oooo.
Eh-Eh-Eh-Eh...
Eh-Eh-Eh-Eh-Eh-Eh-Eh-
Eh-Eh-Eh
Eh-Eh-
Eh-Eh-Eh-Eh
Eh-Eh-

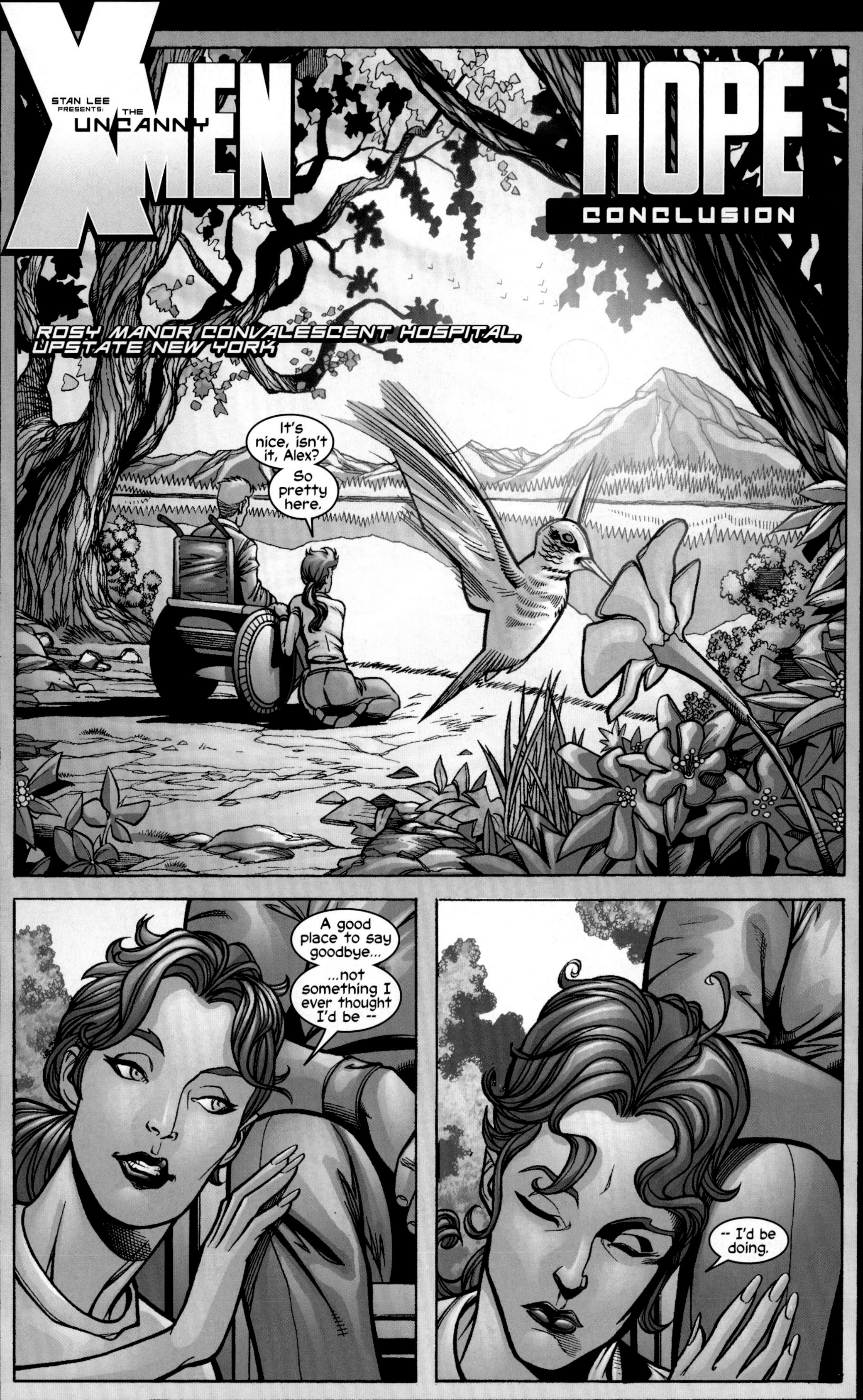
STAN LEE PRESENTS: THE UNCANNY X-MEN
HOPE
CONCLUSION
ROSY MANOR CONVALESCENT HOSPITAL, UPSTATE NEW YORK
It's nice, isn't it, Alex?
So pretty here.
A good place to say goodbye...
...not something I ever thought I'd be --
-- I'd be doing.

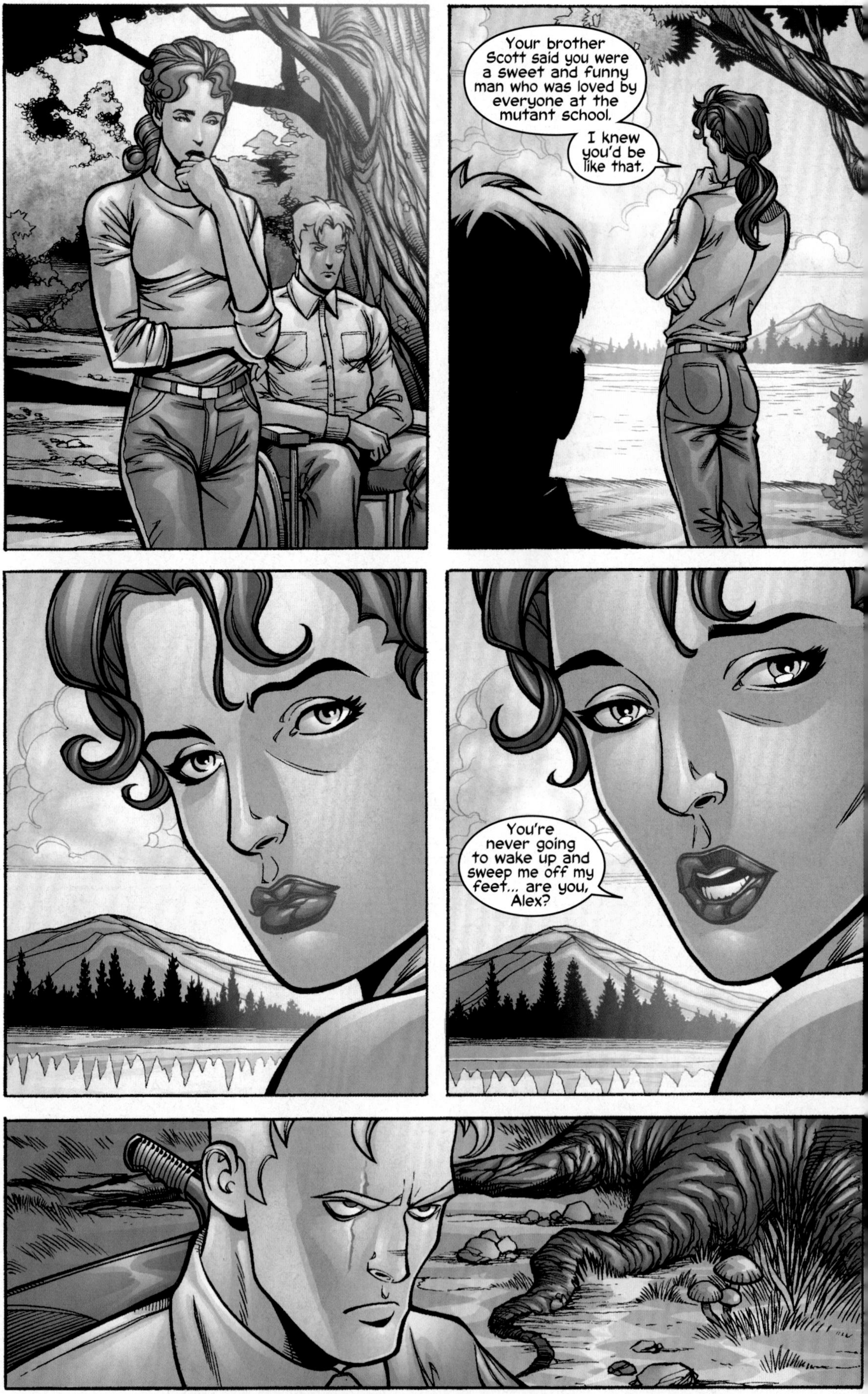

Your brother Scott said you were a sweet and funny man who was loved by everyone at the mutant school.
I knew you'd be like that.
You're never going to wake up and sweep me off my feet... are you, Alex?

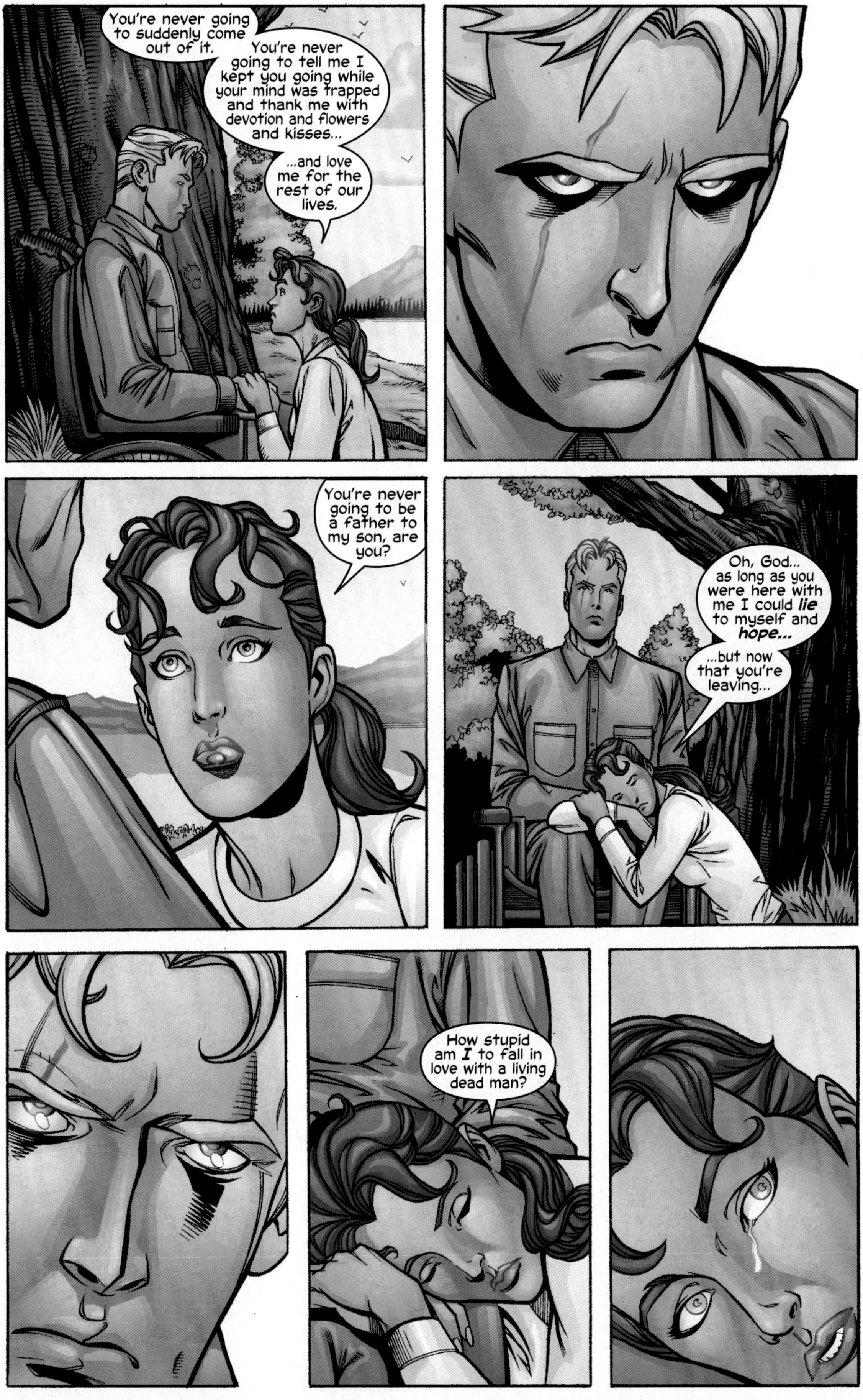
You're never going to suddenly come out of it.
You're never going to tell me I kept you going while your mind was trapped and thank me with devotion and flowers and kisses...
...and love me for the rest of our lives.
You're never going to be a father to my son, are you?
Oh, God... as long as you were here with me I could *lie* to myself and ***hope...***
...but now that you're leaving...
How stupid am ***I*** to fall in love with a living dead man?

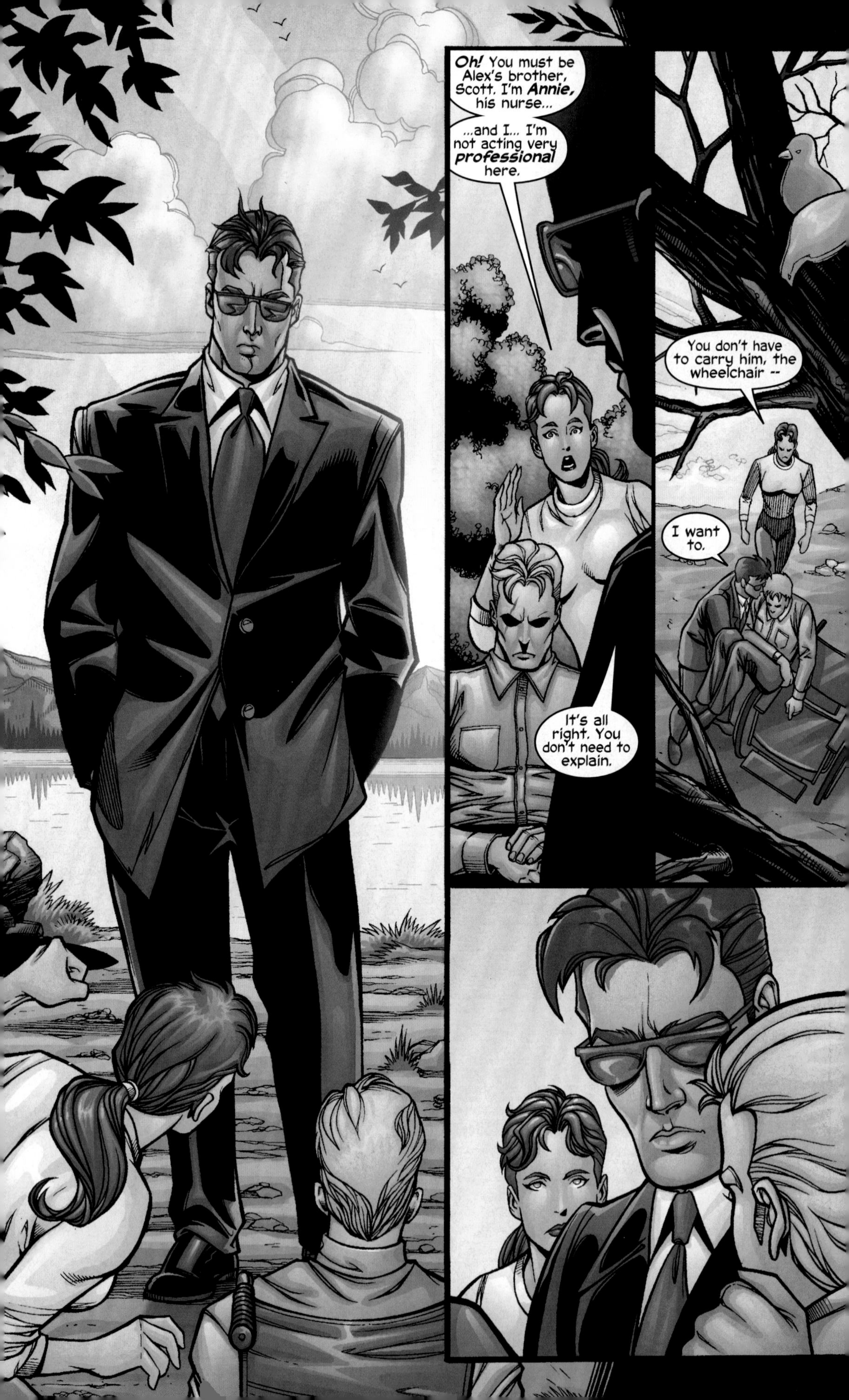
Oh! You must be Alex's brother, Scott. I'm Annie, his nurse...
...and I... I'm not acting very professional here.
It's all right. You don't need to explain.
You don't have to carry him, the wheelchair --
I want to.

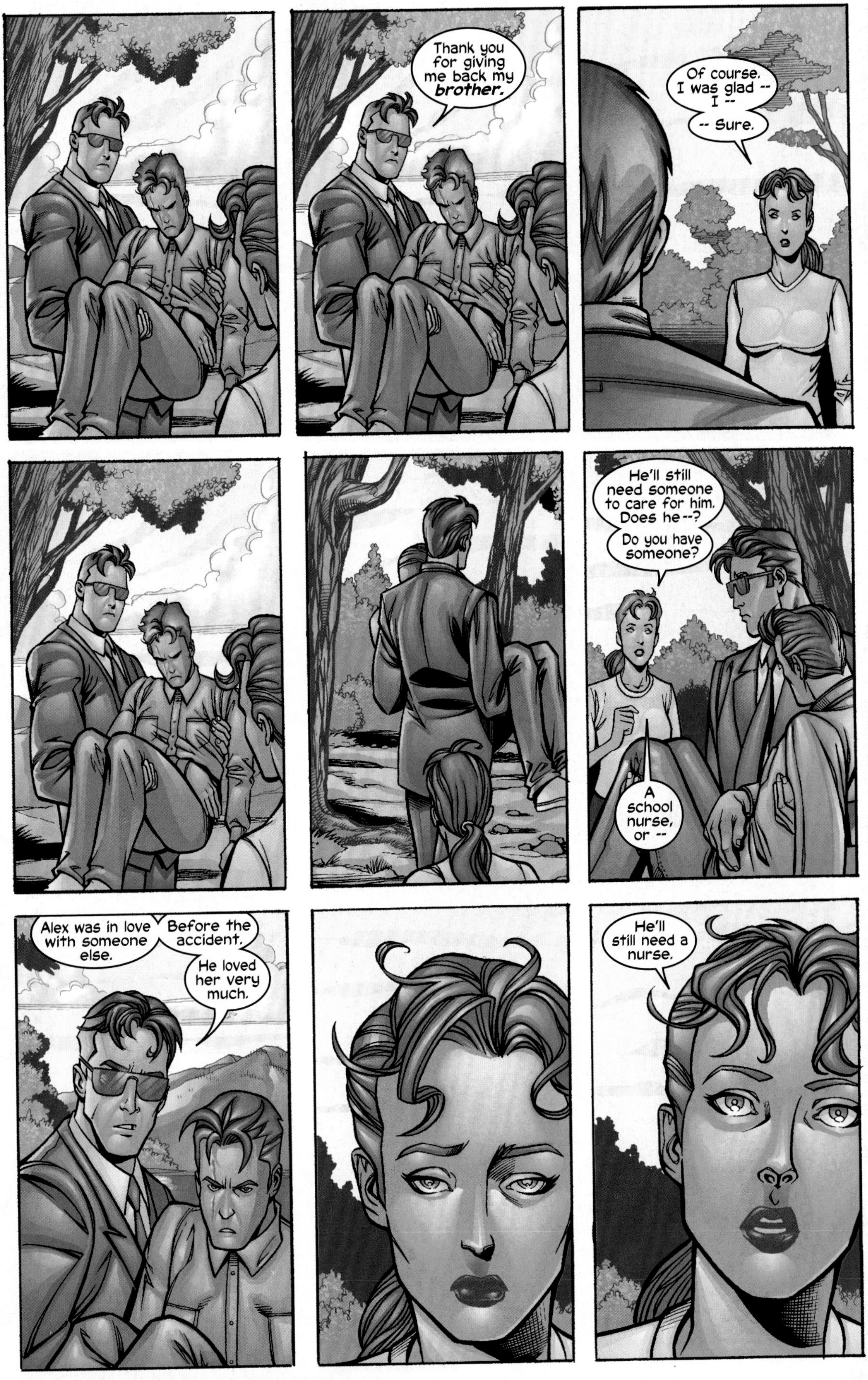
Thank you for giving me back my **brother.**
Of course. I was glad -- I --
-- Sure.
He'll still need someone to care for him. Does he --?
Do you have someone?
A school nurse, or --
Alex was in love with someone else.
Before the accident.
He loved her very much.
He'll still need a nurse.

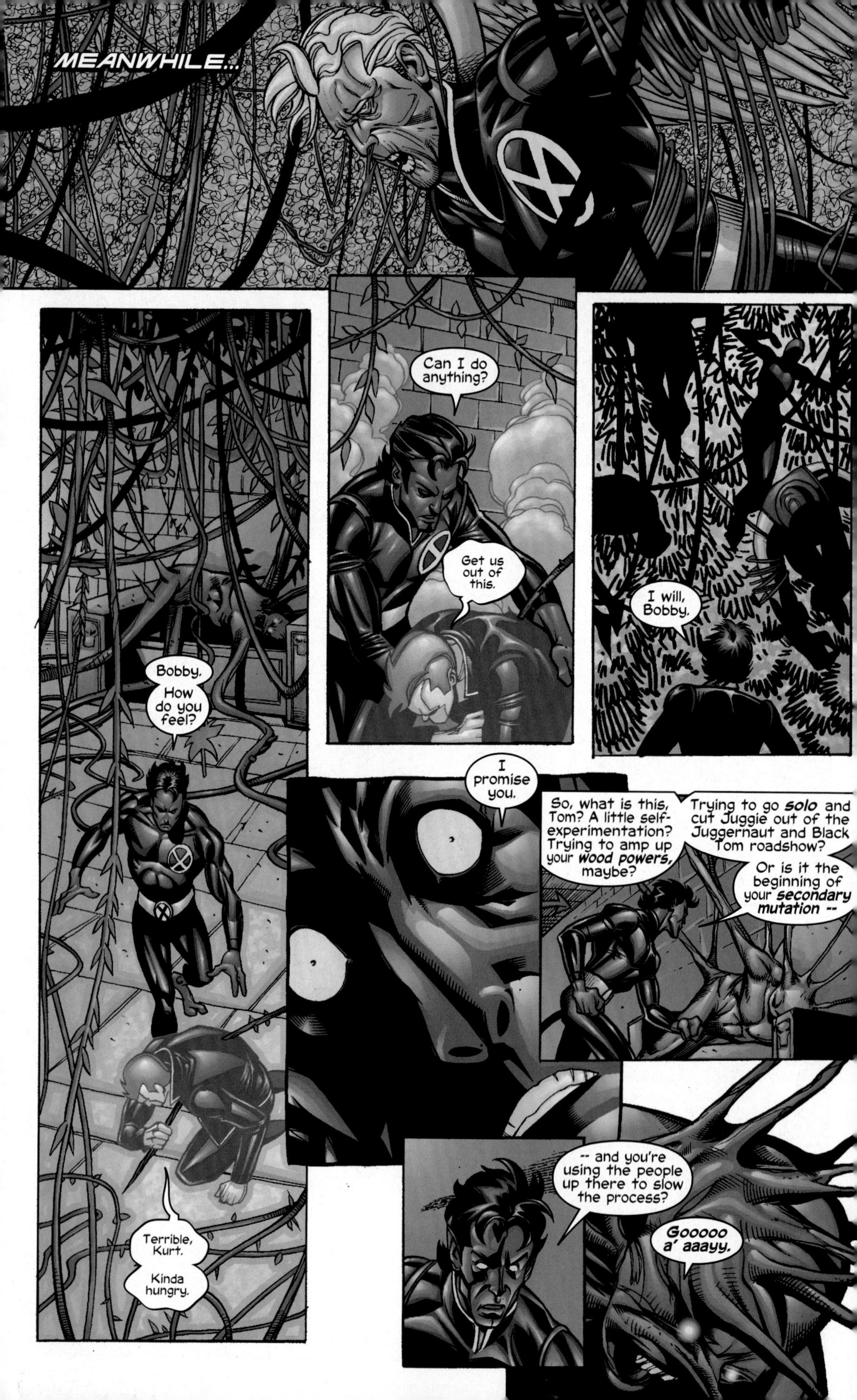
MEANWHILE...
Bobby. How do you feel?
Terrible, Kurt.
Kinda hungry.
Can I do anything?
Get us out of this.
I will, Bobby.
I promise you.
So, what is this, Tom? A little self-experimentation? Trying to amp up your wood powers, maybe?
Trying to go solo and cut Juggie out of the Juggernaut and Black Tom roadshow?
Or is it the beginning of your secondary mutation --
-- and you're using the people up there to slow the process?
Gooooo a' aaayy.

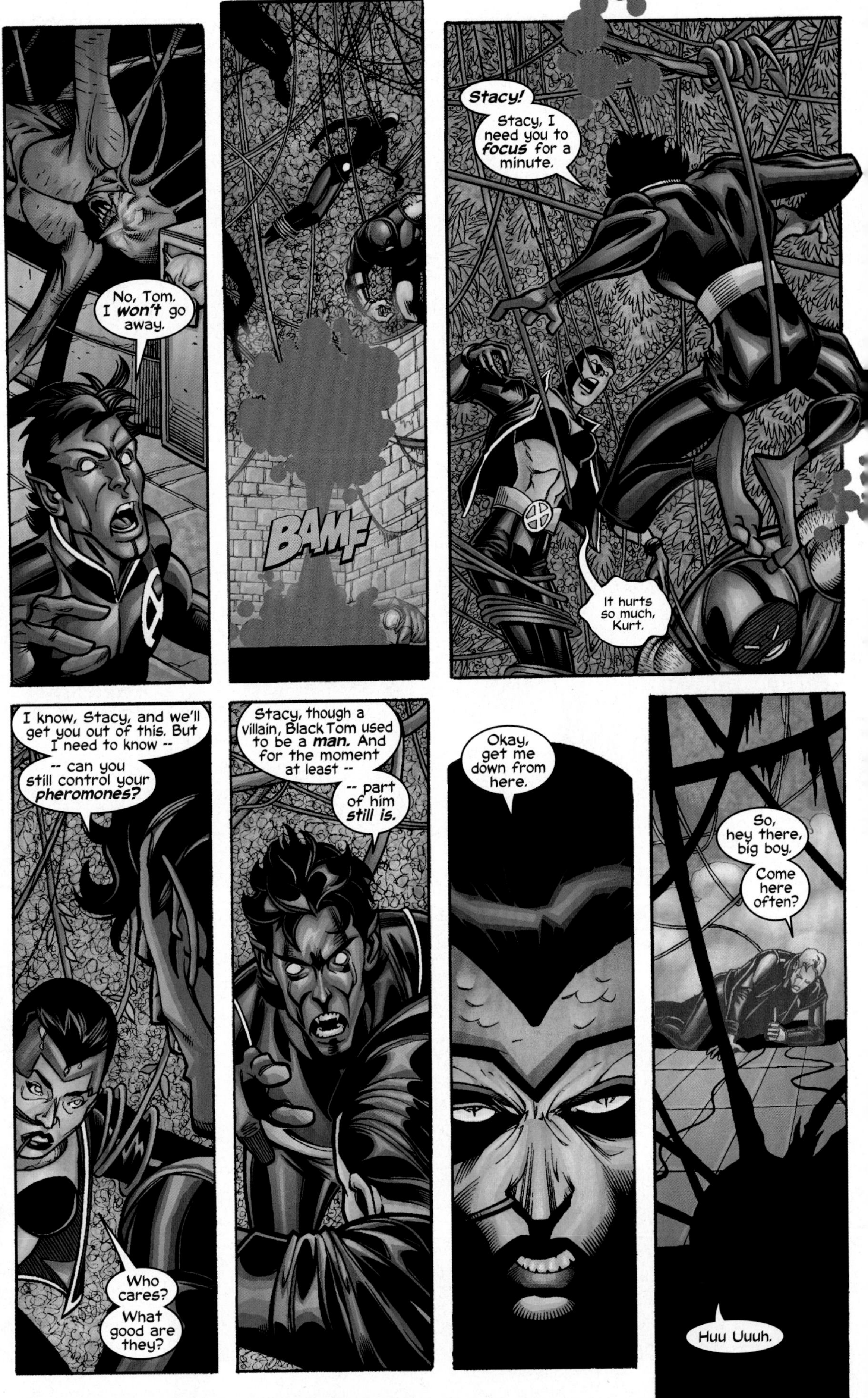
No, Tom. I *won't* go away.
BAMF
Stacy!
Stacy, I need you to *focus* for a minute.
It hurts so much, Kurt.
I know, Stacy, and we'll get you out of this. But I need to know --
-- can you still control your *pheromones?*
Who cares? What good are they?
Stacy, though a villain, Black Tom used to be a *man.* And for the moment at least --
-- part of him *still is.*
Okay, get me down from here.
So, hey there, big boy.
Come here often?
Huu Uuuh.

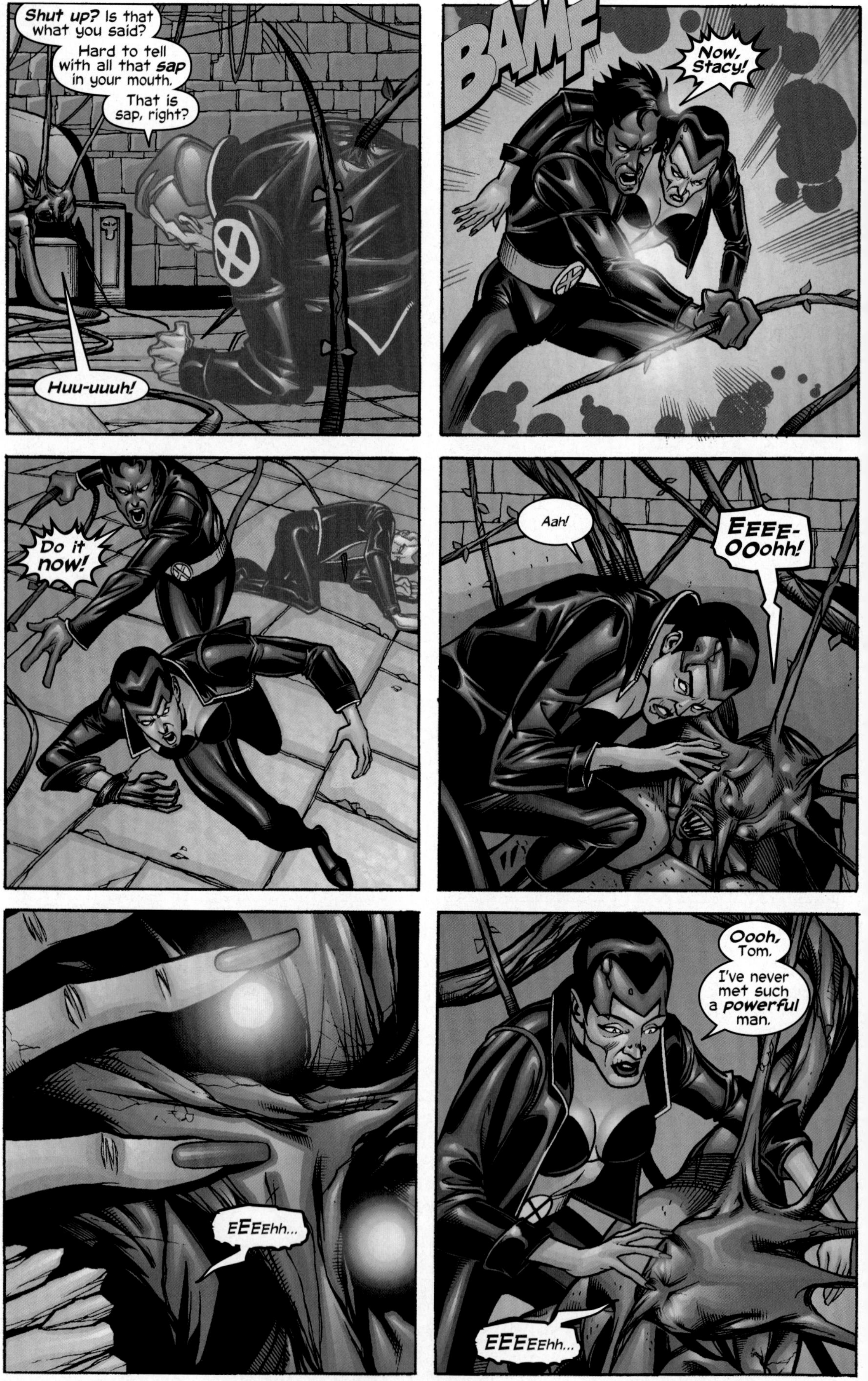

Shut up? Is that what you said?
Hard to tell with all that sap in your mouth.
That is sap, right?
Huu-uuuh!
BAMF
Now, Stacy!
Do it now!
Aah!
EEEE-OOohh!
EEEehh...
Oooh, Tom.
I've never met such a powerful man.
EEEEehh...

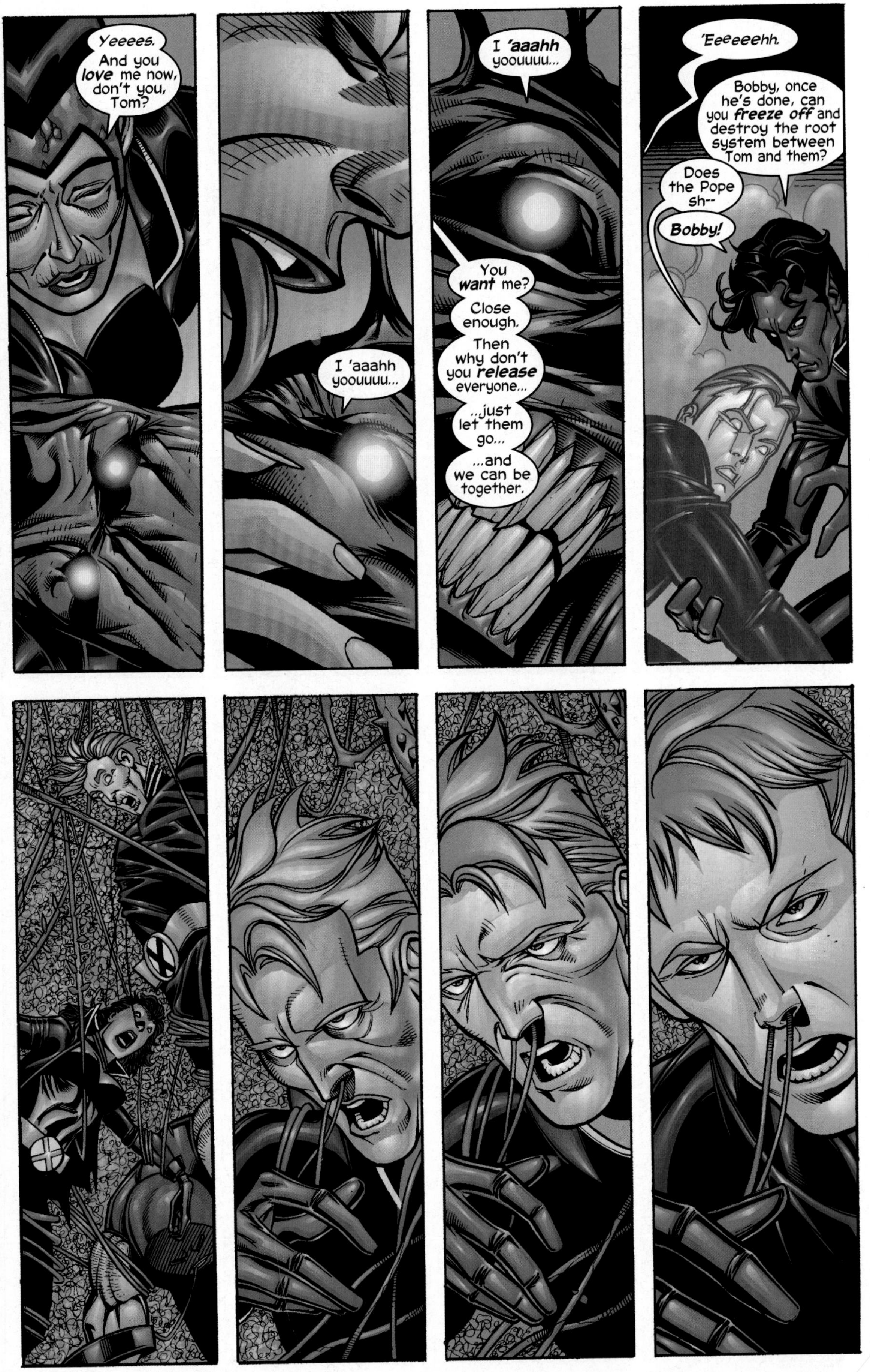
Yeeees.
And you love me now, don't you, Tom?
I 'aaahh yoouuuu...
I 'aaahh yoouuuu...
You want me?
Close enough.
Then why don't you release everyone...
...just let them go...
...and we can be together.
'Eeeeeehh.
Bobby, once he's done, can you freeze off and destroy the root system between Tom and them?
Does the Pope sh--
Bobby!

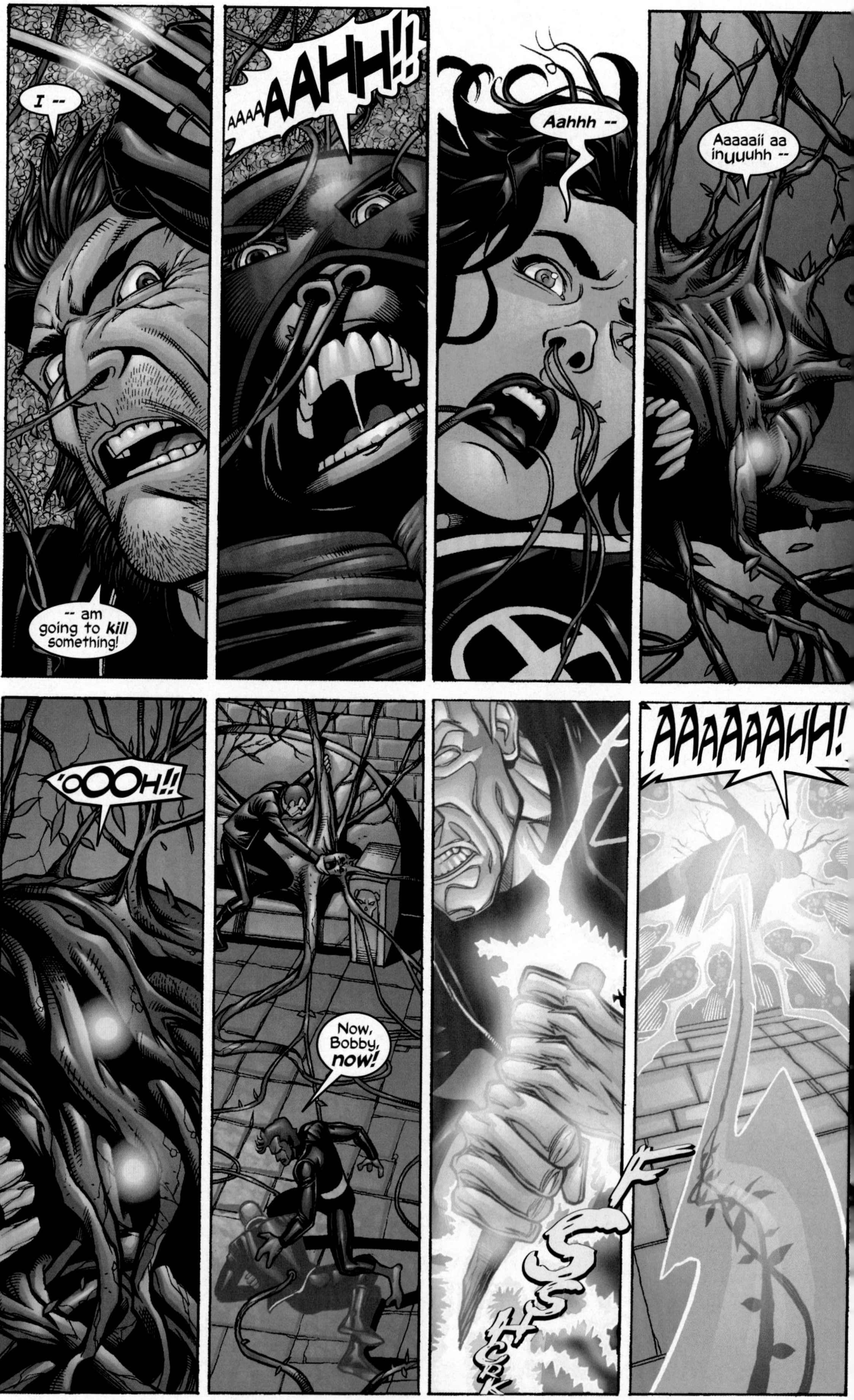

I --
-- am going to **kill** something!
AAAAAAHH!!
Aahhh --
Aaaaaii aa inyuuhh --
'OOOH!!
Now, Bobby, **now!**
SSHCRK
AAAAAAHH!

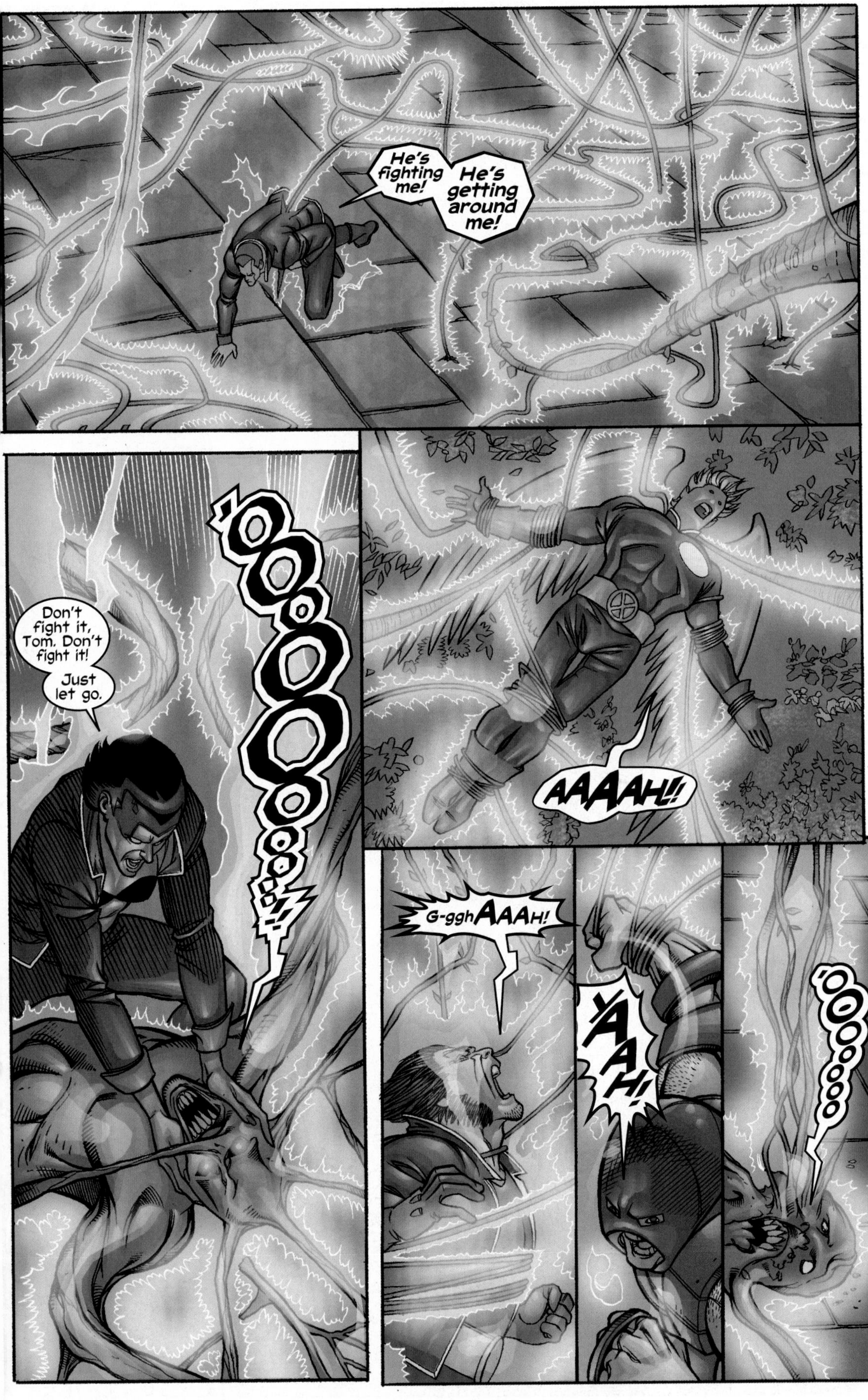
He's fighting me!
He's getting around me!
Don't fight it, Tom. Don't fight it!
Just let go.
'OOOOOOOOOOO!!
AAAAH!!
G-gghAAAH!
YAAH!
'OOOOOOOO

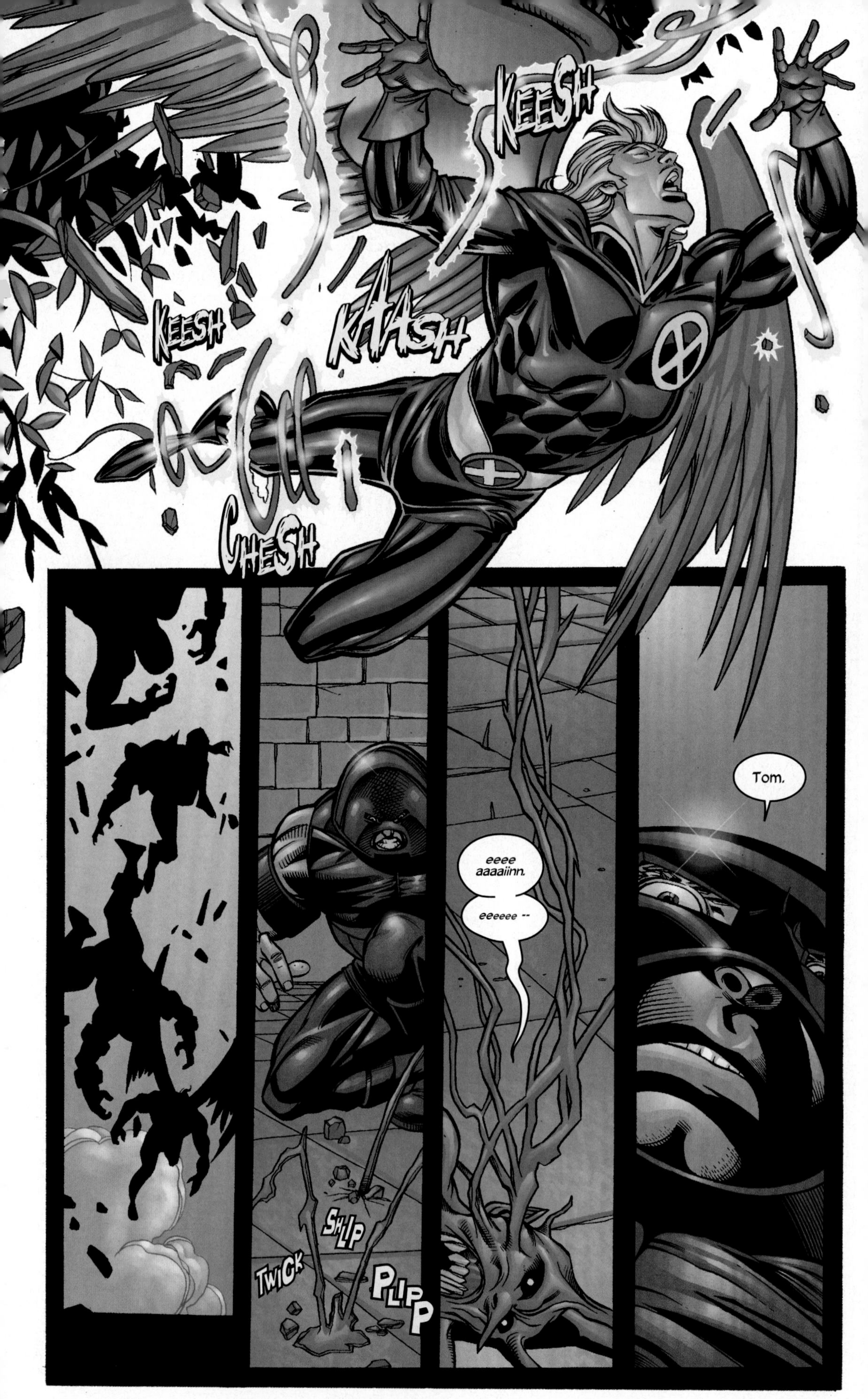

KEESH
KEESH
KAASH
CHESH
TWICK
SHLIP
PLIPP
eeee aaaaiinn.
eeeee --
Tom.

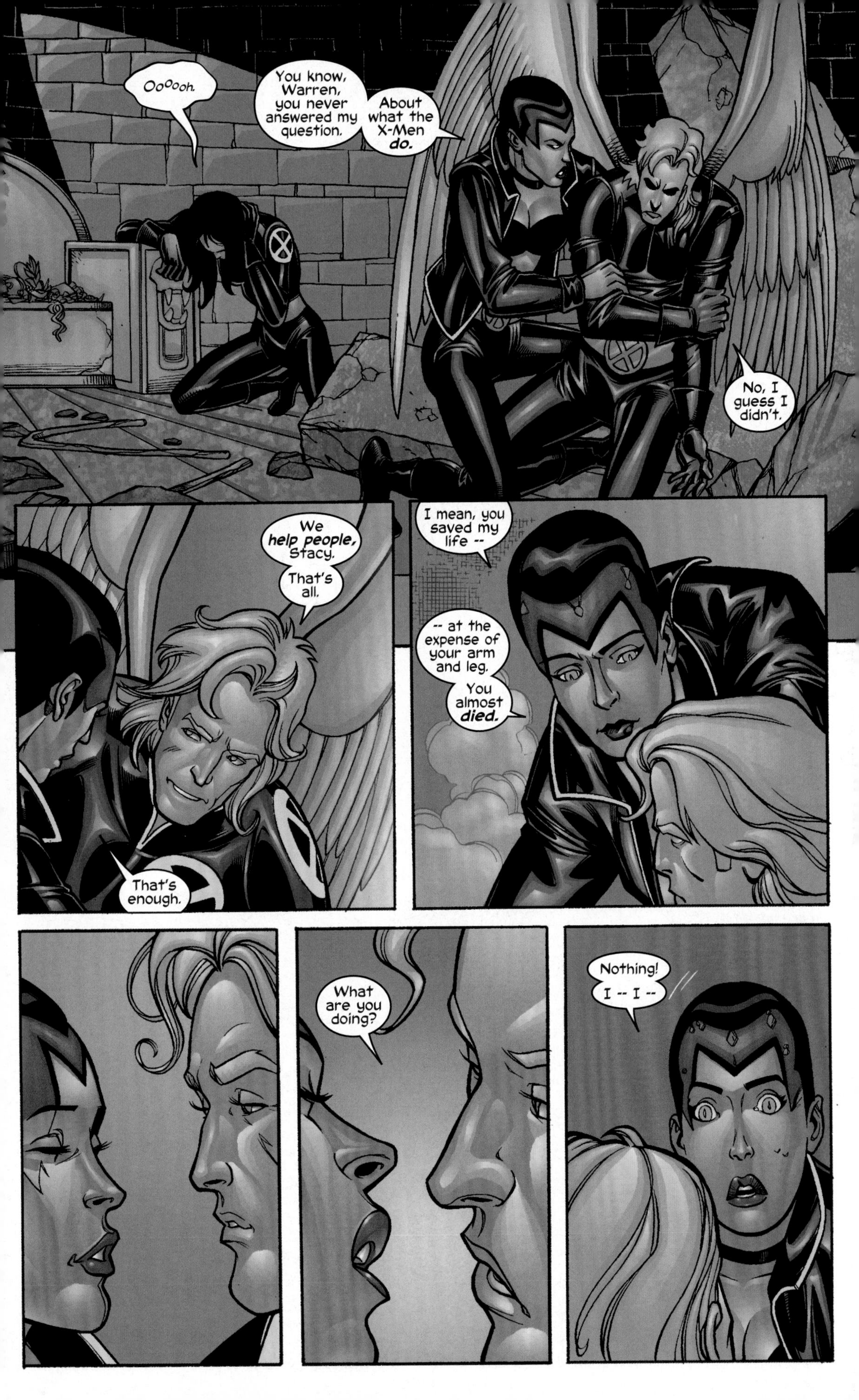

Ooooooh.
You know, Warren, you never answered my question.
About what the X-Men do.
No, I guess I didn't.
We help people, Stacy.
That's all.
That's enough.
I mean, you saved my life --
-- at the expense of your arm and leg.
You almost died.
What are you doing?
Nothing!
I -- I --

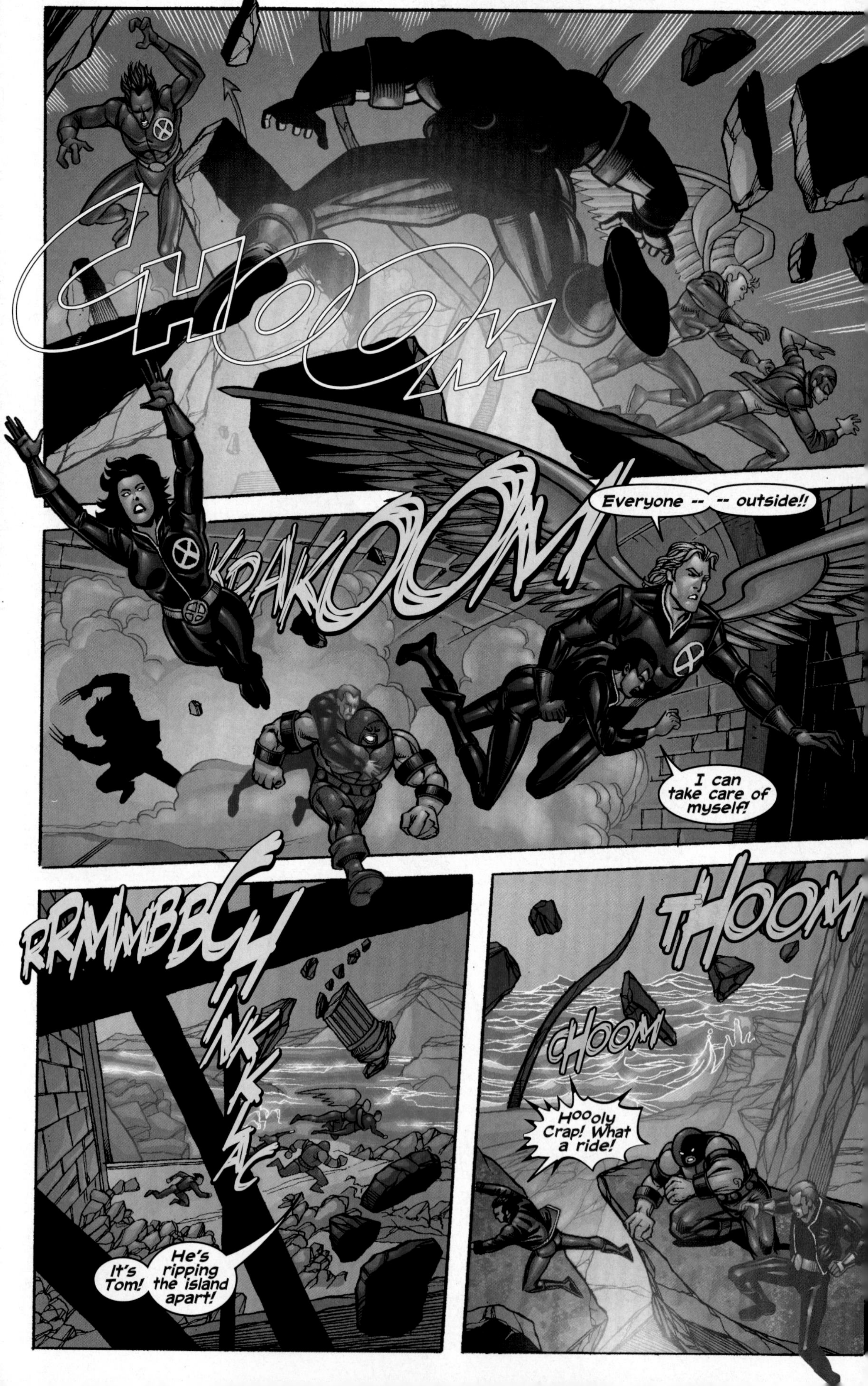
CHOOOOM
KRAKOOM
Everyone -- -- outside!!
I can take care of myself!
RRMMBBCH
INKKLAK
It's Tom!
He's ripping the island apart!
THOOM
CHOOM
Hoooly Crap! What a ride!

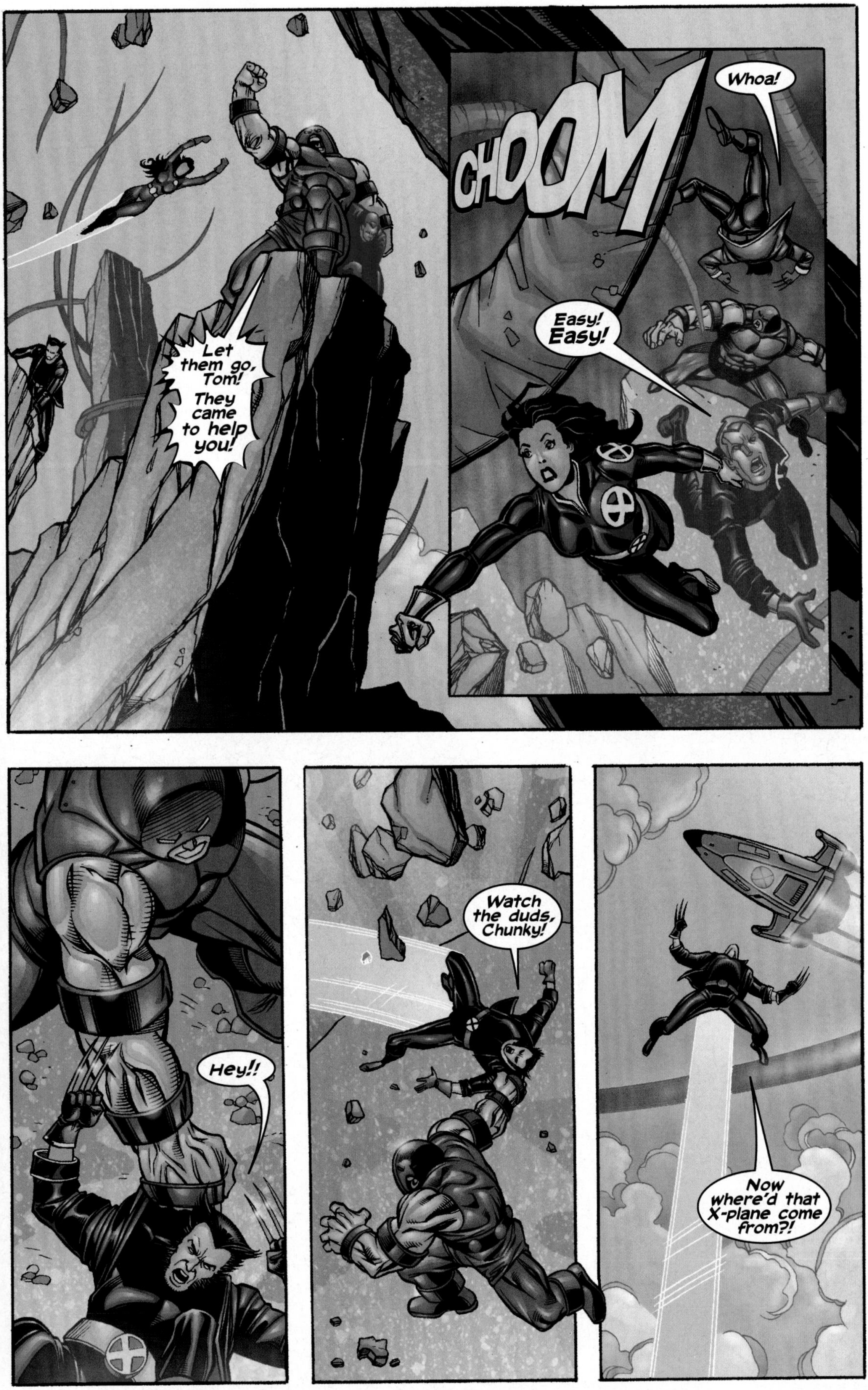
Let them go, Tom! They came to help you!
CHOOM
Whoa!
Easy! Easy!
Hey!!
Watch the duds, Chunky!
Now where'd that X-plane come from?!

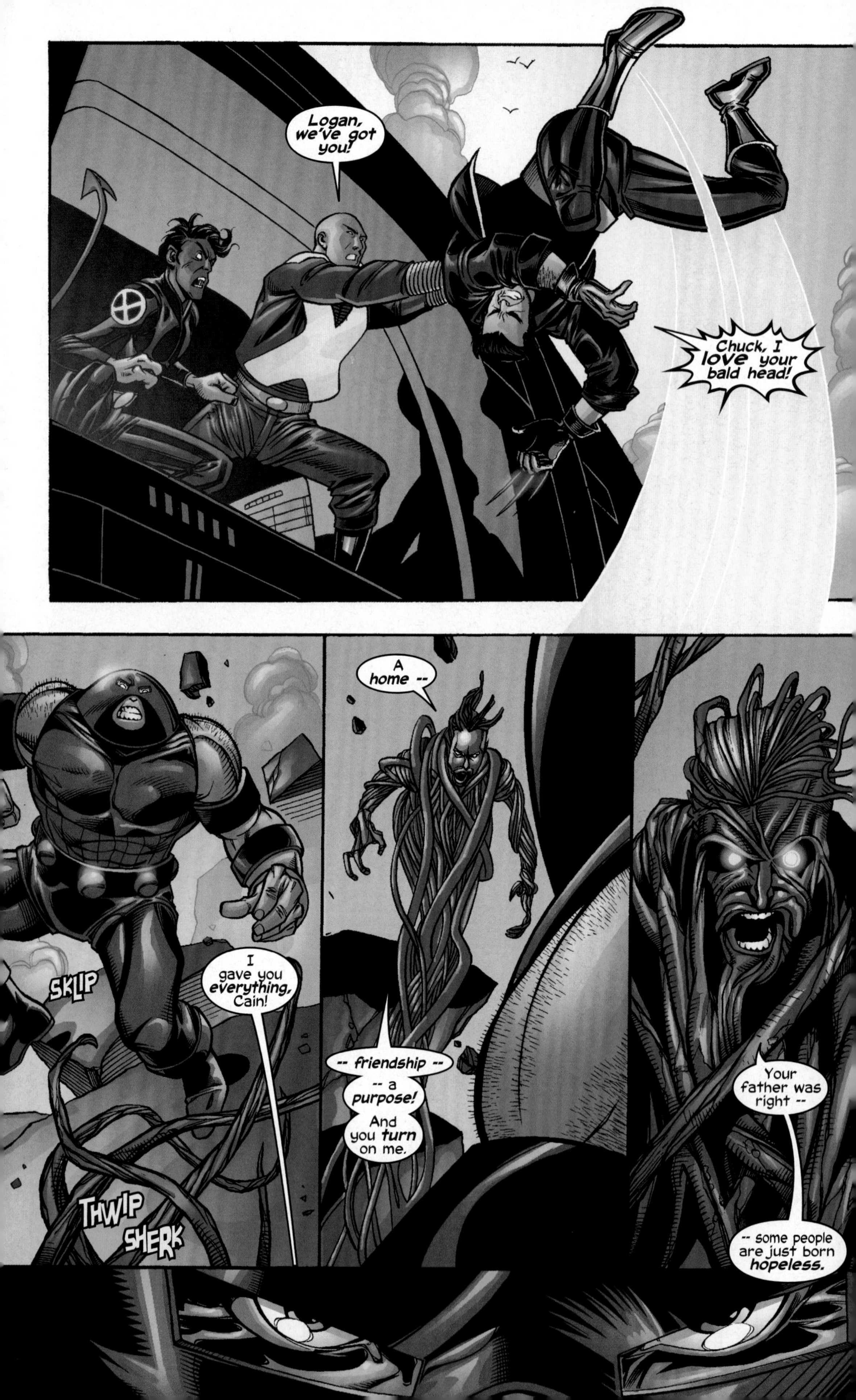
Logan, we've got you!
Chuck, I love your bald head!
SKLIP
I gave you everything, Cain!
THWIP
SHERK
A home --
-- friendship --
-- a purpose!
And you turn on me.
Your father was right --
-- some people are just born hopeless.

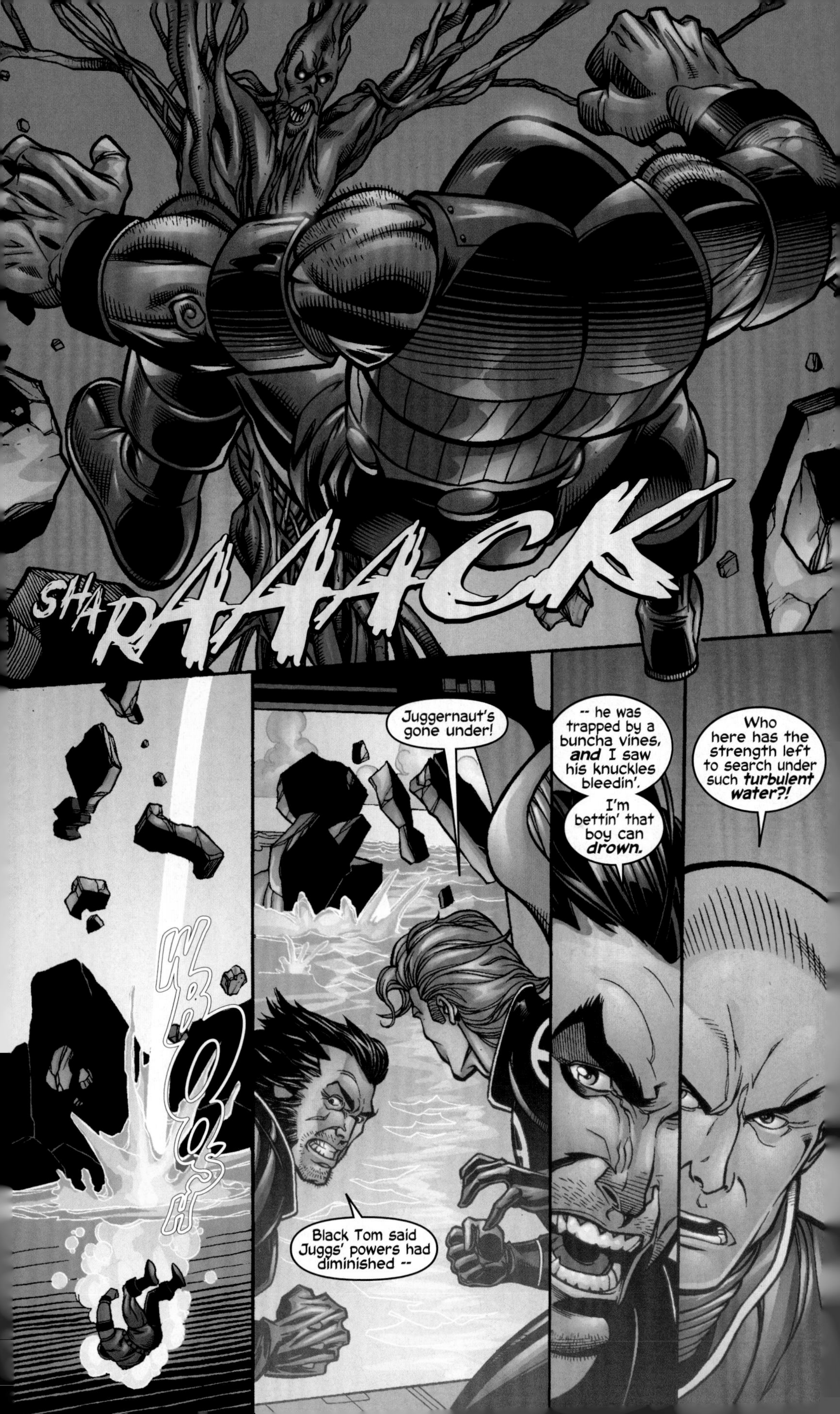
SHRAAACK
WHOOSH
Juggernaut's gone under!
Black Tom said Juggs' powers had diminished --
-- he was trapped by a buncha vines, and I saw his knuckles bleedin'.
I'm bettin' that boy can drown.
Who here has the strength left to search under such turbulent water?!

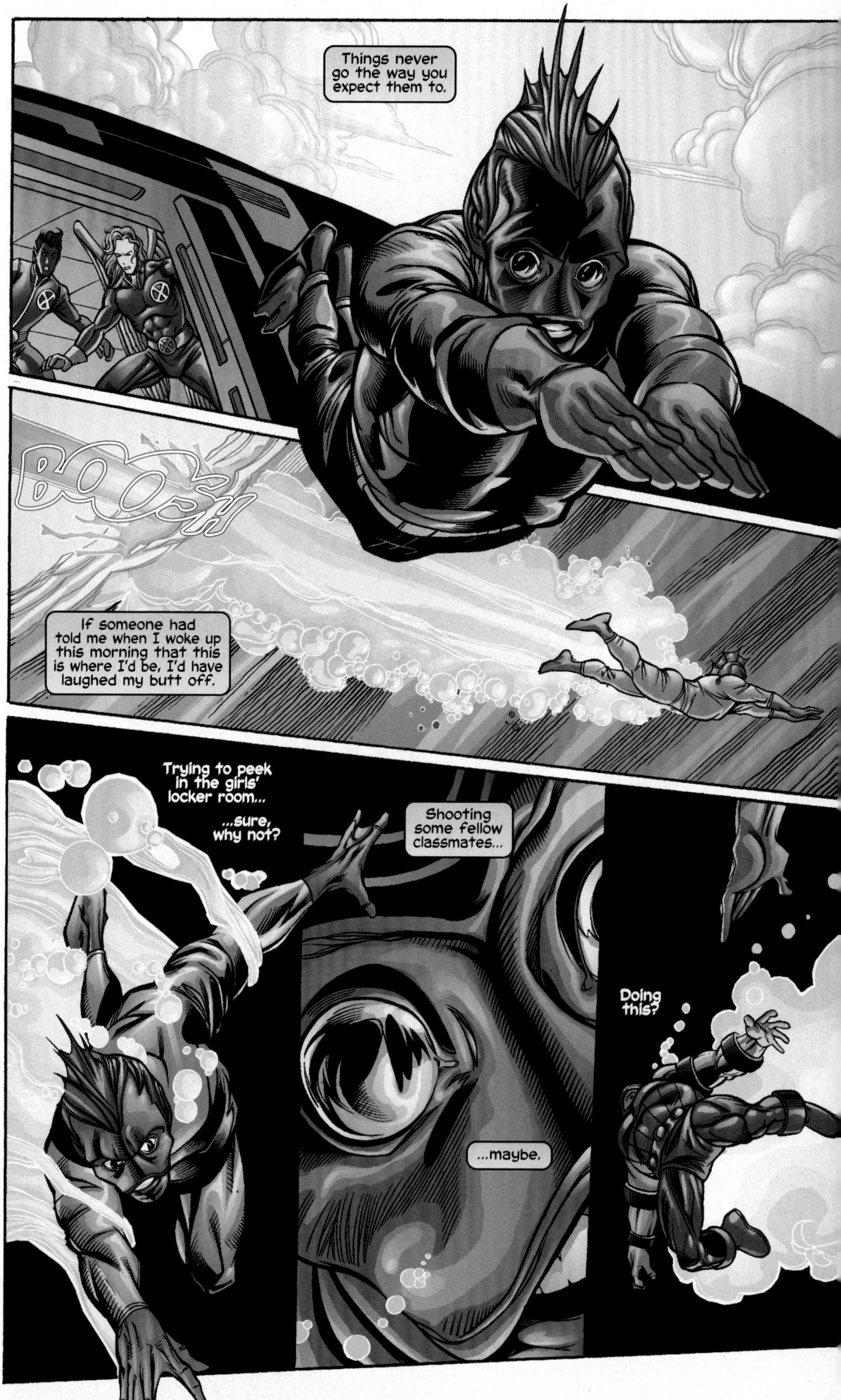
Things never go the way you expect them to.
BLOOSH
If someone had told me when I woke up this morning that this is where I'd be, I'd have laughed my butt off.
Trying to peek in the girls' locker room...
...sure, why not?
Shooting some fellow classmates...
...maybe.
Doing this?

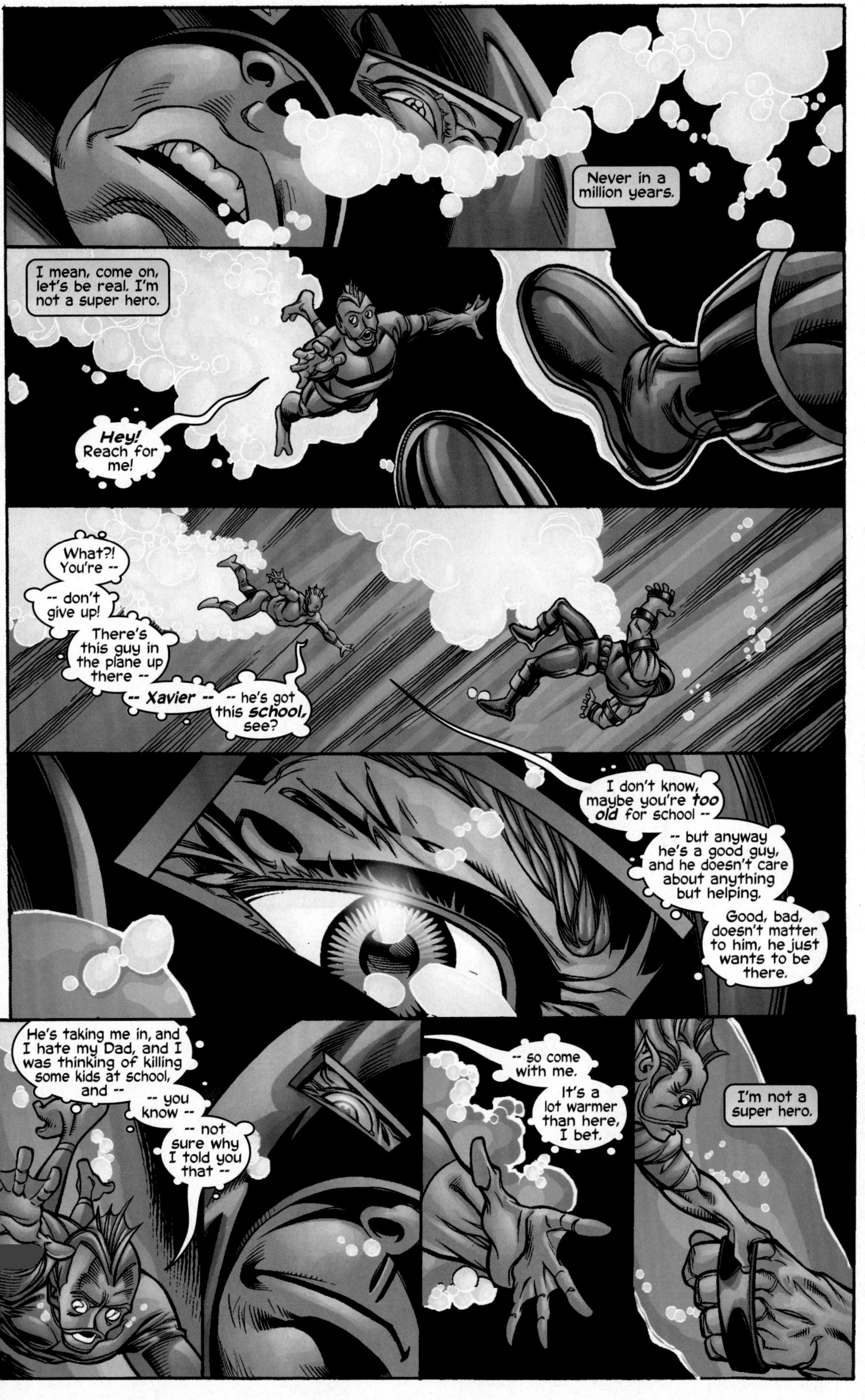
Never in a million years.
I mean, come on, let's be real. I'm not a super hero.
Hey! Reach for me!
What?! You're --
-- don't give up!
There's this guy in the plane up there --
-- Xavier --
-- he's got this school, see?
I don't know, maybe you're too old for school --
-- but anyway he's a good guy, and he doesn't care about anything but helping.
Good, bad, doesn't matter to him, he just wants to be there.
He's taking me in, and I hate my Dad, and I was thinking of killing some kids at school, and --
-- you know --
-- not sure why I told you that --
-- so come with me.
It's a lot warmer than here, I bet.
I'm not a super hero.

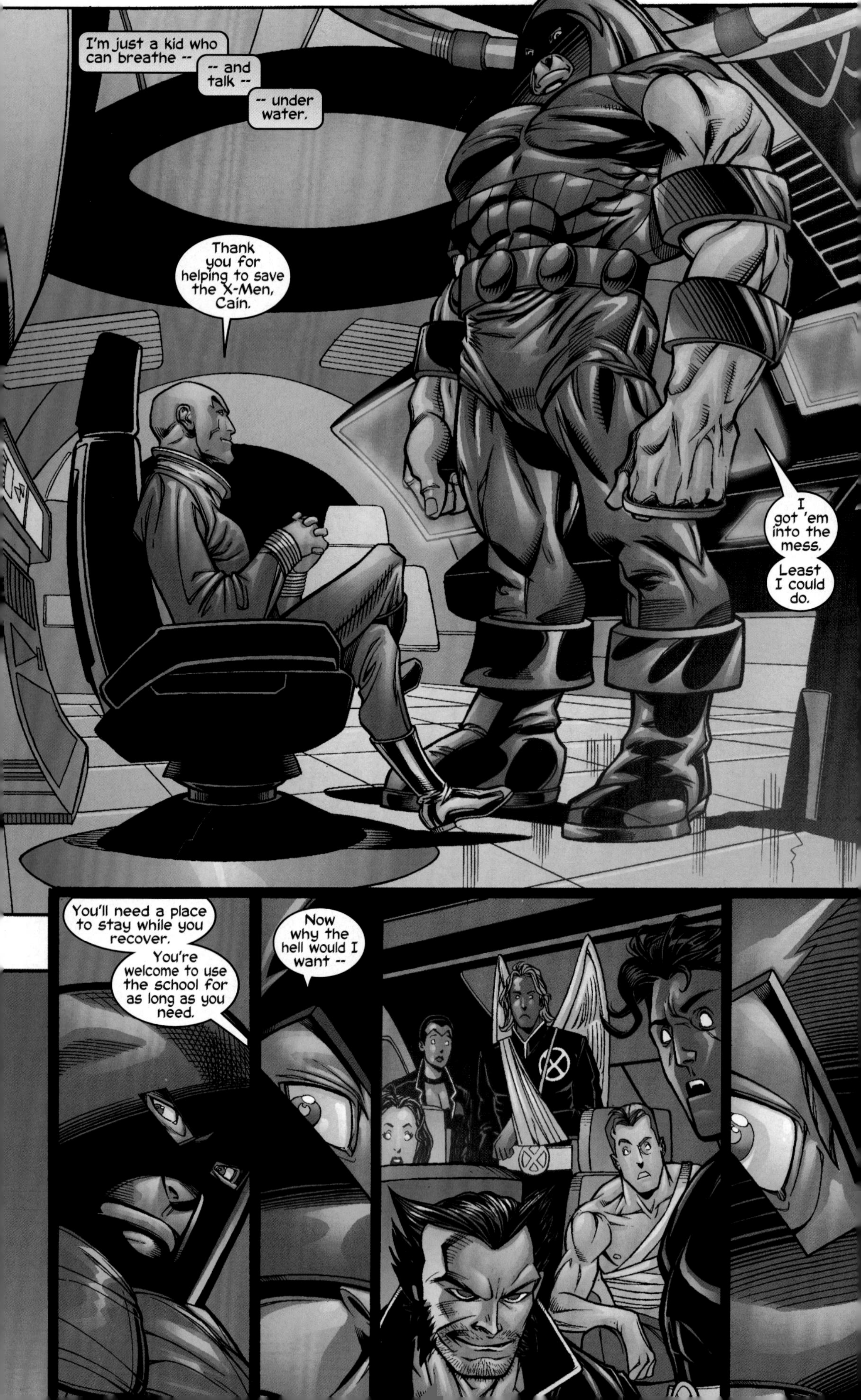
I'm just a kid who can breathe --
-- and talk --
-- under water.
Thank you for helping to save the X-Men, Cain.
I got 'em into the mess.
Least I could do.
You'll need a place to stay while you recover.
You're welcome to use the school for as long as you need.
Now why the hell would I want --

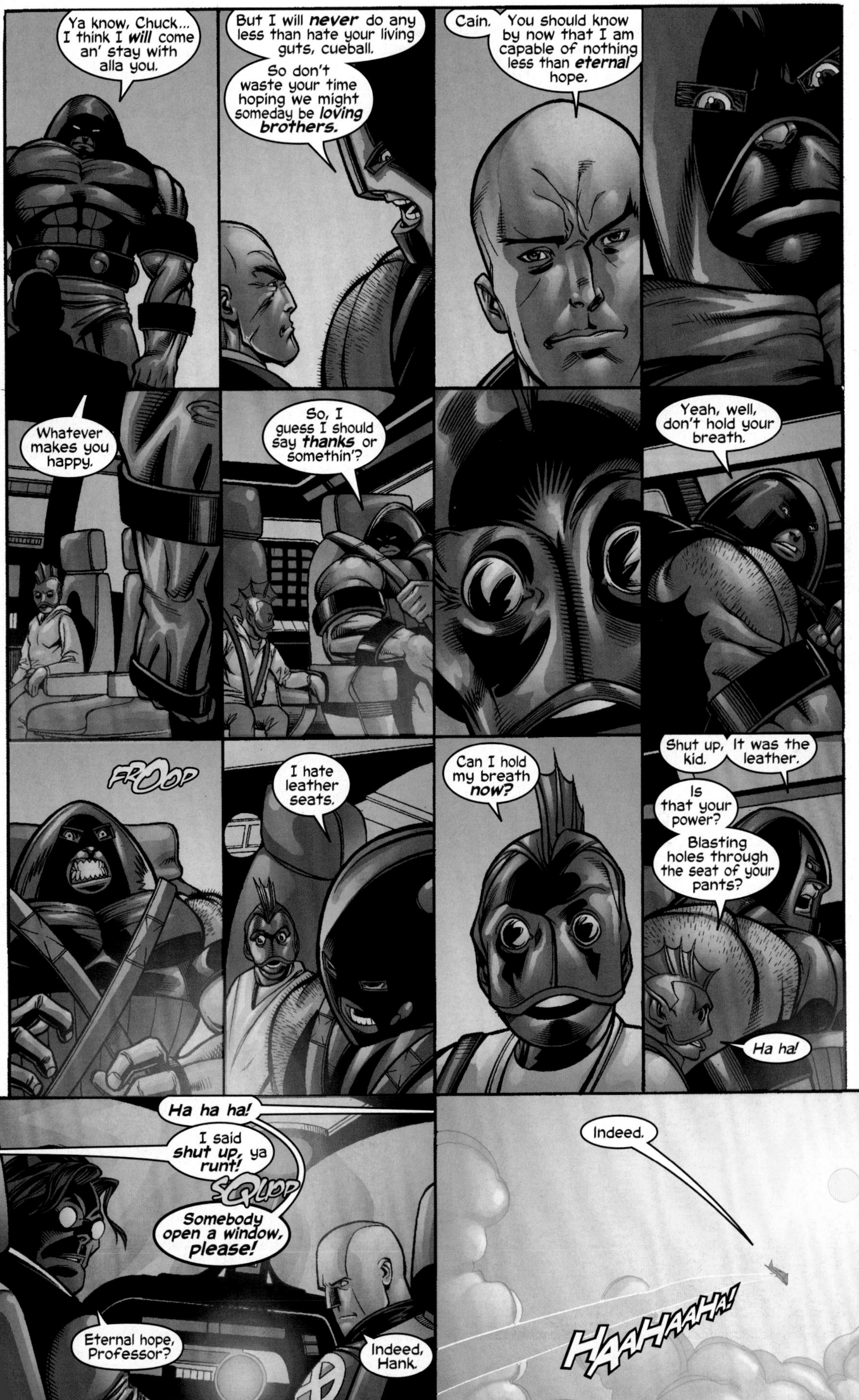
Ya know, Chuck... I think I will come an' stay with alla you.
But I will never do any less than hate your living guts, cueball.
So don't waste your time hoping we might someday be loving brothers.
Cain.
You should know by now that I am capable of nothing less than eternal hope.
Whatever makes you happy.
So, I guess I should say thanks or somethin'?
Yeah, well, don't hold your breath.
FROOP
I hate leather seats.
Can I hold my breath now?
Shut up, kid.
It was the leather.
Is that your power?
Blasting holes through the seat of your pants?
Ha ha!
Ha ha ha!
I said shut up, ya runt!
SQUPP
Somebody open a window, please!
Eternal hope, Professor?
Indeed, Hank.
Indeed.
HAAHAAHA!

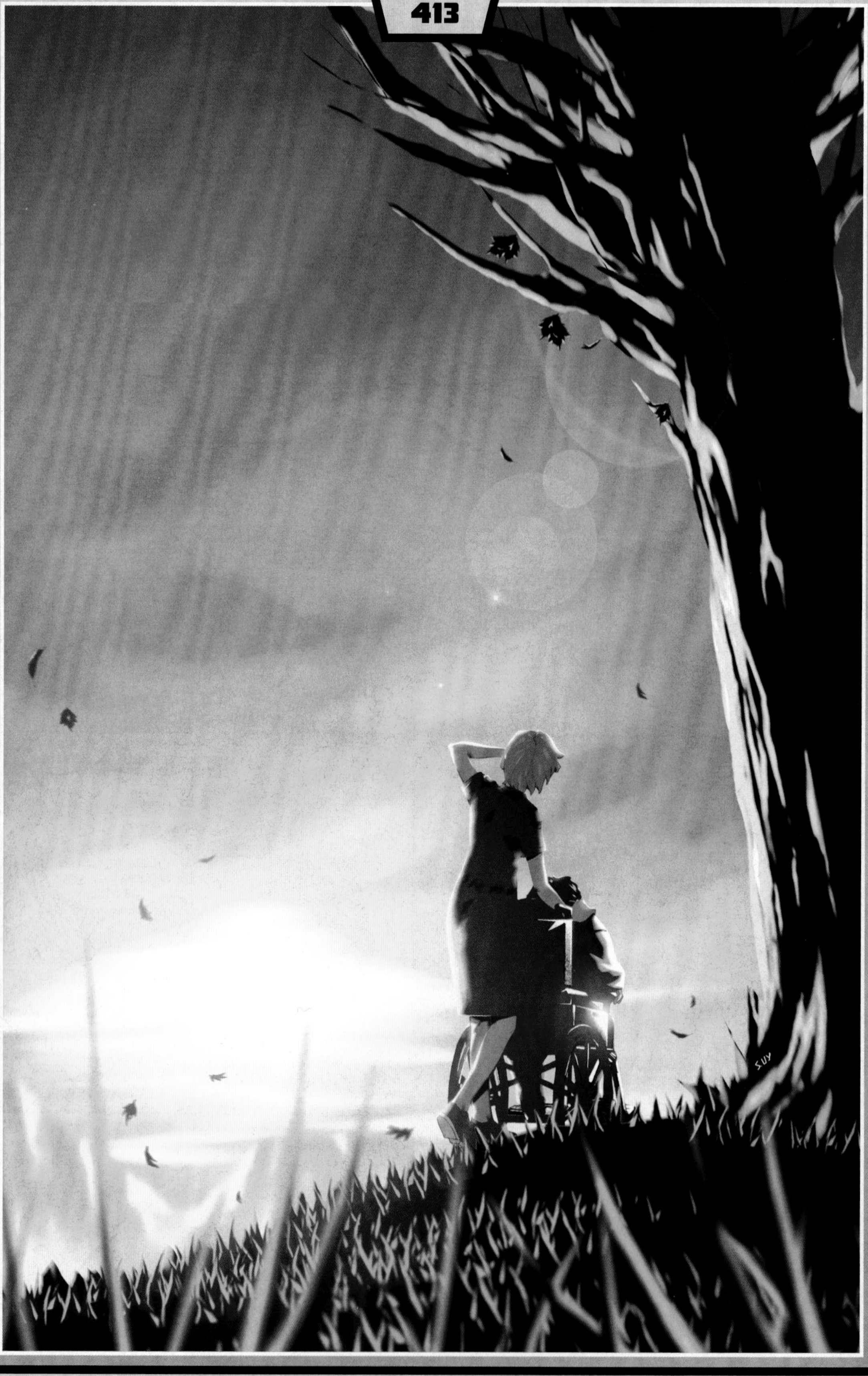

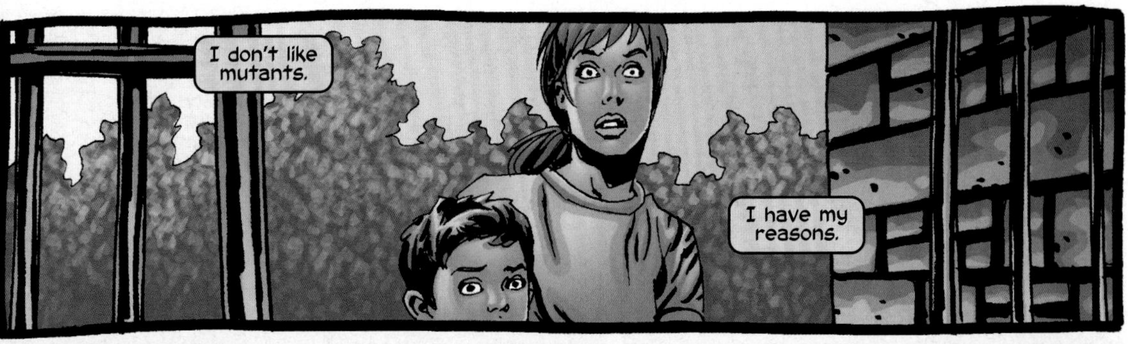
I don't like mutants.
I have my reasons.

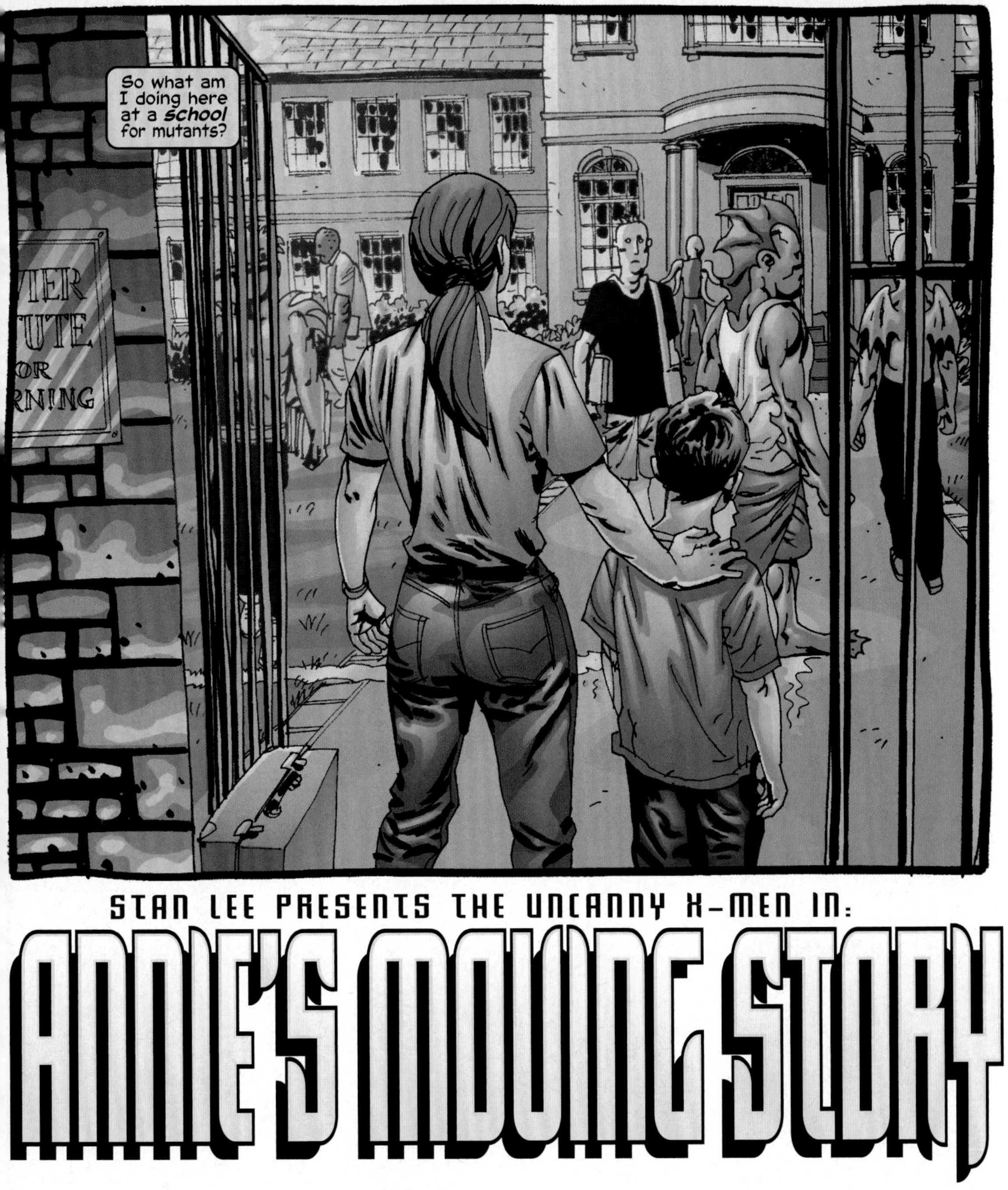
So what am I doing here at a *school* for mutants?

STAN LEE PRESENTS THE UNCANNY X-MEN IN:

ANNIE'S MOVING STORY

Don't **stare**, Carter.

I'm not staring, Mommy.

I feel guilty about my "racism". I'm a nurse. I'm supposed to be **above** such things.

But I **do** have my reasons.

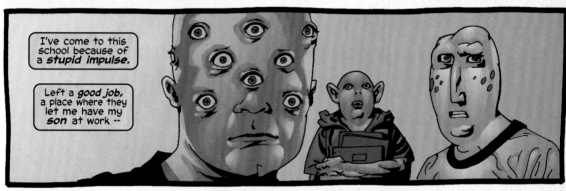

I've come to this school because of a **stupid impulse.**

Left a **good job**, a place where they let me have my **son** at work --

--and came to "Mutant High".

Hi, you must be **Annie.** I'm Paige Guthrie.

Scott asked me to meet you.

Hello. How are you?

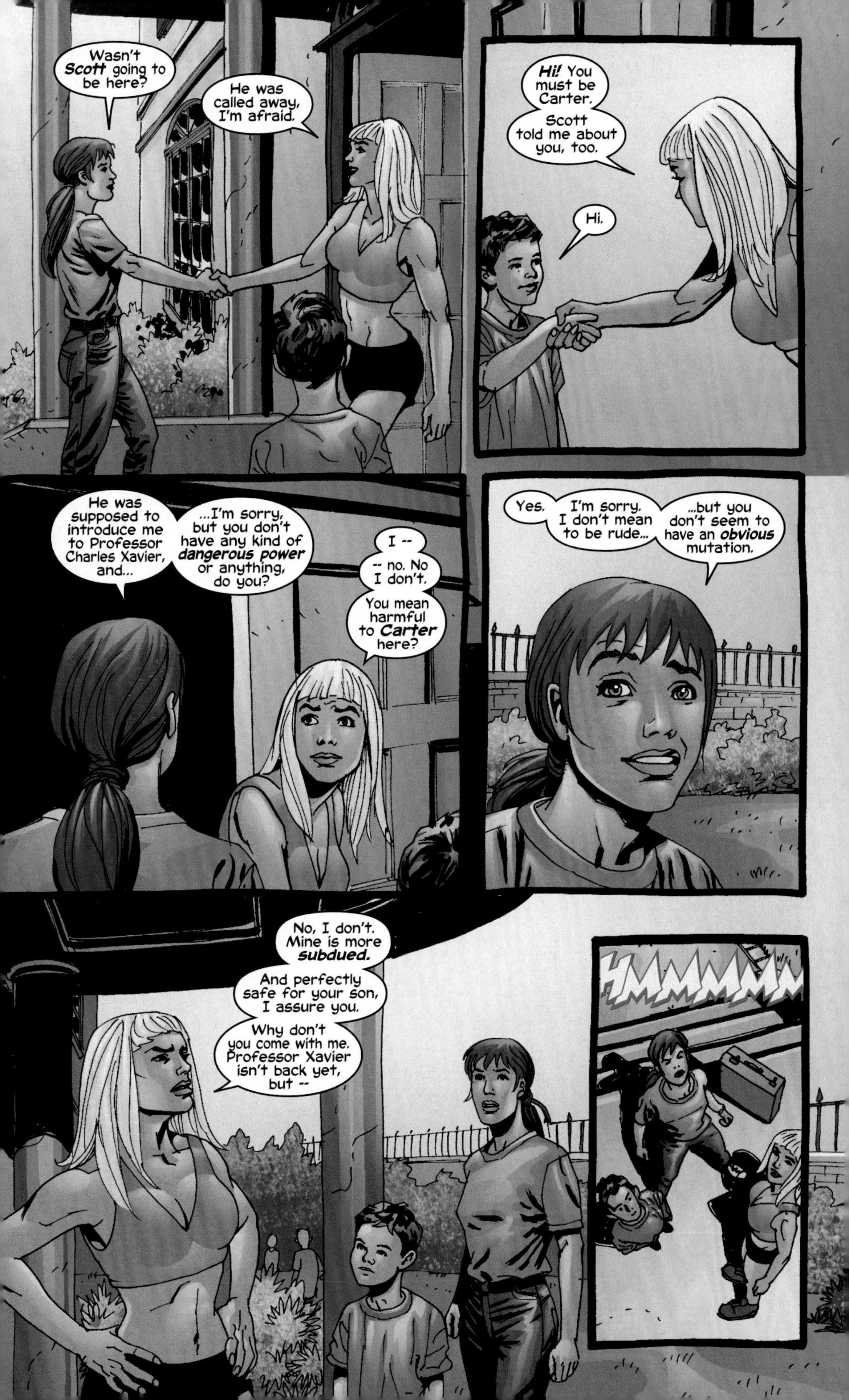
Wasn't Scott going to be here?
He was called away, I'm afraid.
Hi! You must be Carter.
Scott told me about you, too.
Hi.
He was supposed to introduce me to Professor Charles Xavier, and...
...I'm sorry, but you don't have any kind of dangerous power or anything, do you?
I --
-- no. No I don't.
You mean harmful to Carter here?
Yes.
I'm sorry. I don't mean to be rude...
...but you don't seem to have an obvious mutation.
No, I don't. Mine is more subdued.
And perfectly safe for your son, I assure you.
Why don't you come with me. Professor Xavier isn't back yet, but --
HMMMMM

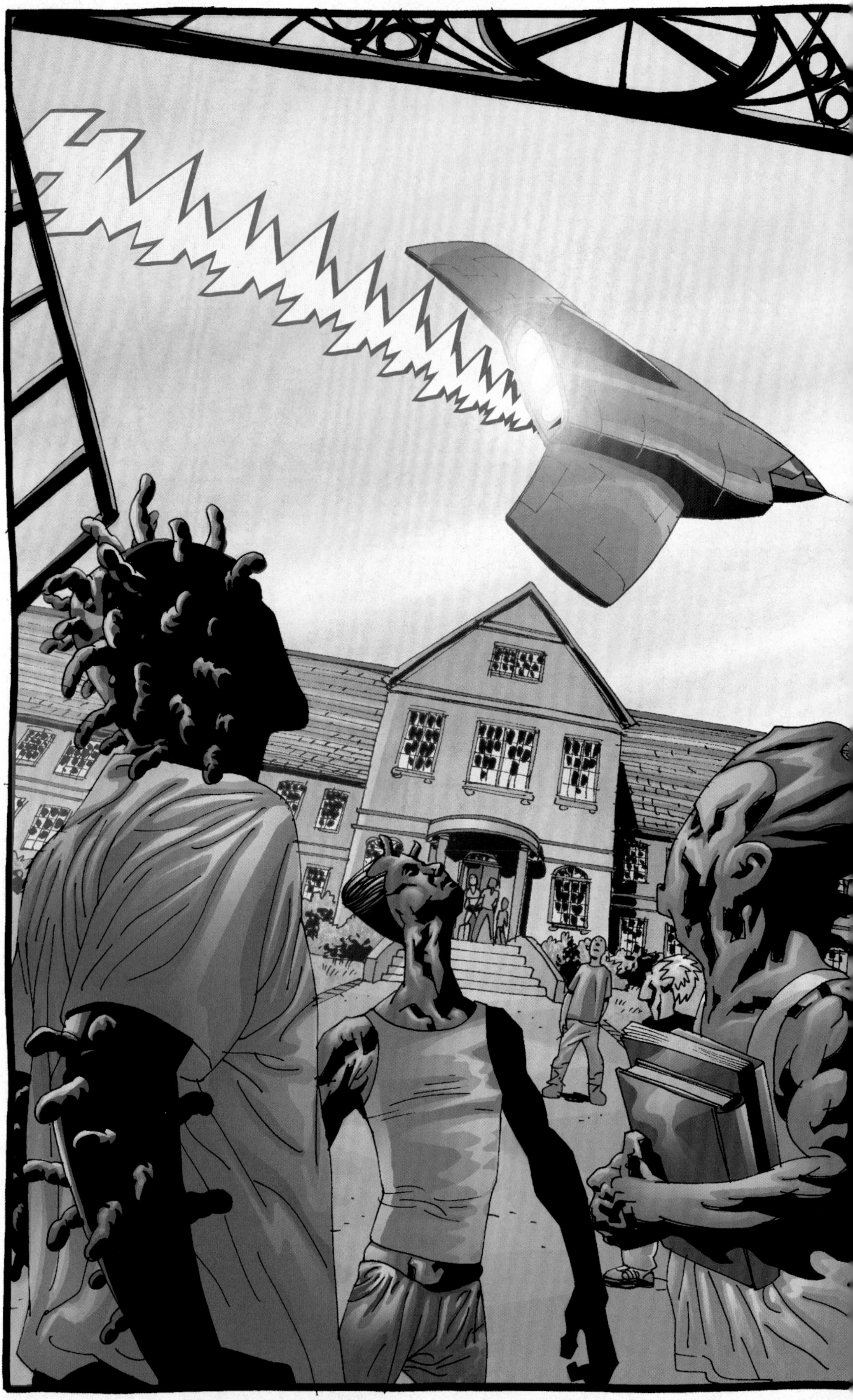

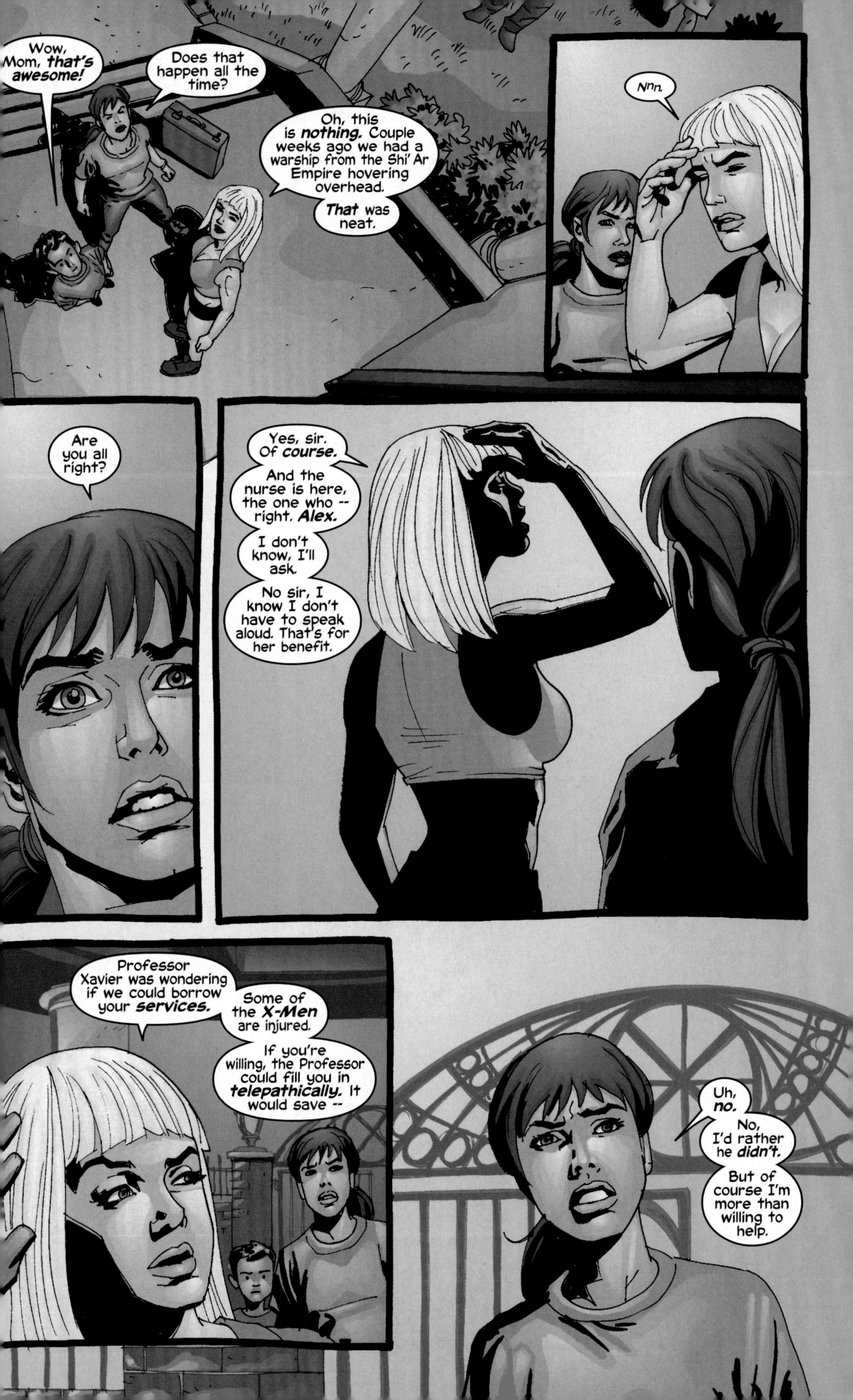

Wow, Mom, that's awesome!
Does that happen all the time?
Oh, this is nothing. Couple weeks ago we had a warship from the Shi'Ar Empire hovering overhead.
That was neat.
Nnn.
Are you all right?
Yes, sir. Of course.
And the nurse is here, the one who -- right. Alex.
I don't know, I'll ask.
No sir, I know I don't have to speak aloud. That's for her benefit.
Professor Xavier was wondering if we could borrow your services.
Some of the X-Men are injured.
If you're willing, the Professor could fill you in telepathically. It would save --
Uh, no.
No, I'd rather he didn't.
But of course I'm more than willing to help.

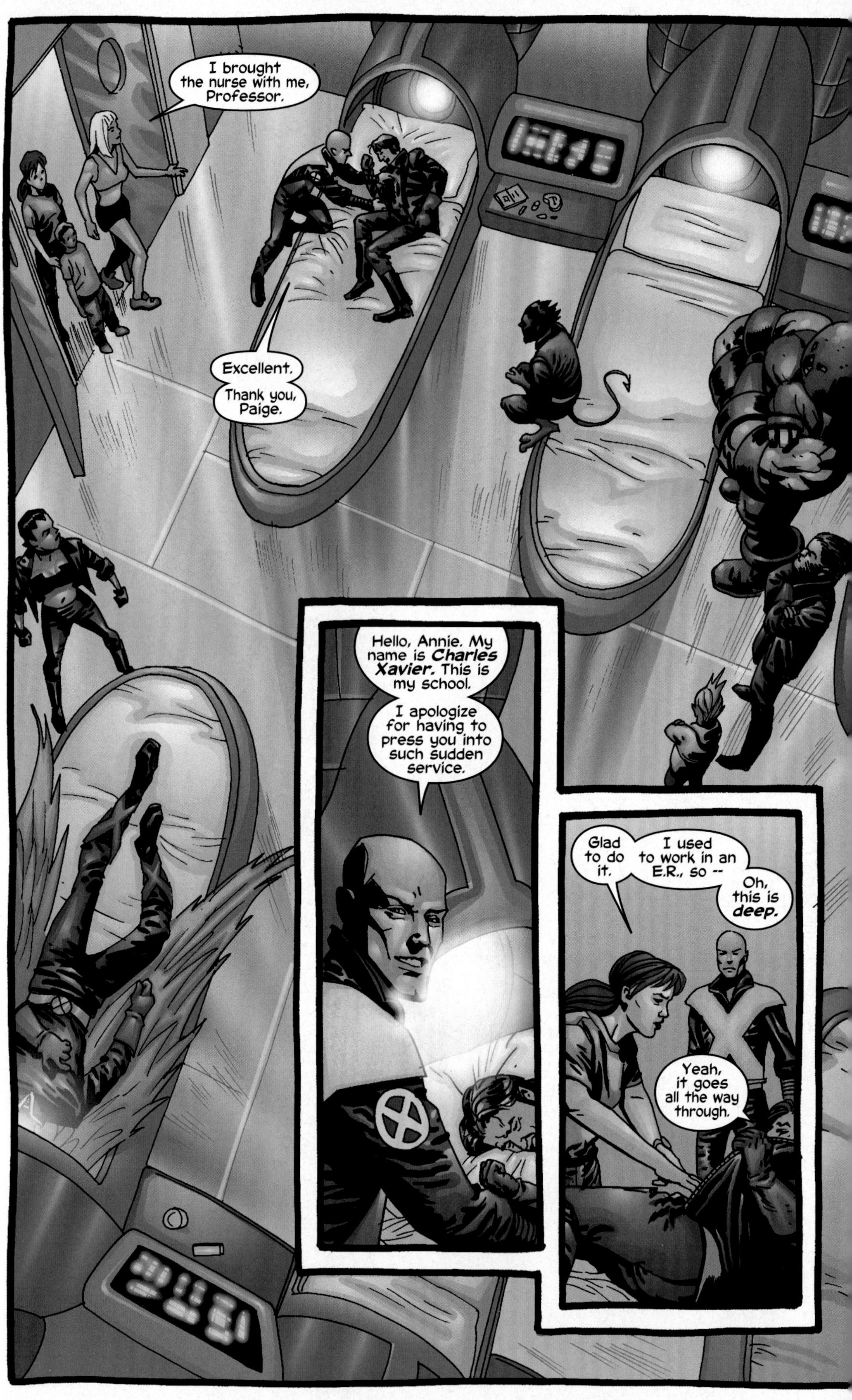

I brought the nurse with me, Professor.
Excellent.
Thank you, Paige.
Hello, Annie. My name is Charles Xavier. This is my school.
I apologize for having to press you into such sudden service.
Glad to do it.
I used to work in an E.R., so --
Oh, this is deep.
Yeah, it goes all the way through.

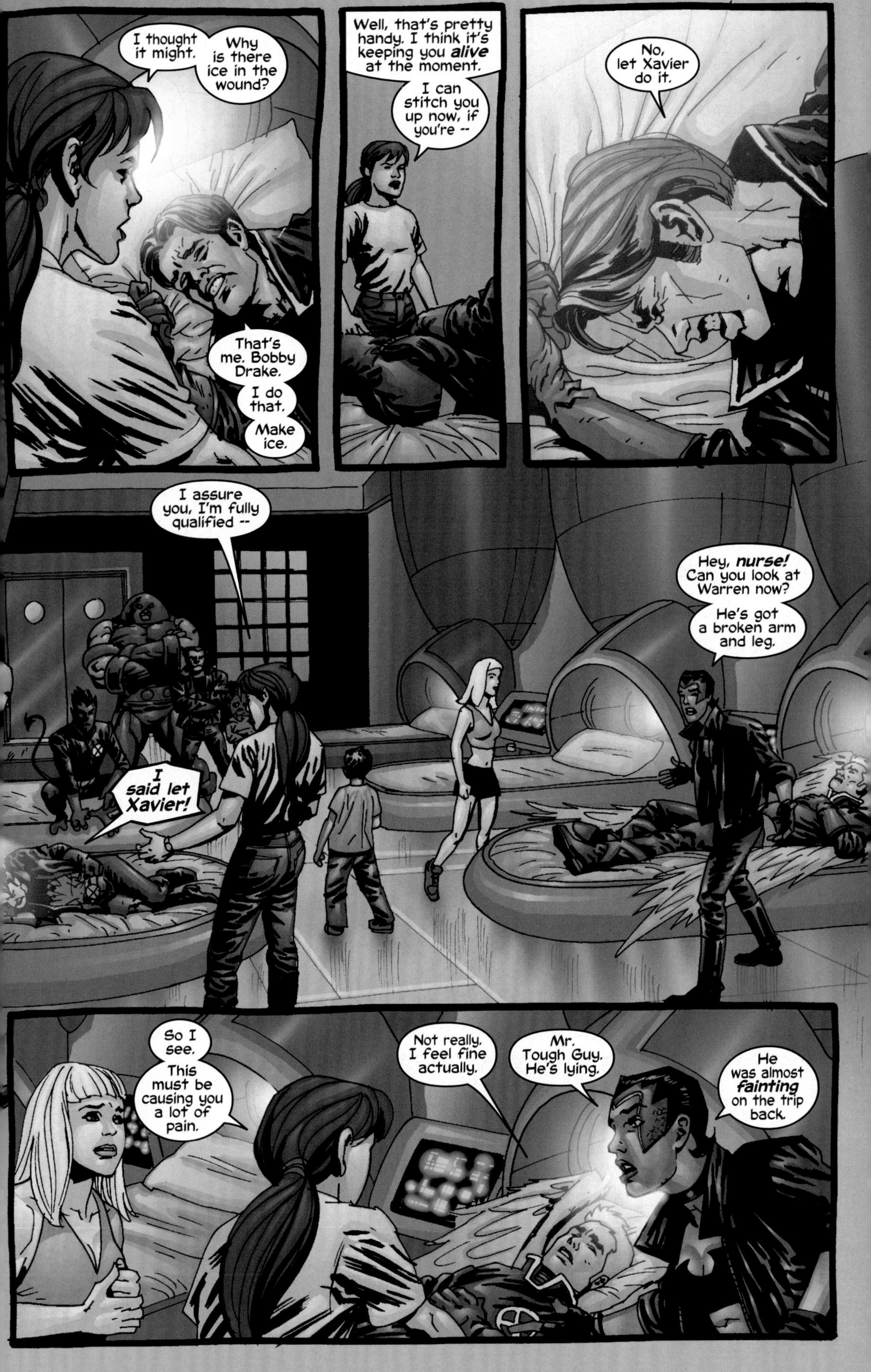
I thought it might.
Why is there ice in the wound?
That's me. Bobby Drake.
I do that.
Make ice.
Well, that's pretty handy. I think it's keeping you *alive* at the moment.
I can stitch you up now, if you're --
No, let Xavier do it.
I assure you, I'm fully qualified --
I said let Xavier!
Hey, *nurse!* Can you look at Warren now?
He's got a broken arm and leg.
So I see.
This must be causing you a lot of pain.
Not really. I feel fine actually.
Mr. Tough Guy. He's lying.
He was almost *fainting* on the trip back.

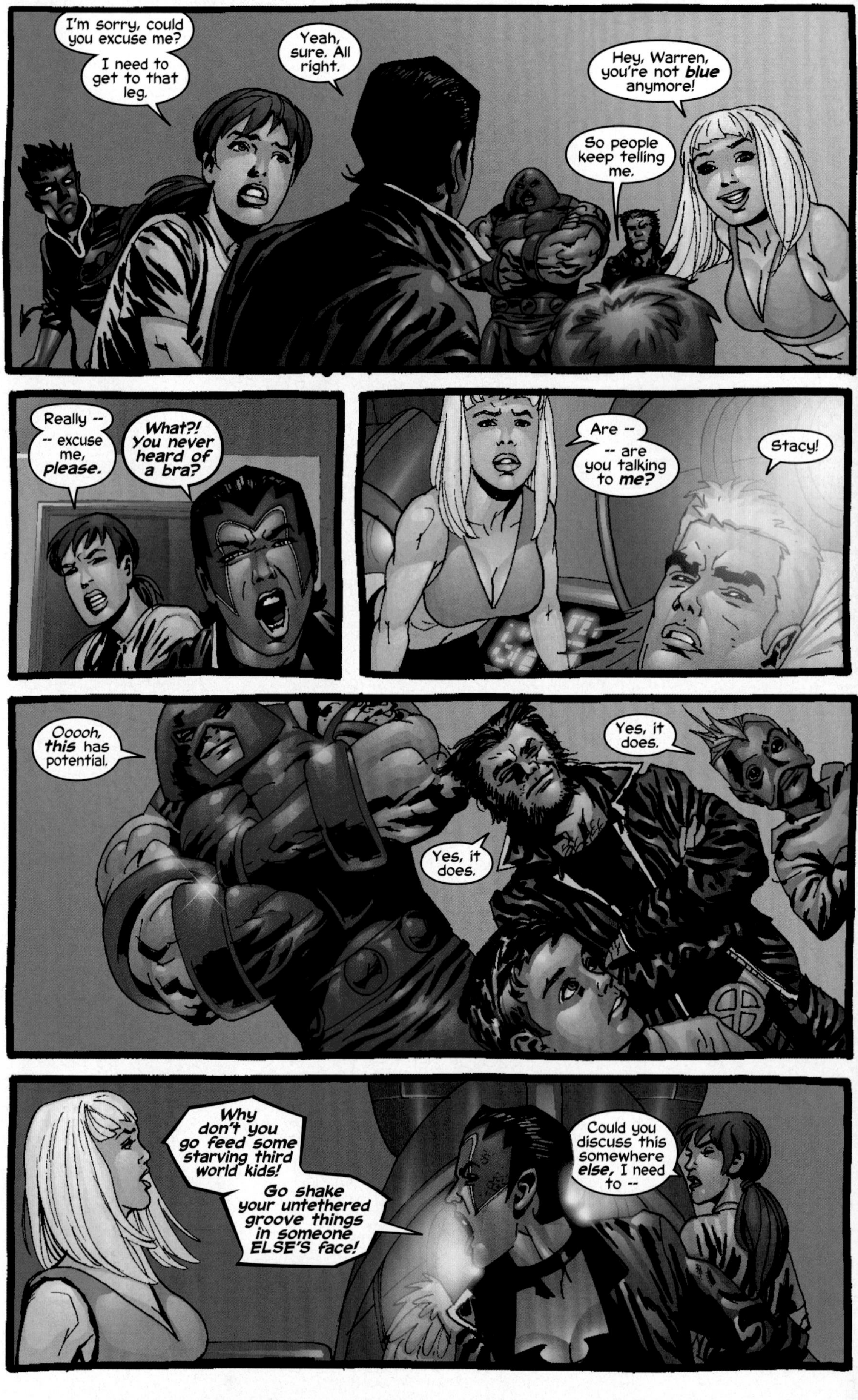

I'm sorry, could you excuse me?
I need to get to that leg.
Yeah, sure. All right.
Hey, Warren, you're not *blue* anymore!
So people keep telling me.
Really --
-- excuse me, *please.*
What?! You never heard of a bra?
Are --
-- are you talking to *me?*
Stacy!
Ooooh, *this* has potential.
Yes, it does.
Yes, it does.
Why don't you go feed some starving third world kids!
Go shake your untethered groove things in someone ELSE'S face!
Could you discuss this somewhere *else,* I need to --

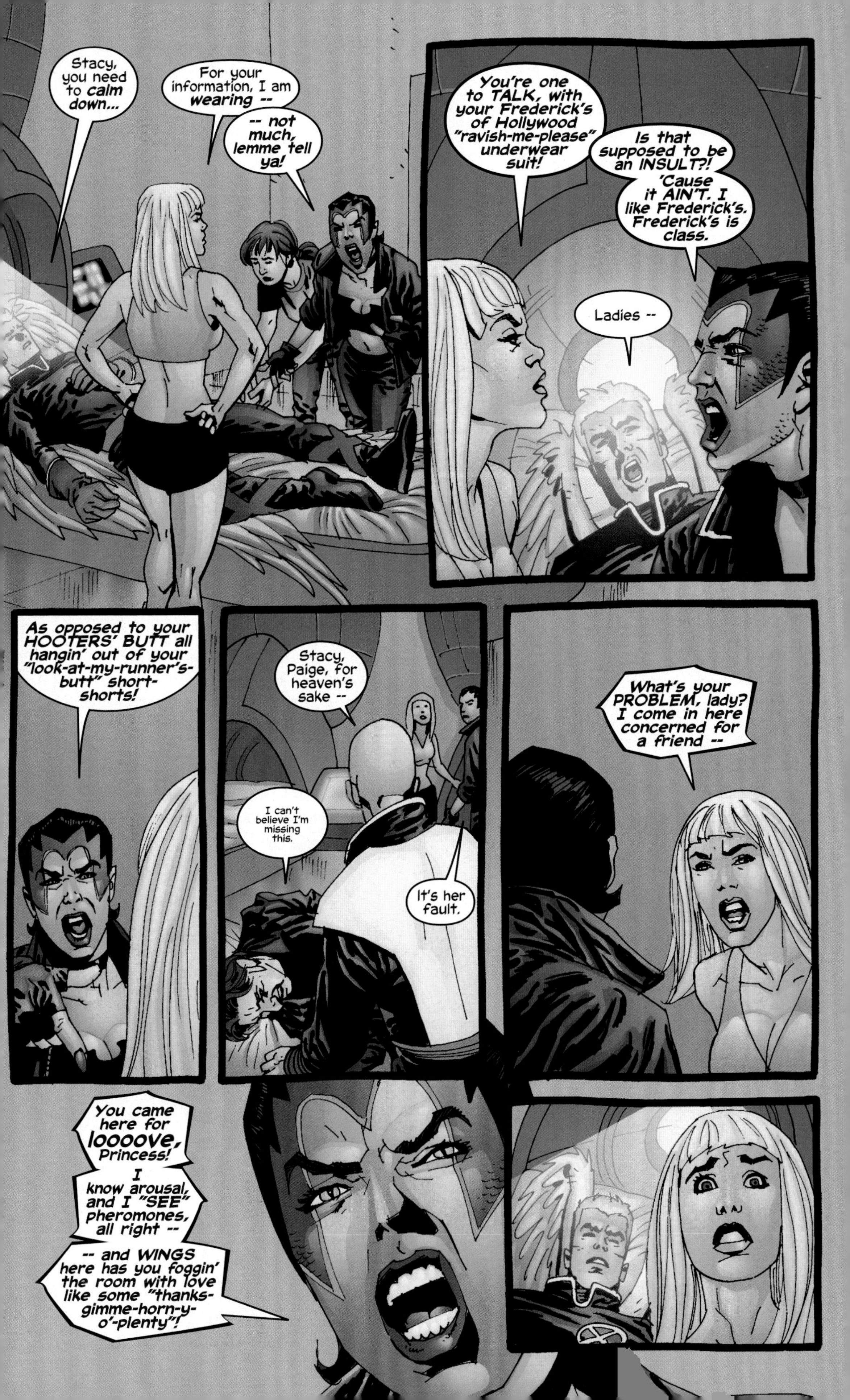
Stacy, you need to calm down...
For your information, I am wearing --
-- not much, lemme tell ya!
You're one to TALK, with your Frederick's of Hollywood "ravish-me-please" underwear suit!
Is that supposed to be an INSULT?!
'Cause it AIN'T. I like Frederick's. Frederick's is class.
Ladies --
As opposed to your HOOTERS' BUTT all hangin' out of your "look-at-my-runner's-butt" short-shorts!
Stacy, Paige, for heaven's sake --
I can't believe I'm missing this.
It's her fault.
What's your PROBLEM, lady? I come in here concerned for a friend --
You came here for loooove, Princess!
I know arousal, and I "SEE" pheromones, all right --
-- and WINGS here has you foggin' the room with love like some "thanks-gimme-horn-y-o'-plenty"!

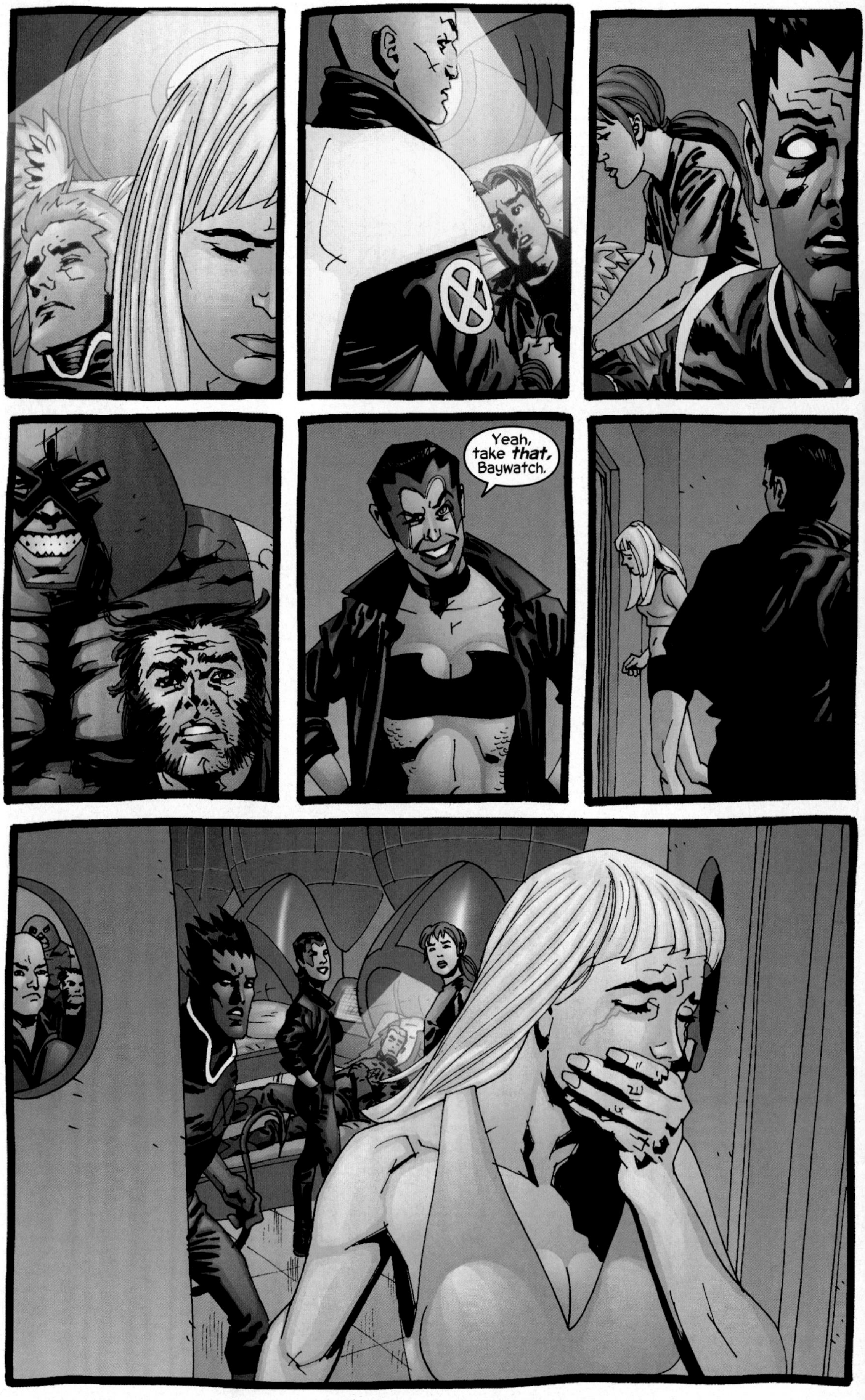
Yeah, take *that,* Baywatch.

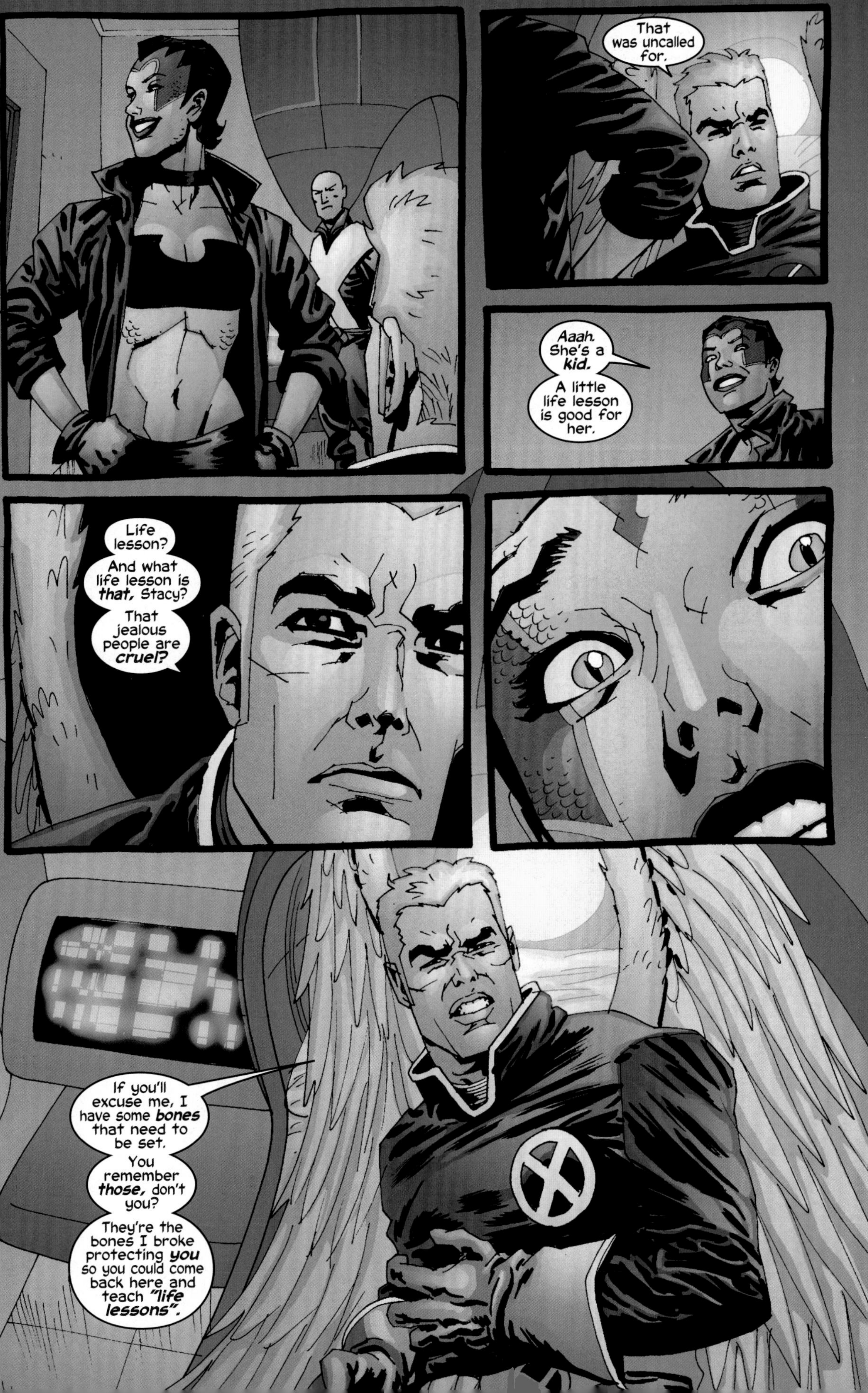
That was uncalled for.
Aaah. She's a kid.
A little life lesson is good for her.
Life lesson?
And what life lesson is that, Stacy?
That jealous people are cruel?
If you'll excuse me, I have some bones that need to be set.
You remember those, don't you?
They're the bones I broke protecting you so you could come back here and teach "life lessons".

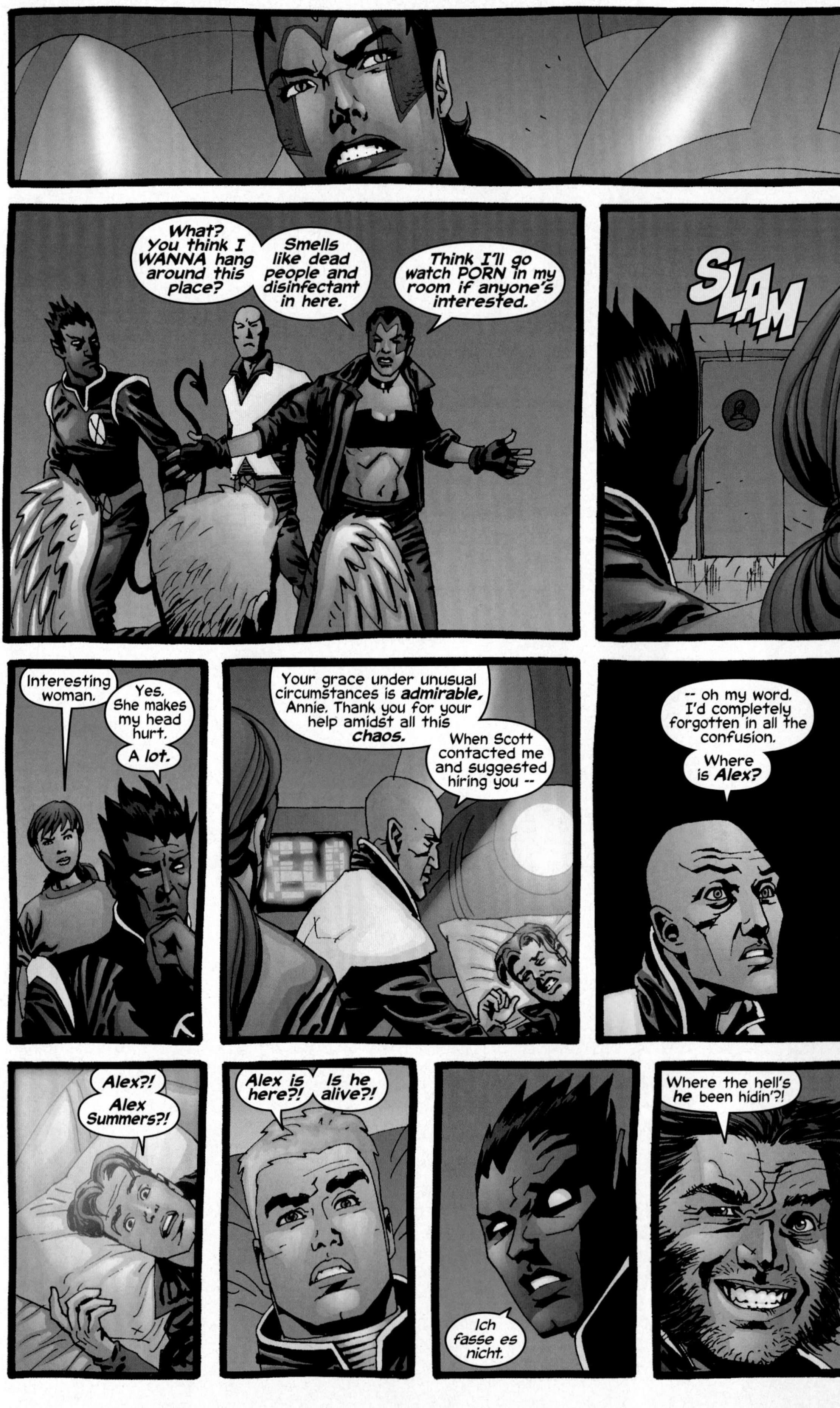
What? You think I WANNA hang around this place?
Smells like dead people and disinfectant in here.
Think I'll go watch PORN in my room if anyone's interested.
SLAM
Interesting woman.
Yes. She makes my head hurt.
A lot.
Your grace under unusual circumstances is admirable, Annie. Thank you for your help amidst all this chaos.
When Scott contacted me and suggested hiring you --
-- oh my word. I'd completely forgotten in all the confusion.
Where is Alex?
Alex?! Alex Summers?!
Alex is here?!
Is he alive?!
Ich fasse es nicht.
Where the hell's he been hidin'?!

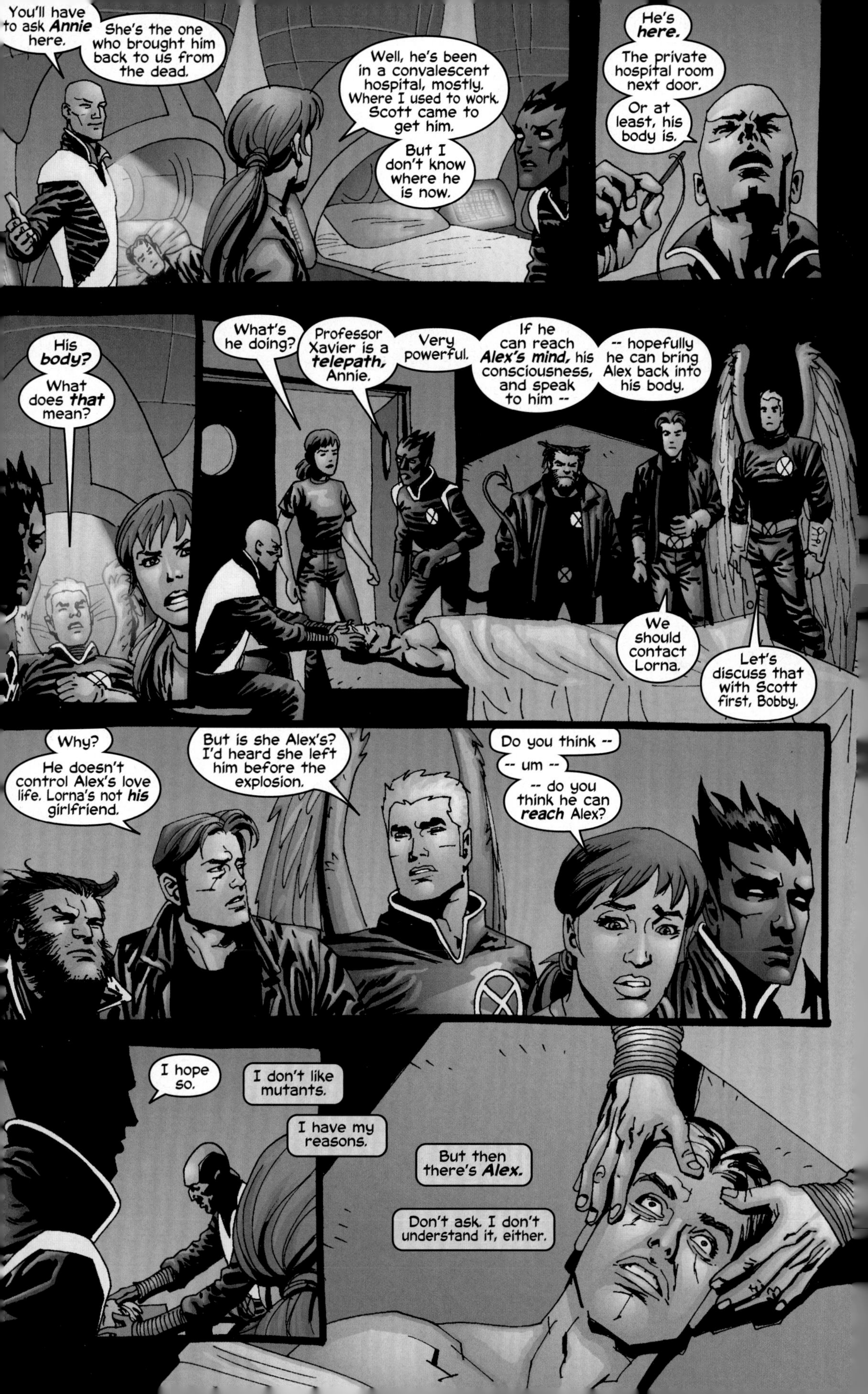
You'll have to ask Annie here.
She's the one who brought him back to us from the dead.
Well, he's been in a convalescent hospital, mostly. Where I used to work. Scott came to get him.
But I don't know where he is now.
He's here.
The private hospital room next door.
Or at least, his body is.
His body?
What does that mean?
What's he doing?
Professor Xavier is a telepath, Annie.
Very powerful.
If he can reach Alex's mind, his consciousness, and speak to him --
-- hopefully he can bring Alex back into his body.
We should contact Lorna.
Let's discuss that with Scott first, Bobby.
Why?
He doesn't control Alex's love life. Lorna's not his girlfriend.
But is she Alex's? I'd heard she left him before the explosion.
Do you think --
-- um --
-- do you think he can reach Alex?
I hope so.
I don't like mutants.
I have my reasons.
But then there's Alex.
Don't ask. I don't understand it, either.

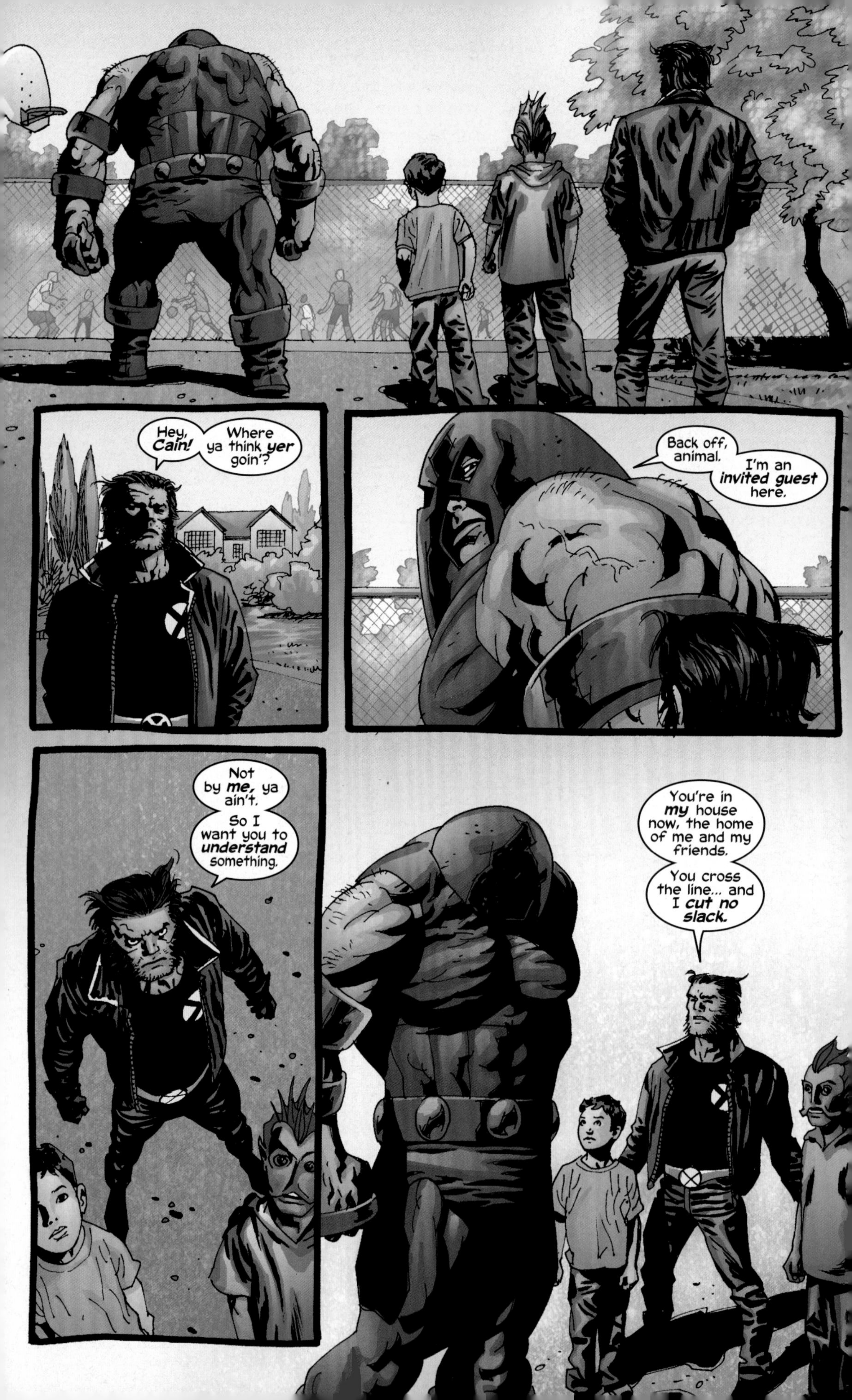

Hey, Cain!
Where ya think yer goin'?
Back off, animal.
I'm an invited guest here.
Not by me, ya ain't.
So I want you to understand something.
You're in my house now, the home of me and my friends.
You cross the line... and I cut no slack.

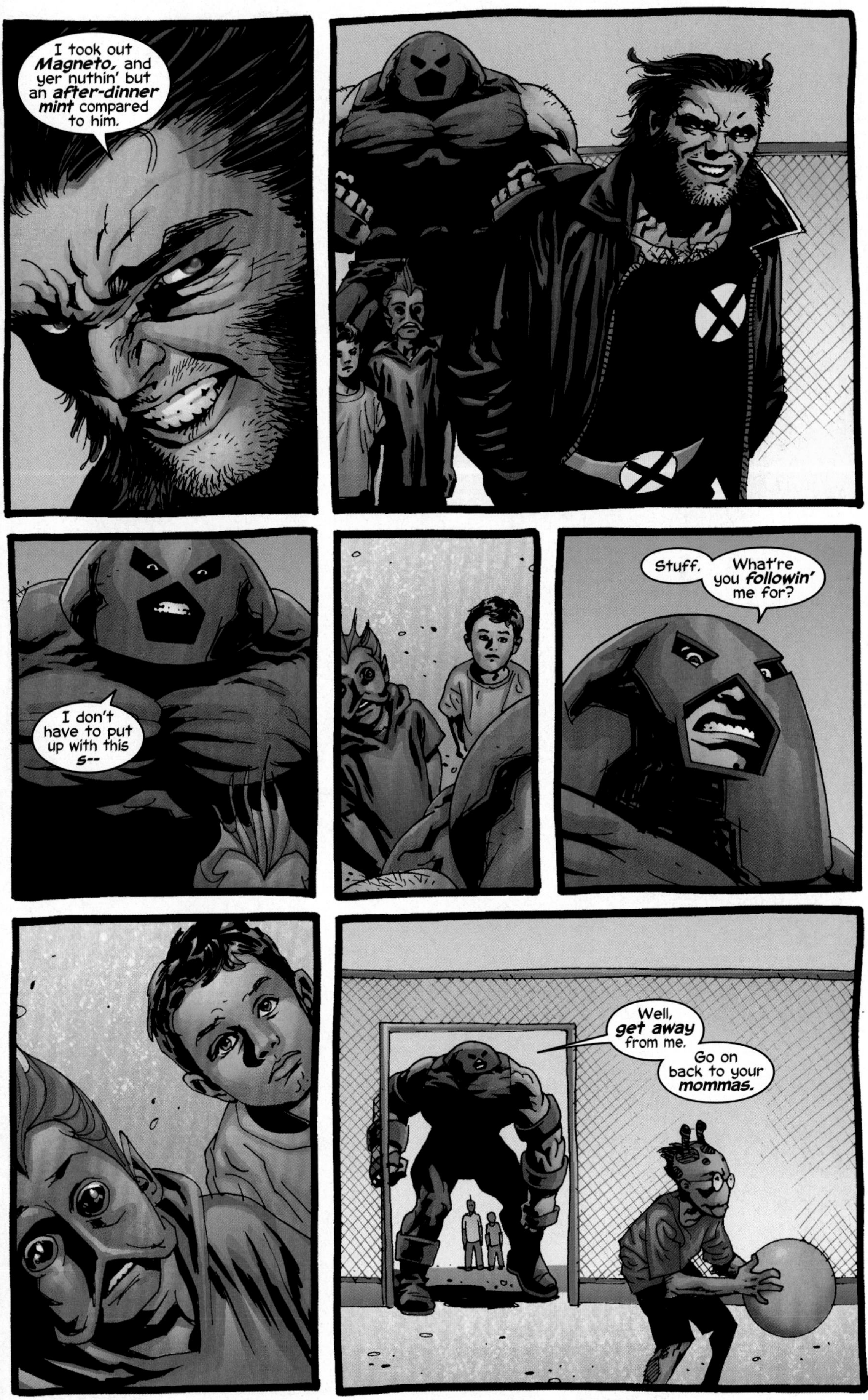
I took out Magneto, and yer nuthin' but an after-dinner mint compared to him.
I don't have to put up with this s--
Stuff.
What're you followin' me for?
Well, get away from me.
Go on back to your mommas.

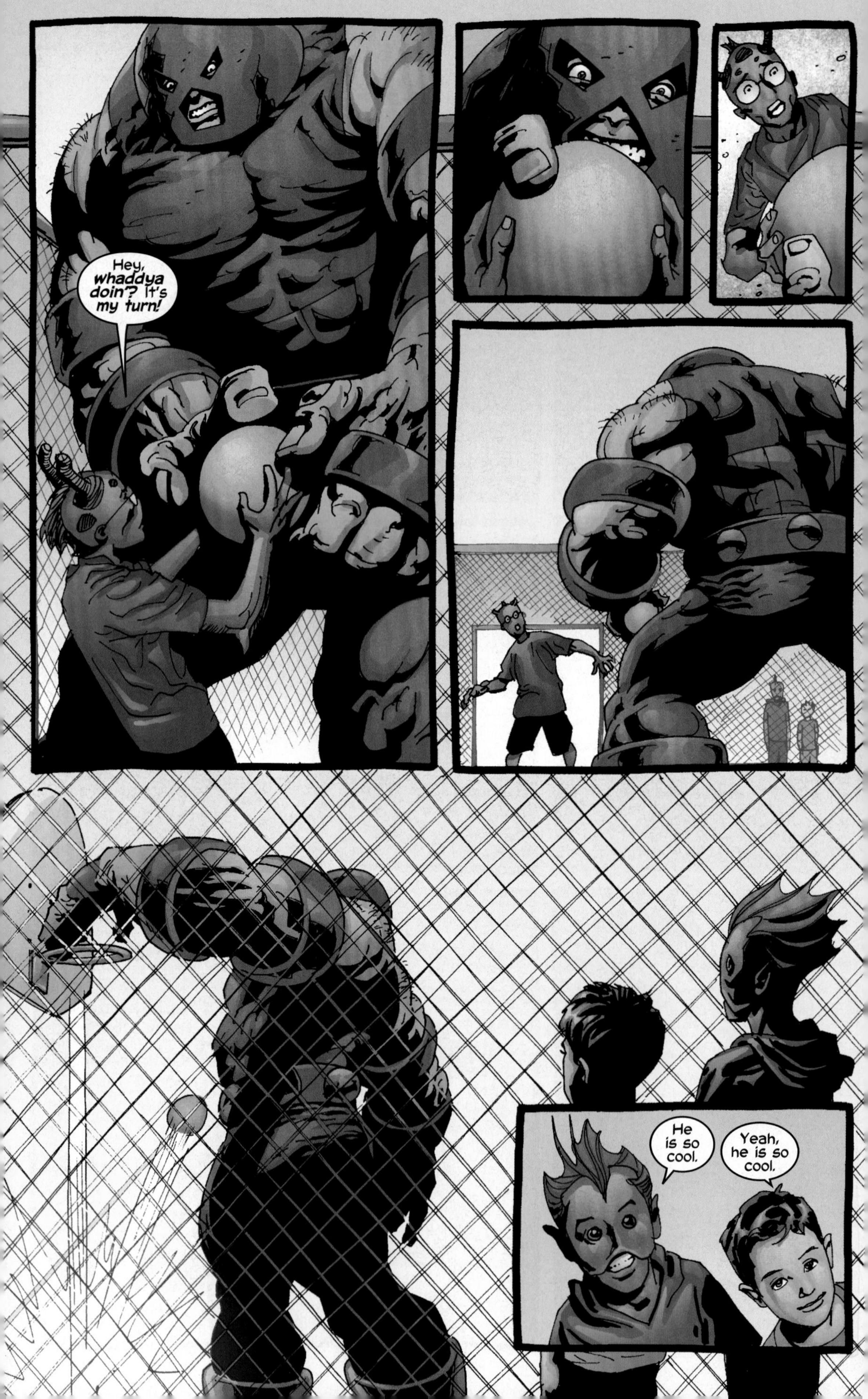
Hey, whaddya doin? It's my turn!
He is so cool.
Yeah, he is so cool.

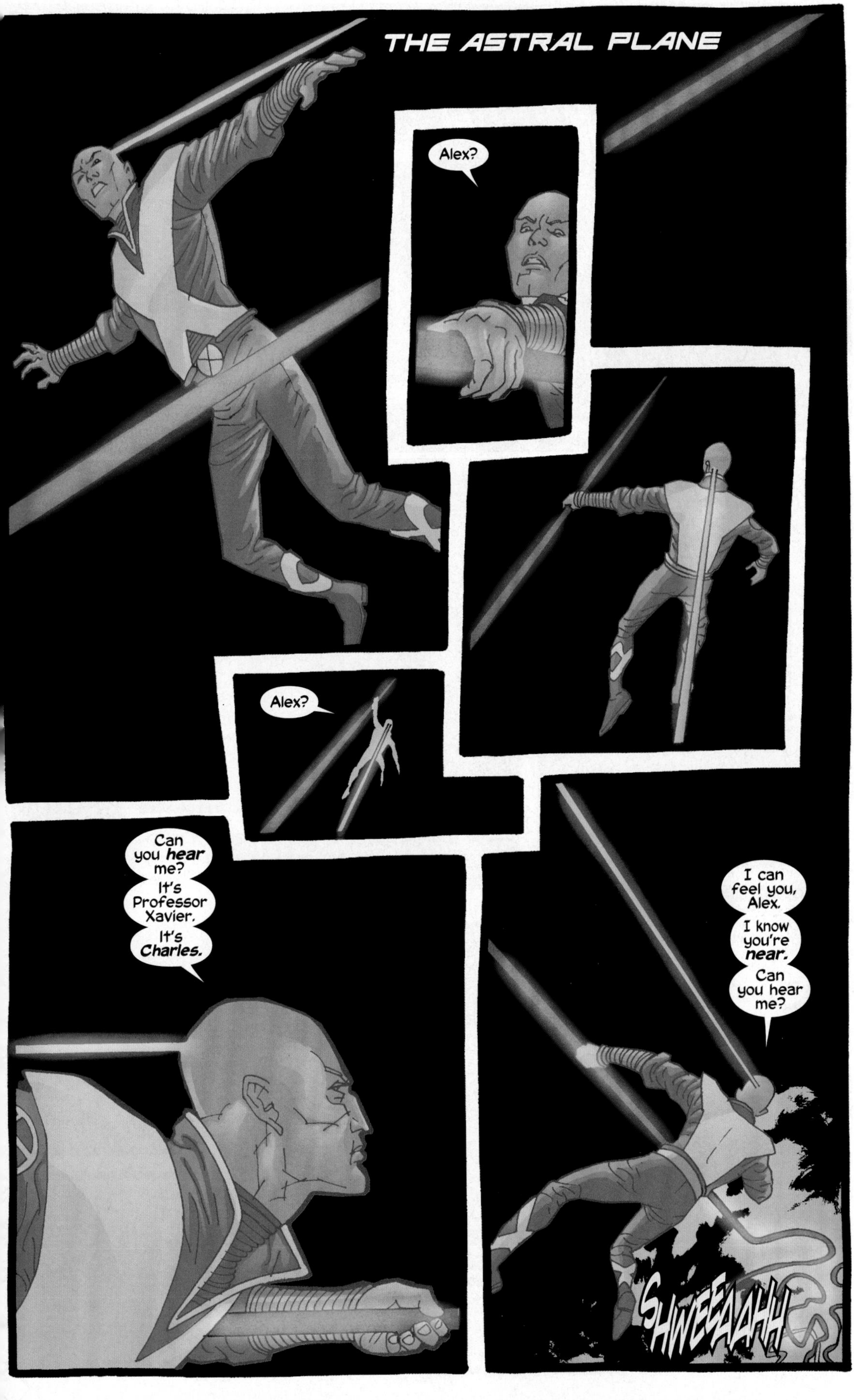
THE ASTRAL PLANE
Alex?
Alex?
Can you *hear* me?
It's Professor Xavier.
It's *Charles.*
I can feel you, Alex.
I know you're *near.*
Can you hear me?
SHWEEAAHH

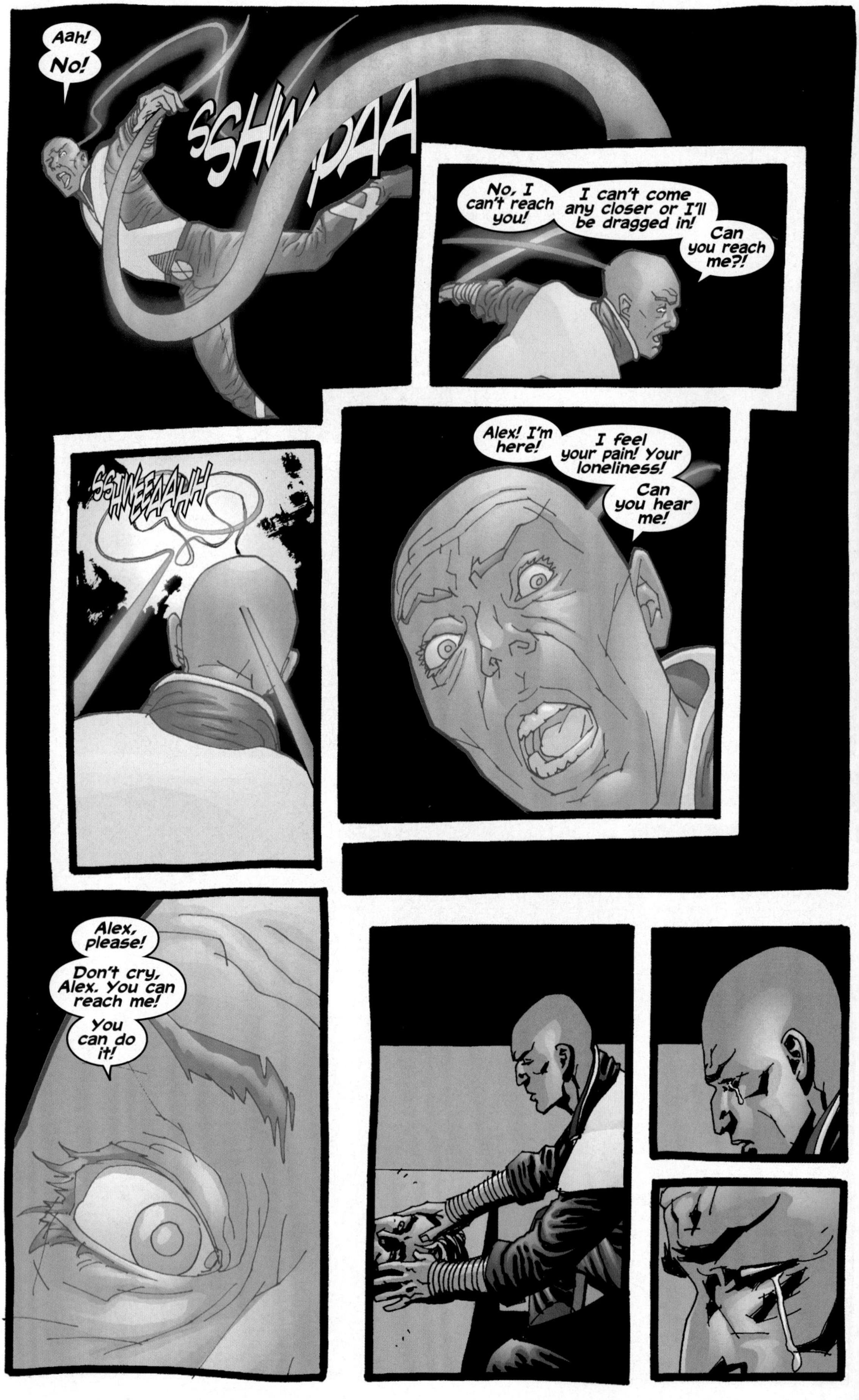
Aah!
No!
SSHWPAA
No, I can't reach you!
I can't come any closer or I'll be dragged in!
Can you reach me?!
SSHWEEAAHH
Alex! I'm here!
I feel your pain! Your loneliness!
Can you hear me!
Alex, please!
Don't cry, Alex. You can reach me!
You can do it!

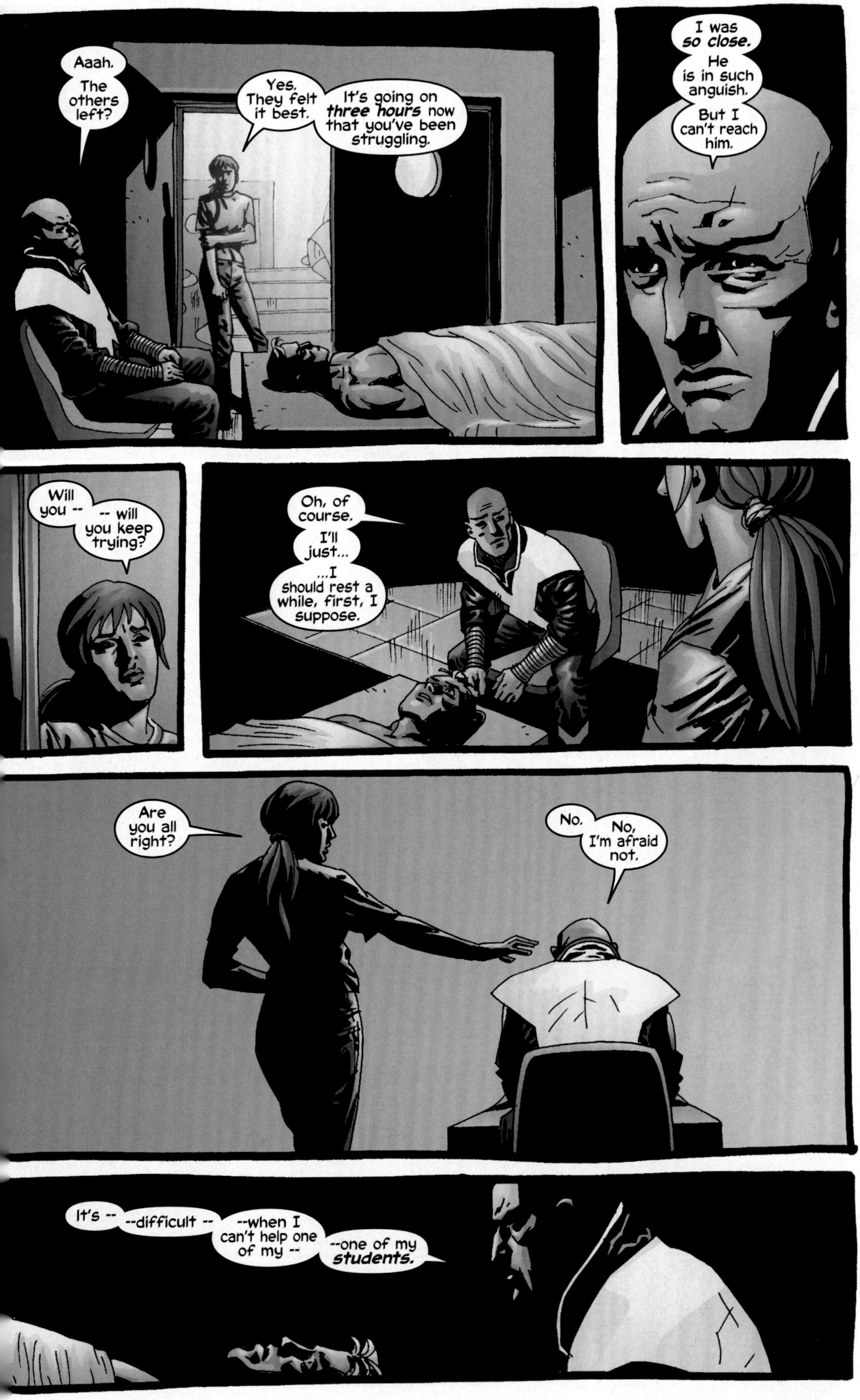
Aaah.
The others left?
Yes. They felt it best.
It's going on *three hours* now that you've been struggling.
I was *so close.*
He is in such anguish.
But I can't reach him.
Will you --
-- will you keep trying?
Oh, of course.
I'll just...
...I should rest a while, first, I suppose.
Are you all right?
No.
No, I'm afraid not.
It's --
--difficult --
--when I can't help one of my --
--one of my *students.*

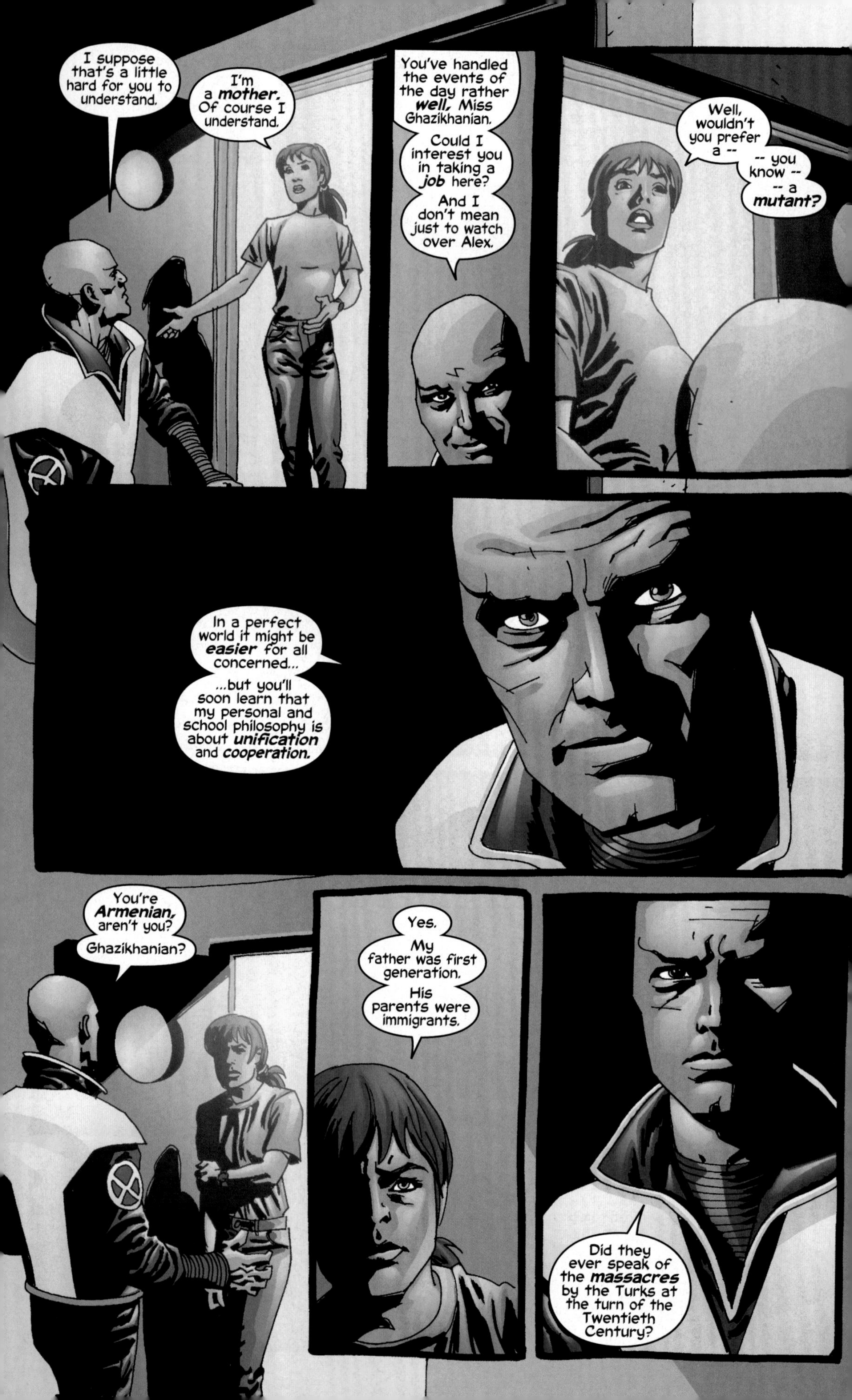

I suppose that's a little hard for you to understand.
I'm a **mother.** Of course I understand.
You've handled the events of the day rather **well,** Miss Ghazikhanian.
Could I interest you in taking a **job** here?
And I don't mean just to watch over Alex.
Well, wouldn't you prefer a --
-- you know --
-- a **mutant?**
In a perfect world it might be **easier** for all concerned...
...but you'll soon learn that my personal and school philosophy is about **unification** and **cooperation.**
You're **Armenian,** aren't you?
Ghazikhanian?
Yes.
My father was first generation.
His parents were immigrants.
Did they ever speak of the **massacres** by the Turks at the turn of the Twentieth Century?

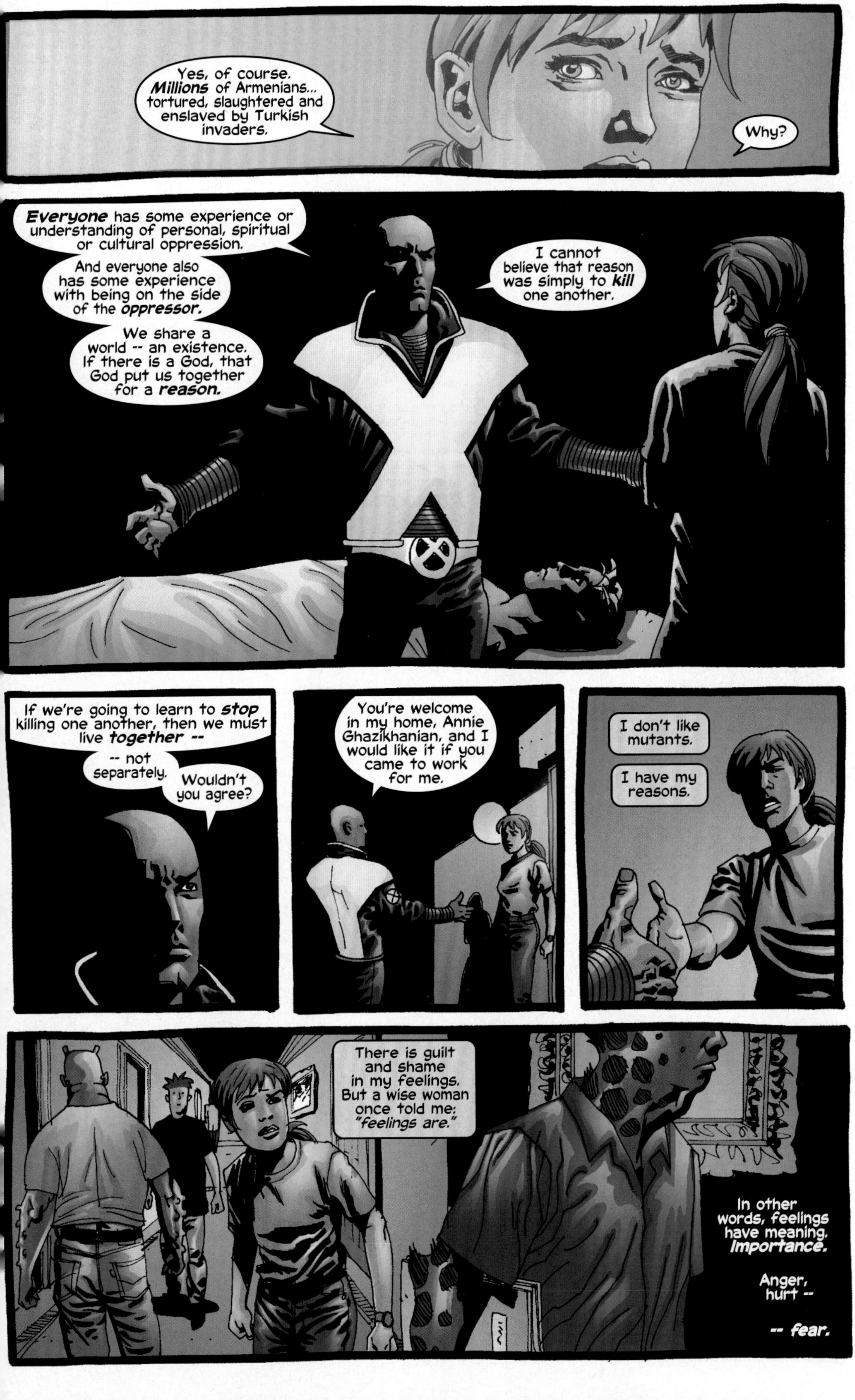
Yes, of course. Millions of Armenians... tortured, slaughtered and enslaved by Turkish invaders.
Why?
Everyone has some experience or understanding of personal, spiritual or cultural oppression.
And everyone also has some experience with being on the side of the oppressor.
We share a world -- an existence. If there is a God, that God put us together for a reason.
I cannot believe that reason was simply to kill one another.
If we're going to learn to stop killing one another, then we must live together --
-- not separately.
Wouldn't you agree?
You're welcome in my home, Annie Ghazikhanian, and I would like it if you came to work for me.
I don't like mutants.
I have my reasons.
There is guilt and shame in my feelings. But a wise woman once told me: "feelings are."
In other words, feelings have meaning. Importance.
Anger, hurt --
-- fear.

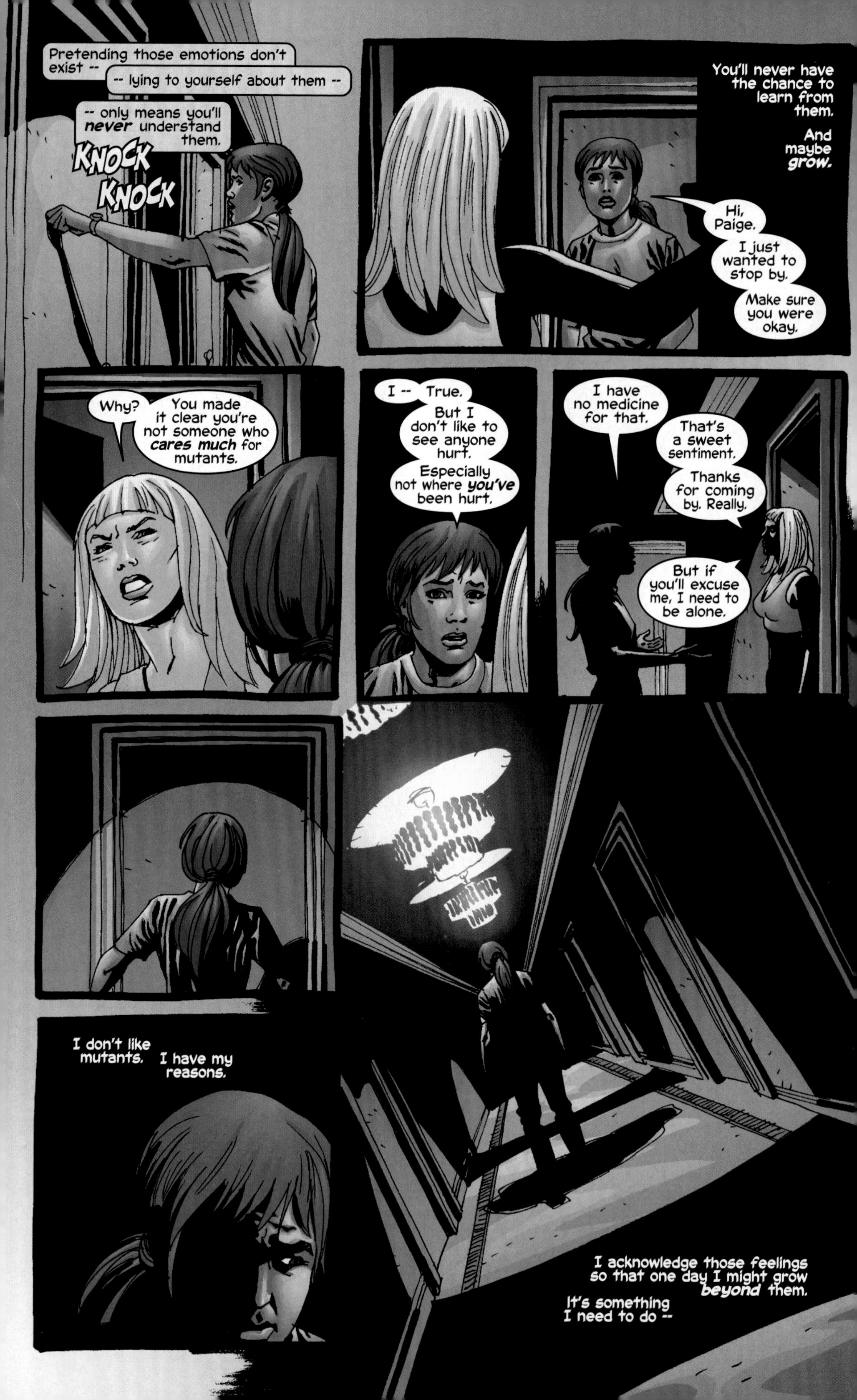
Pretending those emotions don't exist --
-- lying to yourself about them --
-- only means you'll **never** understand them.
KNOCK
KNOCK
You'll never have the chance to learn from them.
And maybe **grow.**
Hi, Paige.
I just wanted to stop by.
Make sure you were okay.
Why?
You made it clear you're not someone who **cares much** for mutants.
I -- True.
But I don't like to see anyone hurt.
Especially not where **you've** been hurt.
I have no medicine for that.
That's a sweet sentiment.
Thanks for coming by. Really.
But if you'll excuse me, I need to be alone.
I don't like mutants.
I have my reasons.
I acknowledge those feelings so that one day I might grow **beyond** them.
It's something I need to do --

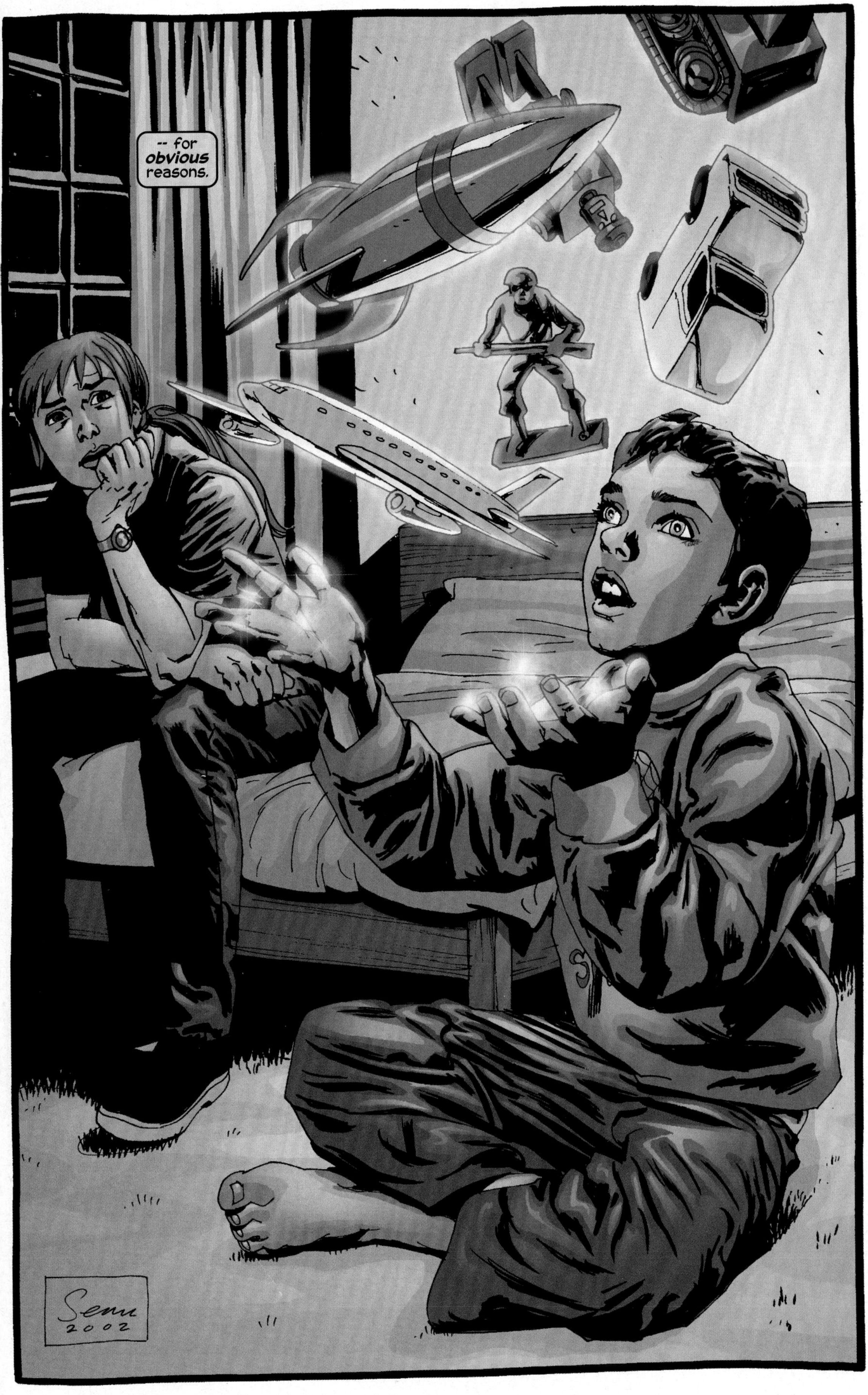
-- for *obvious* reasons.
Senn
2002

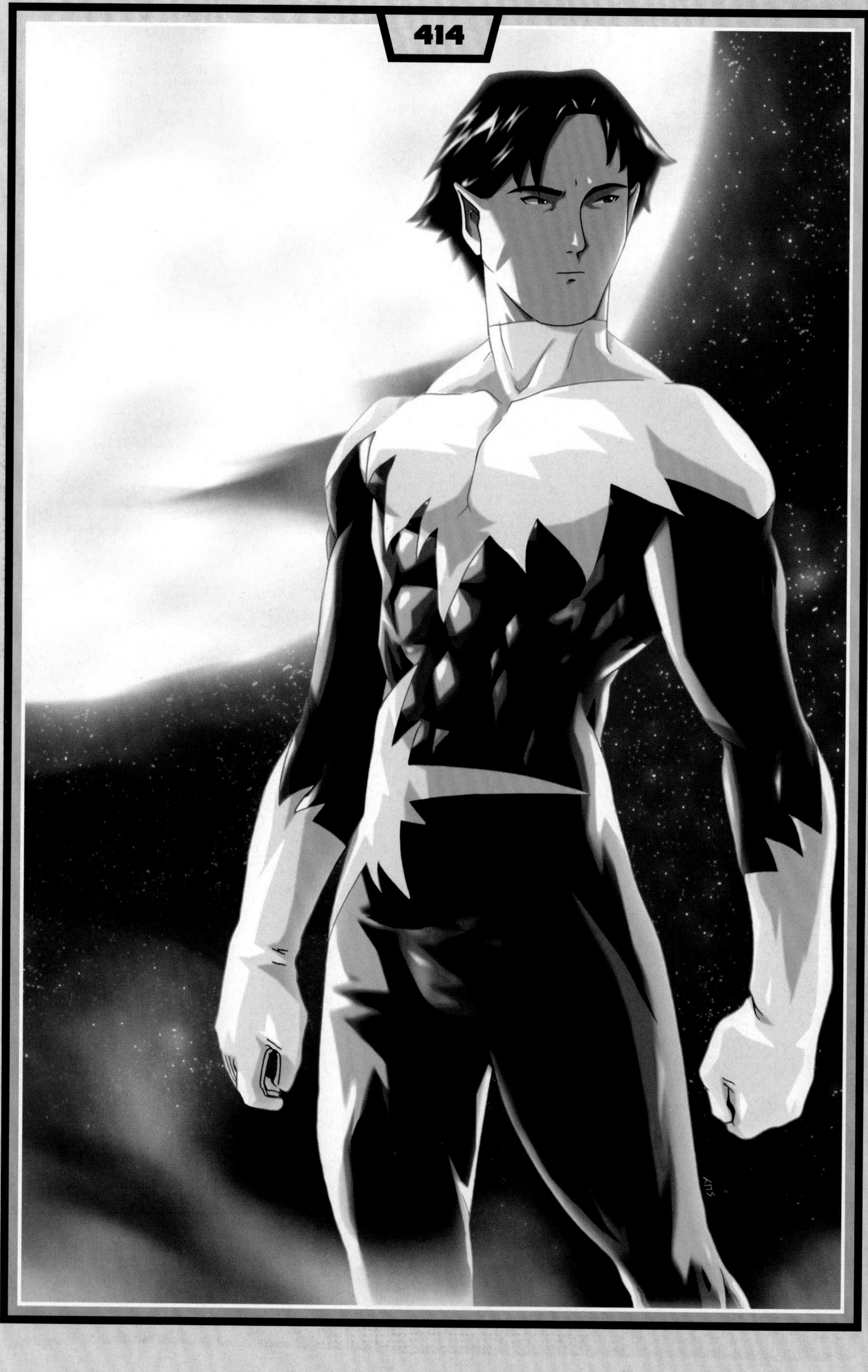
414

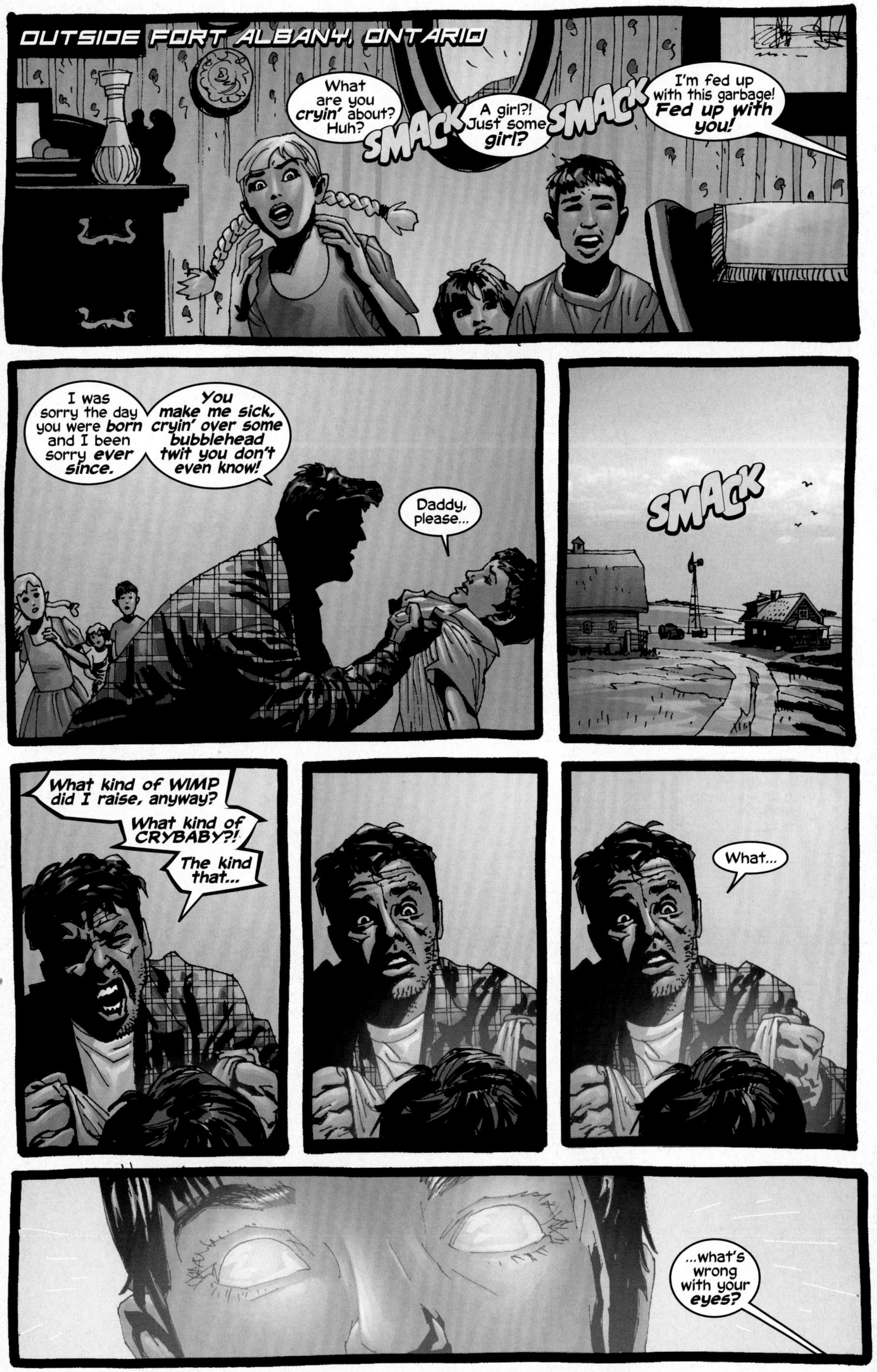
OUTSIDE FORT ALBANY, ONTARIO
What are you cryin' about? Huh?
SMACK
A girl?! Just some girl?
SMACK
I'm fed up with this garbage! Fed up with you!
I was sorry the day you were born and I been sorry ever since.
You make me sick, cryin' over some bubblehead twit you don't even know!
Daddy, please...
SMACK
What kind of WIMP did I raise, anyway?
What kind of CRYBABY?!
The kind that...
What...
...what's wrong with your eyes?

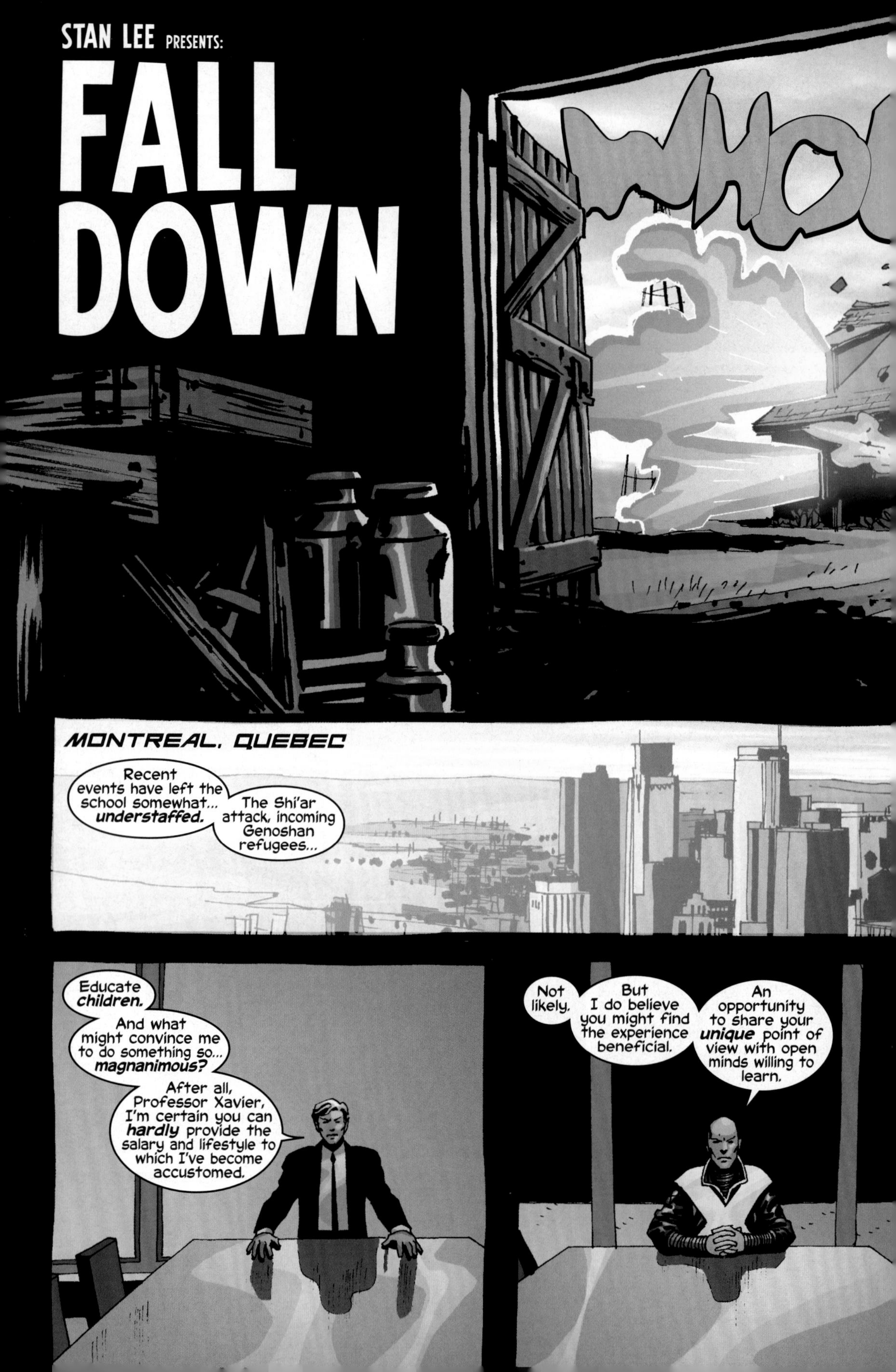
STAN LEE PRESENTS:
FALL DOWN
MONTREAL, QUEBEC
Recent events have left the school somewhat... understaffed.
The Shi'ar attack, incoming Genoshan refugees...
Educate children.
And what might convince me to do something so... magnanimous?
After all, Professor Xavier, I'm certain you can hardly provide the salary and lifestyle to which I've become accustomed.
Not likely.
But I do believe you might find the experience beneficial.
An opportunity to share your unique point of view with open minds willing to learn.

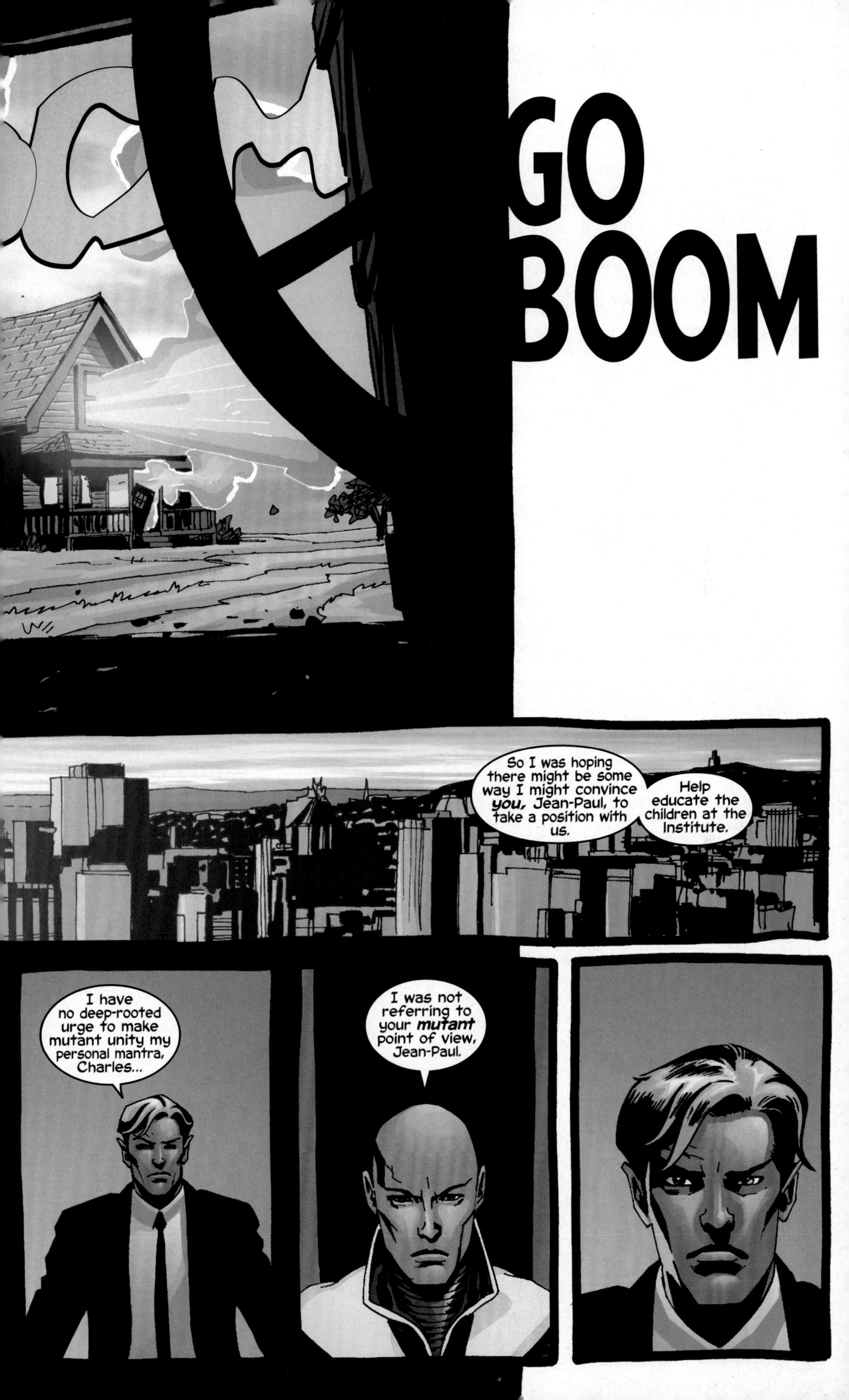
GO BOOM
So I was hoping there might be some way I might convince you, Jean-Paul, to take a position with us.
Help educate the children at the Institute.
I have no deep-rooted urge to make mutant unity my personal mantra, Charles...
I was not referring to your mutant point of view, Jean-Paul.

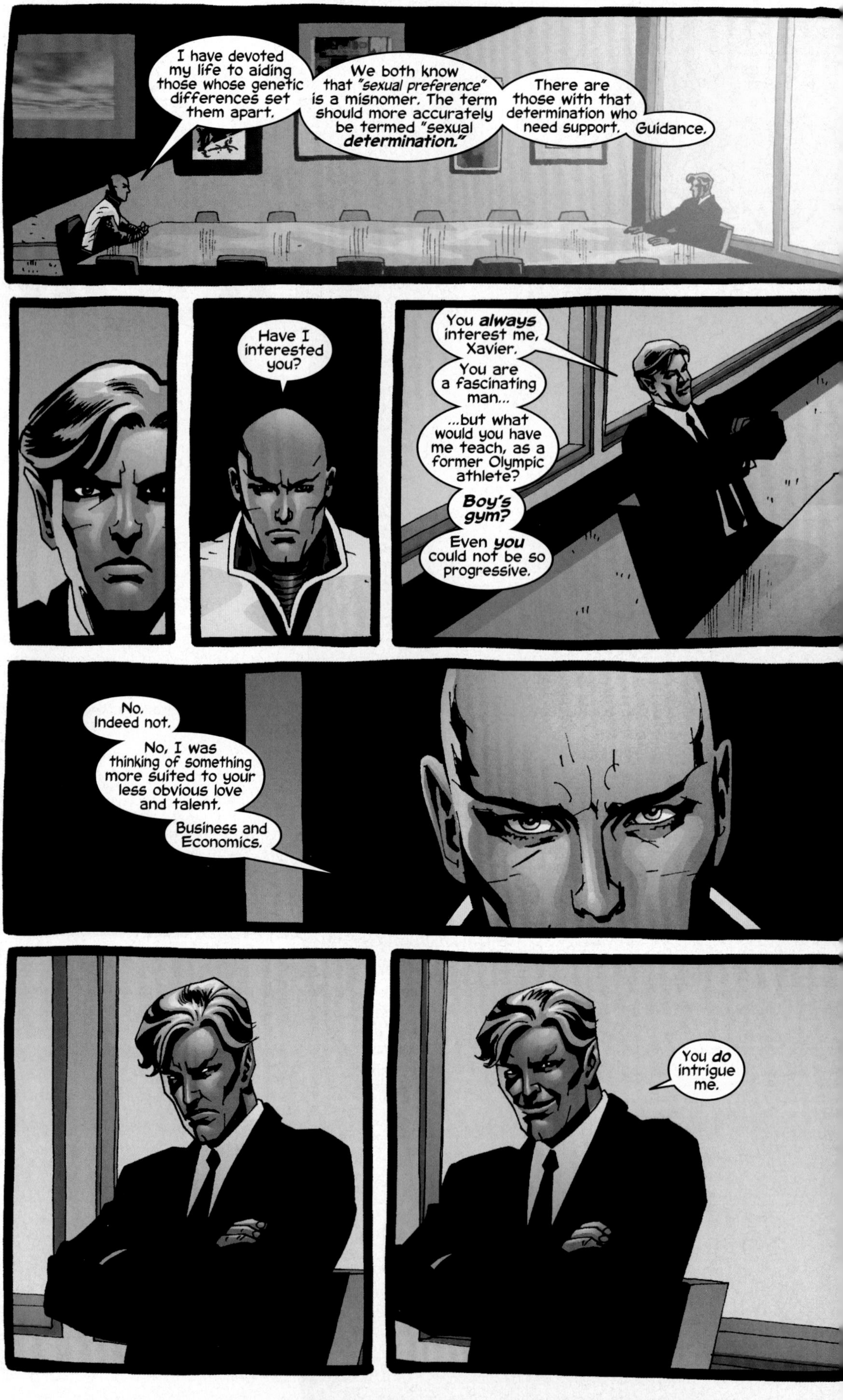

I have devoted my life to aiding those whose genetic differences set them apart.
We both know that "sexual preference" is a misnomer. The term should more accurately be termed "sexual determination."
There are those with that determination who need support.
Guidance.
Have I interested you?
You always interest me, Xavier.
You are a fascinating man...
...but what would you have me teach, as a former Olympic athlete?
Boy's gym?
Even you could not be so progressive.
No. Indeed not.
No, I was thinking of something more suited to your less obvious love and talent.
Business and Economics.
You do intrigue me.

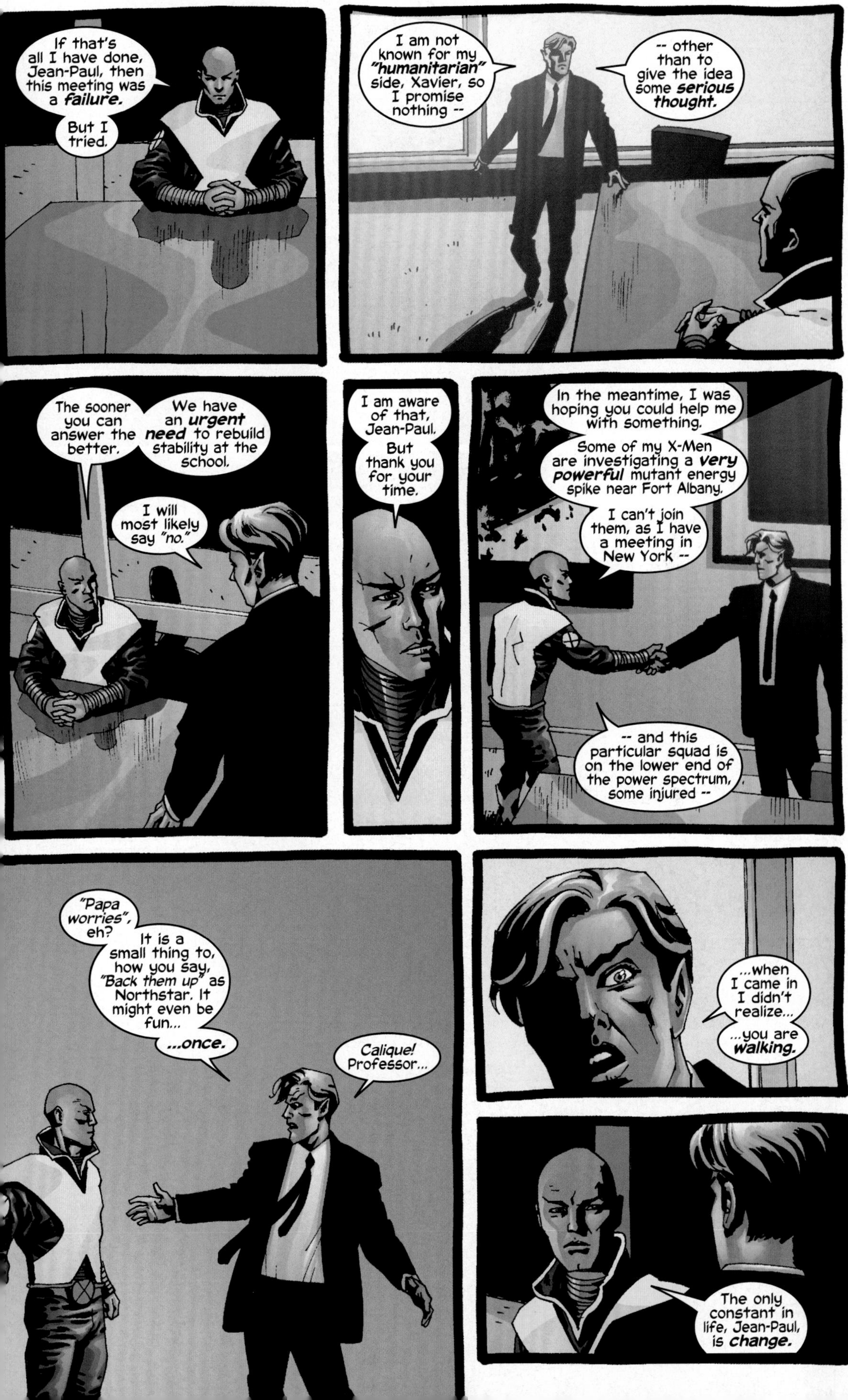
If that's all I have done, Jean-Paul, then this meeting was a *failure.*
But I tried.
I am not known for my *"humanitarian"* side, Xavier, so I promise nothing --
-- other than to give the idea some *serious thought.*
The sooner you can answer the better.
We have an *urgent need* to rebuild stability at the school.
I will most likely say *"no."*
I am aware of that, Jean-Paul.
But thank you for your time.
In the meantime, I was hoping you could help me with something.
Some of my X-Men are investigating a *very powerful* mutant energy spike near Fort Albany.
I can't join them, as I have a meeting in New York --
-- and this particular squad is on the lower end of the power spectrum, some injured --
"Papa worries", eh?
It is a small thing to, how you say, *"Back them up"* as Northstar. It might even be fun...
...once.
Calique! Professor...
...when I came in I didn't realize...
...you are *walking.*
The only constant in life, Jean-Paul, is *change.*

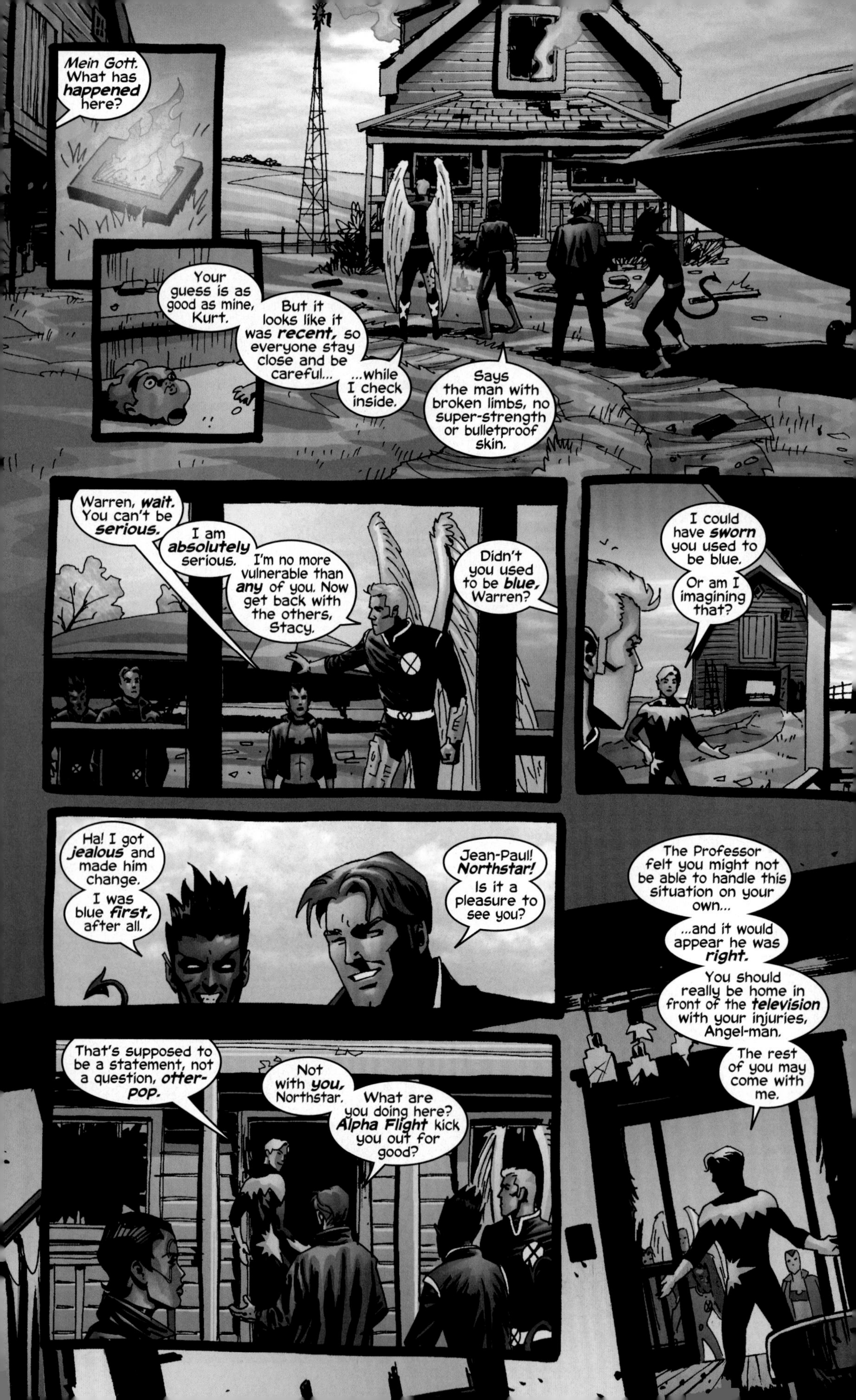
Mein Gott. What has happened here?
Your guess is as good as mine, Kurt.
But it looks like it was recent, so everyone stay close and be careful...
...while I check inside.
Says the man with broken limbs, no super-strength or bulletproof skin.
Warren, wait. You can't be serious.
I am absolutely serious.
I'm no more vulnerable than any of you. Now get back with the others, Stacy.
Didn't you used to be blue, Warren?
I could have sworn you used to be blue.
Or am I imagining that?
Ha! I got jealous and made him change.
I was blue first, after all.
Jean-Paul! Northstar!
Is it a pleasure to see you?
That's supposed to be a statement, not a question, otter-pop.
Not with you, Northstar.
What are you doing here? Alpha Flight kick you out for good?
The Professor felt you might not be able to handle this situation on your own...
...and it would appear he was right.
You should really be home in front of the television with your injuries, Angel-man.
The rest of you may come with me.

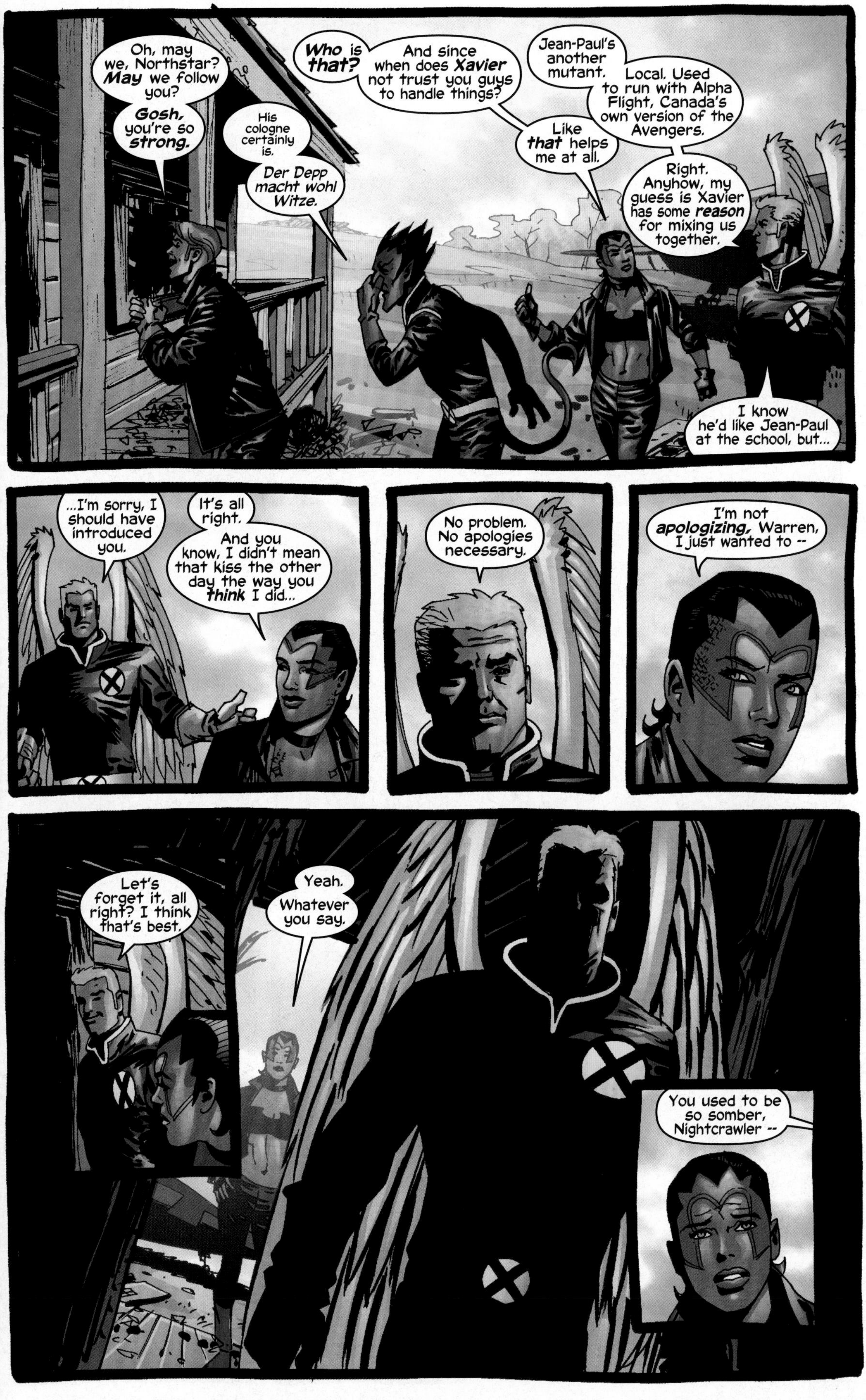

Oh, may we, Northstar? May we follow you?
Gosh, you're so strong.
His cologne certainly is.
Der Depp macht wohl Witze.
Who is that?
And since when does Xavier not trust you guys to handle things?
Jean-Paul's another mutant.
Local. Used to run with Alpha Flight, Canada's own version of the Avengers.
Like that helps me at all.
Right. Anyhow, my guess is Xavier has some reason for mixing us together.
I know he'd like Jean-Paul at the school, but...
...I'm sorry, I should have introduced you.
It's all right.
And you know, I didn't mean that kiss the other day the way you think I did...
No problem. No apologies necessary.
I'm not apologizing, Warren, I just wanted to --
Let's forget it, all right? I think that's best.
Yeah. Whatever you say.
You used to be so somber, Nightcrawler --

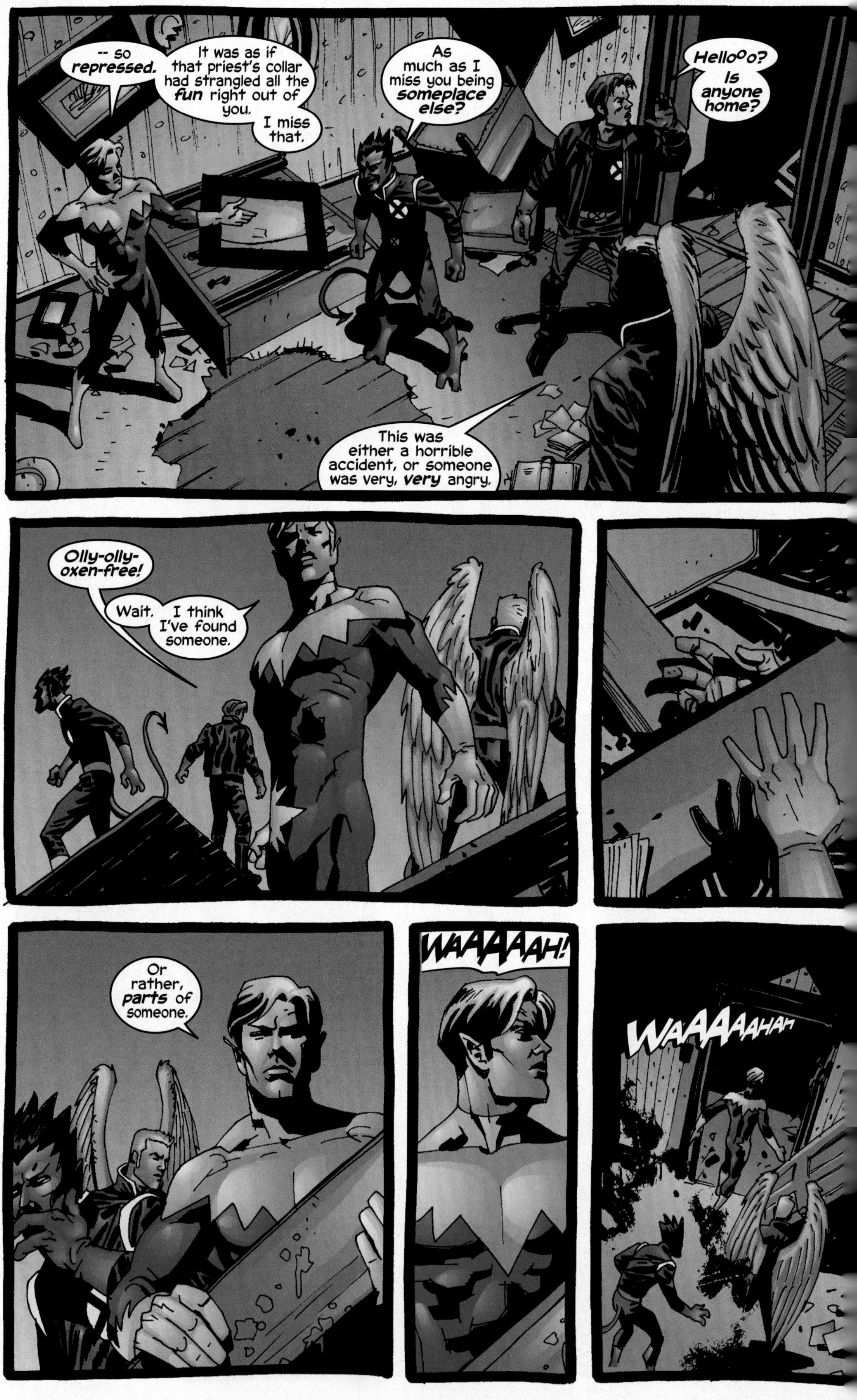

-- so repressed.
It was as if that priest's collar had strangled all the fun right out of you.
I miss that.
As much as I miss you being someplace else?
Hello°o?
Is anyone home?
This was either a horrible accident, or someone was very, very angry.
Olly-olly-oxen-free!
Wait.
I think I've found someone.
Or rather, parts of someone.
WAAAAAH!
WAAAAAHAH

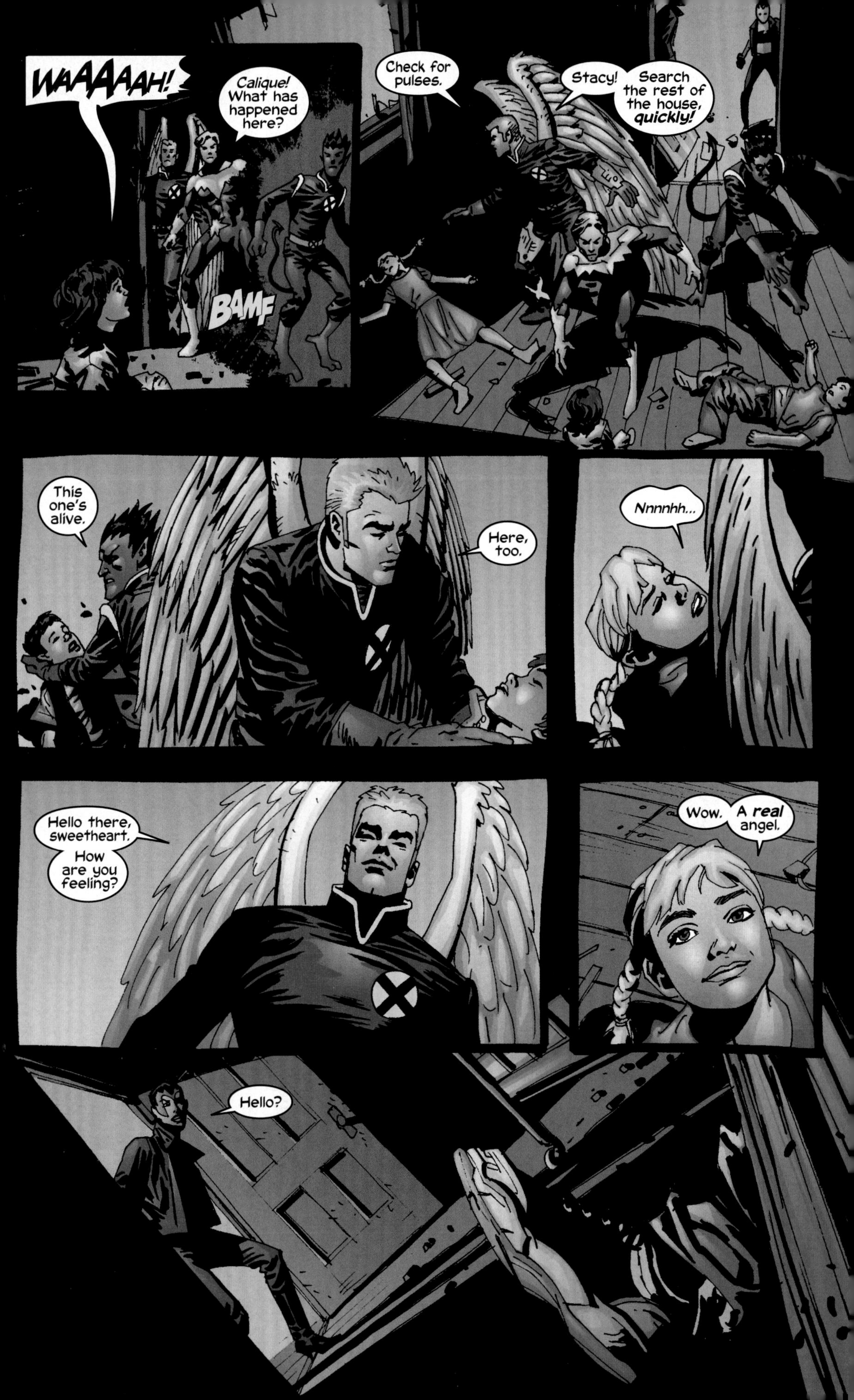
WAAAAAH!
Calique! What has happened here?
BAMF
Check for pulses.
Stacy! Search the rest of the house, quickly!
This one's alive.
Here, too.
Nnnnhh...
Hello there, sweetheart.
How are you feeling?
Wow. A real angel.
Hello?

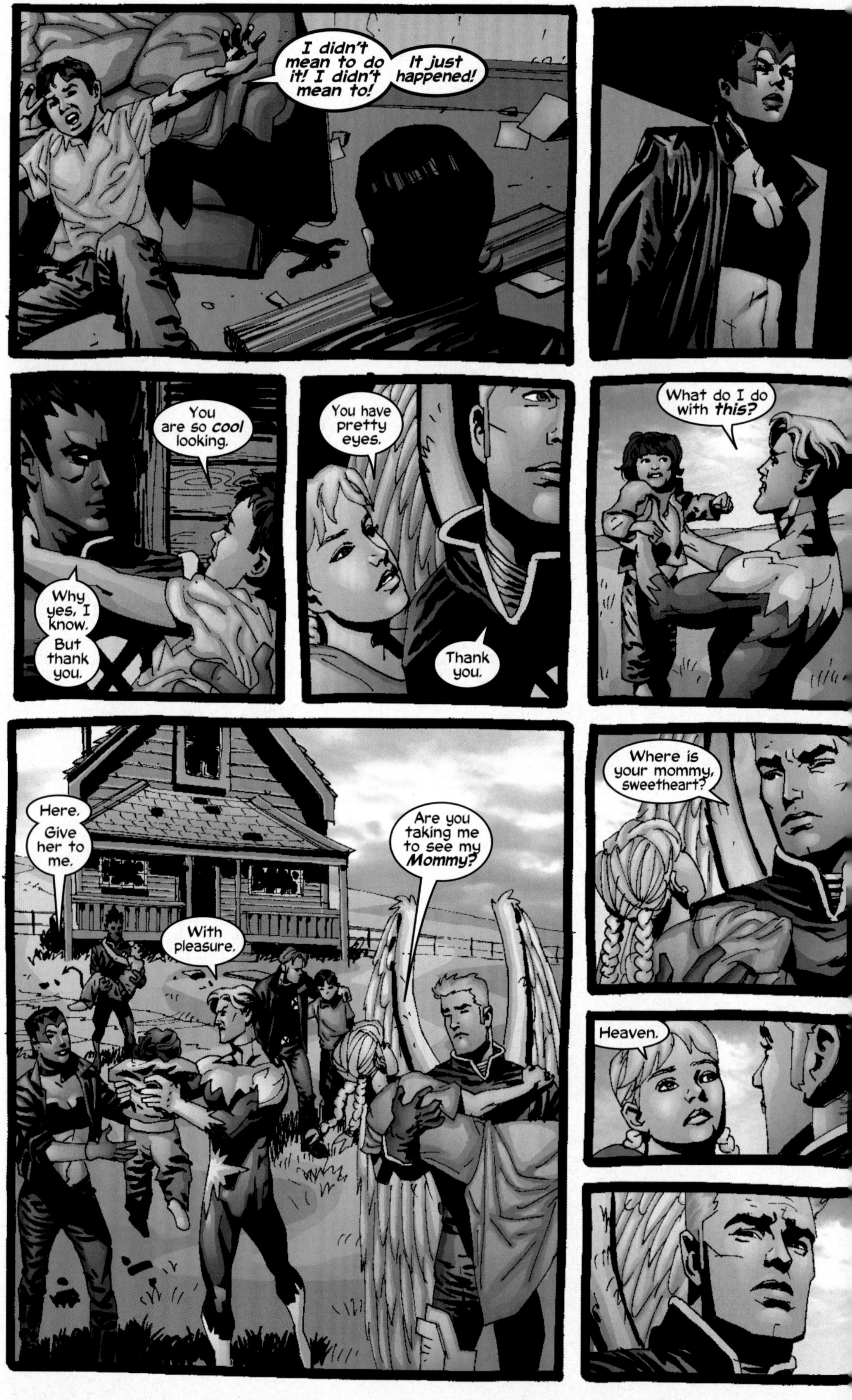

I didn't mean to do it! I didn't mean to!
It just happened!
You are so cool looking.
Why yes, I know.
But thank you.
You have pretty eyes.
Thank you.
What do I do with this?
Here. Give her to me.
With pleasure.
Are you taking me to see my Mommy?
Where is your mommy, sweetheart?
Heaven.

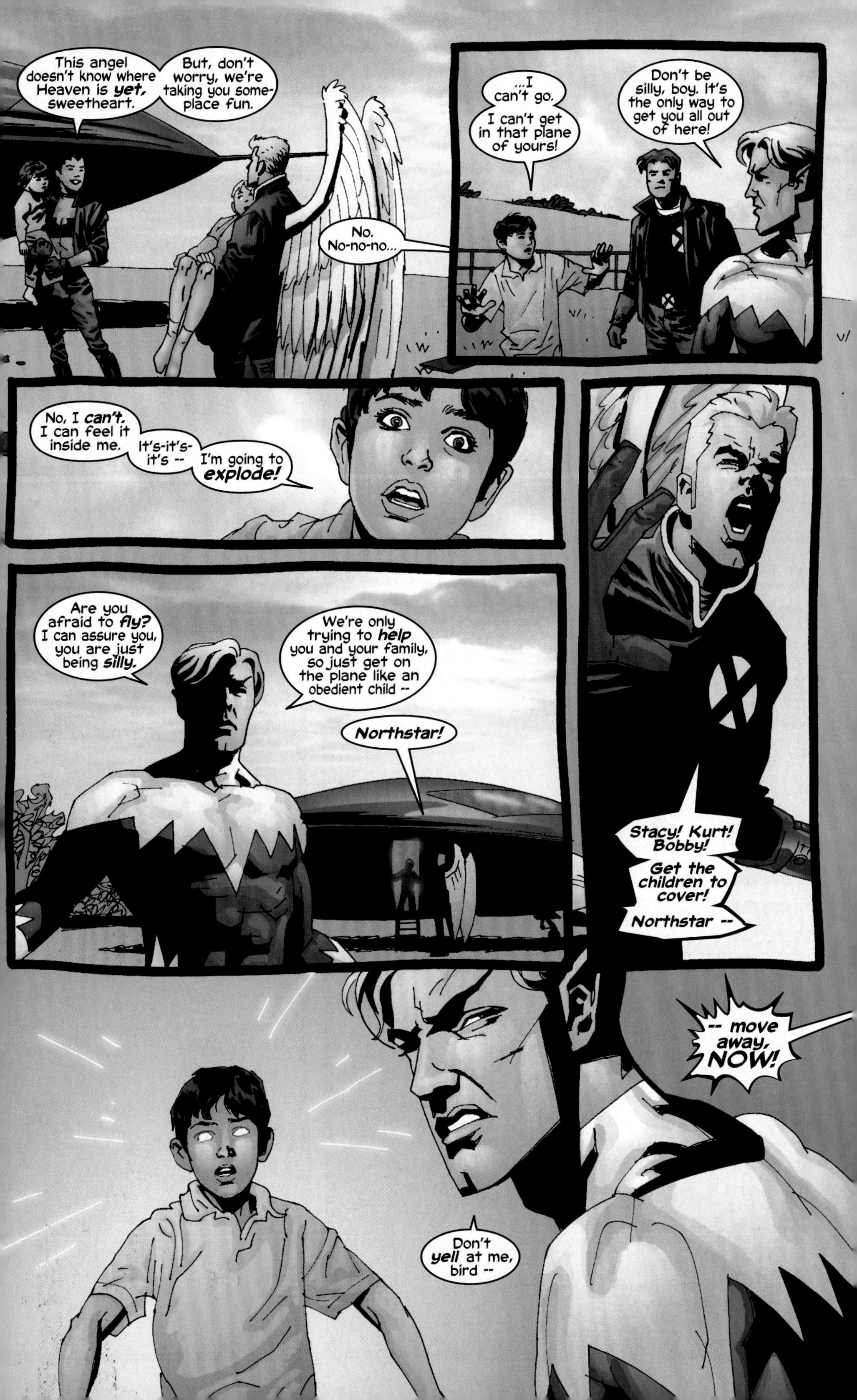
This angel doesn't know where Heaven is yet, sweetheart.
But, don't worry, we're taking you someplace fun.
No, No-no-no...
...I can't go.
I can't get in that plane of yours!
Don't be silly, boy. It's the only way to get you all out of here!
No, I can't. I can feel it inside me.
It's-it's-it's --
I'm going to explode!
Are you afraid to fly? I can assure you, you are just being silly.
We're only trying to help you and your family, so just get on the plane like an obedient child --
Northstar!
Stacy! Kurt! Bobby!
Get the children to cover!
Northstar --
-- move away, NOW!
Don't yell at me, bird --

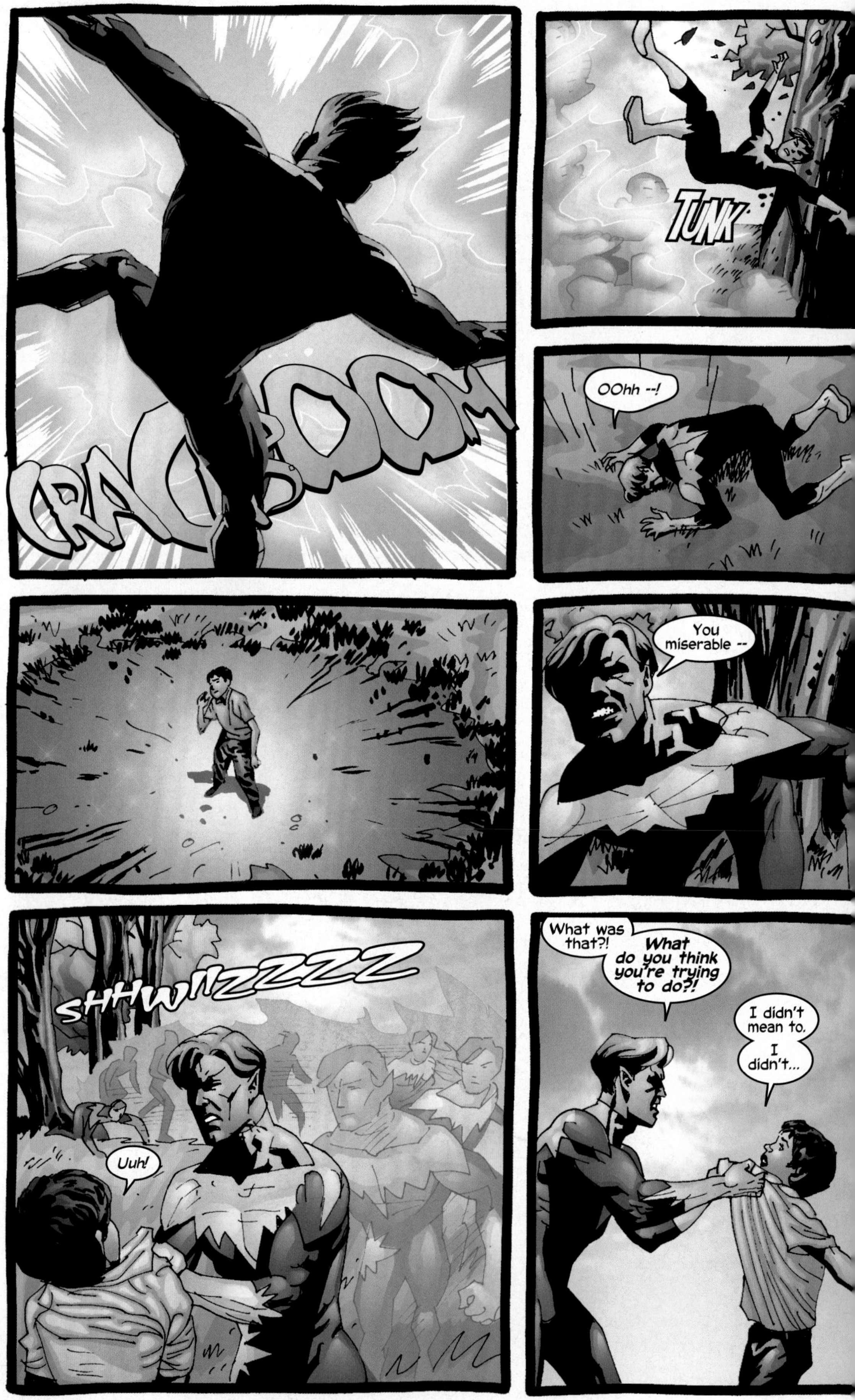
CRACKBOOOM
TUNK
OOhh --!
You miserable --
SHHWIIZZZZZ
Uuh!
What was that?!
What do you think you're trying to do?!
I didn't mean to. I didn't...

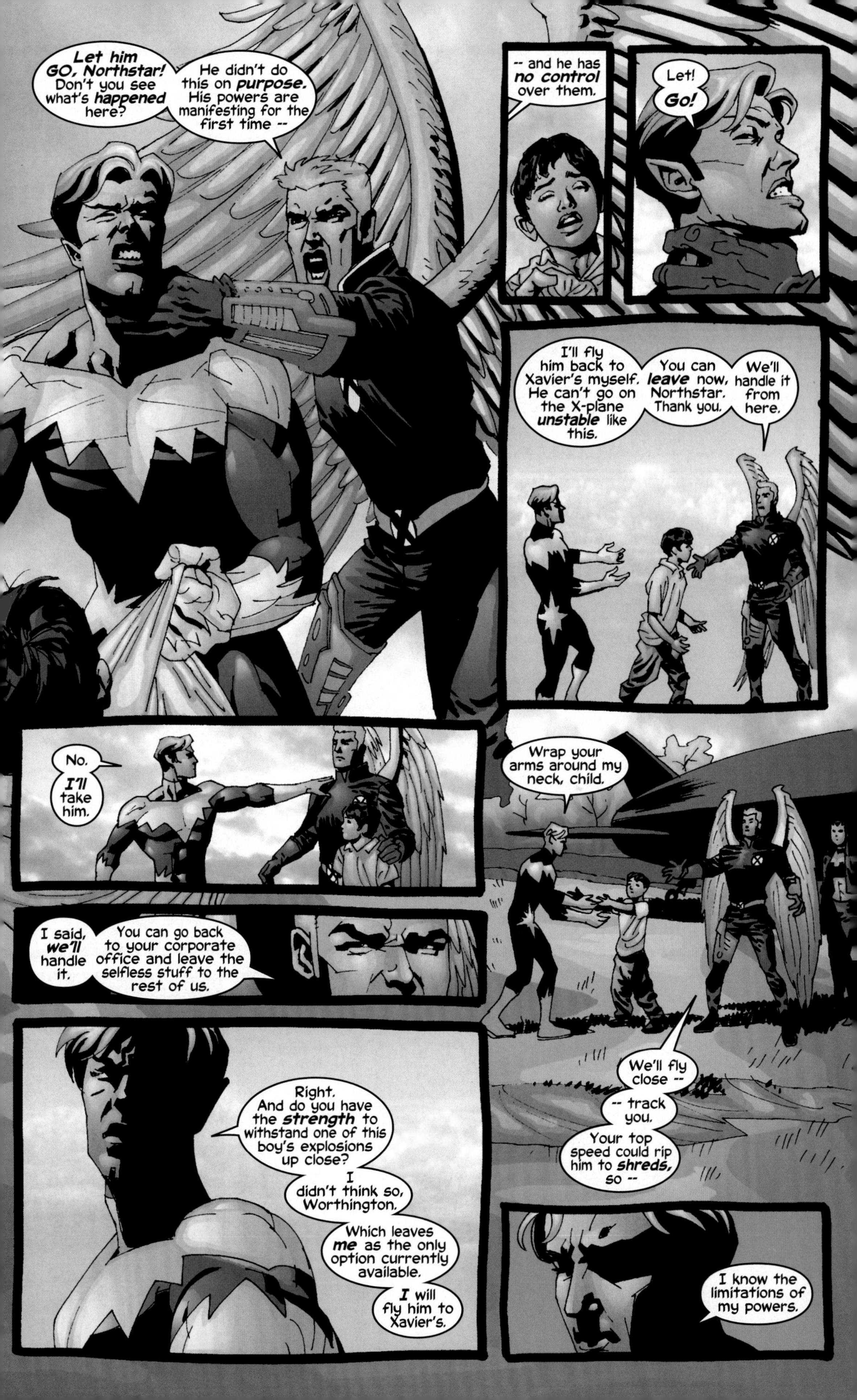
Let him GO, Northstar! Don't you see what's happened here?
He didn't do this on purpose. His powers are manifesting for the first time --
-- and he has no control over them.
Let! Go!
I'll fly him back to Xavier's myself. He can't go on the X-plane unstable like this.
You can leave now, Northstar. Thank you.
We'll handle it from here.
No. I'll take him.
I said, we'll handle it.
You can go back to your corporate office and leave the selfless stuff to the rest of us.
Right. And do you have the strength to withstand one of this boy's explosions up close?
I didn't think so, Worthington.
Which leaves me as the only option currently available.
I will fly him to Xavier's.
Wrap your arms around my neck, child.
We'll fly close --
-- track you.
Your top speed could rip him to shreds, so --
I know the limitations of my powers.

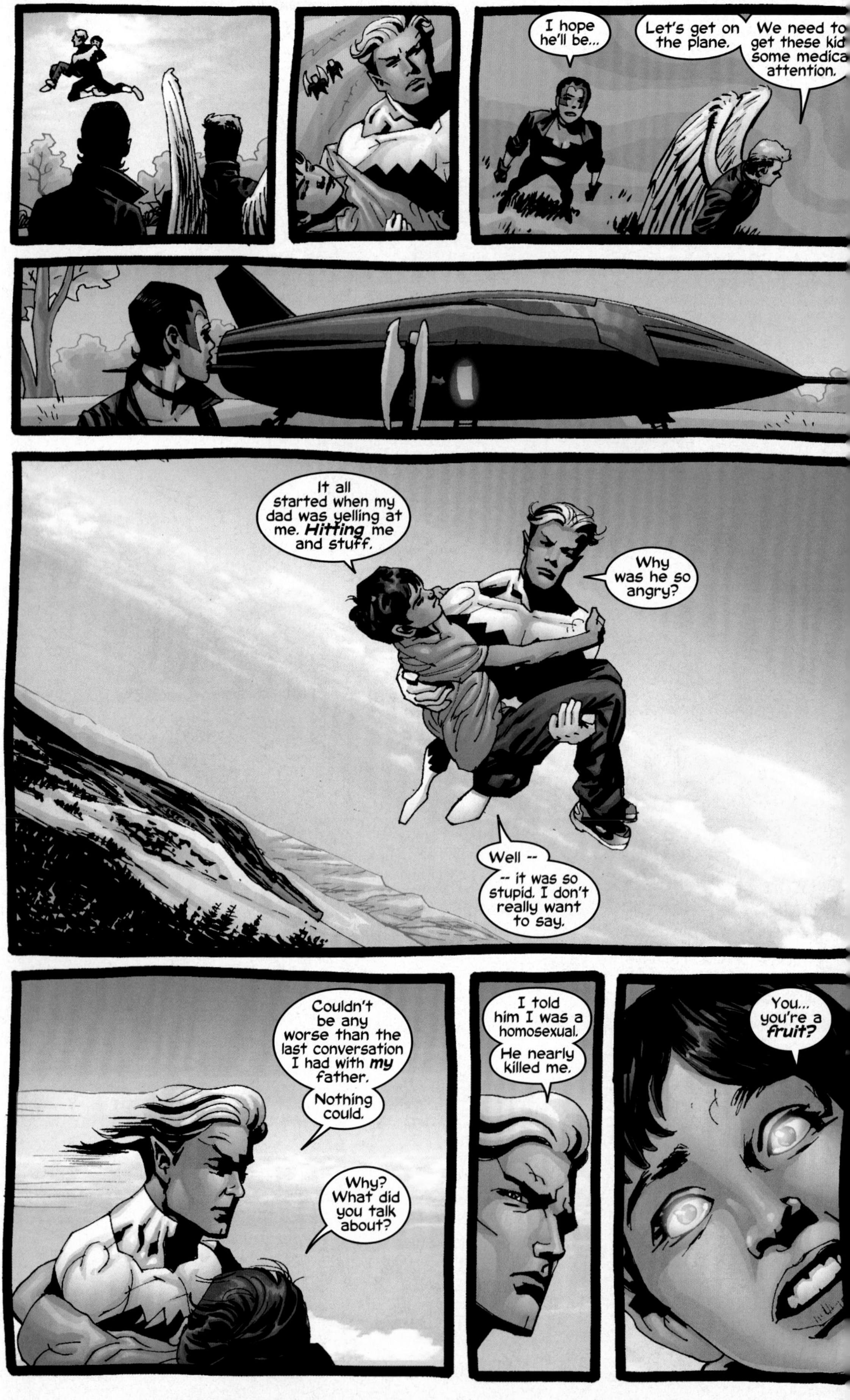
I hope he'll be...
Let's get on the plane.
We need to get these kid some medica attention.
It all started when my dad was yelling at me. Hitting me and stuff.
Why was he so angry?
Well --
-- it was so stupid. I don't really want to say.
Couldn't be any worse than the last conversation I had with my father.
Nothing could.
Why? What did you talk about?
I told him I was a homosexual.
He nearly killed me.
You... you're a fruit?

Put me down! Put me DOWN!

Stop moving! You're throwing me off balance!

Idiot! Look how high you are! Stop being stupid and climb onto my back!

I'm not a queer and you can't make me!

I'm not trying to make you into anything, you little fool. I'm trying to save your life! For what lunatic reason at the moment I cannot recall, and --

SWA DOO

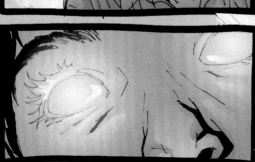

Calvasse --

AAAhh--

Dammit.

SHWOOOC

HWOO

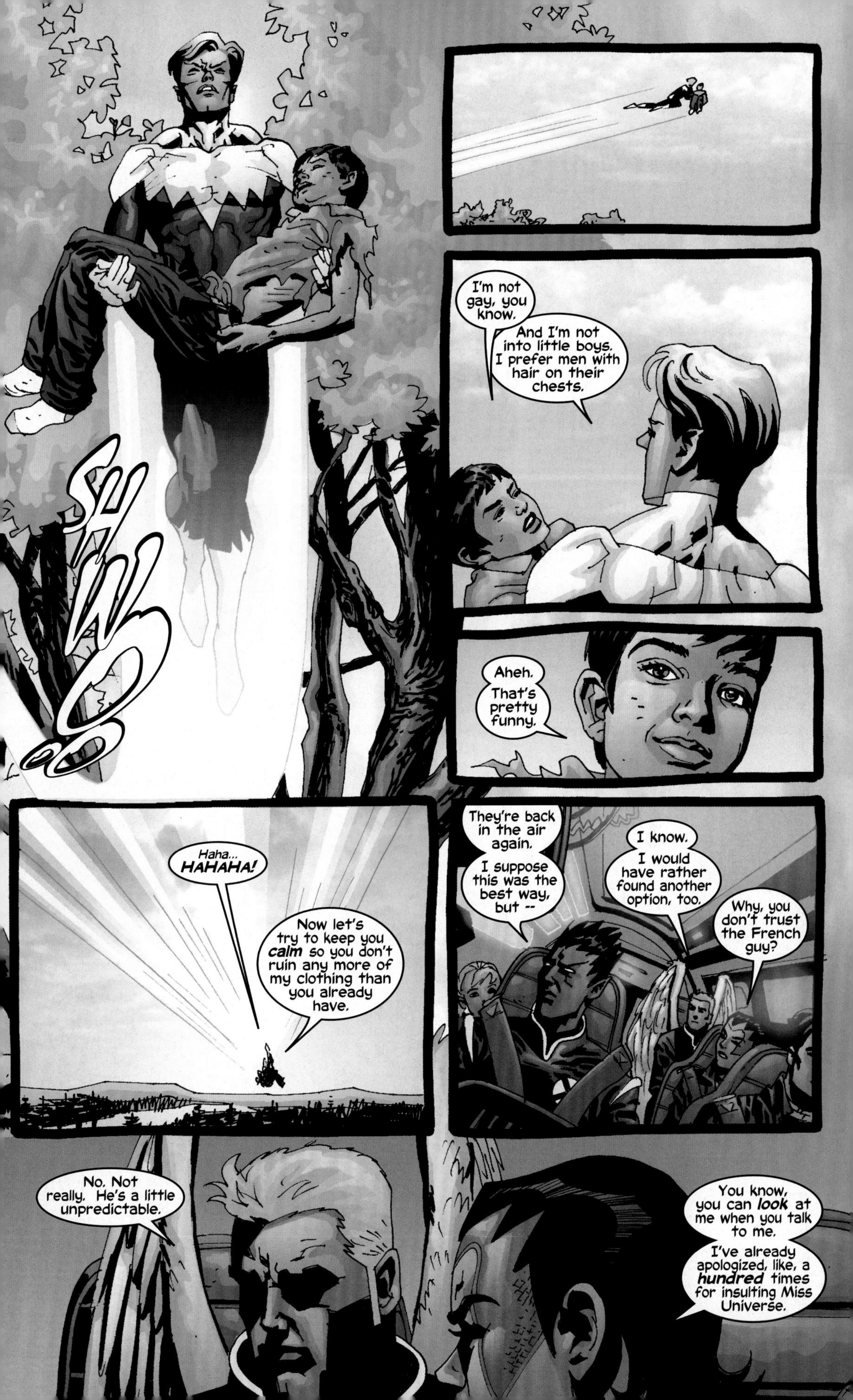
SHWOOO
I'm not gay, you know.
And I'm not into little boys. I prefer men with hair on their chests.
Aheh. That's pretty funny.
Haha... HAHAHA!
Now let's try to keep you *calm* so you don't ruin any more of my clothing than you already have.
They're back in the air again.
I suppose this was the best way, but --
I know. I would have rather found another option, too.
Why, you don't trust the French guy?
No. Not really. He's a little unpredictable.
You know, you can *look* at me when you talk to me.
I've already apologized, like, a *hundred* times for insulting Miss Universe.

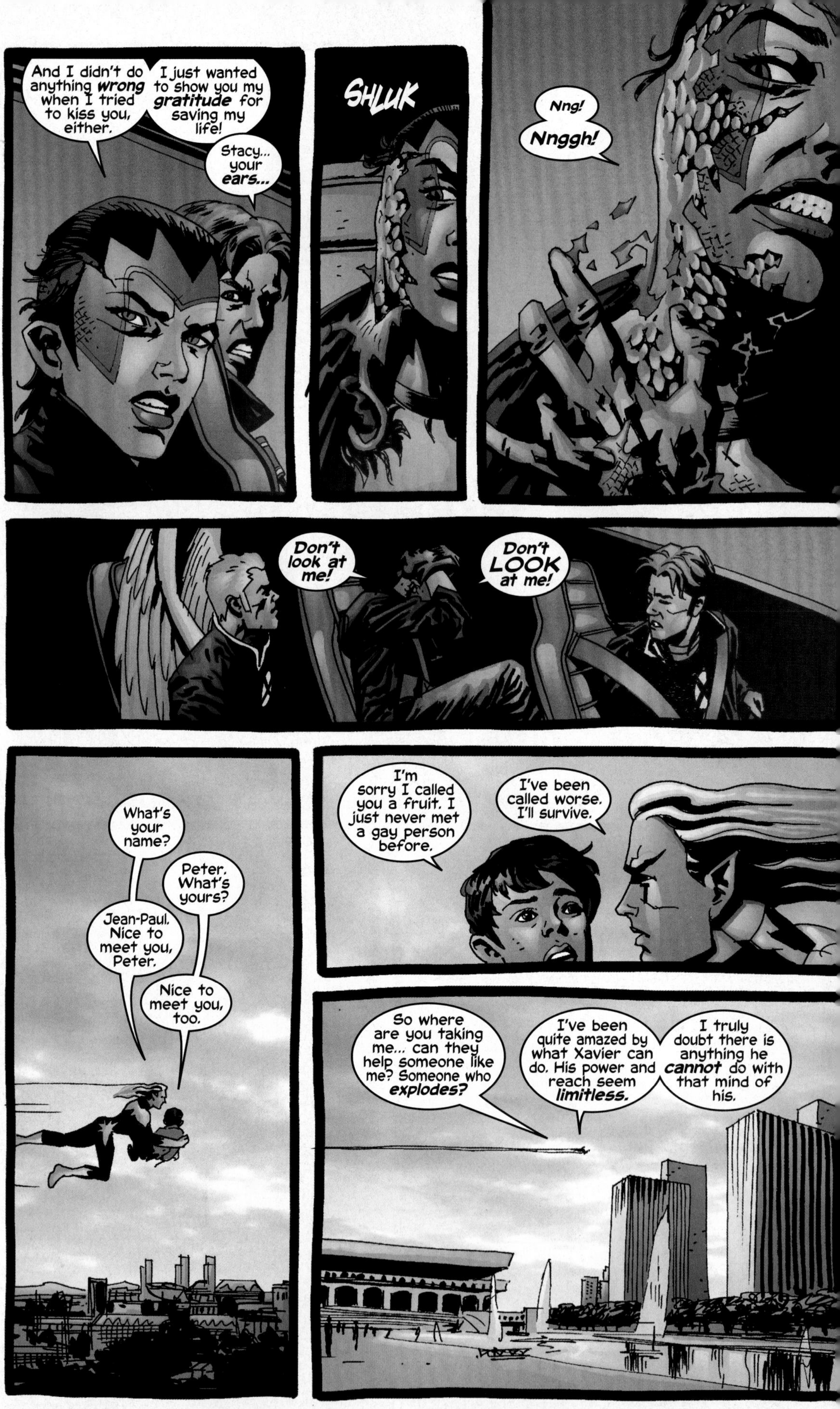
And I didn't do anything wrong when I tried to kiss you, either.
I just wanted to show you my gratitude for saving my life!
Stacy... your ears...
SHLUK
Nng!
Nnggh!
Don't look at me!
Don't LOOK at me!
What's your name?
Peter. What's yours?
Jean-Paul. Nice to meet you, Peter.
Nice to meet you, too.
I'm sorry I called you a fruit. I just never met a gay person before.
I've been called worse. I'll survive.
So where are you taking me... can they help someone like me? Someone who explodes?
I've been quite amazed by what Xavier can do. His power and reach seem limitless.
I truly doubt there is anything he cannot do with that mind of his.

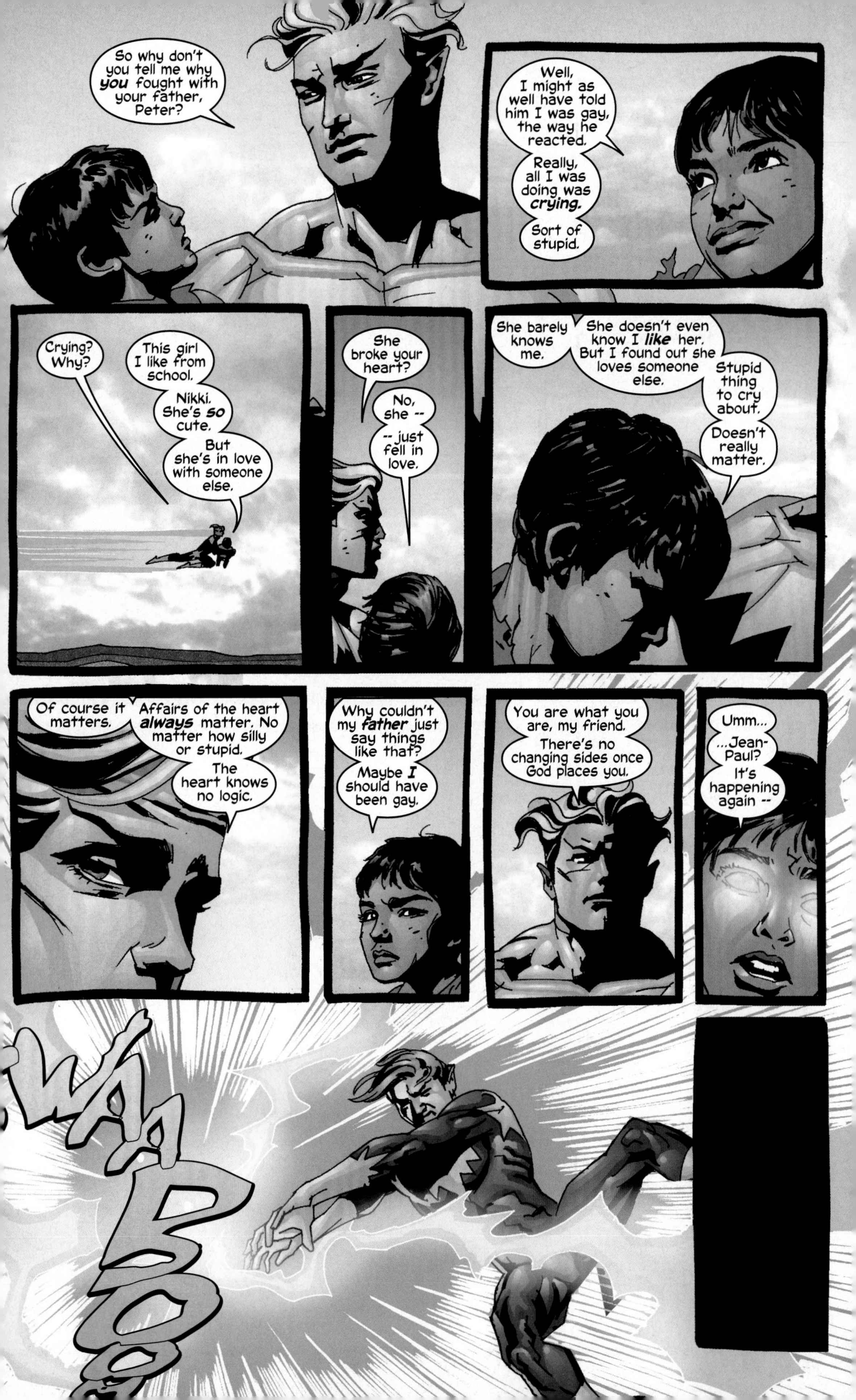
So why don't you tell me why *you* fought with your father, Peter?
Well, I might as well have told him I was gay, the way he reacted.
Really, all I was doing was *crying.*
Sort of stupid.
Crying? Why?
This girl I like from school.
Nikki. She's *so* cute.
But she's in love with someone else.
She broke your heart?
No, she --
-- just fell in love.
She barely knows me.
She doesn't even know I *like* her. But I found out she loves someone else.
Stupid thing to cry about.
Doesn't really matter.
Of course it matters.
Affairs of the heart *always* matter. No matter how silly or stupid.
The heart knows no logic.
Why couldn't my *father* just say things like that?
Maybe *I* should have been gay.
You are what you are, my friend.
There's no changing sides once God places you.
Umm...
...Jean-Paul?
It's happening again --
WAABOO

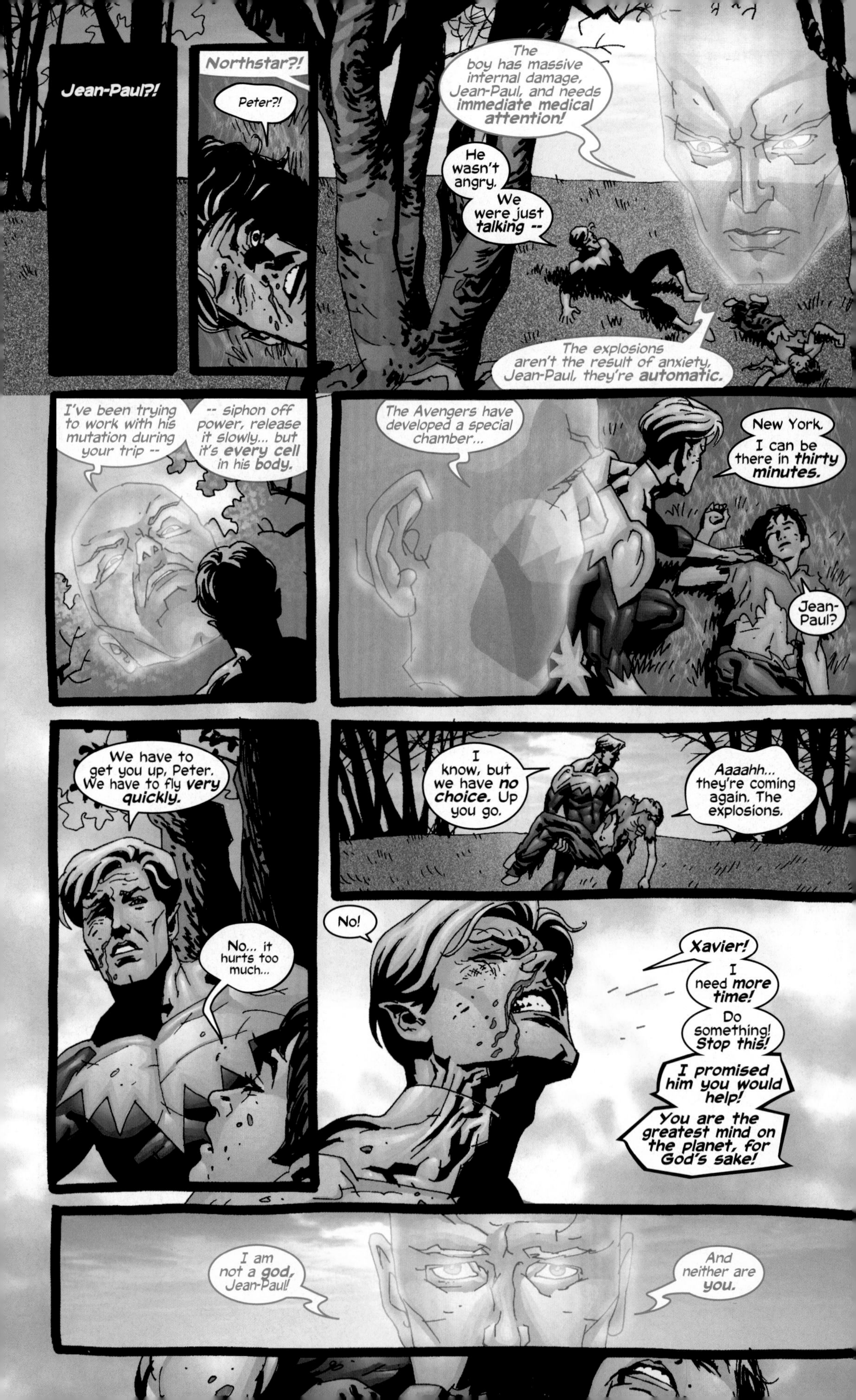
Jean-Paul?!
Northstar?!
Peter?!
The boy has massive internal damage, Jean-Paul, and needs immediate medical attention!
He wasn't angry.
We were just talking --
The explosions aren't the result of anxiety, Jean-Paul, they're automatic.
I've been trying to work with his mutation during your trip --
-- siphon off power, release it slowly... but it's every cell in his body.
The Avengers have developed a special chamber...
New York.
I can be there in thirty minutes.
Jean-Paul?
We have to get you up, Peter. We have to fly very quickly.
I know, but we have no choice. Up you go.
Aaaahh... they're coming again. The explosions.
No... it hurts too much...
No!
Xavier!
I need more time!
Do something! Stop this!
I promised him you would help!
You are the greatest mind on the planet, for God's sake!
I am not a god, Jean-Paul!
And neither are you.

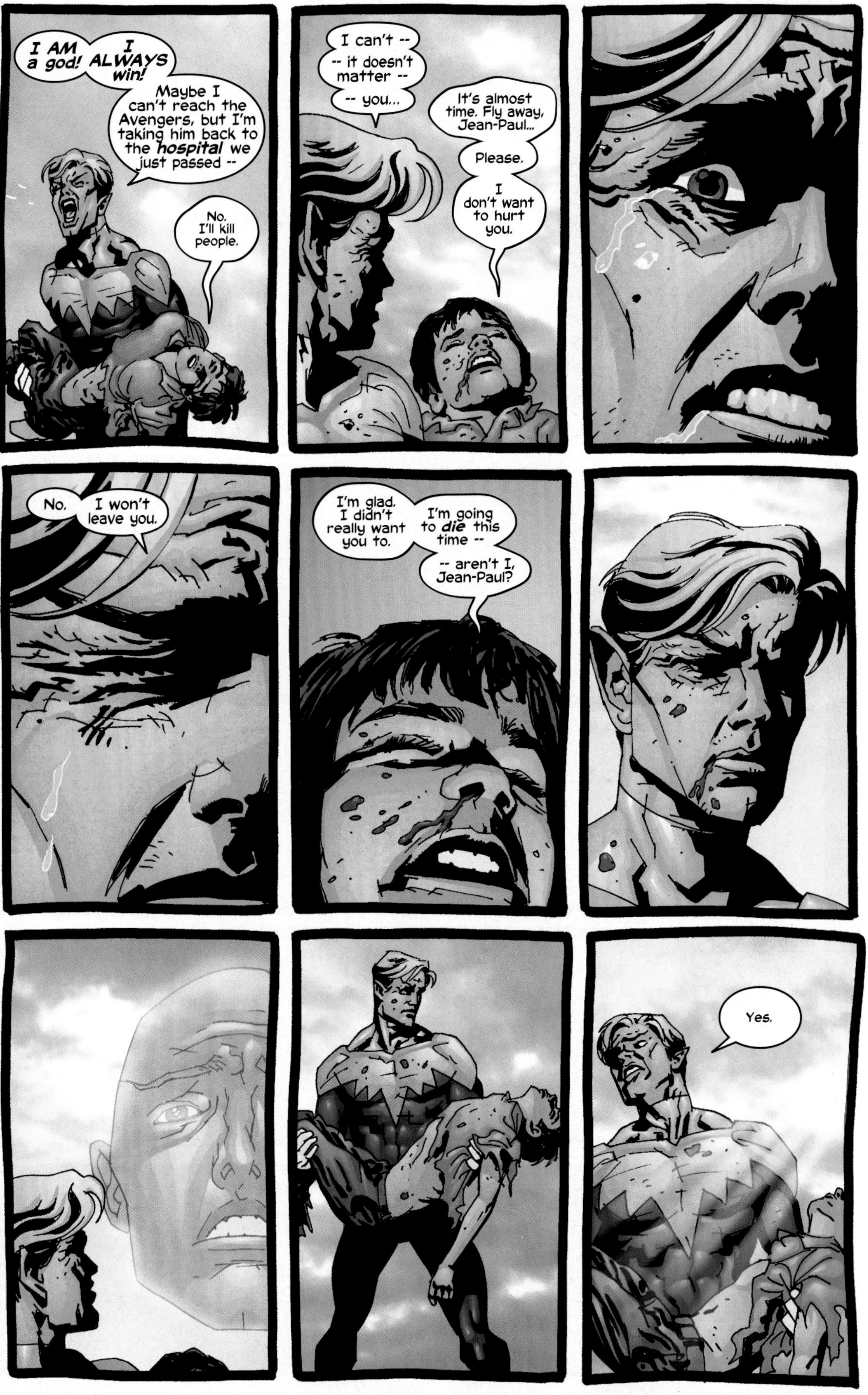
I AM a god!
I ALWAYS win!
Maybe I can't reach the Avengers, but I'm taking him back to the *hospital* we just passed --
No. I'll kill people.
I can't --
-- it doesn't matter --
-- you...
It's almost time. Fly away, Jean-Paul...
Please.
I don't want to hurt you.
No.
I won't leave you.
I'm glad. I didn't really want you to.
I'm going to *die* this time --
-- aren't I, Jean-Paul?
Yes.

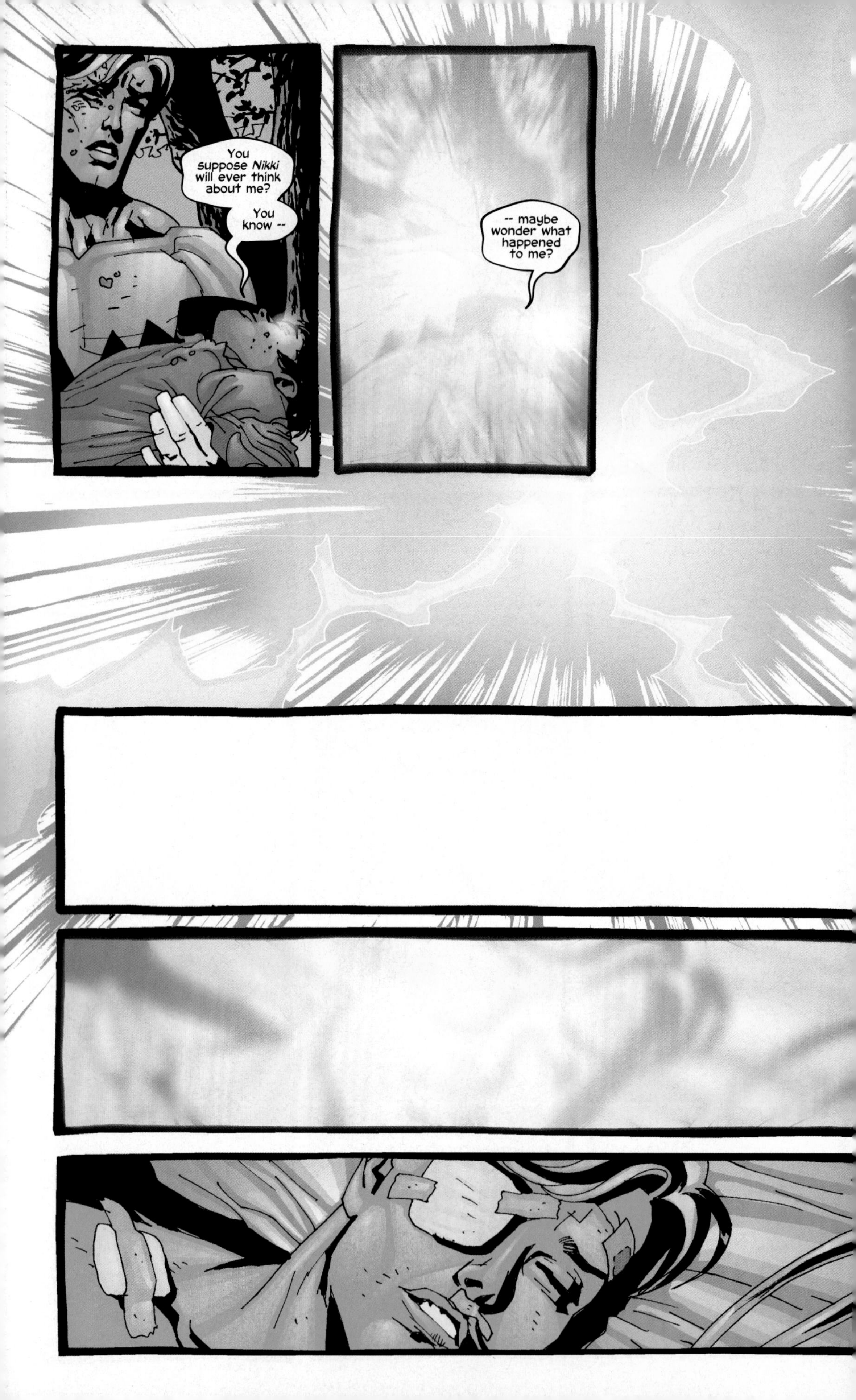
You suppose Nikki will ever think about me?
You know --
-- maybe wonder what happened to me?

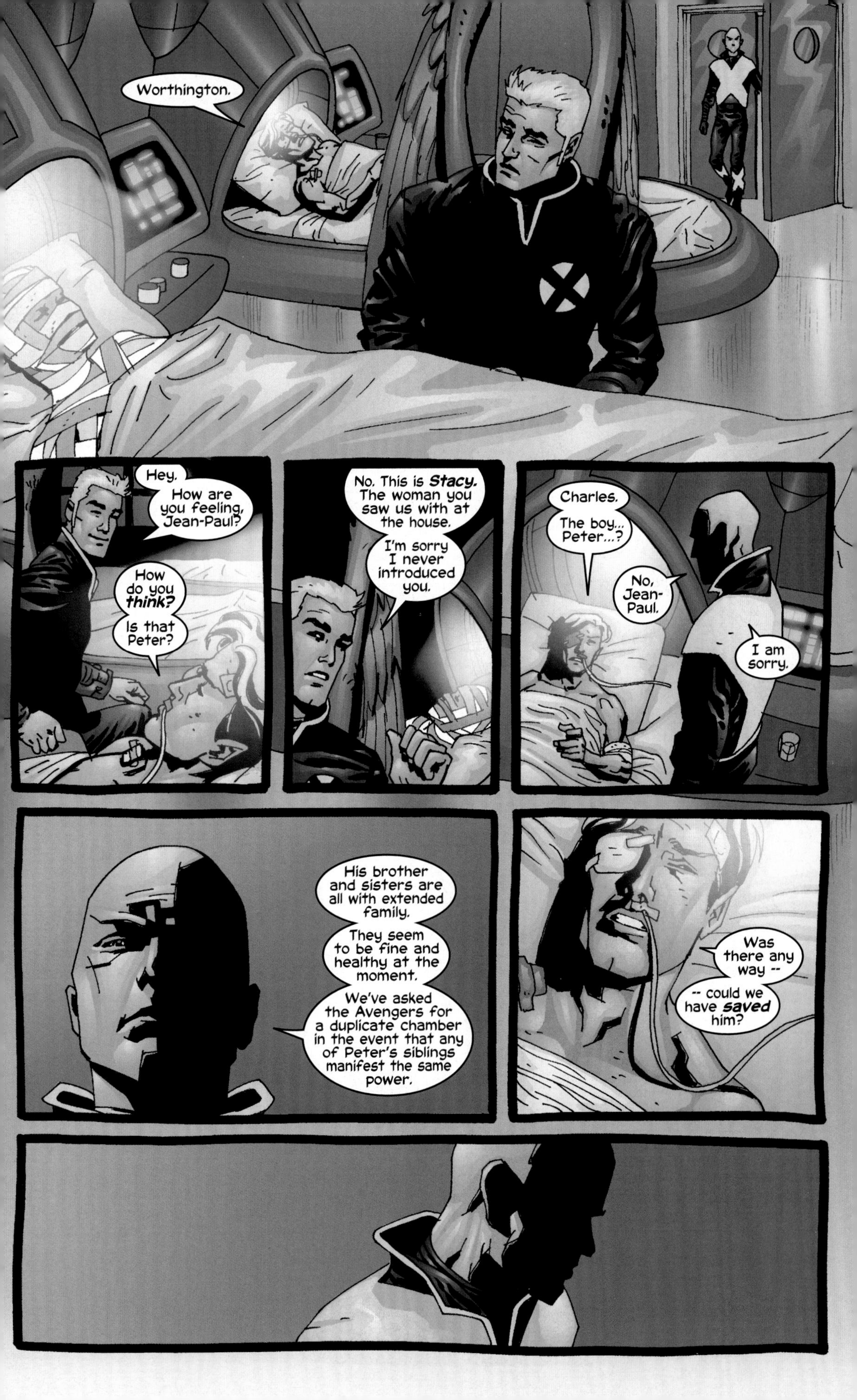
Worthington.
Hey.
How are you feeling, Jean-Paul?
How do you *think?*
Is that Peter?
No. This is *Stacy.* The woman you saw us with at the house.
I'm sorry I never introduced you.
Charles.
The boy... Peter...?
No, Jean-Paul.
I am sorry.
His brother and sisters are all with extended family.
They seem to be fine and healthy at the moment.
We've asked the Avengers for a duplicate chamber in the event that any of Peter's siblings manifest the same power.
Was there any way --
-- could we have *saved* him?

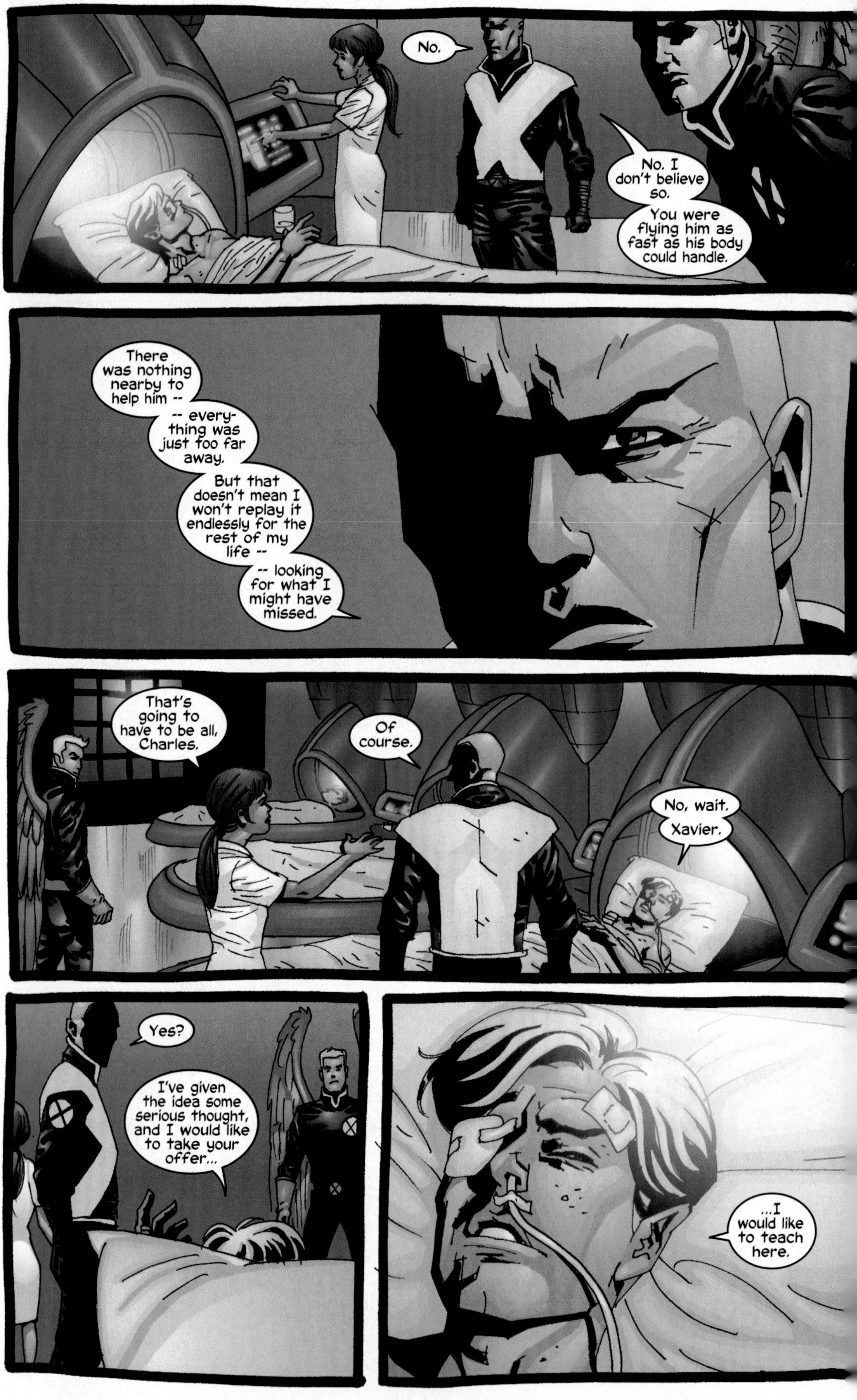
No.
No. I don't believe so.
You were flying him as fast as his body could handle.
There was nothing nearby to help him --
-- every-thing was just too far away.
But that doesn't mean I won't replay it endlessly for the rest of my life --
-- looking for what I might have missed.
That's going to have to be all, Charles.
Of course.
No, wait, Xavier.
Yes?
I've given the idea some serious thought, and I would like to take your offer...
...I would like to teach here.

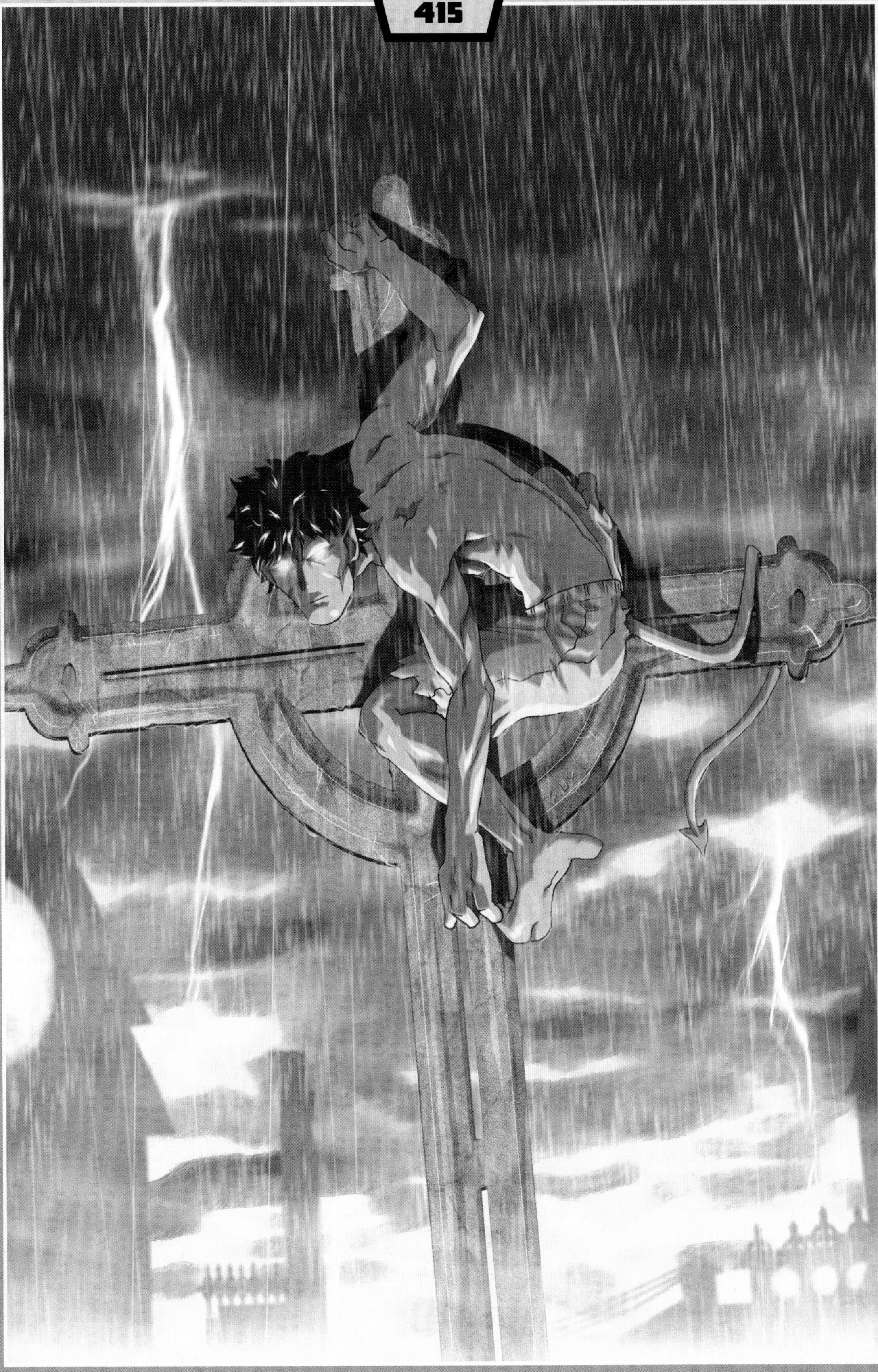

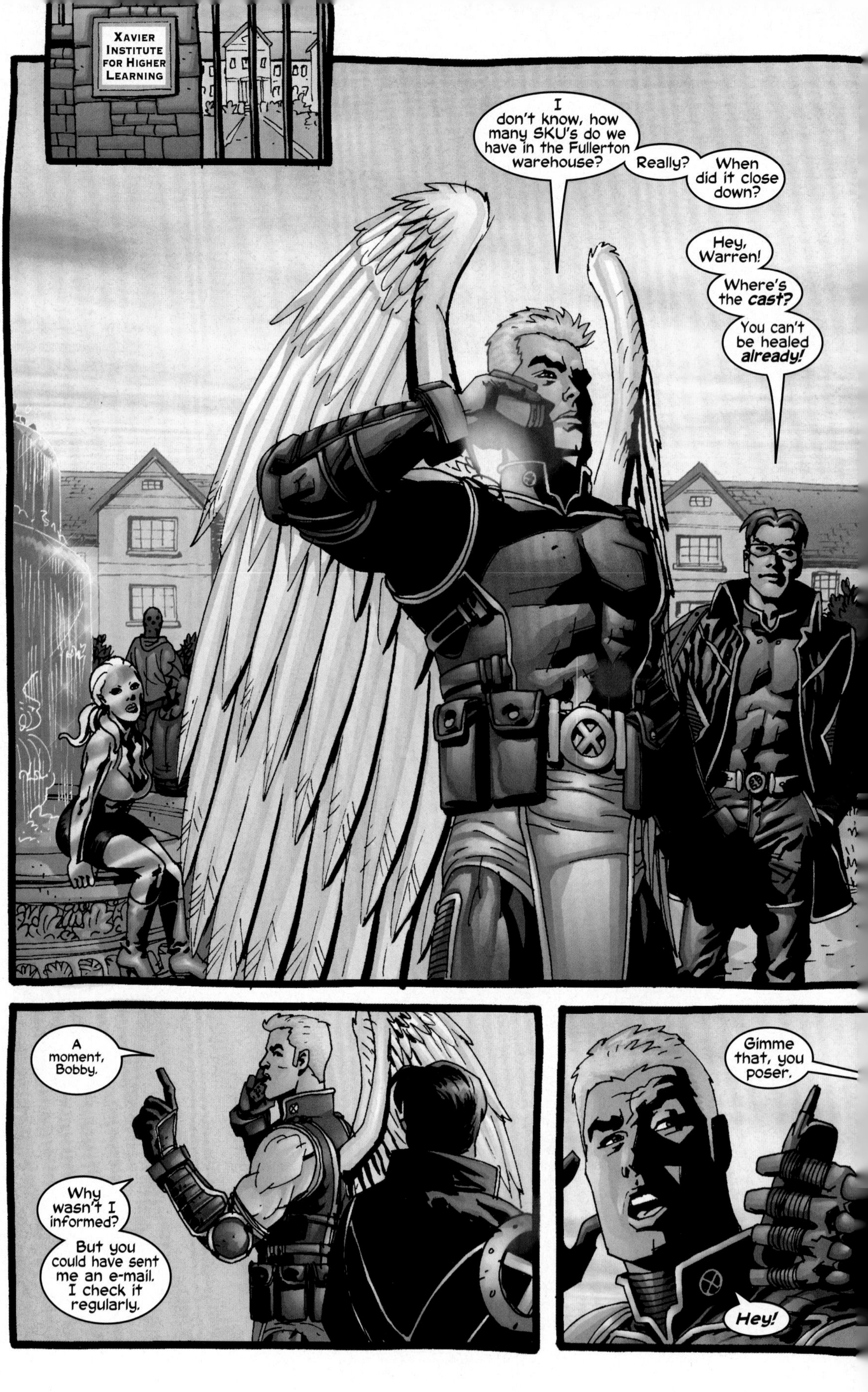
XAVIER INSTITUTE FOR HIGHER LEARNING
I don't know, how many SKU's do we have in the Fullerton warehouse?
Really?
When did it close down?
Hey, Warren!
Where's the cast?
You can't be healed already!
A moment, Bobby.
Why wasn't I informed?
But you could have sent me an e-mail. I check it regularly.
Gimme that, you poser.
Hey!

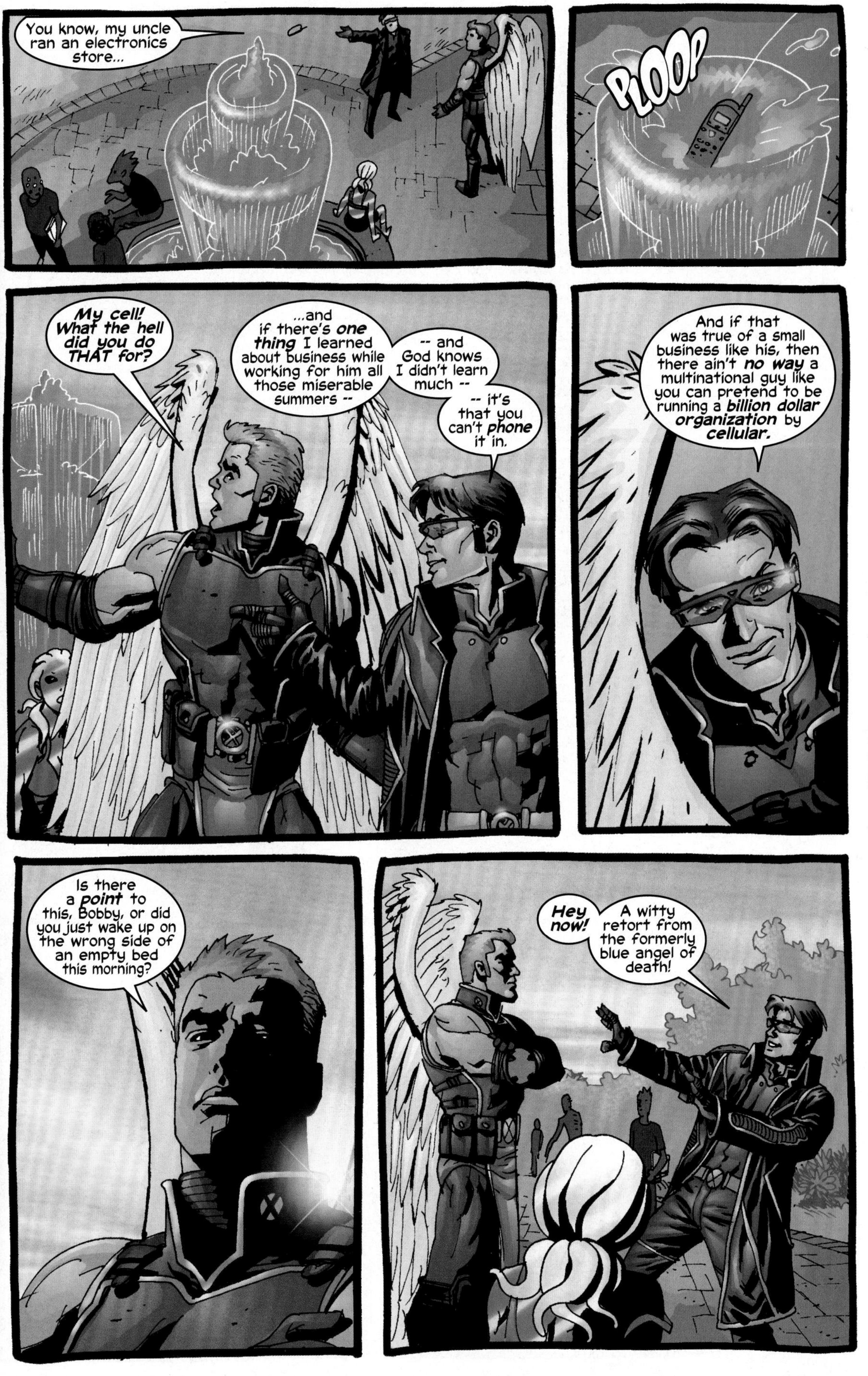
You know, my uncle ran an electronics store...
PLOOP
My cell! What the hell did you do THAT for?
...and if there's one thing I learned about business while working for him all those miserable summers --
-- and God knows I didn't learn much --
-- it's that you can't phone it in.
And if that was true of a small business like his, then there ain't no way a multinational guy like you can pretend to be running a billion dollar organization by cellular.
Is there a point to this, Bobby, or did you just wake up on the wrong side of an empty bed this morning?
Hey now!
A witty retort from the formerly blue angel of death!

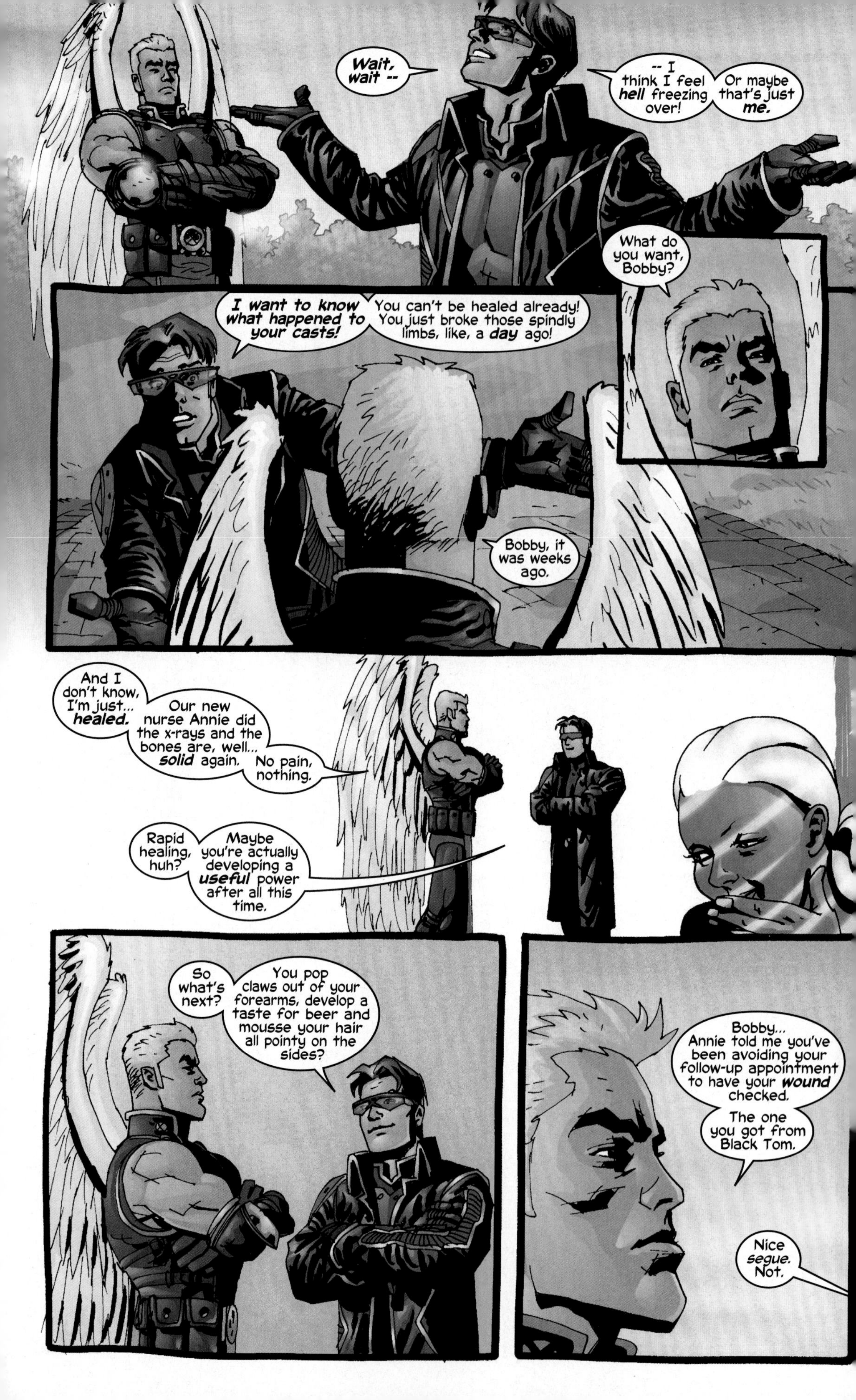

Wait, wait --
-- I think I feel hell freezing over!
Or maybe that's just me.
What do you want, Bobby?
I want to know what happened to your casts!
You can't be healed already! You just broke those spindly limbs, like, a day ago!
Bobby, it was weeks ago.
And I don't know, I'm just... healed.
Our new nurse Annie did the x-rays and the bones are, well... solid again.
No pain, nothing.
Rapid healing, huh?
Maybe you're actually developing a useful power after all this time.
So what's next?
You pop claws out of your forearms, develop a taste for beer and mousse your hair all pointy on the sides?
Bobby... Annie told me you've been avoiding your follow-up appointment to have your wound checked.
The one you got from Black Tom.
Nice segue. Not.

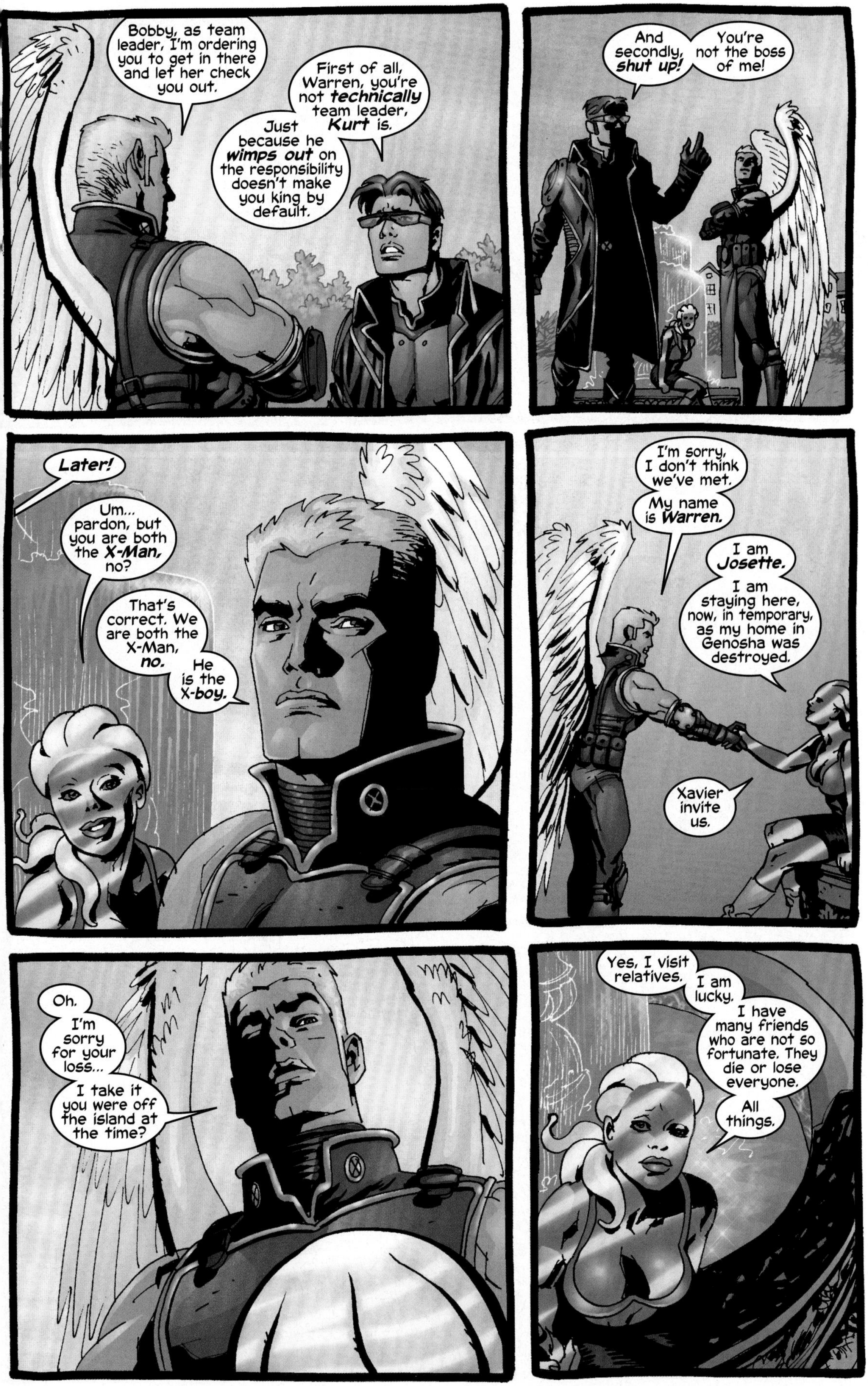
Bobby, as team leader, I'm ordering you to get in there and let her check you out.
First of all, Warren, you're not **technically** team leader, **Kurt** is.
Just because he **wimps out** on the responsibility doesn't make you king by default.
And secondly, **shut up!**
You're not the boss of me!
Later!
Um... pardon, but you are both the **X-Man,** no?
That's correct. We are both the X-Man, **no.**
He is the X-**boy.**
I'm sorry, I don't think we've met.
My name is **Warren.**
I am **Josette.**
I am staying here, now, in temporary, as my home in Genosha was destroyed.
Xavier invite us.
Oh.
I'm sorry for your loss...
I take it you were off the island at the time?
Yes, I visit relatives.
I am lucky.
I have many friends who are not so fortunate. They die or lose everyone.
All things.

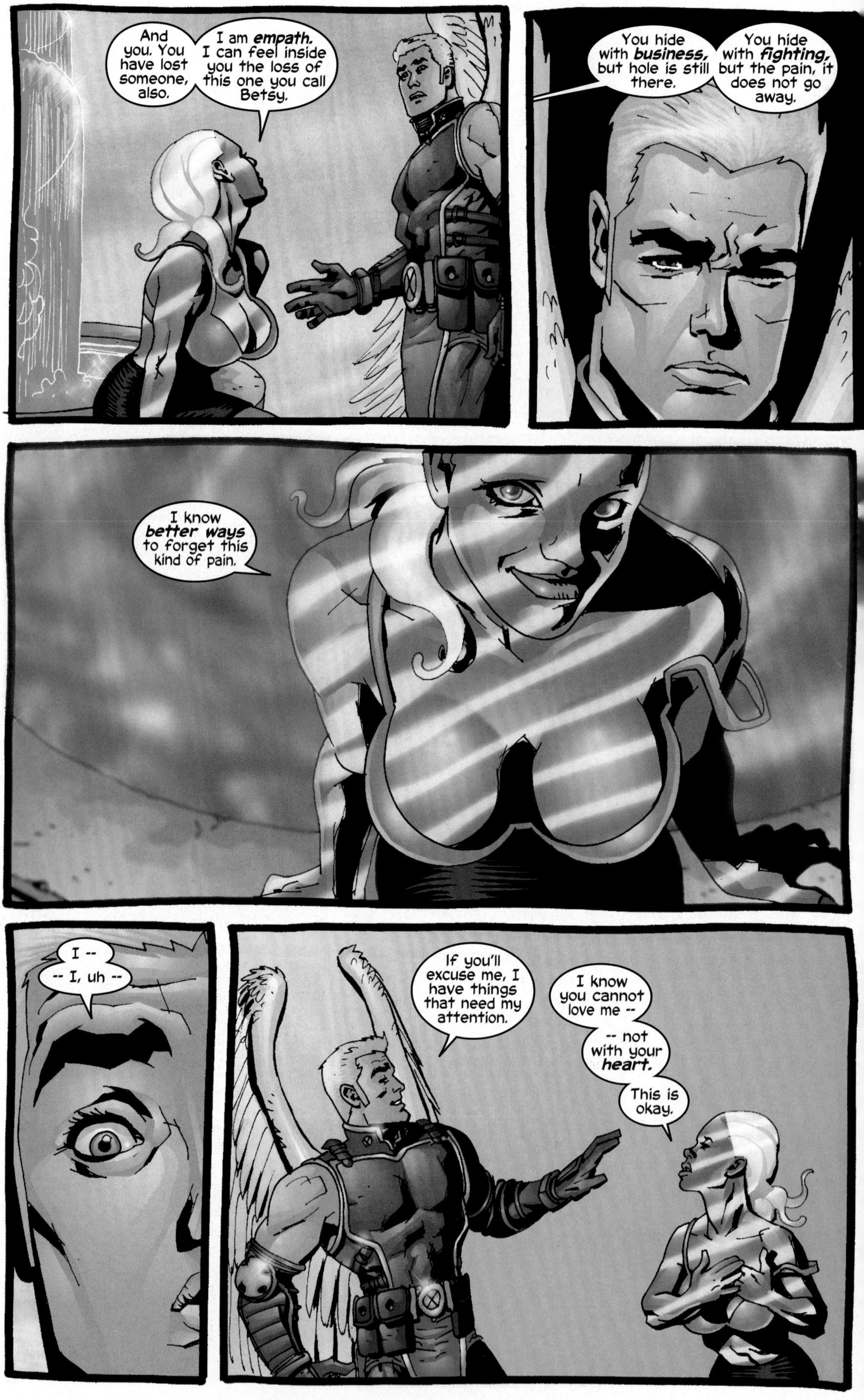
And you. You have lost someone, also.
I am *empath.* I can feel inside you the loss of this one you call Betsy.
You hide with *business,* but hole is still there.
You hide with *fighting,* but the pain, it does not go away.
I know *better ways* to forget this kind of pain.
I --
-- I, uh --
If you'll excuse me, I have things that need my attention.
I know you cannot love me --
-- not with your *heart.*
This is okay.

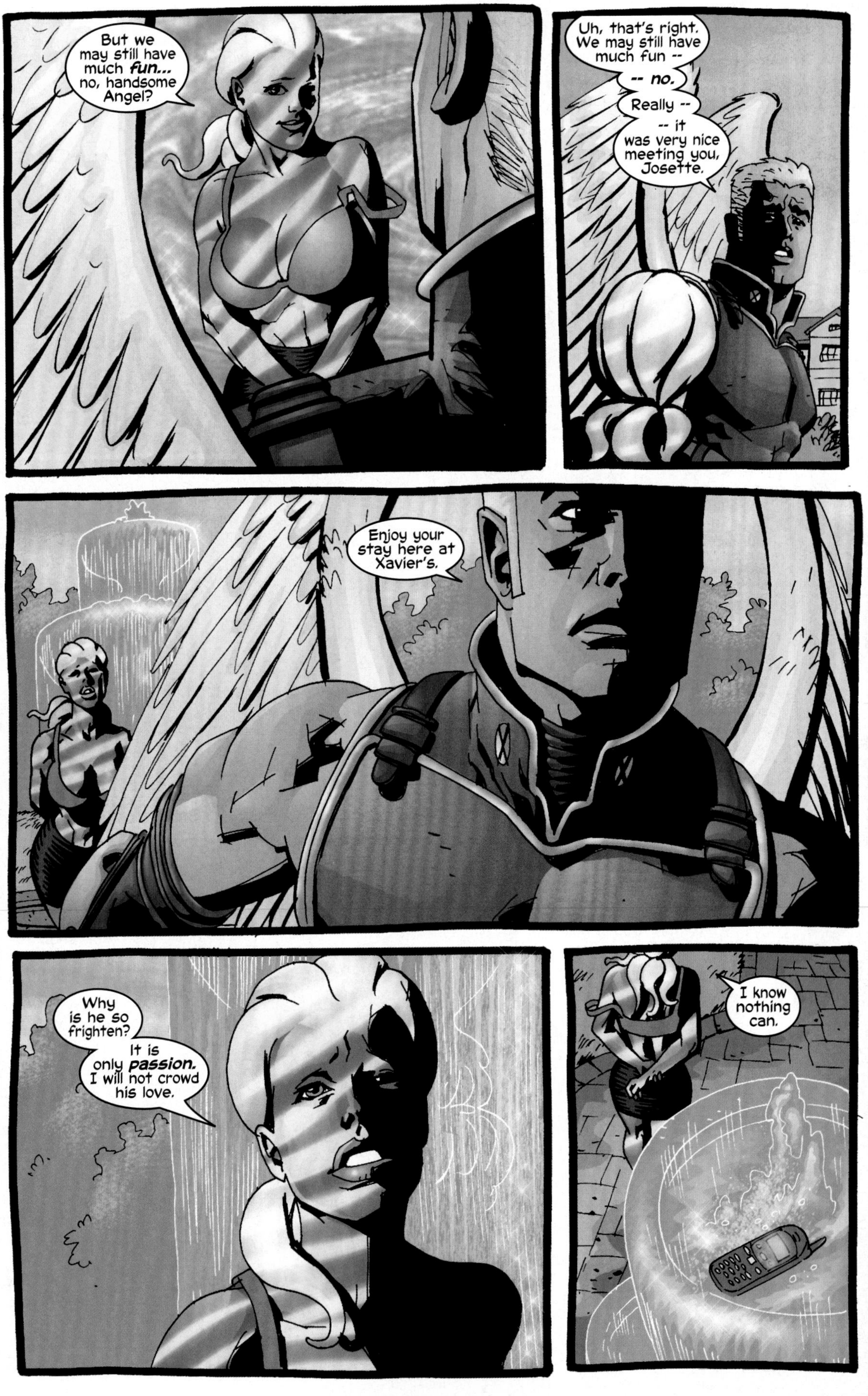
But we may still have much **fun...** no, handsome Angel?
Uh, that's right. We may still have much fun --
-- no.
Really --
-- it was very nice meeting you, Josette.
Enjoy your stay here at Xavier's.
Why is he so frighten?
It is only **passion.** I will not crowd his love.
I know nothing can.

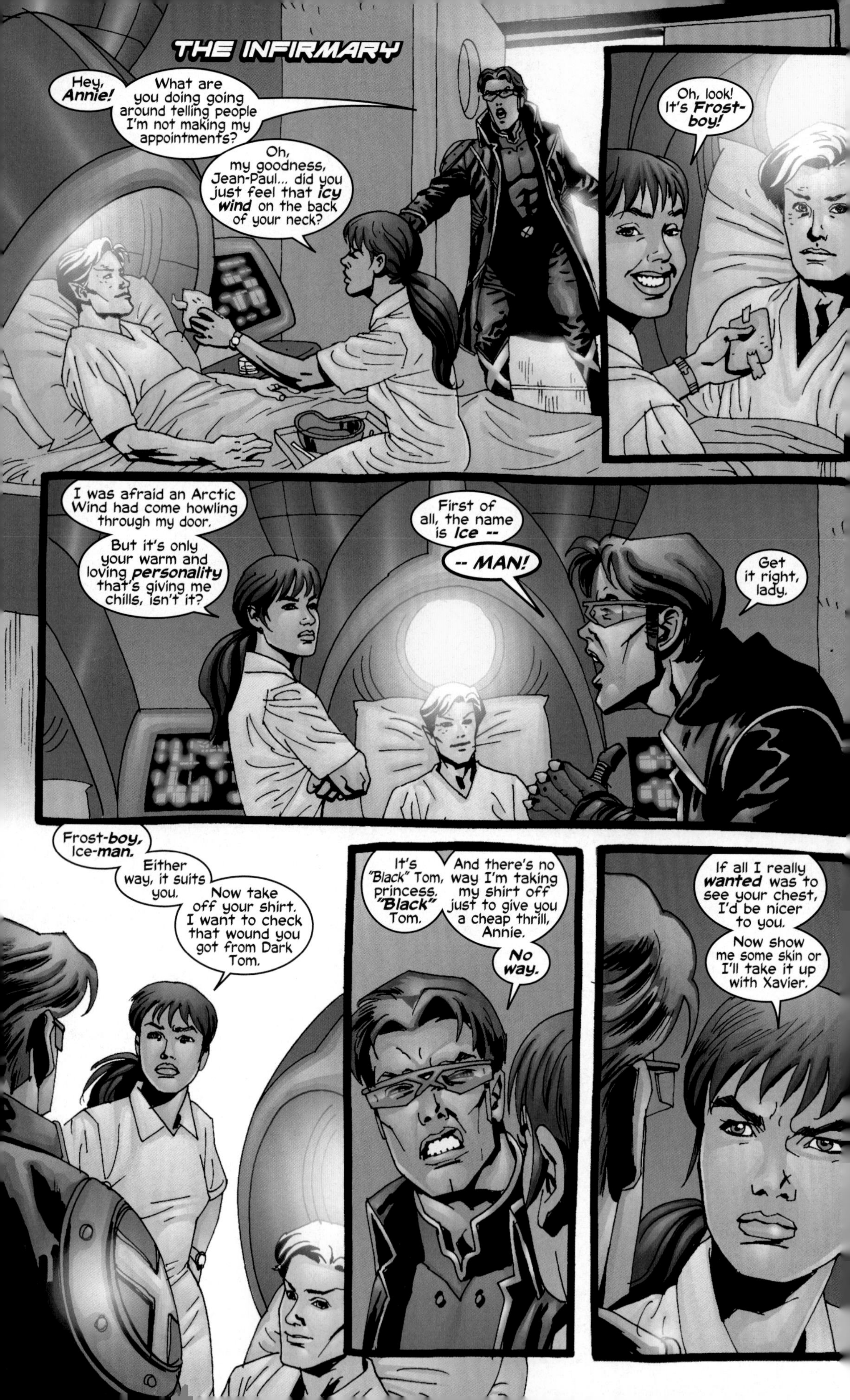
THE INFIRMARY
Hey, Annie!
What are you doing going around telling people I'm not making my appointments?
Oh, my goodness, Jean-Paul... did you just feel that icy wind on the back of your neck?
Oh, look! It's Frost-boy!
I was afraid an Arctic Wind had come howling through my door.
But it's only your warm and loving personality that's giving me chills, isn't it?
First of all, the name is Ice --
-- MAN!
Get it right, lady.
Frost-boy, Ice-man.
Either way, it suits you.
Now take off your shirt. I want to check that wound you got from Dark Tom.
It's "Black" Tom, princess. "Black" Tom.
And there's no way I'm taking my shirt off just to give you a cheap thrill, Annie.
No way.
If all I really wanted was to see your chest, I'd be nicer to you.
Now show me some skin or I'll take it up with Xavier.

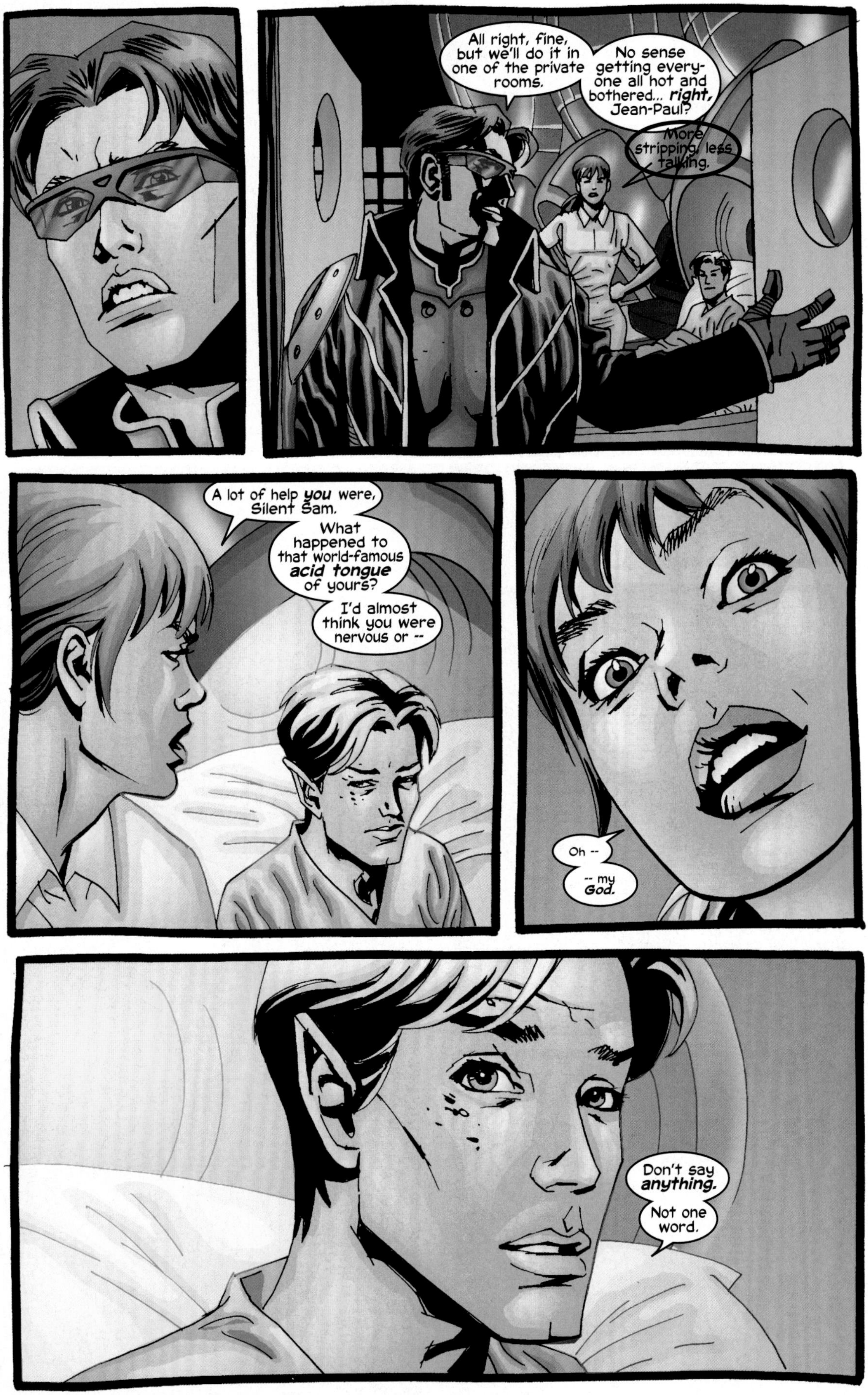
All right, fine, but we'll do it in one of the private rooms.
No sense getting every-one all hot and bothered... *right,* Jean-Paul?
More stripping, less talking.
A lot of help *you* were, Silent Sam.
What happened to that world-famous *acid tongue* of yours?
I'd almost think you were nervous or --
Oh --
-- my *God.*
Don't say *anything.*
Not one word.

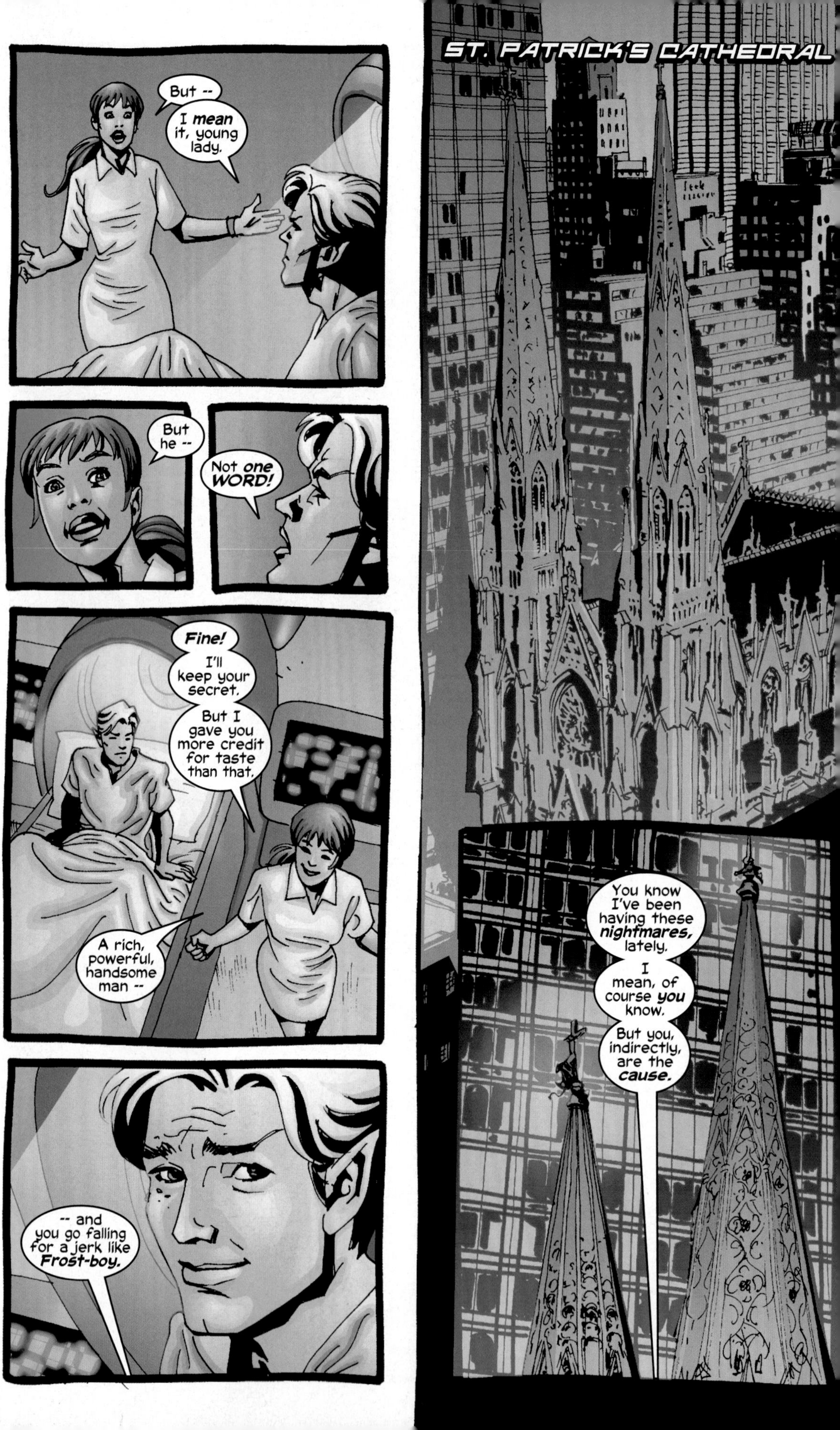
But --
I mean it, young lady.
But he --
Not one WORD!
Fine!
I'll keep your secret.
But I gave you more credit for taste than that.
A rich, powerful, handsome man --
-- and you go falling for a jerk like Frost-boy.
ST. PATRICK'S CATHEDRAL
You know I've been having these nightmares, lately.
I mean, of course you know.
But you, indirectly, are the cause.

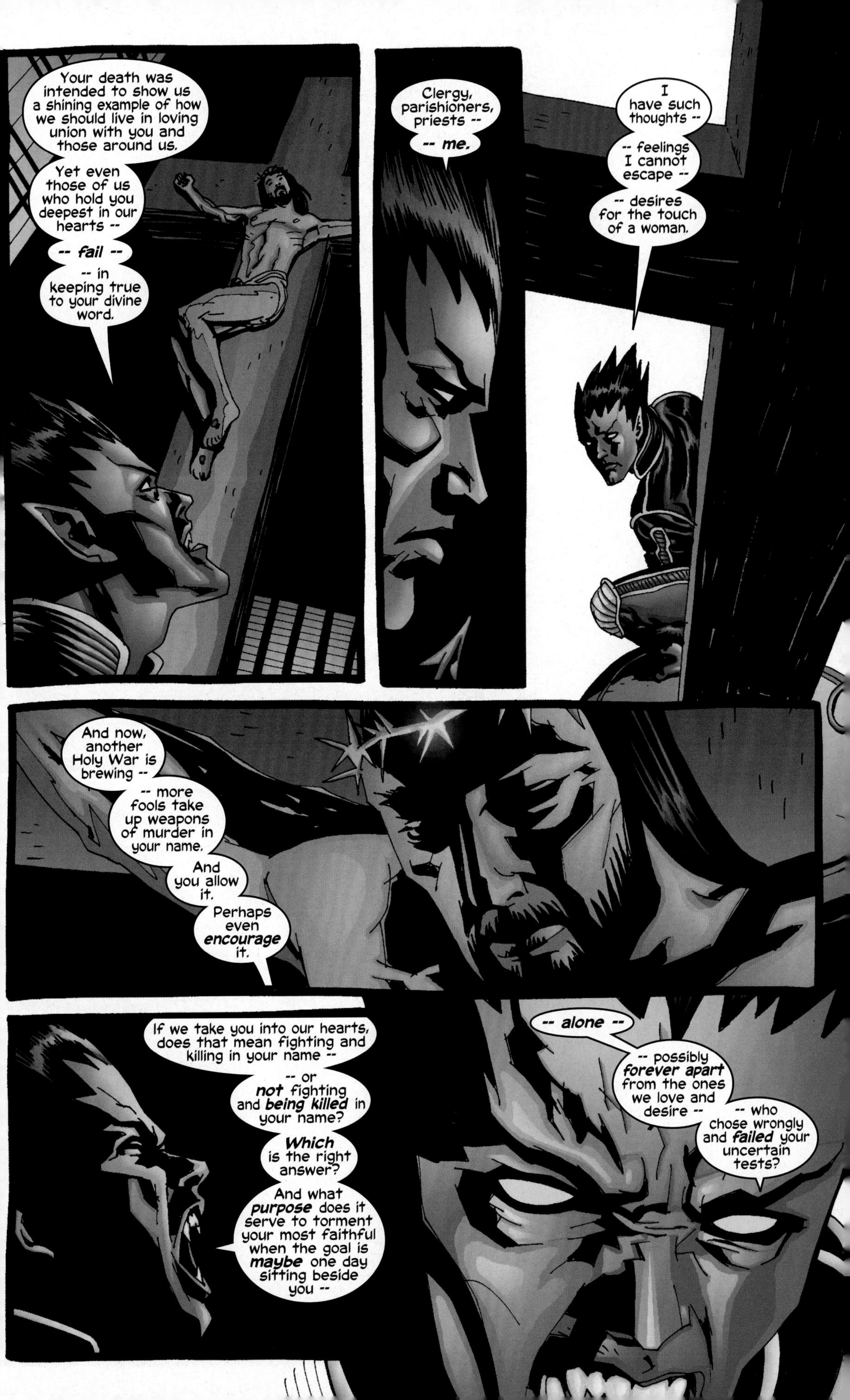
Your death was intended to show us a shining example of how we should live in loving union with you and those around us.
Yet even those of us who hold you deepest in our hearts --
-- fail --
-- in keeping true to your divine word.
Clergy, parishioners, priests --
-- me.
I have such thoughts --
-- feelings I cannot escape --
-- desires for the touch of a woman.
And now, another Holy War is brewing --
-- more fools take up weapons of murder in your name.
And you allow it.
Perhaps even encourage it.
If we take you into our hearts, does that mean fighting and killing in your name --
-- or not fighting and being killed in your name?
Which is the right answer?
And what purpose does it serve to torment your most faithful when the goal is maybe one day sitting beside you --
-- alone --
-- possibly forever apart from the ones we love and desire --
-- who chose wrongly and failed your uncertain tests?

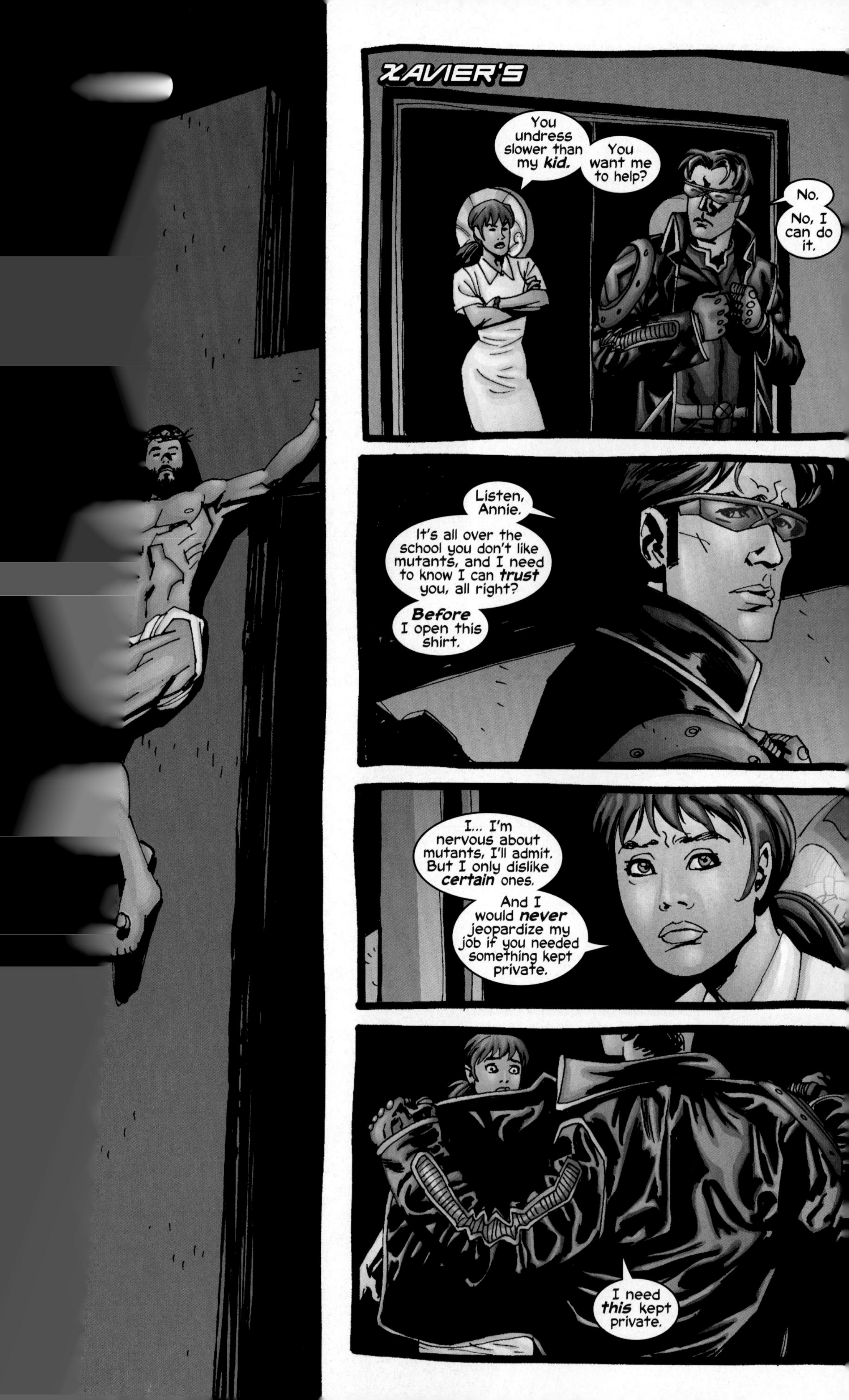
XAVIER'S
You undress slower than my *kid.*
You want me to help?
No.
No, I can do it.
Listen, Annie.
It's all over the school you don't like mutants, and I need to know I can *trust* you, all right?
Before I open this shirt.
I... I'm nervous about mutants, I'll admit. But I only dislike *certain* ones.
And I would *never* jeopardize my job if you needed something kept private.
I need *this* kept private.

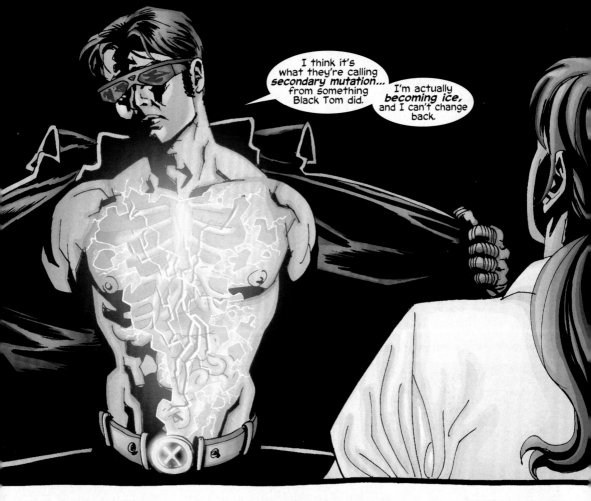

I think it's what they're calling *secondary mutation...* from something Black Tom did. I'm actually *becoming ice,* and I can't change back.

LATER...

Thanks for the check-up, Annie.

So... when you gonna get up off your lazy butt and start doing some *work* around this place, Northstar?

He can actually leave the infirmary now, for walks and meals, as long as it's not too strenuous.

If he wants.

Why don't you two go get something to eat? Grab some *dinner* together?

Well, I -- -- uh --

Yeah, come on. The Dining Commons is still open.

I'll buy.

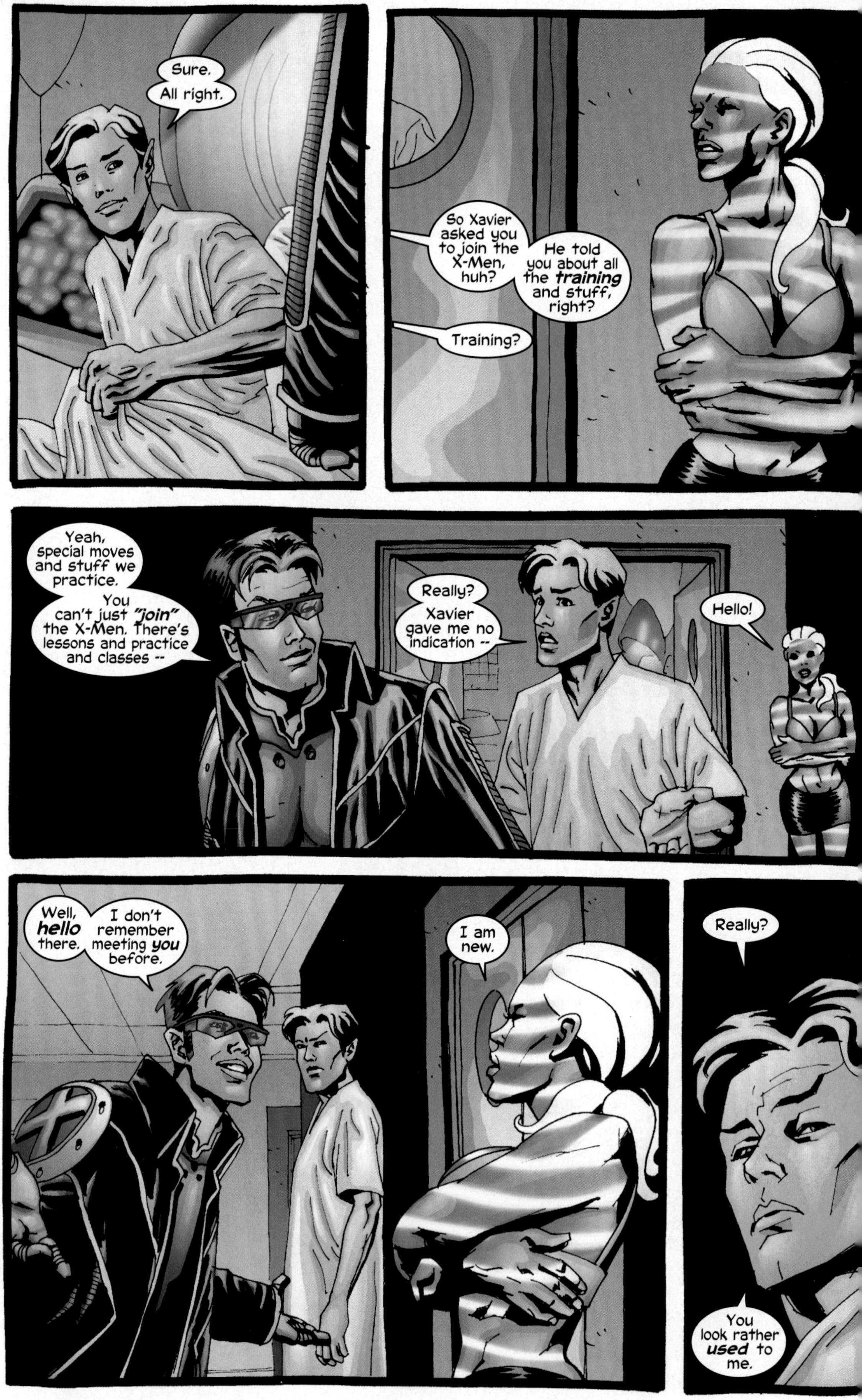
Sure.
All right.
So Xavier asked you to join the X-Men, huh?
He told you about all the **training** and stuff, right?
Training?
Yeah, special moves and stuff we practice.
You can't just ***"join"*** the X-Men. There's lessons and practice and classes --
Really? Xavier gave me no indication --
Hello!
Well, **hello** there.
I don't remember meeting **you** before.
I am new.
Really?
You look rather **used** to me.

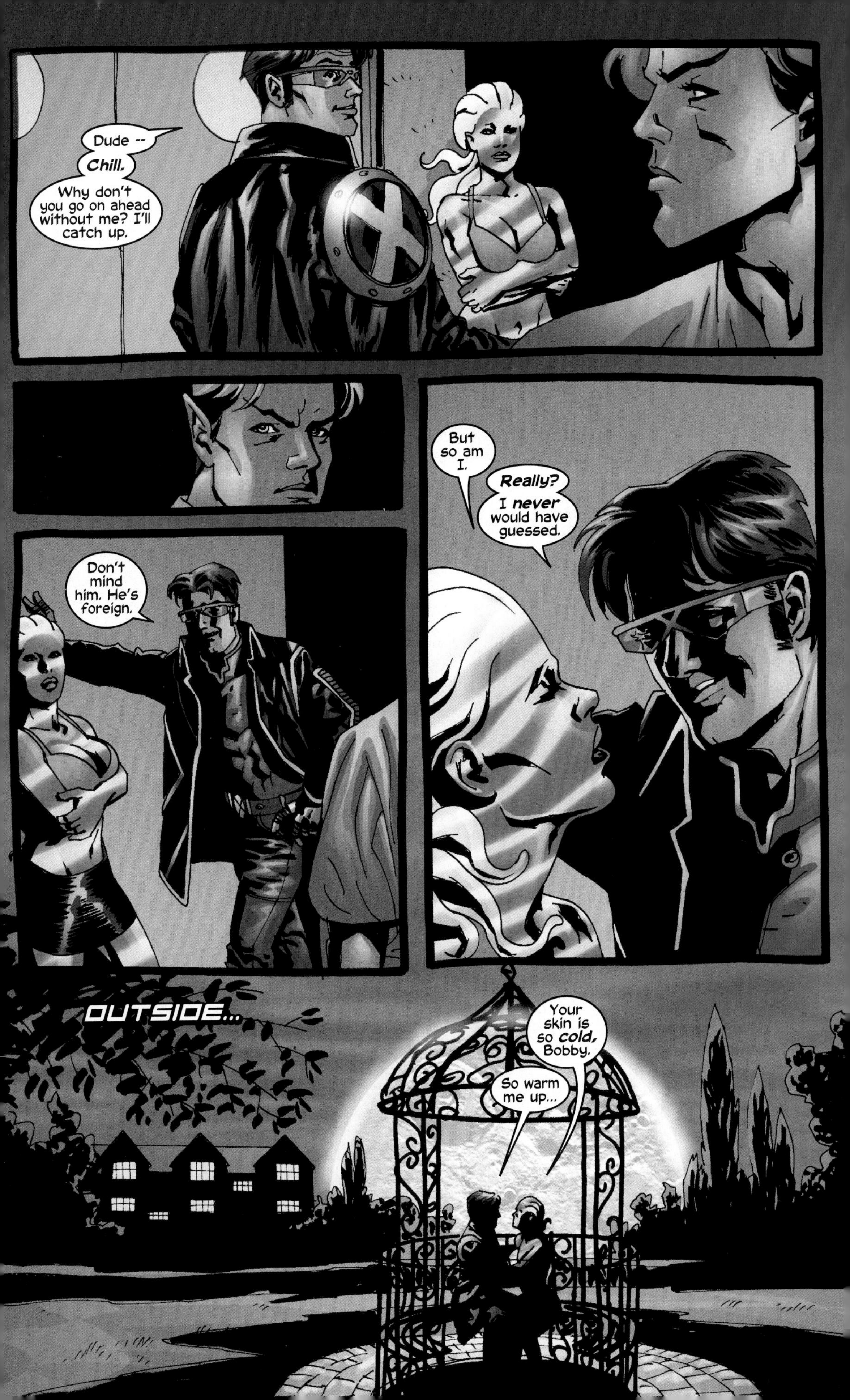
Dude --
Chill.
Why don't you go on ahead without me? I'll catch up.
Don't mind him. He's foreign.
But so am I.
Really? I never would have guessed.
OUTSIDE...
Your skin is so cold, Bobby.
So warm me up...

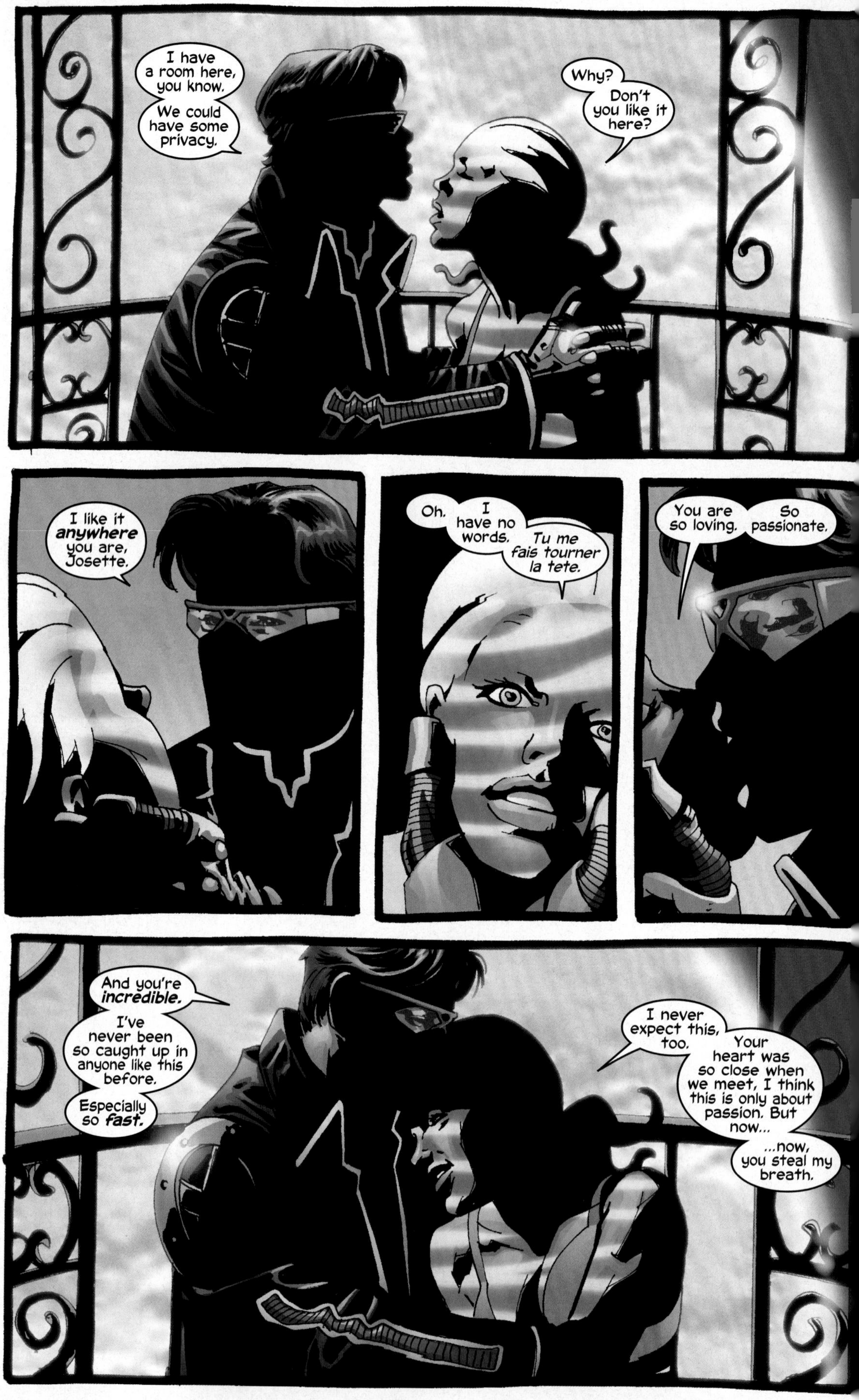

I have a room here, you know.
We could have some privacy.
Why?
Don't you like it here?
I like it *anywhere* you are, Josette.
Oh.
I have no words.
Tu me fais tourner la tete.
You are so loving.
So passionate.
And you're *incredible.*
I've never been so caught up in anyone like this before.
Especially so *fast.*
I never expect this, too.
Your heart was so close when we meet, I think this is only about passion. But now...
...now, you steal my breath.

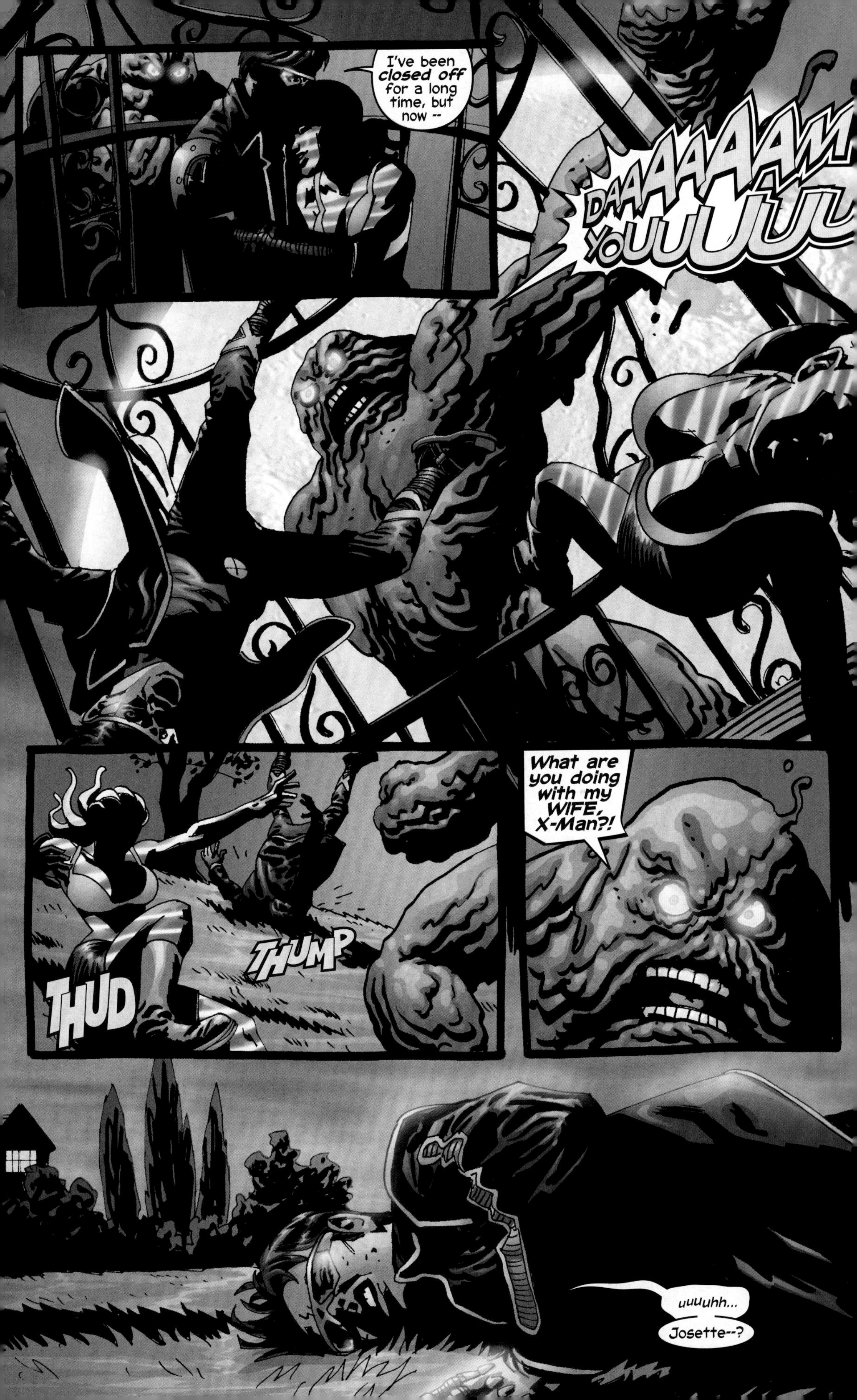
I've been closed off for a long time, but now --
DAAAAAAM YOUUUUU
What are you doing with my WIFE, X-Man?!
THUMP
THUD
uuuuhh...
Josette--?

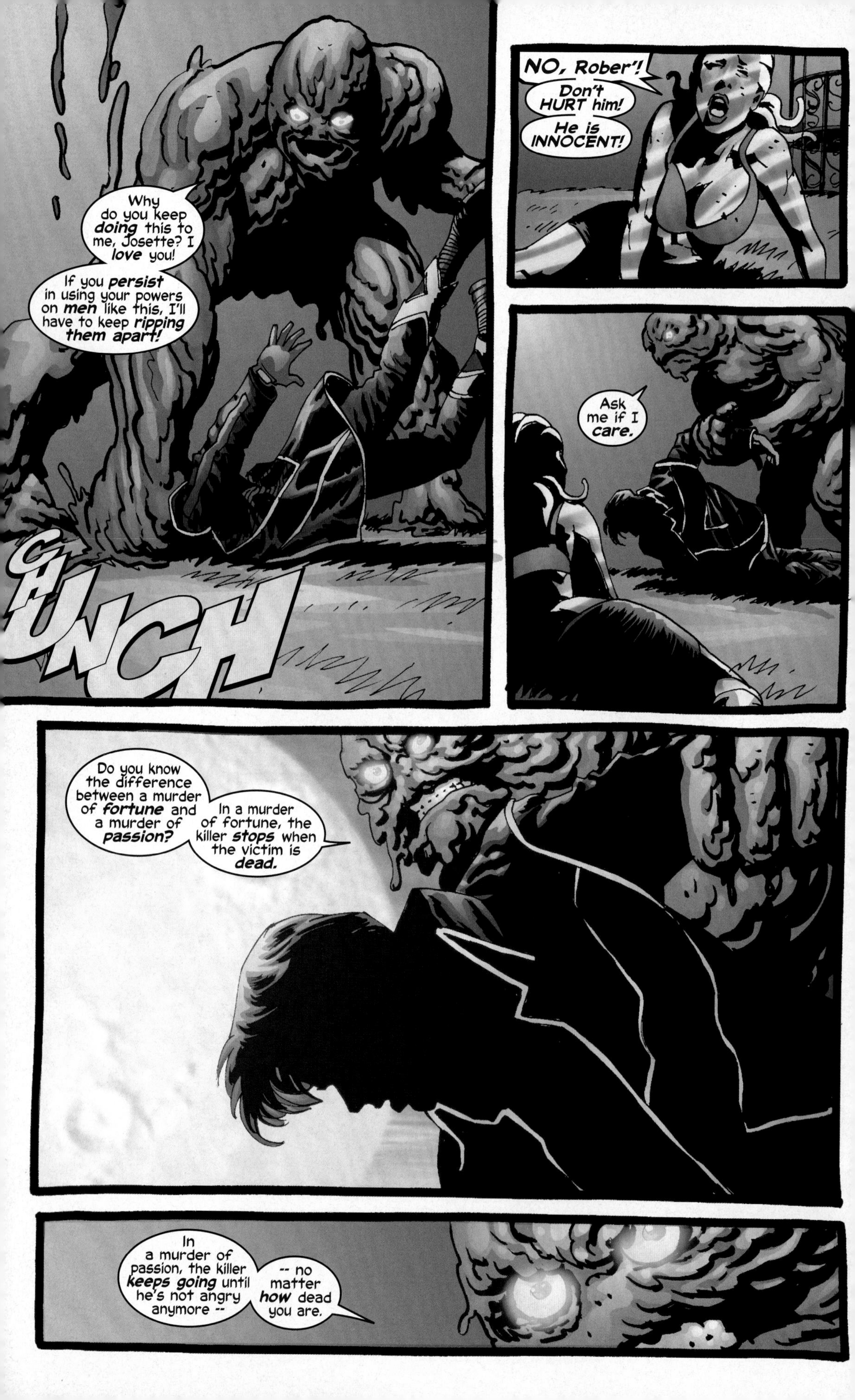
Why do you keep doing this to me, Josette? I love you!
If you persist in using your powers on men like this, I'll have to keep ripping them apart!
CHUNCH
NO, Rober'!
Don't HURT him!
He is INNOCENT!
Ask me if I care.
Do you know the difference between a murder of fortune and a murder of passion?
In a murder of fortune, the killer stops when the victim is dead.
In a murder of passion, the killer keeps going until he's not angry anymore --
-- no matter how dead you are.

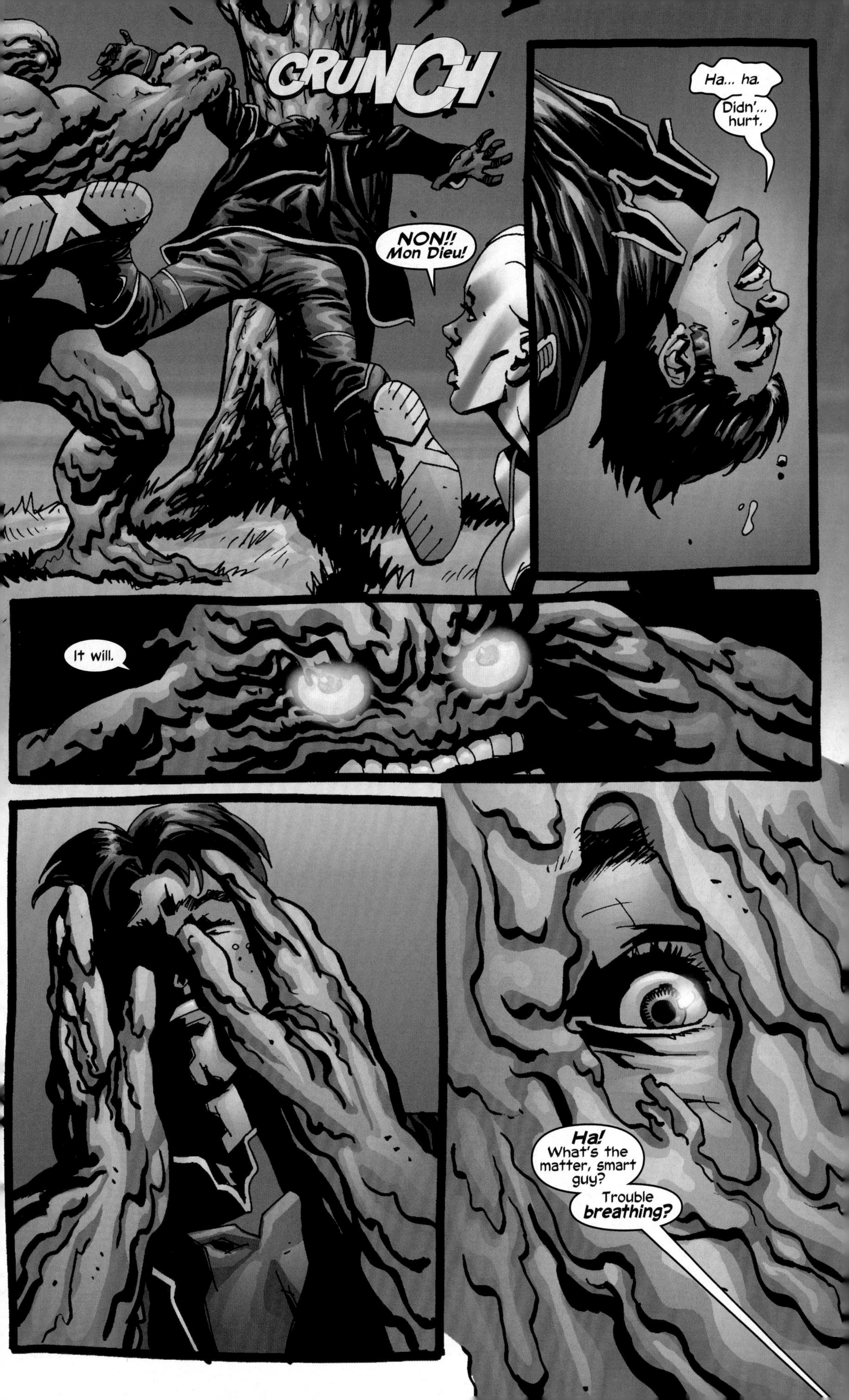
CRUNCH
NON!! Mon Dieu!
Ha... ha.
Didn'... hurt.
It will.
Ha! What's the matter, smart guy?
Trouble breathing?

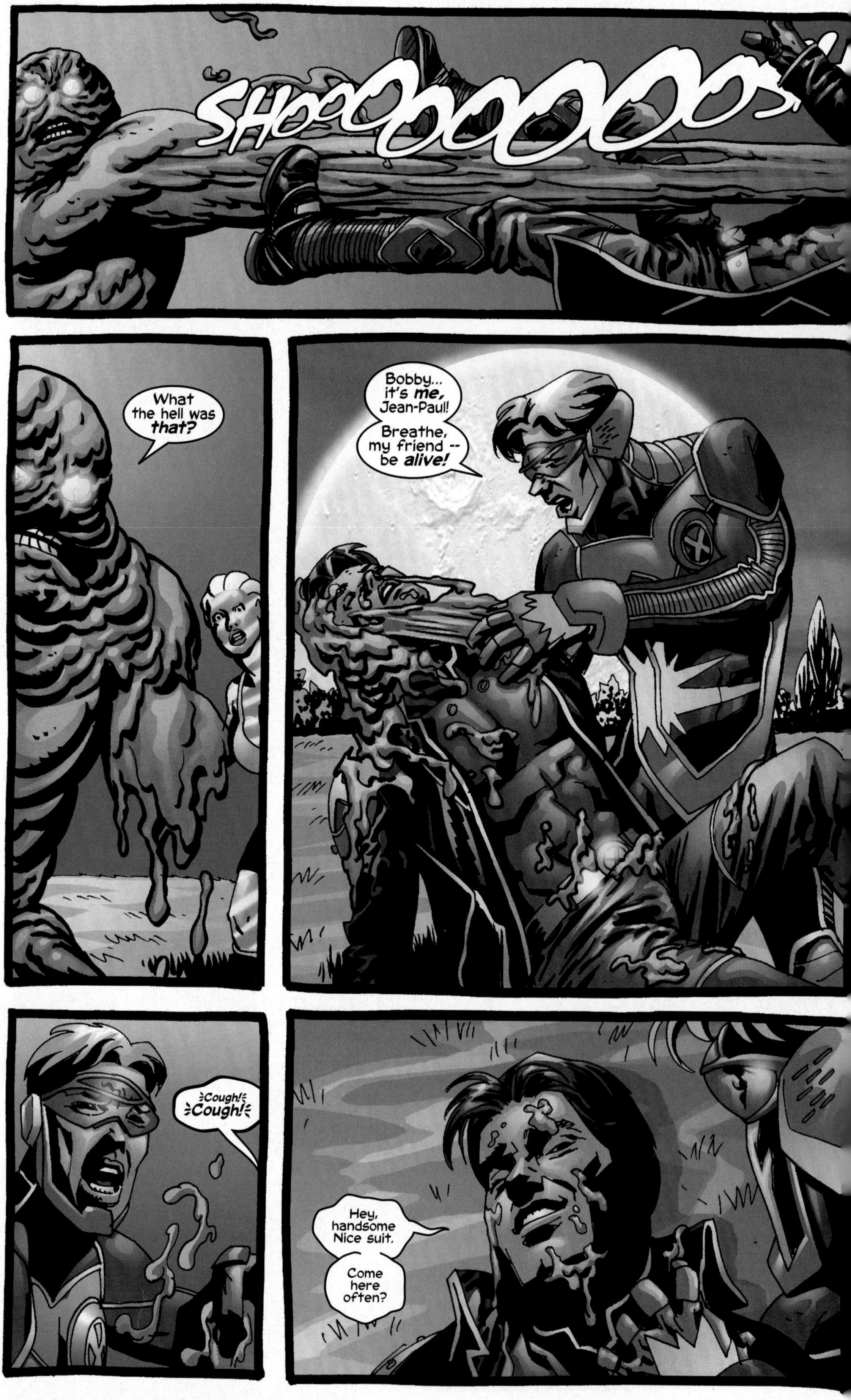
SHOOOOOOOOOSH
What the hell was that?
Bobby... it's me, Jean-Paul!
Breathe, my friend -- be alive!
Cough! Cough!
Hey, handsome Nice suit.
Come here often?

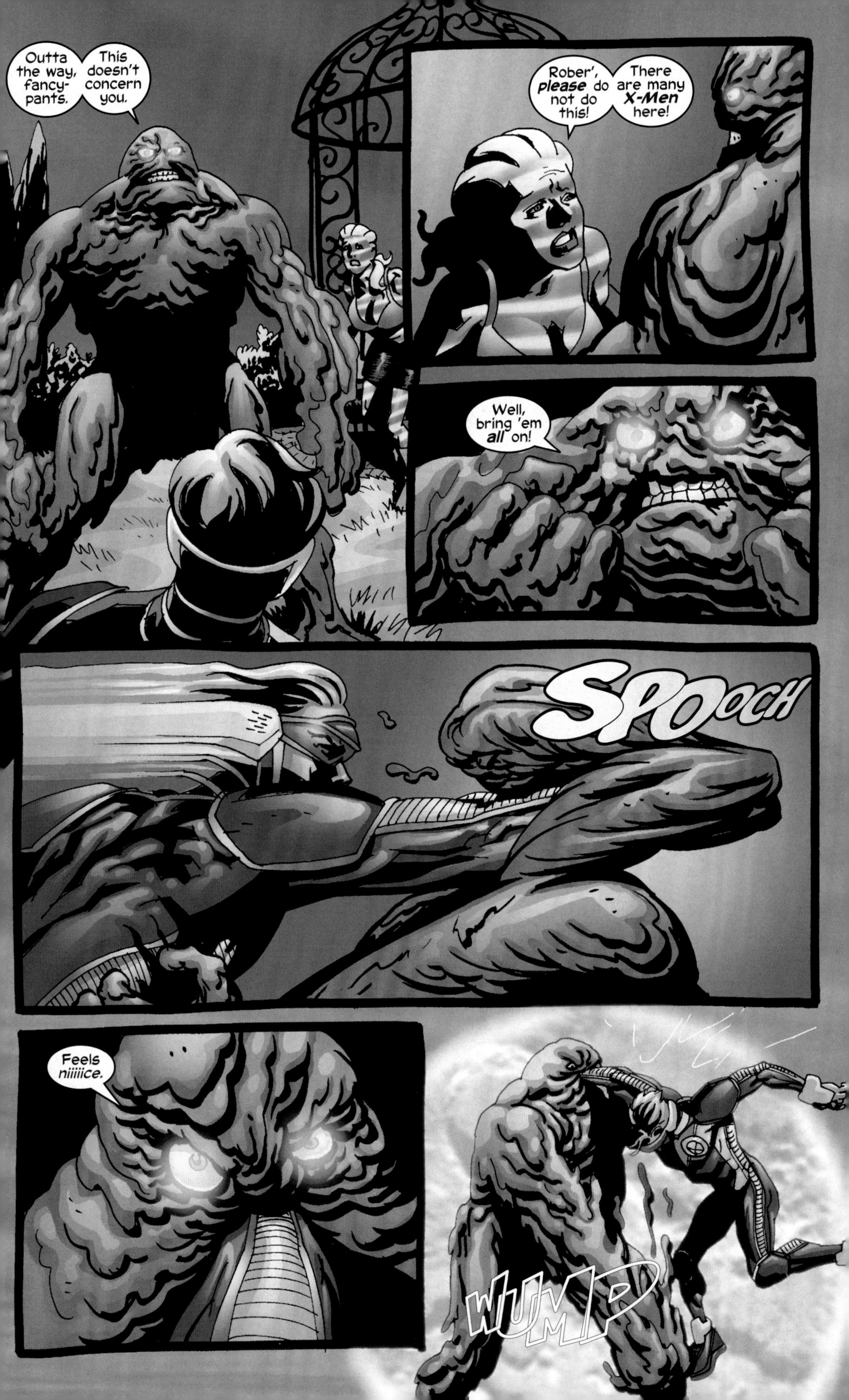

Outta the way, fancy-pants.
This doesn't concern you.
Rober', *please* do not do this!
There are many *X-Men* here!
Well, bring 'em *all* on!
SPOOCH
Feels *niiiiice.*
WUMP

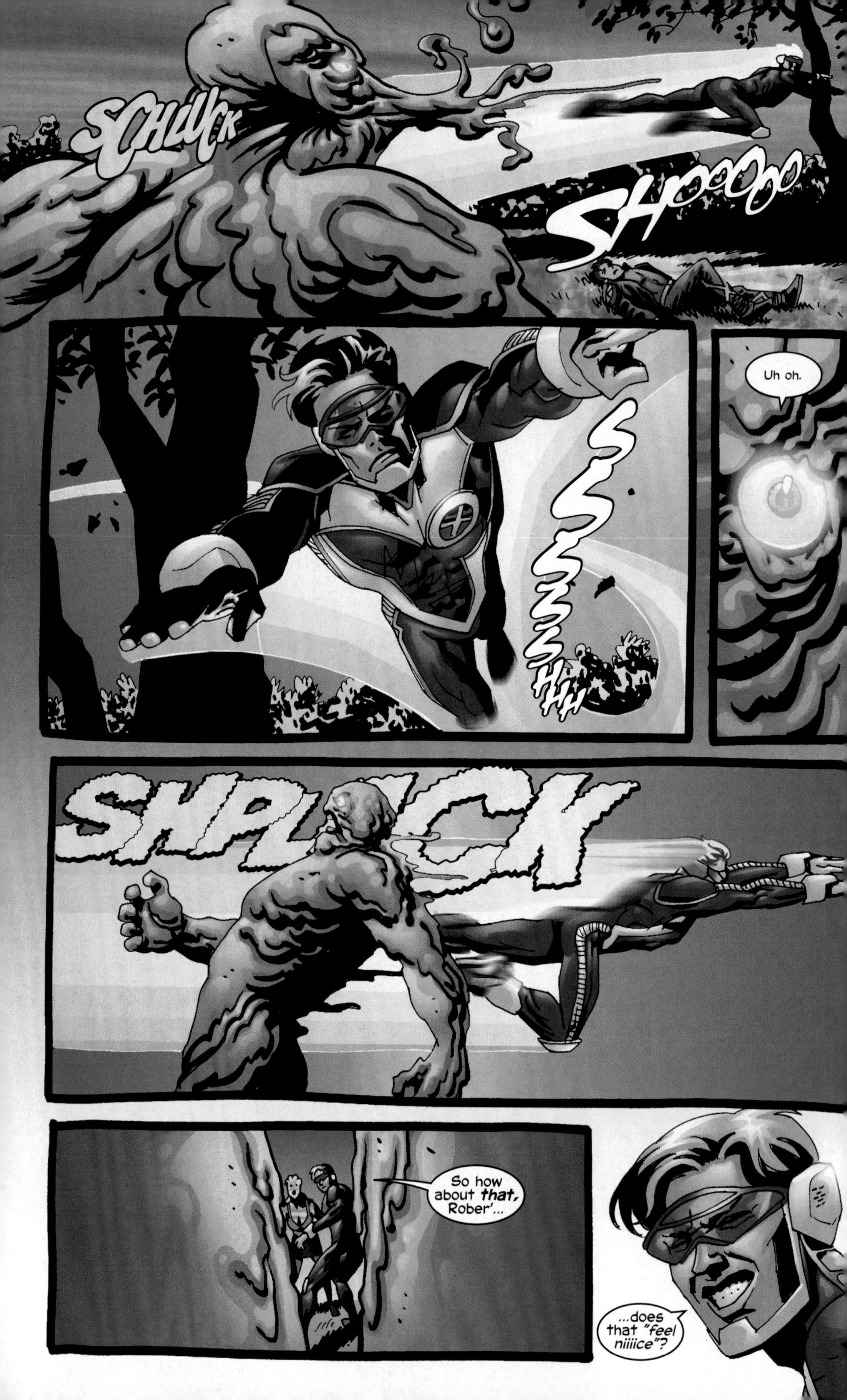
SCHLUCK
SHOOOOO
SSSSSSHHH
Uh oh.
SHLACK
So how about that, Rober'...
...does that "feel niiiice"?

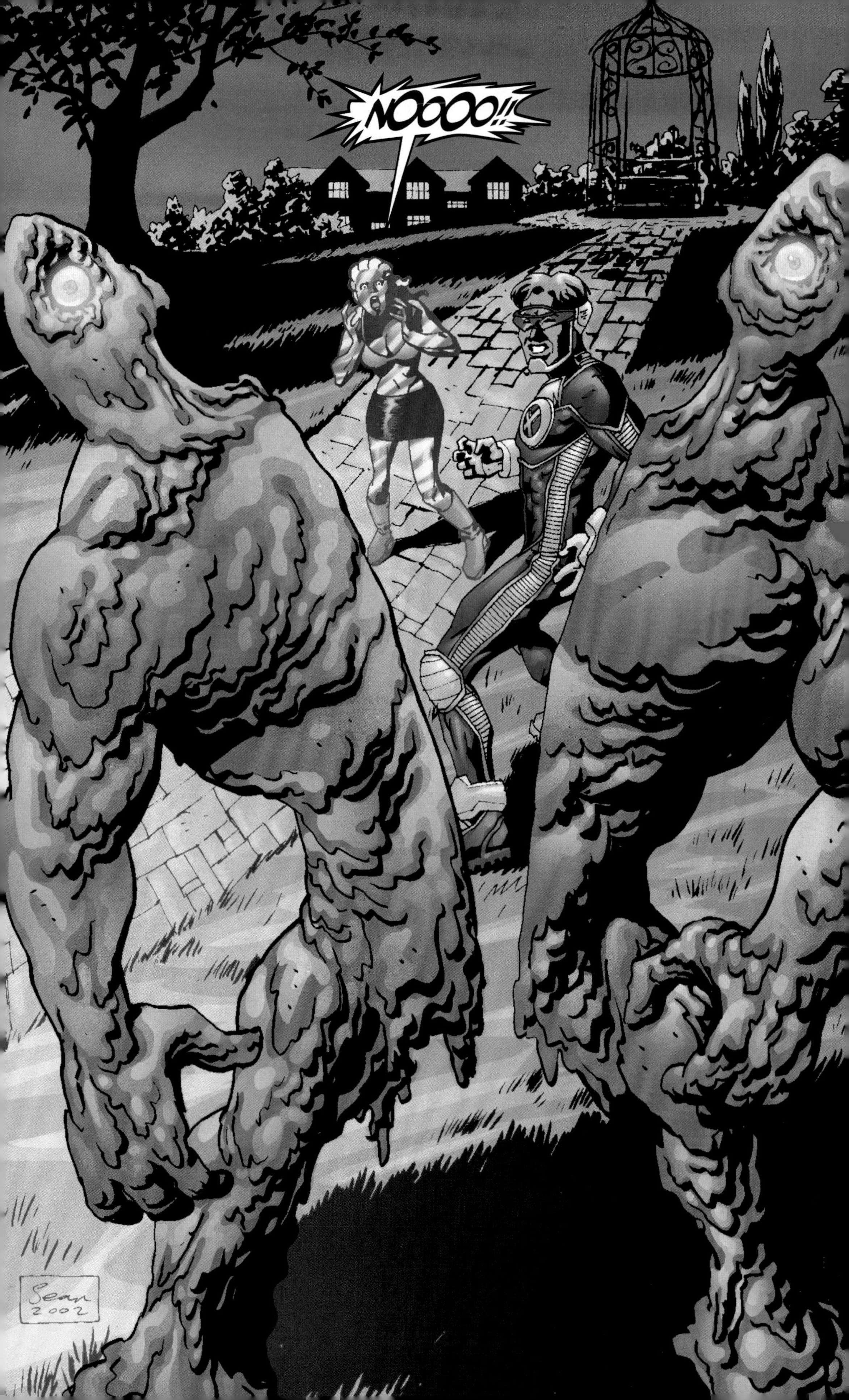
NOOOO!!
Sean 2002

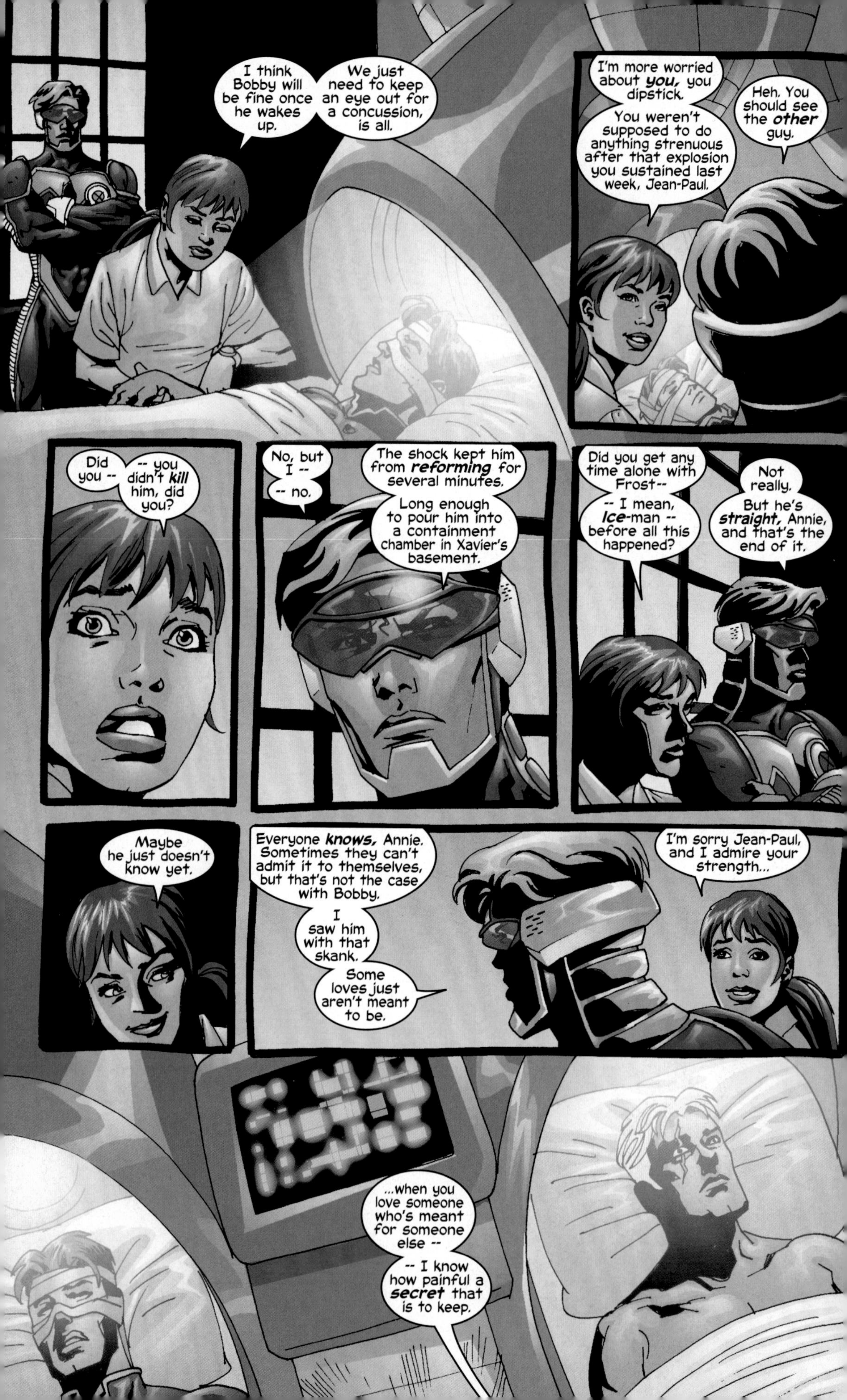
I think Bobby will be fine once he wakes up.
We just need to keep an eye out for a concussion, is all.
I'm more worried about you, you dipstick.
You weren't supposed to do anything strenuous after that explosion you sustained last week, Jean-Paul.
Heh. You should see the other guy.
Did you --
-- you didn't kill him, did you?
No, but I --
-- no.
The shock kept him from reforming for several minutes.
Long enough to pour him into a containment chamber in Xavier's basement.
Did you get any time alone with Frost--
-- I mean, Ice-man -- before all this happened?
Not really.
But he's straight, Annie, and that's the end of it.
Maybe he just doesn't know yet.
Everyone knows, Annie. Sometimes they can't admit it to themselves, but that's not the case with Bobby.
I saw him with that skank.
Some loves just aren't meant to be.
I'm sorry Jean-Paul, and I admire your strength...
...when you love someone who's meant for someone else --
-- I know how painful a secret that is to keep.

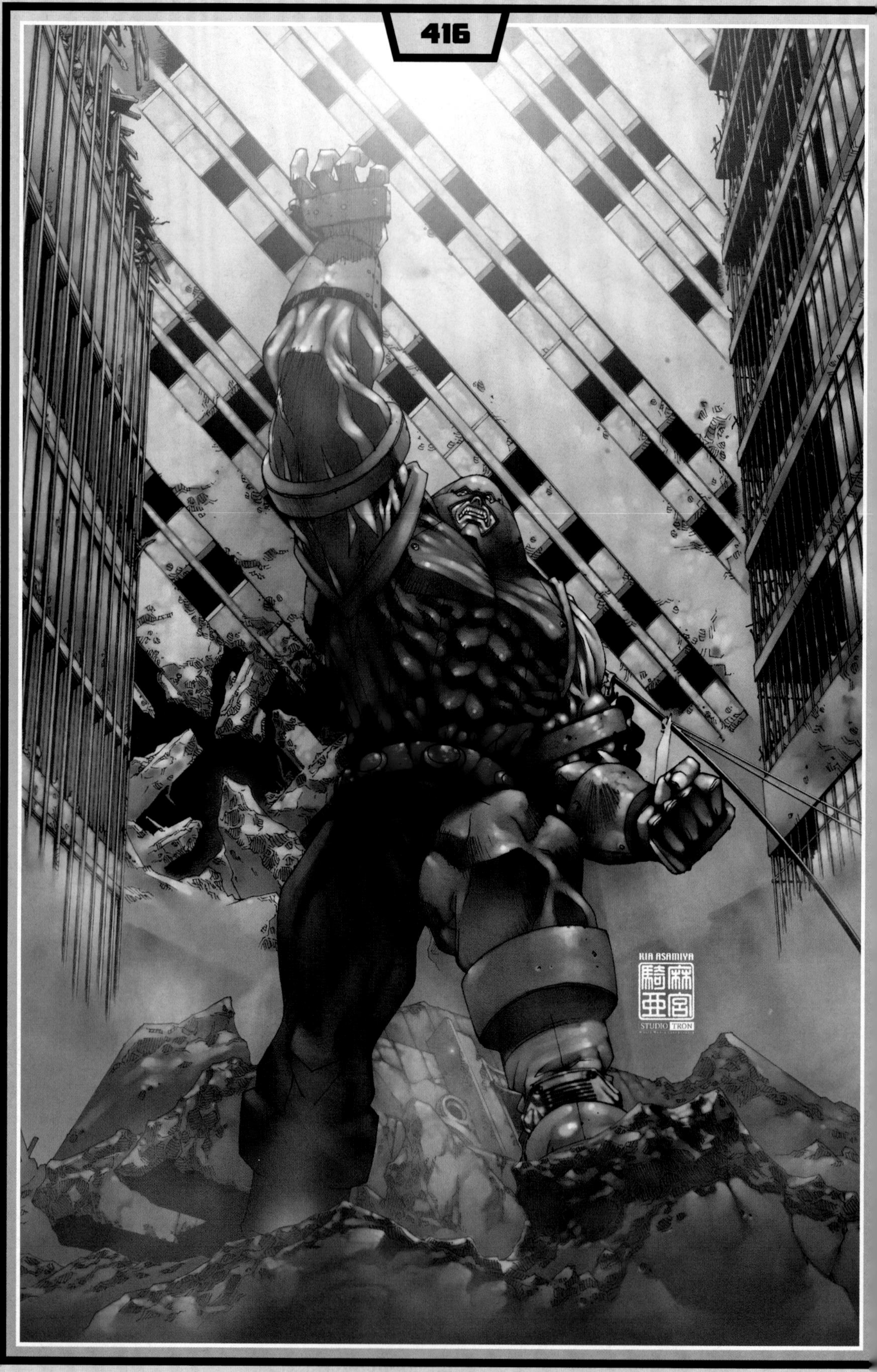
416
KIA ASAMIYA
麻宮騎亜
STUDIO TRON

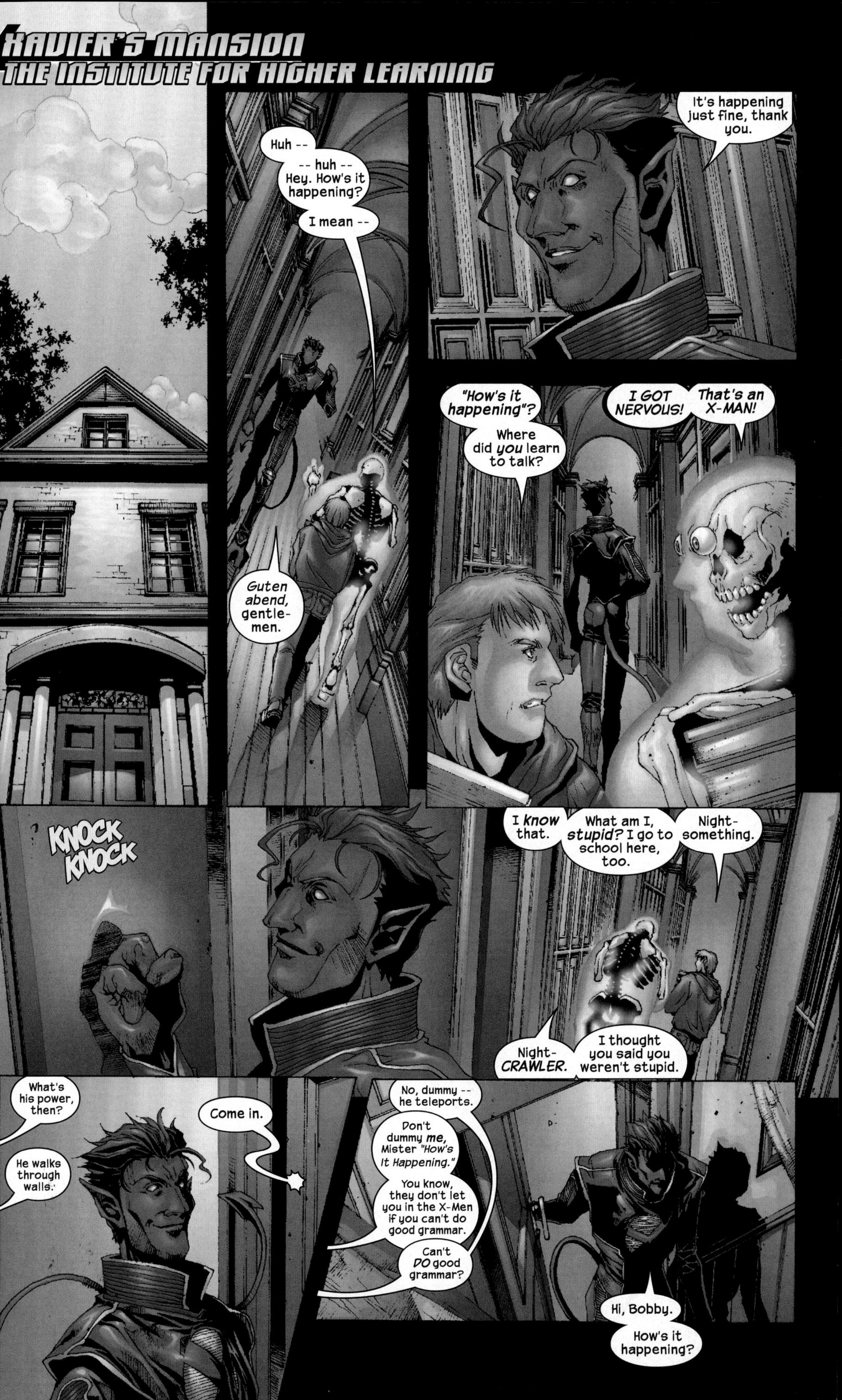
XAVIER'S MANSION
THE INSTITUTE FOR HIGHER LEARNING
Huh --
-- huh -- Hey. How's it happening?
I mean --
Guten abend, gentle-men.
It's happening just fine, thank you.
"How's it happening"?
Where did *you* learn to talk?
I GOT NERVOUS!
That's an X-MAN!
KNOCK KNOCK
I *know* that.
What am I, *stupid?* I go to school here, too.
Night-something.
Night-*CRAWLER.*
I thought you said you weren't stupid.
What's his power, then?
He walks through walls.
Come in.
No, dummy -- he teleports.
Don't dummy *me*, Mister *"How's It Happening."*
You know, they don't let you in the X-Men if you can't do good grammar.
Can't *DO* good grammar?
Hi, Bobby.
How's it happening?

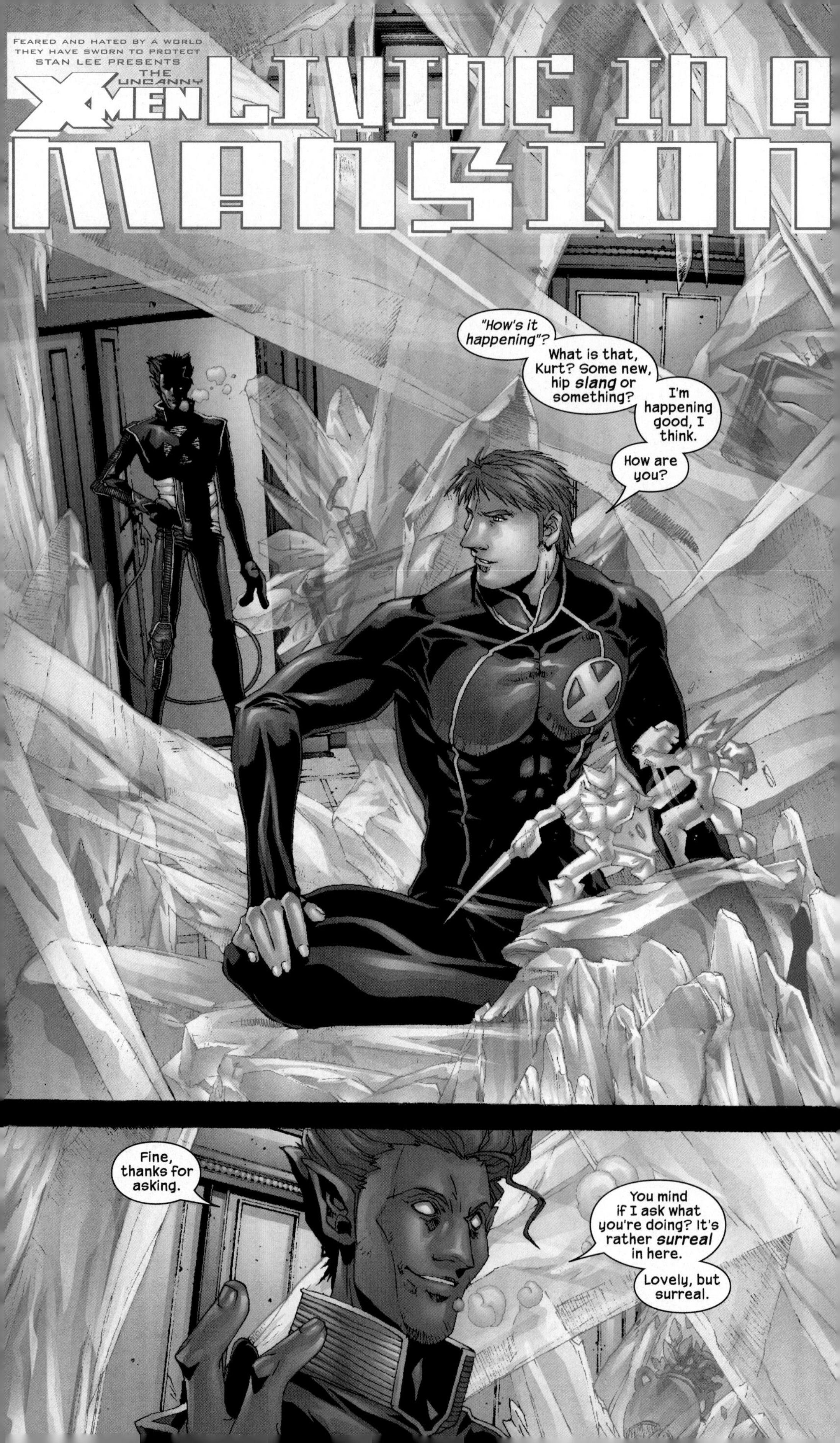
FEARED AND HATED BY A WORLD THEY HAVE SWORN TO PROTECT
STAN LEE PRESENTS
THE UNCANNY X-MEN
LIVING IN A MANSION
"How's it happening"?
What is that, Kurt? Some new, hip slang or something?
I'm happening good, I think.
How are you?
Fine, thanks for asking.
You mind if I ask what you're doing? It's rather surreal in here.
Lovely, but surreal.

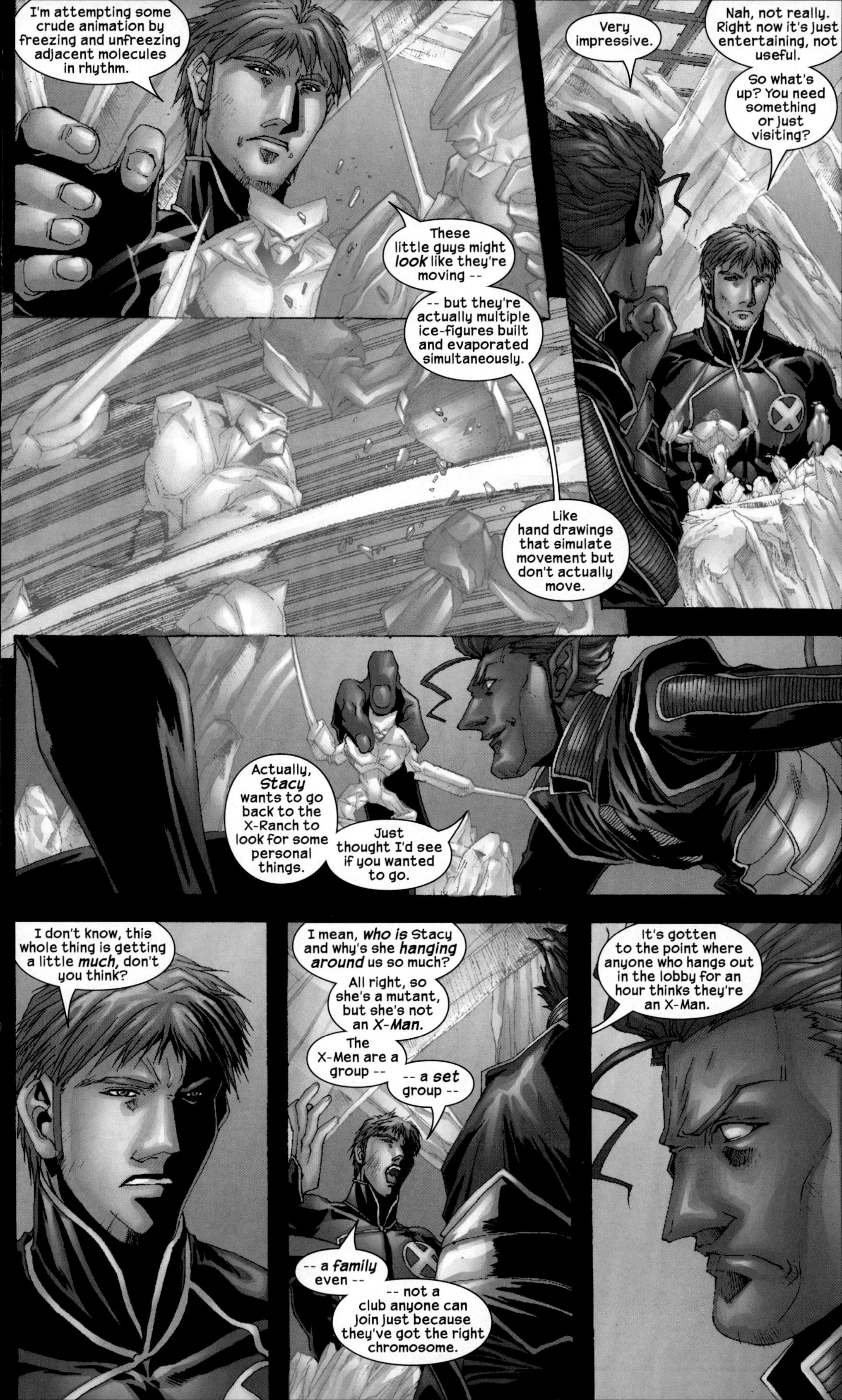

I'm attempting some crude animation by freezing and unfreezing adjacent molecules in rhythm.
These little guys might *look* like they're moving --
-- but they're actually multiple ice-figures built and evaporated simultaneously.
Like hand drawings that simulate movement but don't actually move.
Very impressive.
Nah, not really. Right now it's just entertaining, not useful.
So what's up? You need something or just visiting?
Actually, *Stacy* wants to go back to the X-Ranch to look for some personal things.
Just thought I'd see if you wanted to go.
I don't know, this whole thing is getting a little *much*, don't you think?
I mean, *who is* Stacy and why's she *hanging around* us so much?
All right, so she's a mutant, but she's not an *X-Man*.
The X-Men are a group --
-- a *set* group --
-- a *family* even --
-- not a club anyone can join just because they've got the right chromosome.
It's gotten to the point where anyone who hangs out in the lobby for an hour thinks they're an X-Man.

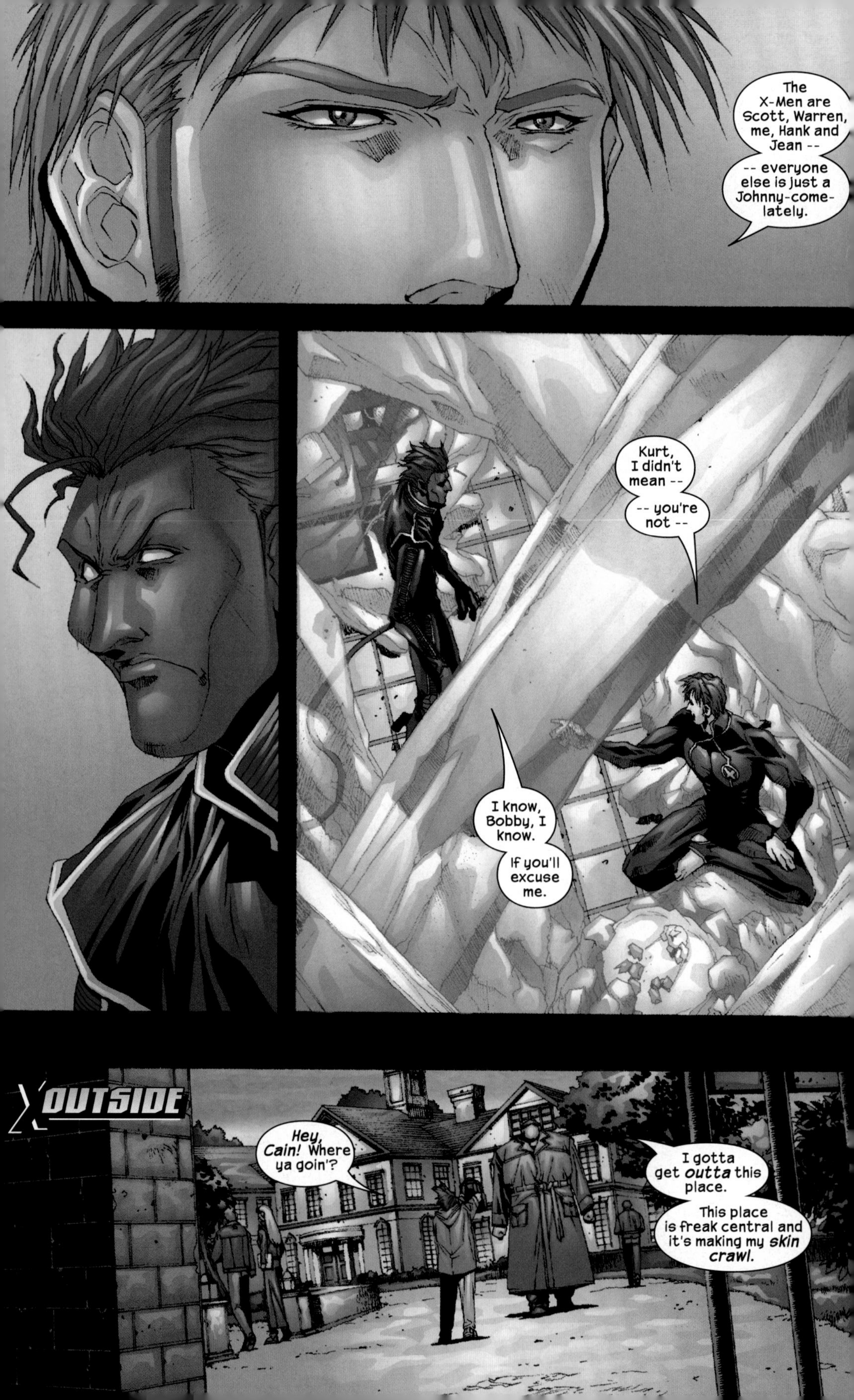
The X-Men are Scott, Warren, me, Hank and Jean --
-- everyone else is just a Johnny-come-lately.
Kurt, I didn't mean --
-- you're not --
I know, Bobby, I know.
If you'll excuse me.
OUTSIDE
Hey, Cain! Where ya goin'?
I gotta get outta this place.
This place is freak central and it's making my skin crawl.

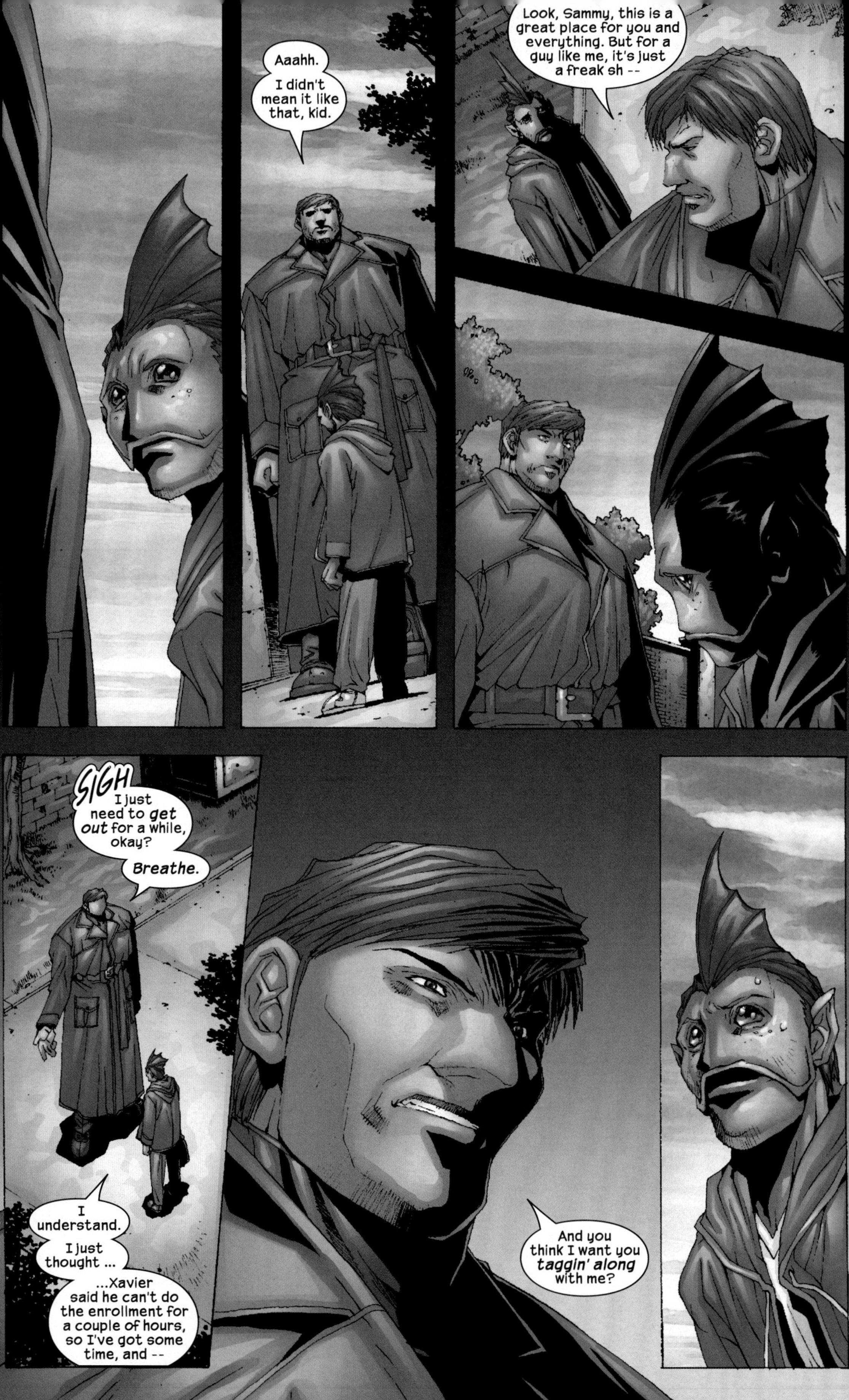

Aaahh.
I didn't mean it like that, kid.
Look, Sammy, this is a great place for you and everything. But for a guy like me, it's just a freak sh --
SIGH
I just need to *get out* for a while, okay?
Breathe.
I understand.
I just thought ...
...Xavier said he can't do the enrollment for a couple of hours, so I've got some time, and --
And you think I want you *taggin' along* with me?

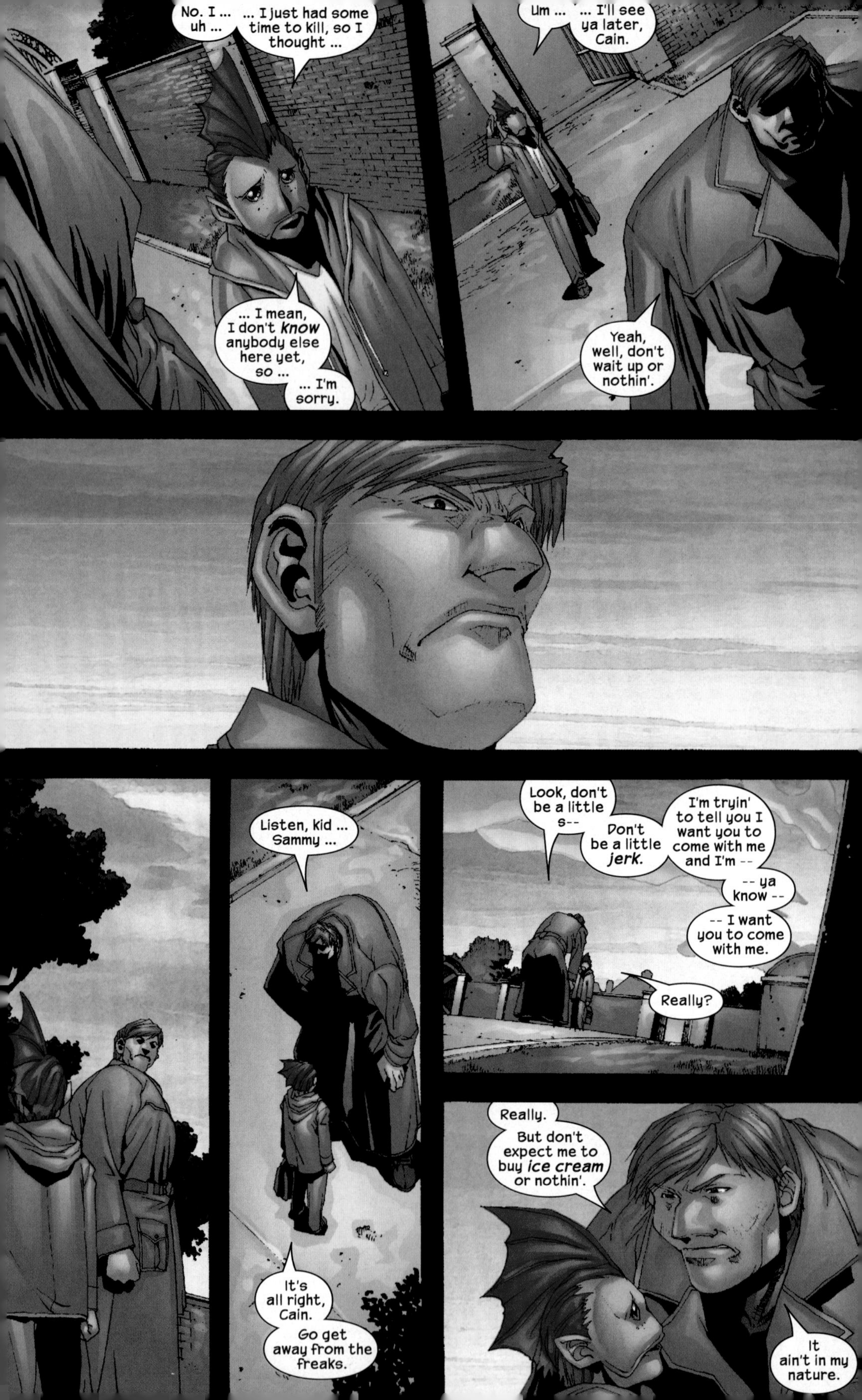
No. I ... uh ...
... I just had some time to kill, so I thought ...
... I mean, I don't *know* anybody else here yet, so ...
... I'm sorry.
Um ...
... I'll see ya later, Cain.
Yeah, well, don't wait up or nothin'.
Listen, kid ... Sammy ...
It's all right, Cain.
Go get away from the freaks.
Look, don't be a little s--
Don't be a little *jerk.*
I'm tryin' to tell you I want you to come with me and I'm --
-- ya know --
-- I want you to come with me.
Really?
Really.
But don't expect me to buy *ice cream* or nothin'.
It ain't in my nature.

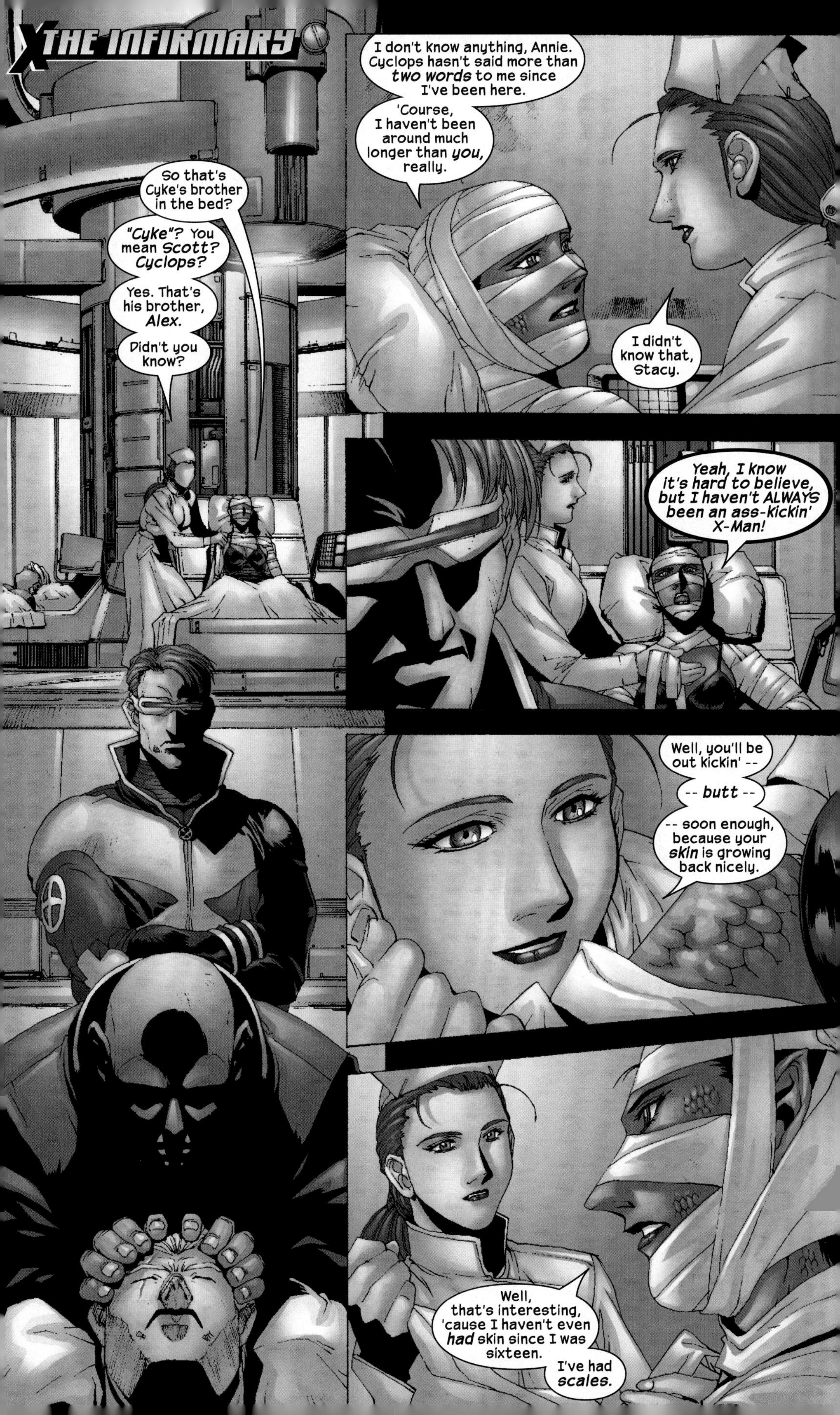
THE INFIRMARY
So that's Cyke's brother in the bed?
"Cyke"? You mean Scott? Cyclops?
Yes. That's his brother, Alex.
Didn't you know?
I don't know anything, Annie. Cyclops hasn't said more than two words to me since I've been here.
'Course, I haven't been around much longer than you, really.
I didn't know that, Stacy.
Yeah, I know it's hard to believe, but I haven't ALWAYS been an ass-kickin' X-Man!
Well, you'll be out kickin' --
-- butt --
-- soon enough, because your skin is growing back nicely.
Well, that's interesting, 'cause I haven't even had skin since I was sixteen.
I've had scales.

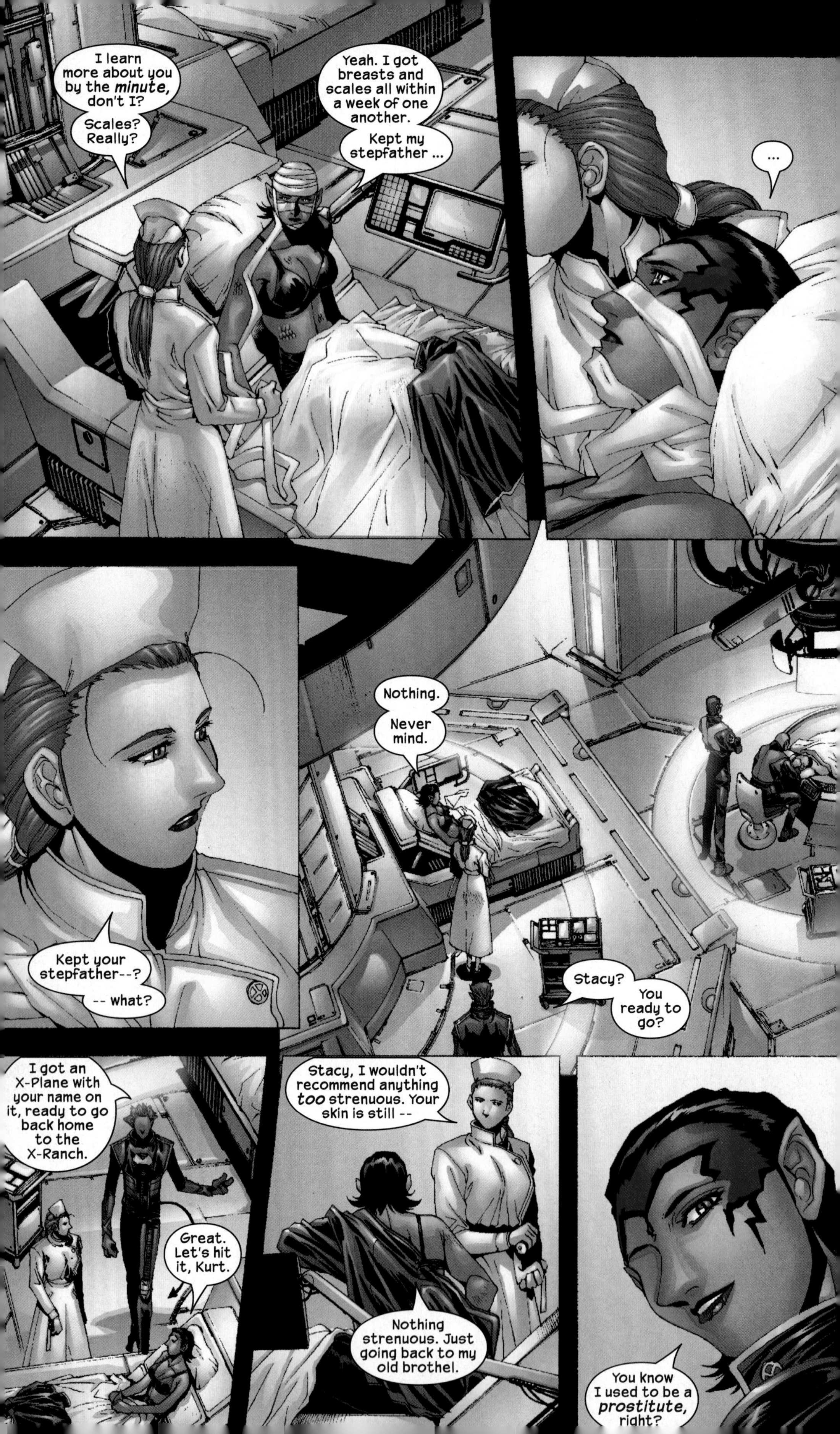
I learn more about you by the *minute,* don't I?
Scales? Really?
Yeah. I got breasts and scales all within a week of one another.
Kept my stepfather ...
...
Kept your stepfather--?
-- what?
Nothing.
Never mind.
Stacy?
You ready to go?
I got an X-Plane with your name on it, ready to go back home to the X-Ranch.
Great. Let's hit it, Kurt.
Stacy, I wouldn't recommend anything *too* strenuous. Your skin is still --
Nothing strenuous. Just going back to my old brothel.
You know I used to be a *prostitute,* right?

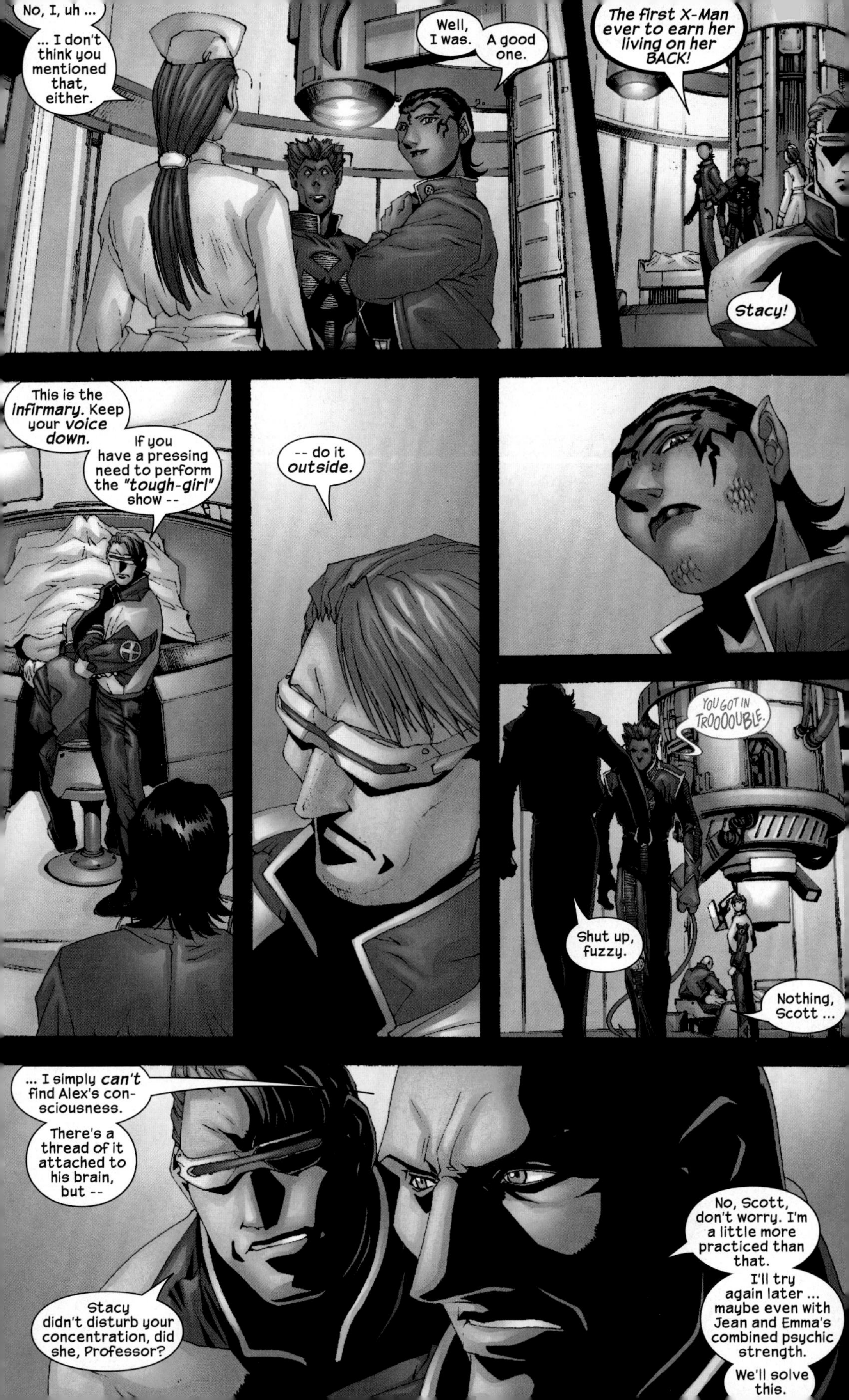
No, I, uh ...
... I don't think you mentioned that, either.
Well, I was.
A good one.
The first X-Man ever to earn her living on her BACK!
Stacy!
This is the infirmary. Keep your voice down.
If you have a pressing need to perform the "tough-girl" show --
-- do it outside.
YOU GOT IN TROOOOUBLE.
Shut up, fuzzy.
Nothing, Scott ...
... I simply can't find Alex's consciousness.
There's a thread of it attached to his brain, but --
Stacy didn't disturb your concentration, did she, Professor?
No, Scott, don't worry. I'm a little more practiced than that.
I'll try again later ... maybe even with Jean and Emma's combined psychic strength.
We'll solve this.

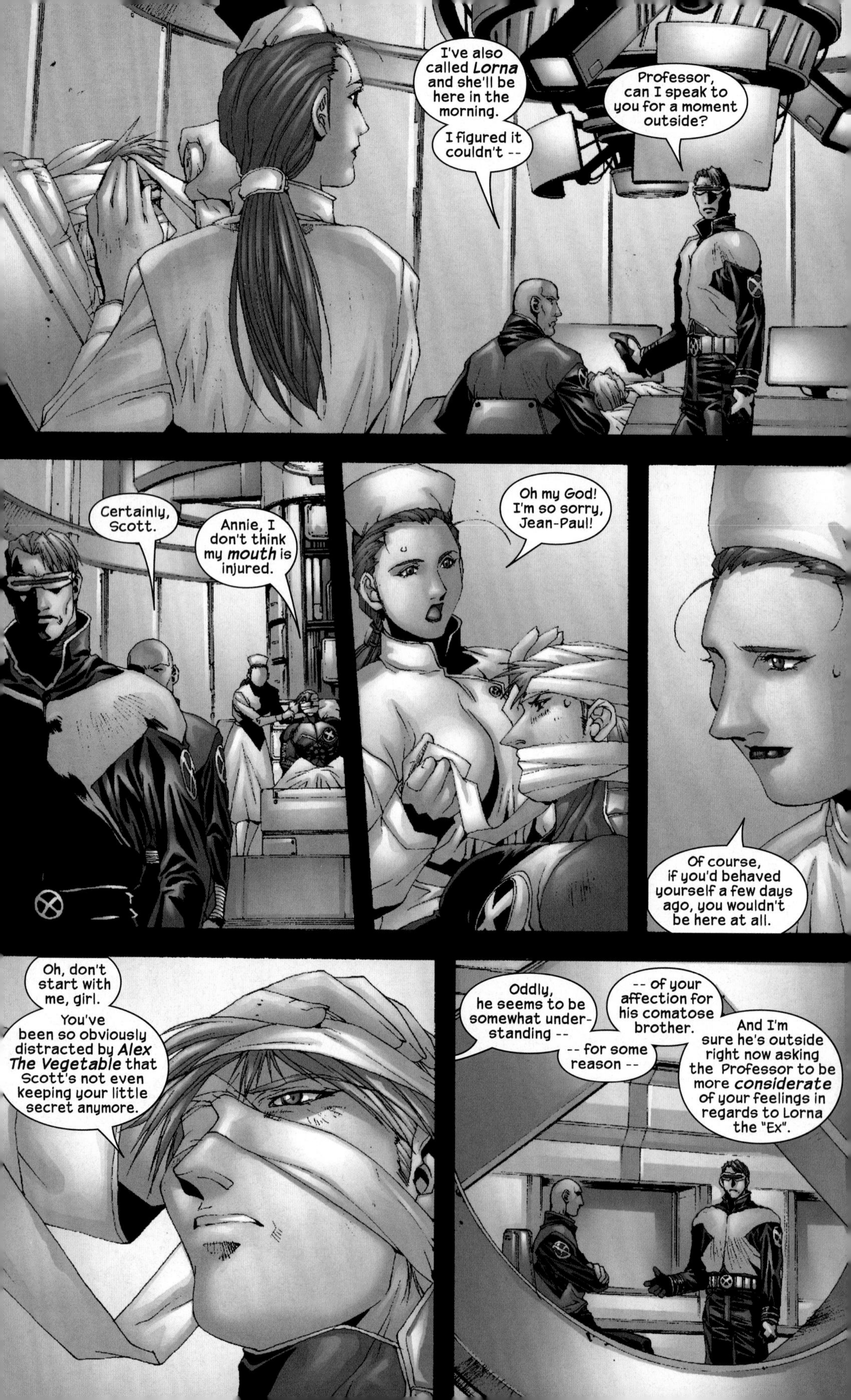
I've also called Lorna and she'll be here in the morning.
I figured it couldn't --
Professor, can I speak to you for a moment outside?
Certainly, Scott.
Annie, I don't think my mouth is injured.
Oh my God! I'm so sorry, Jean-Paul!
Of course, if you'd behaved yourself a few days ago, you wouldn't be here at all.
Oh, don't start with me, girl.
You've been so obviously distracted by Alex The Vegetable that Scott's not even keeping your little secret anymore.
Oddly, he seems to be somewhat under-standing --
-- for some reason --
-- of your affection for his comatose brother.
And I'm sure he's outside right now asking the Professor to be more considerate of your feelings in regards to Lorna the "Ex".

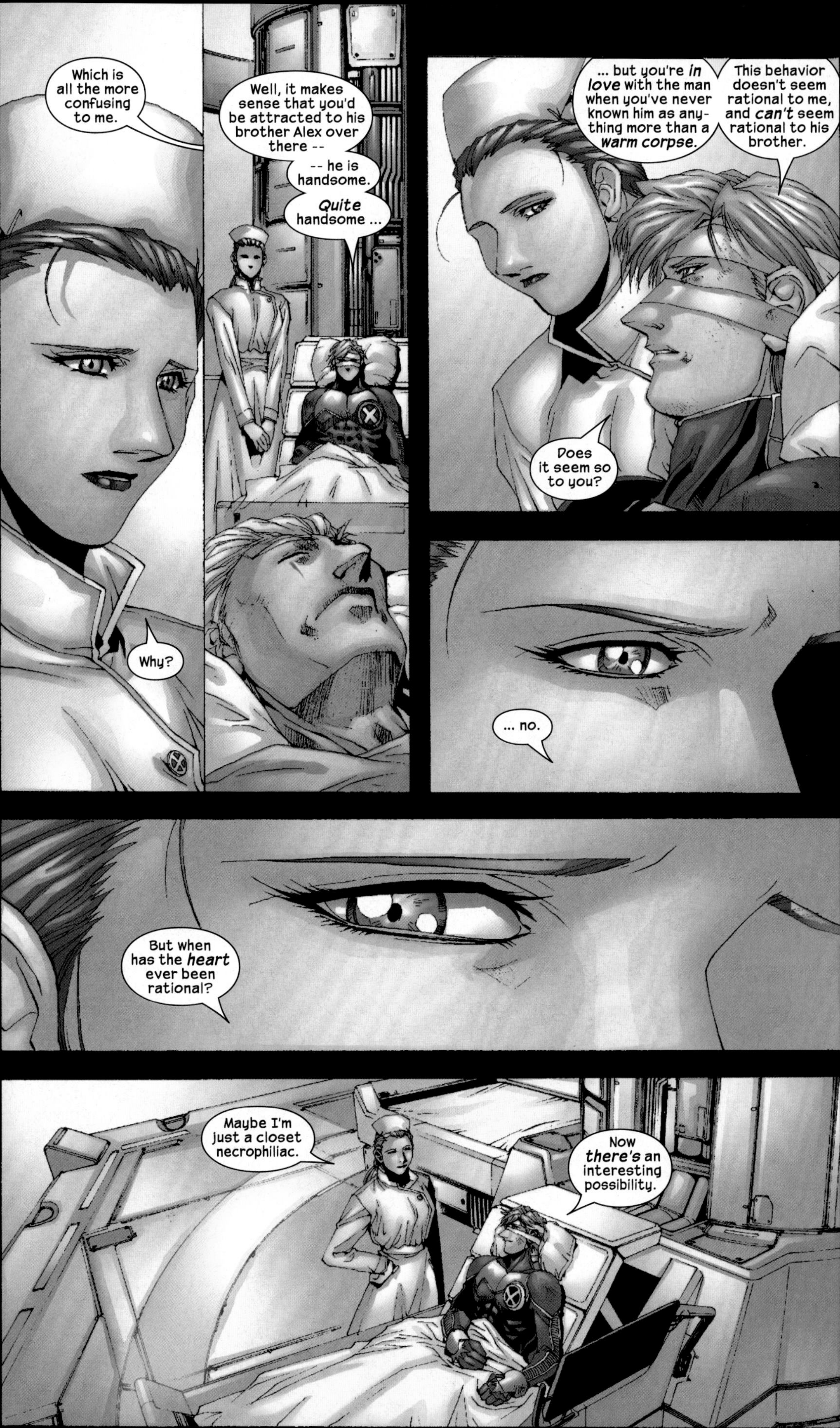

Which is all the more confusing to me.
Well, it makes sense that you'd be attracted to his brother Alex over there --
-- he is handsome.
Quite handsome ...
Why?
... but you're *in love* with the man when you've never known him as anything more than a *warm corpse.*
This behavior doesn't seem rational to me, and *can't* seem rational to his brother.
Does it seem so to you?
... no.
But when has the *heart* ever been rational?
Maybe I'm just a closet necrophiliac.
Now *there's* an interesting possibility.

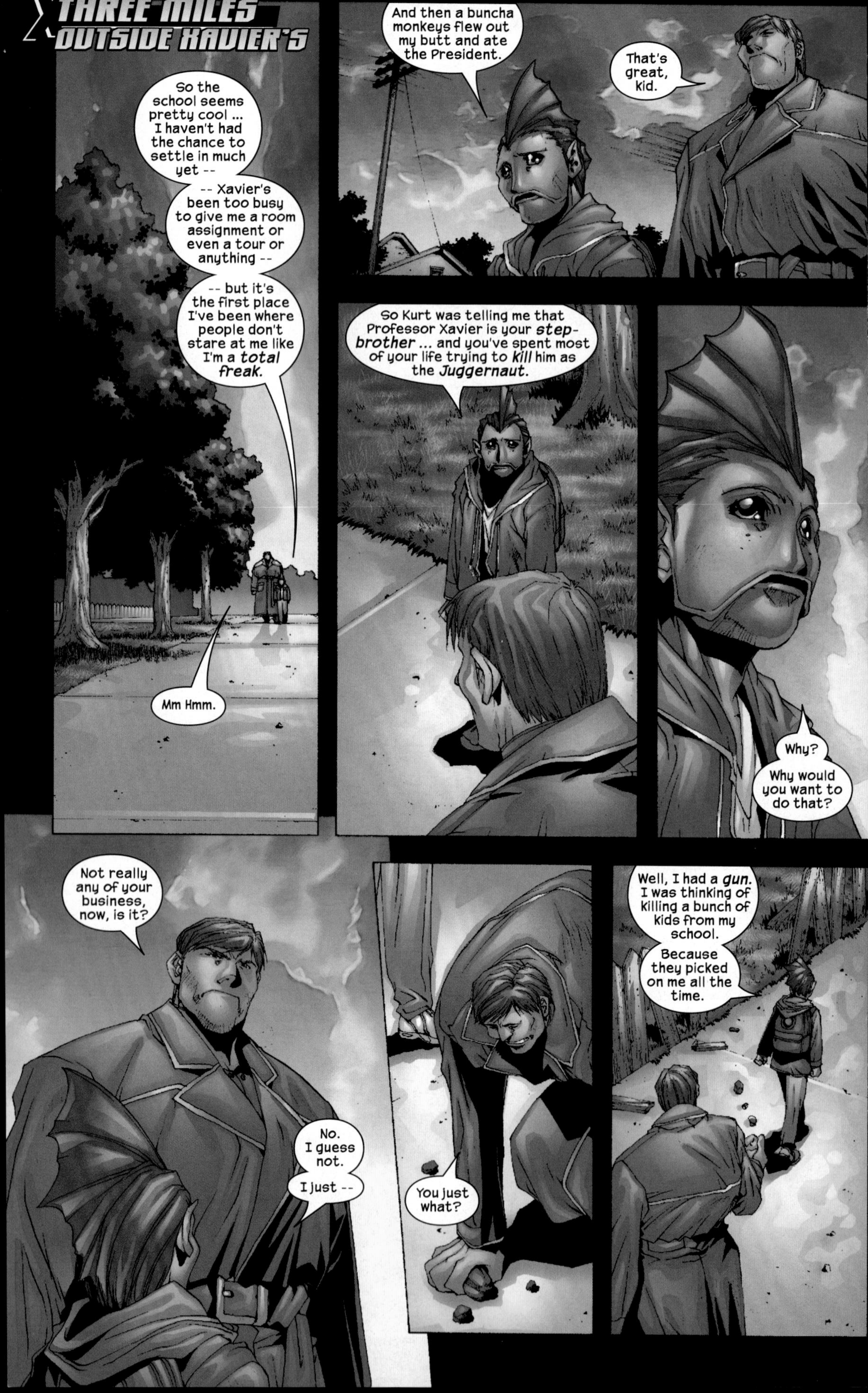
THREE MILES OUTSIDE XAVIER'S
So the school seems pretty cool ... I haven't had the chance to settle in much yet --
-- Xavier's been too busy to give me a room assignment or even a tour or anything --
-- but it's the first place I've been where people don't stare at me like I'm a *total freak*.
Mm Hmm.
And then a buncha monkeys flew out my butt and ate the President.
That's great, kid.
So Kurt was telling me that Professor Xavier is your *step-brother* ... and you've spent most of your life trying to *kill* him as the *Juggernaut*.
Why?
Why would you want to do that?
Not really any of your business, now, is it?
No. I guess not.
I just --
You just what?
Well, I had a *gun*. I was thinking of killing a bunch of kids from my school.
Because they picked on me all the time.

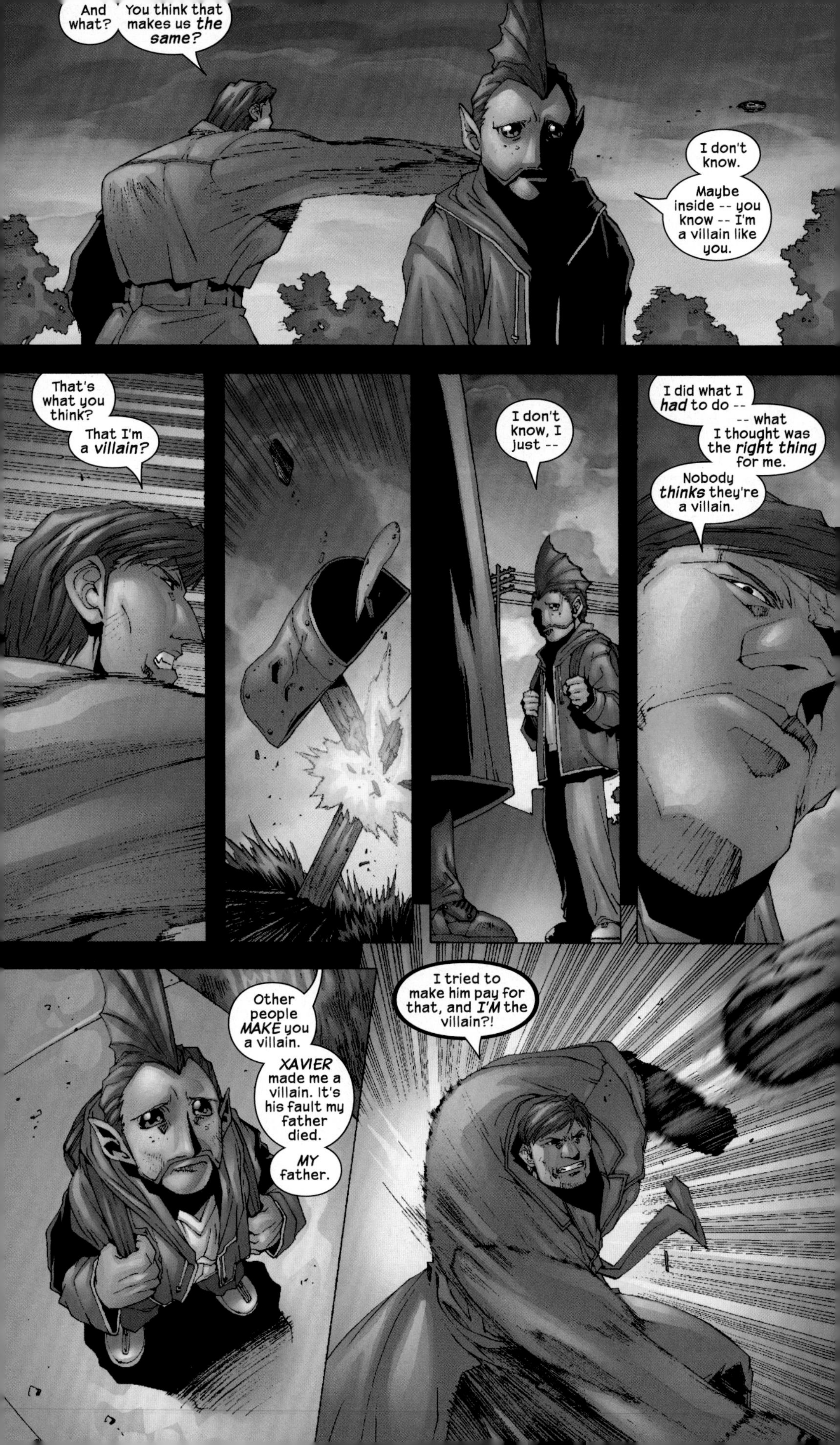
And what?
You think that makes us the same?
I don't know.
Maybe inside -- you know -- I'm a villain like you.
That's what you think?
That I'm a villain?
I don't know, I just --
I did what I had to do --
-- what I thought was the right thing for me.
Nobody thinks they're a villain.
Other people MAKE you a villain.
XAVIER made me a villain. It's his fault my father died.
MY father.
I tried to make him pay for that, and I'M the villain?!

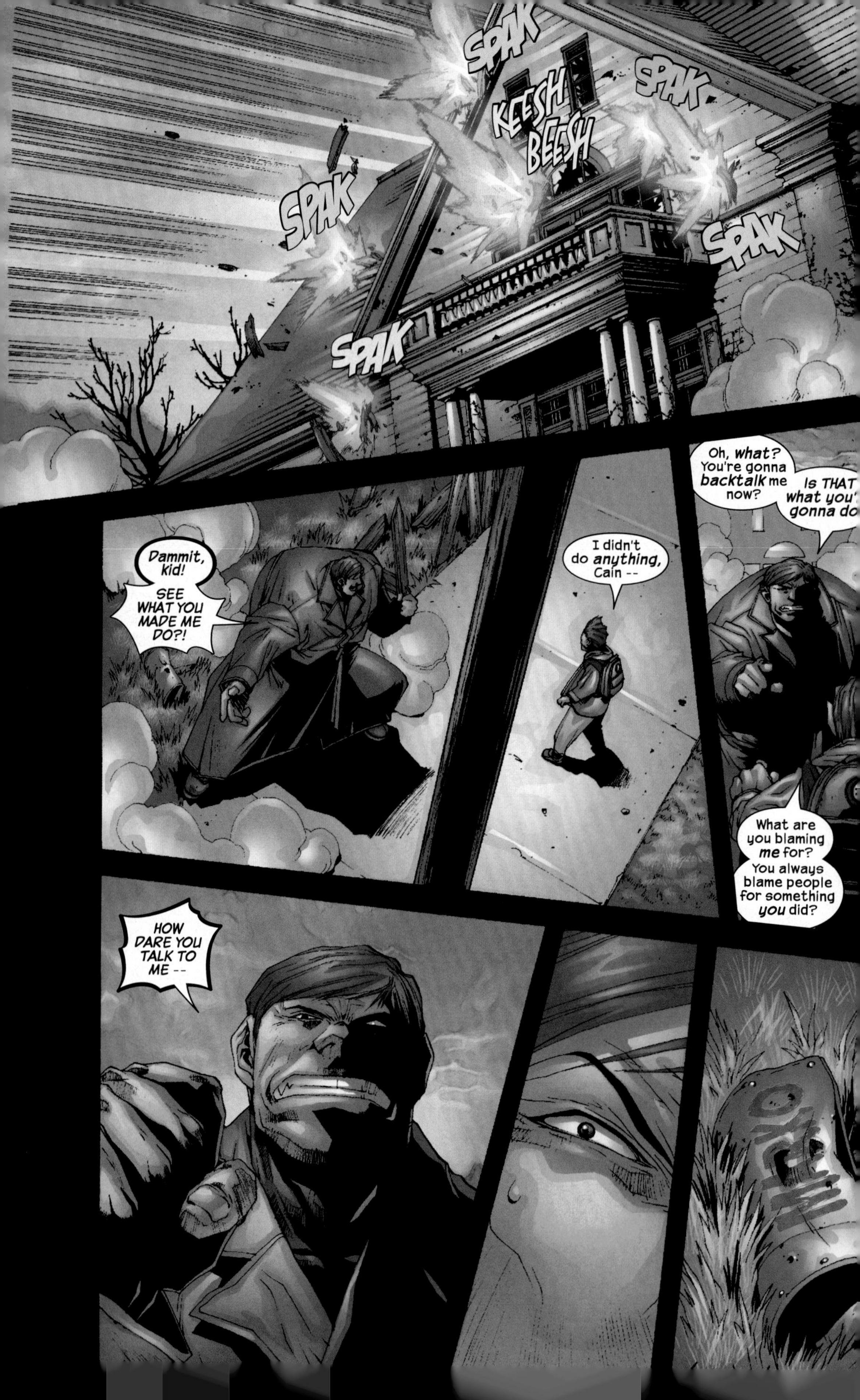
SPAK
KEESH
BEESH
SPAK
SPAK
SPAK
SPAK
Dammit, kid!
SEE WHAT YOU MADE ME DO?!
I didn't do anything, Cain --
Oh, what? You're gonna backtalk me now?
What are you blaming me for? You always blame people for something you did?
HOW DARE YOU TALK TO ME --

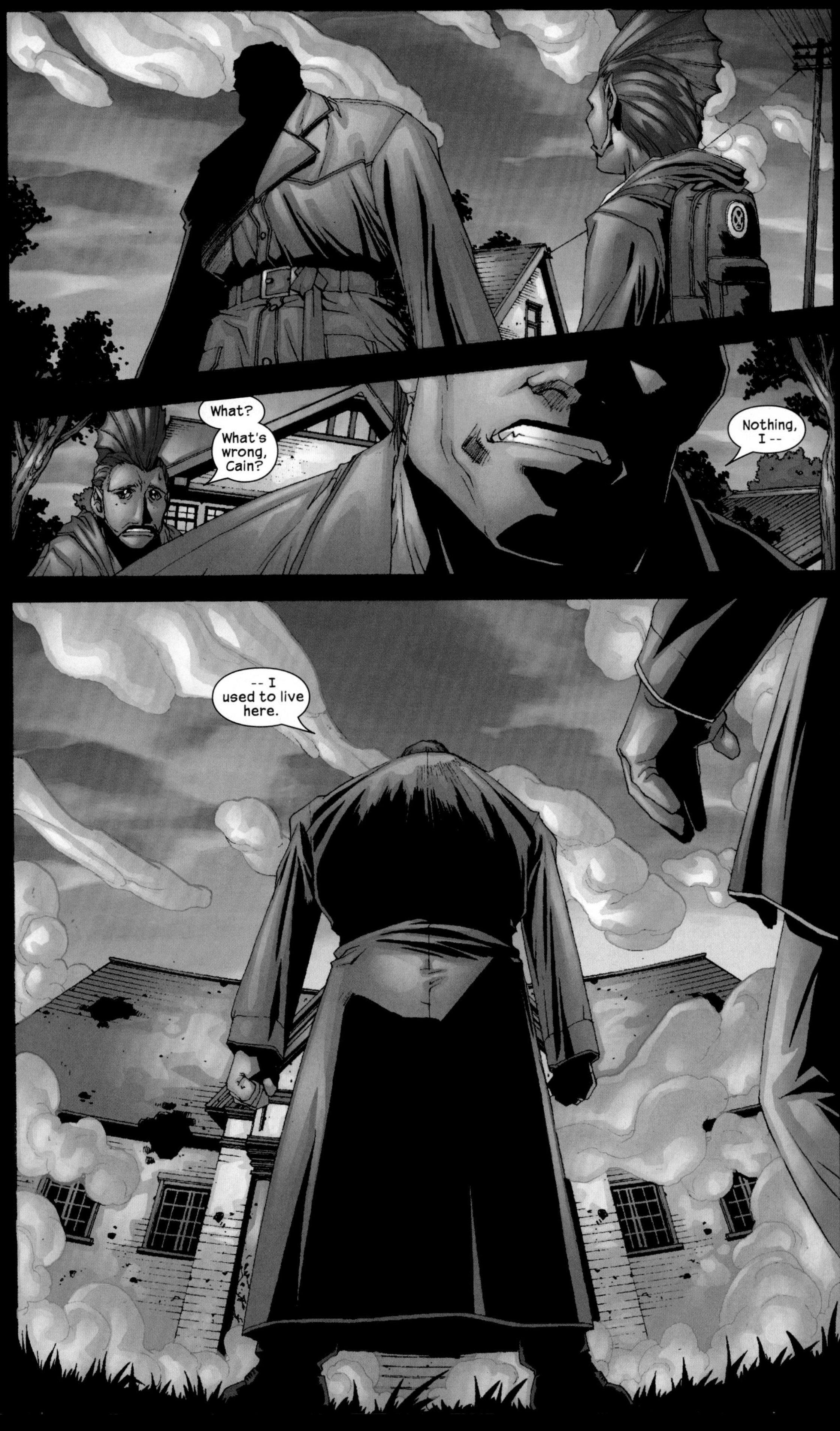
What?
What's wrong, Cain?
Nothing, I --
-- I used to live here.

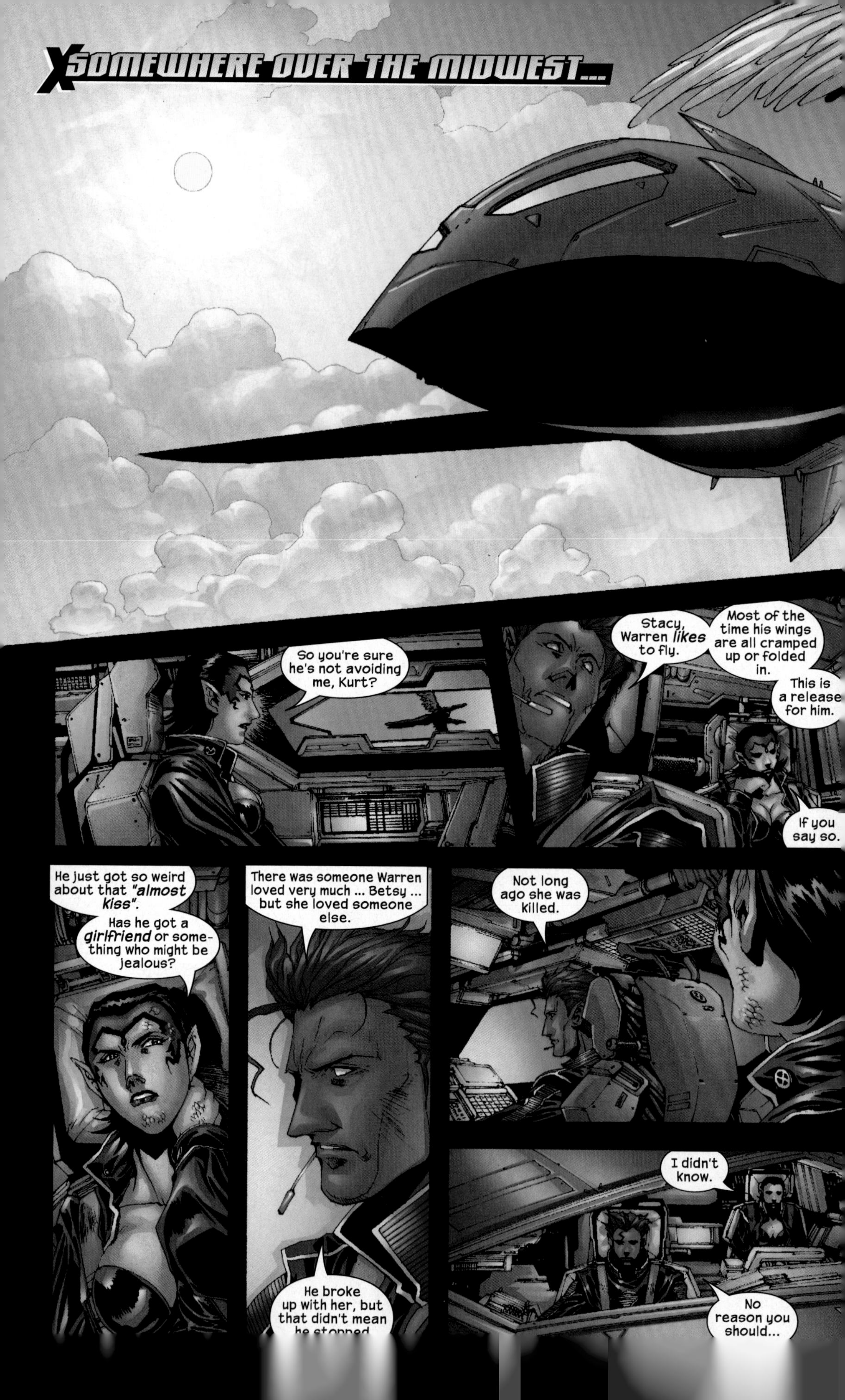
SOMEWHERE OVER THE MIDWEST...
So you're sure he's not avoiding me, Kurt?
Stacy, Warren *likes* to fly.
Most of the time his wings are all cramped up or folded in.
This is a release for him.
If you say so.
He just got so weird about that *"almost kiss"*.
Has he got a *girlfriend* or something who might be jealous?
There was someone Warren loved very much ... Betsy ... but she loved someone else.
He broke up with her, but that didn't mean
Not long ago she was killed.
I didn't know.
No reason you should...

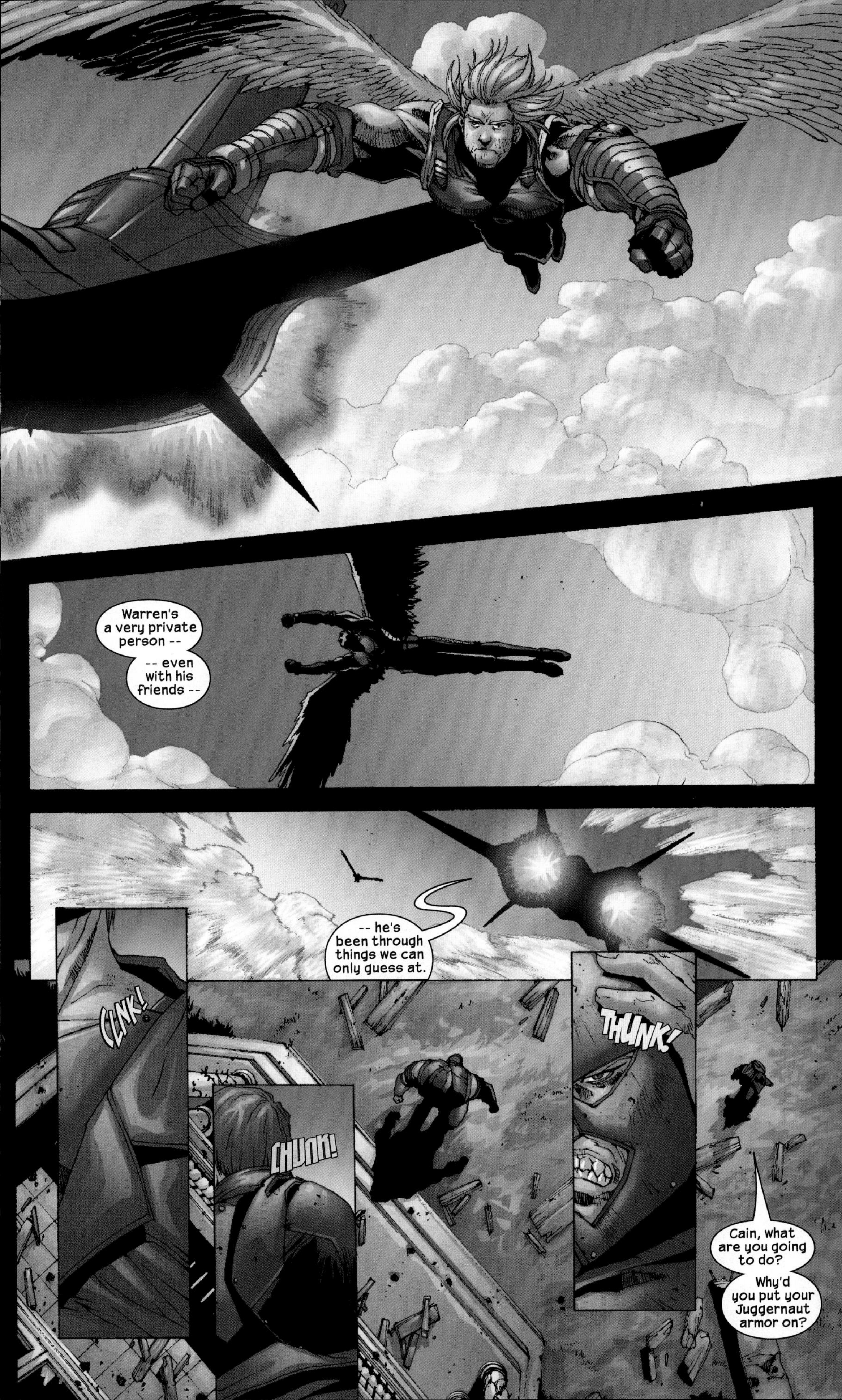
Warren's a very private person --
-- even with his friends --
-- he's been through things we can only guess at.
CLNK!
CHUNK!
THUNK!
Cain, what are you going to do?
Why'd you put your Juggernaut armor on?

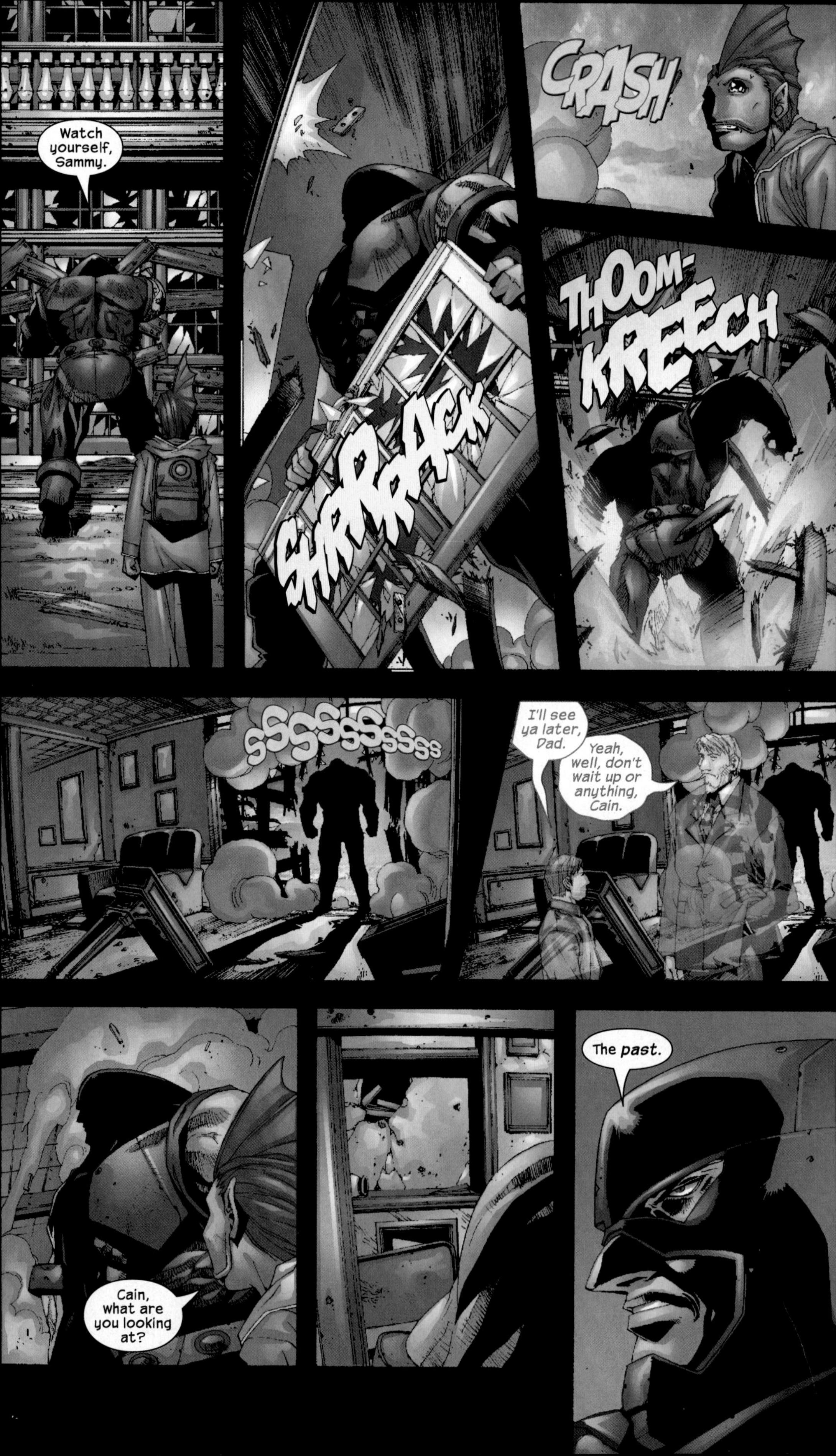
Watch yourself, Sammy.
SHRRACK
CRASH
THOOM-KREECH
SSSSSSsssss
I'll see ya later, Dad.
Yeah, well, don't wait up or anything, Cain.
Cain, what are you looking at?
The past.

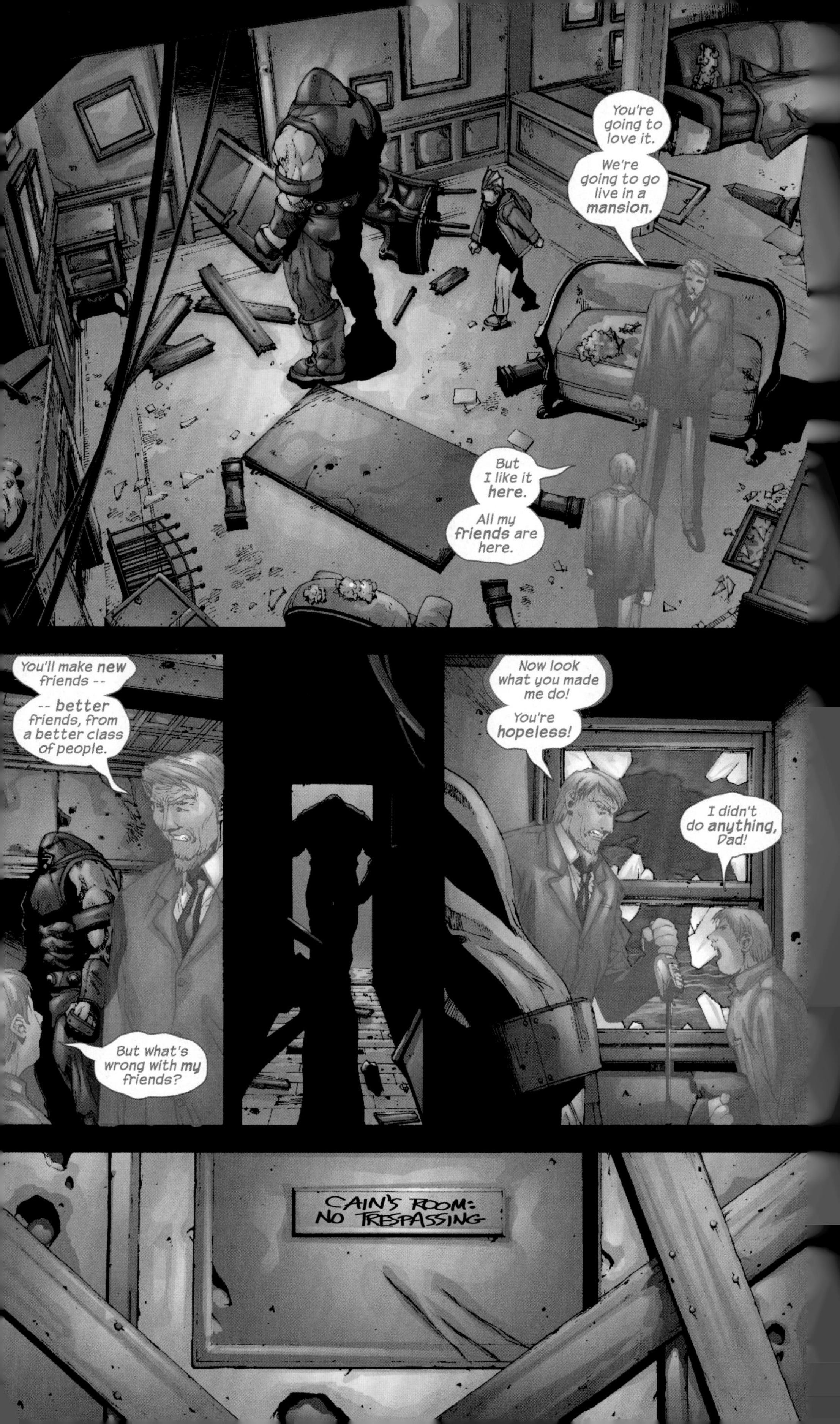

You're going to love it.
We're going to go live in a mansion.
But I like it here.
All my friends are here.
You'll make new friends --
-- better friends, from a better class of people.
But what's wrong with my friends?
Now look what you made me do!
You're hopeless!
I didn't do anything, Dad!
CAIN'S ROOM: NO TRESPASSING

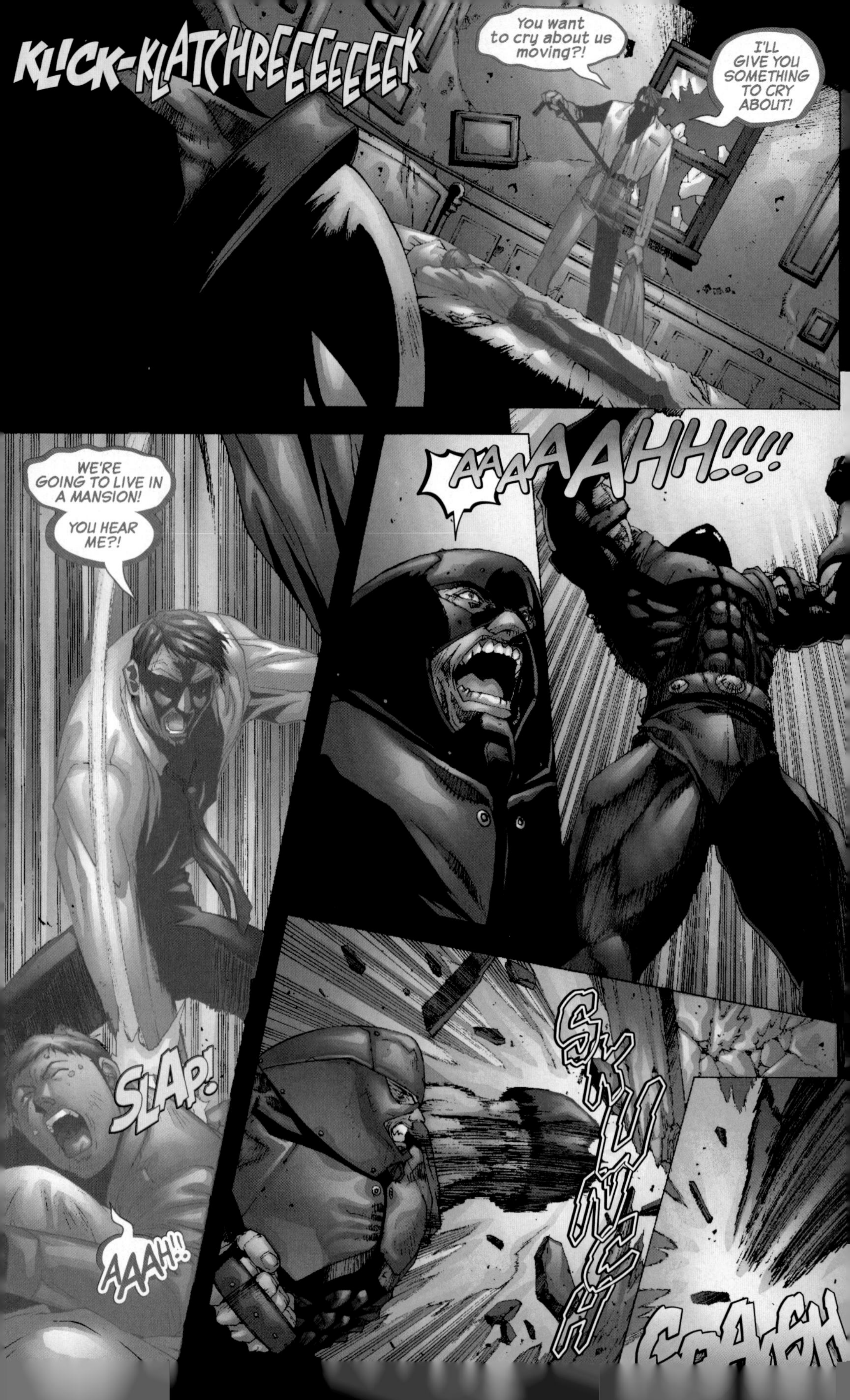

KLICK-KLATCHREEEEEEEK
You want to cry about us moving?!
I'LL GIVE YOU SOMETHING TO CRY ABOUT!
WE'RE GOING TO LIVE IN A MANSION!
YOU HEAR ME?!
AAAAAHH!!!!
SLAP!
AAAH!!
SHUNCH

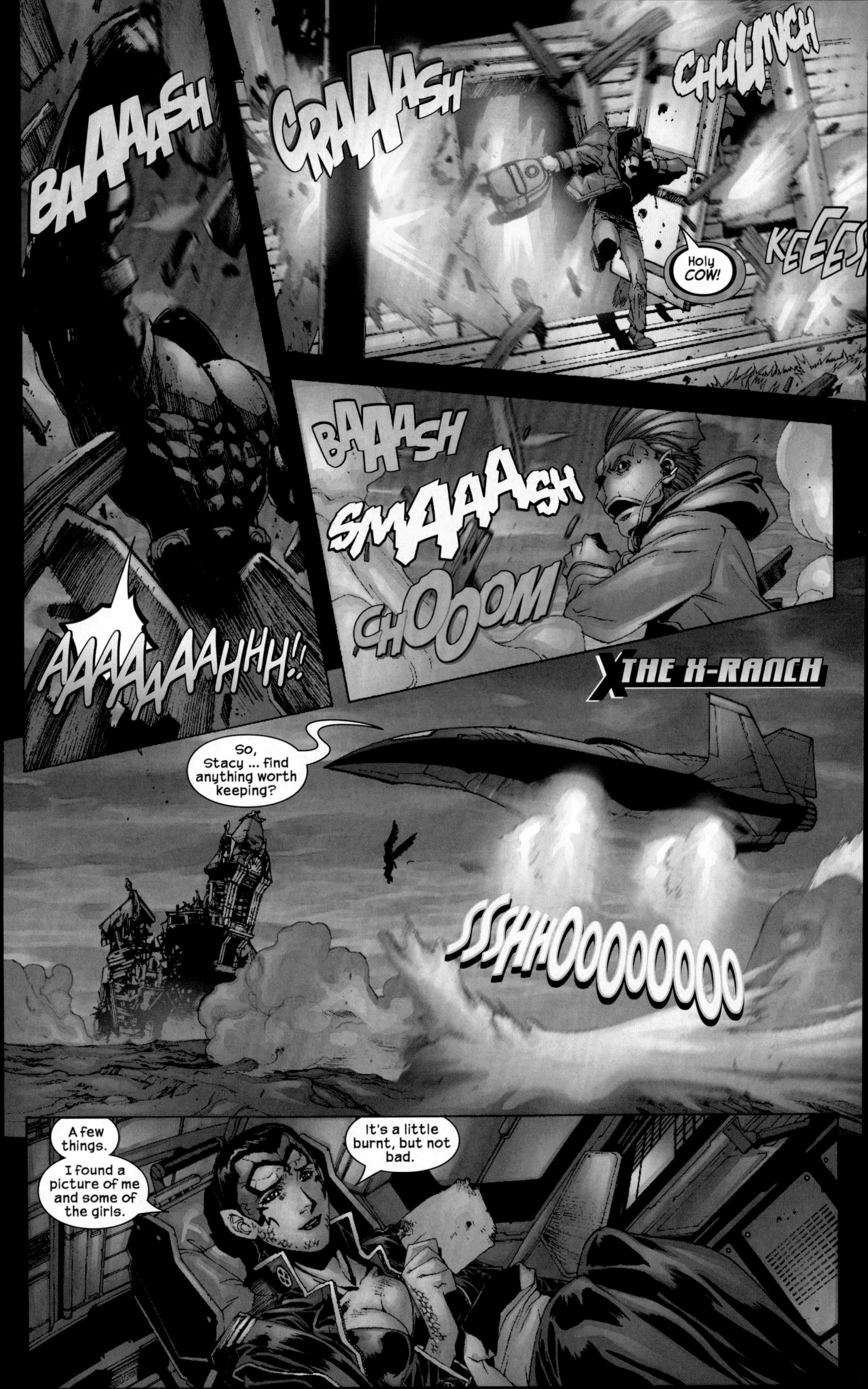
BAAAASH
CRAAASH
CHUUNCH
Holy COW!
KEEES
AAAAAAAHHH!!
BAAASH
SMAAASH
CHOOOM
THE X-RANCH
So, Stacy ... find anything worth keeping?
SSSHHOOOOOOOO
A few things.
I found a picture of me and some of the girls.
It's a little burnt, but not bad.

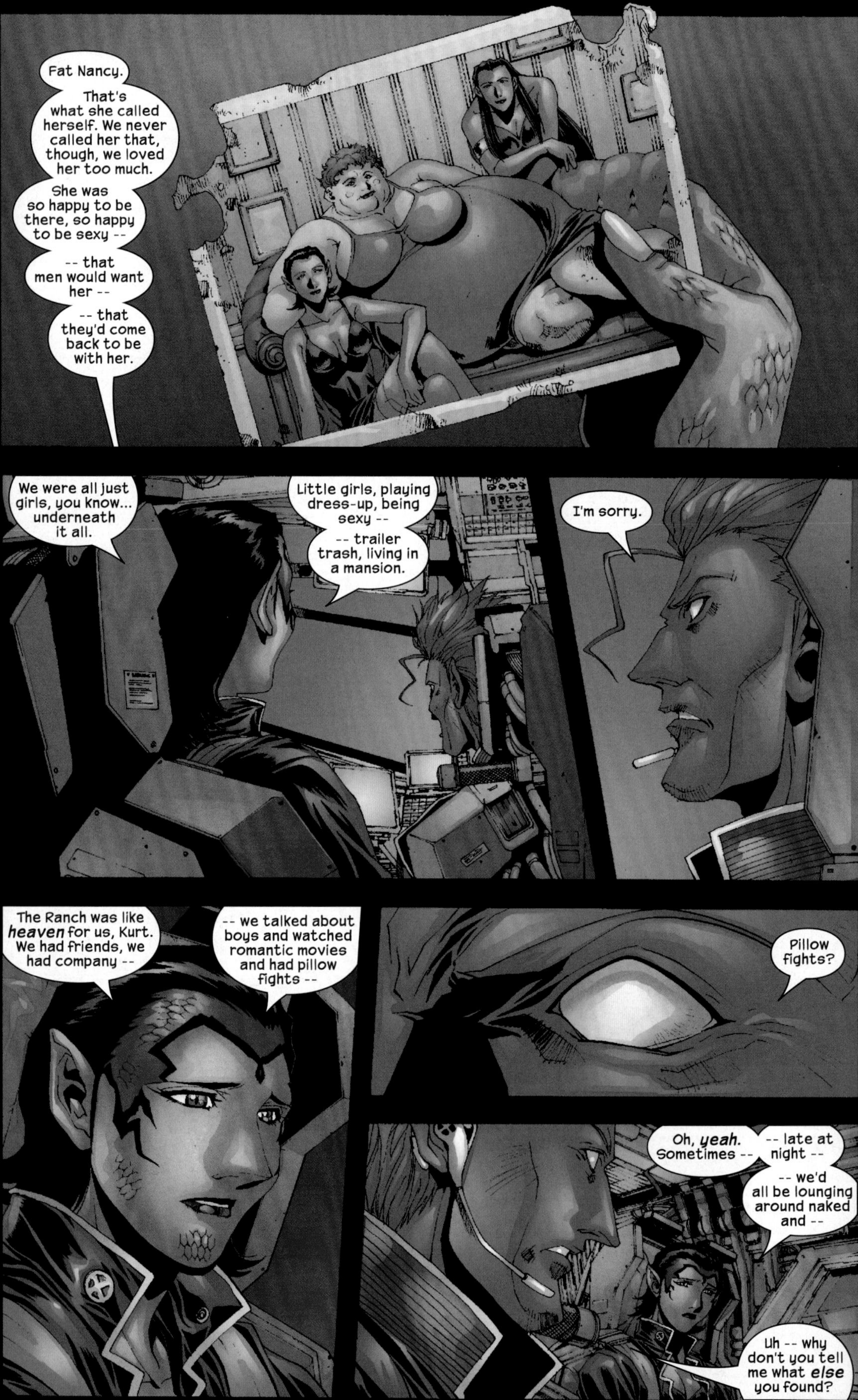
Fat Nancy.
That's what she called herself. We never called her that, though, we loved her too much.
She was so happy to be there, so happy to be sexy --
-- that men would want her --
-- that they'd come back to be with her.
We were all just girls, you know... underneath it all.
Little girls, playing dress-up, being sexy --
-- trailer trash, living in a mansion.
I'm sorry.
The Ranch was like *heaven* for us, Kurt. We had friends, we had company --
-- we talked about boys and watched romantic movies and had pillow fights --
Pillow fights?
Oh, *yeah.* Sometimes --
-- late at night --
-- we'd all be lounging around naked and --
Uh -- why don't you tell me what *else* you found?

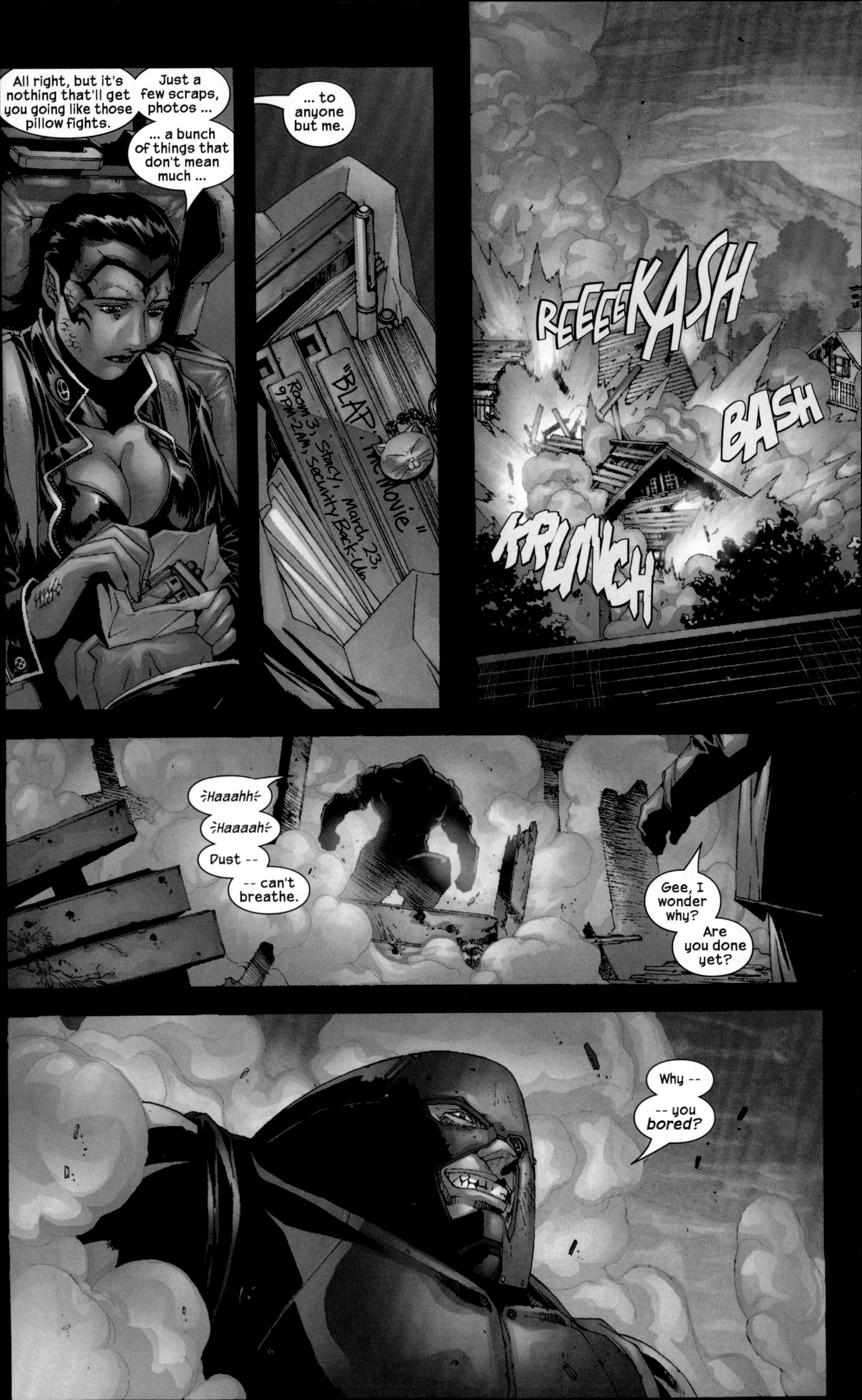
All right, but it's nothing that'll get you going like those pillow fights.
Just a few scraps, photos ...
... a bunch of things that don't mean much ...
... to anyone but me.
"BLAP": The Movie"
Room 3, Stacy, March 23, 9PM-2AM, Security Back-Up
REEEEEKASH
BASH
KRUNCH
Haaahh
Haaaah
Dust --
-- can't breathe.
Gee, I wonder why?
Are you done yet?
Why --
-- you *bored?*

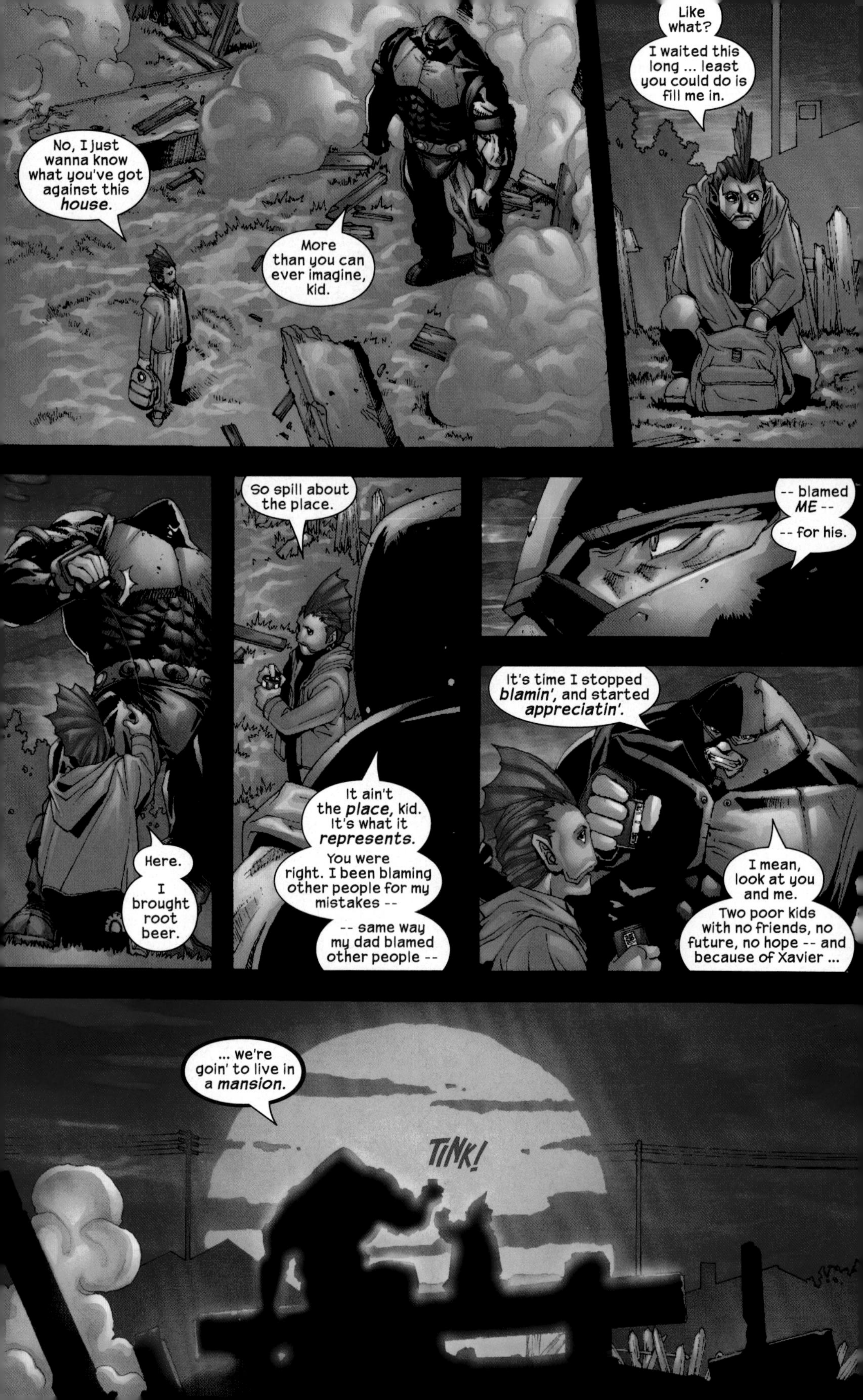
No, I just wanna know what you've got against this *house*.
More than you can ever imagine, kid.
Like what?
I waited this long ... least you could do is fill me in.
Here.
I brought root beer.
So spill about the place.
It ain't the *place*, kid. It's what it *represents*.
You were right. I been blaming other people for my mistakes --
-- same way my dad blamed other people --
-- blamed *ME* --
-- for his.
It's time I stopped *blamin'*, and started *appreciatin'*.
I mean, look at you and me.
Two poor kids with no friends, no future, no hope -- and because of Xavier ...
... we're goin' to live in a *mansion*.
TINK!

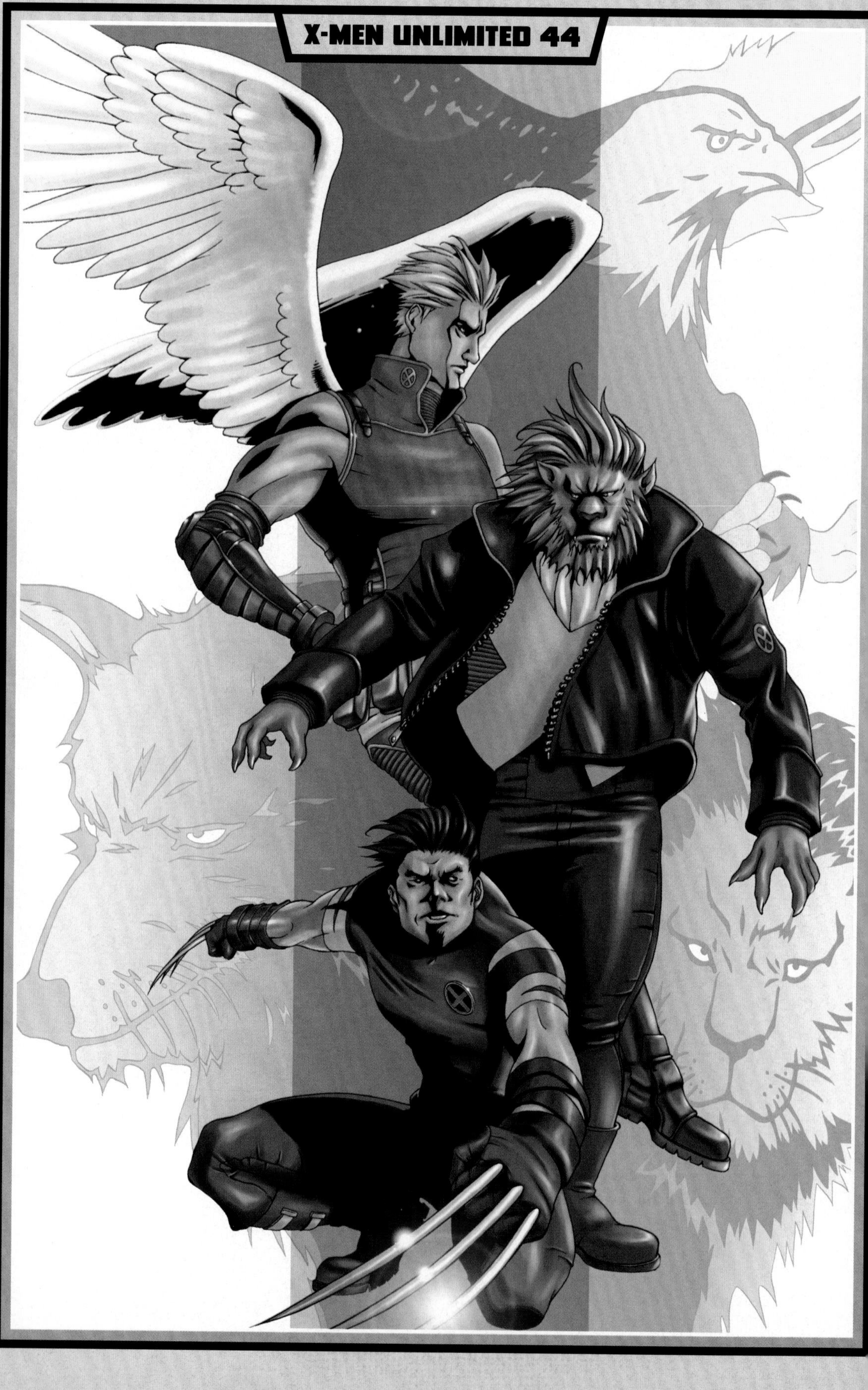
X-MEN UNLIMITED 44

"The day may come when the rest of animal creation may acquire those rights which never could have been witholden from them but by the hand of tyranny.

"The French have already discovered that the blackness of the skin is no reason why a human being should be abandoned without redress to the caprice of a tormentor. It may one day come to be recognized that the number of the legs, the villosity of the skin, or the termination of the os sacrum, are reasons equally insufficient for abandoning a sensitive being to the same fate.

"What else is it that should trace the insuperable line? Is it the faculty of reason, or perhaps the faculty of discourse?

"But a full-grown horse or dog is beyond comparison a more rational, as well as more conversable animal, than an infant of a day, or even, a month old. But suppose they were otherwise, what would it avail? "The question is not, 'Can they reason?' Nor 'Can they talk?'

"But, 'Can they suffer?'"

- Jeremy Bentham

Can They Suffer?

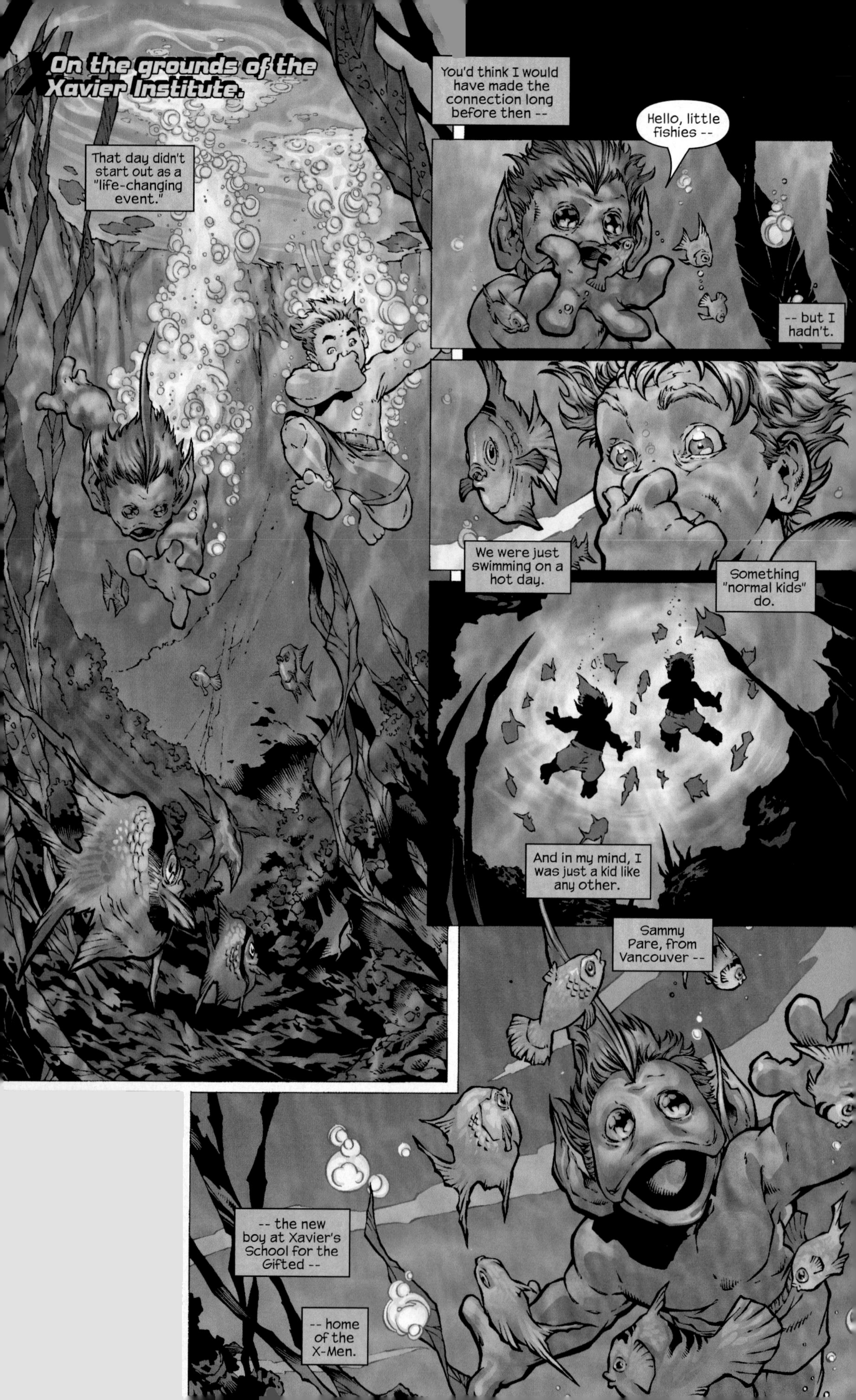
On the grounds of the Xavier Institute.
That day didn't start out as a "life-changing event."
You'd think I would have made the connection long before then --
Hello, little fishies --
-- but I hadn't.
We were just swimming on a hot day.
Something "normal kids" do.
And in my mind, I was just a kid like any other.
Sammy Pare, from Vancouver --
-- the new boy at Xavier's School for the Gifted --
-- home of the X-Men.

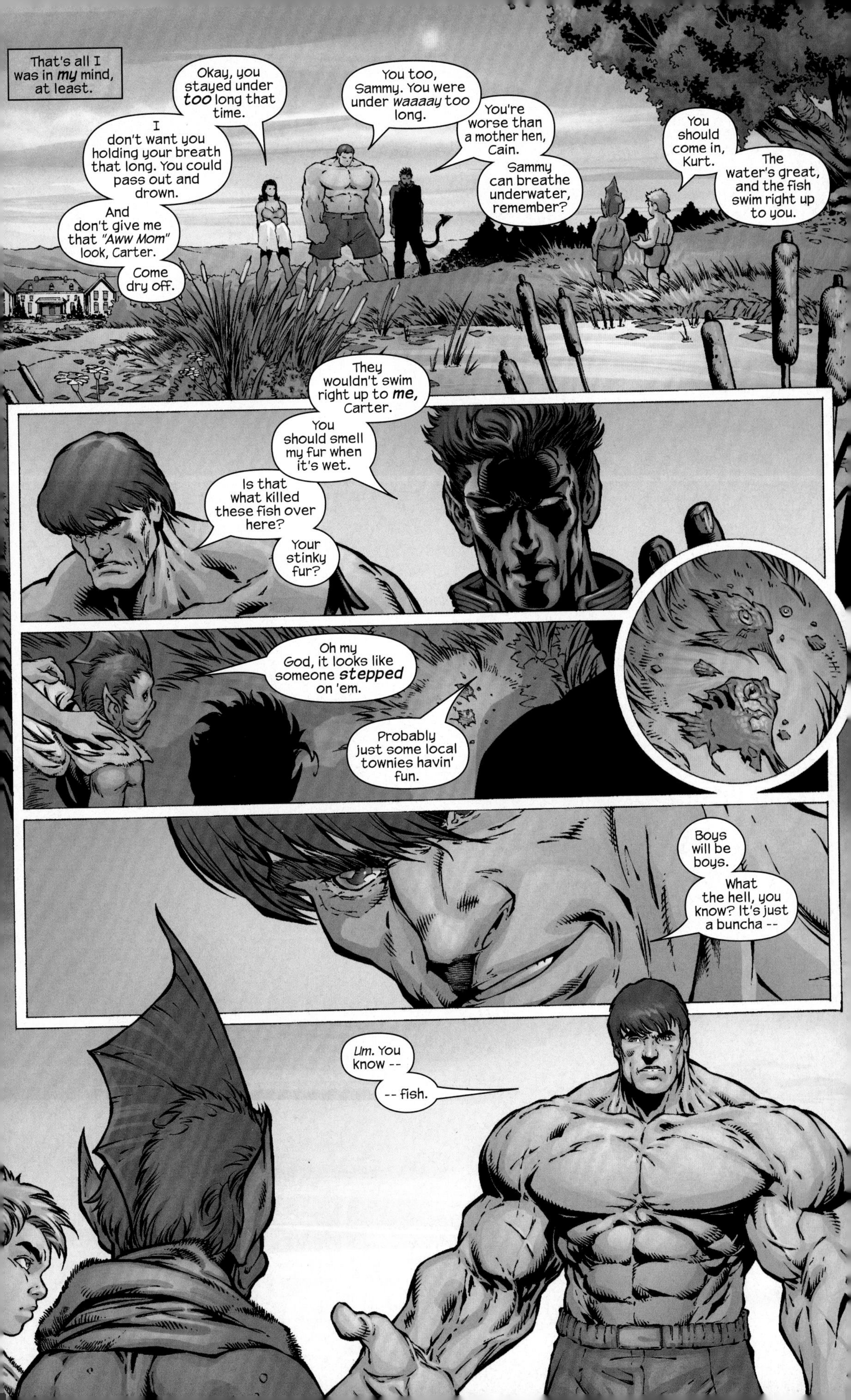

That's all I was in *my* mind, at least.
Okay, you stayed under *too* long that time.
I don't want you holding your breath that long. You could pass out and drown.
And don't give me that "Aww Mom" look, Carter.
Come dry off.
You too, Sammy. You were under waaaay too long.
You're worse than a mother hen, Cain.
Sammy can breathe underwater, remember?
You should come in, Kurt.
The water's great, and the fish swim right up to you.
They wouldn't swim right up to *me*, Carter.
You should smell my fur when it's wet.
Is that what killed these fish over here?
Your stinky fur?
Oh my God, it looks like someone *stepped* on 'em.
Probably just some local townies havin' fun.
Boys will be boys.
What the hell, you know? It's just a buncha --
Um. You know --
-- fish.

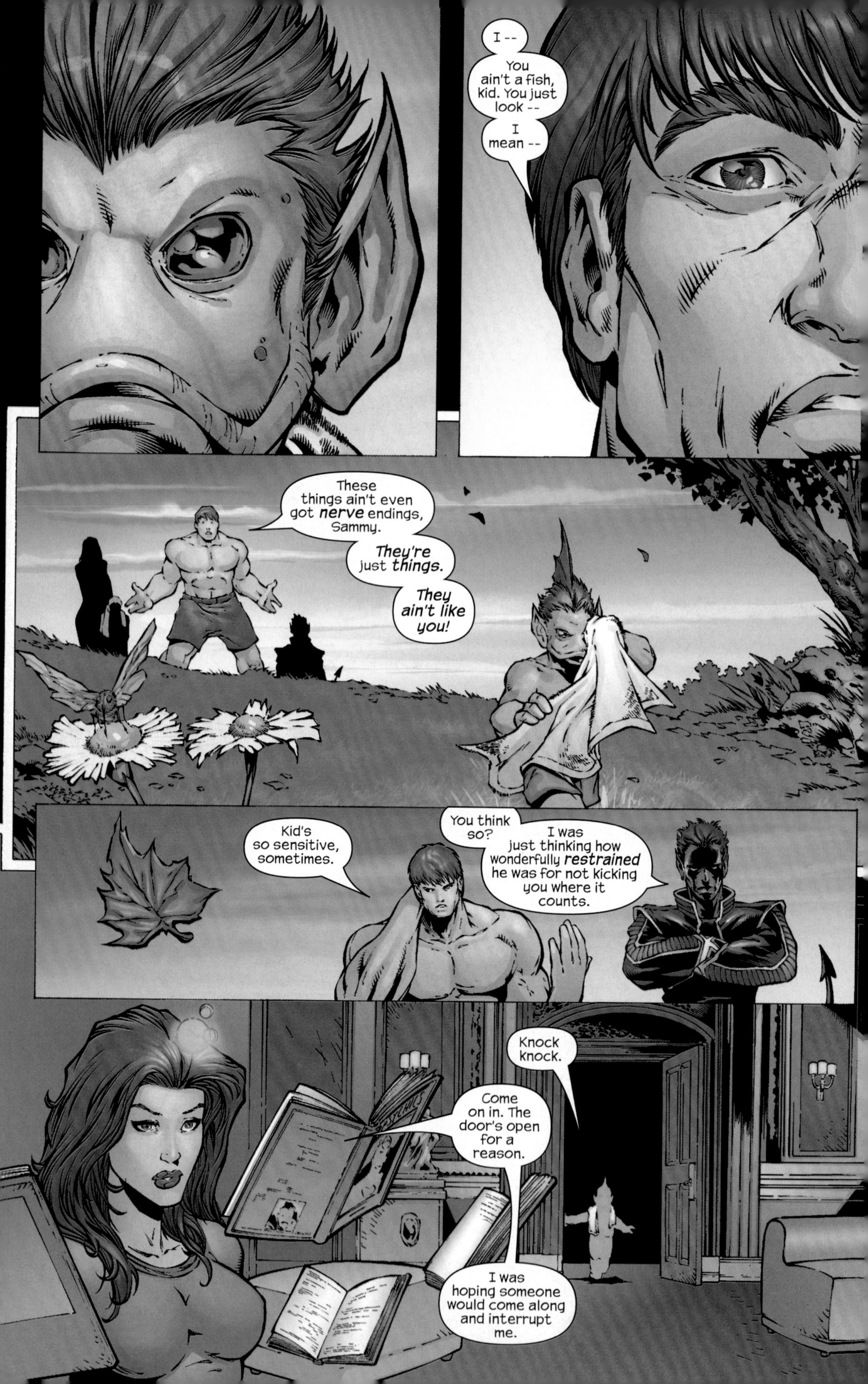
I --
You ain't a fish, kid. You just look --
I mean --
These things ain't even got nerve endings, Sammy.
They're just things.
They ain't like you!
Kid's so sensitive, sometimes.
You think so?
I was just thinking how wonderfully restrained he was for not kicking you where it counts.
Knock knock.
Come on in. The door's open for a reason.
I was hoping someone would come along and interrupt me.

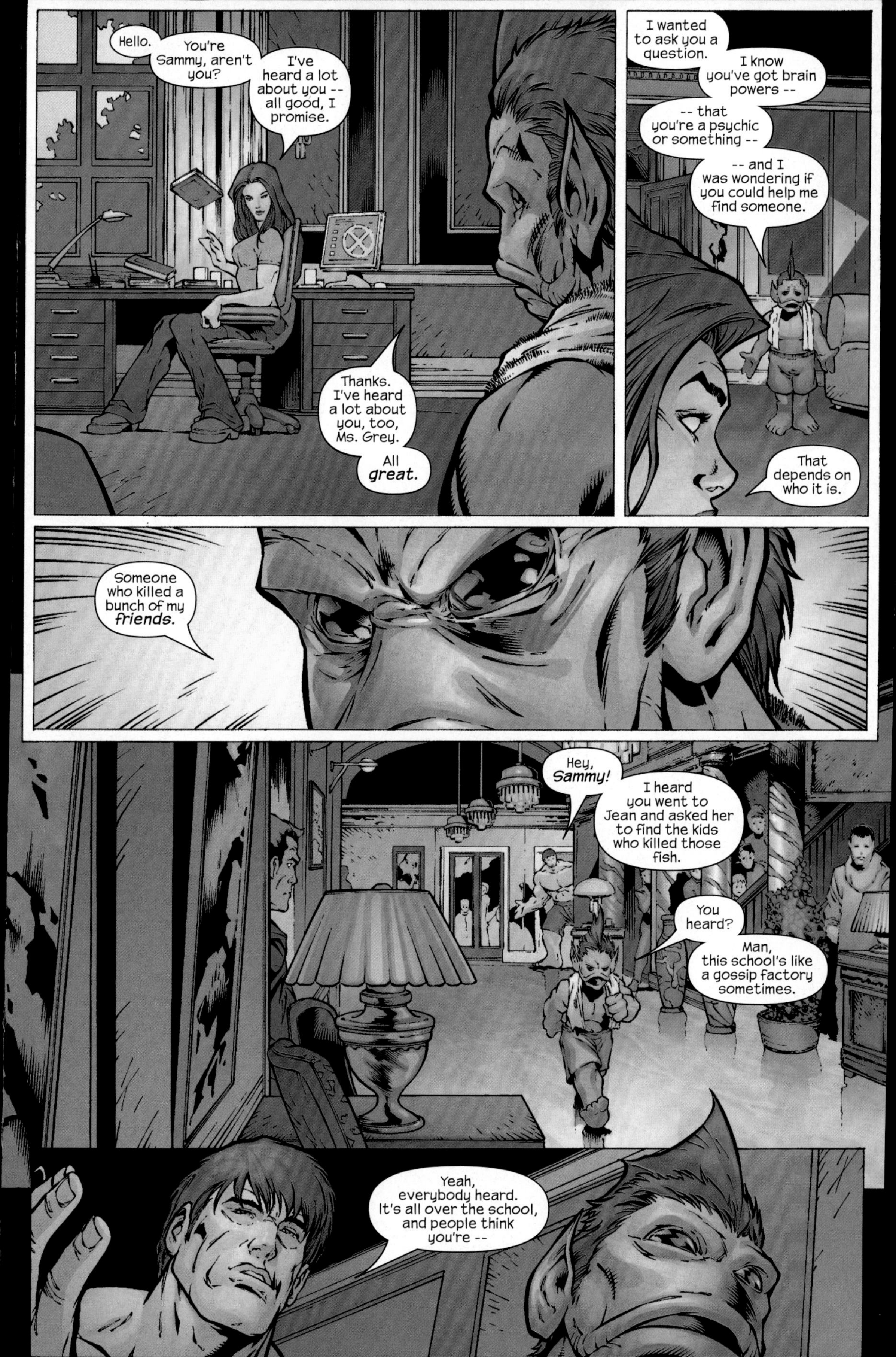

Hello.
You're Sammy, aren't you?
I've heard a lot about you -- all good, I promise.
Thanks. I've heard a lot about you, too, Ms. Grey.
All *great.*
I wanted to ask you a question.
I know you've got brain powers --
-- that you're a psychic or something --
-- and I was wondering if you could help me find someone.
That depends on who it is.
Someone who killed a bunch of my *friends.*
Hey, *Sammy!*
I heard you went to Jean and asked her to find the kids who killed those fish.
You heard?
Man, this school's like a gossip factory sometimes.
Yeah, everybody heard. It's all over the school, and people think you're --

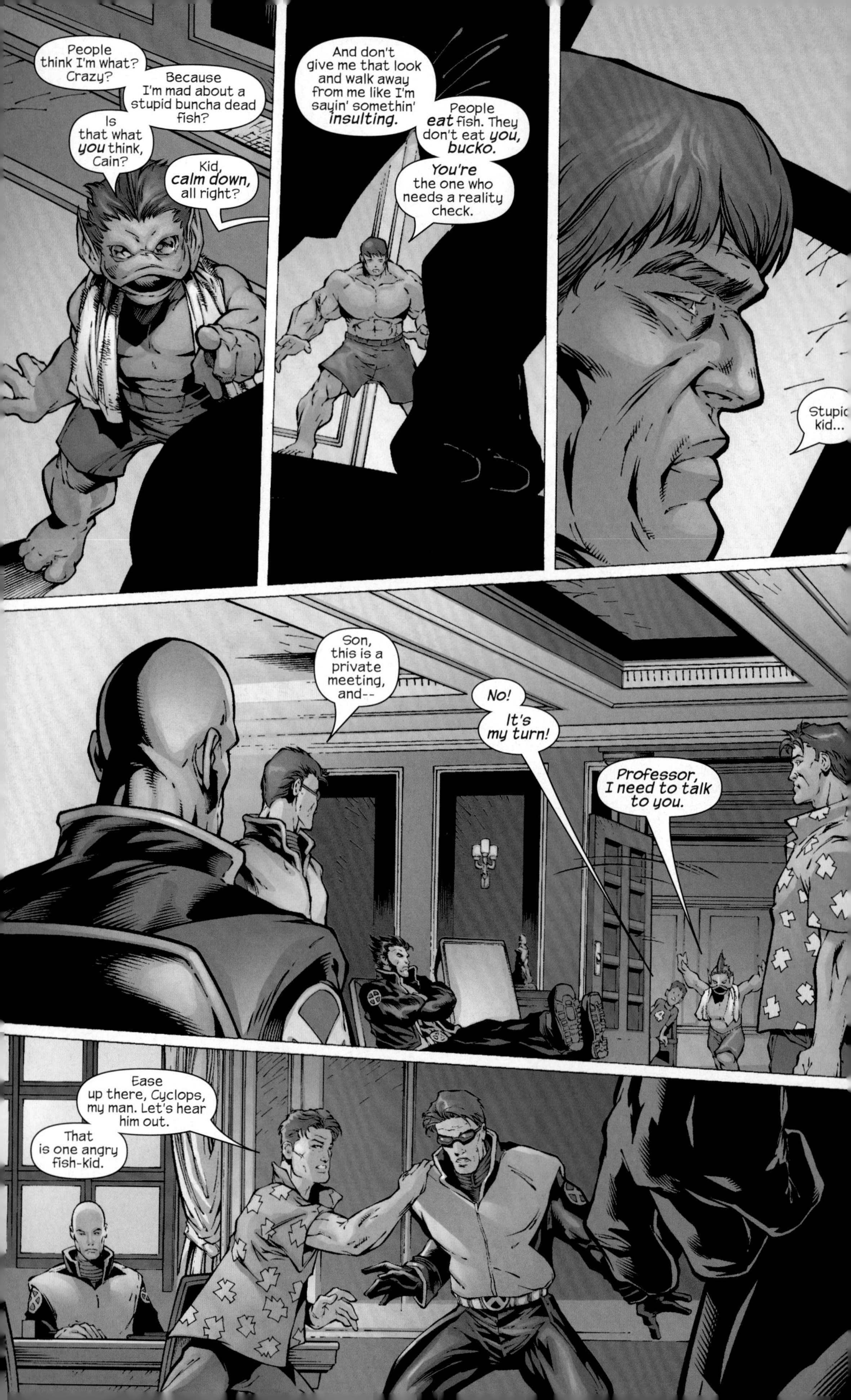
People think I'm what? Crazy?
Because I'm mad about a stupid buncha dead fish?
Is that what *you* think, Cain?
Kid, **calm down,** all right?
And don't give me that look and walk away from me like I'm sayin' somethin' *insulting.*
People *eat* fish. They don't eat *you, bucko.*
You're the one who needs a reality check.
Stupid kid...
Son, this is a private meeting, and--
No!
It's my turn!
Professor, I need to talk to you.
Ease up there, Cyclops, my man. Let's hear him out.
That is one angry fish-kid.

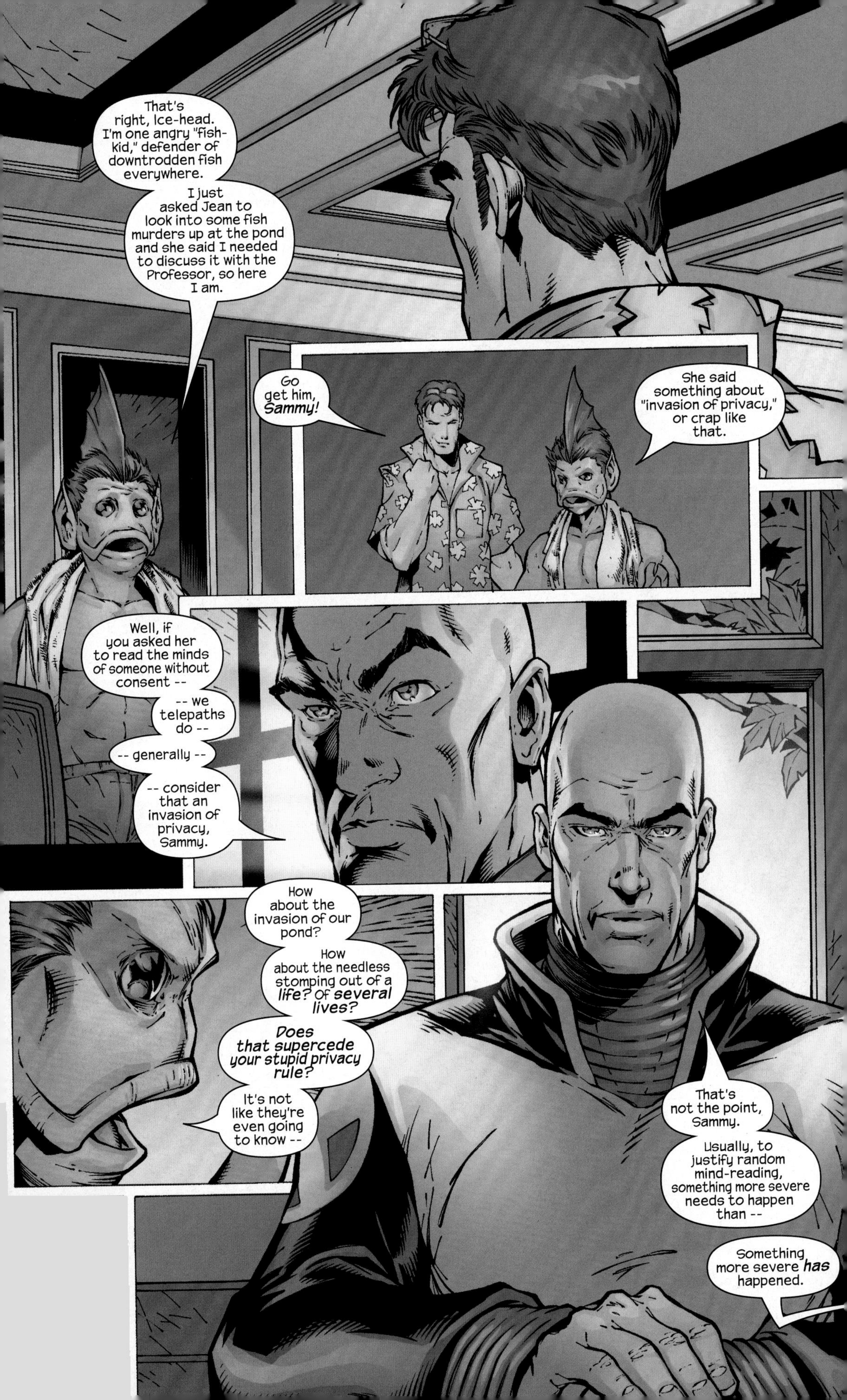
That's right, Ice-head. I'm one angry "fish-kid," defender of downtrodden fish everywhere.
I just asked Jean to look into some fish murders up at the pond and she said I needed to discuss it with the Professor, so here I am.
Go get him, Sammy!
She said something about "invasion of privacy," or crap like that.
Well, if you asked her to read the minds of someone without consent --
-- we telepaths do --
-- generally --
-- consider that an invasion of privacy, Sammy.
How about the invasion of our pond?
How about the needless stomping out of a *life?* Of *several lives?*
Does that supercede your stupid privacy rule?
It's not like they're even going to know --
That's not the point, Sammy.
Usually, to justify random mind-reading, something more severe needs to happen than --
Something more severe *has* happened.

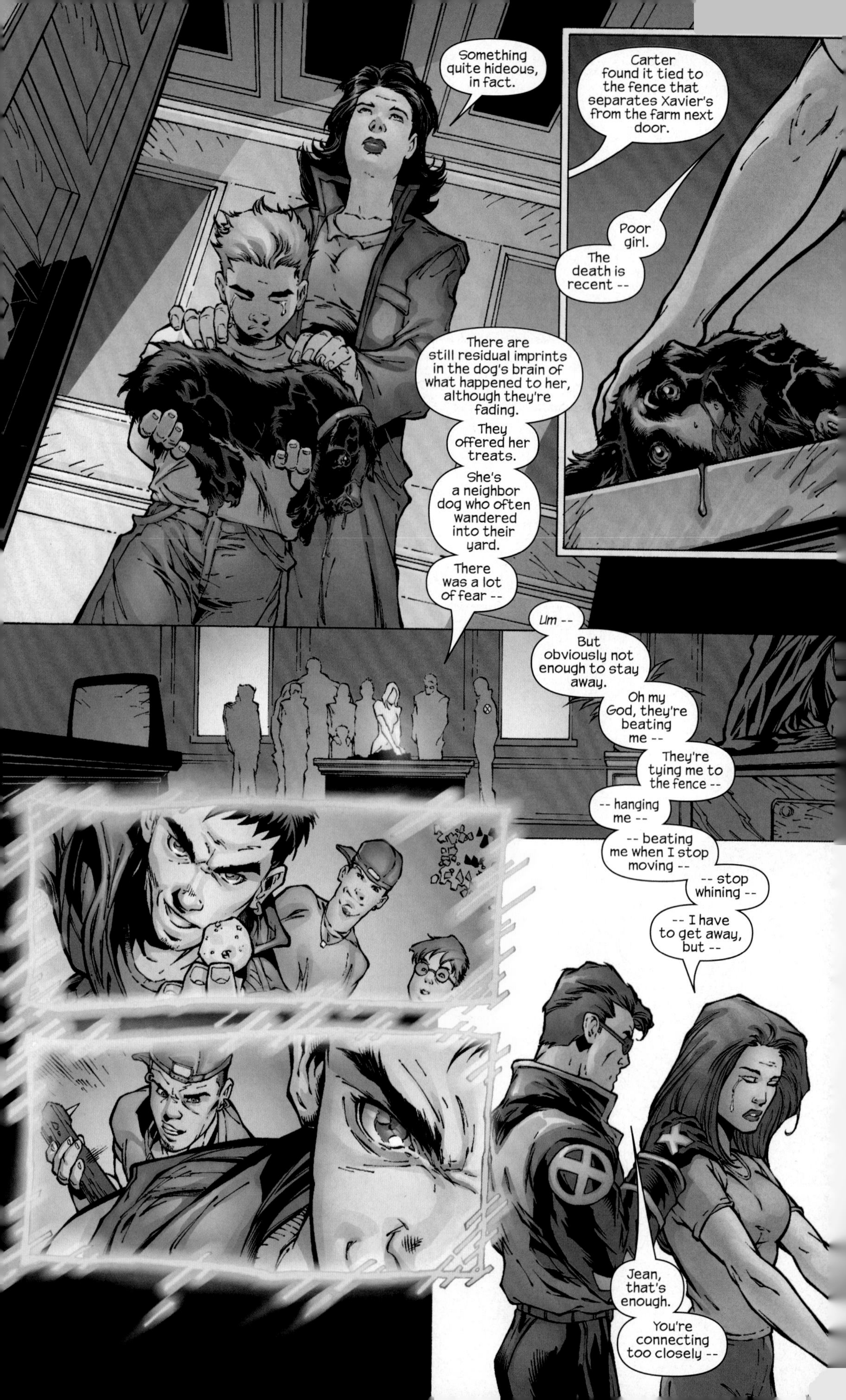
Something quite hideous, in fact.
Carter found it tied to the fence that separates Xavier's from the farm next door.
Poor girl.
The death is recent --
There are still residual imprints in the dog's brain of what happened to her, although they're fading.
They offered her treats.
She's a neighbor dog who often wandered into their yard.
There was a lot of fear --
Um --
But obviously not enough to stay away.
Oh my God, they're beating me --
They're tying me to the fence --
-- hanging me --
-- beating me when I stop moving --
-- stop whining --
-- I have to get away, but --
Jean, that's enough.
You're connecting too closely --

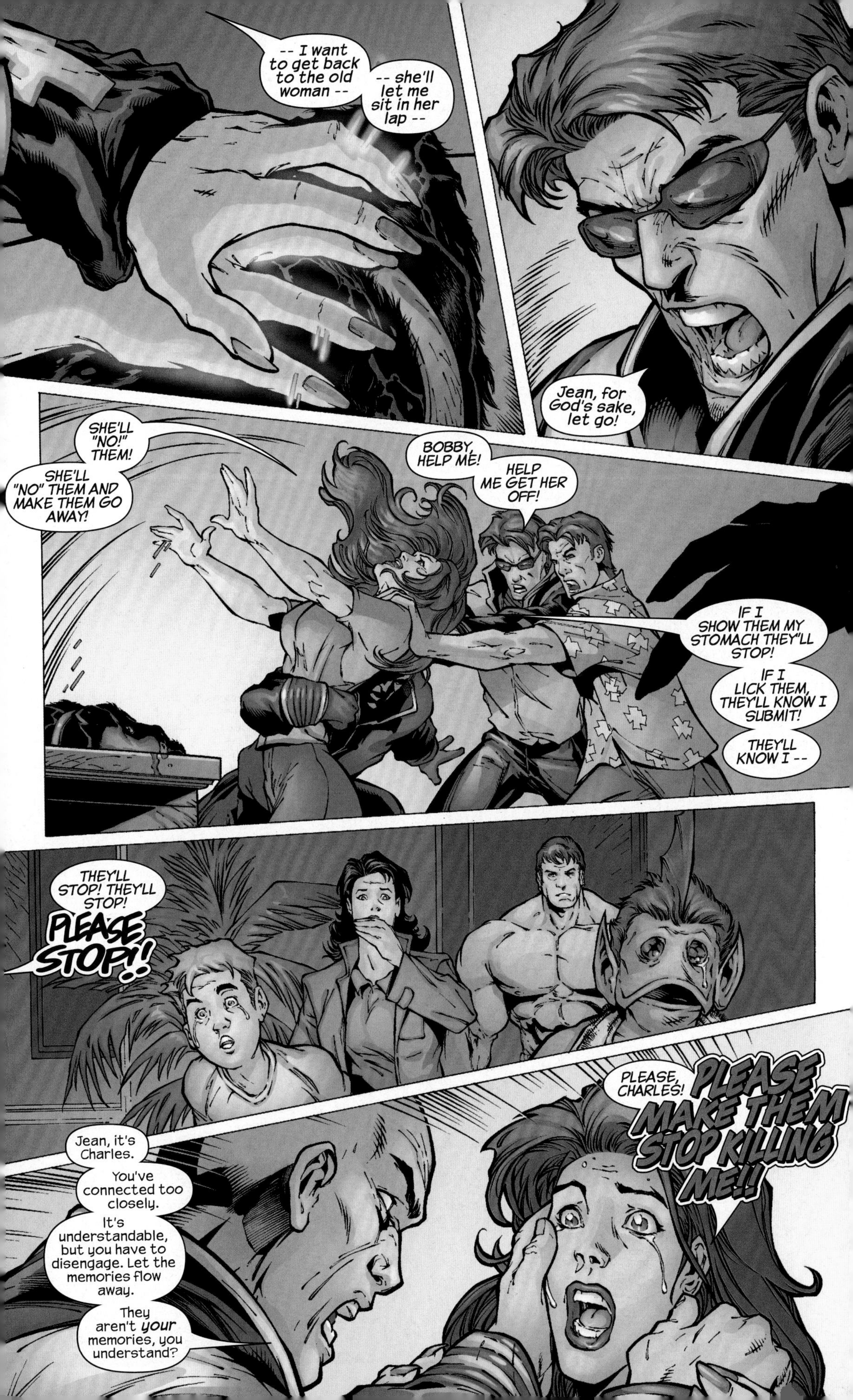

-- I want to get back to the old woman --
-- she'll let me sit in her lap --
Jean, for God's sake, let go!
SHE'LL "NO!" THEM!
SHE'LL "NO" THEM AND MAKE THEM GO AWAY!
BOBBY, HELP ME!
HELP ME GET HER OFF!
IF I SHOW THEM MY STOMACH THEY'LL STOP!
IF I LICK THEM, THEY'LL KNOW I SUBMIT!
THEY'LL KNOW I --
THEY'LL STOP! THEY'LL STOP!
PLEASE STOP!!
PLEASE, CHARLES!
PLEASE MAKE THEM STOP KILLING ME!!
Jean, it's Charles.
You've connected too closely.
It's understandable, but you have to disengage. Let the memories flow away.
They aren't *your* memories, you understand?

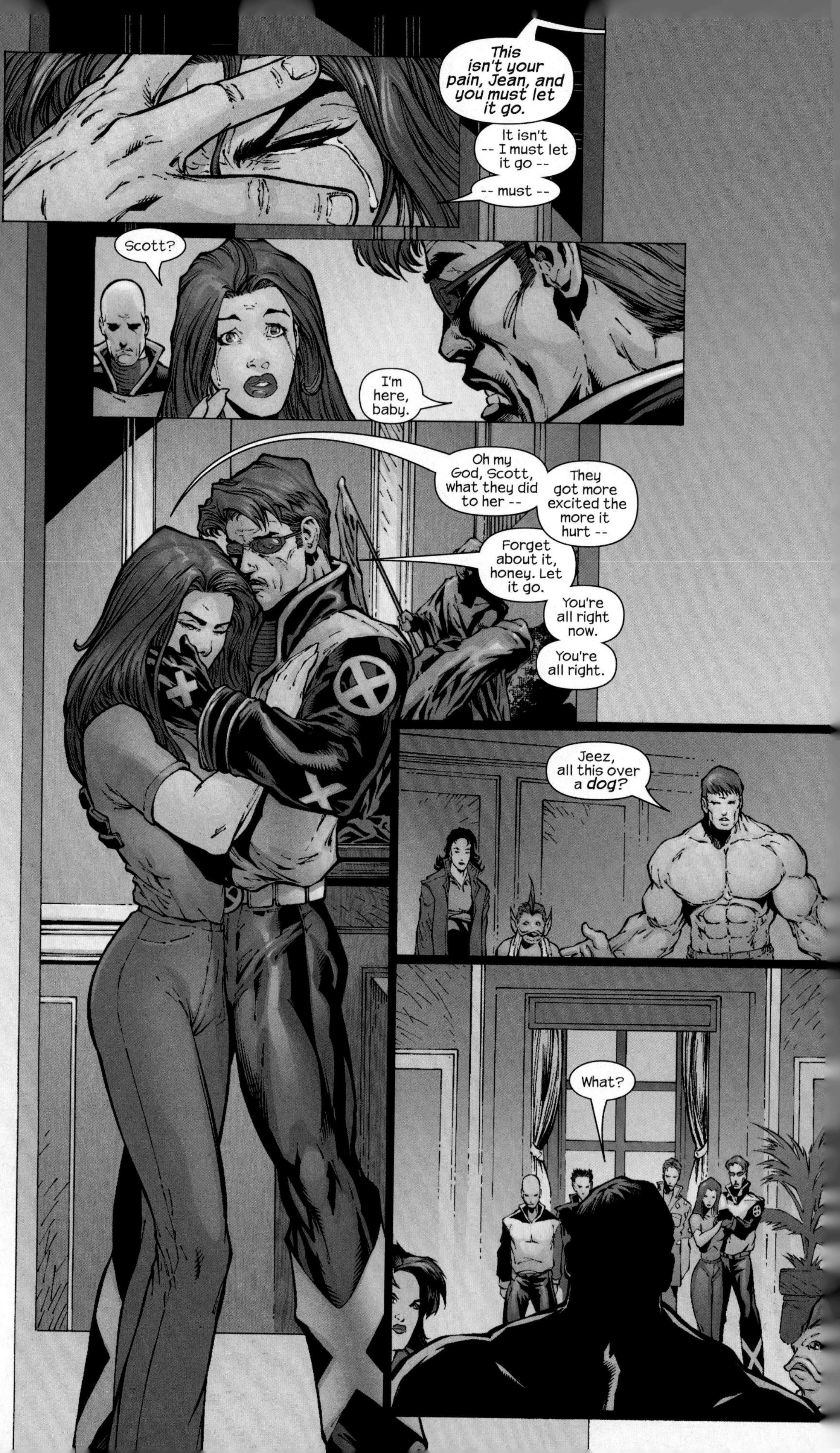
This isn't your pain, Jean, and you must let it go.
It isn't -- I must let it go --
-- must --
Scott?
I'm here, baby.
Oh my God, Scott, what they did to her --
They got more excited the more it hurt --
Forget about it, honey. Let it go.
You're all right now.
You're all right.
Jeez, all this over a *dog?*
What?

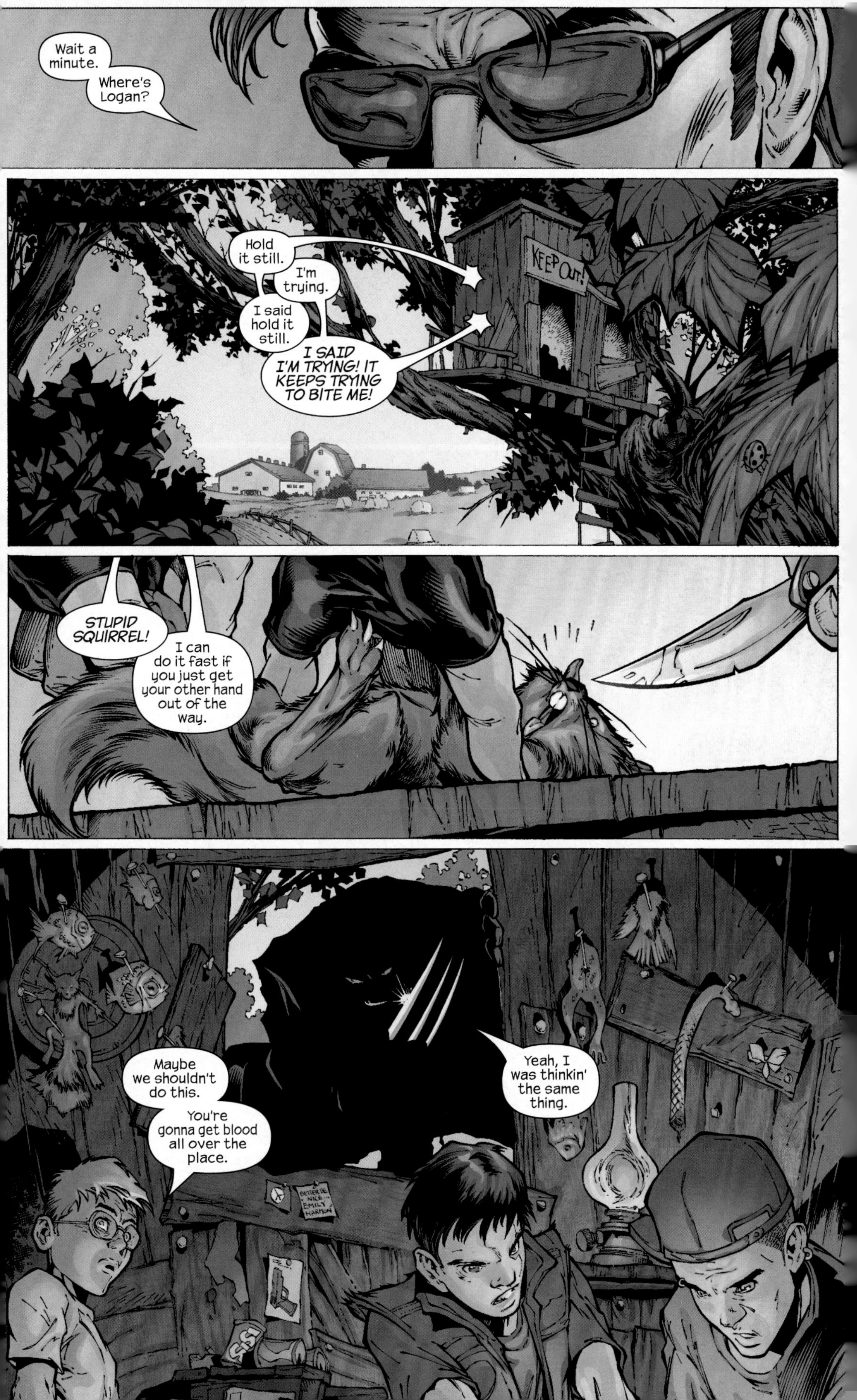
Wait a minute.
Where's Logan?
KEEP OUT!
Hold it still.
I'm trying.
I said hold it still.
I SAID I'M TRYING! IT KEEPS TRYING TO BITE ME!
STUPID SQUIRREL!
I can do it fast if you just get your other hand out of the way.
Maybe we shouldn't do this.
You're gonna get blood all over the place.
Yeah, I was thinkin' the same thing.
BETTER BE NICE EMILY HARMON

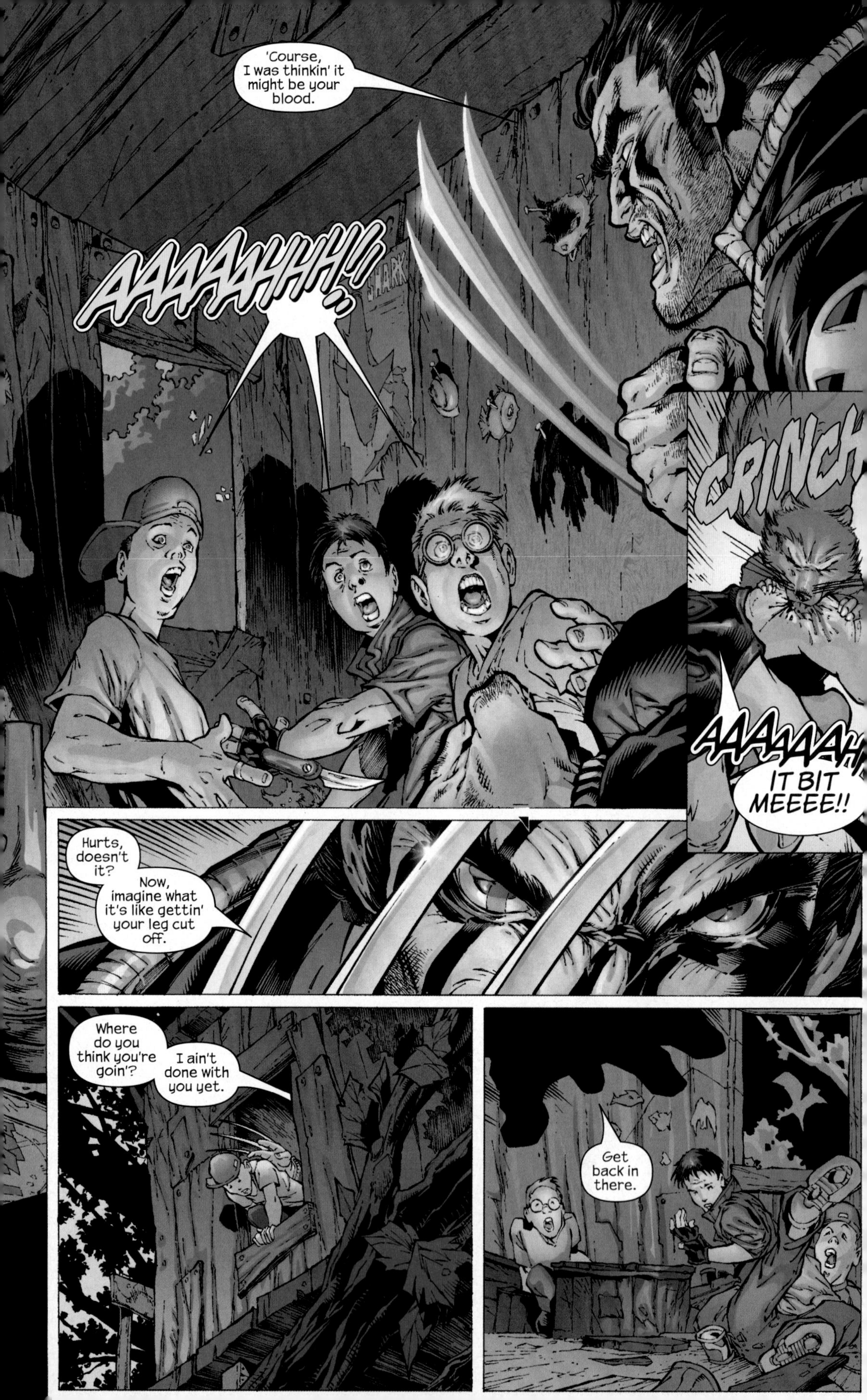

'Course, I was thinkin' it might be your blood.
AAAAAHHH!!
CRINCH
AAAAAAH, IT BIT MEEEE!!
Hurts, doesn't it?
Now, imagine what it's like gettin' your leg cut off.
Where do you think you're goin'?
I ain't done with you yet.
Get back in there.

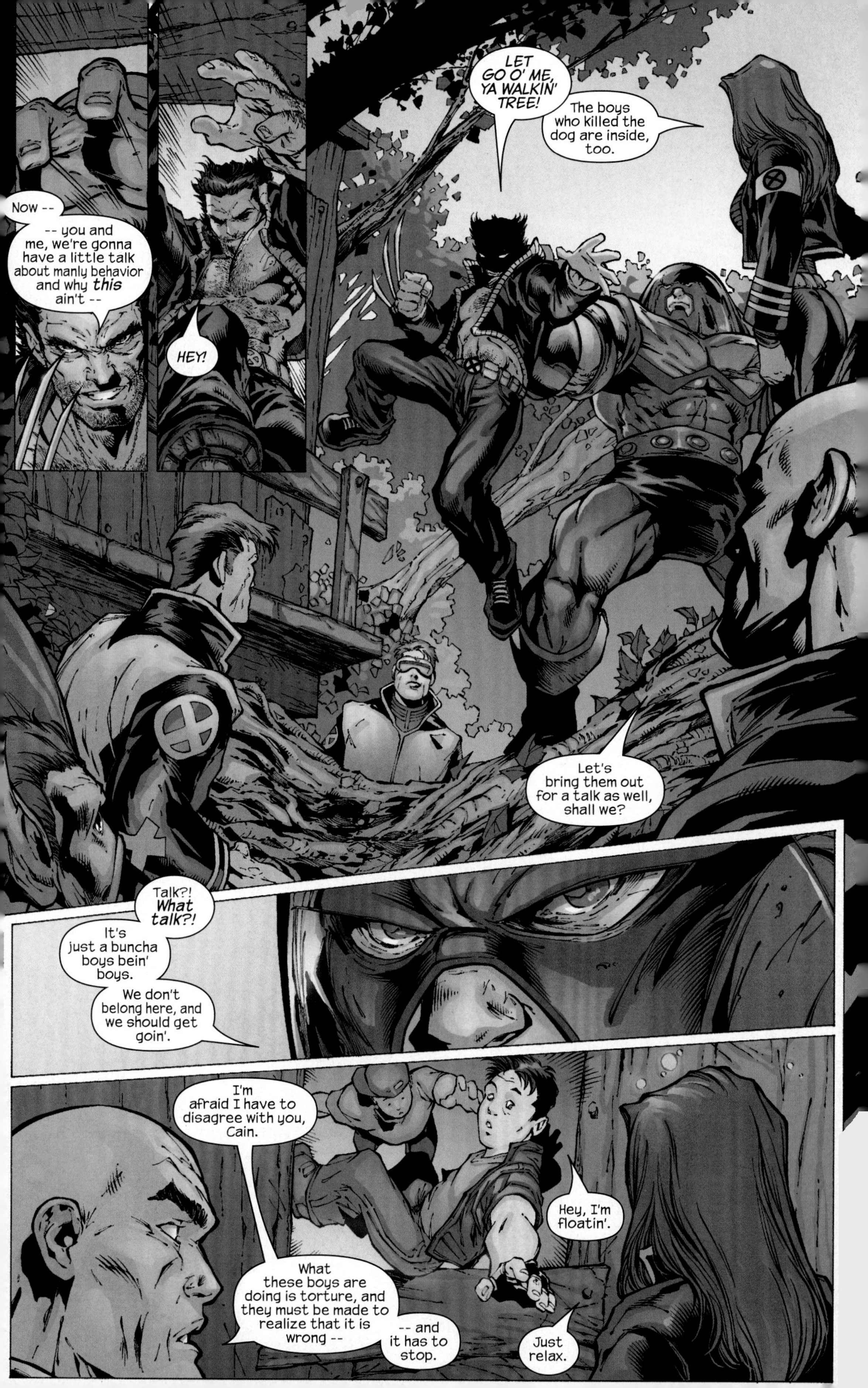
Now --
-- you and me, we're gonna have a little talk about manly behavior and why *this* ain't --
HEY!
LET GO O' ME, YA WALKIN' TREE!
The boys who killed the dog are inside, too.
Let's bring them out for a talk as well, shall we?
Talk?! *What talk?!*
It's just a buncha boys bein' boys.
We don't belong here, and we should get goin'.
I'm afraid I have to disagree with you, Cain.
Hey, I'm floatin'.
What these boys are doing is torture, and they must be made to realize that it is wrong --
-- and it has to stop.
Just relax.

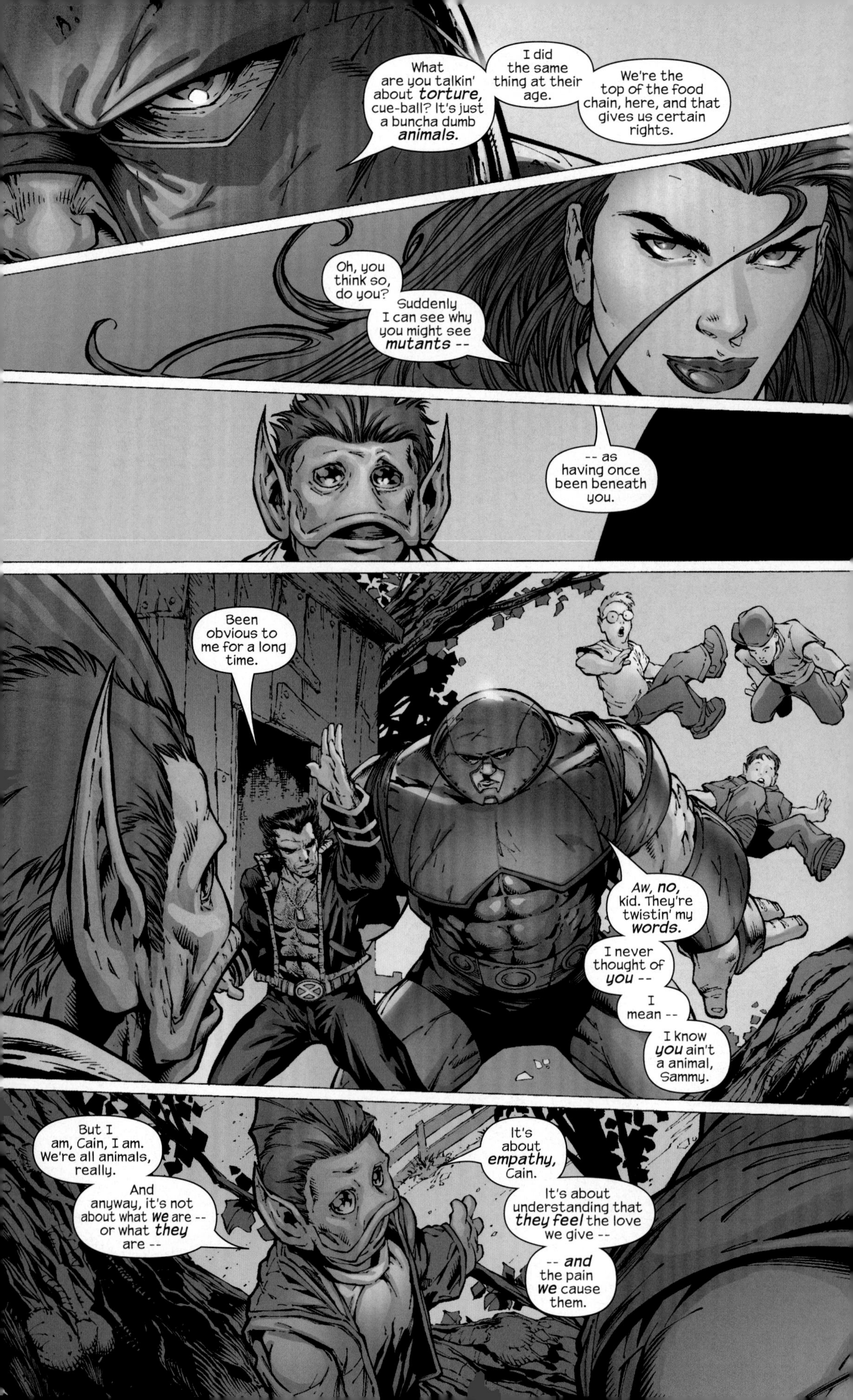
What are you talkin' about torture, cue-ball? It's just a buncha dumb animals.
I did the same thing at their age.
We're the top of the food chain, here, and that gives us certain rights.
Oh, you think so, do you?
Suddenly I can see why you might see mutants --
-- as having once been beneath you.
Been obvious to me for a long time.
Aw, no, kid. They're twistin' my words.
I never thought of you --
I mean --
I know you ain't a animal, Sammy.
But I am, Cain, I am. We're all animals, really.
And anyway, it's not about what we are -- or what they are --
It's about empathy, Cain.
It's about understanding that they feel the love we give --
-- and the pain we cause them.

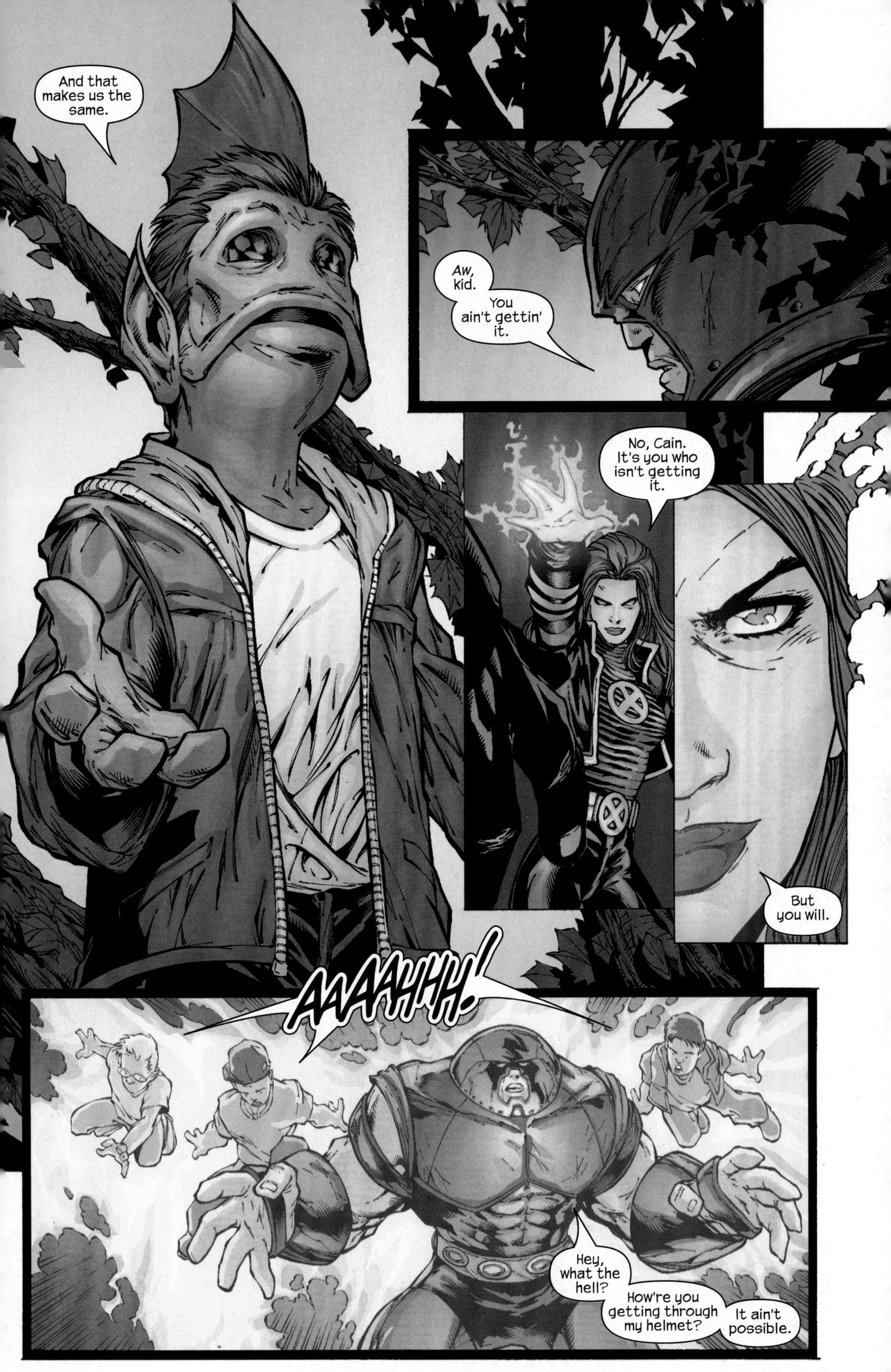
And that makes us the same.
Aw, kid.
You ain't gettin' it.
No, Cain. It's you who isn't getting it.
But you will.
AAAAHHH!
Hey, what the hell?
How're you getting through my helmet?
It ain't possible.

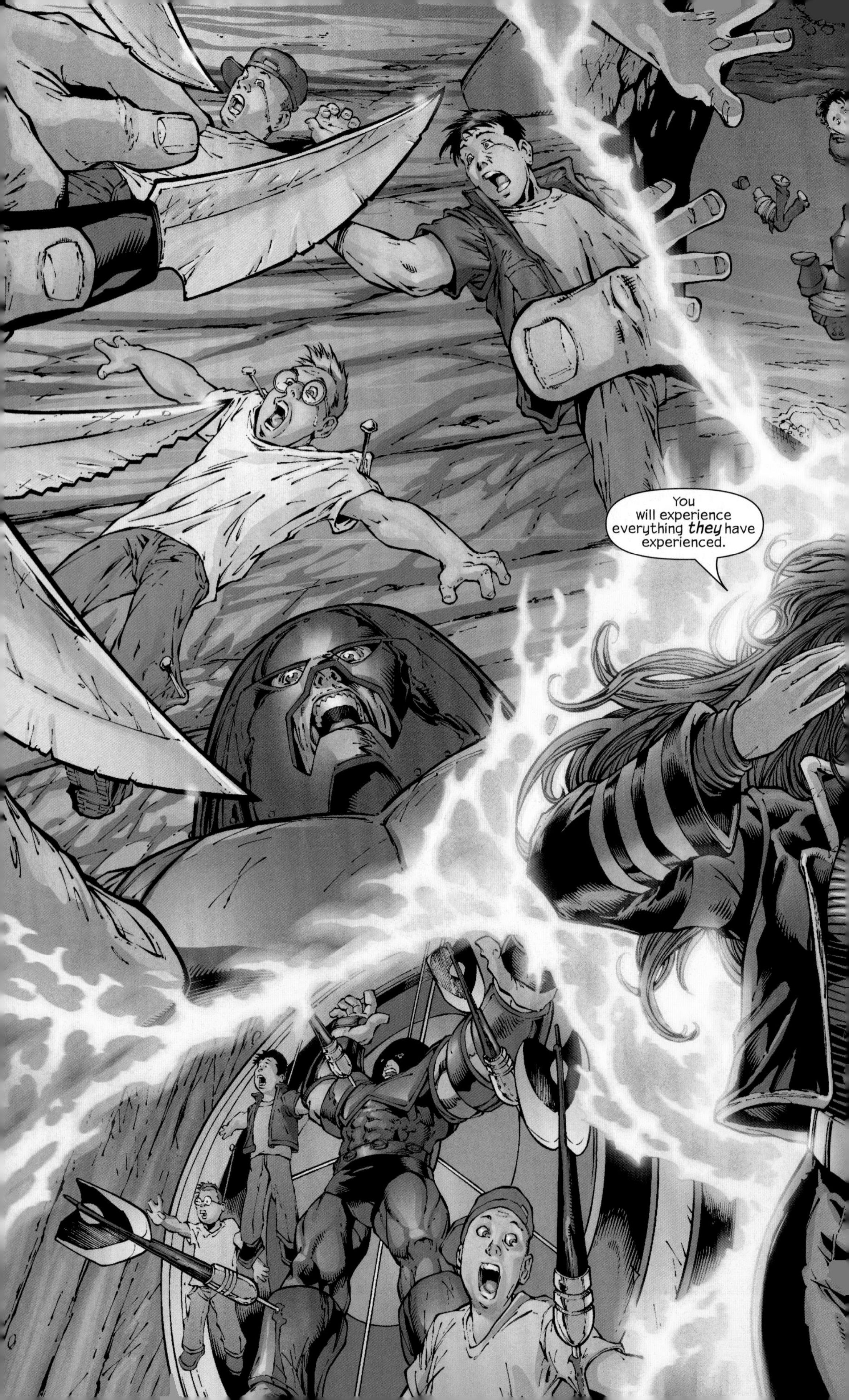
You will experience everything *they* have experienced.

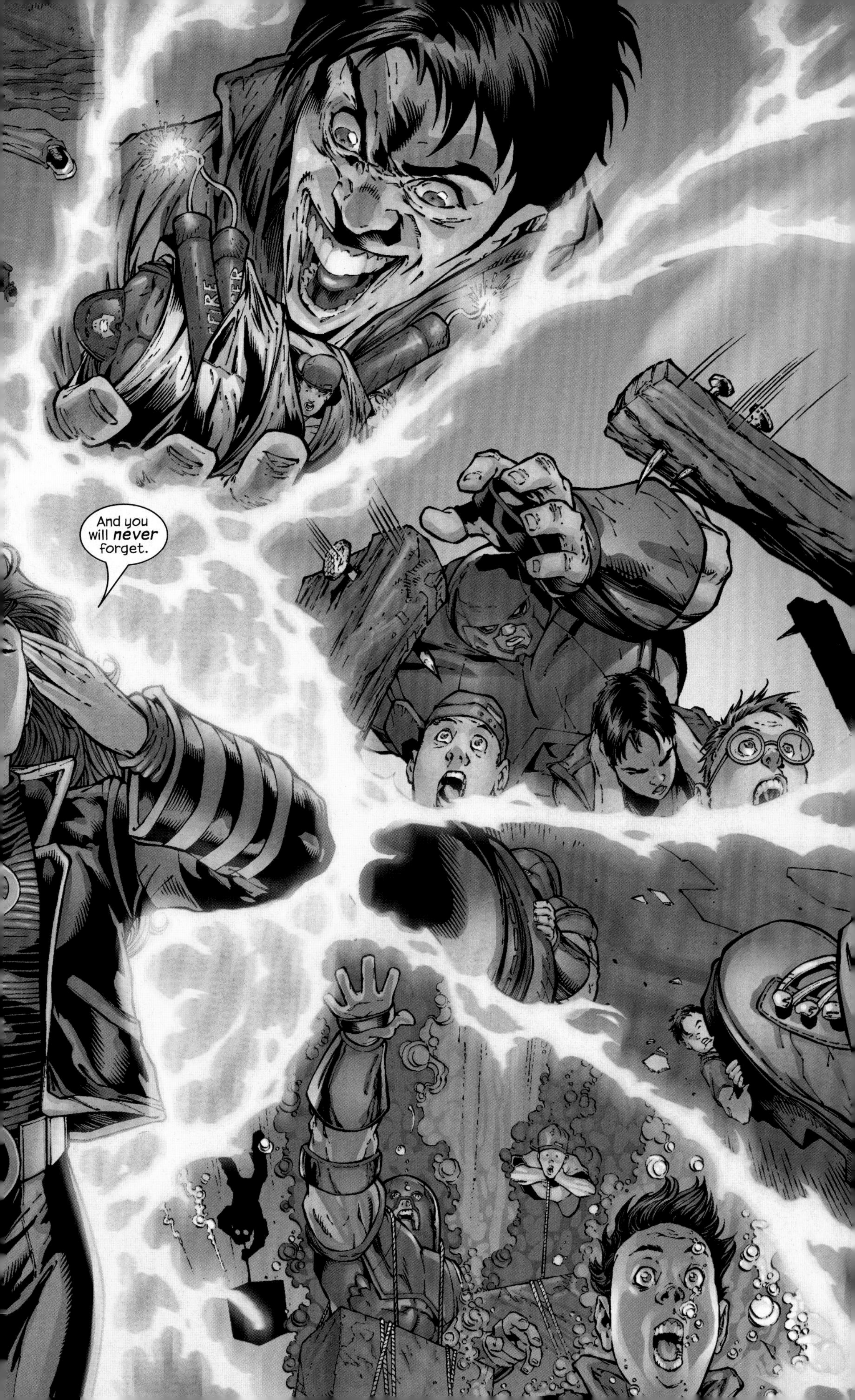
And you will never forget.

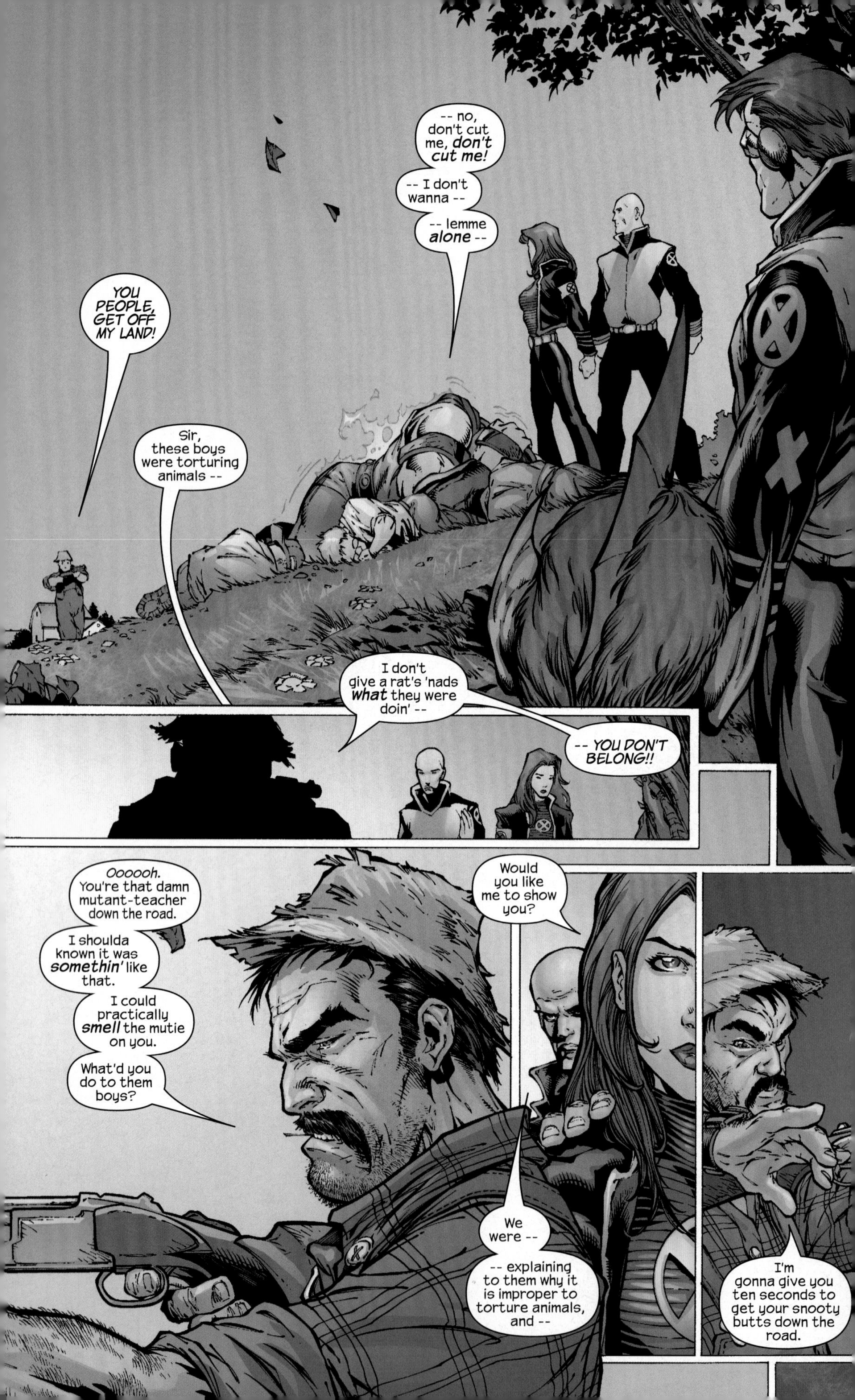
-- no, don't cut me, don't cut me!
-- I don't wanna --
-- lemme alone --
YOU PEOPLE, GET OFF MY LAND!
Sir, these boys were torturing animals --
I don't give a rat's 'nads what they were doin' --
-- YOU DON'T BELONG!!
Oooooh. You're that damn mutant-teacher down the road.
I shoulda known it was somethin' like that.
I could practically smell the mutie on you.
What'd you do to them boys?
Would you like me to show you?
We were --
-- explaining to them why it is improper to torture animals, and --
I'm gonna give you ten seconds to get your snooty butts down the road.

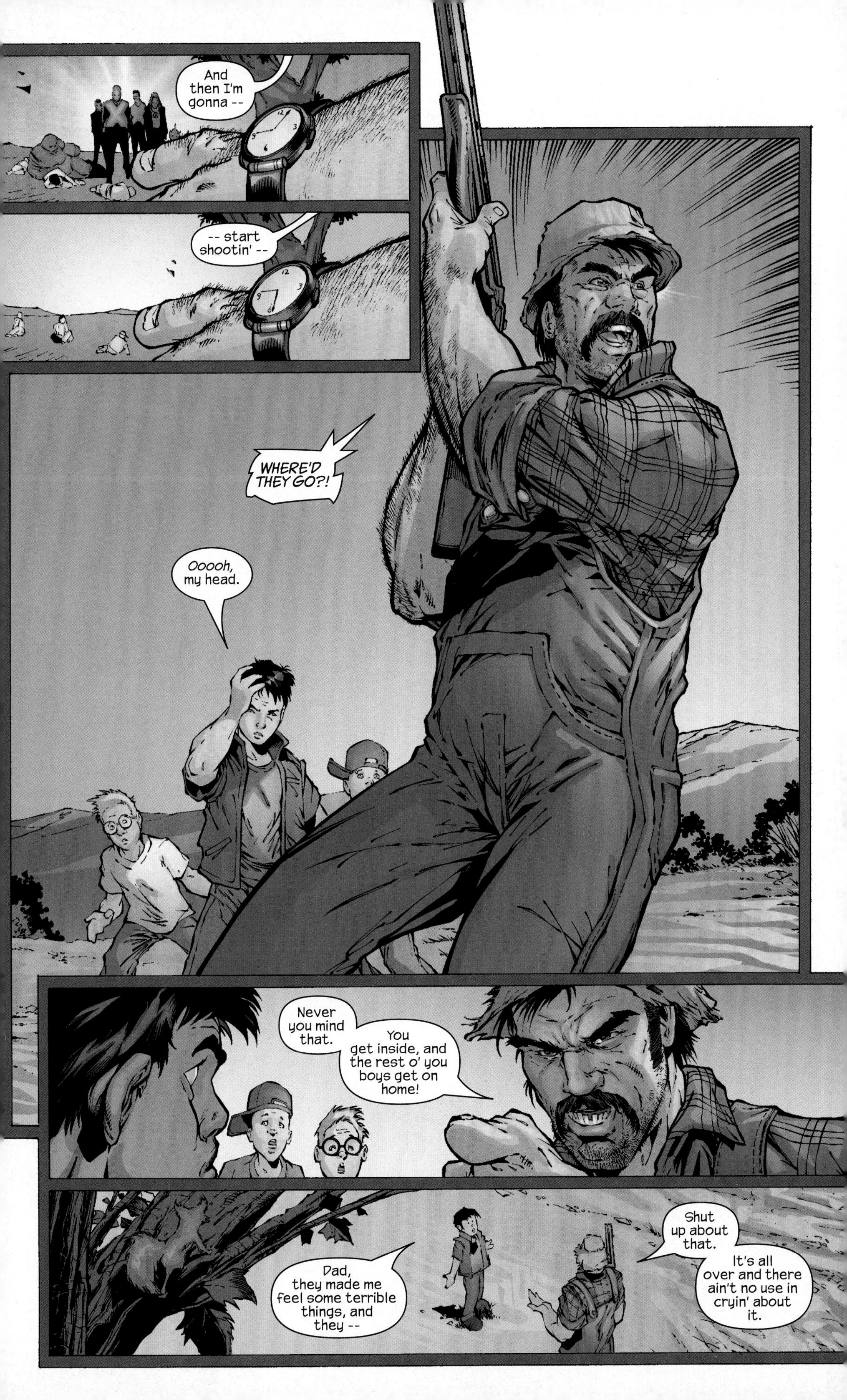

And then I'm gonna --
-- start shootin' --
WHERE'D THEY GO?!
Ooooh, my head.
Never you mind that.
You get inside, and the rest o' you boys get on home!
Dad, they made me feel some terrible things, and they --
Shut up about that.
It's all over and there ain't no use in cryin' about it.

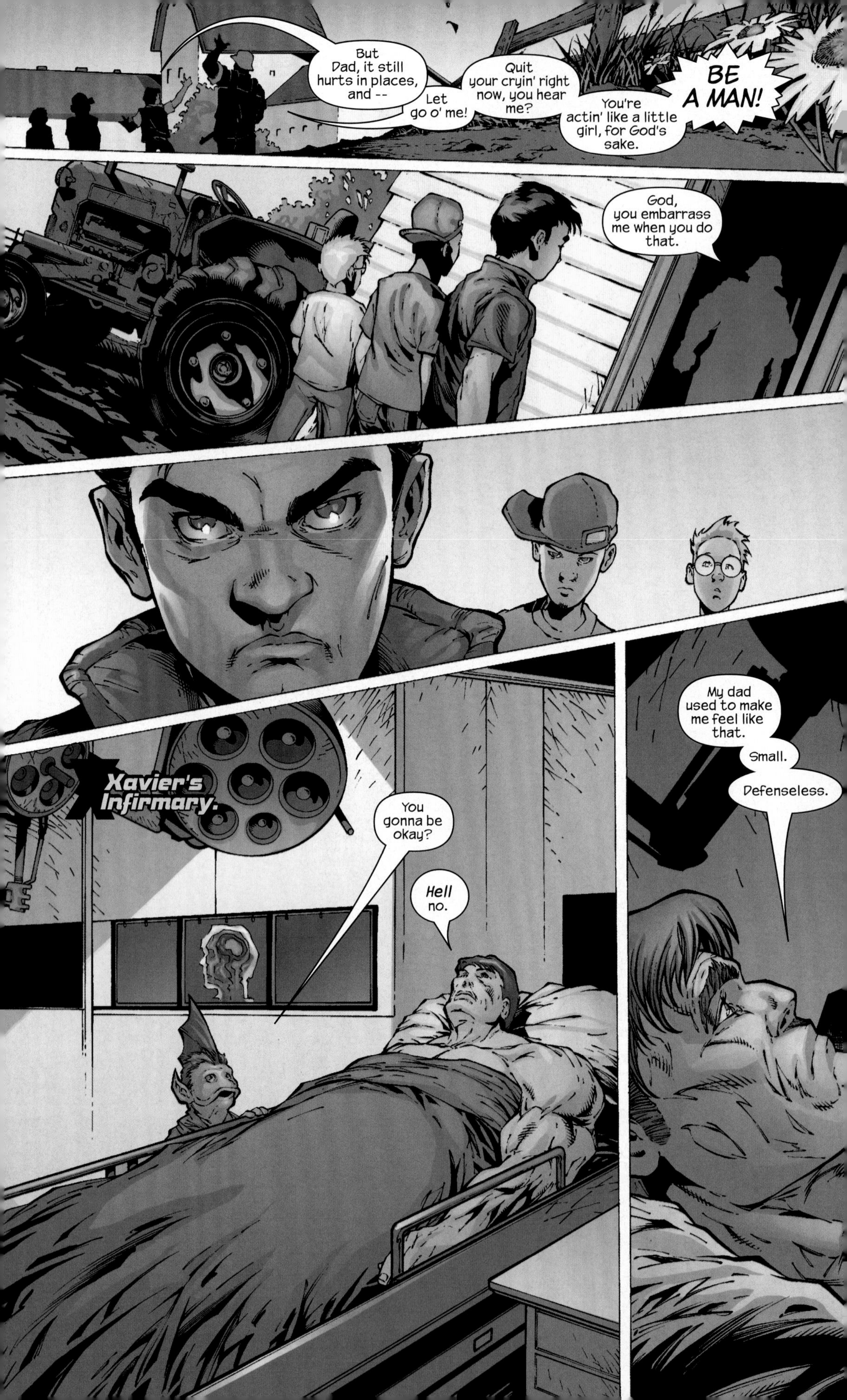
But Dad, it still hurts in places, and --
Let go o' me!
Quit your cryin' right now, you hear me?
You're actin' like a little girl, for God's sake.
BE A MAN!
God, you embarrass me when you do that.
Xavier's Infirmary.
You gonna be okay?
Hell no.
My dad used to make me feel like that.
Small.
Defenseless.

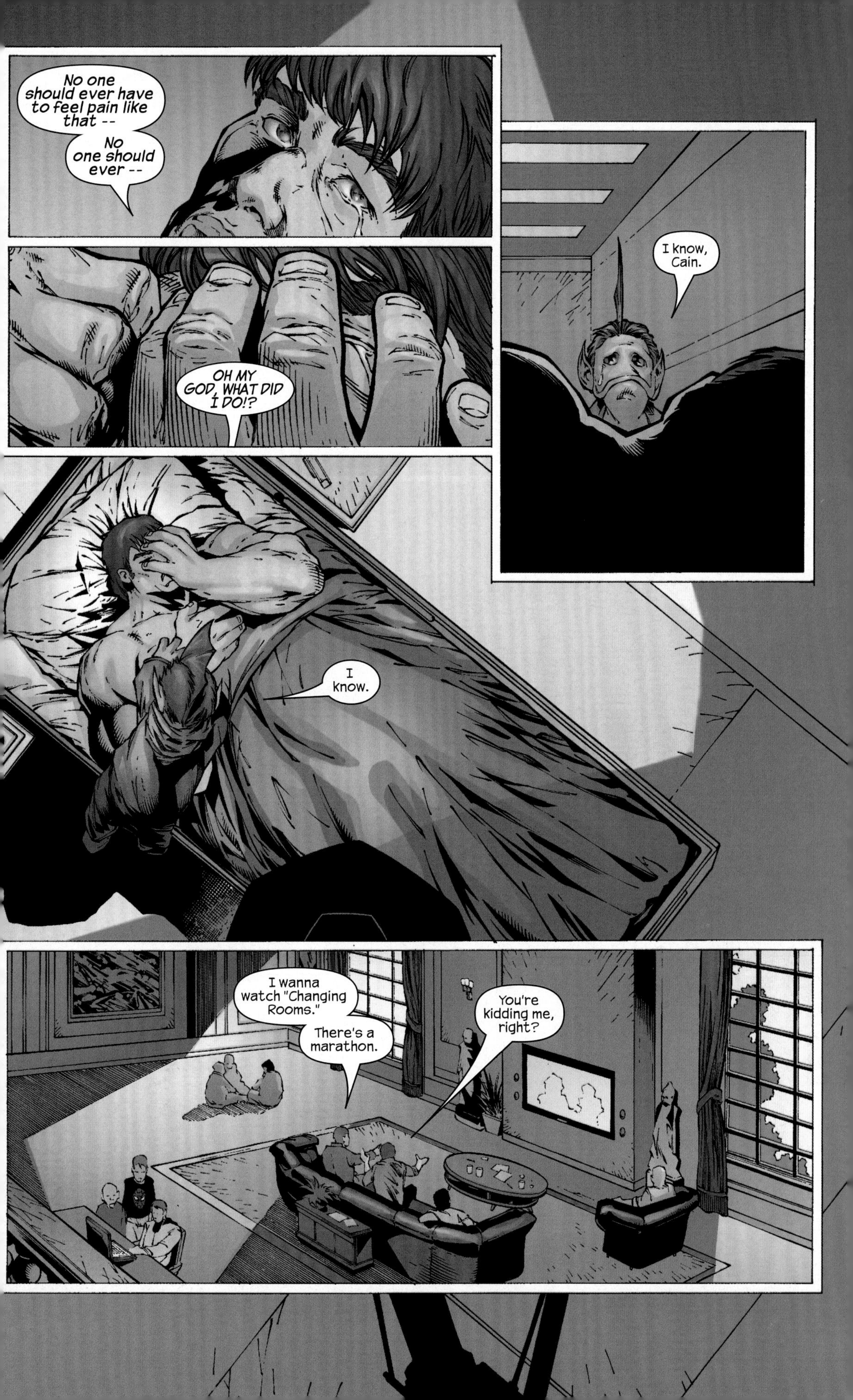
No one should ever have to feel pain like that --
No one should ever --
I know, Cain.
OH MY GOD, WHAT DID I DO!?
I know.
I wanna watch "Changing Rooms."
There's a marathon.
You're kidding me, right?

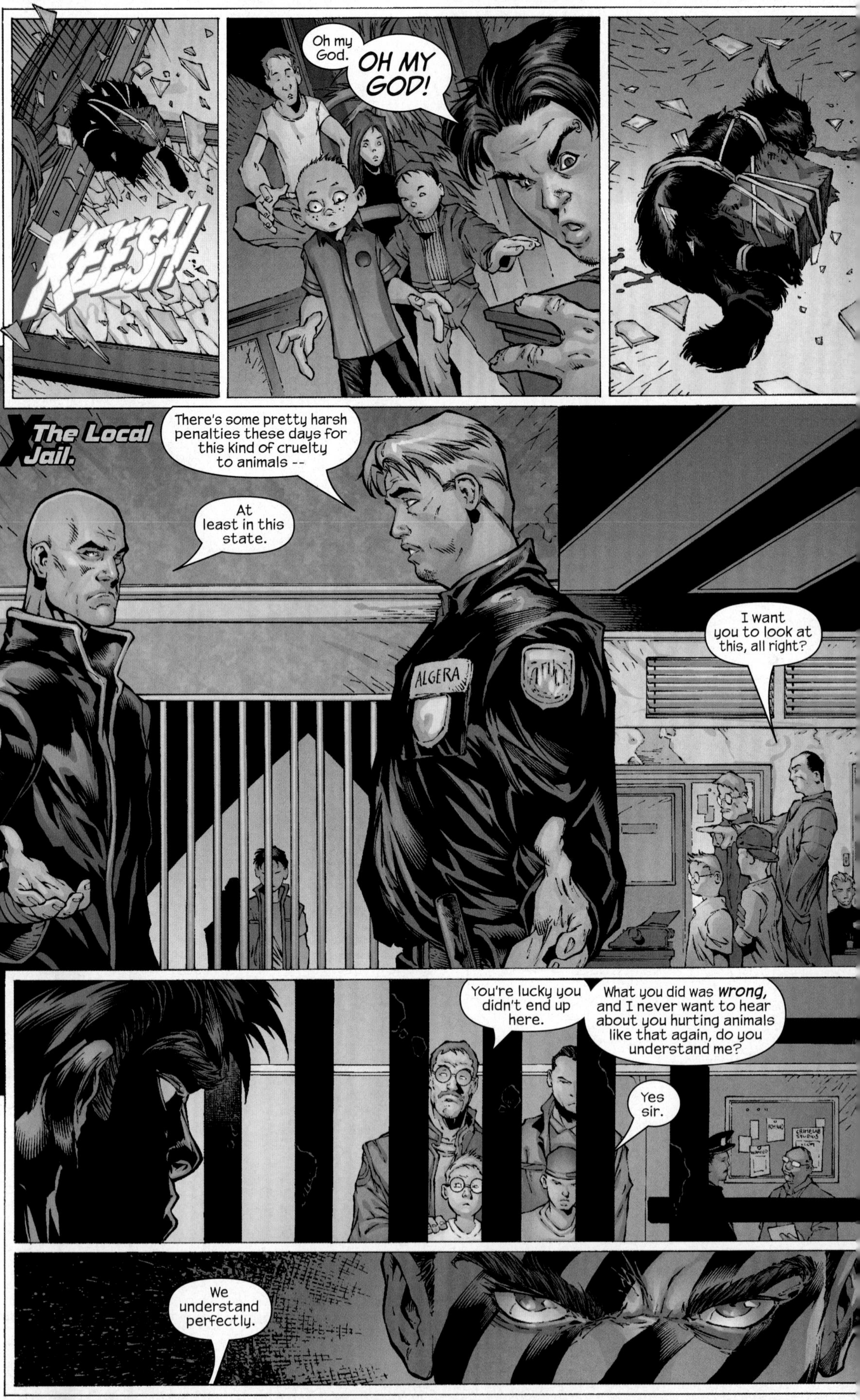
KEESH!
Oh my God.
OH MY GOD!
The Local Jail.
There's some pretty harsh penalties these days for this kind of cruelty to animals --
At least in this state.
ALGERA
I want you to look at this, all right?
You're lucky you didn't end up here.
What you did was wrong, and I never want to hear about you hurting animals like that again, do you understand me?
Yes sir.
We understand perfectly.

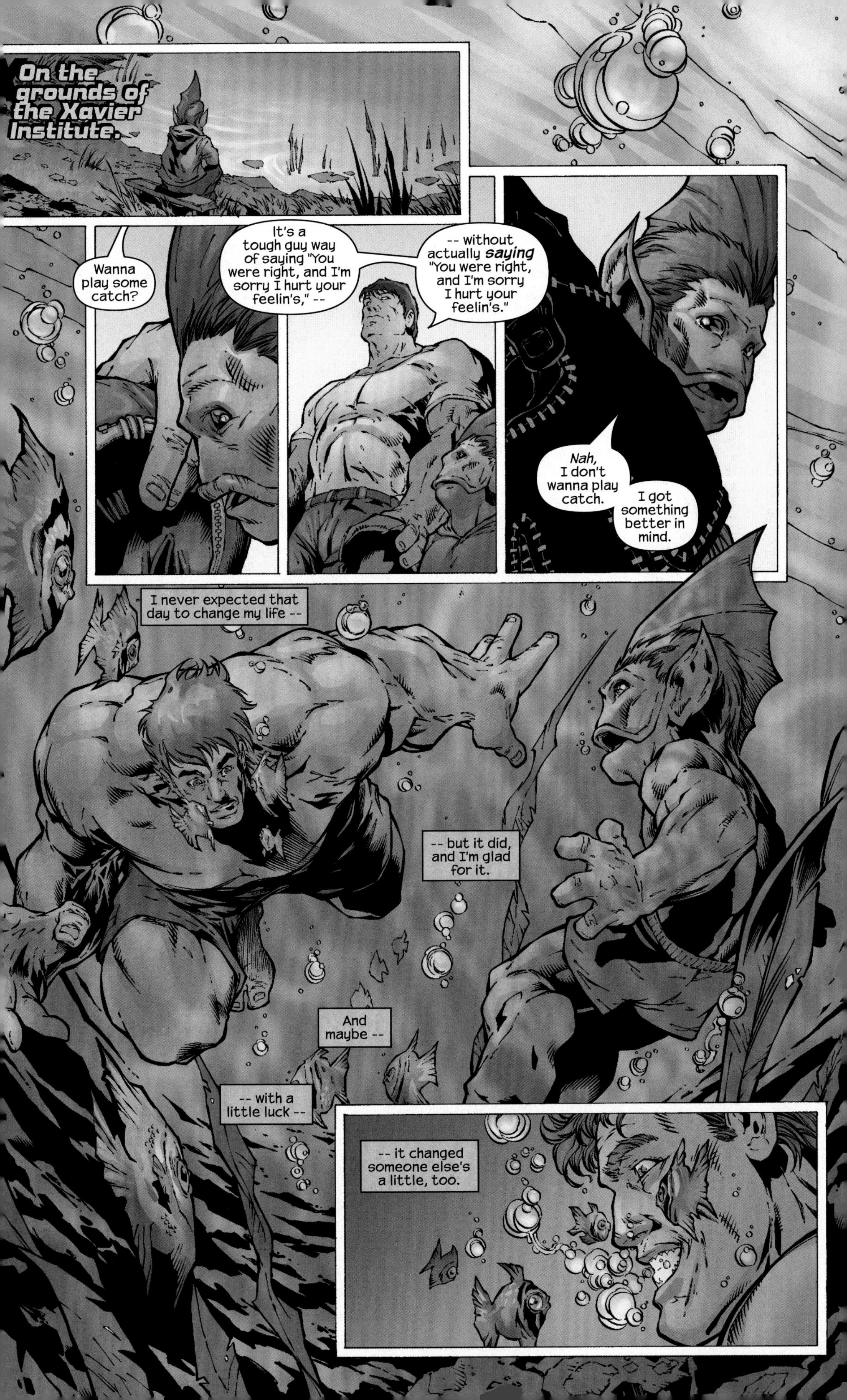

On the grounds of the Xavier Institute.
Wanna play some catch?
It's a tough guy way of saying "You were right, and I'm sorry I hurt your feelin's," --
-- without actually *saying* "You were right, and I'm sorry I hurt your feelin's."
Nah, I don't wanna play catch.
I got something better in mind.
I never expected that day to change my life --
-- but it did, and I'm glad for it.
And maybe --
-- with a little luck --
-- it changed someone else's a little, too.

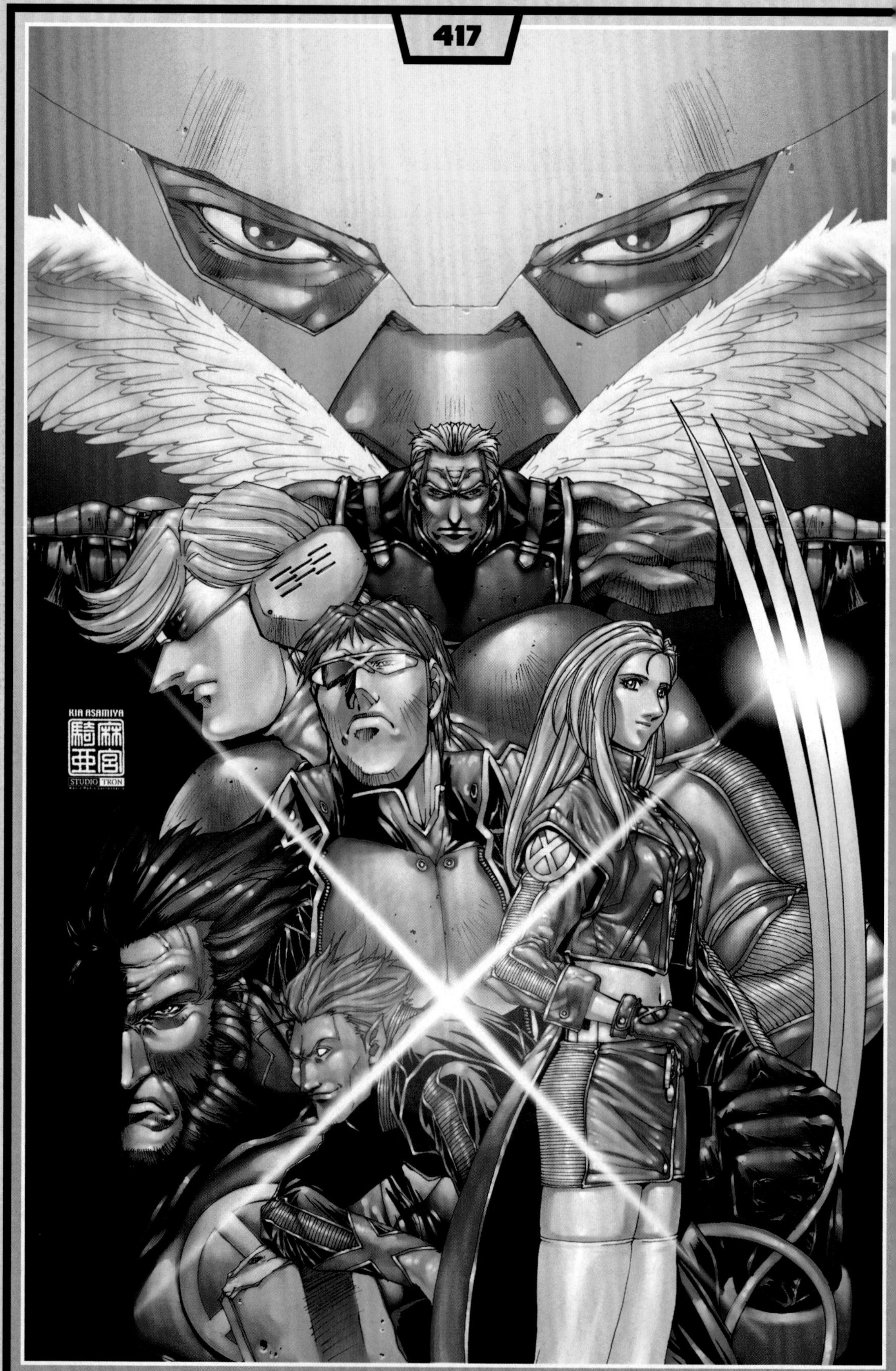
417
KIA ASAMIYA
STUDIO TRON

DOMINANT SPECIES, PART I

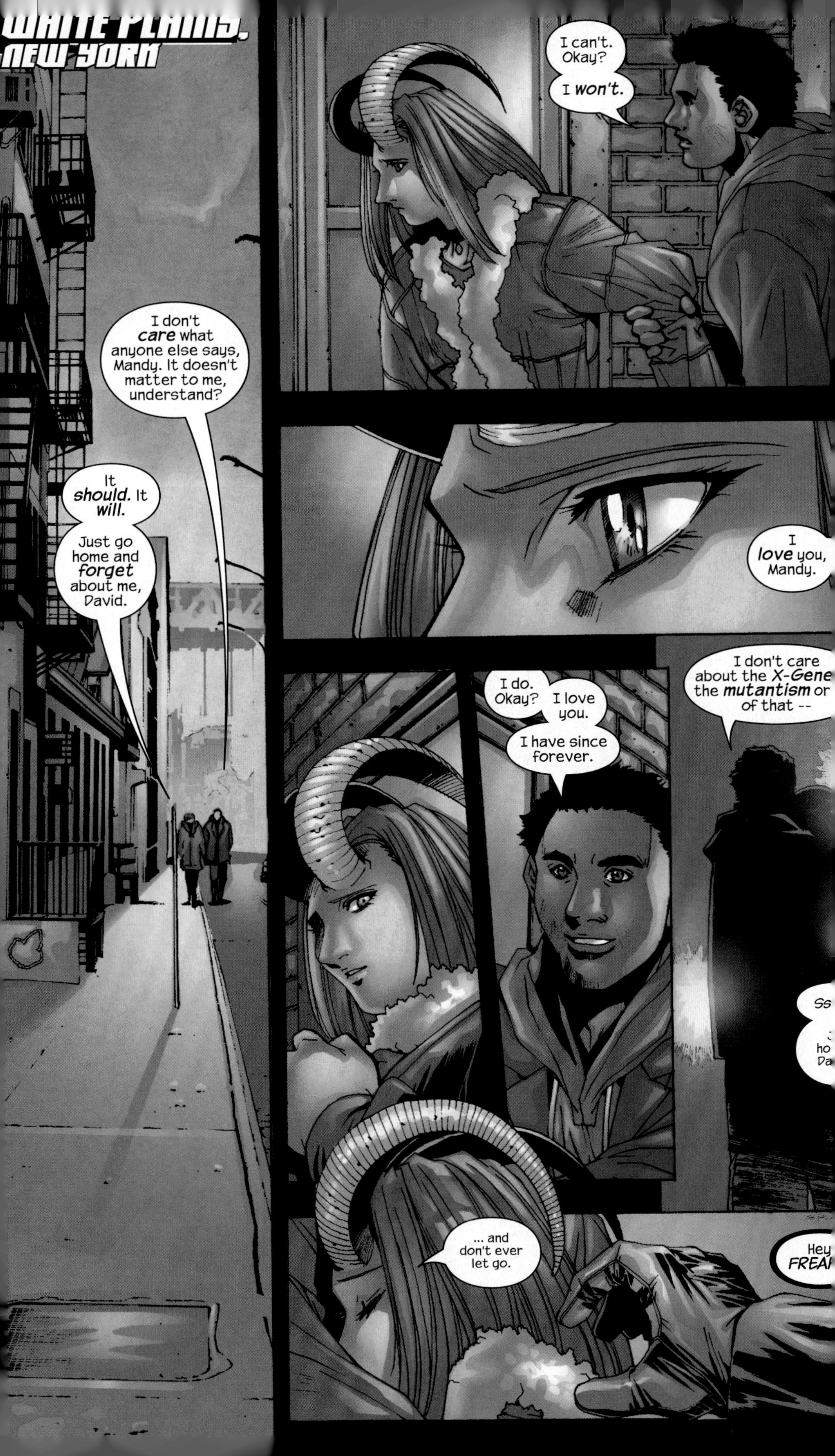
WHITE PLAINS, NEW YORK
I don't care what anyone else says, Mandy. It doesn't matter to me, understand?
It should. It will.
Just go home and forget about me, David.
I can't. Okay?
I won't.
I love you, Mandy.
I do. Okay?
I love you.
I have since forever.
... and don't ever let go.

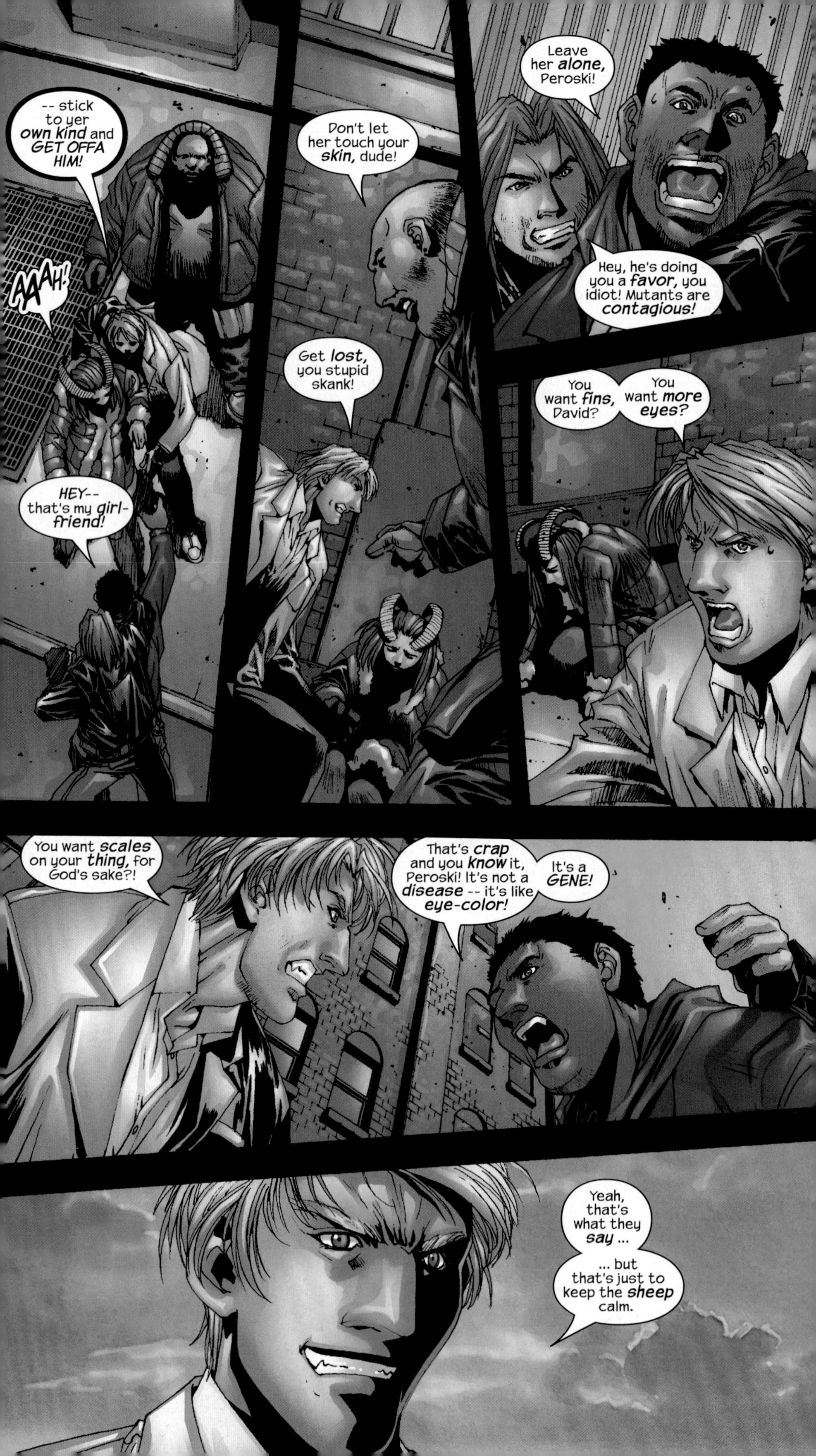
-- stick to yer own kind and GET OFFA HIM!
AAAH!
HEY-- that's my girl-friend!
Don't let her touch your skin, dude!
Get lost, you stupid skank!
Leave her alone, Peroski!
Hey, he's doing you a favor, you idiot! Mutants are contagious!
You want fins, David?
You want more eyes?
You want scales on your thing, for God's sake?!
That's crap and you know it, Peroski! It's not a disease -- it's like eye-color!
It's a GENE!
Yeah, that's what they say ...
... but that's just to keep the sheep calm.

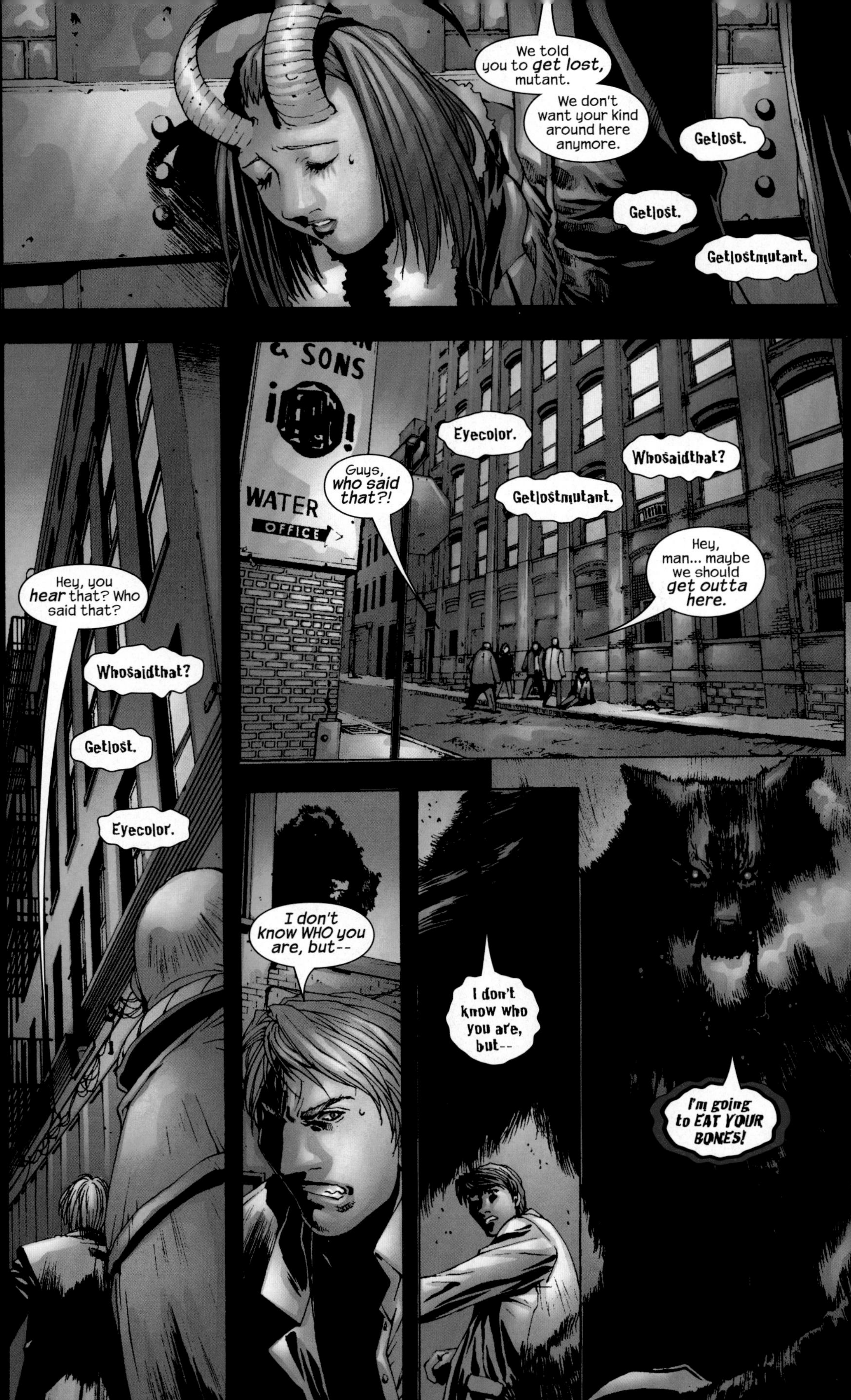
We told you to get lost, mutant.
We don't want your kind around here anymore.
Getlost.
Getlost.
Getlostmutant.
Hey, you hear that? Who said that?
Whosaidthat?
Getlost.
Eyecolor.
& SONS
WATER
OFFICE
Guys, who said that?!
Eyecolor.
Whosaidthat?
Getlostmutant.
Hey, man... maybe we should get outta here.
I don't know WHO you are, but--
I don't know who you are, but--
I'm going to EAT YOUR BONES!

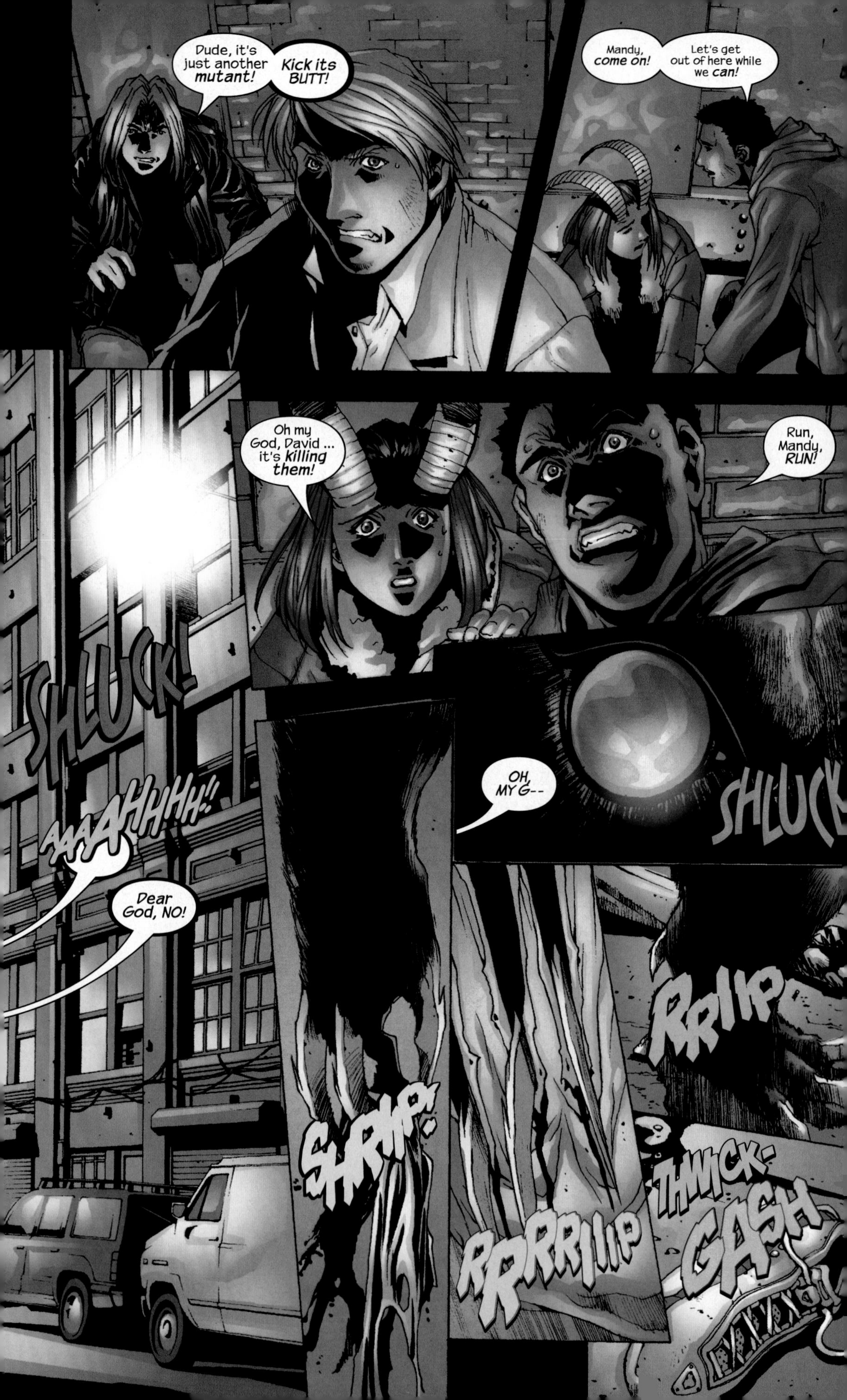
Dude, it's just another mutant!
Kick its BUTT!
Mandy, come on!
Let's get out of here while we can!
Oh my God, David ... it's killing them!
Run, Mandy, RUN!
SHLUCK!
AAAAHHHH!!
Dear God, NO!
OH, MY G--
SHLUCK
SHRIP!
RRRRIIIIP
RRIIP
THWICK-
GASH

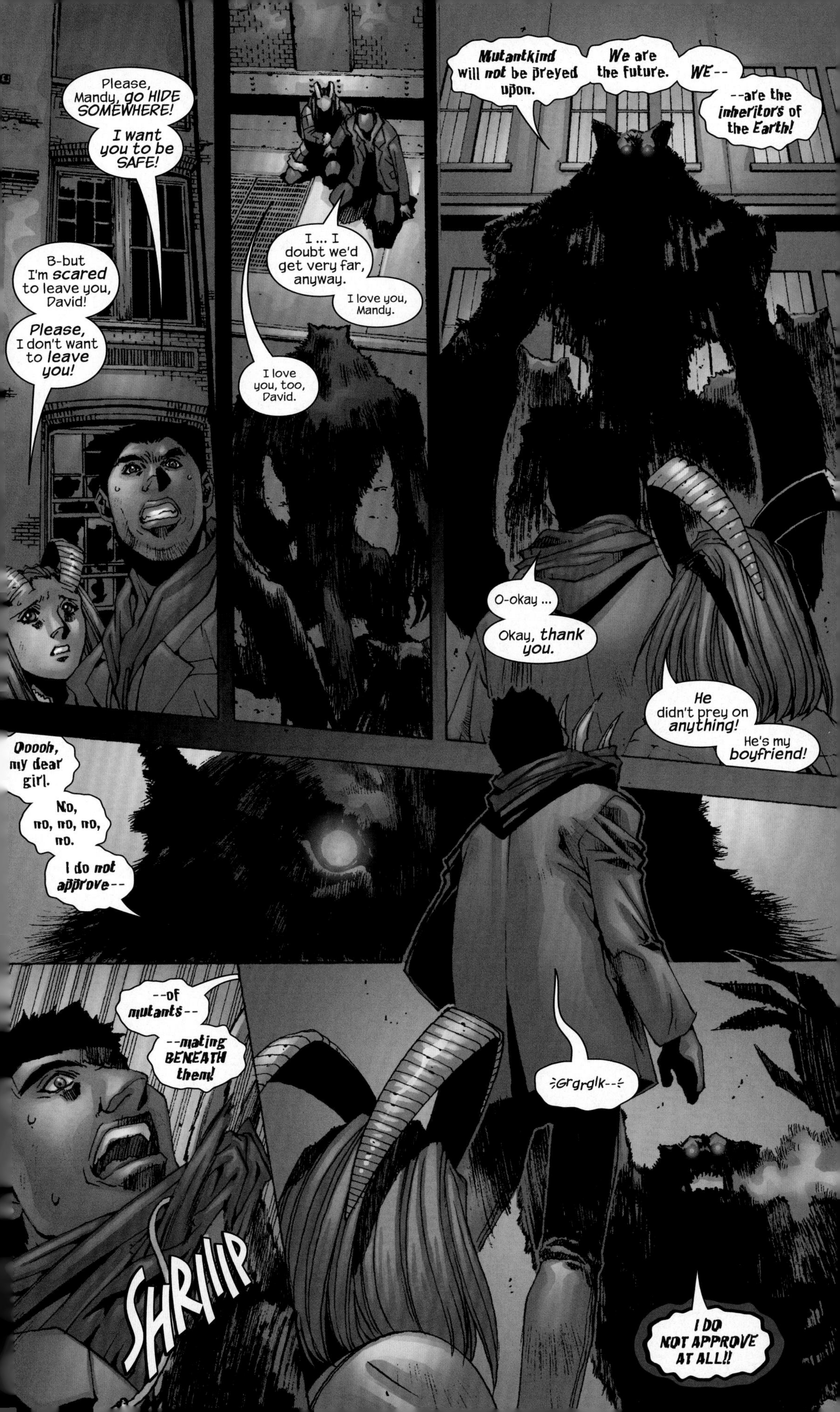
Please, Mandy, go HIDE SOMEWHERE!
I want you to be SAFE!
B-but I'm scared to leave you, David!
Please, I don't want to leave you!
I ... I doubt we'd get very far, anyway.
I love you, Mandy.
I love you, too, David.
Mutantkind will not be preyed upon.
We are the future.
WE--
--are the inheritors of the Earth!
O-okay ...
Okay, thank you.
He didn't prey on anything!
He's my boyfriend!
Ooooh, my dear girl.
No, no, no, no, no.
I do not approve--
--of mutants--
--mating BENEATH them!
Grgrglk--
SHRIIIP
I DO NOT APPROVE AT ALL!!

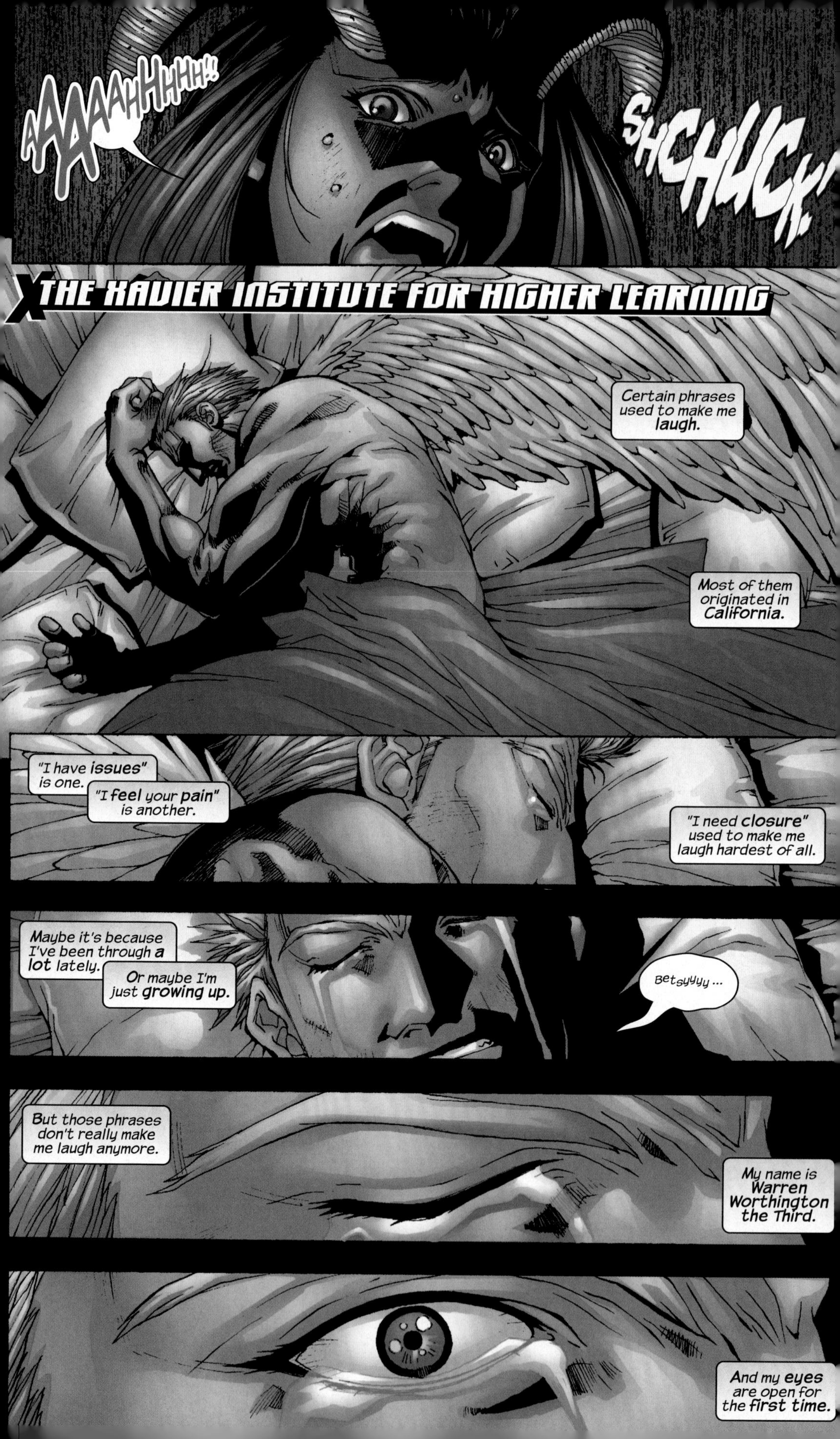
AAAAAHHHHH!!
SHCHUCK!
THE XAVIER INSTITUTE FOR HIGHER LEARNING
Certain phrases used to make me laugh.
Most of them originated in California.
"I have issues" is one.
"I feel your pain" is another.
"I need closure" used to make me laugh hardest of all.
Maybe it's because I've been through a lot lately.
Or maybe I'm just growing up.
Betsyyyy...
But those phrases don't really make me laugh anymore.
My name is Warren Worthington the Third.
And my eyes are open for the first time.

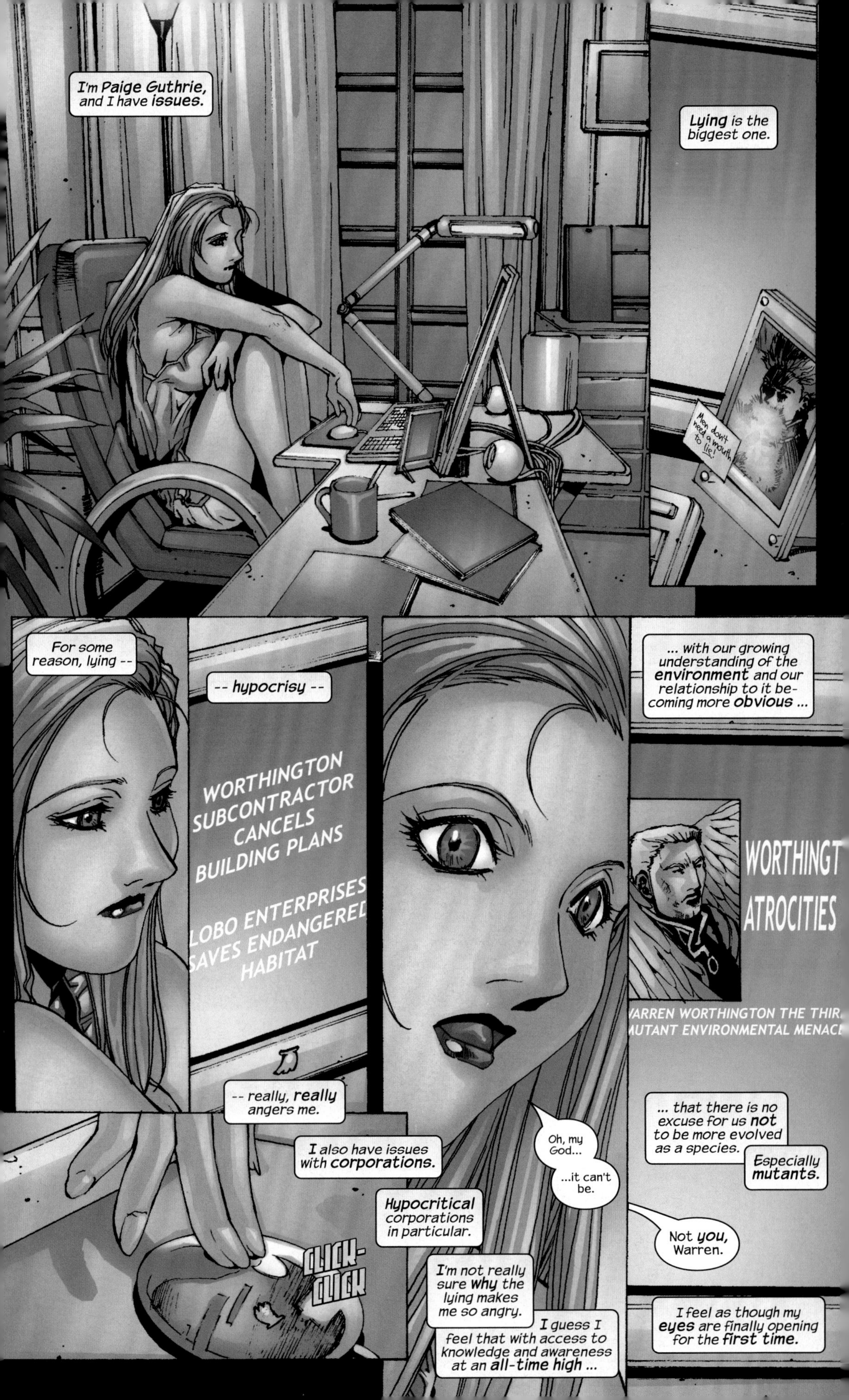
I'm Paige Guthrie, and I have issues.
Lying is the biggest one.
Men don't need a mouth to lie!
For some reason, lying --
-- hypocrisy --
WORTHINGTON SUBCONTRACTOR CANCELS BUILDING PLANS
LOBO ENTERPRISES SAVES ENDANGERED HABITAT
-- really, really angers me.
I also have issues with corporations.
Hypocritical corporations in particular.
CLICK-CLICK
I'm not really sure why the lying makes me so angry.
I guess I feel that with access to knowledge and awareness at an all-time high ...
... with our growing understanding of the environment and our relationship to it be-coming more obvious ...
WORTHINGT
ATROCITIES
WARREN WORTHINGTON THE THIR
MUTANT ENVIRONMENTAL MENACE
... that there is no excuse for us not to be more evolved as a species.
Especially mutants.
Oh, my God...
...it can't be.
Not you, Warren.
I feel as though my eyes are finally opening for the first time.

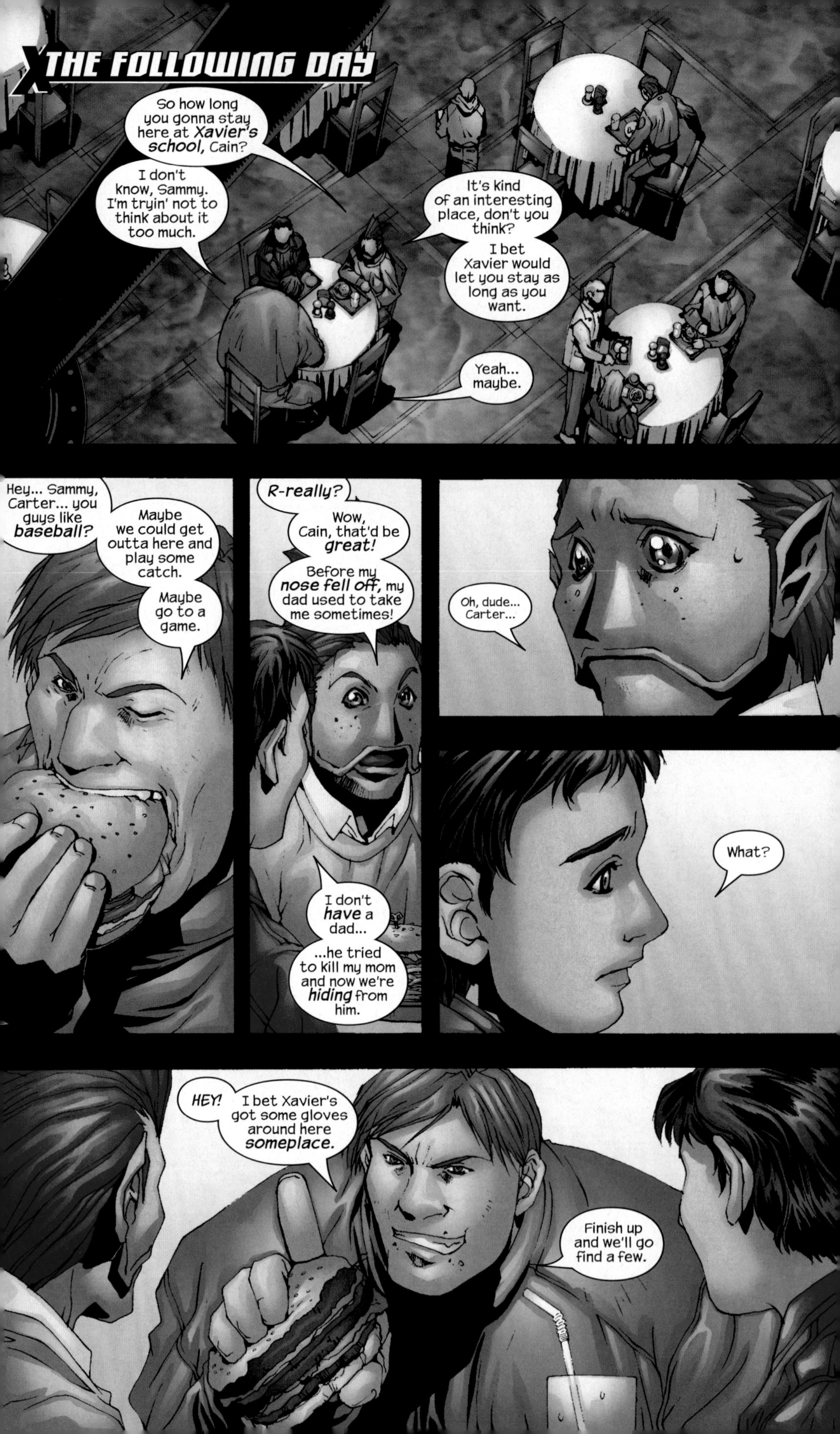
THE FOLLOWING DAY
So how long you gonna stay here at Xavier's school, Cain?
I don't know, Sammy. I'm tryin' not to think about it too much.
It's kind of an interesting place, don't you think?
I bet Xavier would let you stay as long as you want.
Yeah... maybe.
Hey... Sammy, Carter... you guys like baseball?
Maybe we could get outta here and play some catch.
Maybe go to a game.
R-really?
Wow, Cain, that'd be great!
Before my nose fell off, my dad used to take me sometimes!
I don't have a dad...
...he tried to kill my mom and now we're hiding from him.
Oh, dude... Carter...
What?
HEY!
I bet Xavier's got some gloves around here someplace.
Finish up and we'll go find a few.

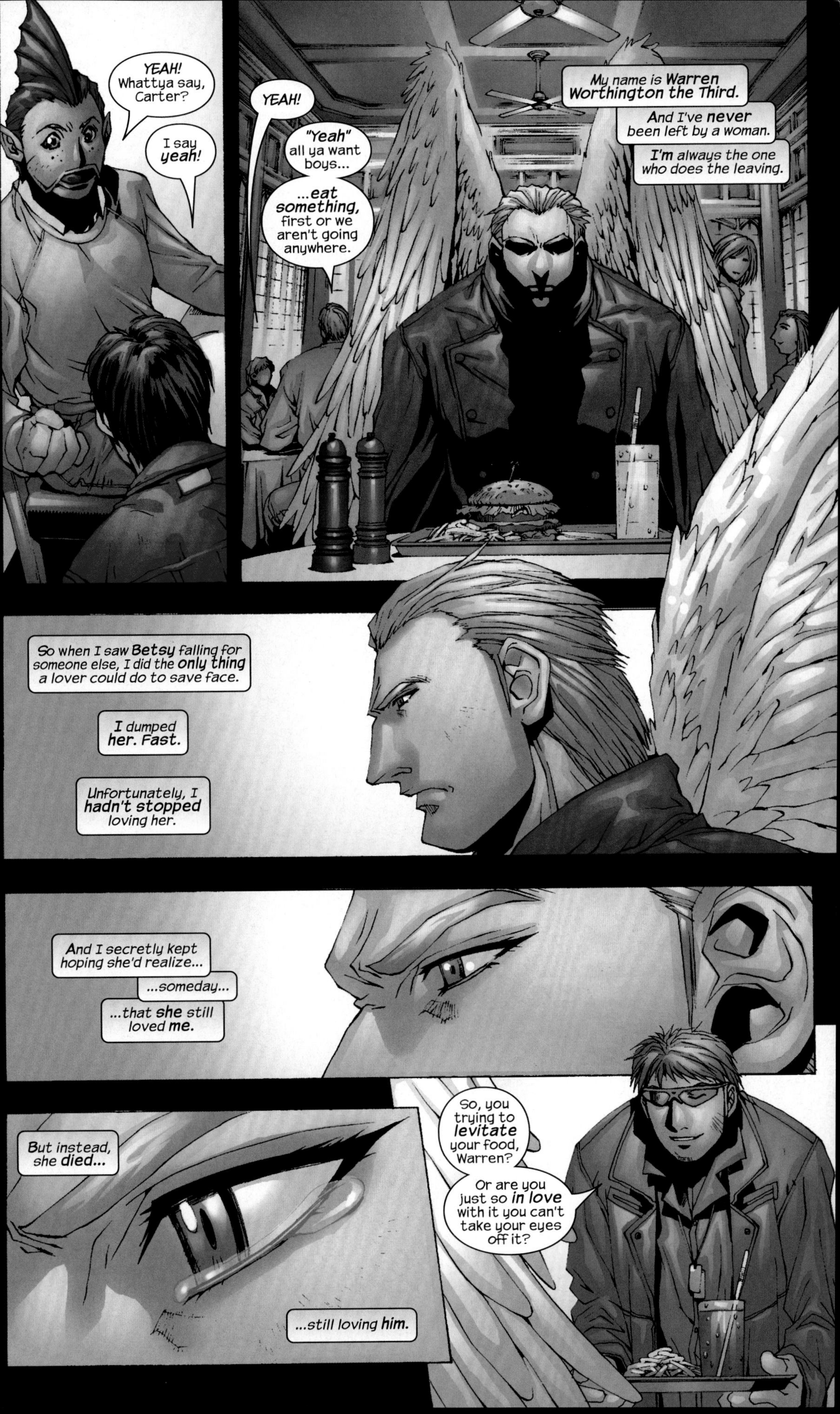

YEAH! Whattya say, Carter?
I say yeah!
YEAH!
"Yeah" all ya want boys...
...eat something, first or we aren't going anywhere.
My name is Warren Worthington the Third.
And I've never been left by a woman.
I'm always the one who does the leaving.
So when I saw Betsy falling for someone else, I did the only thing a lover could do to save face.
I dumped her. Fast.
Unfortunately, I hadn't stopped loving her.
And I secretly kept hoping she'd realize...
...someday...
...that she still loved me.
But instead, she died...
...still loving him.
So, you trying to levitate your food, Warren?
Or are you just so in love with it you can't take your eyes off it?

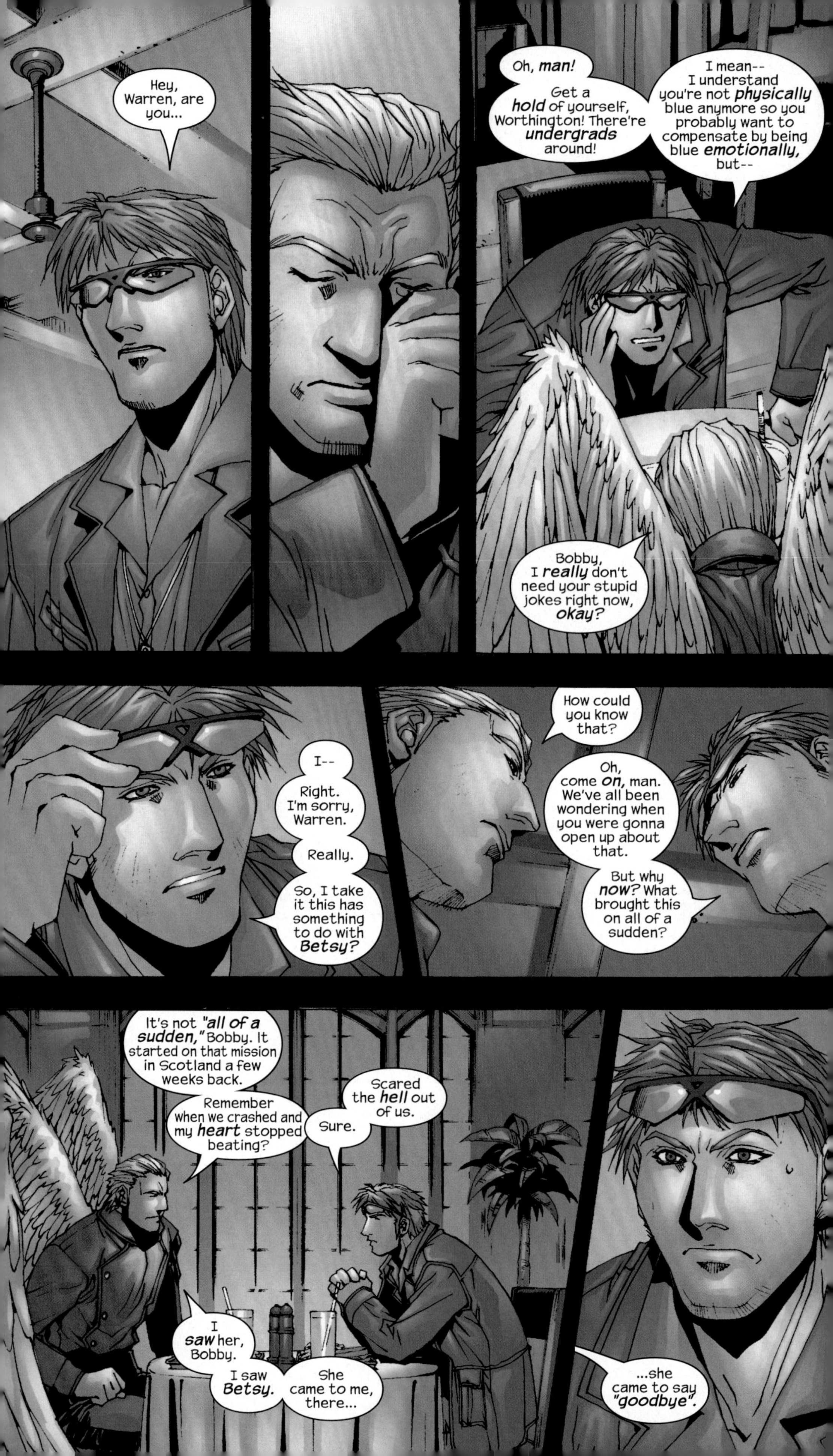
Hey, Warren, are you...
Oh, man!
Get a hold of yourself, Worthington! There're undergrads around!
I mean-- I understand you're not physically blue anymore so you probably want to compensate by being blue emotionally, but--
Bobby, I really don't need your stupid jokes right now, okay?
I--
Right. I'm sorry, Warren.
Really.
So, I take it this has something to do with Betsy?
How could you know that?
Oh, come on, man. We've all been wondering when you were gonna open up about that.
But why now? What brought this on all of a sudden?
It's not "all of a sudden," Bobby. It started on that mission in Scotland a few weeks back.
Remember when we crashed and my heart stopped beating?
Sure.
Scared the hell out of us.
I saw her, Bobby.
I saw Betsy.
She came to me, there...
...she came to say "goodbye".

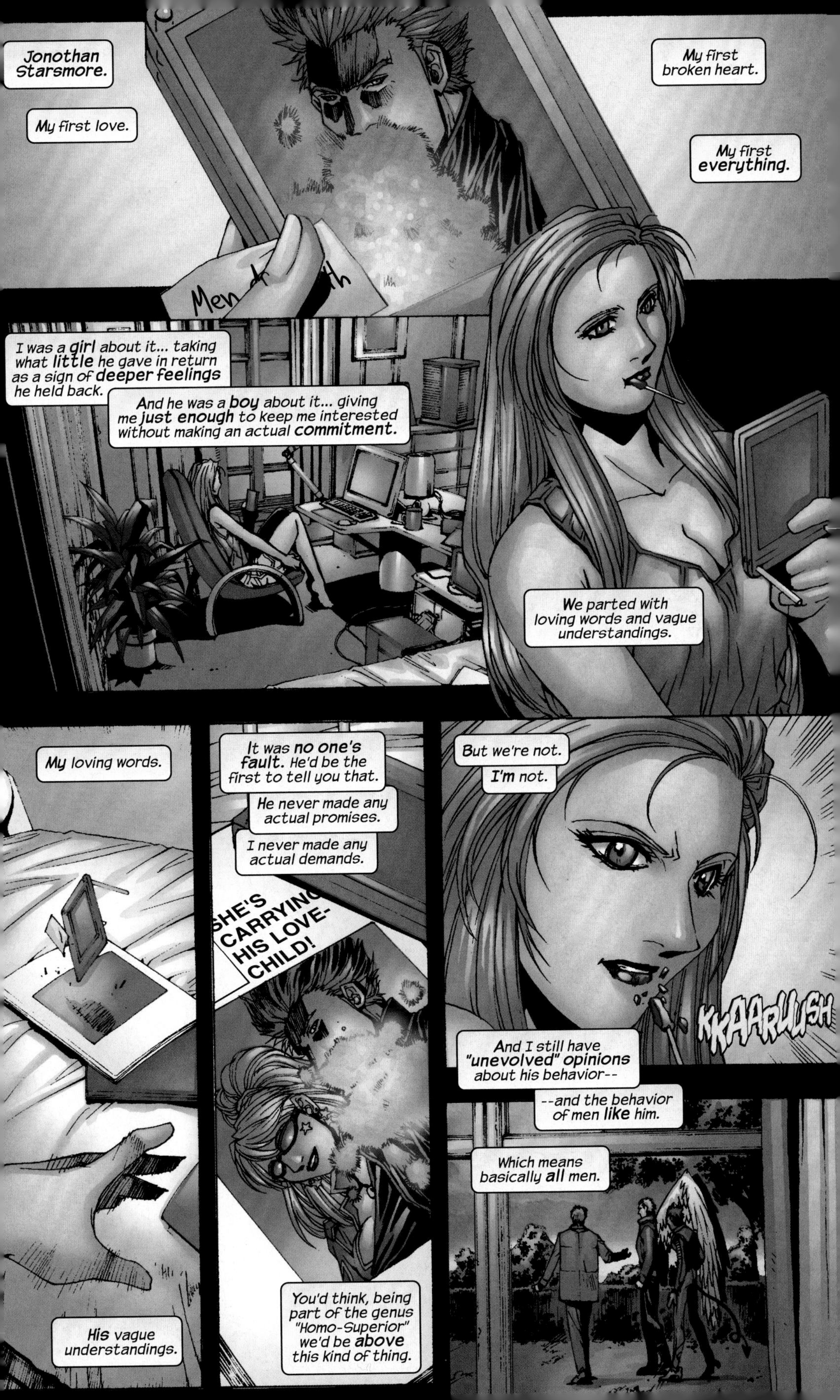
Jonothan Starsmore.
My first love.
My first broken heart.
My first everything.
Men
I was a girl about it... taking what little he gave in return as a sign of deeper feelings he held back.
And he was a boy about it... giving me just enough to keep me interested without making an actual commitment.
We parted with loving words and vague understandings.
My loving words.
His vague understandings.
It was no one's fault. He'd be the first to tell you that.
He never made any actual promises.
I never made any actual demands.
SHE'S CARRYING HIS LOVE-CHILD!
You'd think, being part of the genus "Homo-Superior" we'd be above this kind of thing.
But we're not.
I'm not.
KKAARUUSH
And I still have "unevolved" opinions about his behavior--
--and the behavior of men like him.
Which means basically all men.

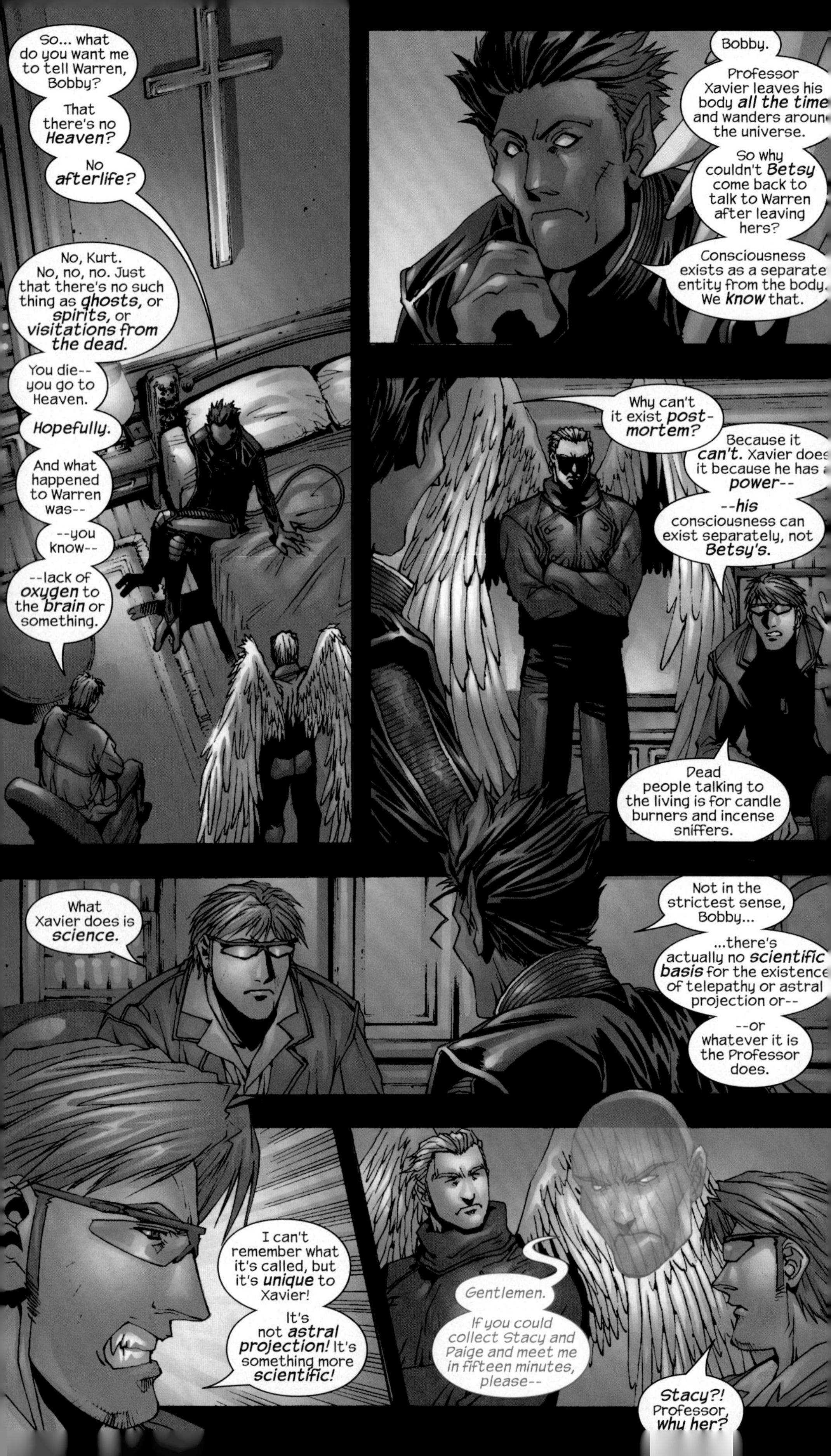

So... what do you want me to tell Warren, Bobby?
That there's no Heaven?
No afterlife?
No, Kurt. No, no, no. Just that there's no such thing as ghosts, or spirits, or visitations from the dead.
You die-- you go to Heaven.
Hopefully.
And what happened to Warren was--
--you know--
--lack of oxygen to the brain or something.
Bobby.
Professor Xavier leaves his body all the time and wanders around the universe.
So why couldn't Betsy come back to talk to Warren after leaving hers?
Consciousness exists as a separate entity from the body. We know that.
Why can't it exist post-mortem?
Because it can't. Xavier does it because he has a power--
--his consciousness can exist separately, not Betsy's.
Dead people talking to the living is for candle burners and incense sniffers.
What Xavier does is science.
Not in the strictest sense, Bobby...
...there's actually no scientific basis for the existence of telepathy or astral projection or--
--or whatever it is the Professor does.
I can't remember what it's called, but it's unique to Xavier!
It's not astral projection! It's something more scientific!
Gentlemen.
If you could collect Stacy and Paige and meet me in fifteen minutes, please--
Stacy?! Professor, why her?

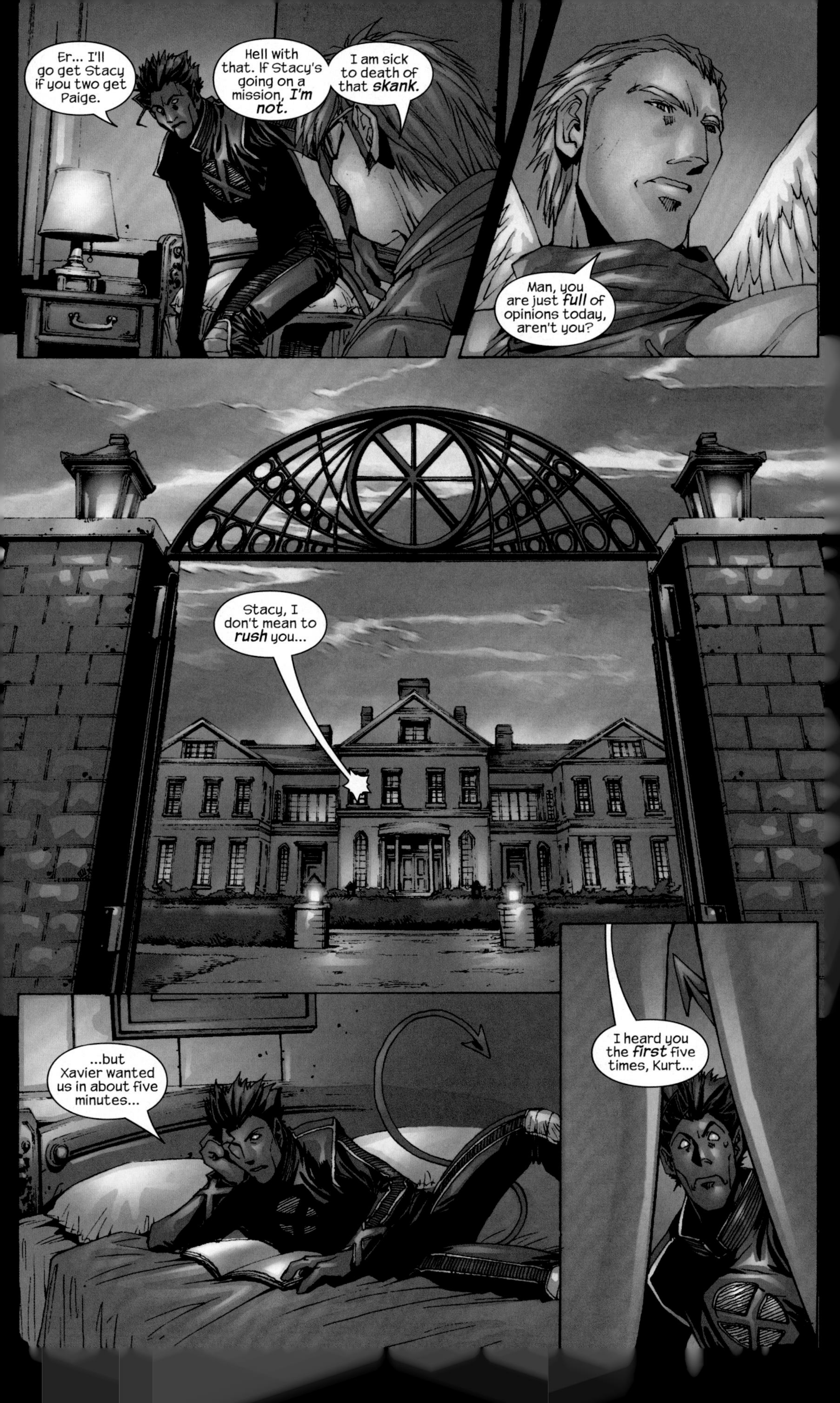

Er... I'll go get Stacy if you two get Paige.
Hell with that. If Stacy's going on a mission, *I'm not.*
I am sick to death of that *skank.*
Man, you are just *full* of opinions today, aren't you?
Stacy, I don't mean to *rush* you...
...but Xavier wanted us in about five minutes...
I heard you the *first* five times, Kurt...

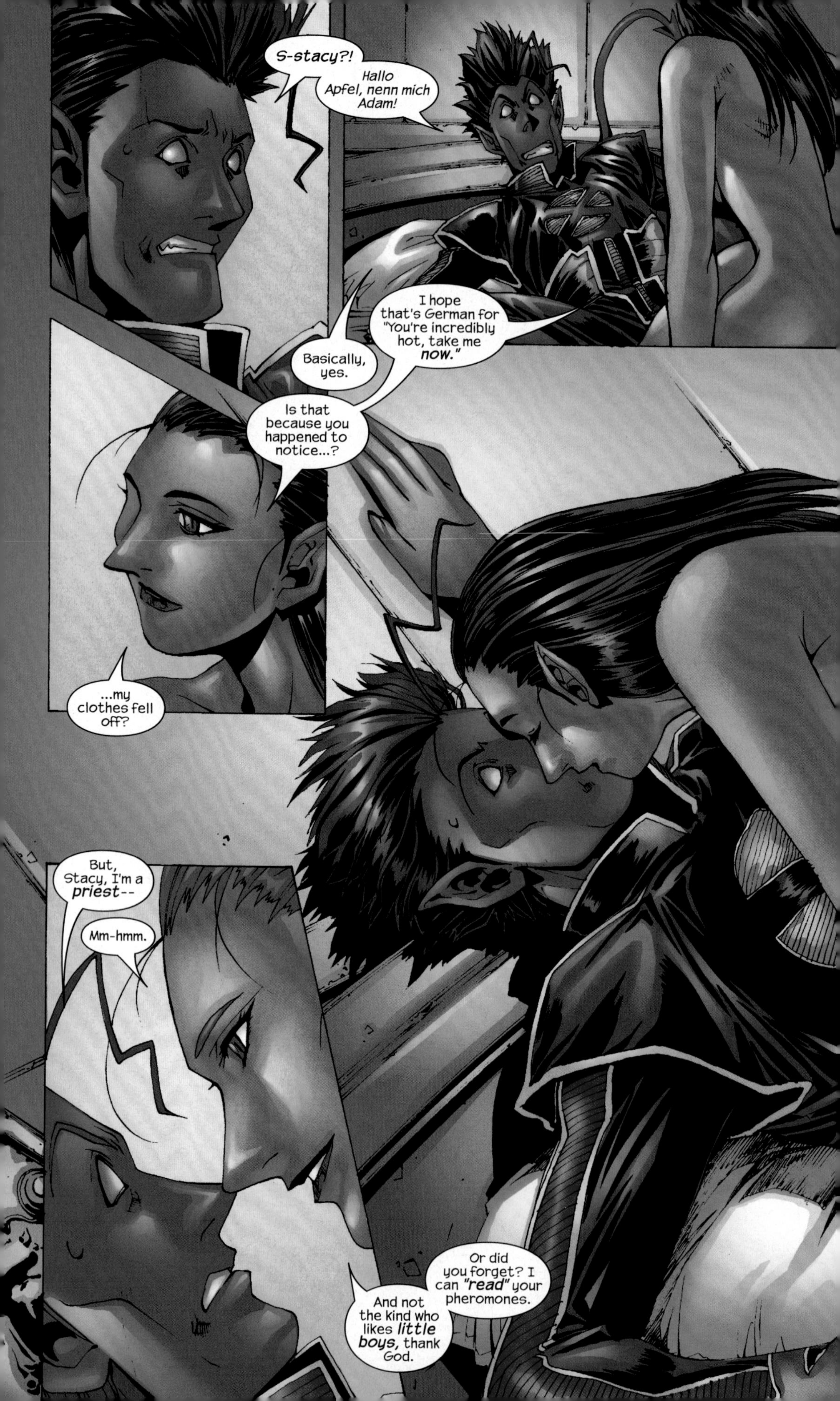
S-stacy?!
Hallo Apfel, nenn mich Adam!
I hope that's German for "You're incredibly hot, take me *now.*"
Basically, yes.
Is that because you happened to notice...?
...my clothes fell off?
But, Stacy, I'm a *priest*--
Mm-hmm.
Or did you forget? I can *"read"* your pheromones.
And not the kind who likes *little boys,* thank God.

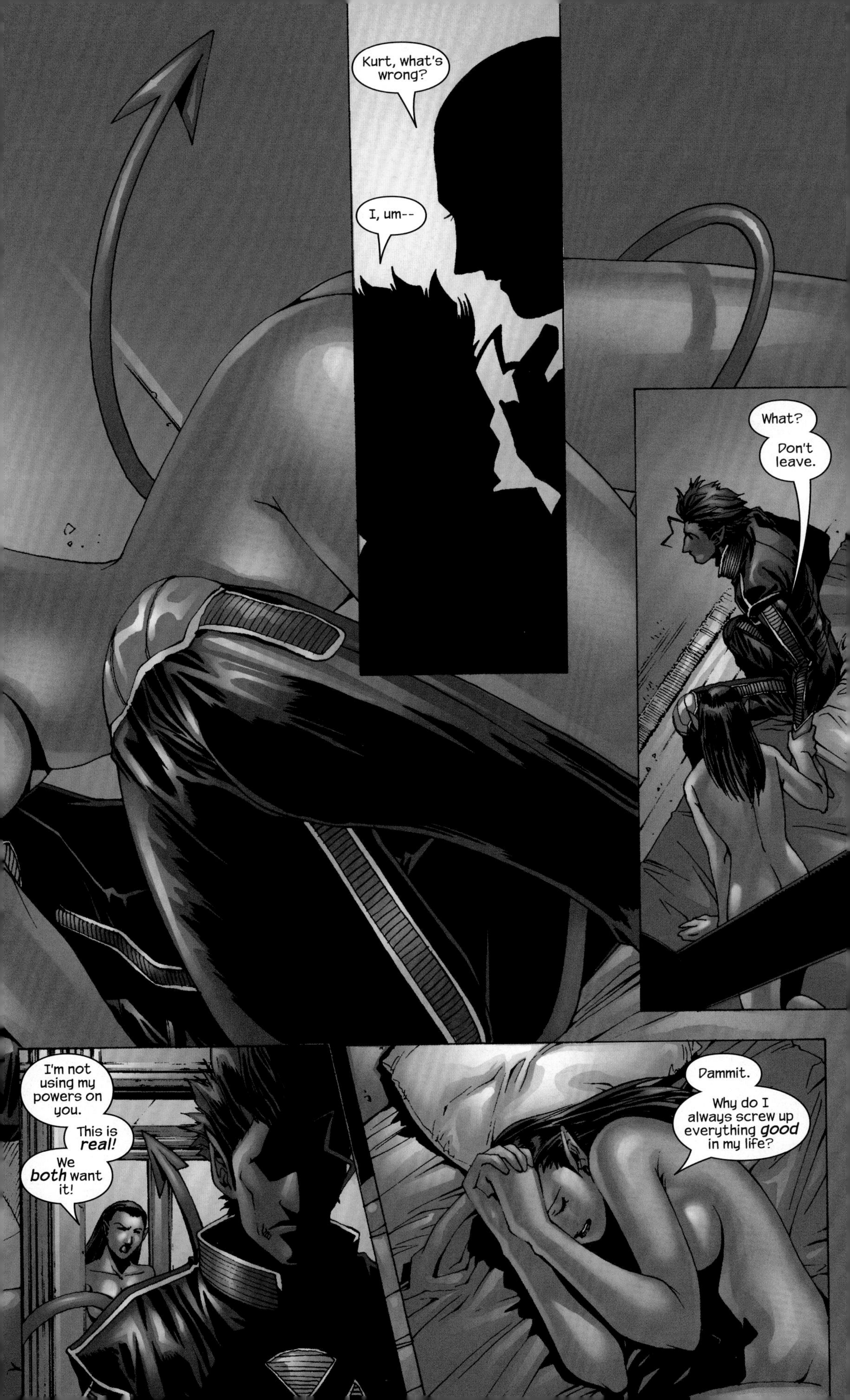
Kurt, what's wrong?
I, um--
What?
Don't leave.
I'm not using my powers on you.
This is *real!*
We *both* want it!
Dammit.
Why do I always screw up everything *good* in my life?

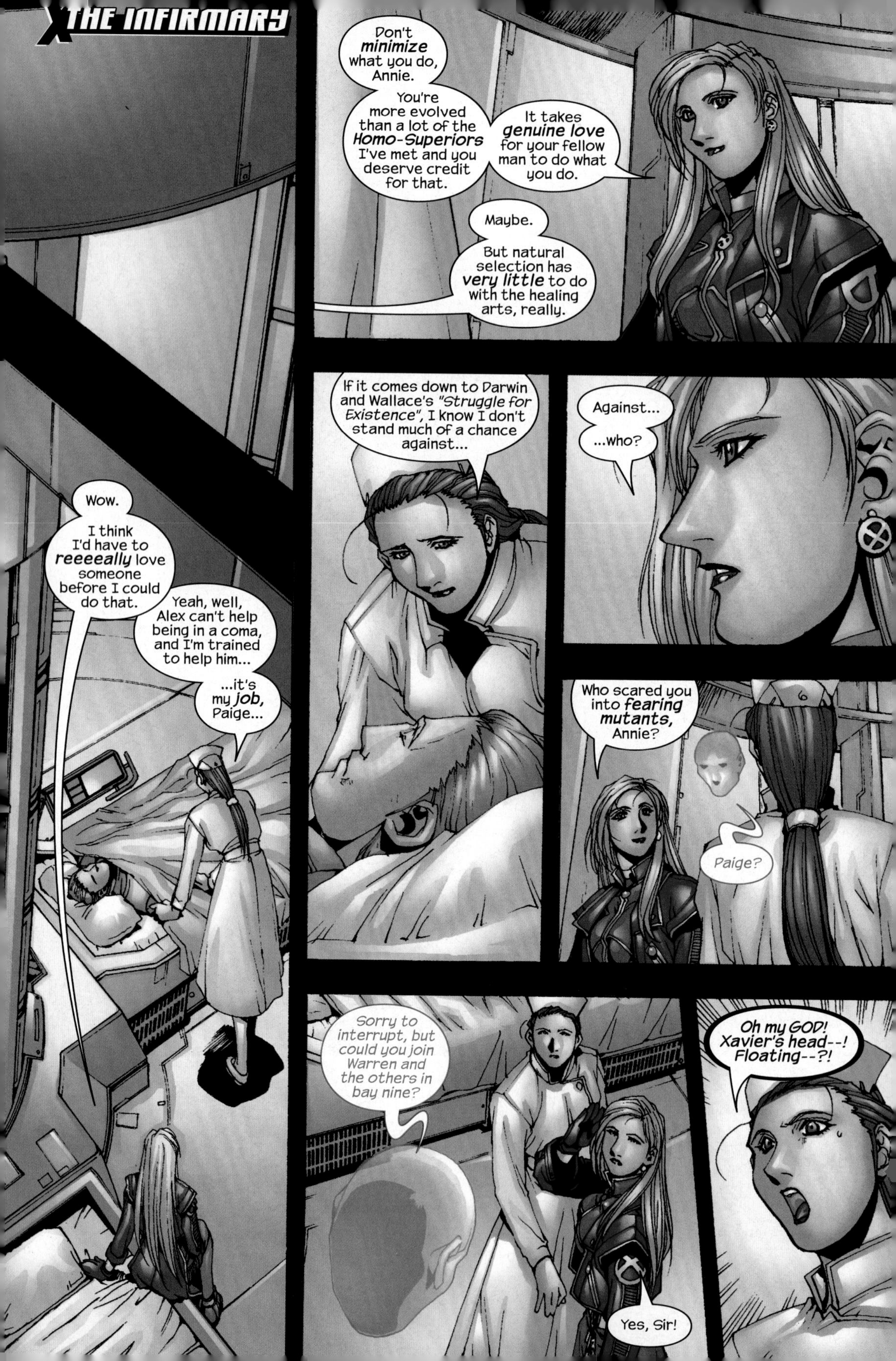
THE INFIRMARY
Don't minimize what you do, Annie.
You're more evolved than a lot of the Homo-Superiors I've met and you deserve credit for that.
It takes genuine love for your fellow man to do what you do.
Maybe.
But natural selection has very little to do with the healing arts, really.
Wow.
I think I'd have to reeeeally love someone before I could do that.
Yeah, well, Alex can't help being in a coma, and I'm trained to help him...
...it's my job, Paige...
If it comes down to Darwin and Wallace's "Struggle for Existence", I know I don't stand much of a chance against...
Against...
...who?
Who scared you into fearing mutants, Annie?
Paige?
Sorry to interrupt, but could you join Warren and the others in bay nine?
Yes, Sir!
Oh my GOD! Xavier's head--! Floating--?!

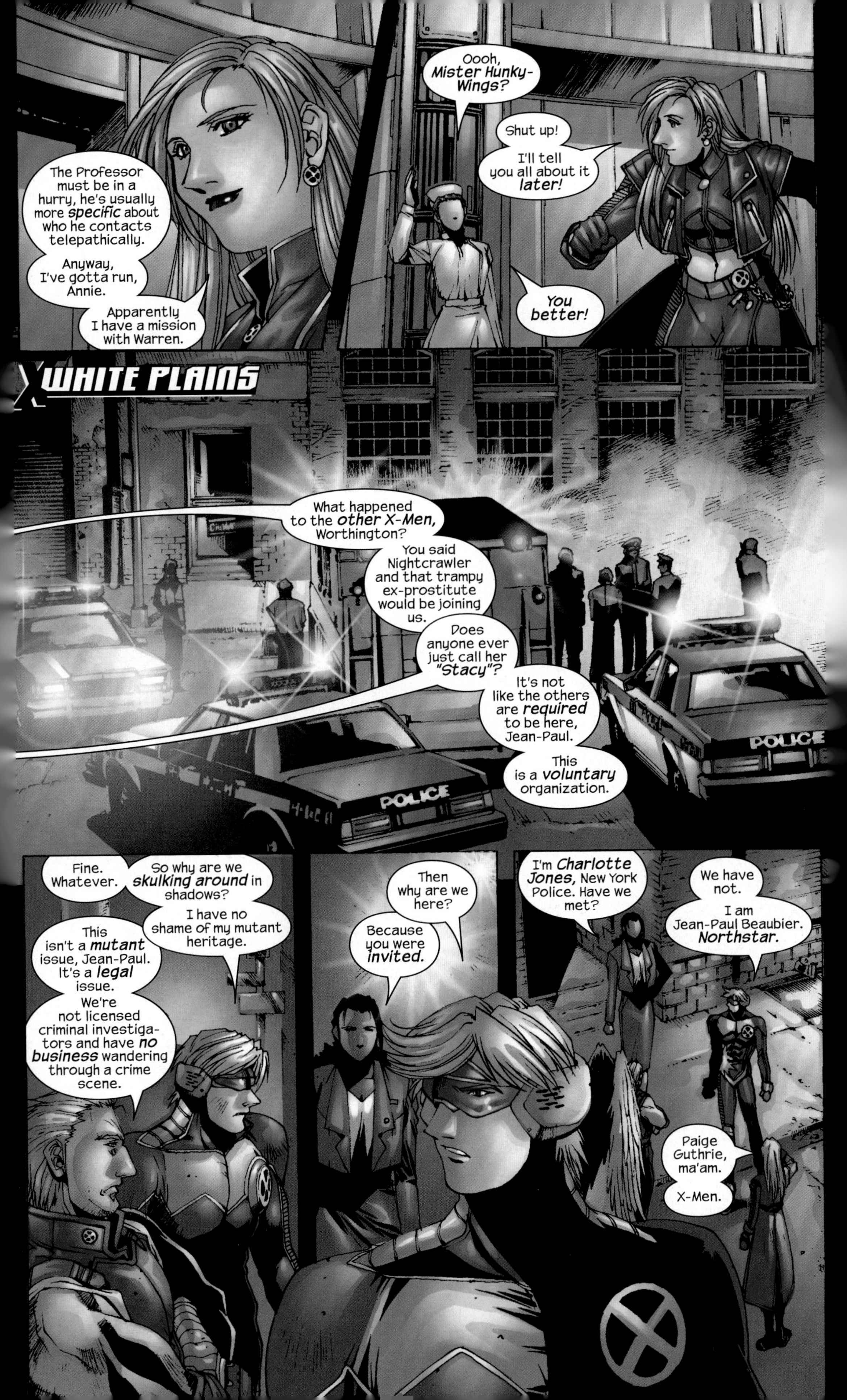
The Professor must be in a hurry, he's usually more *specific* about who he contacts telepathically.
Anyway, I've gotta run, Annie.
Apparently I have a mission with Warren.
Oooh, *Mister Hunky-Wings?*
Shut up!
I'll tell you all about it *later!*
You better!
WHITE PLAINS
What happened to the *other X-Men,* Worthington?
You said Nightcrawler and that trampy ex-prostitute would be joining us.
Does anyone ever just call her *"Stacy"?*
It's not like the others are *required* to be here, Jean-Paul.
This is a *voluntary* organization.
POLICE
POLICE
Fine. Whatever.
So why are we *skulking around* in shadows?
I have no shame of my mutant heritage.
This isn't a *mutant* issue, Jean-Paul. It's a *legal* issue.
We're not licensed criminal investigators and have *no business* wandering through a crime scene.
Then why are we here?
Because you were *invited.*
I'm *Charlotte Jones,* New York Police. Have we met?
We have not.
I am Jean-Paul Beaubier. ***Northstar.***
Paige Guthrie, ma'am.
X-Men.

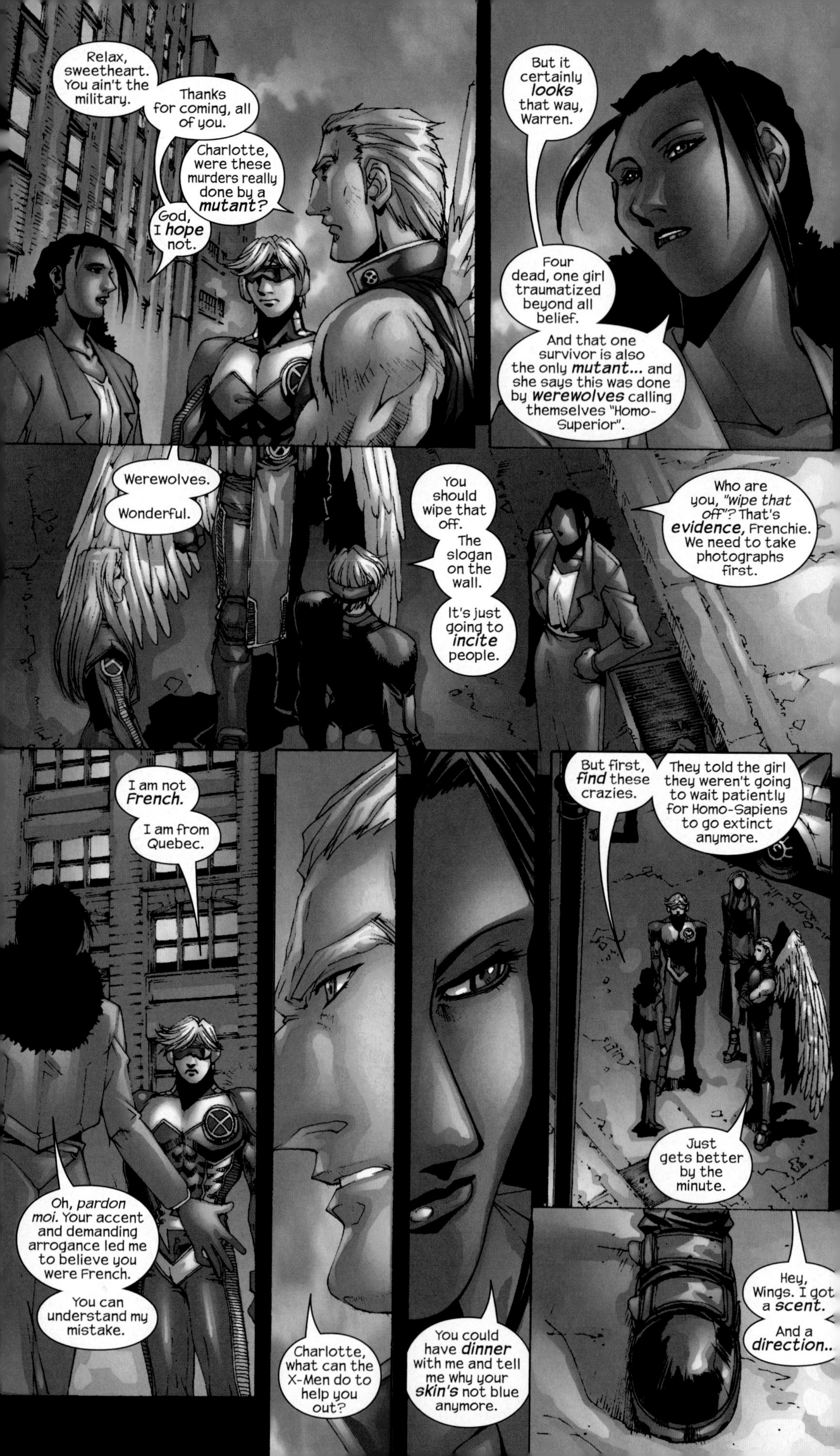
Relax, sweetheart. You ain't the military.
Thanks for coming, all of you.
Charlotte, were these murders really done by a *mutant*?
God, I *hope* not.
But it certainly *looks* that way, Warren.
Four dead, one girl traumatized beyond all belief.
And that one survivor is also the only *mutant...* and she says this was done by *werewolves* calling themselves "Homo-Superior".
Werewolves.
Wonderful.
You should wipe that off.
The slogan on the wall.
It's just going to *incite* people.
Who are you, *"wipe that off"*? That's *evidence,* Frenchie. We need to take photographs first.
I am not *French.*
I am from Quebec.
Oh, *pardon moi.* Your accent and demanding arrogance led me to believe you were French.
You can understand my mistake.
Charlotte, what can the X-Men do to help you out?
You could have *dinner* with me and tell me why your *skin's* not blue anymore.
But first, *find* these crazies.
They told the girl they weren't going to wait patiently for Homo-Sapiens to go extinct anymore.
Just gets better by the minute.
Hey, Wings. I got a *scent.*
And a *direction*...

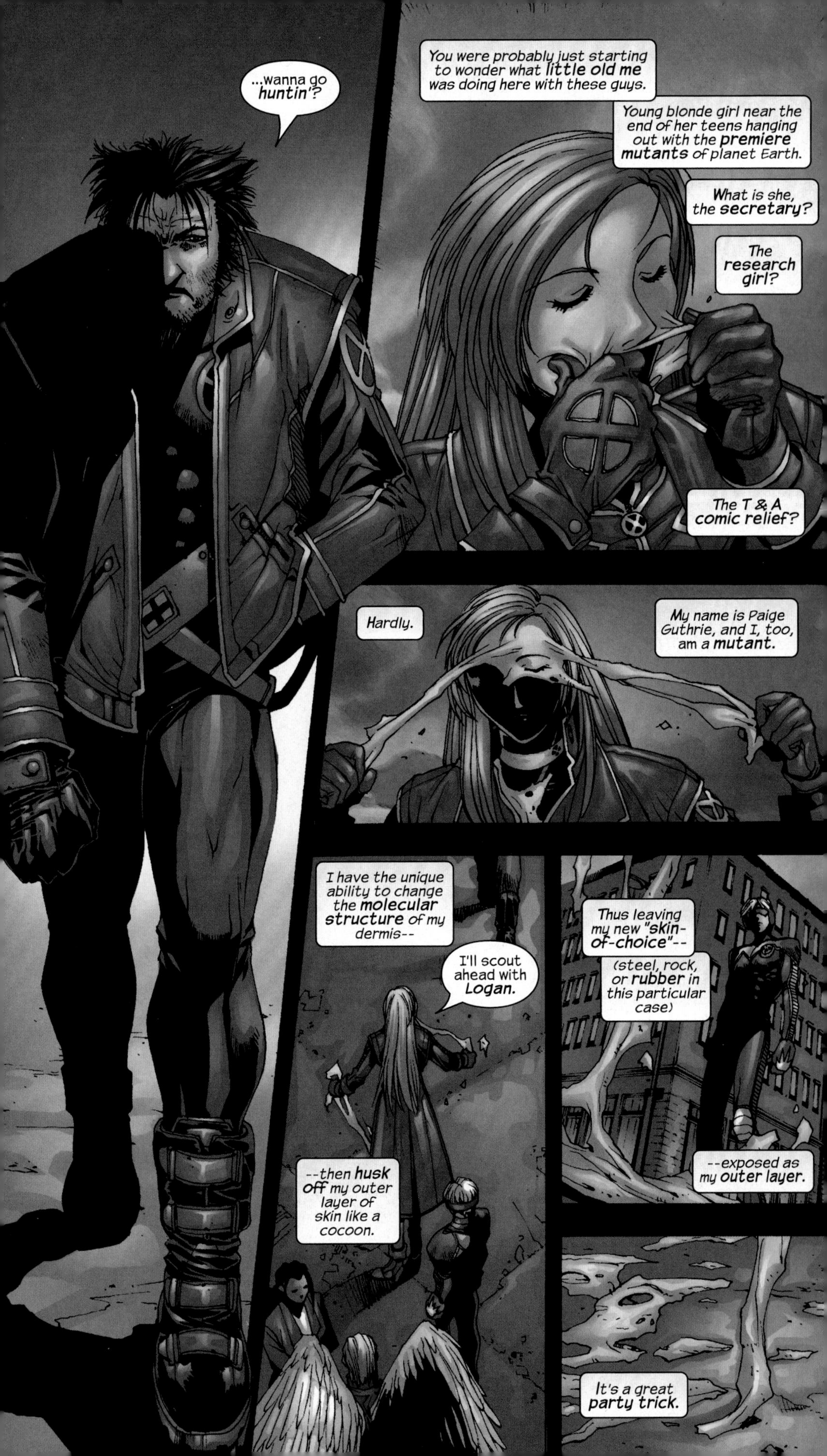

...wanna go huntin'?
You were probably just starting to wonder what little old me was doing here with these guys.
Young blonde girl near the end of her teens hanging out with the premiere mutants of planet Earth.
What is she, the secretary?
The research girl?
The T & A comic relief?
Hardly.
My name is Paige Guthrie, and I, too, am a mutant.
I have the unique ability to change the molecular structure of my dermis--
I'll scout ahead with Logan.
--then husk off my outer layer of skin like a cocoon.
Thus leaving my new "skin-of-choice"--
(steel, rock, or rubber in this particular case)
--exposed as my outer layer.
It's a great party trick.

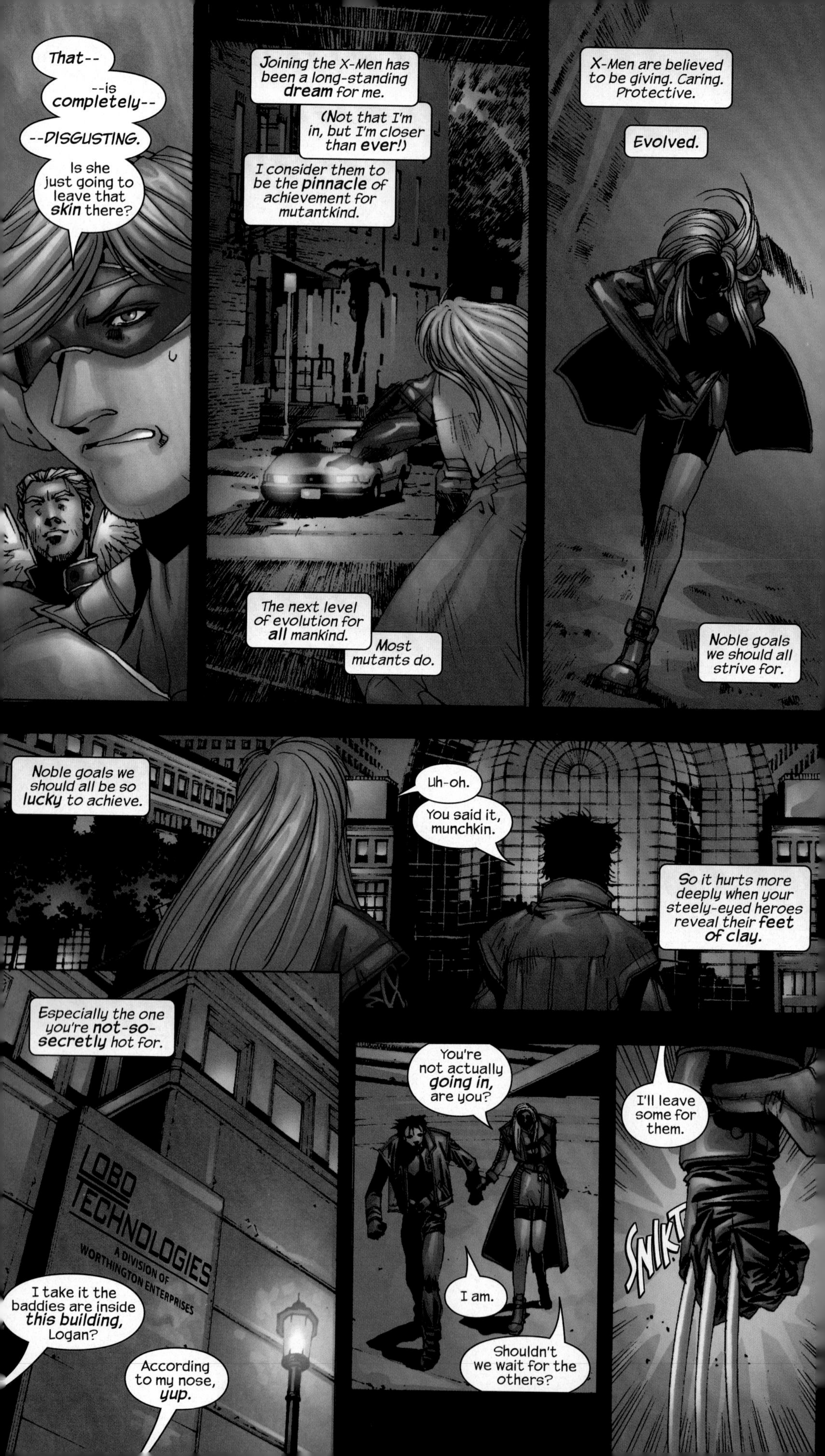
That--
--is completely--
--DISGUSTING.
Is she just going to leave that skin there?
Joining the X-Men has been a long-standing dream for me.
(Not that I'm in, but I'm closer than ever!)
I consider them to be the pinnacle of achievement for mutantkind.
The next level of evolution for all mankind.
Most mutants do.
X-Men are believed to be giving. Caring. Protective.
Evolved.
Noble goals we should all strive for.
Noble goals we should all be so lucky to achieve.
Uh-oh.
You said it, munchkin.
So it hurts more deeply when your steely-eyed heroes reveal their feet of clay.
Especially the one you're not-so-secretly hot for.
LOBO TECHNOLOGIES
A DIVISION OF WORTHINGTON ENTERPRISES
I take it the baddies are inside this building, Logan?
According to my nose, yup.
You're not actually going in, are you?
I am.
Shouldn't we wait for the others?
I'll leave some for them.
SNIKT

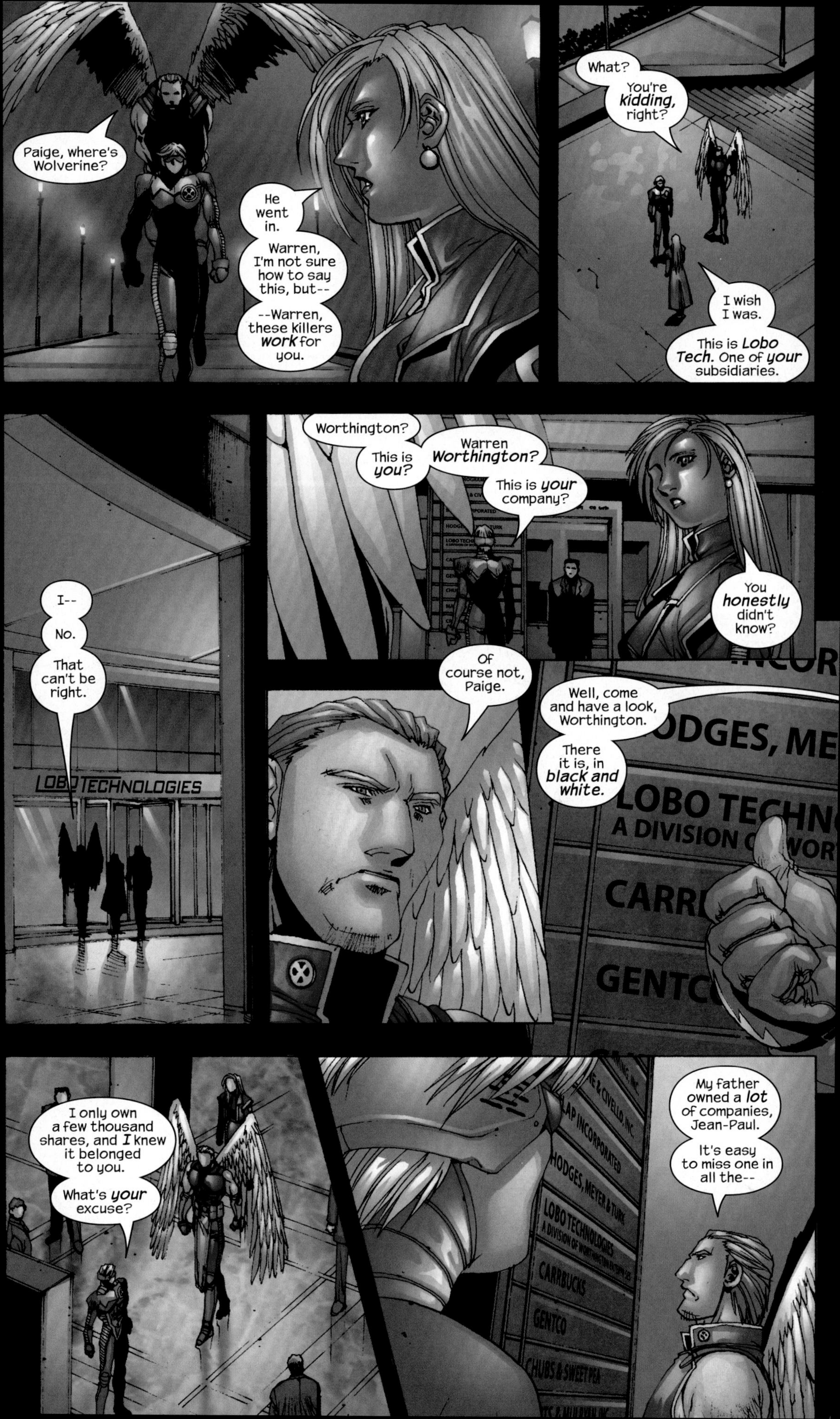
Paige, where's Wolverine?
He went in.
Warren, I'm not sure how to say this, but--
--Warren, these killers work for you.
What? You're kidding, right?
I wish I was.
This is Lobo Tech. One of your subsidiaries.
I--
No.
That can't be right.
LOBO TECHNOLOGIES
Worthington?
This is you?
Warren Worthington?
This is your company?
You honestly didn't know?
Of course not, Paige.
Well, come and have a look, Worthington.
There it is, in black and white.
I only own a few thousand shares, and I knew it belonged to you.
What's your excuse?
LAP INCORPORATED
HODGES, MEYER & TURK
LOBO TECHNOLOGIES
CARRBUCKS
GENTCO
CHUBS & SWEET PEA
My father owned a lot of companies, Jean-Paul.
It's easy to miss one in all the--

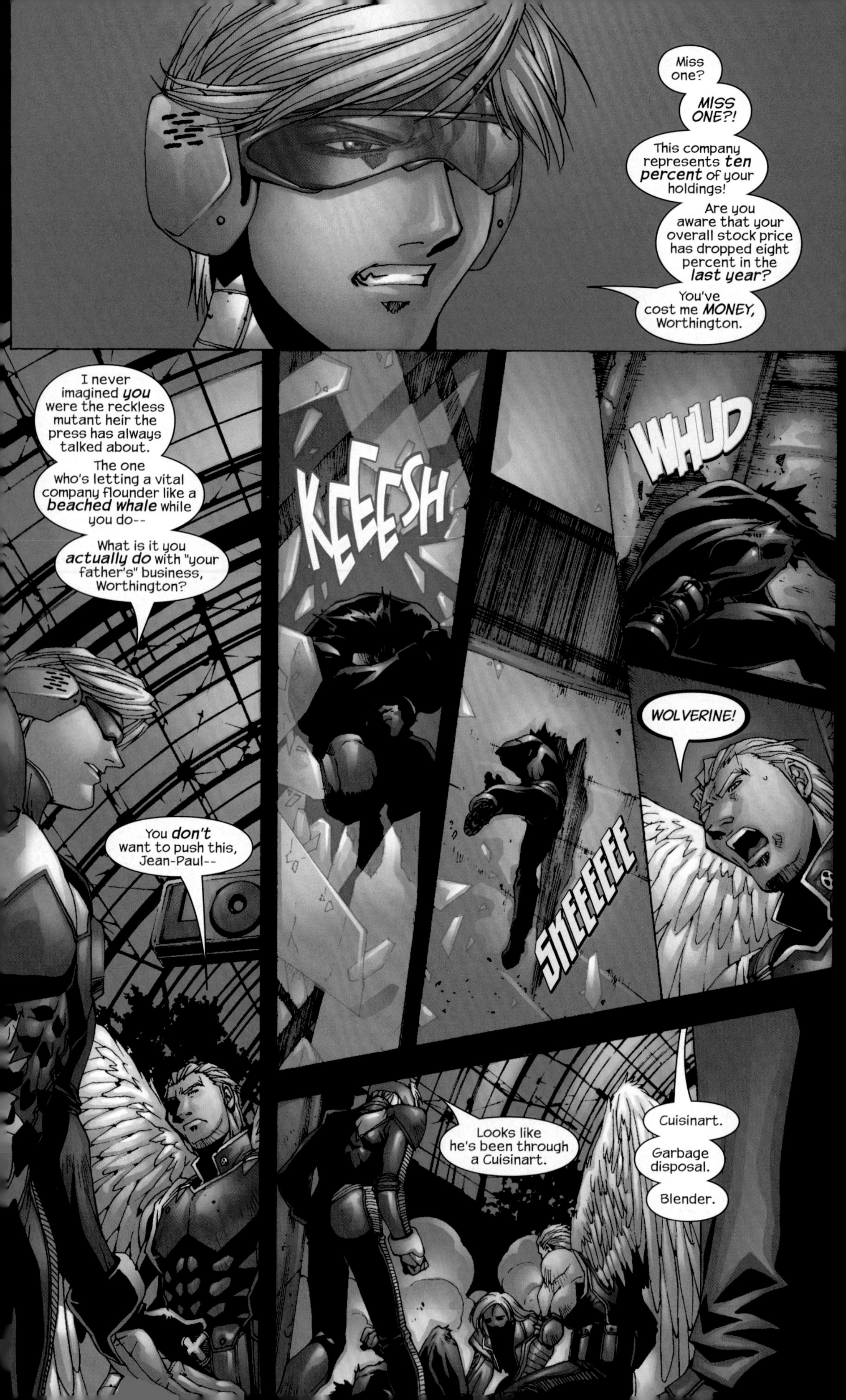
Miss one?
MISS ONE?!
This company represents ten percent of your holdings!
Are you aware that your overall stock price has dropped eight percent in the last year?
You've cost me MONEY, Worthington.
I never imagined you were the reckless mutant heir the press has always talked about.
The one who's letting a vital company flounder like a beached whale while you do--
What is it you actually do with "your father's" business, Worthington?
You don't want to push this, Jean-Paul--
KEEESH
WHUD
SHEEEEEE
WOLVERINE!
Looks like he's been through a Cuisinart.
Cuisinart.
Garbage disposal.
Blender.

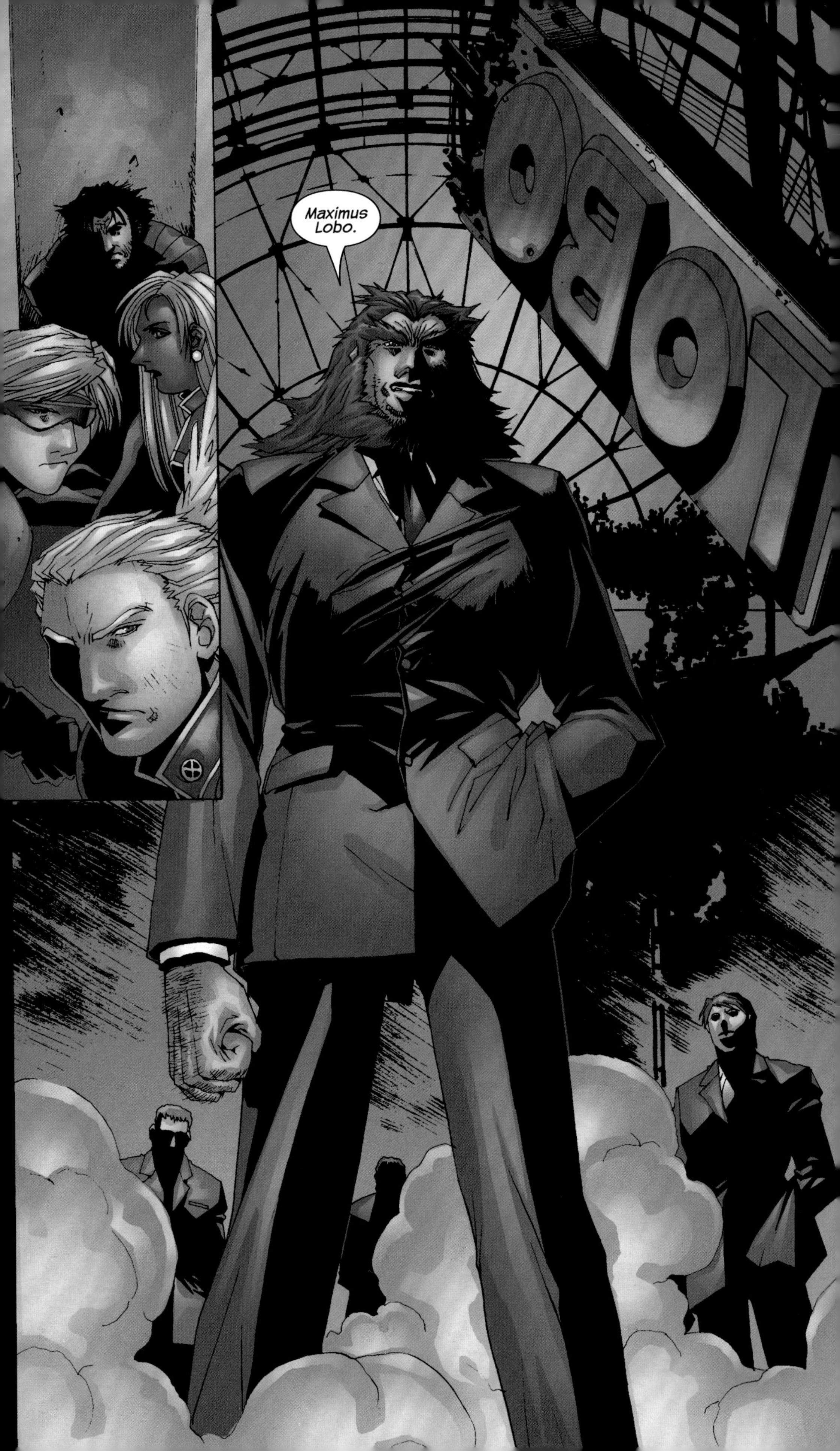
Maximus Lobo.

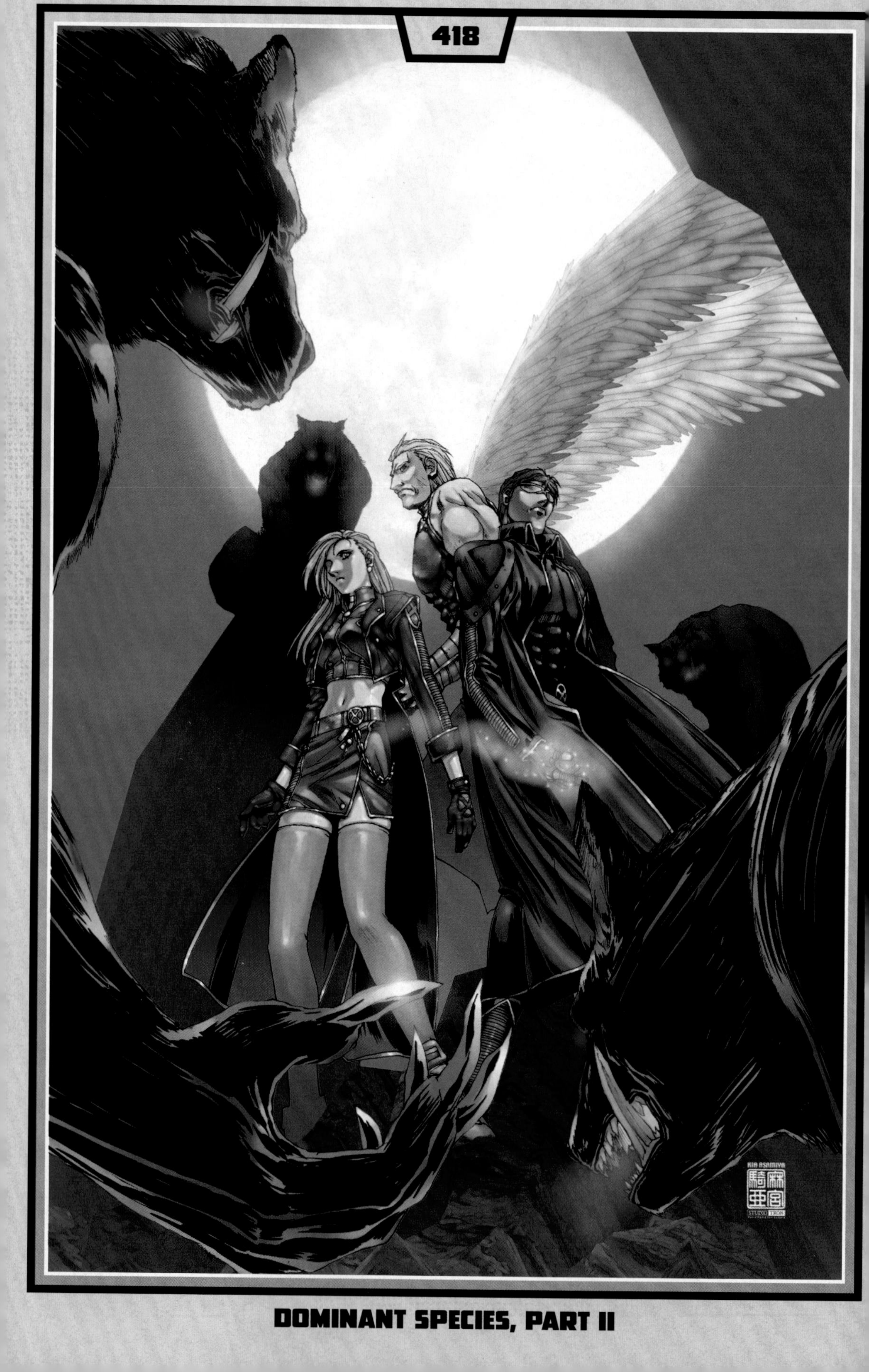
418

DOMINANT SPECIES, PART II

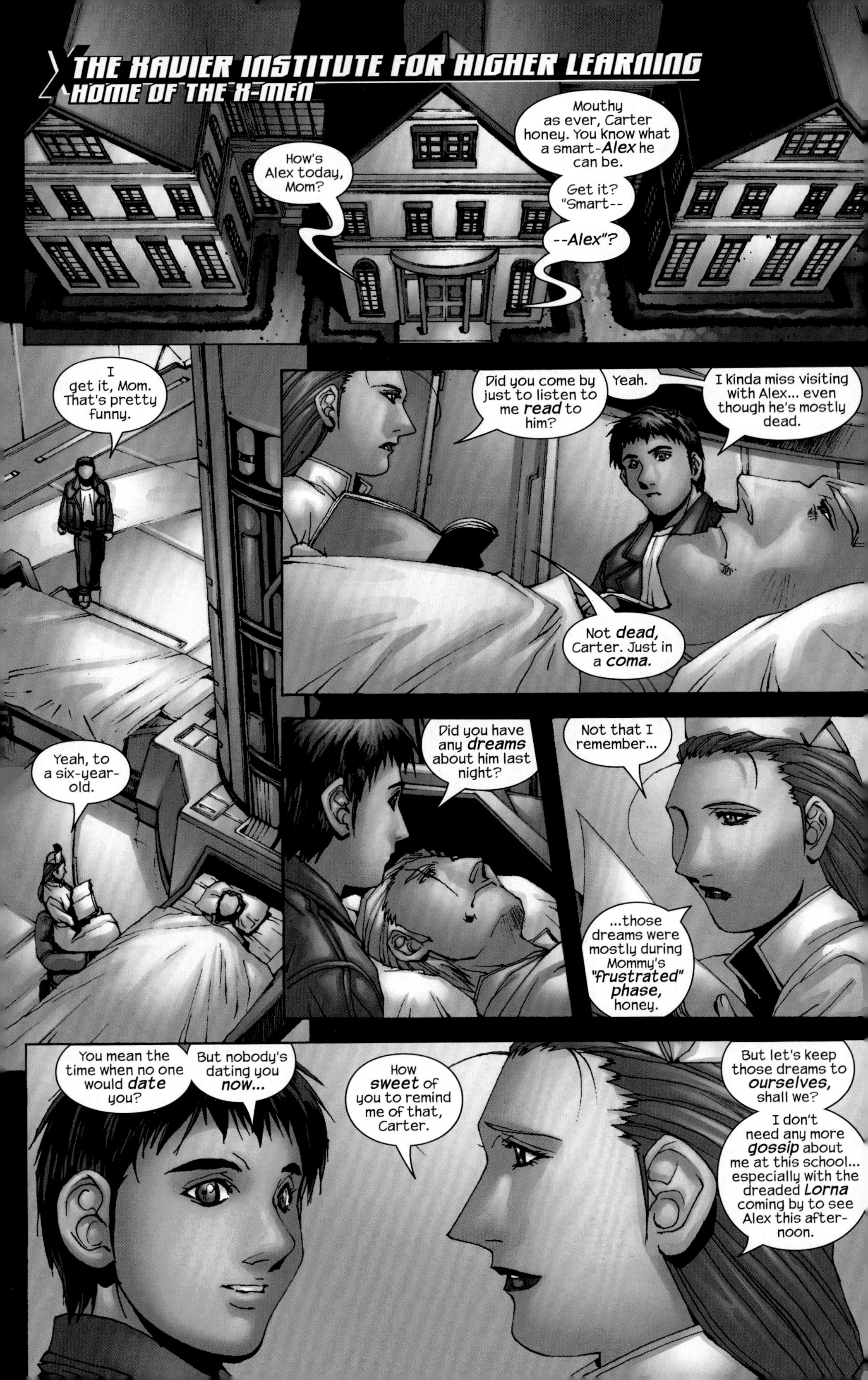
THE XAVIER INSTITUTE FOR HIGHER LEARNING
HOME OF THE X-MEN
How's Alex today, Mom?
Mouthy as ever, Carter honey. You know what a smart-Alex he can be.
Get it? "Smart--
--Alex"?
I get it, Mom. That's pretty funny.
Yeah, to a six-year-old.
Did you come by just to listen to me read to him?
Yeah.
I kinda miss visiting with Alex... even though he's mostly dead.
Not dead, Carter. Just in a coma.
Did you have any dreams about him last night?
Not that I remember...
...those dreams were mostly during Mommy's "frustrated" phase, honey.
You mean the time when no one would date you?
But nobody's dating you now...
How sweet of you to remind me of that, Carter.
But let's keep those dreams to ourselves, shall we?
I don't need any more gossip about me at this school... especially with the dreaded Lorna coming by to see Alex this after-noon.

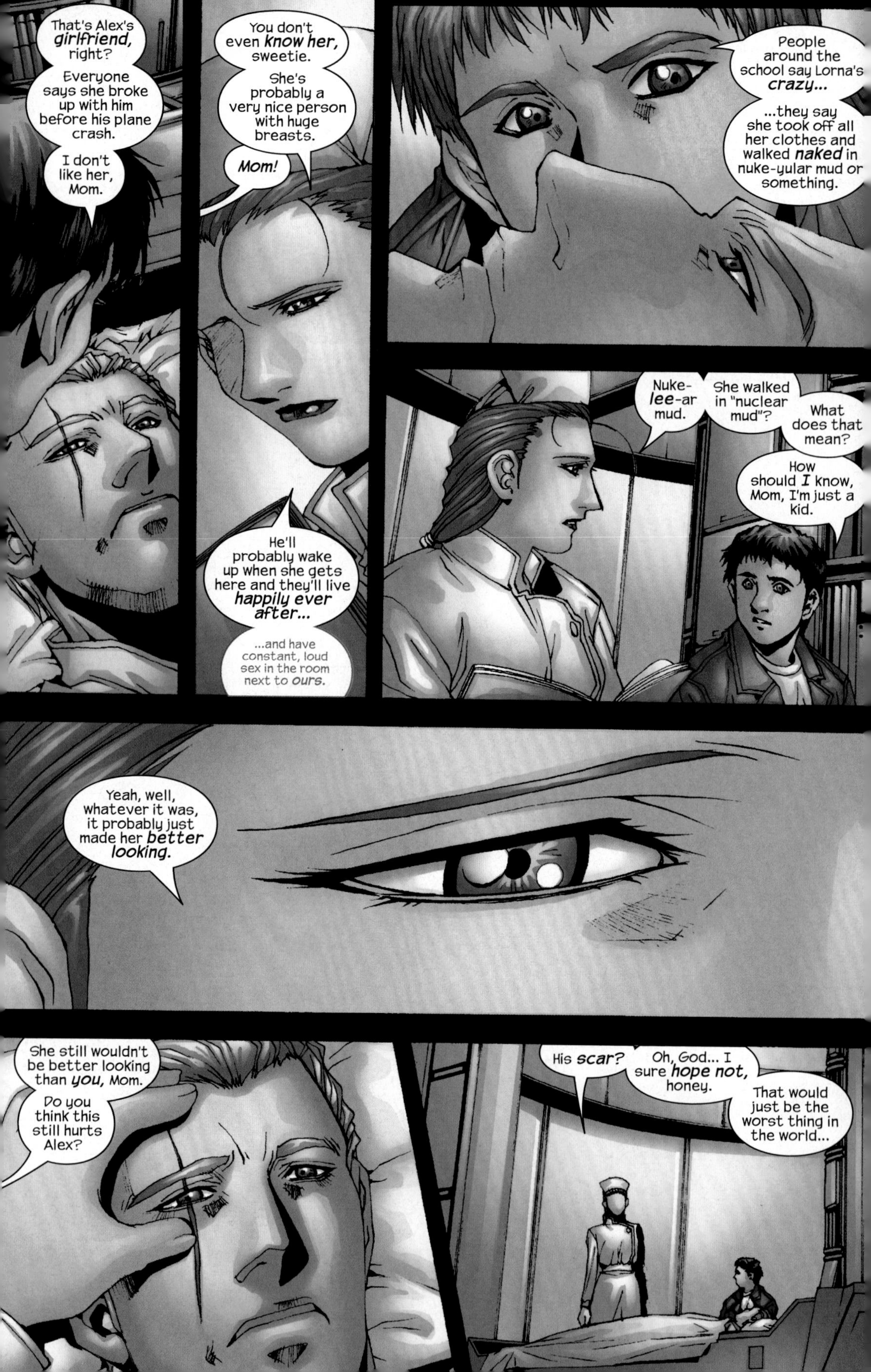
That's Alex's girlfriend, right?
Everyone says she broke up with him before his plane crash.
I don't like her, Mom.
You don't even know her, sweetie.
She's probably a very nice person with huge breasts.
Mom!
He'll probably wake up when she gets here and they'll live happily ever after...
...and have constant, loud sex in the room next to ours.
People around the school say Lorna's crazy...
...they say she took off all her clothes and walked naked in nuke-yular mud or something.
Nuke-lee-ar mud.
She walked in "nuclear mud"?
What does that mean?
How should I know, Mom, I'm just a kid.
Yeah, well, whatever it was, it probably just made her better looking.
She still wouldn't be better looking than you, Mom.
Do you think this still hurts Alex?
His scar?
Oh, God... I sure hope not, honey.
That would just be the worst thing in the world...

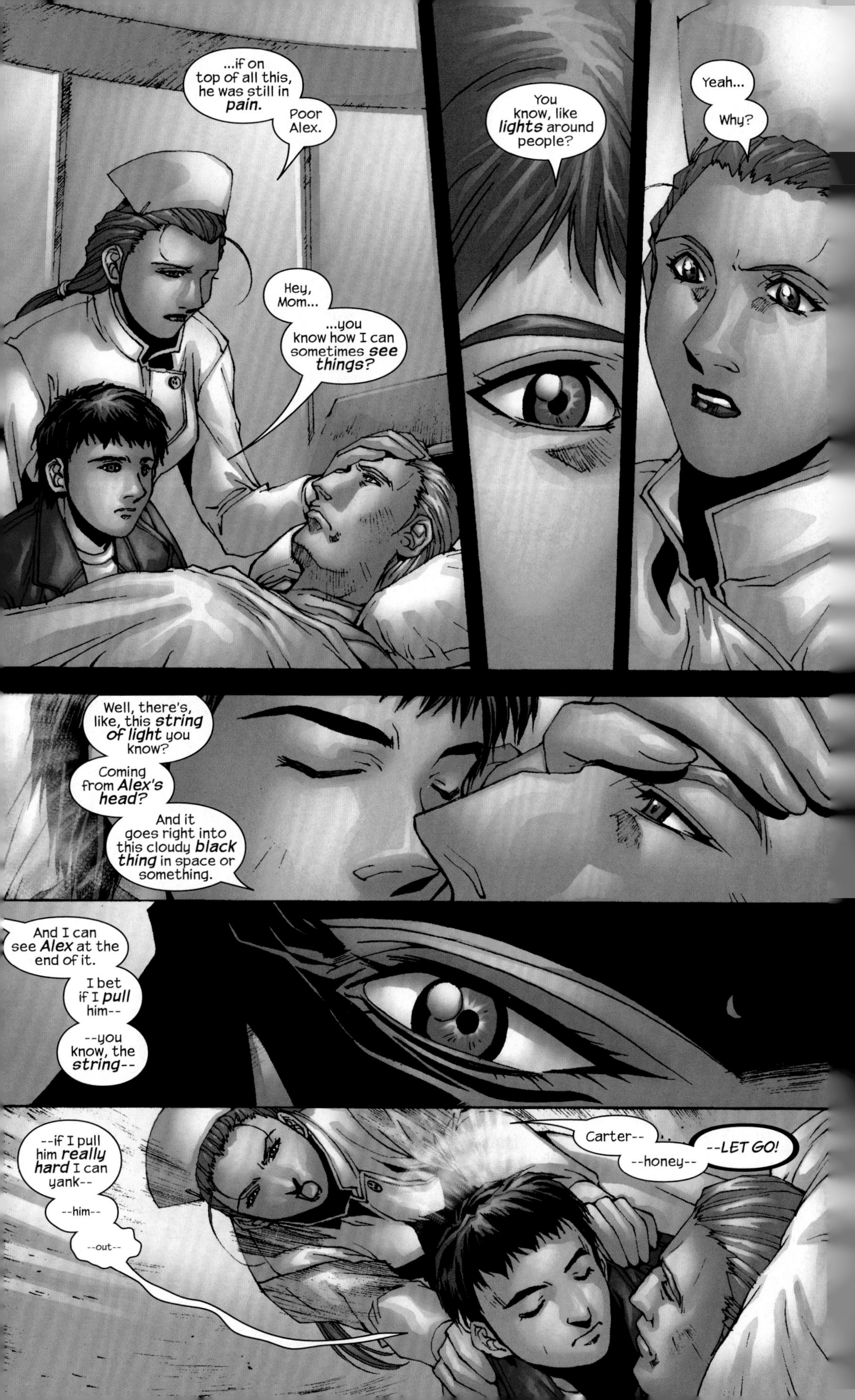

...if on top of all this, he was still in *pain.*
Poor Alex.
Hey, Mom...
...you know how I can sometimes *see things?*
You know, like *lights* around people?
Yeah...
Why?
Well, there's, like, this *string of light* you know?
Coming from *Alex's head?*
And it goes right into this cloudy *black thing* in space or something.
And I can see *Alex* at the end of it.
I bet if I *pull* him--
--you know, the *string*--
--if I pull him *really hard* I can yank--
--him--
--out--
Carter--
--honey--
--*LET GO!*

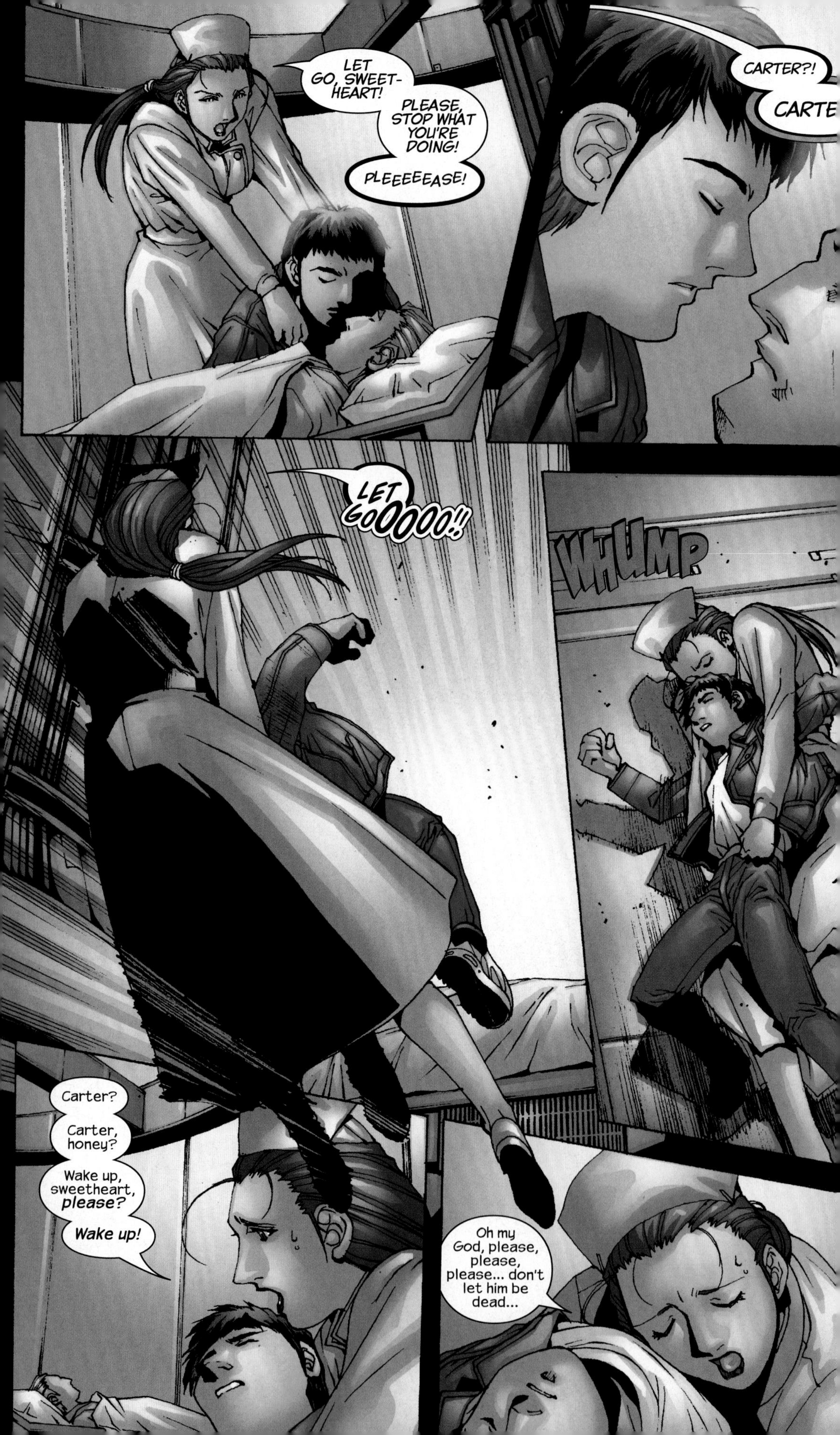

LET GO, SWEET-HEART!
PLEASE, STOP WHAT YOU'RE DOING!
PLEEEEEASE!
CARTER?!
CARTE
LET GOOOOO!!
WHUMP
Carter?
Carter, honey?
Wake up, sweetheart, *please?*
Wake up!
Oh my God, please, please, please... don't let him be dead...

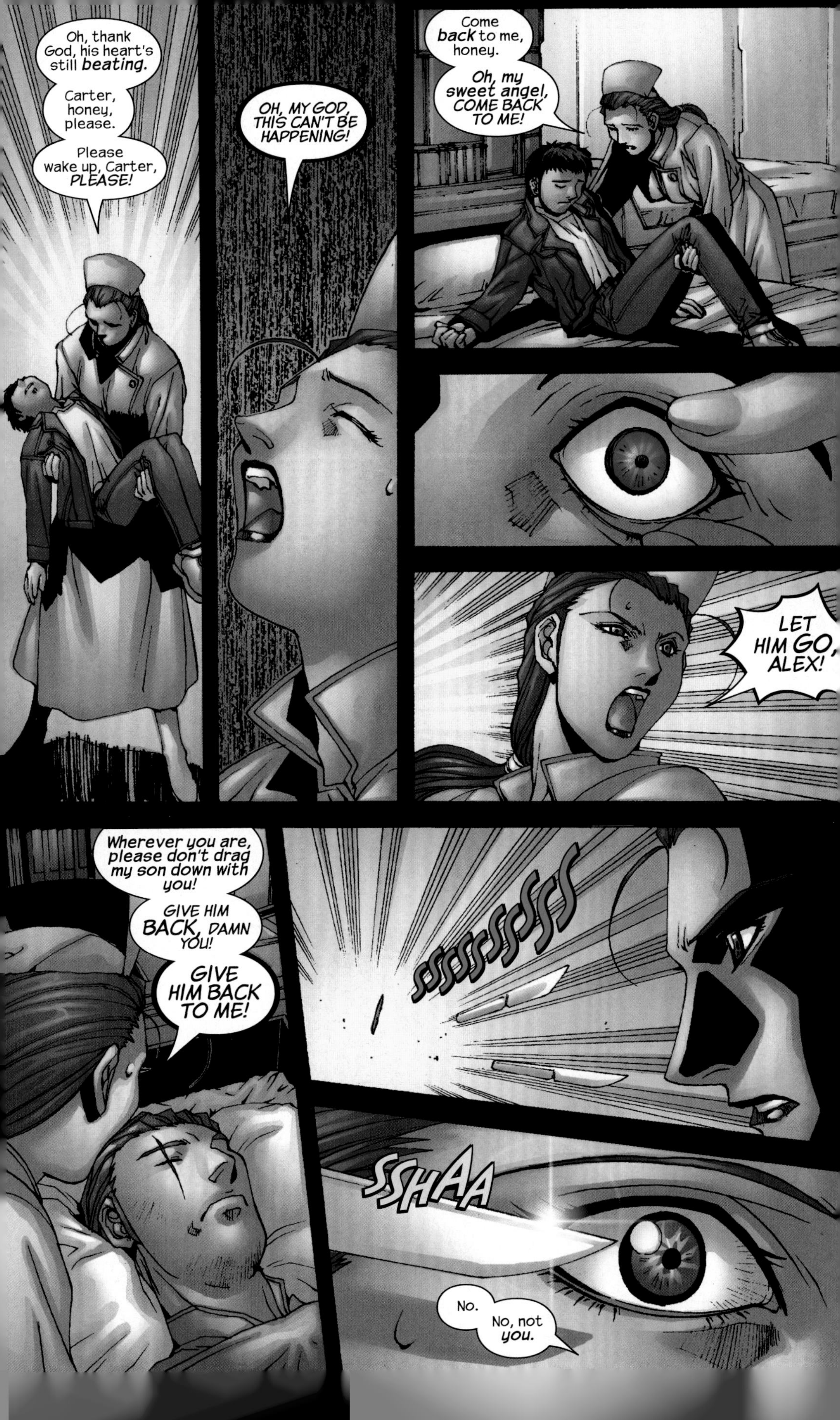
Oh, thank God, his heart's still *beating.*
Carter, honey, please.
Please wake up, Carter, *PLEASE!*
OH, MY GOD, THIS CAN'T BE HAPPENING!
Come *back* to me, honey.
Oh, my sweet angel, COME BACK TO ME!
LET HIM GO, ALEX!
Wherever you are, please don't drag my son down with you!
GIVE HIM BACK, DAMN YOU!
GIVE HIM BACK TO ME!
SSSSSSSSSS
SSHAA
No.
No, not *you.*

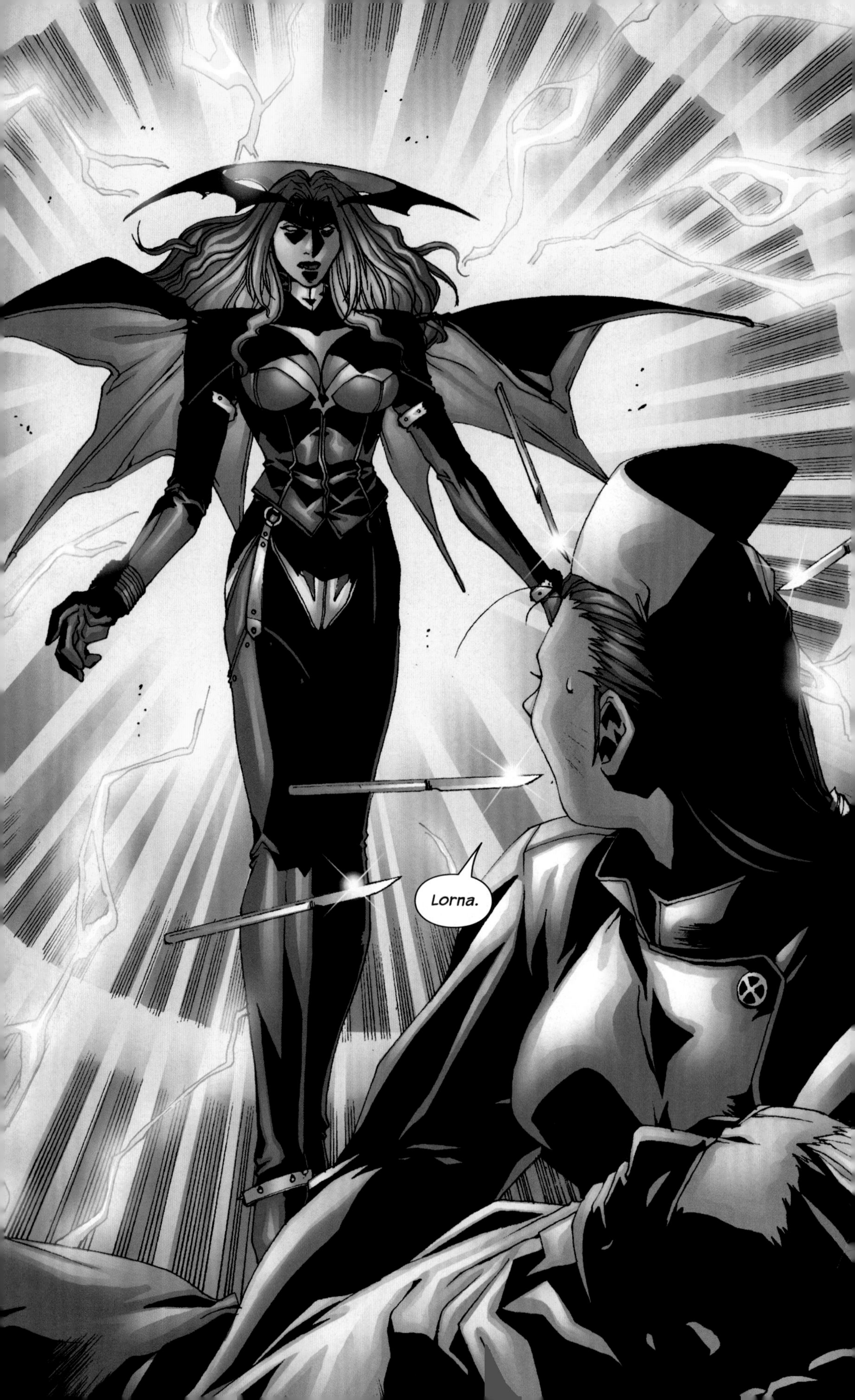
Lorna.

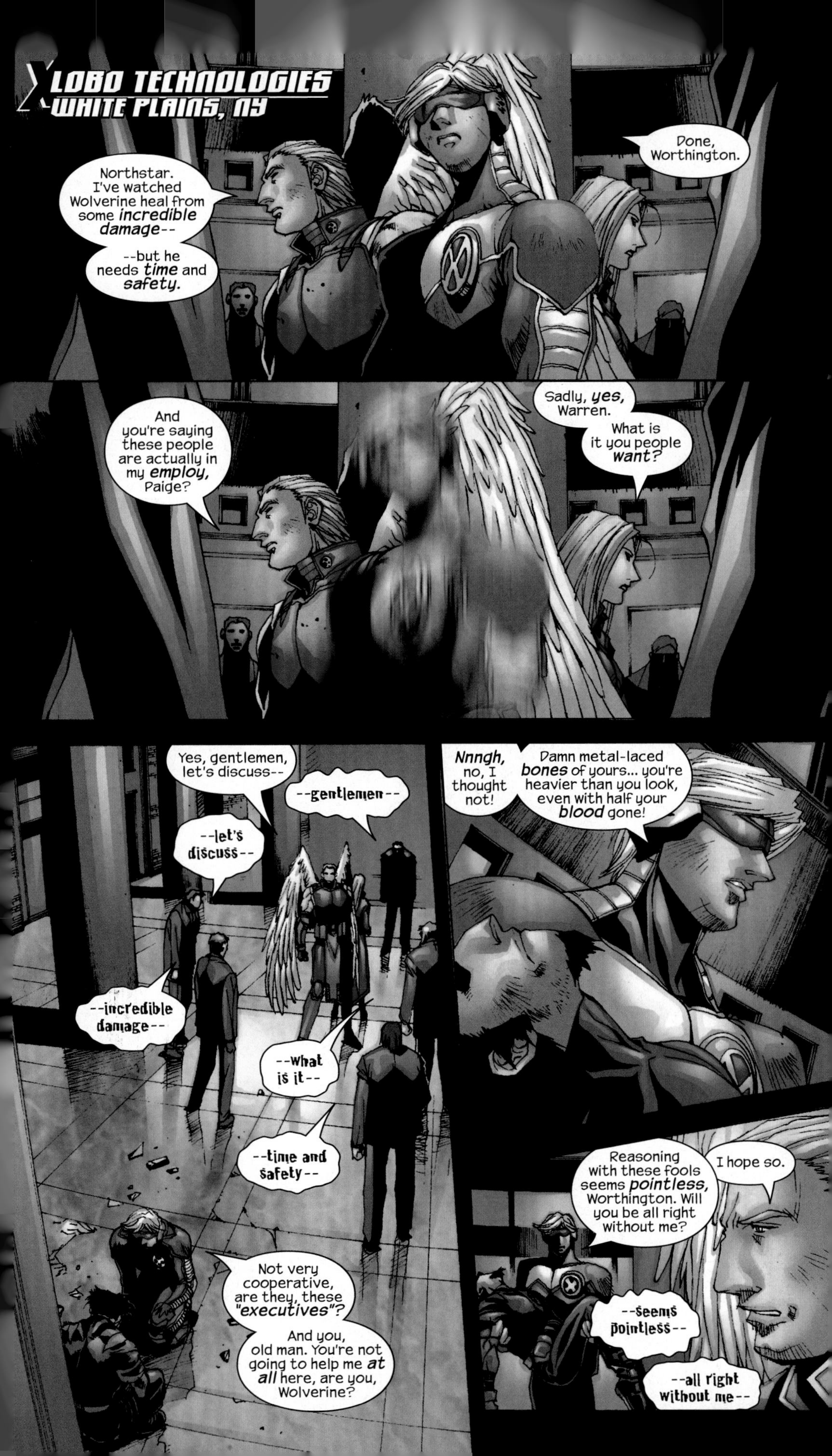

LOBO TECHNOLOGIES -WHITE PLAINS, NY
Northstar. I've watched Wolverine heal from some *incredible damage*--
--but he needs *time* and *safety*.
Done, Worthington.
And you're saying these people are actually in my *employ*, Paige?
Sadly, *yes*, Warren.
What is it you people *want*?
Yes, gentlemen, let's discuss--
--gentlemen--
--let's discuss--
--incredible damage--
--what is it--
--time and safety--
Not very cooperative, are they, these *"executives"*?
And you, old man. You're not going to help me *at all* here, are you, Wolverine?
Nnngh, no, I thought not!
Damn metal-laced *bones* of yours... you're heavier than you look, even with half your *blood* gone!
Reasoning with these fools seems *pointless*, Worthington. Will you be all right without me?
I hope so.
--seems pointless--
--all right without me--

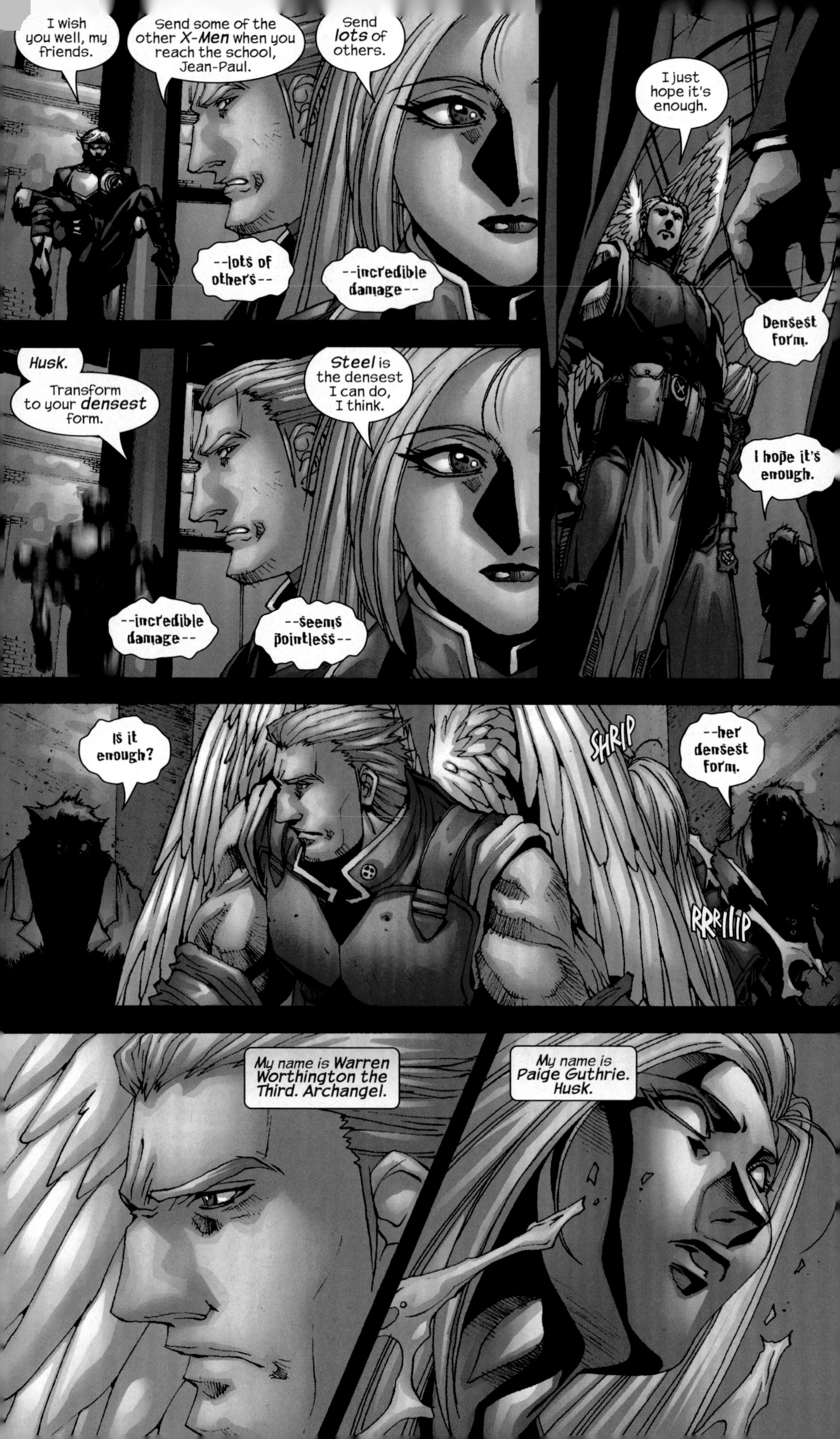
I wish you well, my friends.
Send some of the other X-Men when you reach the school, Jean-Paul.
Send lots of others.
--lots of others--
--incredible damage--
I just hope it's enough.
Densest form.
I hope it's enough.
Husk.
Transform to your densest form.
Steel is the densest I can do, I think.
--incredible damage--
--seems pointless--
Is it enough?
SHRIP
--her densest form.
RRRIIIP
My name is Warren Worthington the Third. Archangel.
My name is Paige Guthrie. Husk.

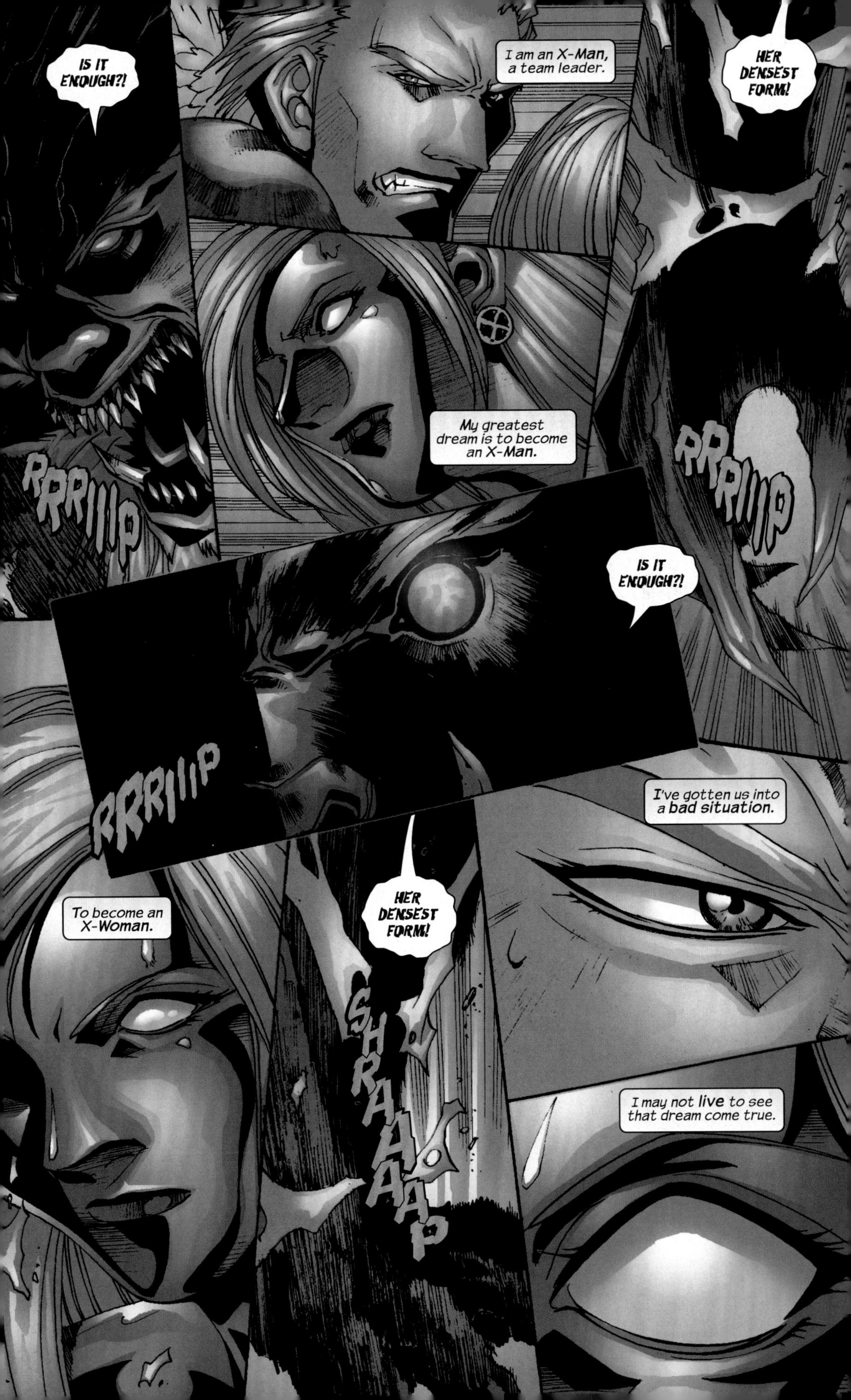
IS IT ENOUGH?!
I am an X-Man, a team leader.
HER DENSEST FORM!
My greatest dream is to become an X-Man.
RRRIIIP
RRRIIIP
IS IT ENOUGH?!
RRRIIIP
I've gotten us into a bad situation.
To become an X-Woman.
HER DENSEST FORM!
SHRAAAAP
I may not live to see that dream come true.

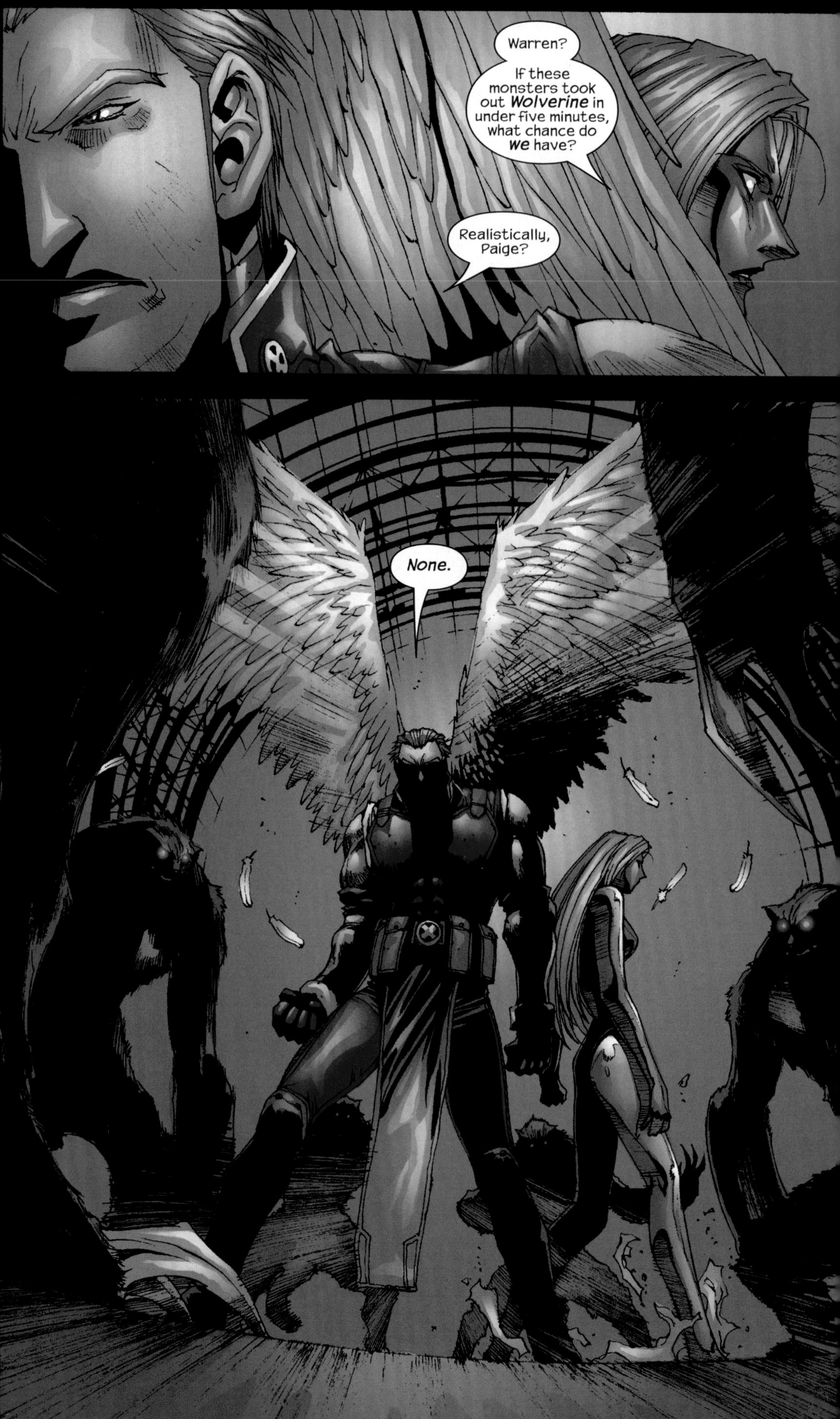
Warren?
If these monsters took out *Wolverine* in under five minutes, what chance do *we* have?
Realistically, Paige?
None.

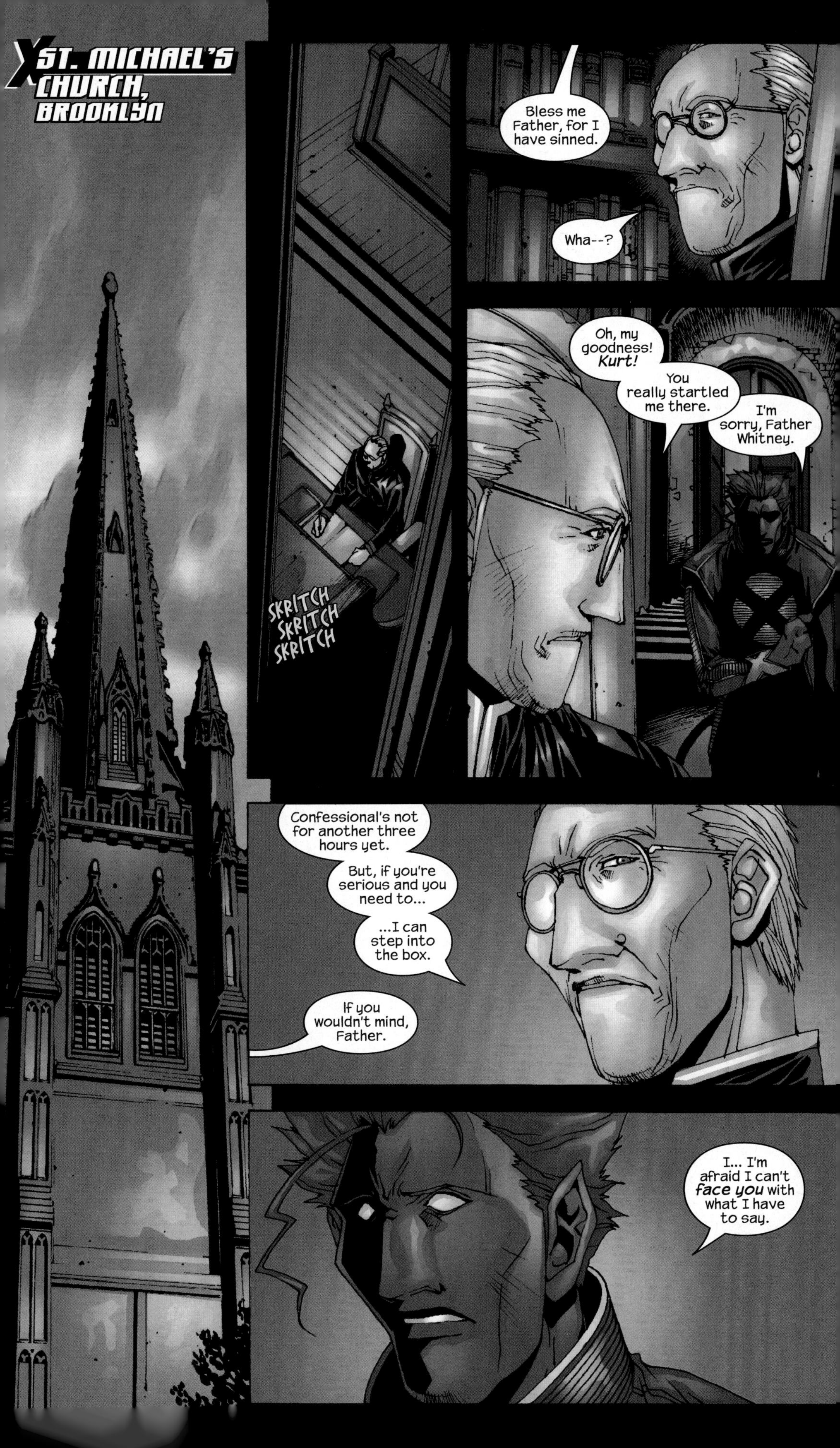
ST. MICHAEL'S CHURCH, BROOKLYN
Bless me Father, for I have sinned.
Wha--?
SKRITCH SKRITCH SKRITCH
Oh, my goodness! *Kurt!*
You really startled me there.
I'm sorry, Father Whitney.
Confessional's not for another three hours yet.
But, if you're serious and you need to...
...I can step into the box.
If you wouldn't mind, Father.
I... I'm afraid I can't *face you* with what I have to say.

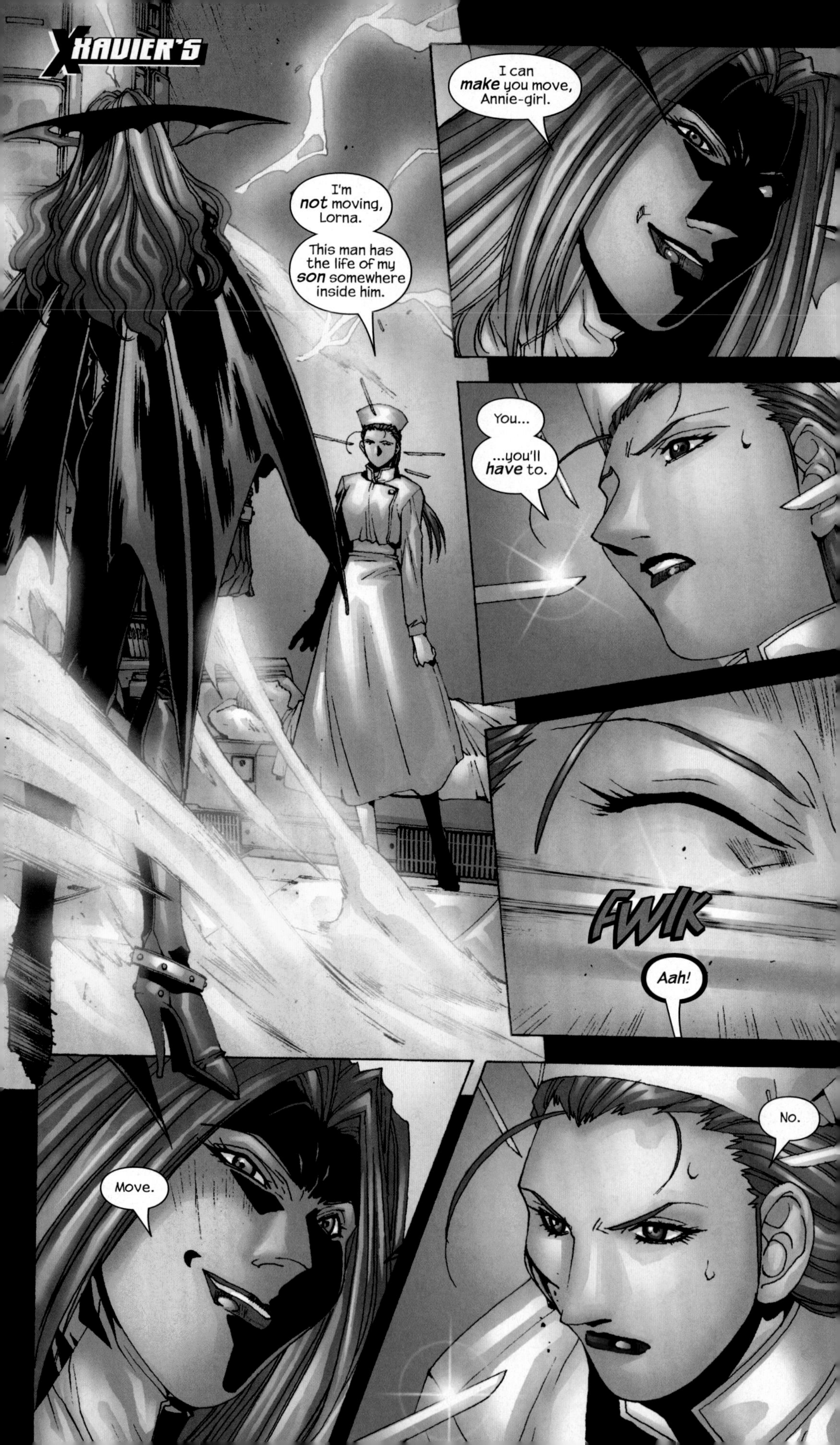
XAVIER'S
I can make you move, Annie-girl.
I'm not moving, Lorna.
This man has the life of my son somewhere inside him.
You...
...you'll have to.
FWIK
Aah!
Move.
No.

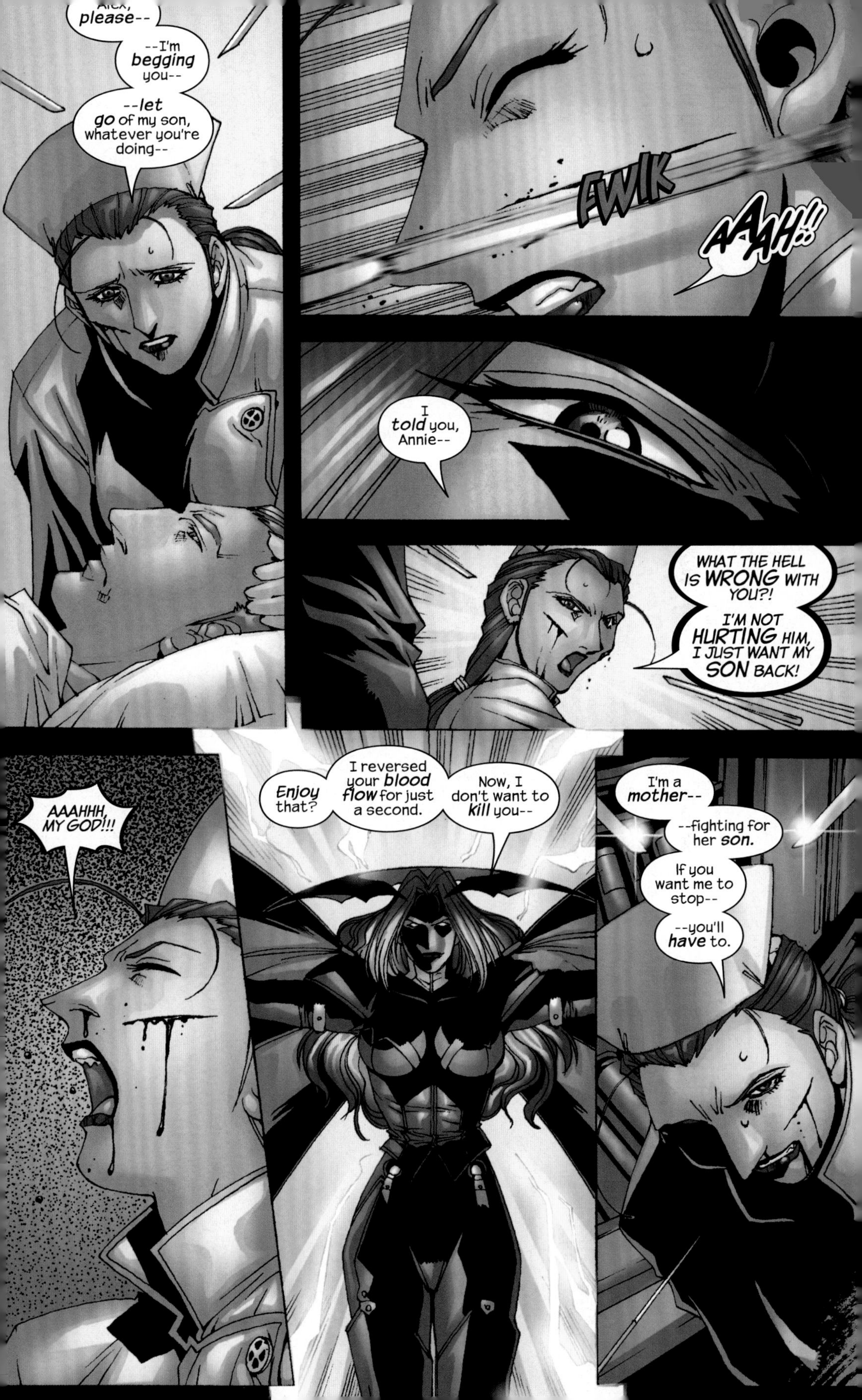
please--
--I'm begging you--
--let go of my son, whatever you're doing--
FWIK
AAAH!!
I told you, Annie--
WHAT THE HELL IS WRONG WITH YOU?!
I'M NOT HURTING HIM, I JUST WANT MY SON BACK!
AAAHHH, MY GOD!!!
Enjoy that?
I reversed your blood flow for just a second.
Now, I don't want to kill you--
I'm a mother--
--fighting for her son.
If you want me to stop--
--you'll have to.

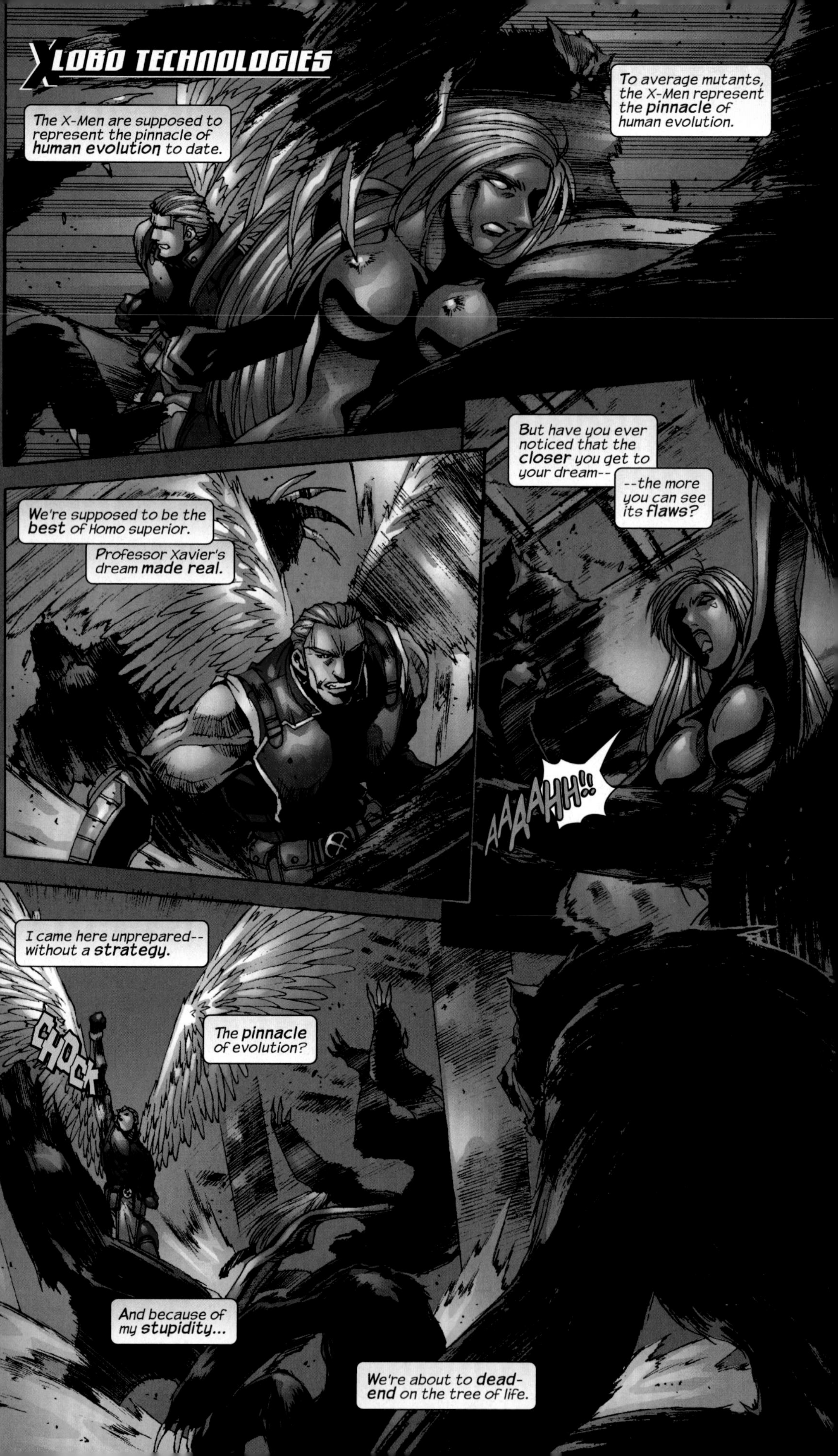
LOBO TECHNOLOGIES
The X-Men are supposed to represent the pinnacle of human evolution to date.
To average mutants, the X-Men represent the pinnacle of human evolution.
We're supposed to be the best of Homo superior.
Professor Xavier's dream made real.
But have you ever noticed that the closer you get to your dream--
--the more you can see its flaws?
AAAAHH!!
I came here unprepared--without a strategy.
CHOCK
The pinnacle of evolution?
And because of my stupidity...
We're about to dead-end on the tree of life.

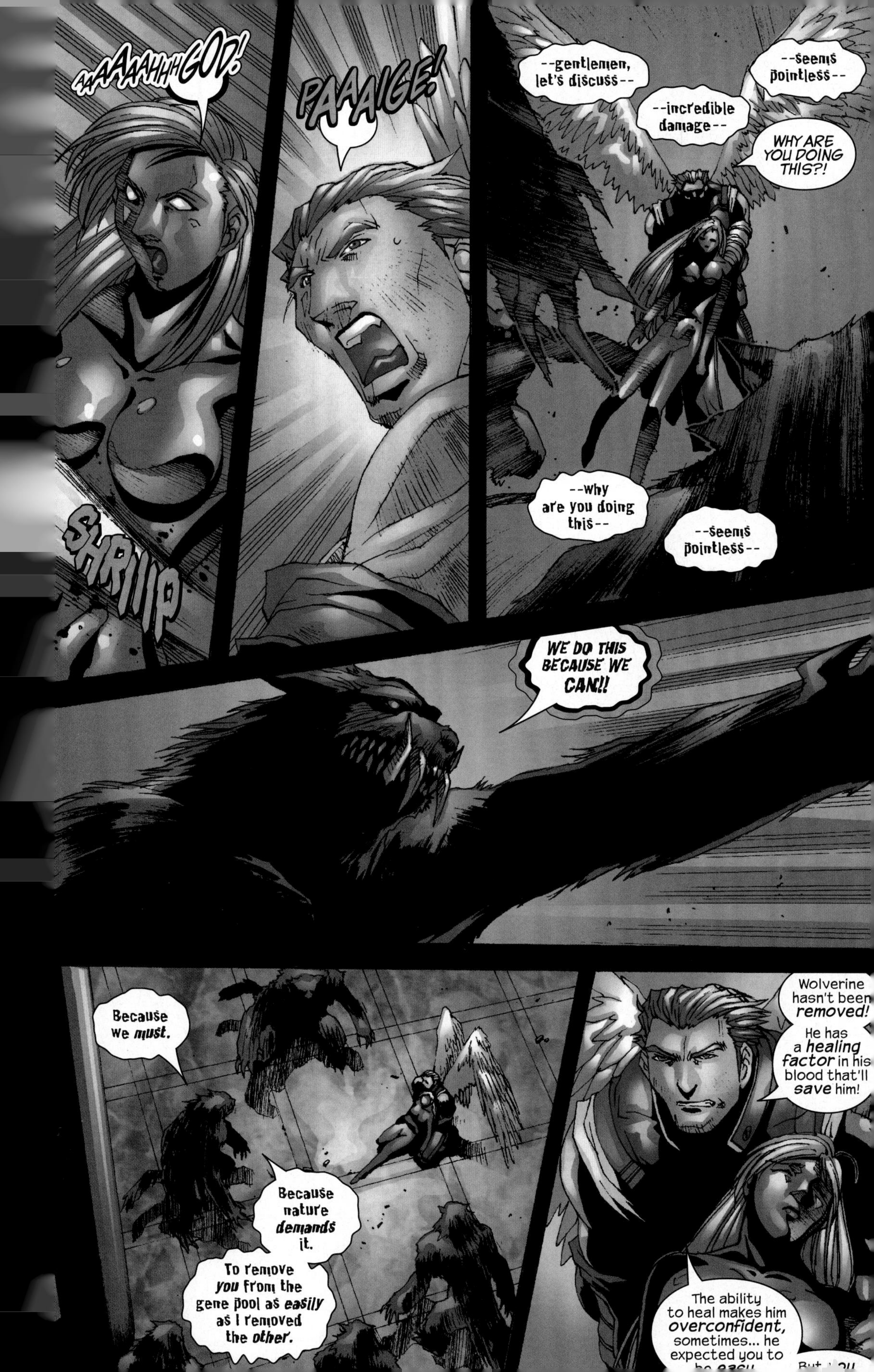
aaAAAAHHGOD!
SHRIIIP
PAAAIGE!
--gentlemen, let's discuss--
--seems pointless--
--incredible damage--
WHY ARE YOU DOING THIS?!
--why are you doing this--
--seems pointless--
WE DO THIS BECAUSE WE CAN!!
Because we must.
Because nature demands it.
To remove you from the gene pool as easily as I removed the other.
Wolverine hasn't been removed!
He has a healing factor in his blood that'll save him!
The ability to heal makes him overconfident, sometimes... he expected you to

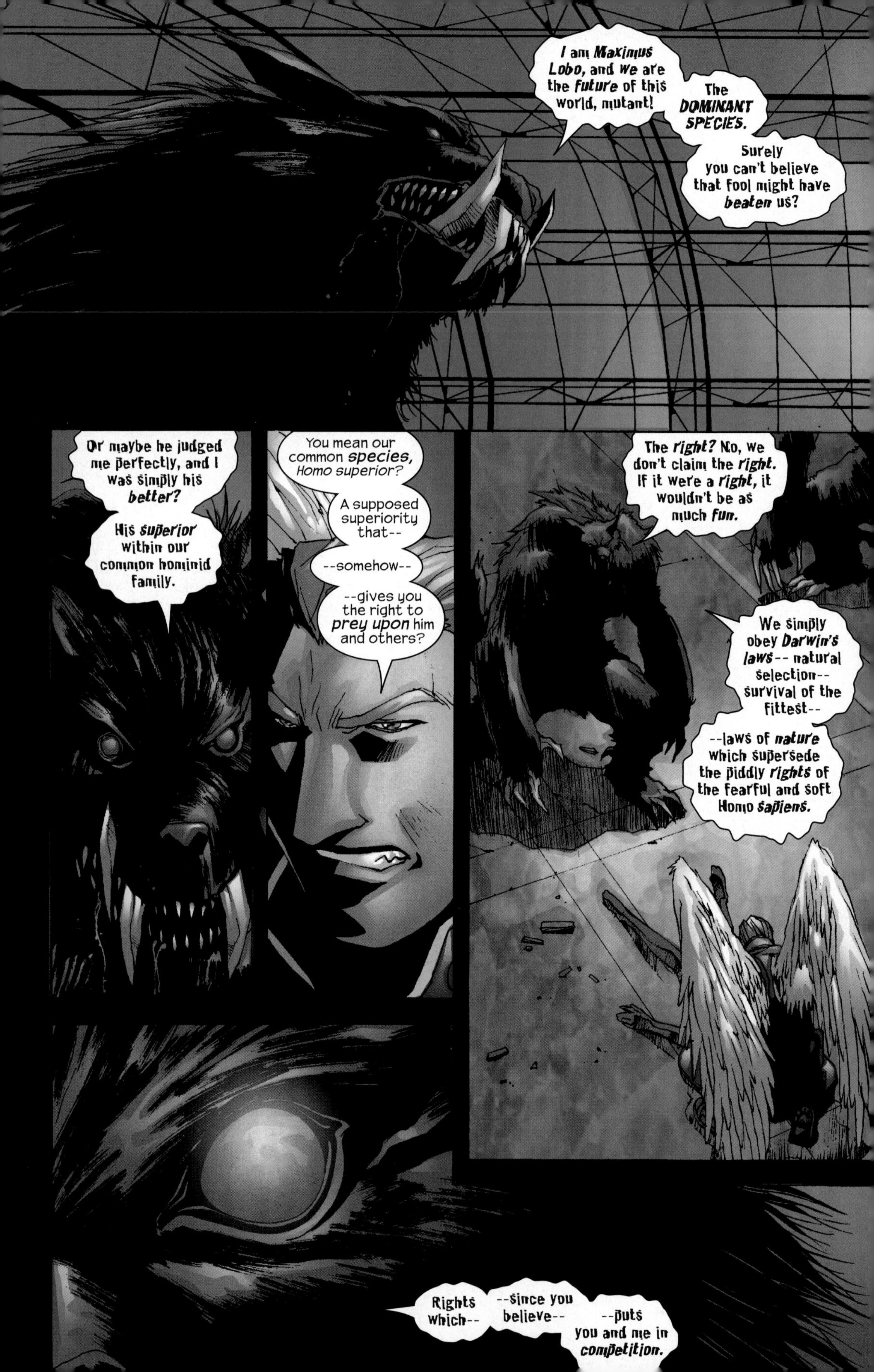
I am Maximus Lobo, and we are the future of this world, mutant!
The DOMINANT SPECIES.
Surely you can't believe that fool might have beaten us?
Or maybe he judged me perfectly, and I was simply his better?
His superior within our common hominid family.
You mean our common species, Homo superior?
A supposed superiority that--
--somehow--
--gives you the right to prey upon him and others?
The right? No, we don't claim the right. If it were a right, it wouldn't be as much fun.
We simply obey Darwin's laws-- natural selection-- survival of the fittest--
--laws of nature which supersede the piddly rights of the fearful and soft Homo sapiens.
Rights which--
--since you believe--
--puts you and me in competition.

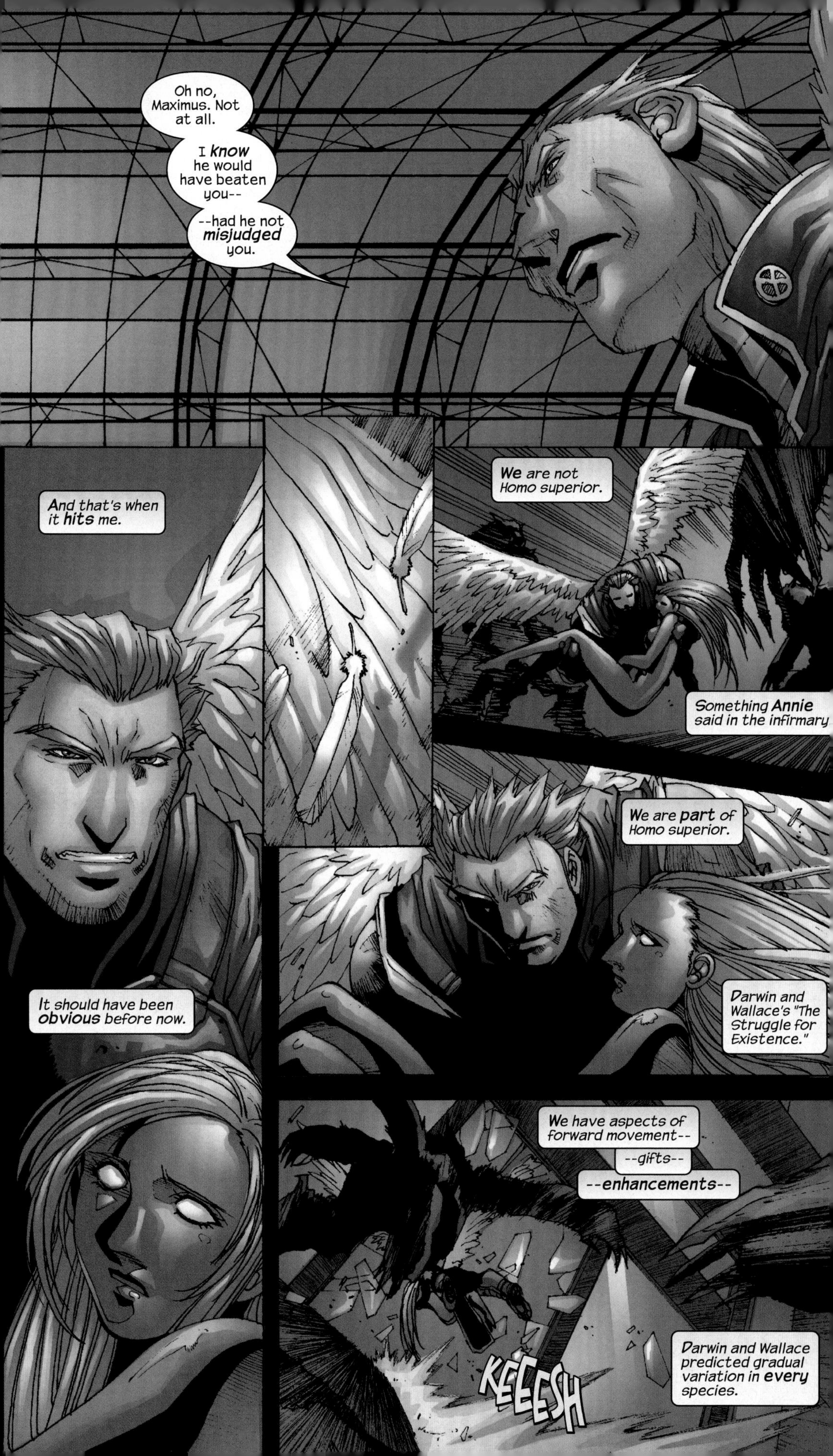
Oh no, Maximus. Not at all.
I know he would have beaten you--
--had he not misjudged you.
And that's when it hits me.
We are not Homo superior.
Something Annie said in the infirmary
It should have been obvious before now.
We are part of Homo superior.
Darwin and Wallace's "The Struggle for Existence."
We have aspects of forward movement--
--gifts--
--enhancements--
Darwin and Wallace predicted gradual variation in every species.
KEEESH

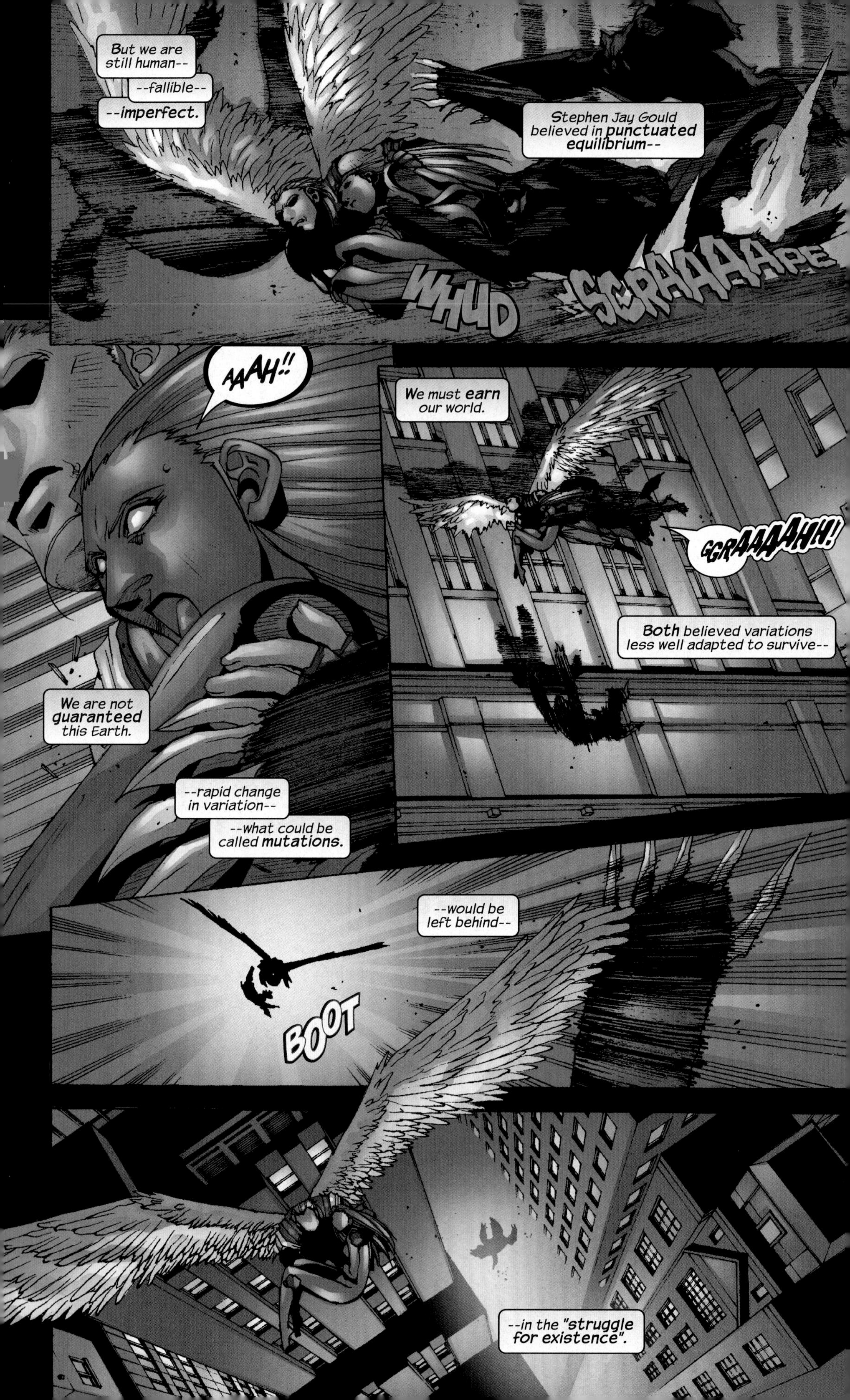
But we are still human--
--fallible--
--imperfect.
Stephen Jay Gould believed in punctuated equilibrium--
WHUD
SCRAAAAAPE
AAAH!!
We must earn our world.
GGRAAAAAHH!
Both believed variations less well adapted to survive--
We are not guaranteed this Earth.
--rapid change in variation--
--what could be called mutations.
--would be left behind--
BOOT
--in the "struggle for existence".

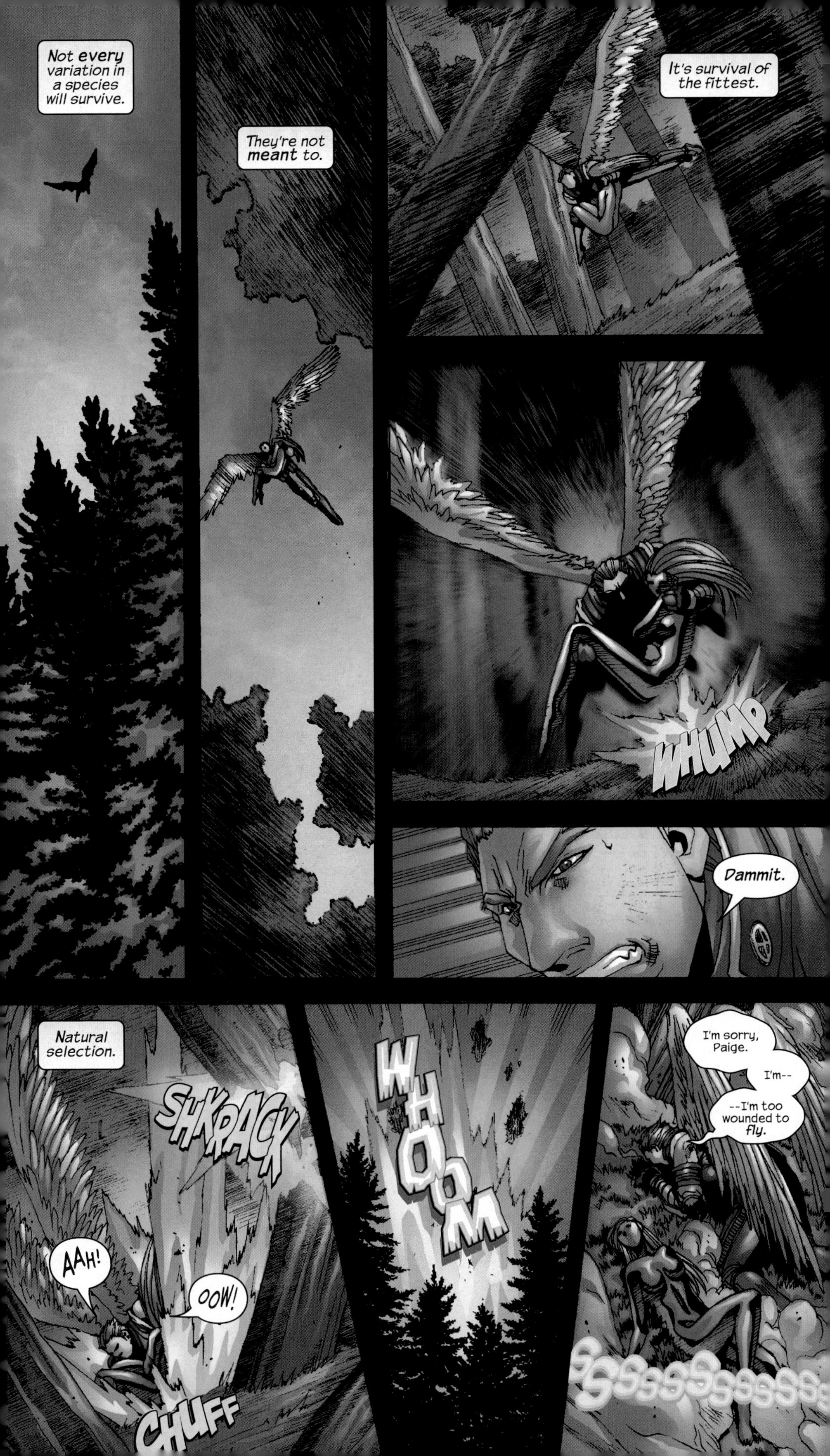
Not every variation in a species will survive.
They're not meant to.
It's survival of the fittest.
WHUMP
Dammit.
Natural selection.
SHKRACK
AAH!
OOW!
CHUFF
WHOOOM
I'm sorry, Paige.
I'm--
--I'm too wounded to fly.
SSSSSSSSSSSSSS

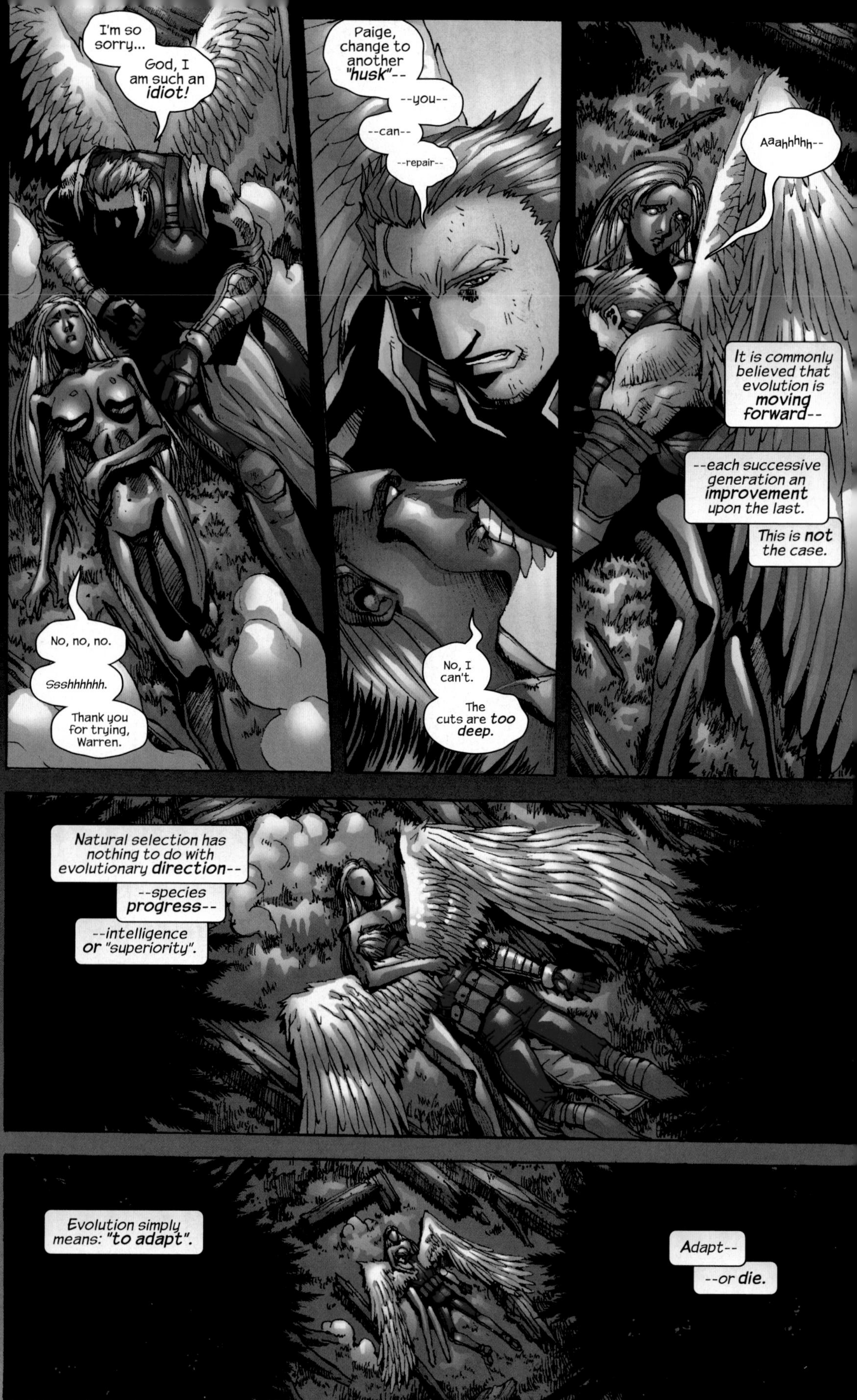

I'm so sorry...
God, I am such an idiot!
No, no, no.
Ssshhhhhh.
Thank you for trying, Warren.
Paige, change to another "husk"--
--you--
--can--
--repair--
No, I can't.
The cuts are too deep.
Aaahhhhh--
It is commonly believed that evolution is moving forward--
--each successive generation an improvement upon the last.
This is not the case.
Natural selection has nothing to do with evolutionary direction--
--species progress--
--intelligence or "superiority".
Evolution simply means: "to adapt".
Adapt--
--or die.

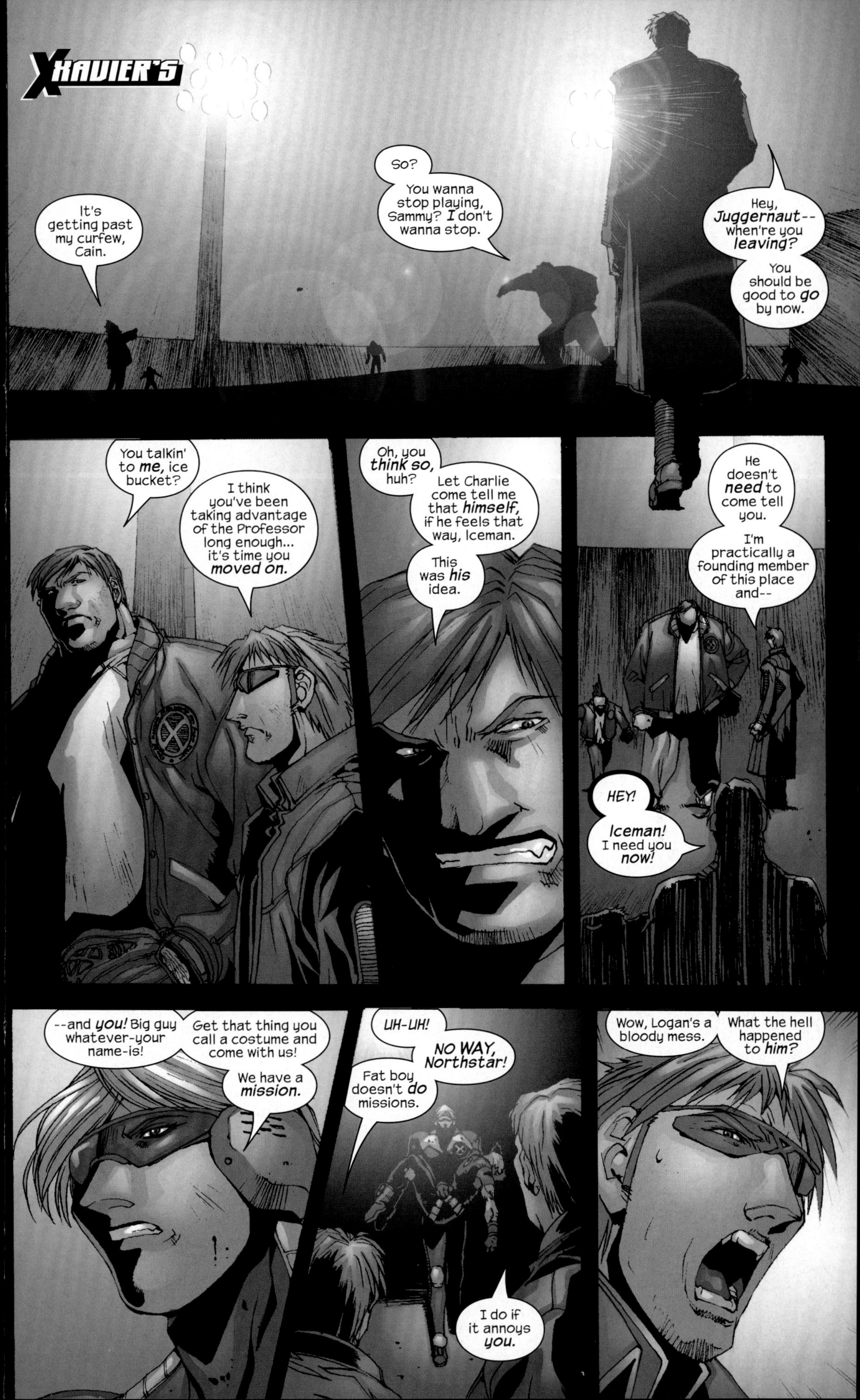
XAVIER'S
It's getting past my curfew, Cain.
So?
You wanna stop playing, Sammy? I don't wanna stop.
Hey, Juggernaut-- when're you leaving?
You should be good to go by now.
You talkin' to me, ice bucket?
I think you've been taking advantage of the Professor long enough... it's time you moved on.
Oh, you think so, huh?
Let Charlie come tell me that himself, if he feels that way, Iceman.
This was his idea.
He doesn't need to come tell you.
I'm practically a founding member of this place and--
HEY!
Iceman! I need you now!
--and you! Big guy whatever-your name-is!
Get that thing you call a costume and come with us!
We have a mission.
UH-UH!
NO WAY, Northstar!
Fat boy doesn't do missions.
I do if it annoys you.
Wow, Logan's a bloody mess.
What the hell happened to him?

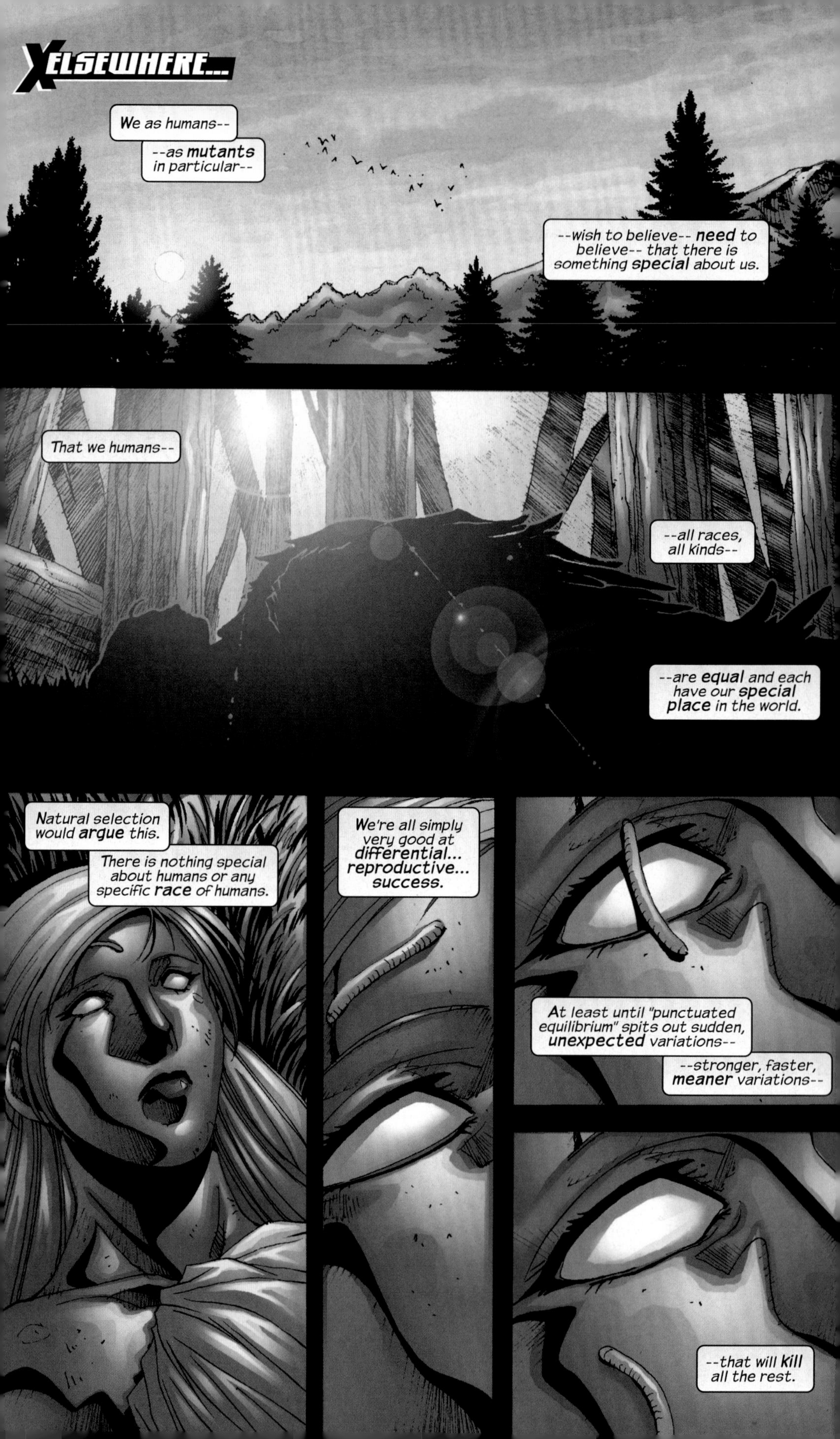
X-ELSEWHERE...
We as humans--
--as mutants in particular--
--wish to believe-- need to believe-- that there is something special about us.
That we humans--
--all races, all kinds--
--are equal and each have our special place in the world.
Natural selection would argue this.
There is nothing special about humans or any specific race of humans.
We're all simply very good at differential... reproductive... success.
At least until "punctuated equilibrium" spits out sudden, unexpected variations--
--stronger, faster, meaner variations--
--that will kill all the rest.

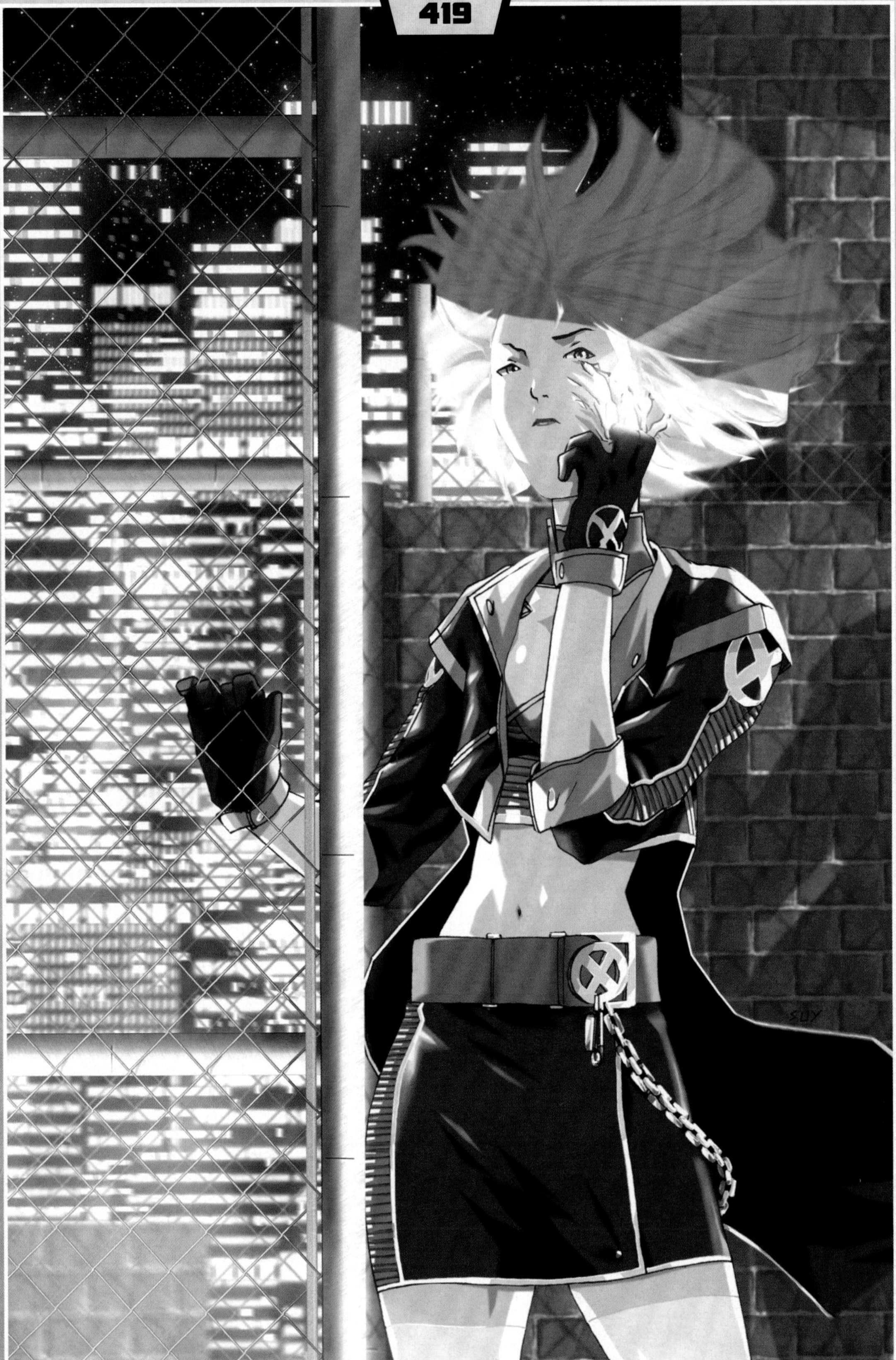
SUY

DOMINANT SPECIES, PART III

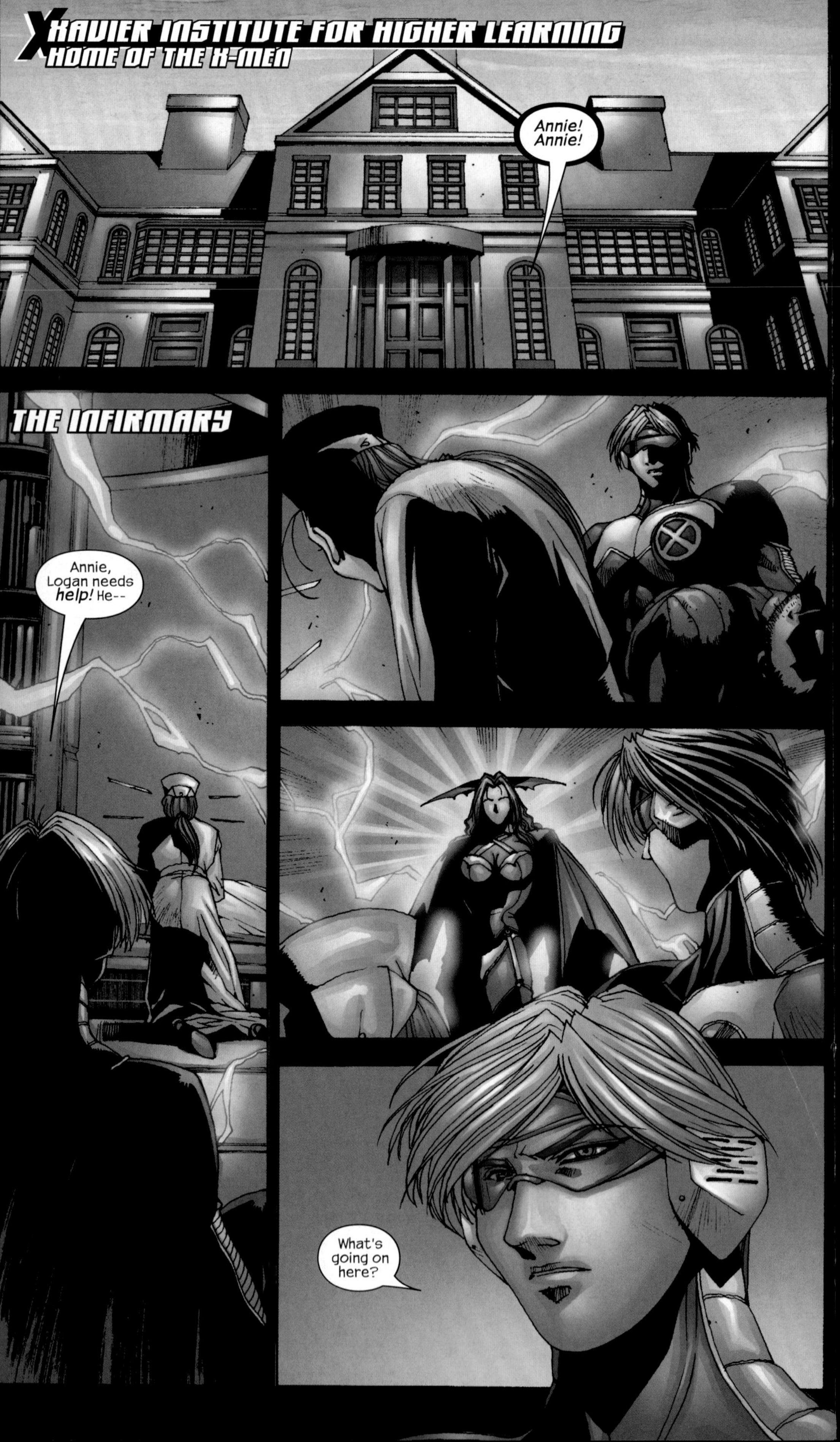
XAVIER INSTITUTE FOR HIGHER LEARNING
HOME OF THE X-MEN
Annie! Annie!
THE INFIRMARY
Annie, Logan needs help! He--
What's going on here?

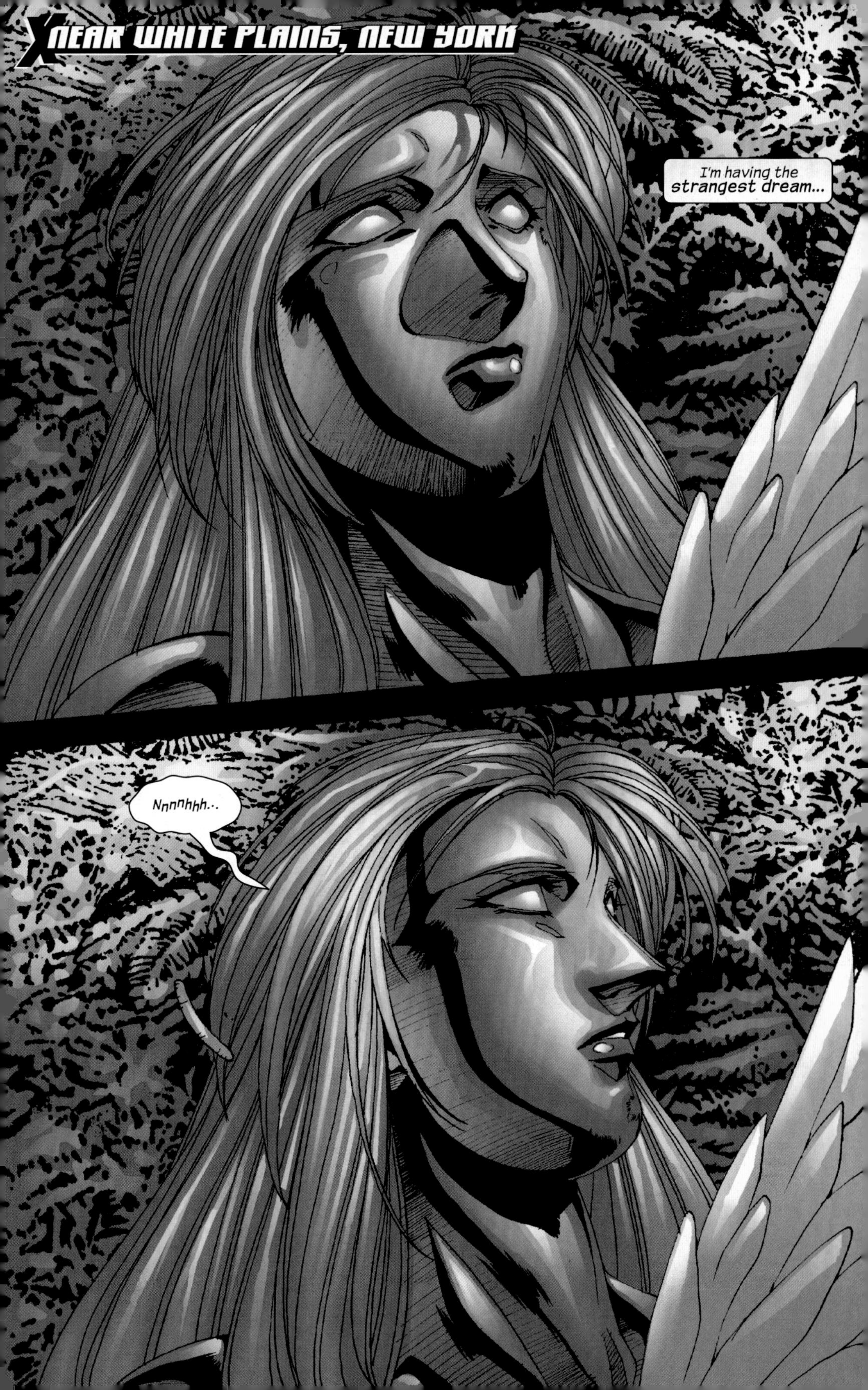
NEAR WHITE PLAINS, NEW YORK
I'm having the strangest dream...
Nnnnhhh...

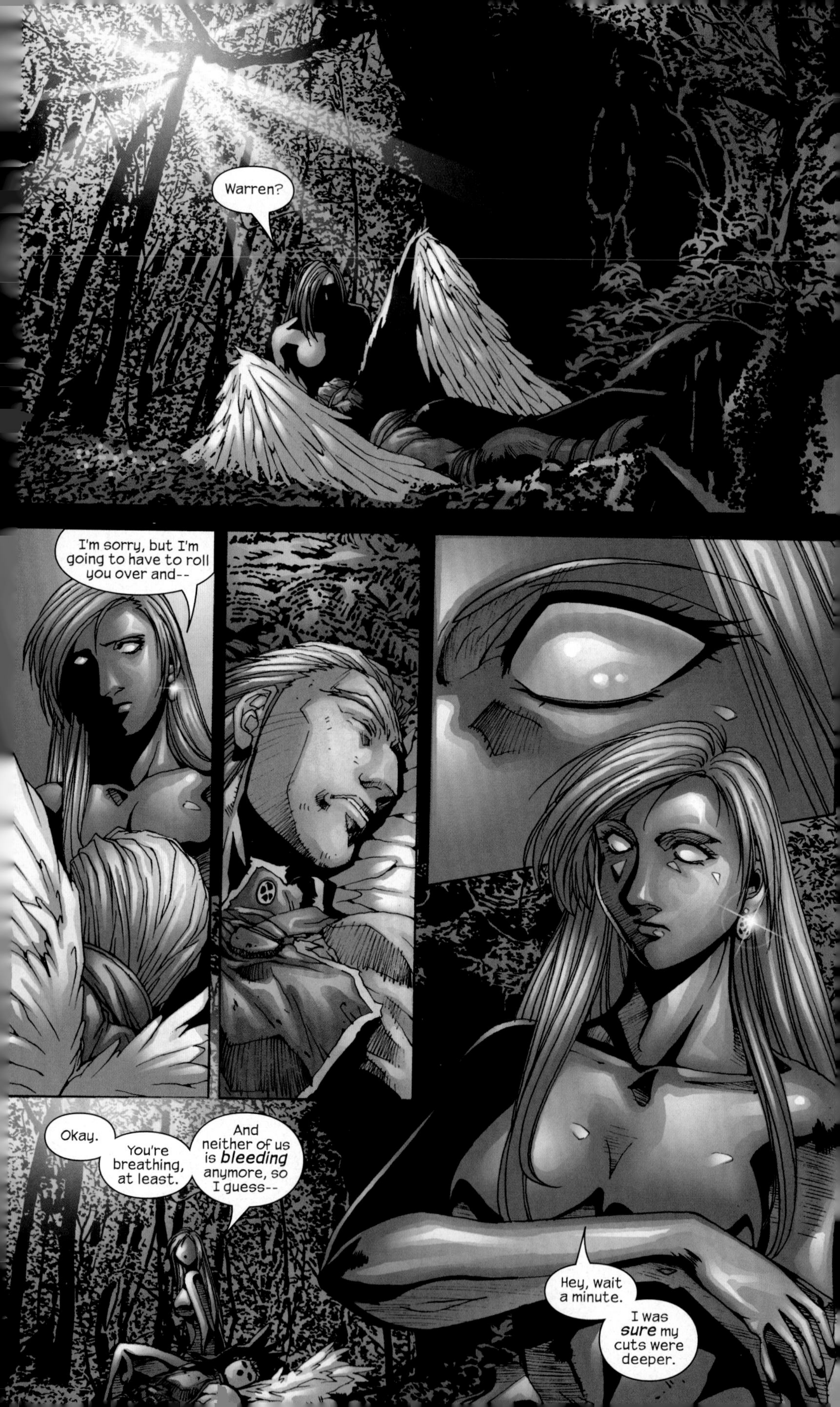
Warren?
I'm sorry, but I'm going to have to roll you over and--
Okay.
You're breathing, at least.
And neither of us is ***bleeding*** anymore, so I guess--
Hey, wait a minute.
I was ***sure*** my cuts were deeper.

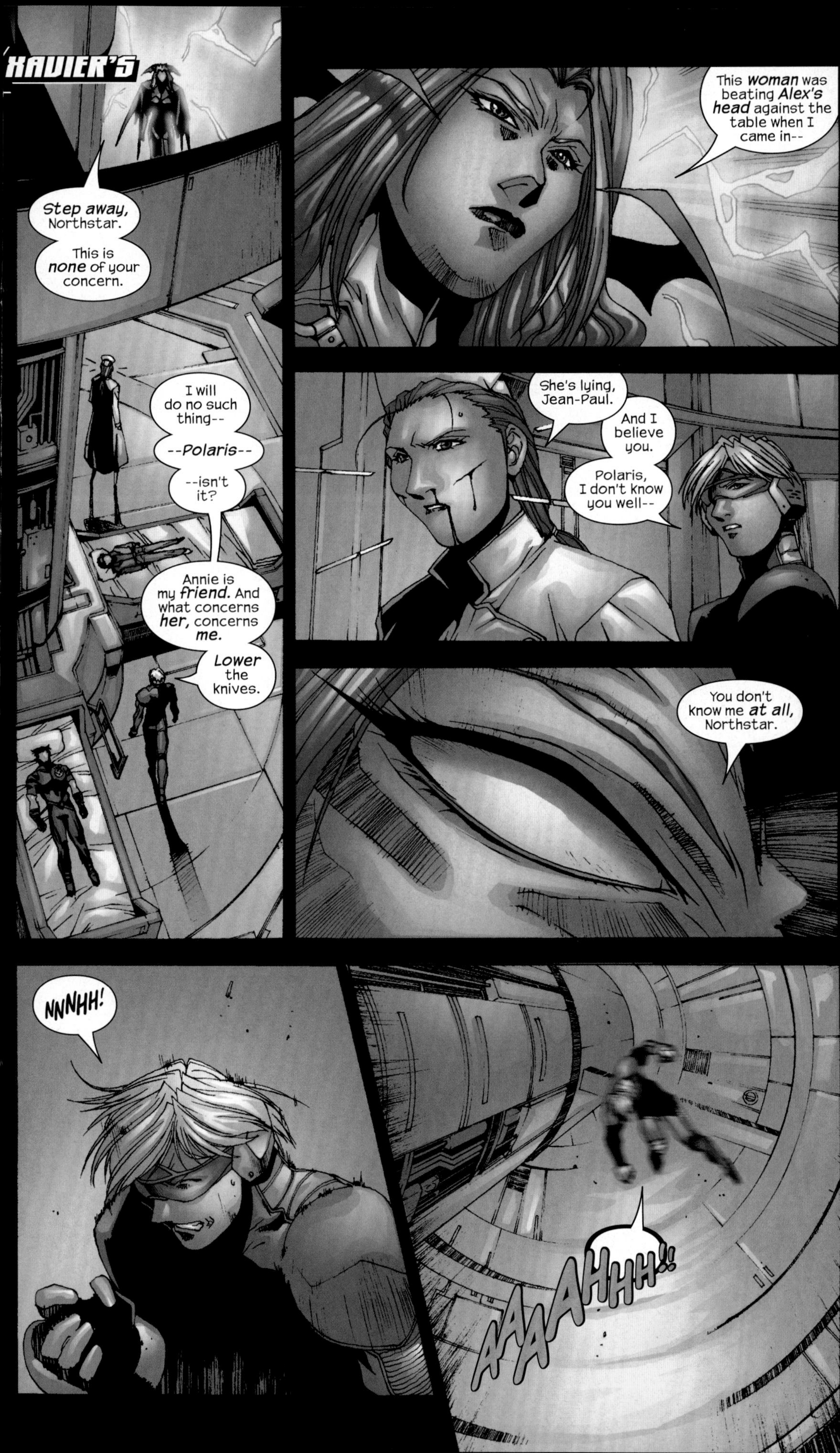
XAVIER'S
Step away, Northstar.
This is none of your concern.
This woman was beating Alex's head against the table when I came in--
I will do no such thing--
--Polaris--
--isn't it?
Annie is my friend. And what concerns her, concerns me.
Lower the knives.
She's lying, Jean-Paul.
And I believe you.
Polaris, I don't know you well--
You don't know me at all, Northstar.
NNNHH!
AAAAAHHH!!

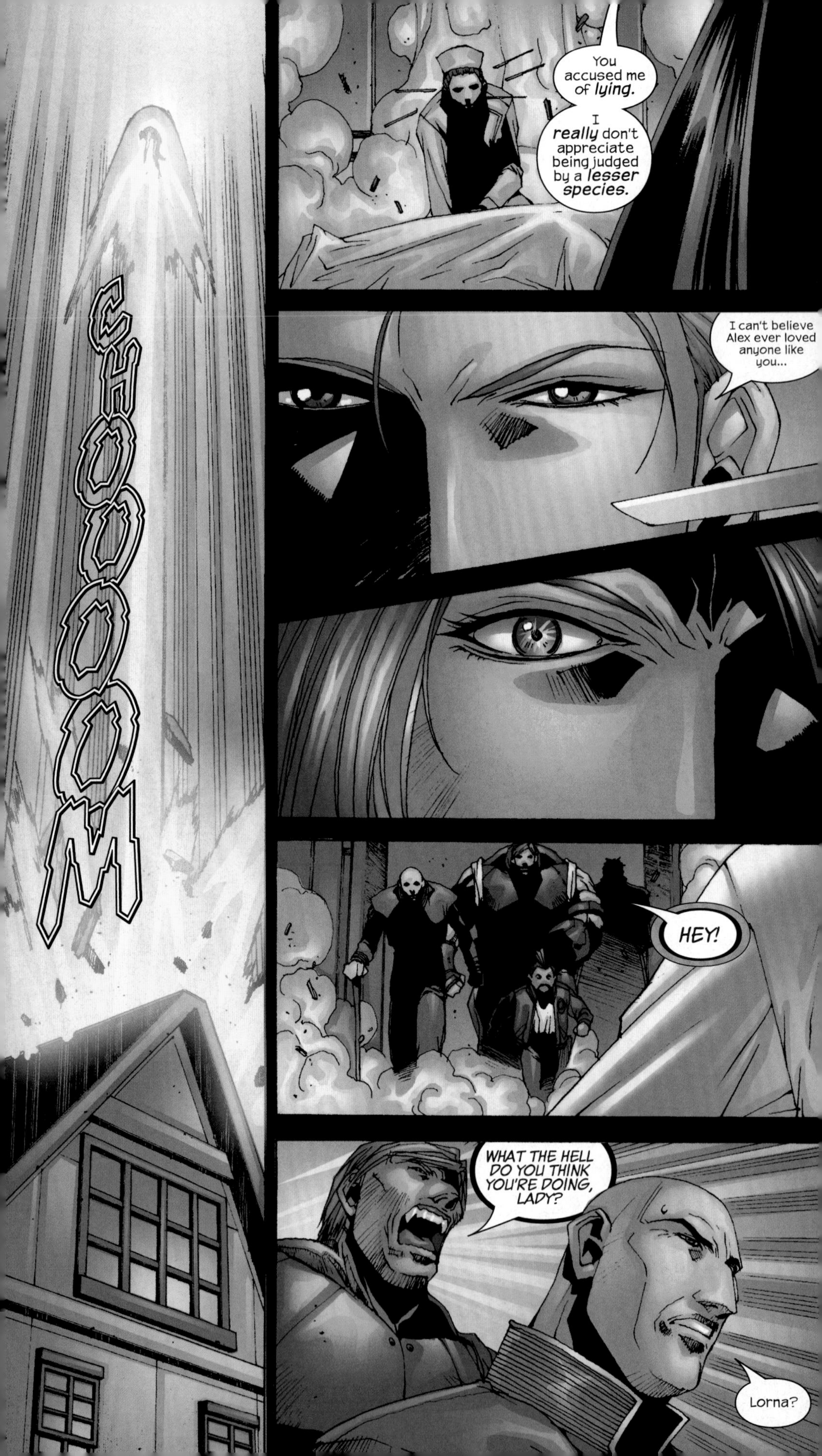
CHOOOOOM
You accused me of lying.
I really don't appreciate being judged by a lesser species.
I can't believe Alex ever loved anyone like you...
HEY!
WHAT THE HELL DO YOU THINK YOU'RE DOING, LADY?
Lorna?

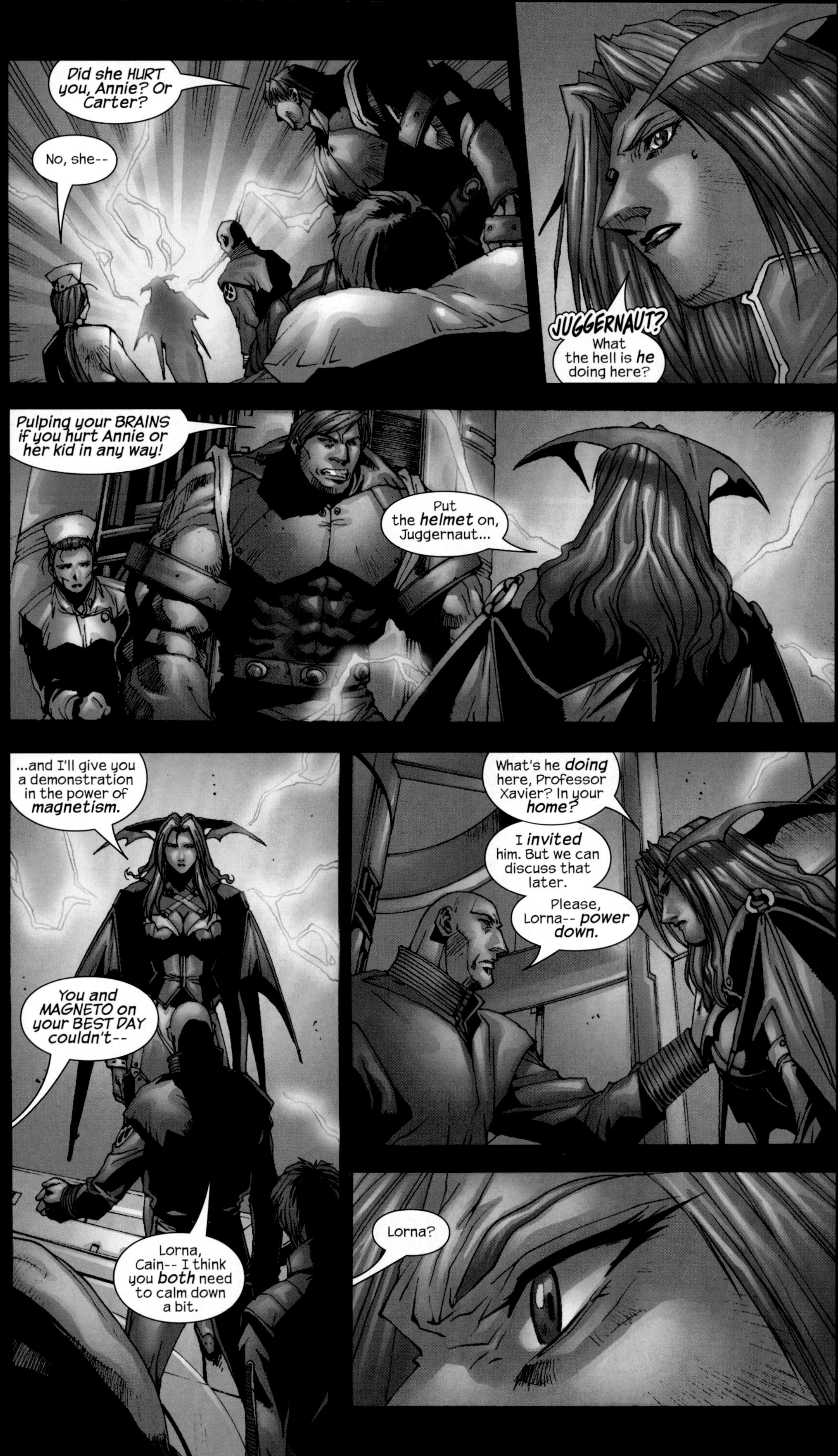

Did she HURT you, Annie? Or Carter?
No, she--
JUGGERNAUT? What the hell is he doing here?
Pulping your BRAINS if you hurt Annie or her kid in any way!
Put the helmet on, Juggernaut...
...and I'll give you a demonstration in the power of magnetism.
You and MAGNETO on your BEST DAY couldn't--
Lorna, Cain-- I think you both need to calm down a bit.
What's he doing here, Professor Xavier? In your home?
I invited him. But we can discuss that later.
Please, Lorna-- power down.
Lorna?

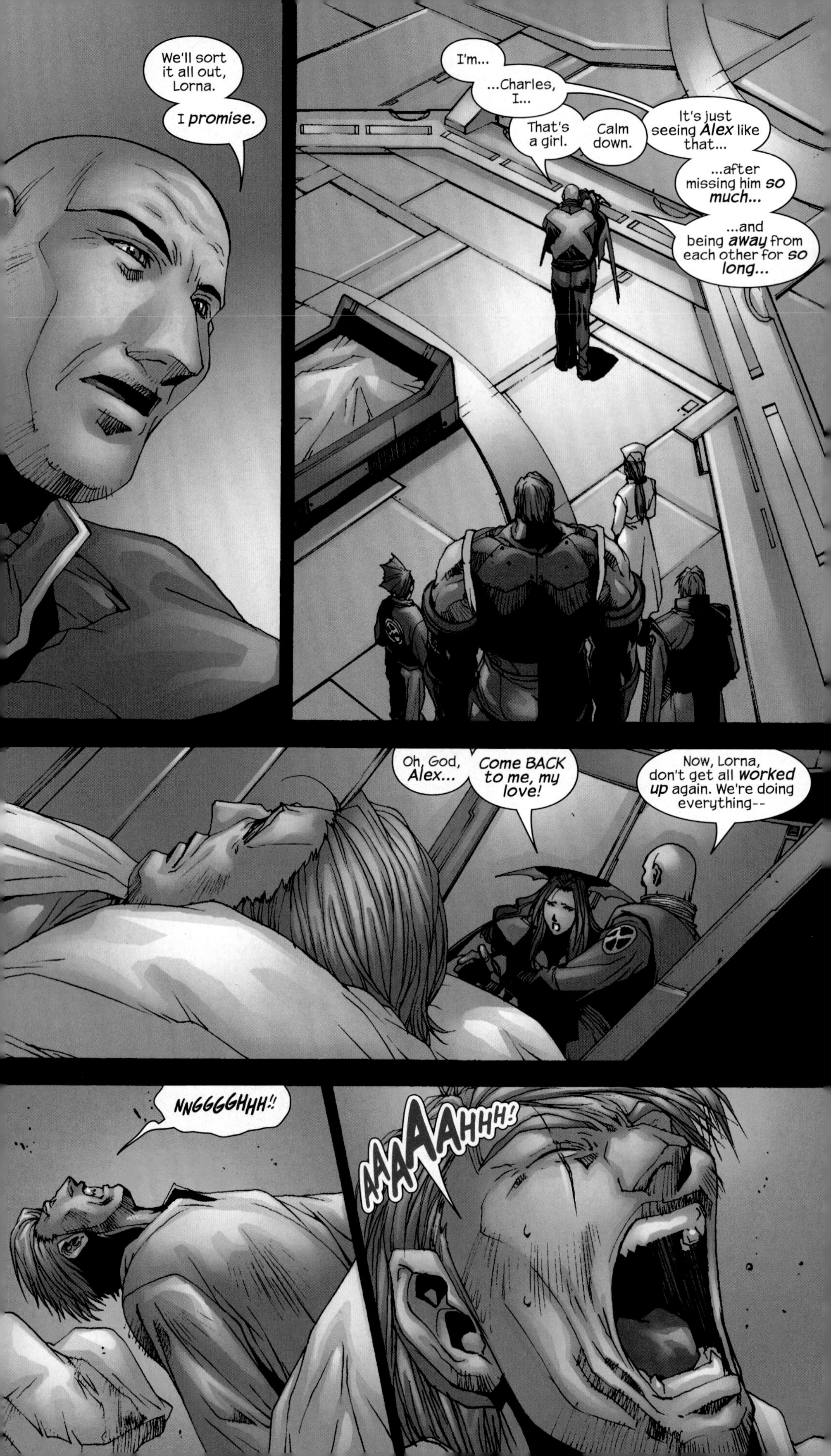
We'll sort it all out, Lorna.
I promise.
I'm...
...Charles, I...
That's a girl.
Calm down.
It's just seeing Alex like that...
...after missing him so much...
...and being away from each other for so long...
Oh, God, Alex...
Come BACK to me, my love!
Now, Lorna, don't get all worked up again. We're doing everything--
NNGGGGHHH!!
AAAAAHHH!

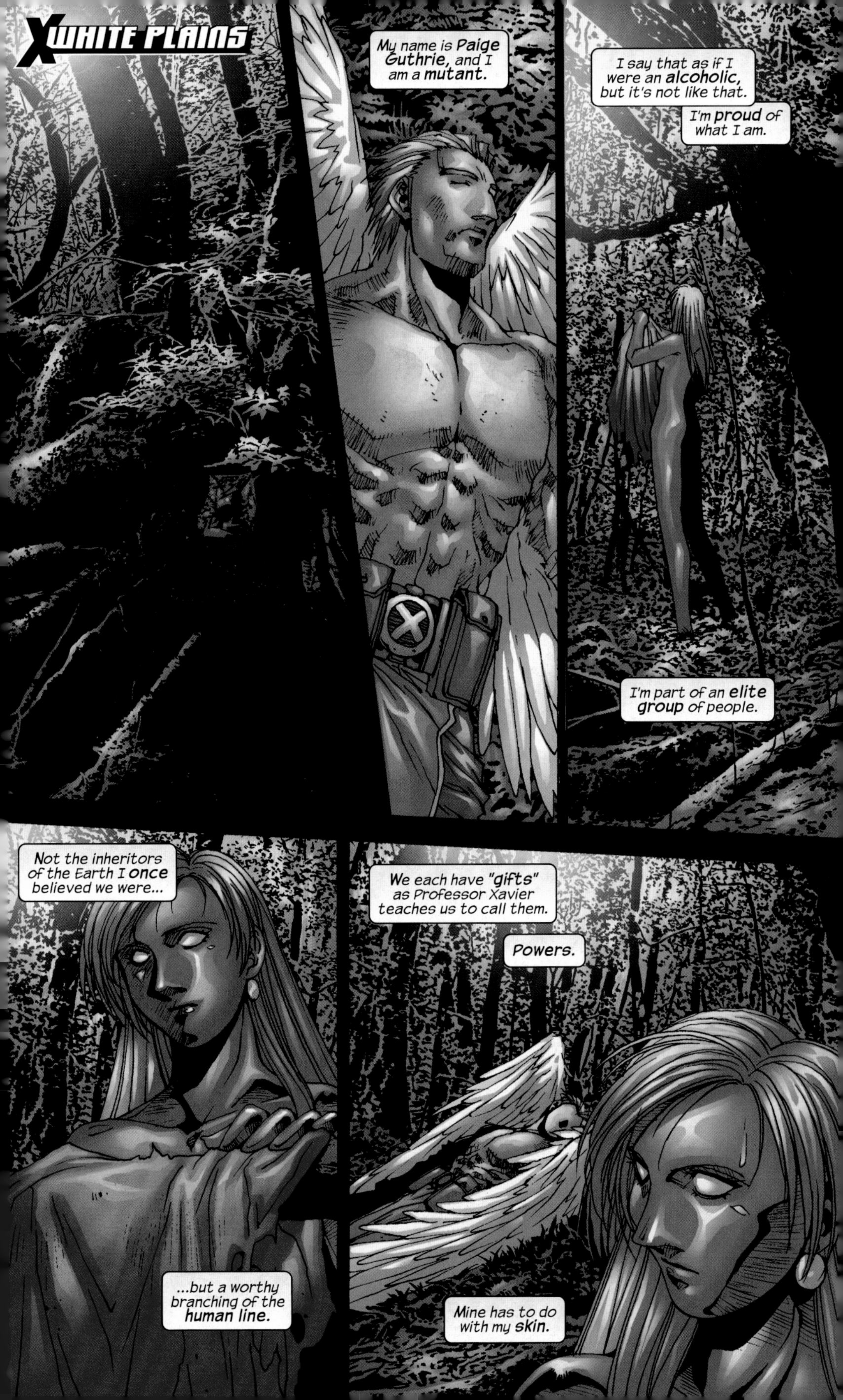
WHITE PLAINS
My name is Paige Guthrie, and I am a mutant.
I say that as if I were an alcoholic, but it's not like that.
I'm proud of what I am.
I'm part of an elite group of people.
Not the inheritors of the Earth I once believed we were...
...but a worthy branching of the human line.
We each have "gifts" as Professor Xavier teaches us to call them.
Powers.
Mine has to do with my skin.

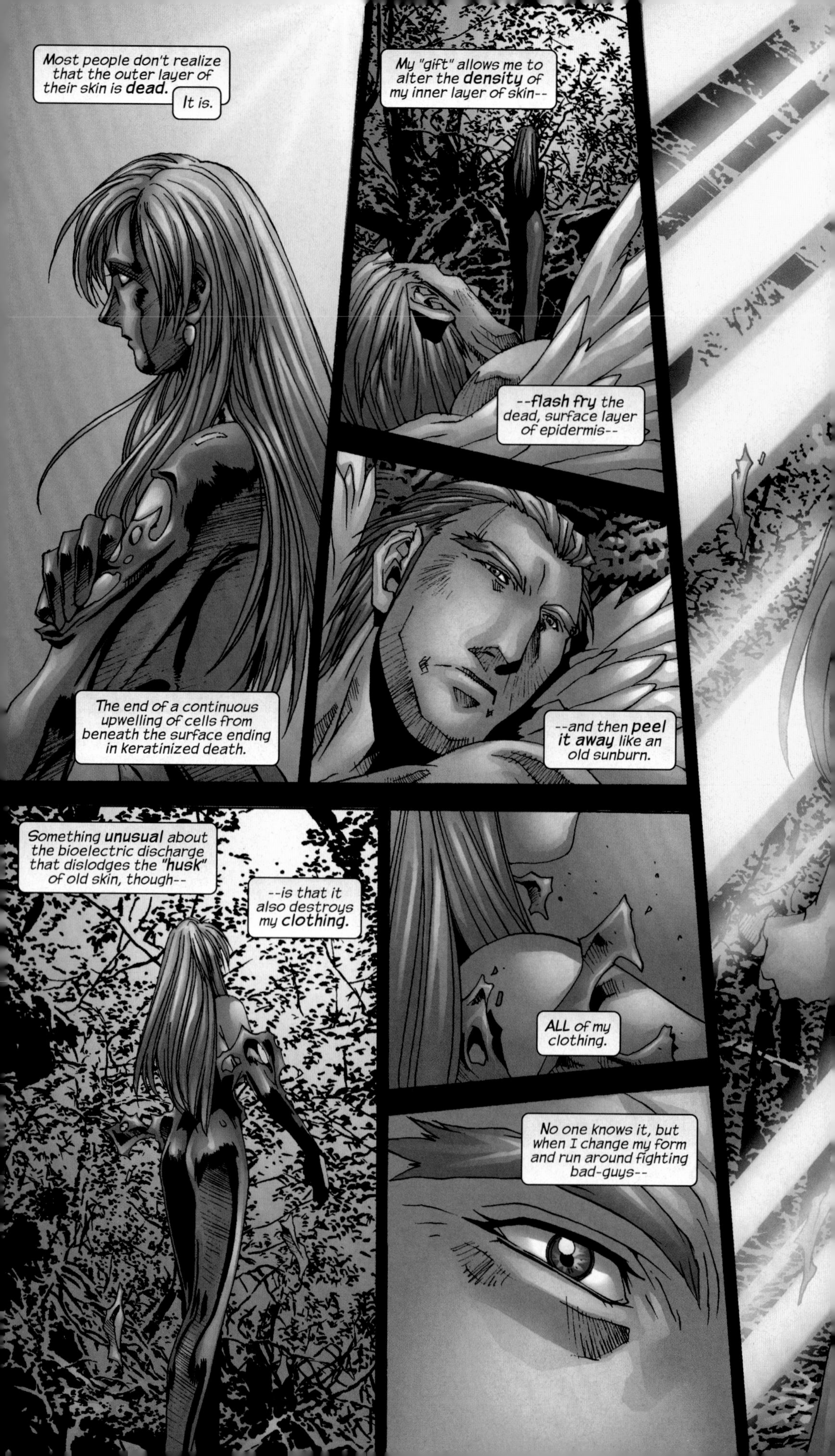
Most people don't realize that the outer layer of their skin is dead.
It is.
My "gift" allows me to alter the density of my inner layer of skin--
--flash fry the dead, surface layer of epidermis--
The end of a continuous upwelling of cells from beneath the surface ending in keratinized death.
--and then peel it away like an old sunburn.
Something unusual about the bioelectric discharge that dislodges the "husk" of old skin, though--
--is that it also destroys my clothing.
ALL of my clothing.
No one knows it, but when I change my form and run around fighting bad-guys--

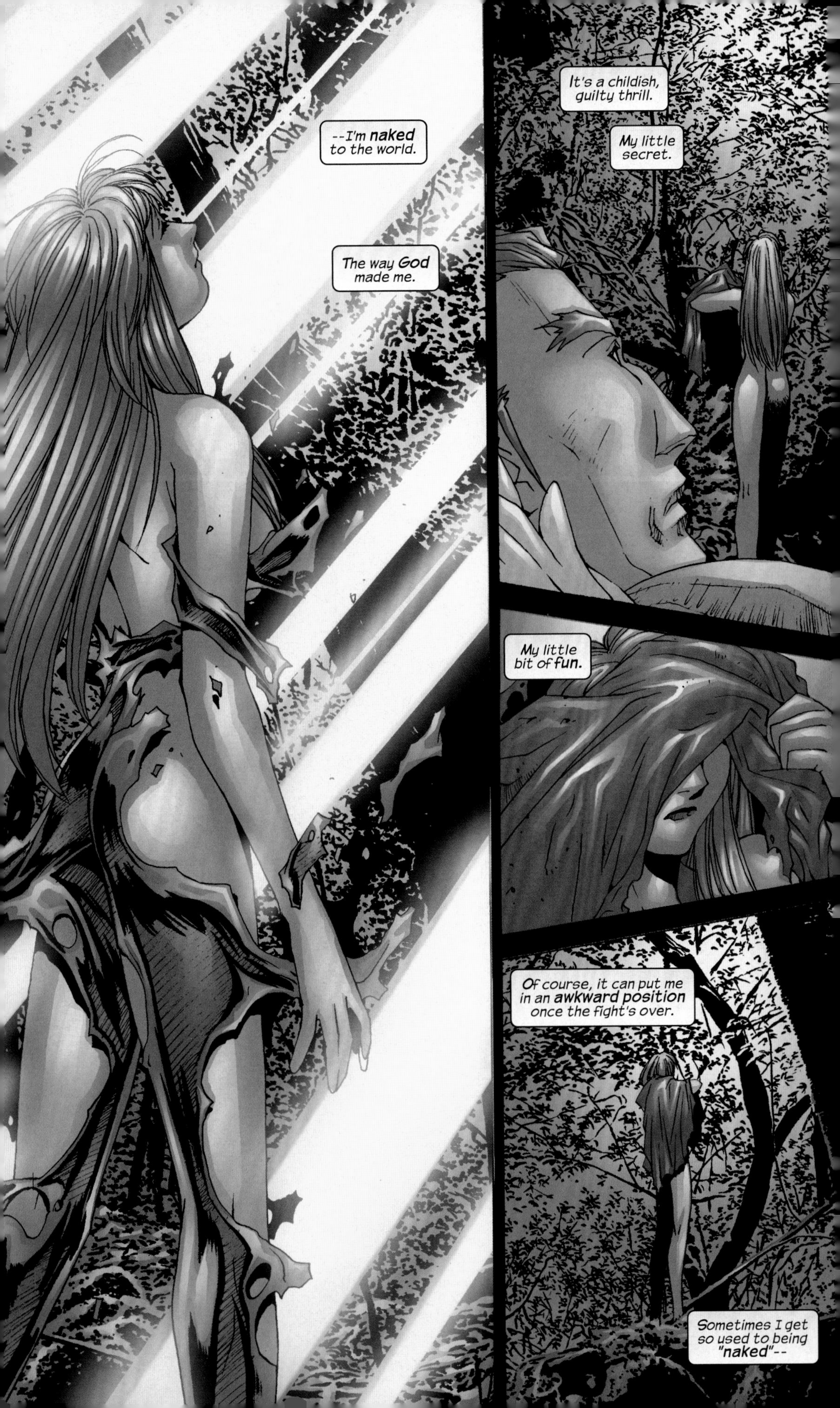

--I'm **naked** to the world.
The way **God** made me.
It's a childish, guilty thrill.
My little secret.
My little bit of **fun.**
Of course, it can put me in an **awkward position** once the fight's over.
Sometimes I get so used to being "**naked**"--

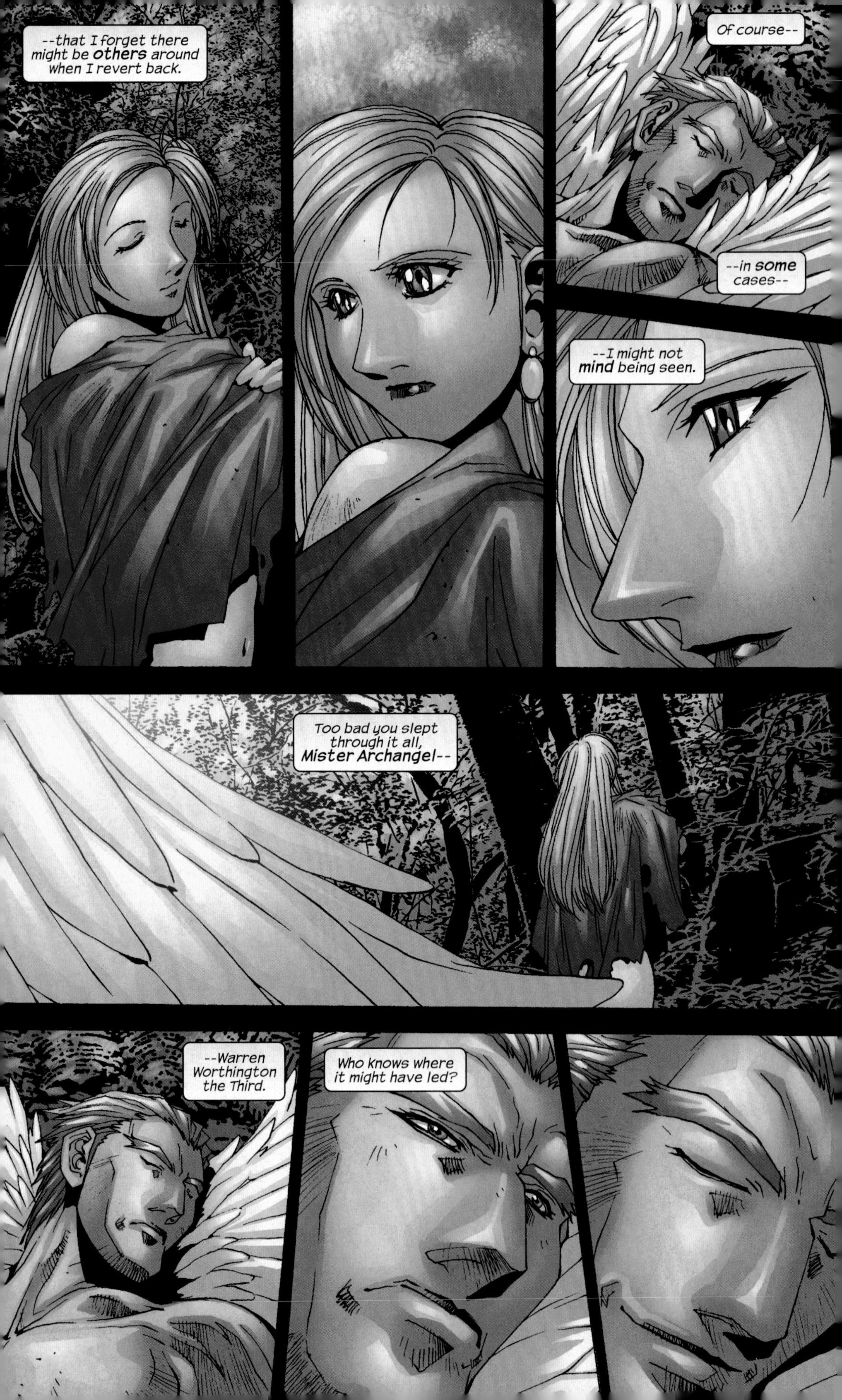
--that I forget there might be others around when I revert back.
Of course--
--in some cases--
--I might not mind being seen.
Too bad you slept through it all, Mister Archangel--
--Warren Worthington the Third.
Who knows where it might have led?

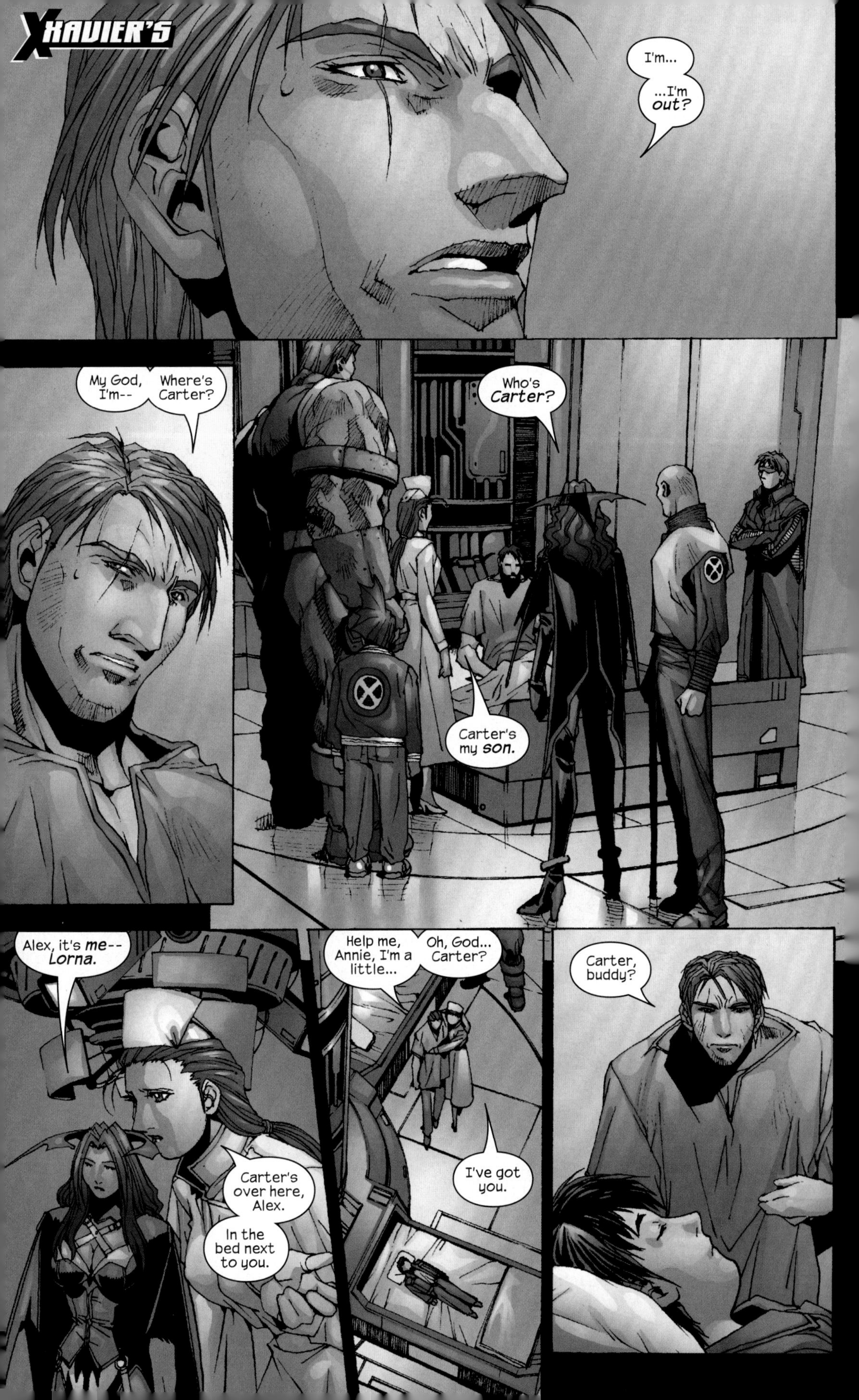
XAVIER'S
I'm...
...I'm out?
My God, I'm--
Where's Carter?
Who's Carter?
Carter's my son.
Alex, it's me-- Lorna.
Carter's over here, Alex.
In the bed next to you.
Help me, Annie, I'm a little...
Oh, God... Carter?
I've got you.
Carter, buddy?

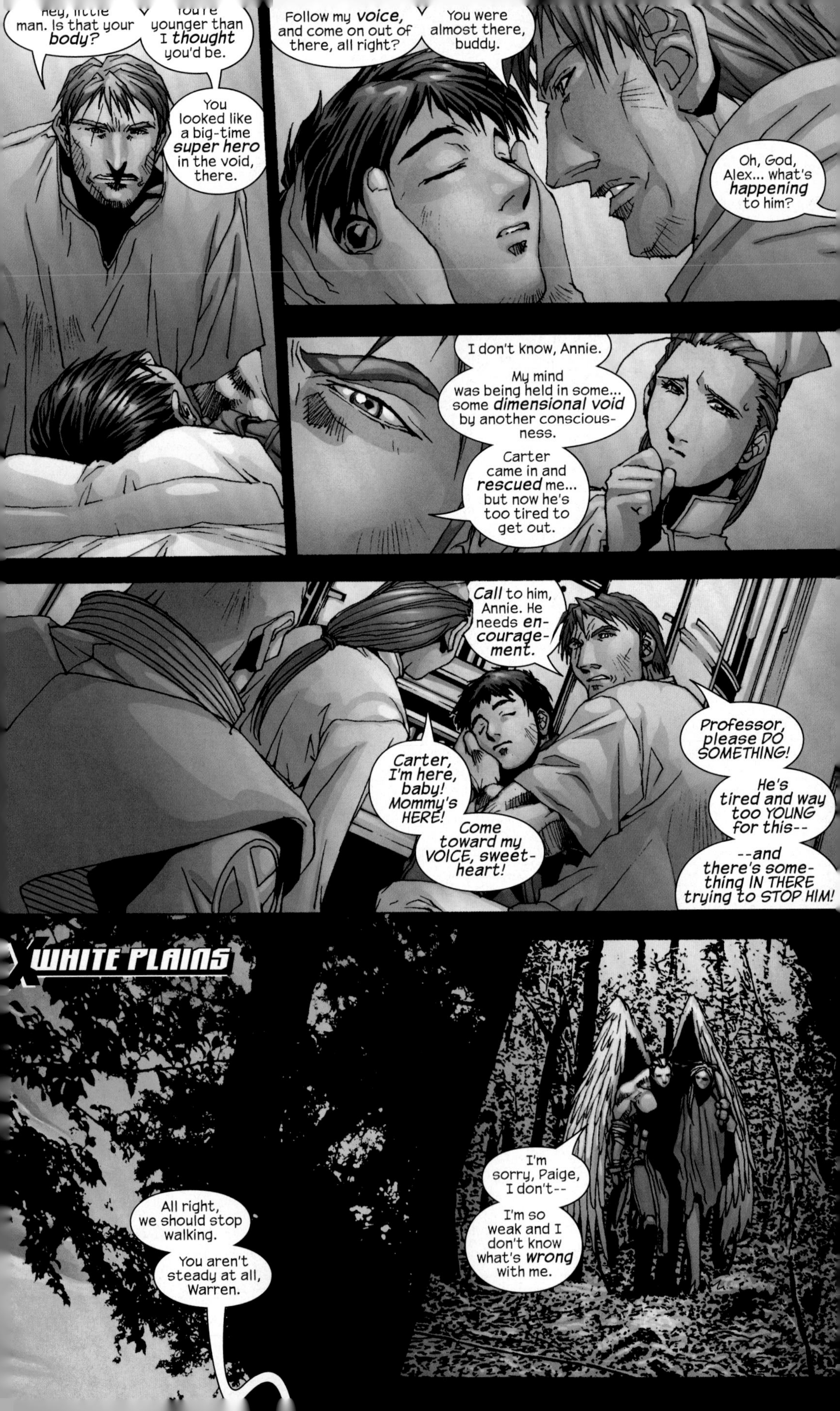
Hey, little man. Is that your body?
You're younger than I thought you'd be.
You looked like a big-time super hero in the void, there.
Follow my voice, and come on out of there, all right?
You were almost there, buddy.
Oh, God, Alex... what's happening to him?
I don't know, Annie.
My mind was being held in some... some dimensional void by another conscious-ness.
Carter came in and rescued me... but now he's too tired to get out.
Call to him, Annie. He needs en-courage-ment.
Carter, I'm here, baby! Mommy's HERE!
Come toward my VOICE, sweet-heart!
Professor, please DO SOMETHING!
He's tired and way too YOUNG for this--
--and there's some-thing IN THERE trying to STOP HIM!
WHITE PLAINS
All right, we should stop walking.
You aren't steady at all, Warren.
I'm sorry, Paige, I don't--
I'm so weak and I don't know what's wrong with me.

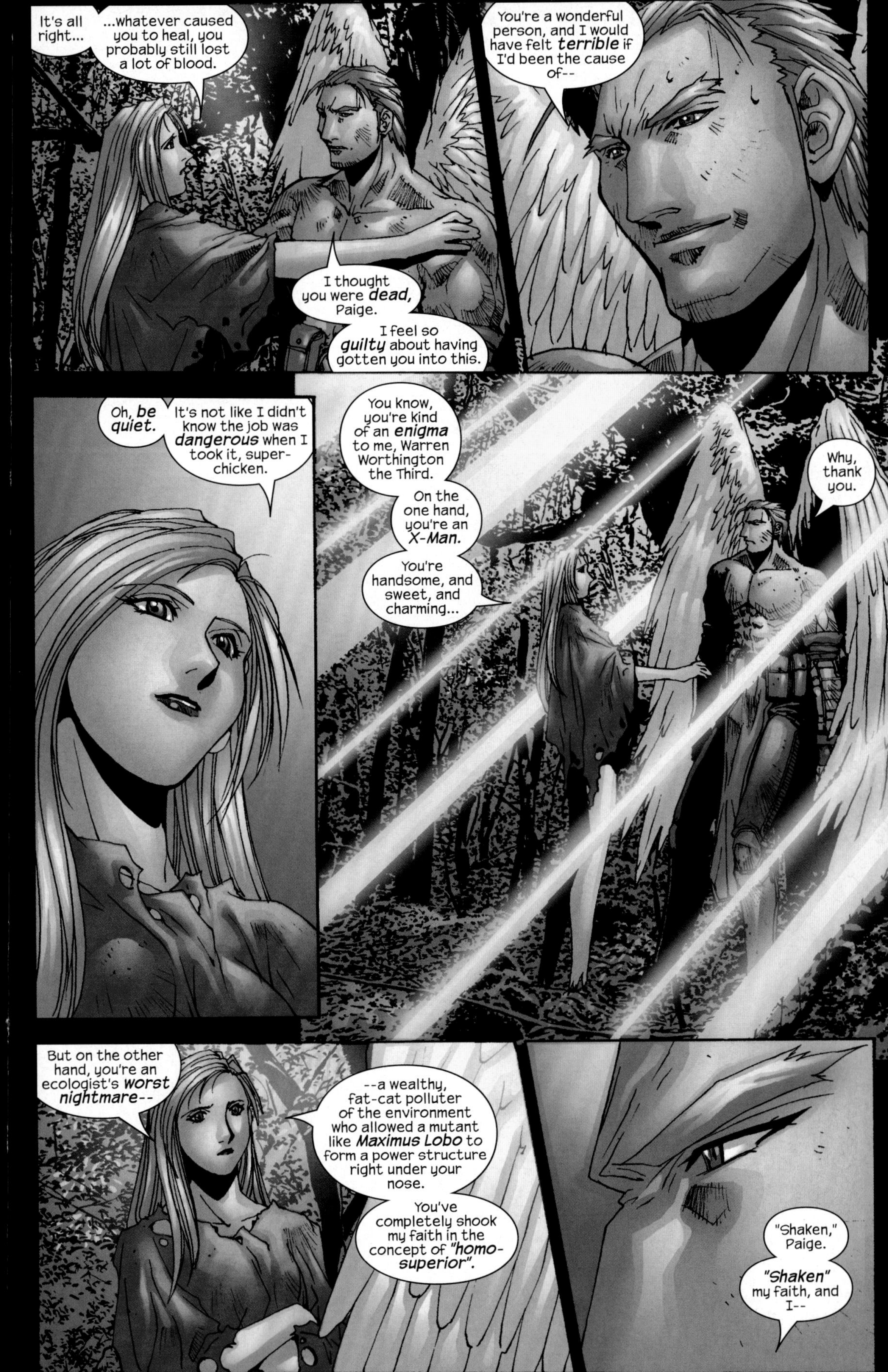
It's all right...
...whatever caused you to heal, you probably still lost a lot of blood.
I thought you were *dead,* Paige.
I feel so *guilty* about having gotten you into this.
You're a wonderful person, and I would have felt *terrible* if I'd been the cause of--
Oh, *be quiet.*
It's not like I didn't know the job was *dangerous* when I took it, super-chicken.
You know, you're kind of an *enigma* to me, Warren Worthington the Third.
On the one hand, you're an *X-Man.*
You're handsome, and sweet, and charming...
Why, thank you.
But on the other hand, you're an ecologist's *worst nightmare*--
--a wealthy, fat-cat polluter of the environment who allowed a mutant like *Maximus Lobo* to form a power structure right under your nose.
You've completely shook my faith in the concept of *"homo-superior".*
"Shaken," Paige.
"Shaken" my faith, and I--

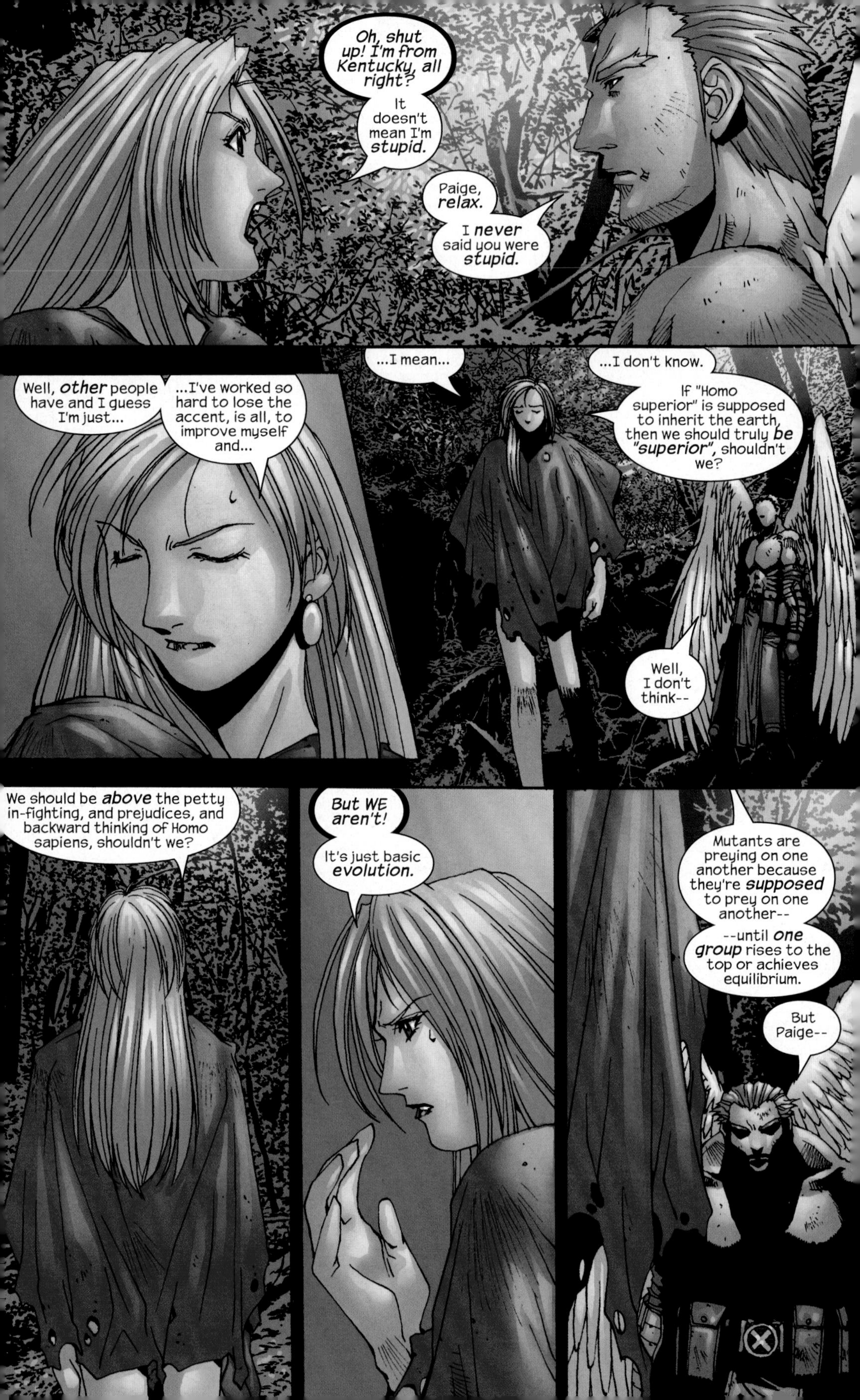
Oh, shut up! I'm from Kentucky, all right?
It doesn't mean I'm stupid.
Paige, relax.
I never said you were stupid.
Well, other people have and I guess I'm just...
...I've worked so hard to lose the accent, is all, to improve myself and...
...I mean...
...I don't know.
If "Homo superior" is supposed to inherit the earth, then we should truly be "superior", shouldn't we?
Well, I don't think--
We should be above the petty in-fighting, and prejudices, and backward thinking of Homo sapiens, shouldn't we?
But WE aren't!
It's just basic evolution.
Mutants are preying on one another because they're supposed to prey on one another--
--until one group rises to the top or achieves equilibrium.
But Paige--

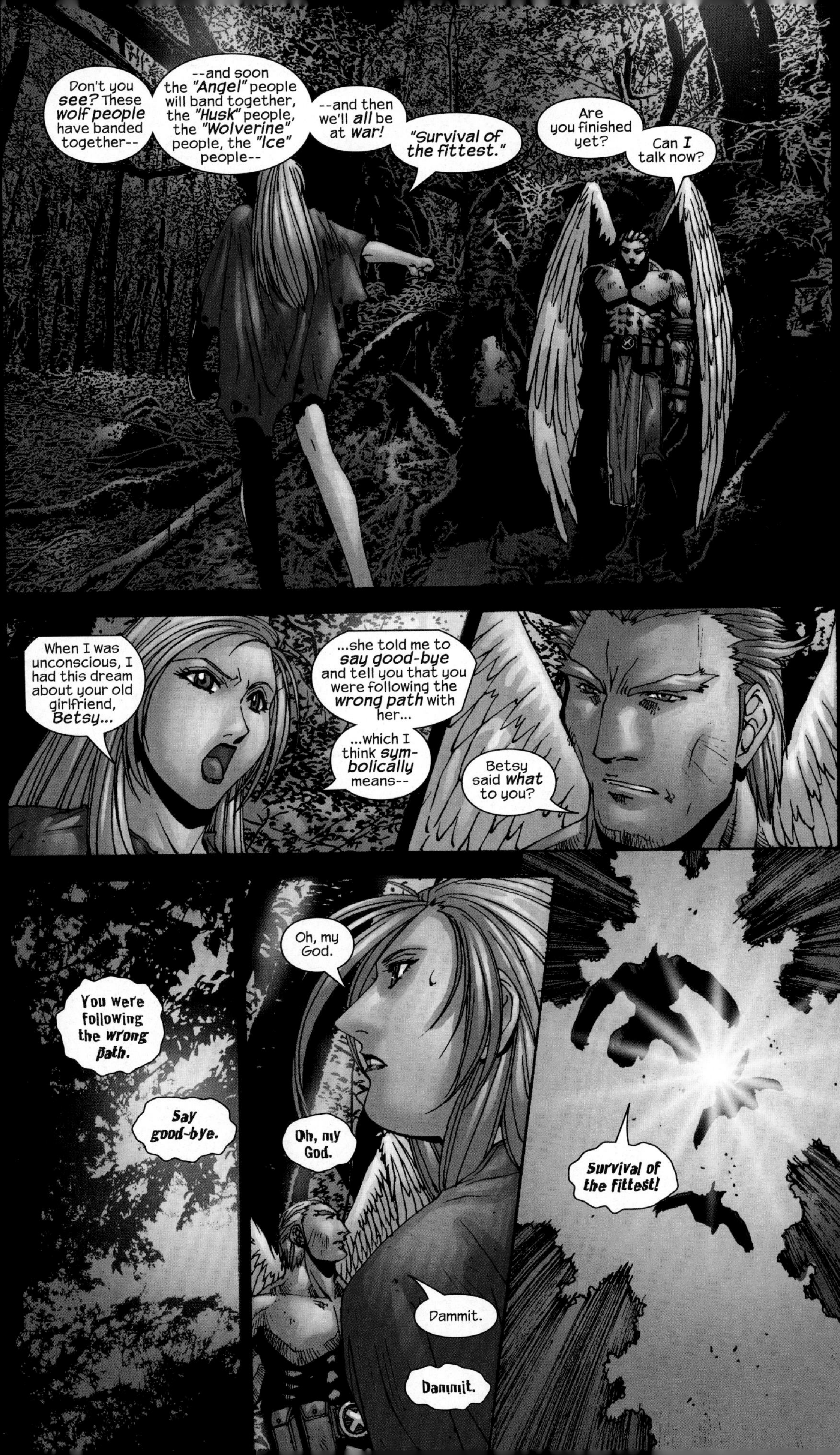

Don't you see? These wolf people have banded together--
--and soon the "Angel" people will band together, the "Husk" people, the "Wolverine" people, the "Ice" people--
--and then we'll all be at war!
"Survival of the fittest."
Are you finished yet?
Can I talk now?
When I was unconscious, I had this dream about your old girlfriend, Betsy...
...she told me to say good-bye and tell you that you were following the wrong path with her...
...which I think sym-bolically means--
Betsy said what to you?
You were following the wrong path.
Say good-bye.
Oh, my God.
Oh, my God.
Dammit.
Dammit.
Survival of the fittest!

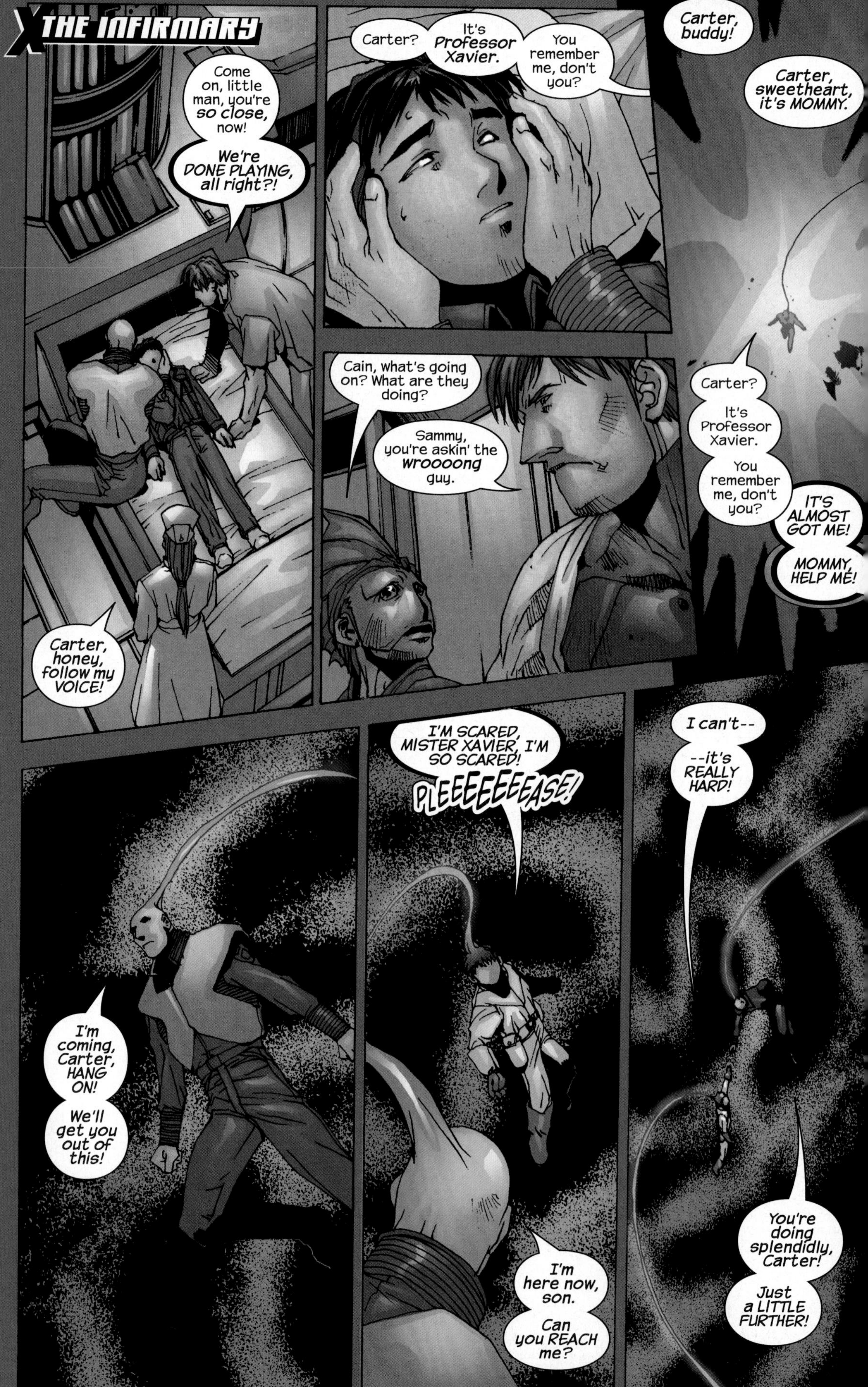
THE INFIRMARY
Come on, little man, you're so close, now!
We're DONE PLAYING, all right?!
Carter, honey, follow my VOICE!
Carter?
It's Professor Xavier.
You remember me, don't you?
Cain, what's going on? What are they doing?
Sammy, you're askin' the wroooong guy.
Carter, buddy!
Carter, sweetheart, it's MOMMY.
Carter?
It's Professor Xavier.
You remember me, don't you?
IT'S ALMOST GOT ME!
MOMMY, HELP ME!
I'm coming, Carter, HANG ON!
We'll get you out of this!
I'M SCARED, MISTER XAVIER, I'M SO SCARED!
PLEEEEEEEASE!
I'm here now, son.
Can you REACH me?
I can't--
--it's REALLY HARD!
You're doing splendidly, Carter!
Just a LITTLE FURTHER!

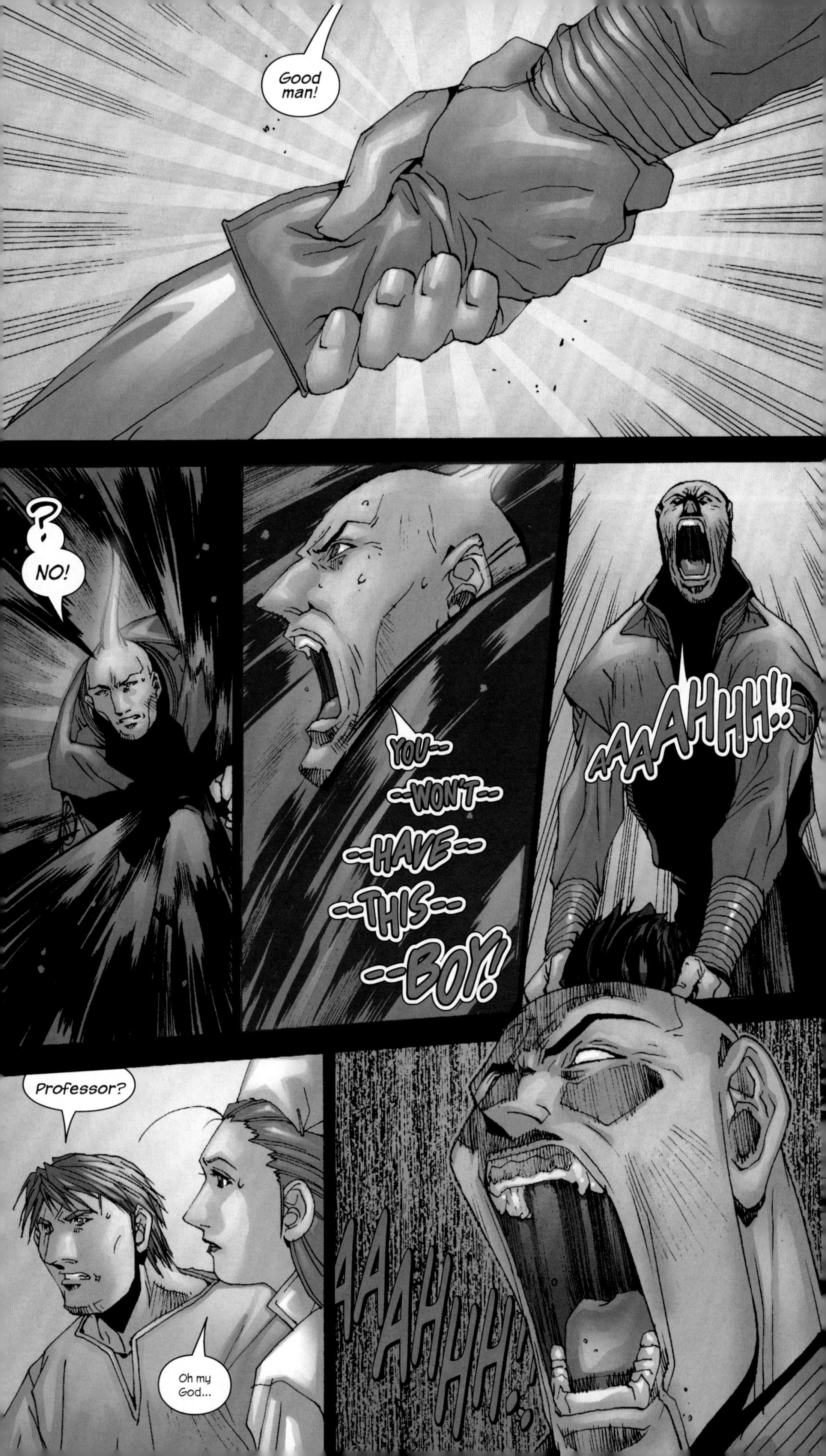
Good man!
?
NO!
YOU-- --WON'T-- --HAVE-- --THIS-- --BOY!
AAAAHHH!!
Professor?
Oh my God...
AAHHH!!

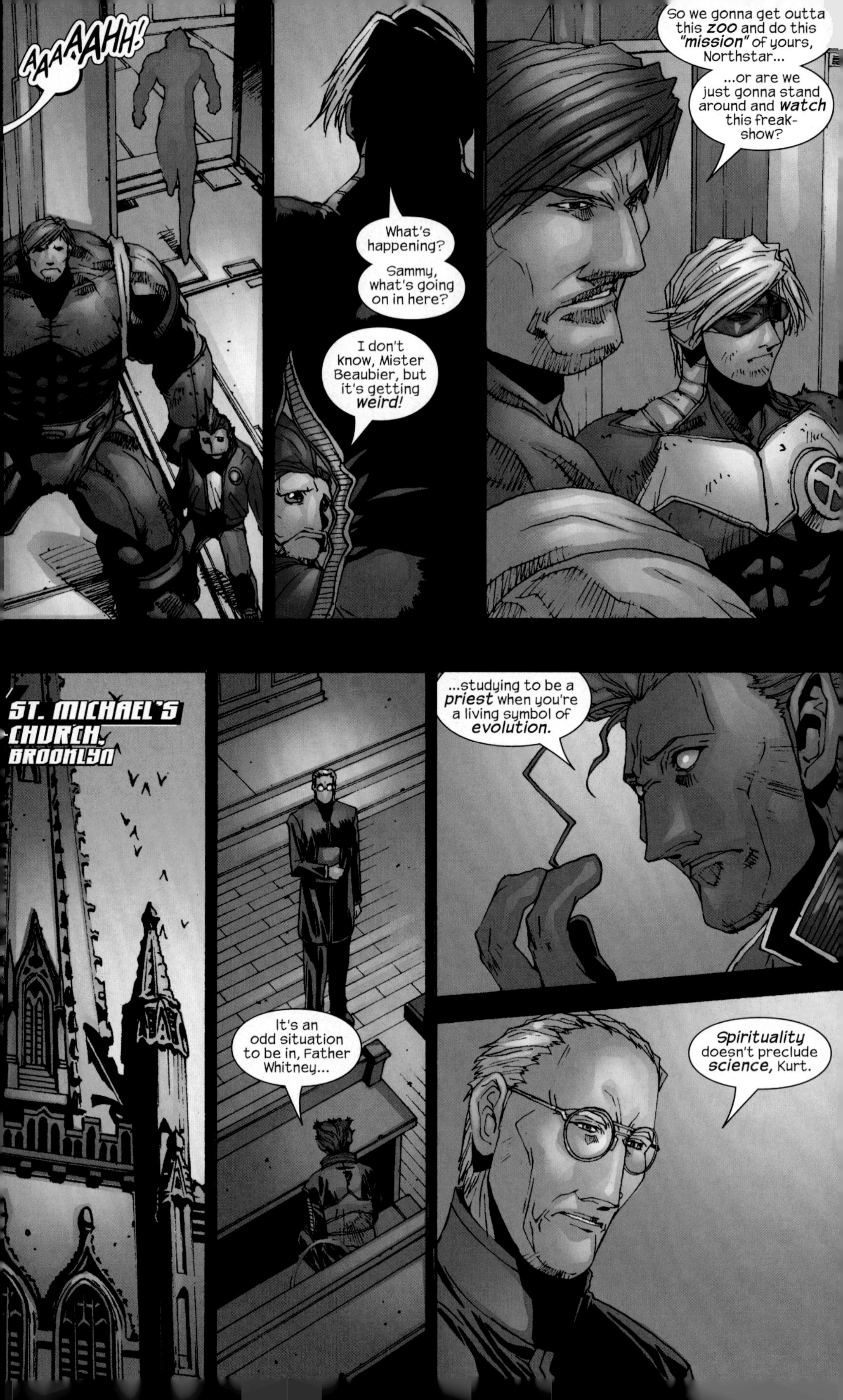
AAAAAHH!
What's happening?
Sammy, what's going on in here?
I don't know, Mister Beaubier, but it's getting weird!
So we gonna get outta this zoo and do this "mission" of yours, Northstar...
...or are we just gonna stand around and watch this freak-show?
ST. MICHAEL'S CHURCH, BROOKLYN
It's an odd situation to be in, Father Whitney...
...studying to be a priest when you're a living symbol of evolution.
Spirituality doesn't preclude science, Kurt.

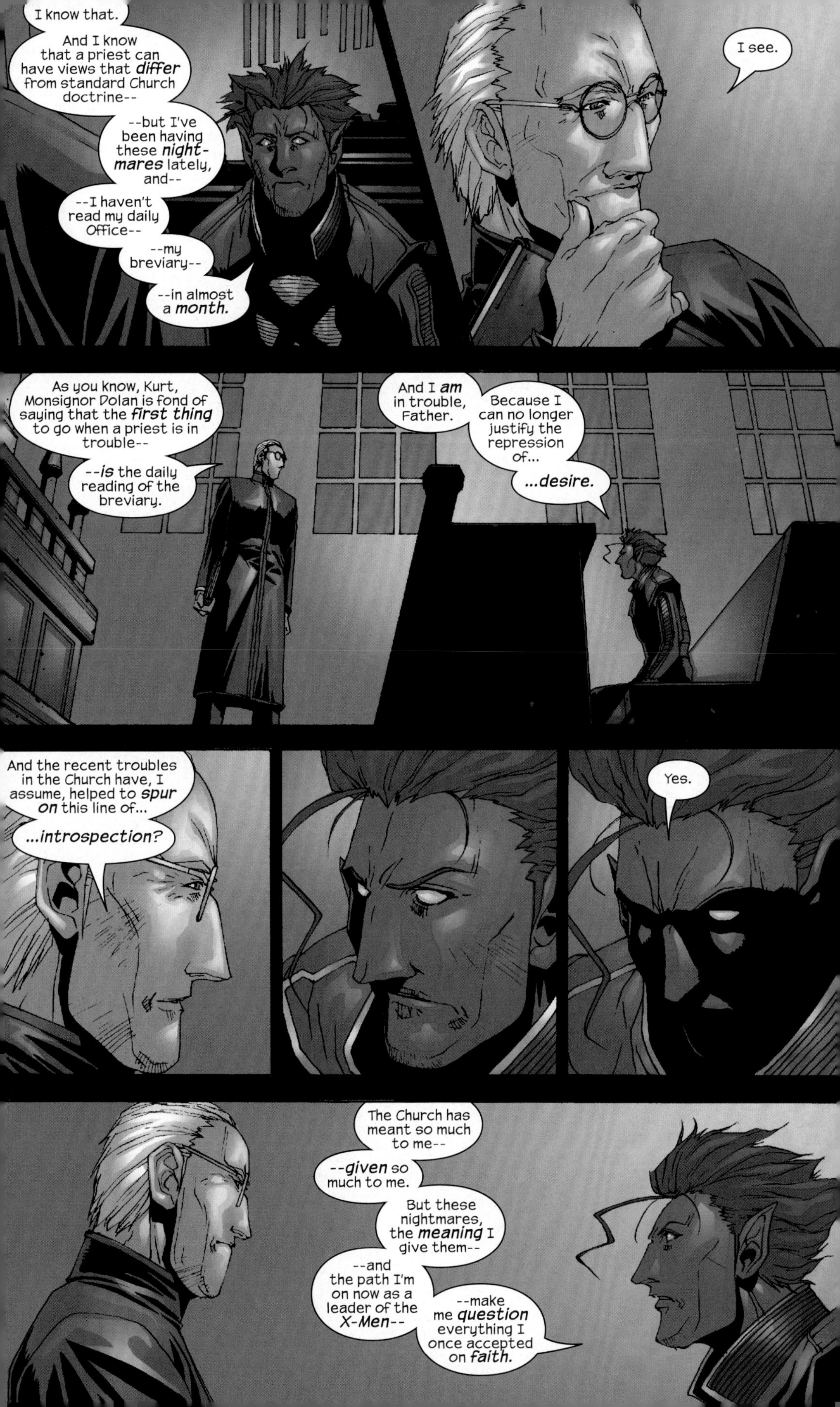
I know that.
And I know that a priest can have views that *differ* from standard Church doctrine--
--but I've been having these *night-mares* lately, and--
--I haven't read my daily Office--
--my breviary--
--in almost a *month.*
I see.
As you know, Kurt, Monsignor Dolan is fond of saying that the *first thing* to go when a priest is in trouble--
--*is* the daily reading of the breviary.
And I *am* in trouble, Father.
Because I can no longer justify the repression of...
...*desire.*
And the recent troubles in the Church have, I assume, helped to *spur on* this line of...
...*introspection?*
Yes.
The Church has meant so much to me--
--*given* so much to me.
But these nightmares, the *meaning* I give them--
--and the path I'm on now as a leader of the *X-Men*--
--make me *question* everything I once accepted on *faith.*

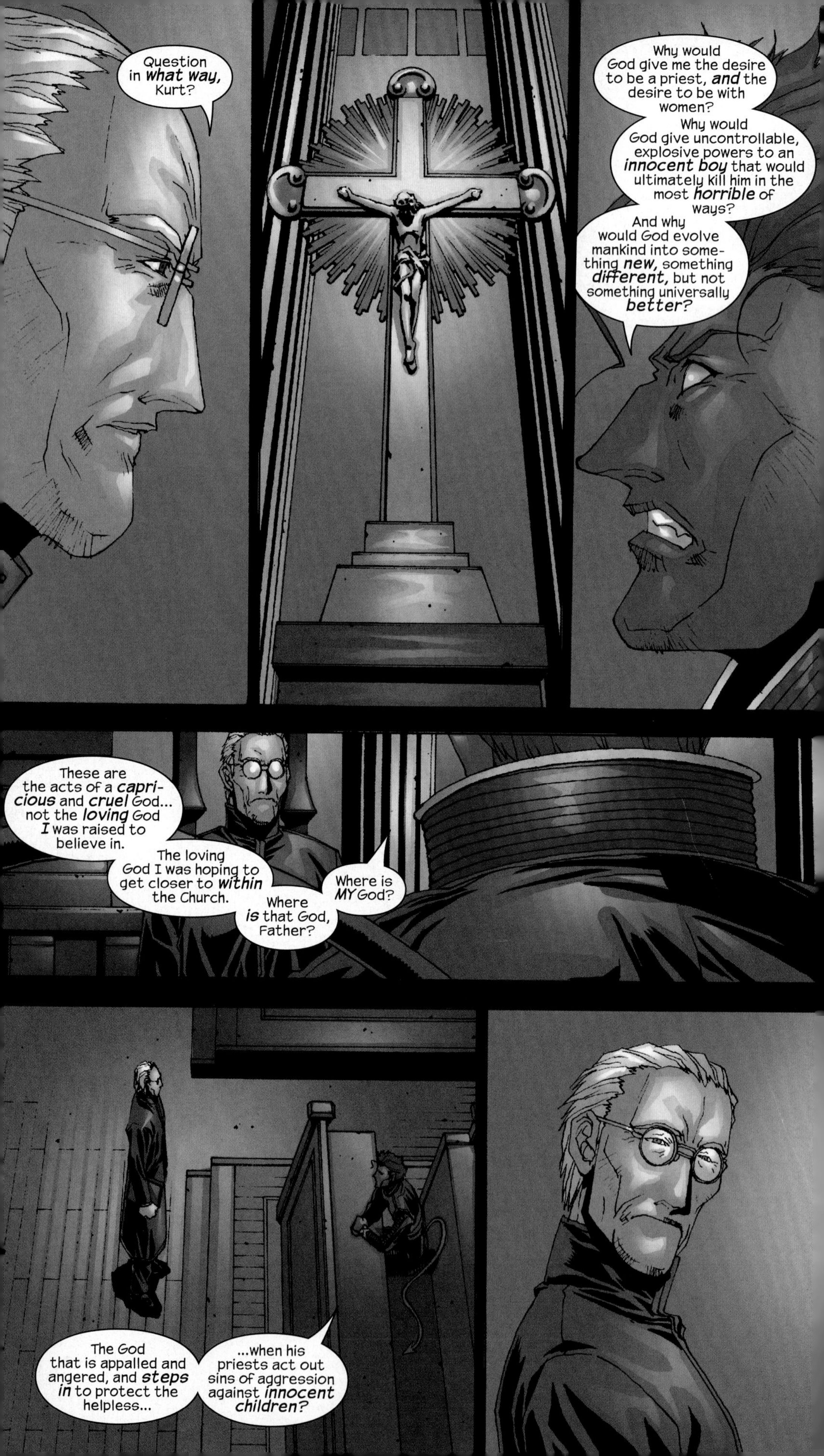

Question in *what way,* Kurt?
Why would God give me the desire to be a priest, *and* the desire to be with women?
Why would God give uncontrollable, explosive powers to an *innocent boy* that would ultimately kill him in the most *horrible* of ways?
And why would God evolve mankind into something *new,* something *different,* but not something universally *better?*
These are the acts of a *capricious* and *cruel* God... not the *loving* God *I* was raised to believe in.
The loving God I was hoping to get closer to *within* the Church.
Where *is* that God, Father?
Where is *MY* God?
The God that is appalled and angered, and *steps in* to protect the helpless...
...when his priests act out sins of aggression against *innocent children?*

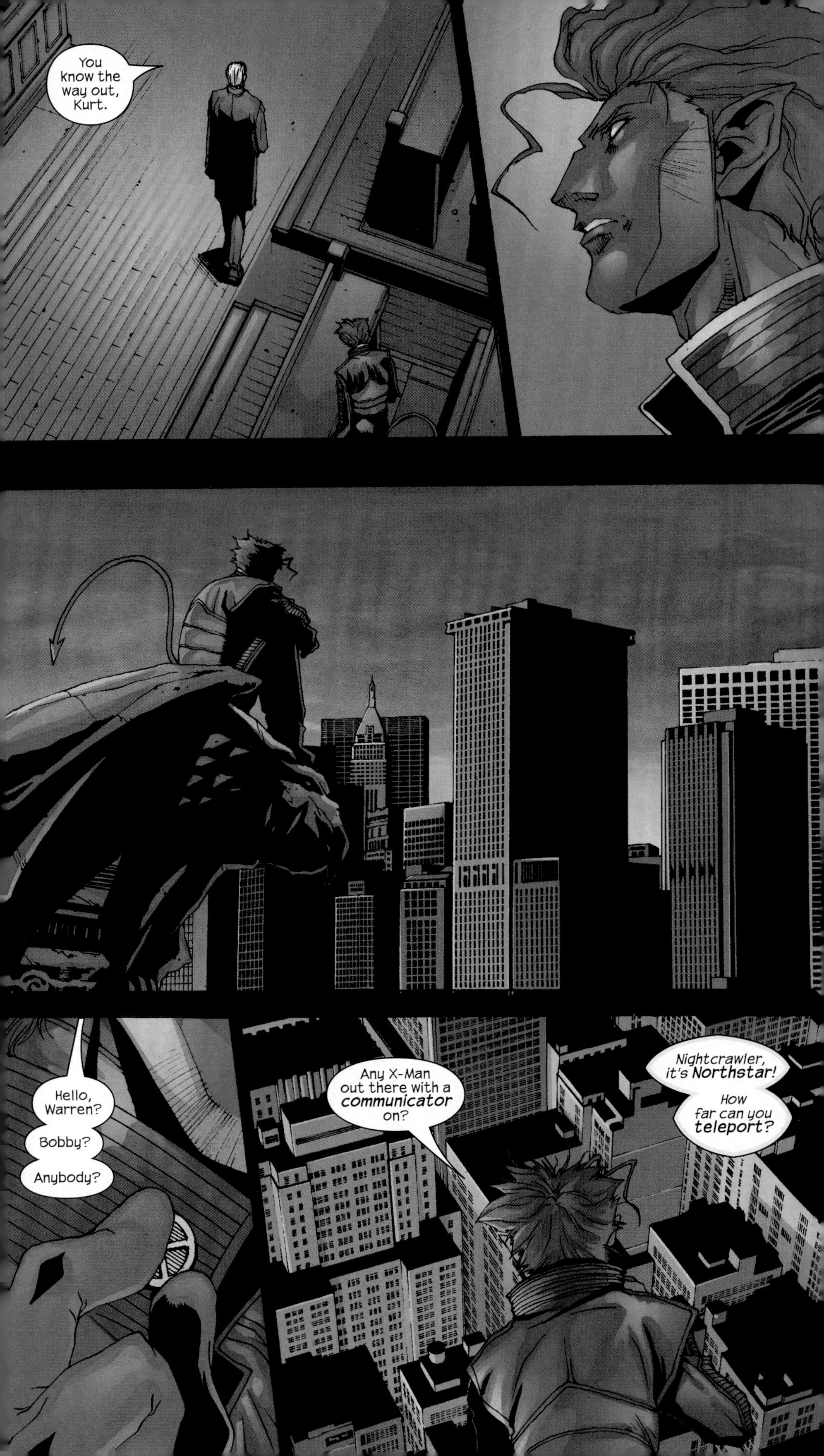

You know the way out, Kurt.
Hello, Warren?
Bobby?
Anybody?
Any X-Man out there with a communicator on?
Nightcrawler, it's Northstar!
How far can you teleport?

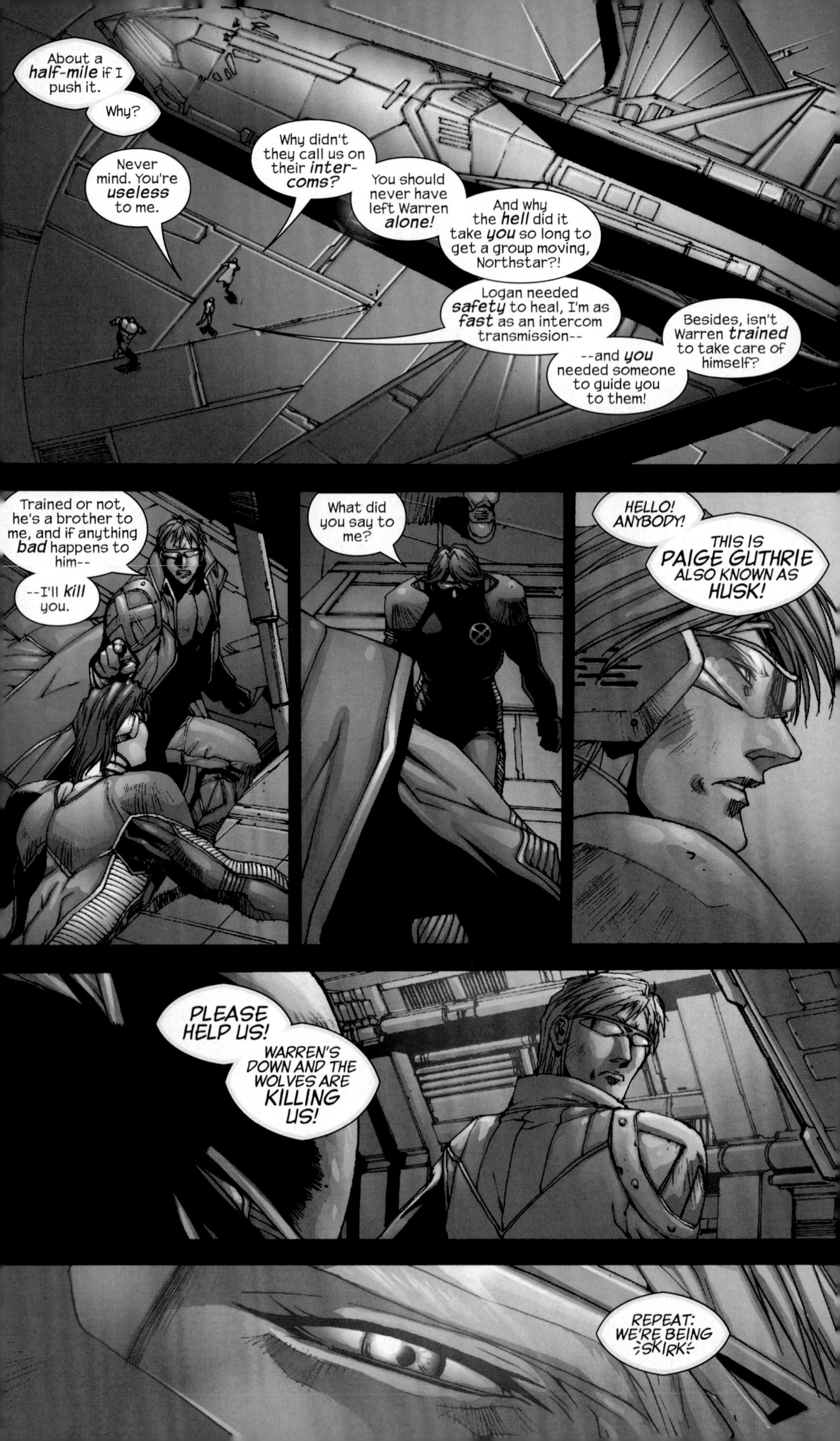

About a half-mile if I push it.
Why?
Never mind. You're useless to me.
Why didn't they call us on their inter-coms?
You should never have left Warren alone!
And why the hell did it take you so long to get a group moving, Northstar?!
Logan needed safety to heal, I'm as fast as an intercom transmission--
--and you needed someone to guide you to them!
Besides, isn't Warren trained to take care of himself?
Trained or not, he's a brother to me, and if anything bad happens to him--
--I'll kill you.
What did you say to me?
HELLO! ANYBODY!
THIS IS PAIGE GUTHRIE ALSO KNOWN AS HUSK!
PLEASE HELP US!
WARREN'S DOWN AND THE WOLVES ARE KILLING US!
REPEAT: WE'RE BEING
SKIRK

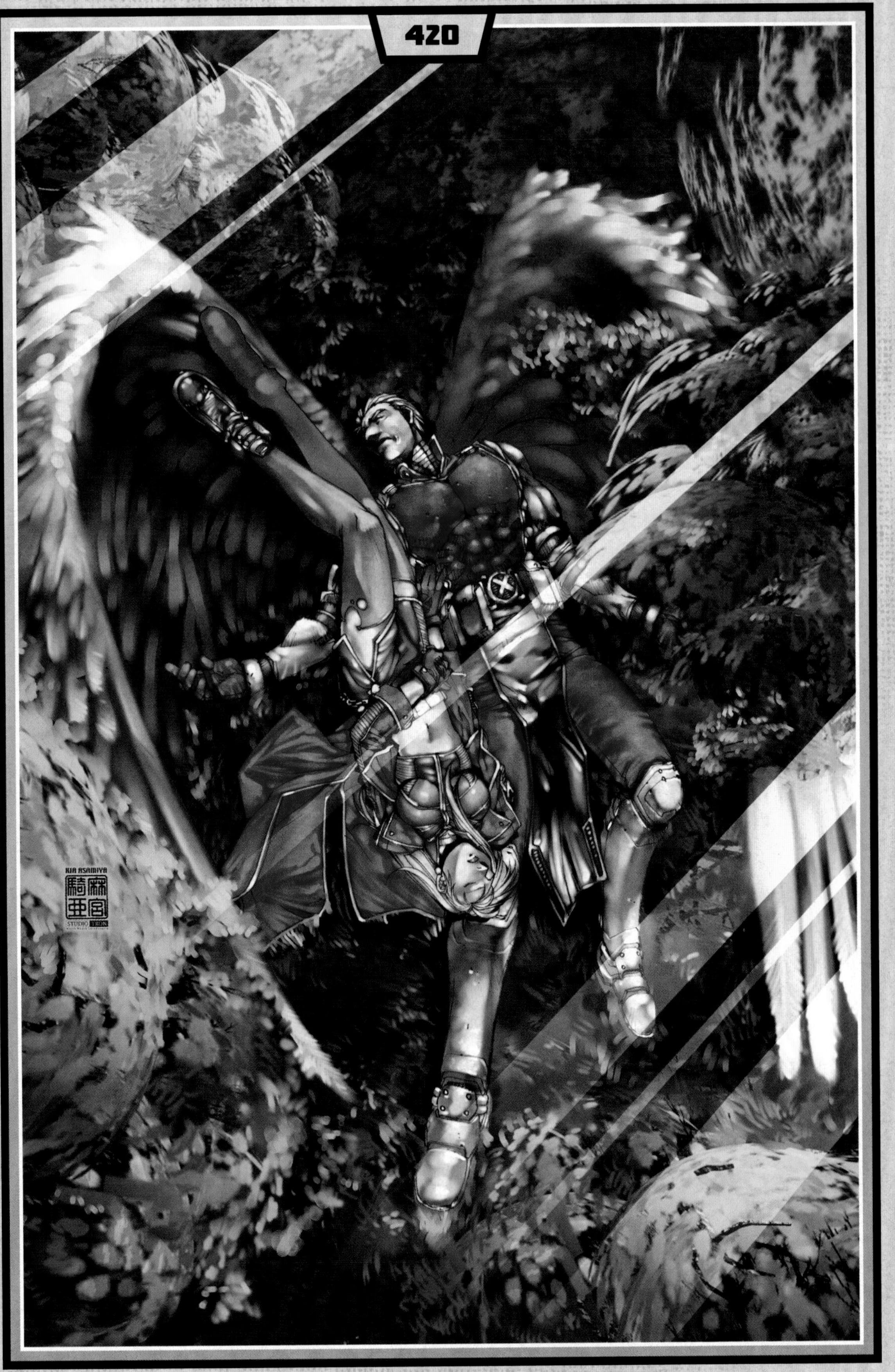
420
KIA ASAMIYA
STUDIO TRON

DOMINANT SPECIES, CONCLUSION

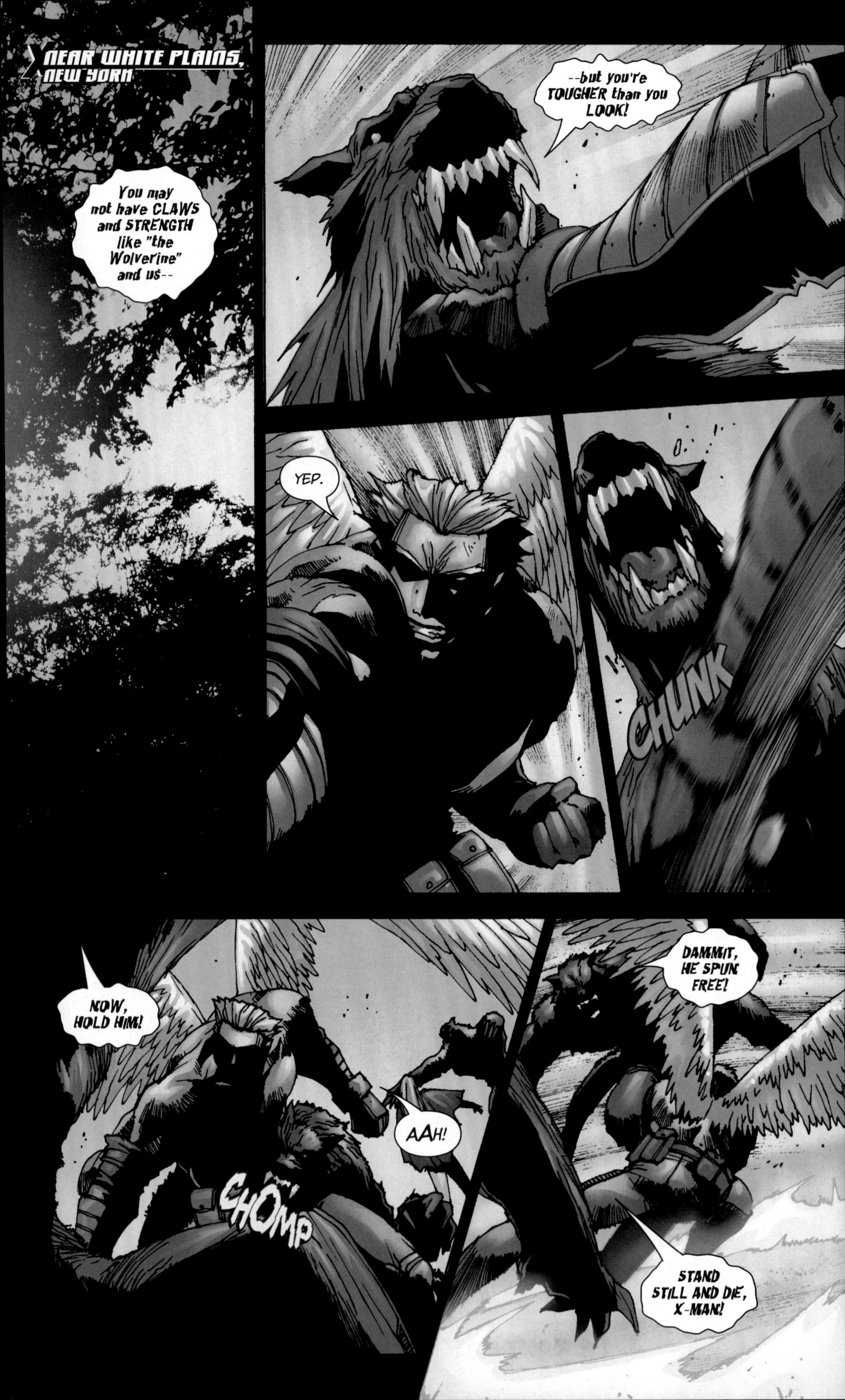
NEAR WHITE PLAINS, NEW YORK
You may not have CLAWS and STRENGTH like "the Wolverine" and us--
--but you're TOUGHER than you LOOK!
YEP.
CHUNK
NOW, HOLD HIM!
AAH!
CHOMP
DAMMIT, HE SPUN FREE!
STAND STILL AND DIE, X-MAN!

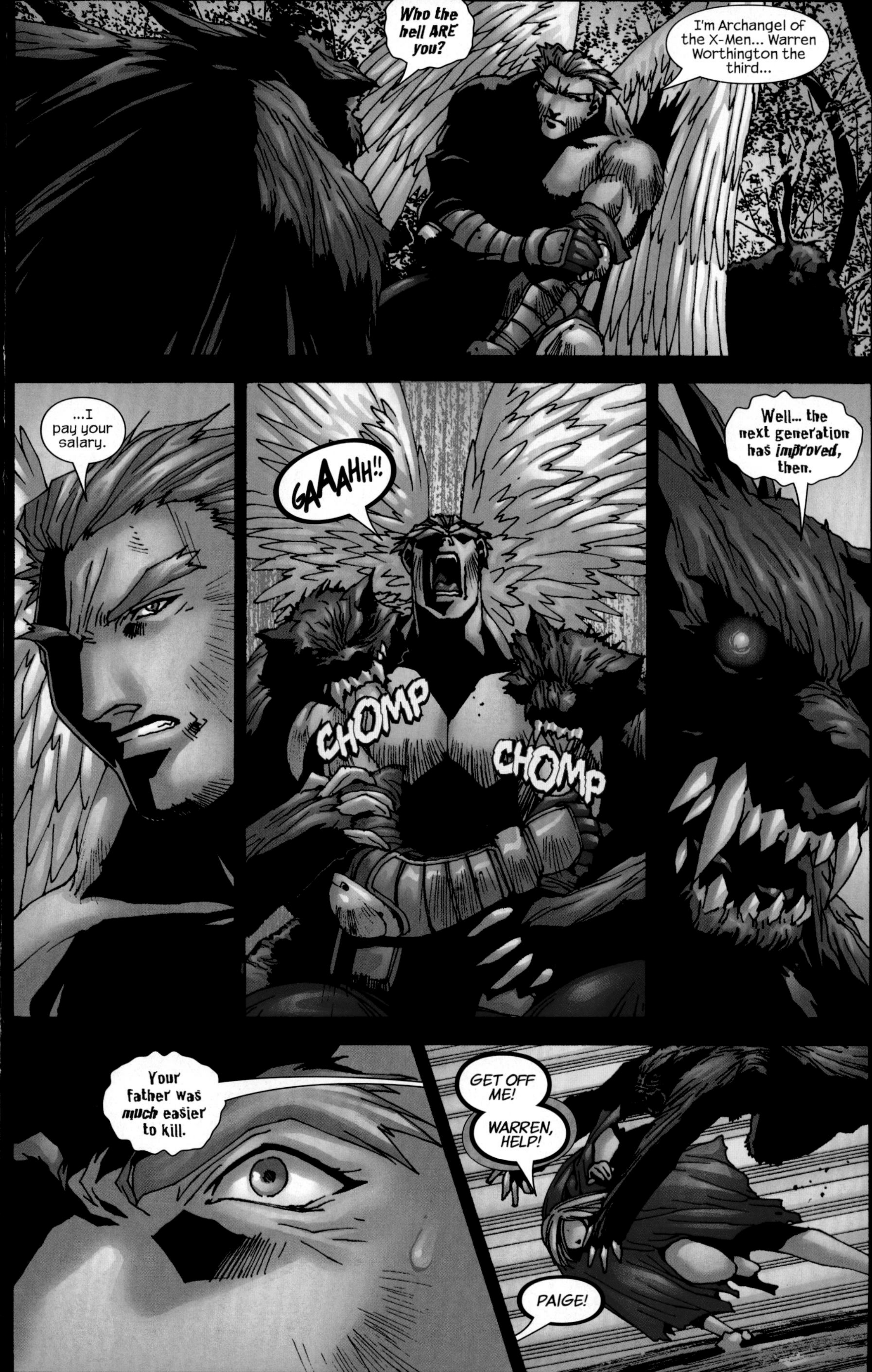

Who the hell ARE you?
I'm Archangel of the X-Men... Warren Worthington the third...
...I pay your salary.
GAAAHH!!
CHOMP
CHOMP
Well... the next generation has improved, then.
Your father was much easier to kill.
GET OFF ME!
WARREN, HELP!
PAIGE!

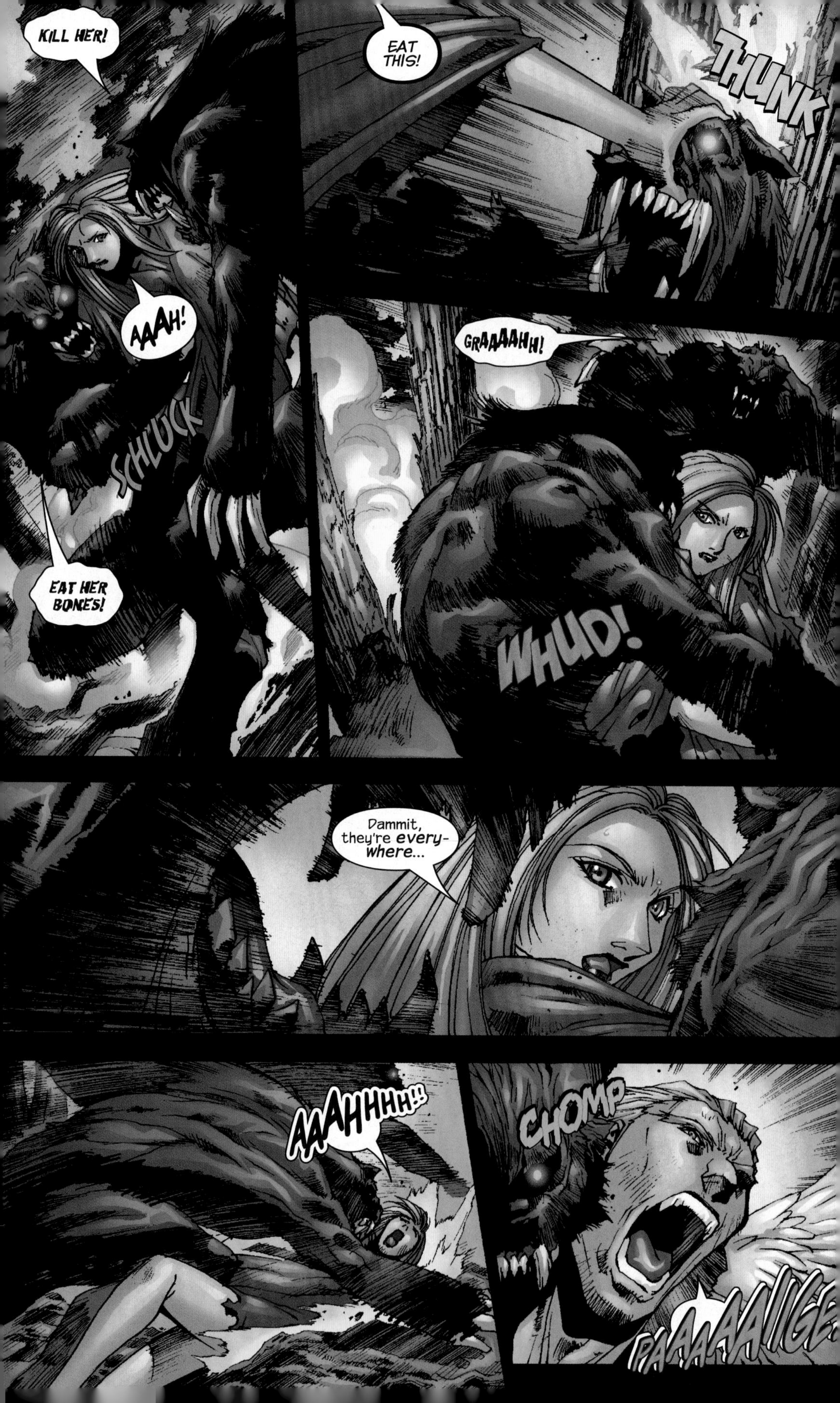
KILL HER!
AAAH!
SCHLUCK
EAT HER BONES!
EAT THIS!
THUNK
GRAAAAHH!
WHUD!
Dammit, they're every-where...
AAAHHHH!!
CHOMP

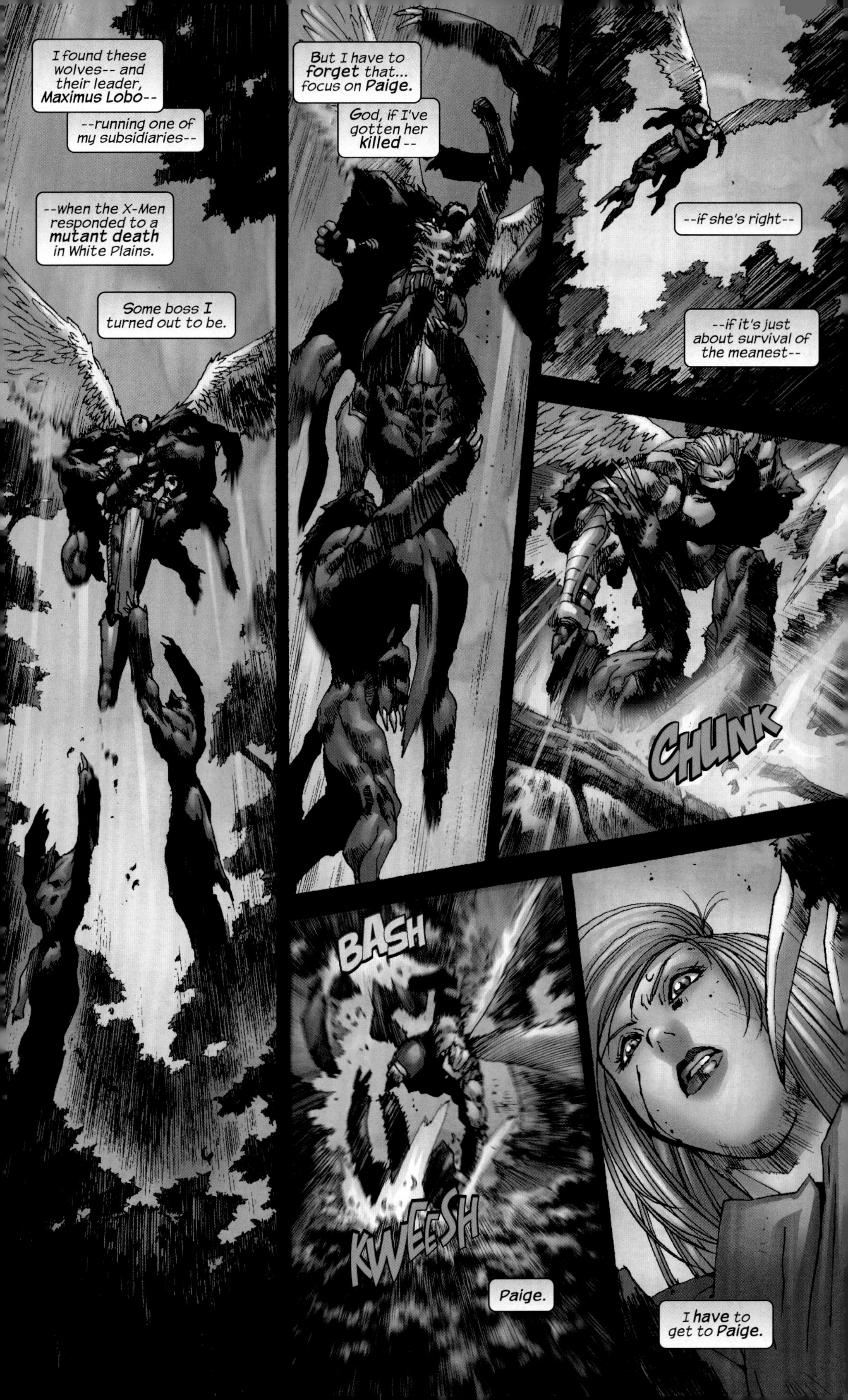

I found these wolves-- and their leader, Maximus Lobo--
--running one of my subsidiaries--
--when the X-Men responded to a mutant death in White Plains.
Some boss I turned out to be.
But I have to forget that... focus on Paige.
God, if I've gotten her killed--
--if she's right--
--if it's just about survival of the meanest--
CHUNK
BASH
KWEESH
Paige.
I have to get to Paige.

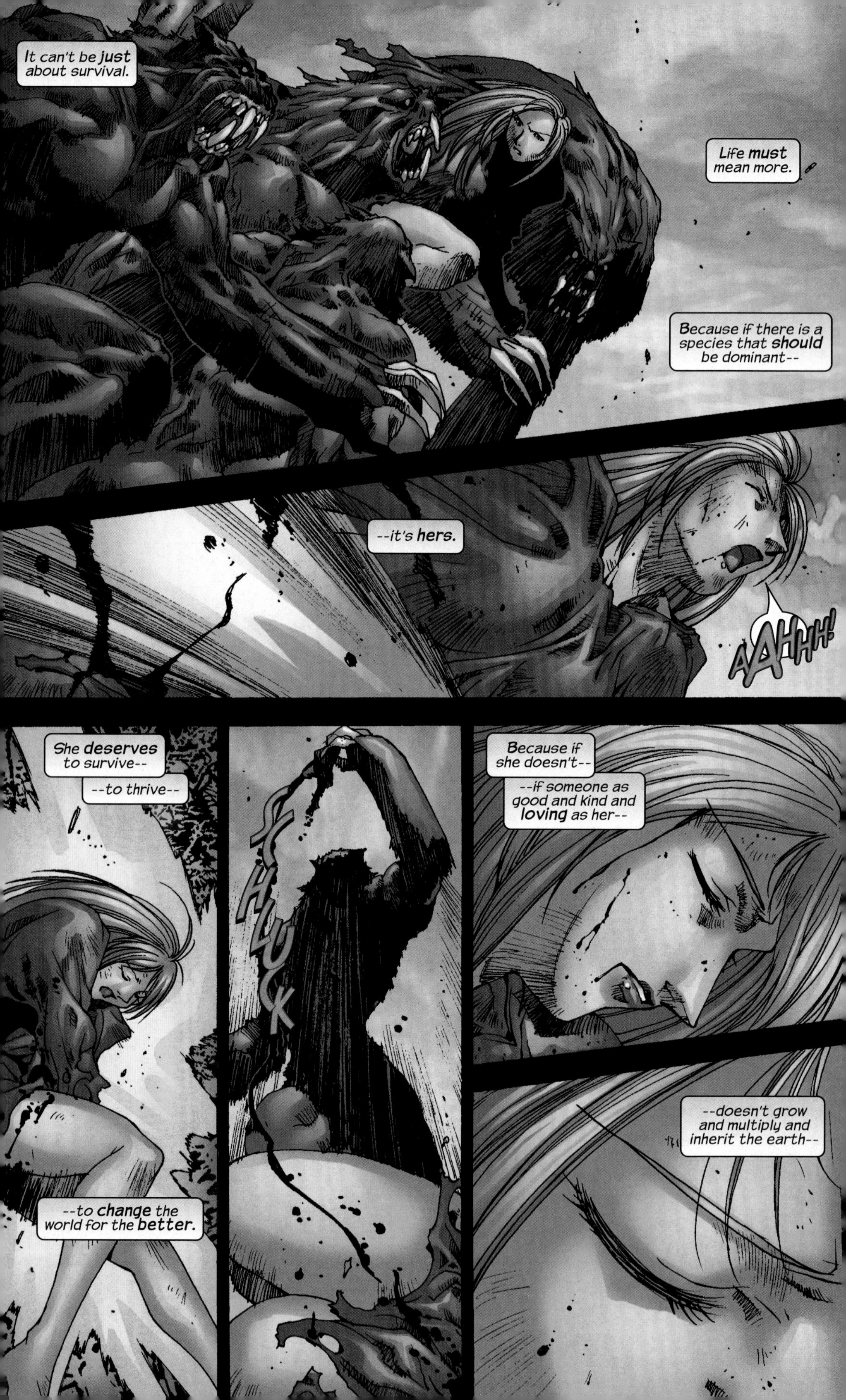
It can't be just about survival.
Life must mean more.
Because if there is a species that should be dominant--
--it's hers.
AAHHH!
She deserves to survive--
--to thrive--
--to change the world for the better.
SHHLUCK
Because if she doesn't--
--if someone as good and kind and loving as her--
--doesn't grow and multiply and inherit the earth--

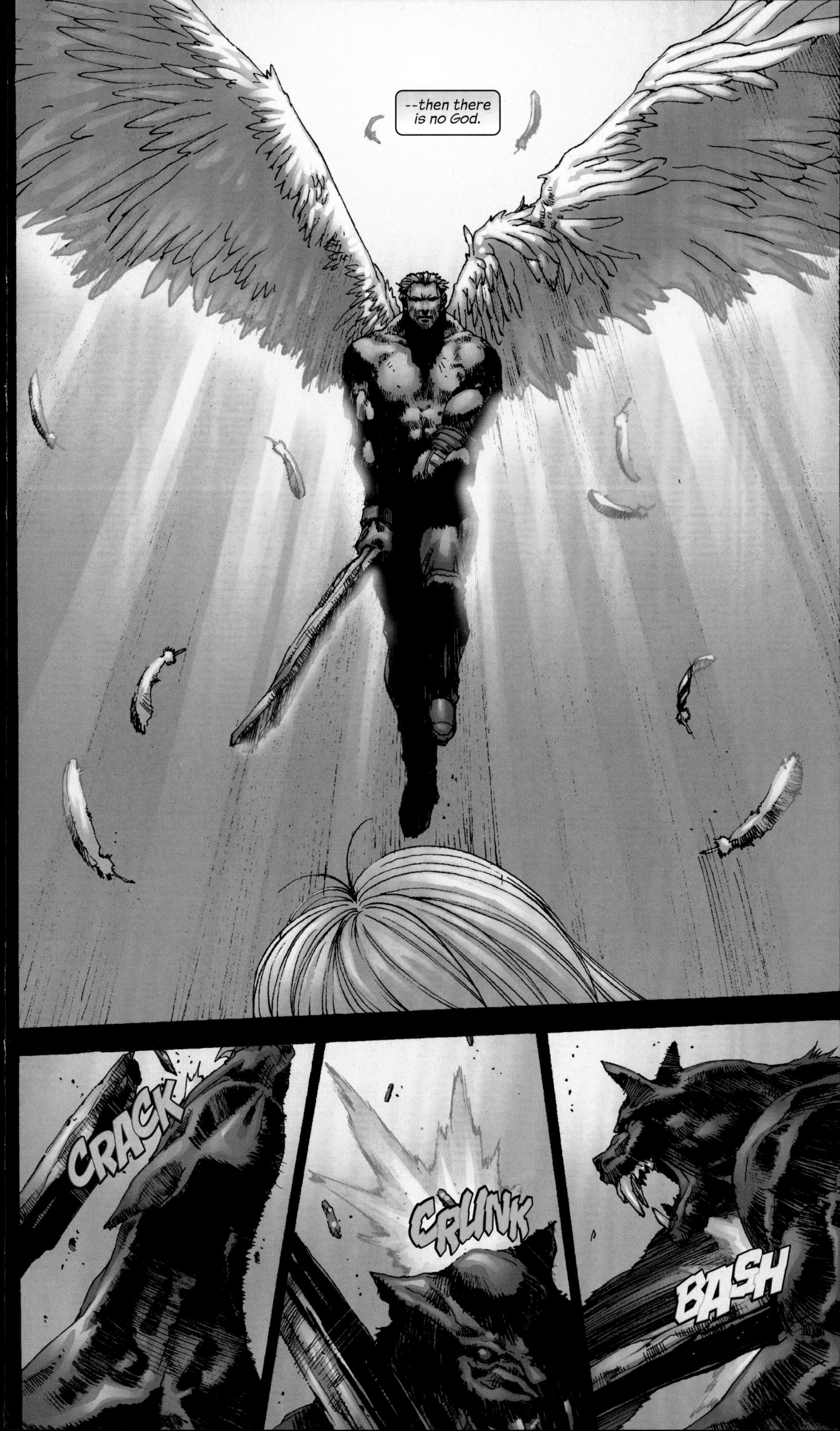
--then there is no God.
CRACK
CRUNK
BASH

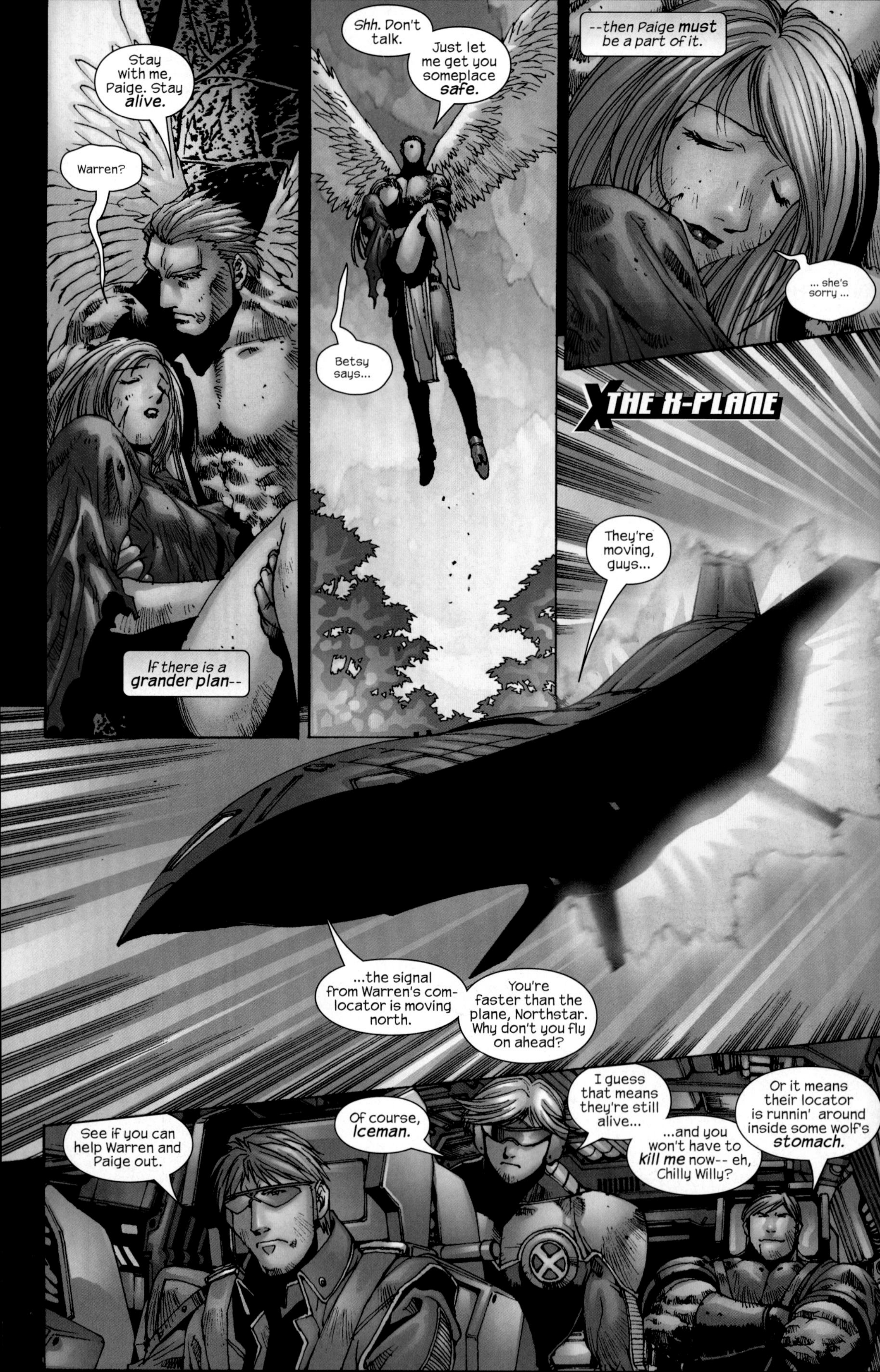
Stay with me, Paige. Stay alive.
Warren?
If there is a grander plan--
Shh. Don't talk.
Just let me get you someplace safe.
Betsy says...
--then Paige must be a part of it.
... she's sorry ...
THE X-PLANE
They're moving, guys...
...the signal from Warren's com-locator is moving north.
You're faster than the plane, Northstar. Why don't you fly on ahead?
See if you can help Warren and Paige out.
Of course, Iceman.
I guess that means they're still alive...
...and you won't have to kill me now-- eh, Chilly Willy?
Or it means their locator is runnin' around inside some wolf's stomach.

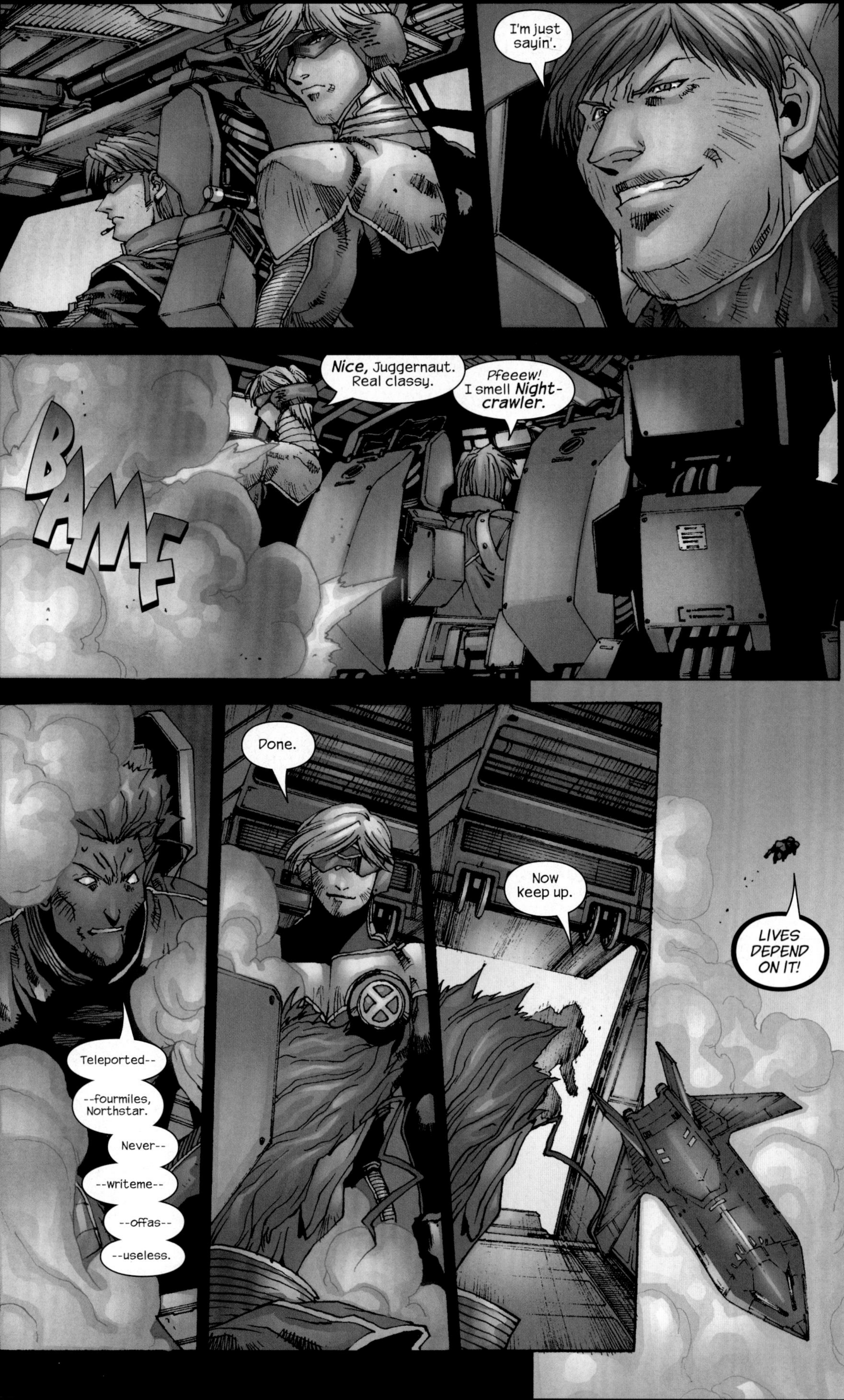
I'm just sayin'.
Nice, Juggernaut. Real classy.
Pfeeew! I smell Night-crawler.
BAMF
Done.
Now keep up.
LIVES DEPEND ON IT!
Teleported--
--fourmiles, Northstar.
Never--
--writeme--
--offas--
--useless.

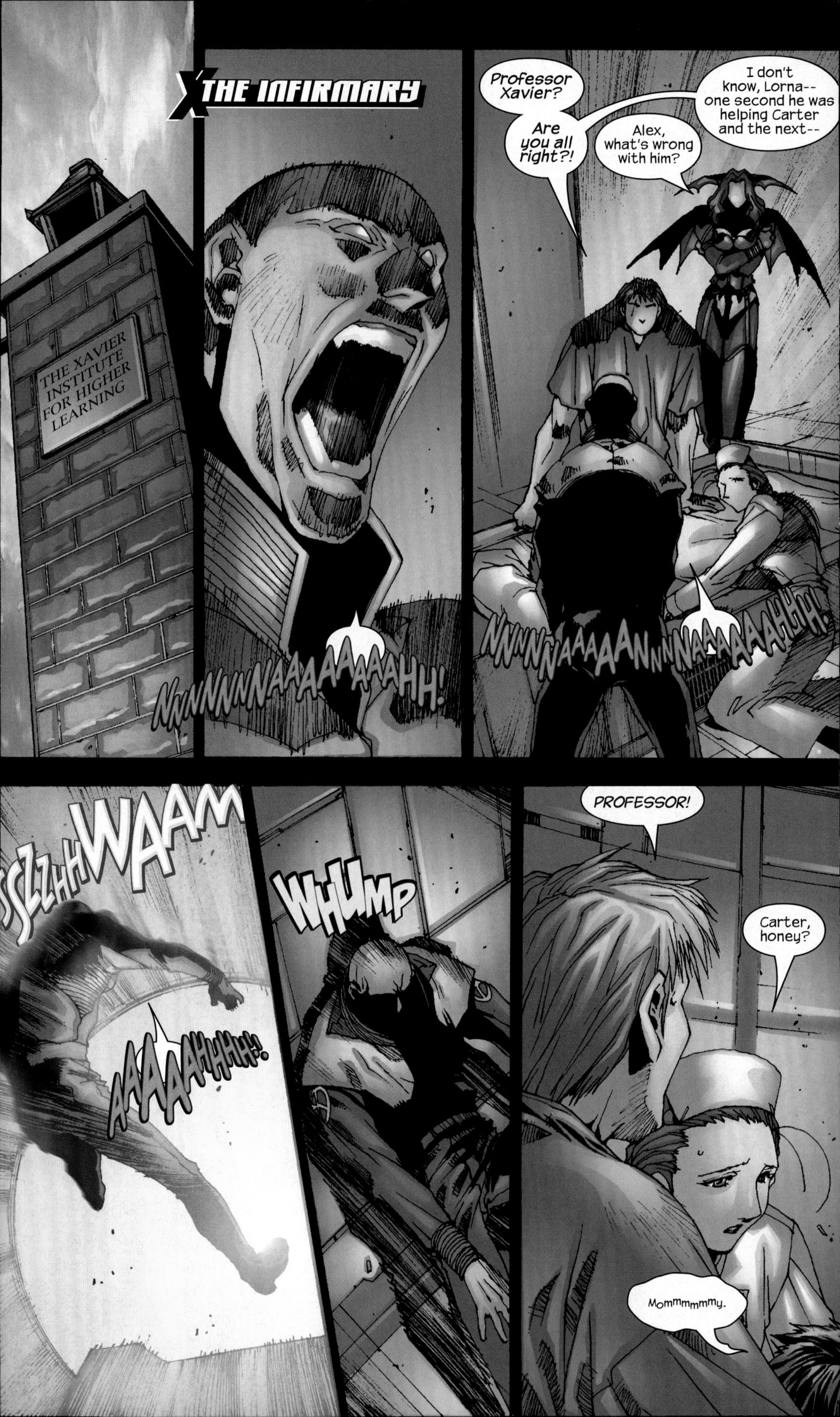
THE INFIRMARY
THE XAVIER INSTITUTE FOR HIGHER LEARNING
NNNNNNNAAAAAAAAAHH!
Professor Xavier?
Are you all right?!
Alex, what's wrong with him?
I don't know, Lorna-- one second he was helping Carter and the next--
NNNNNAAAANNNNAAAAAAAHHH!
SSZZHHWAAM
AAAAAHHHH!
WHUMP
PROFESSOR!
Carter, honey?
Mommmmmmy.

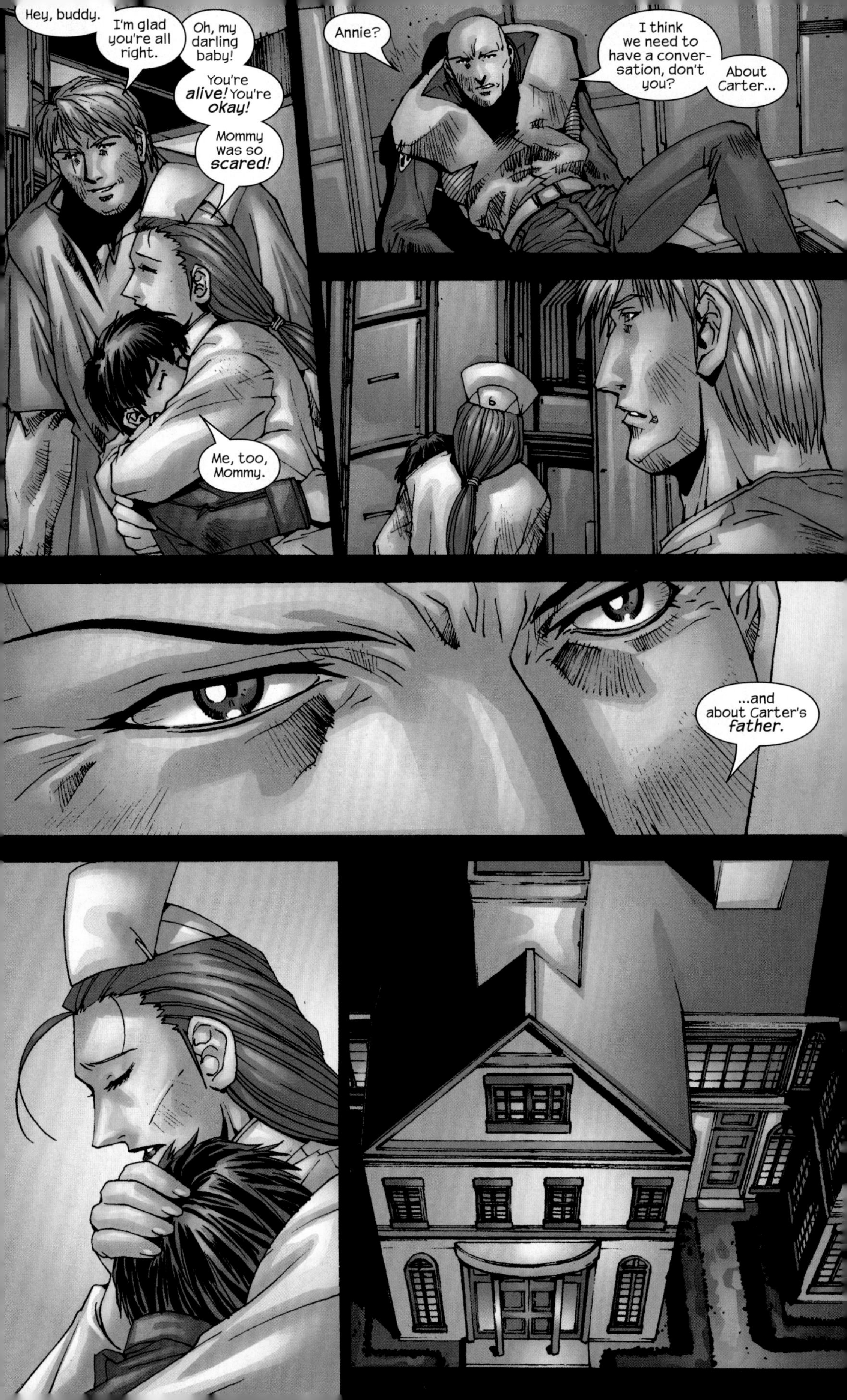
Hey, buddy.
I'm glad you're all right.
Oh, my darling baby!
You're alive! You're okay!
Mommy was so scared!
Me, too, Mommy.
Annie?
I think we need to have a conver-sation, don't you?
About Carter...
...and about Carter's father.

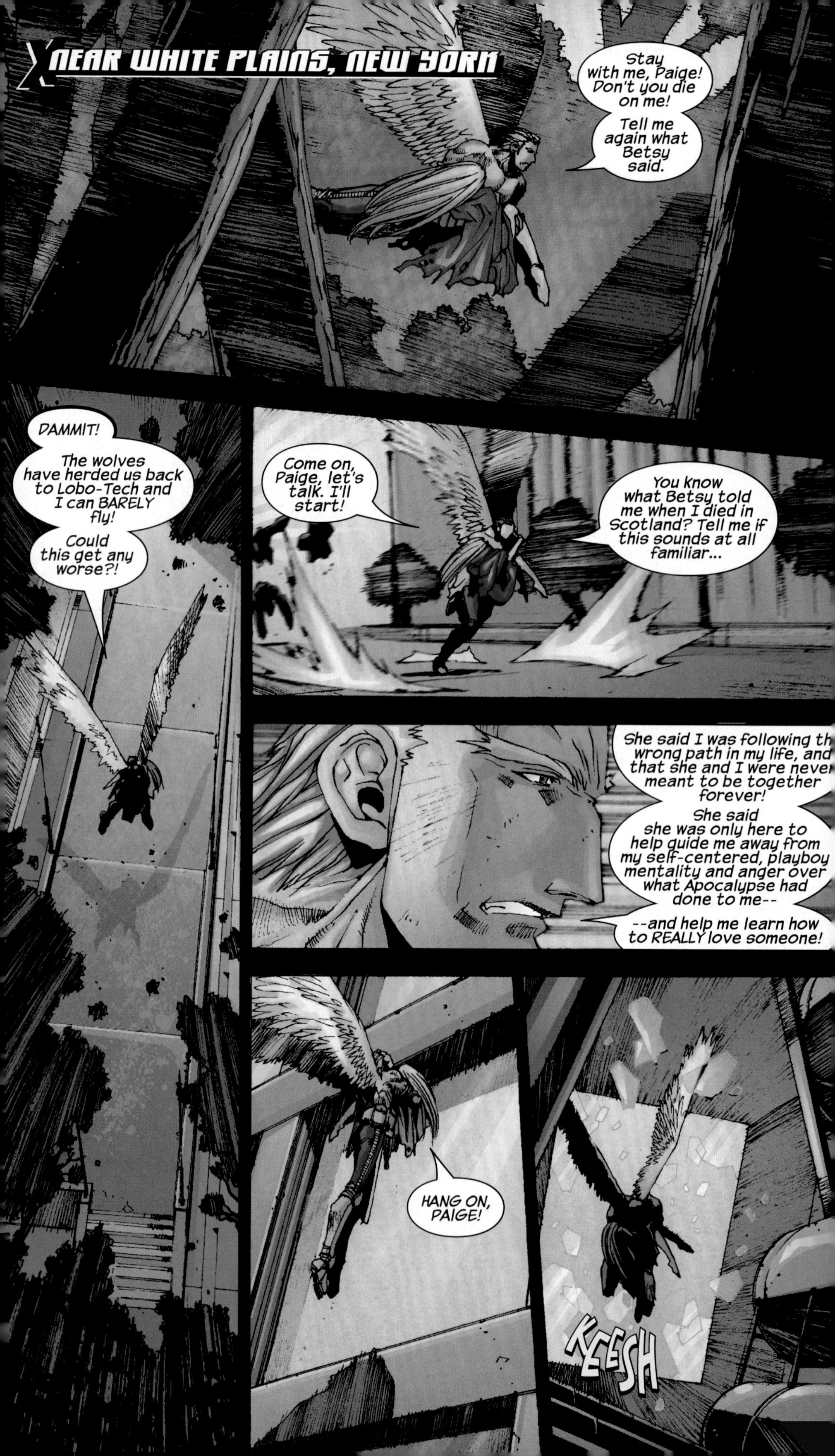
NEAR WHITE PLAINS, NEW YORK
Stay with me, Paige! Don't you die on me!
Tell me again what Betsy said.
DAMMIT!
The wolves have herded us back to Lobo-Tech and I can BARELY fly!
Could this get any worse?!
Come on, Paige, let's talk. I'll start!
You know what Betsy told me when I died in Scotland? Tell me if this sounds at all familiar...
She said I was following th wrong path in my life, and that she and I were neve meant to be together forever!
She said she was only here to help guide me away from my self-centered, playboy mentality and anger over what Apocalypse had done to me--
--and help me learn how to REALLY love someone!
HANG ON, PAIGE!
KEESH

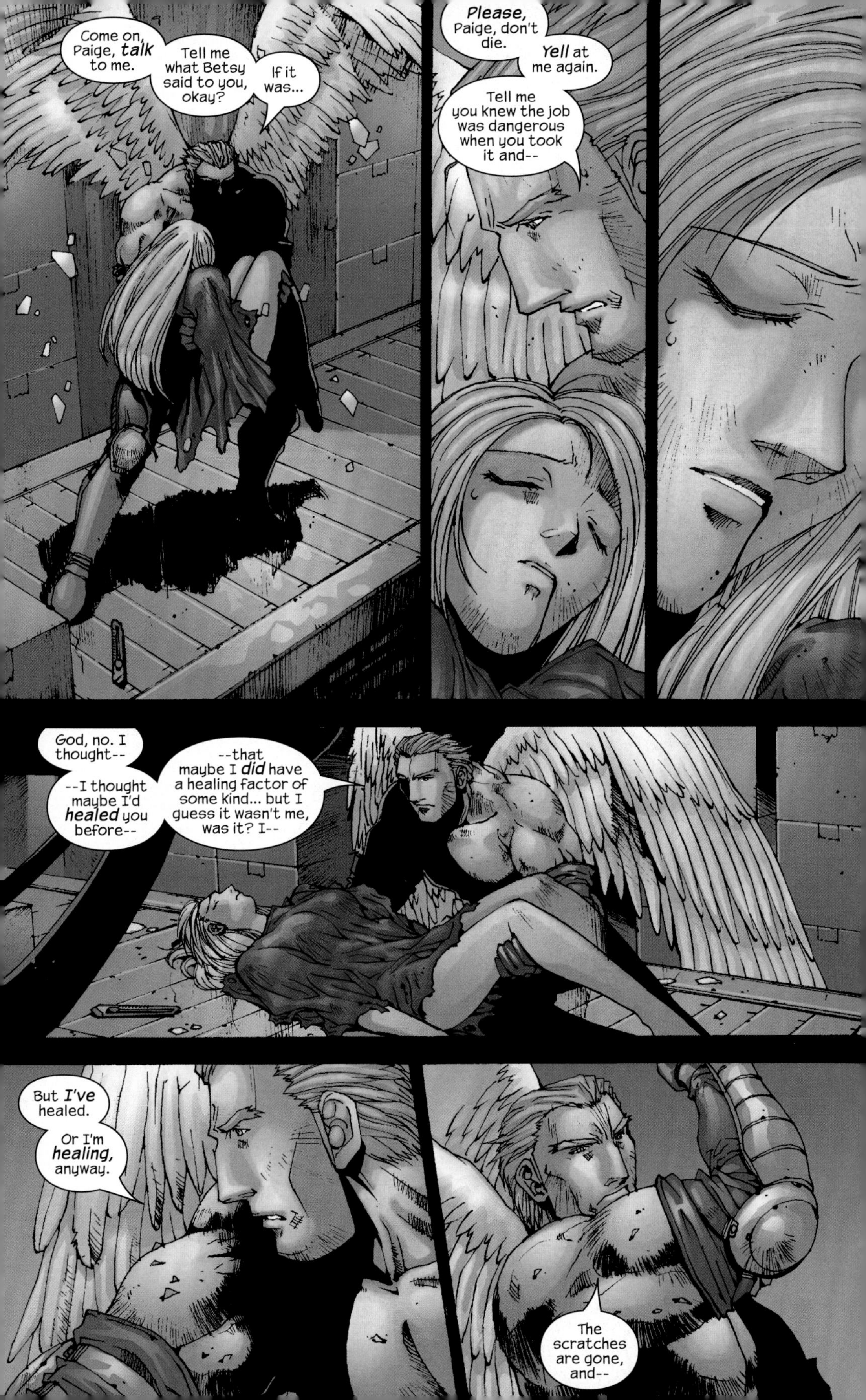

Come on, Paige, *talk* to me.
Tell me what Betsy said to you, okay?
If it was...
Please, Paige, don't die.
Yell at me again.
Tell me you knew the job was dangerous when you took it and--
God, no. I thought--
--I thought maybe I'd *healed* you before--
--that maybe I *did* have a healing factor of some kind... but I guess it wasn't me, was it? I--
But *I've* healed.
Or I'm *healing,* anyway.
The scratches are gone, and--

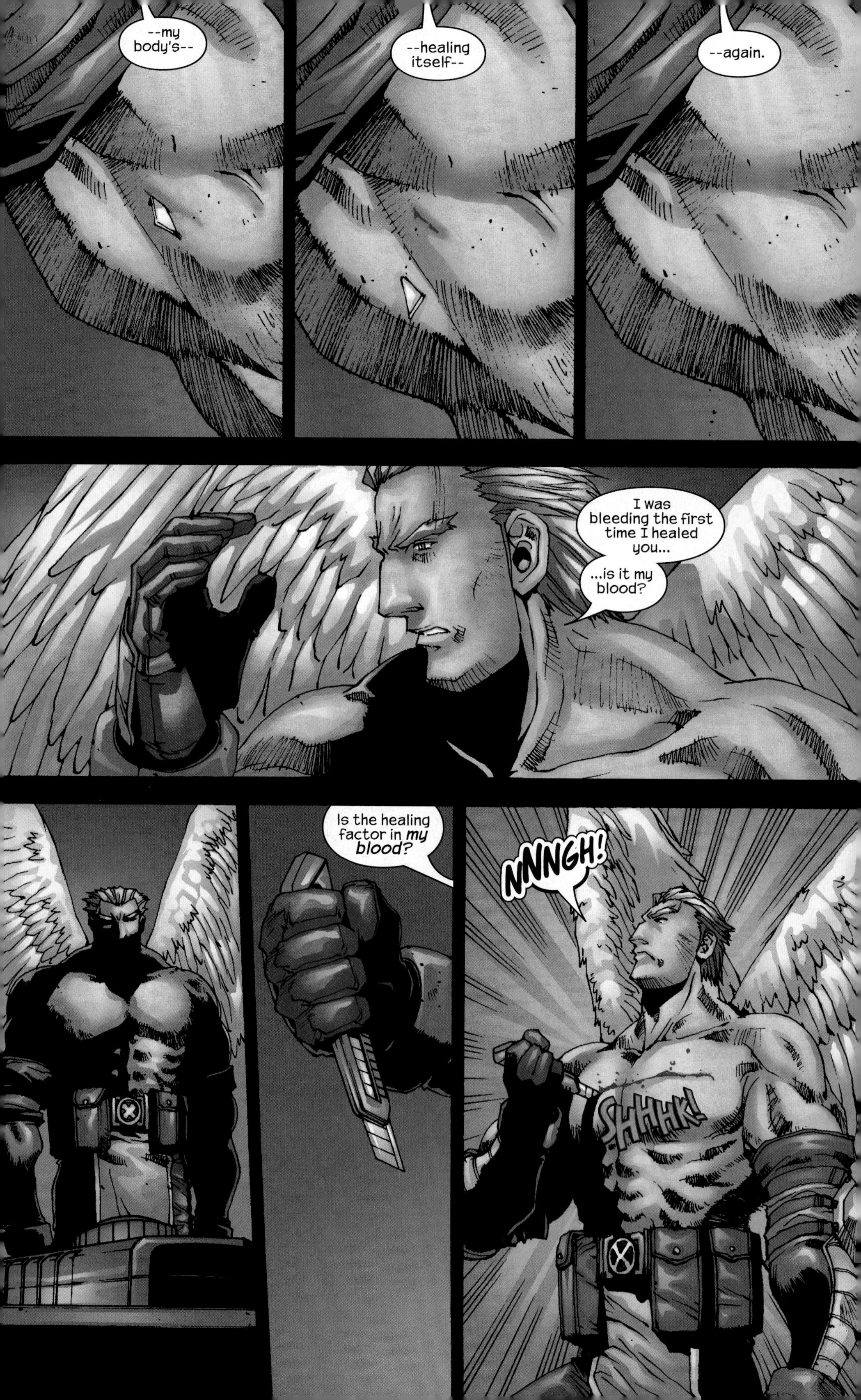
--my body's--
--healing itself--
--again.
I was bleeding the first time I healed you...
...is it my blood?
Is the healing factor in *my blood?*
NNNGH!
SHHHK!

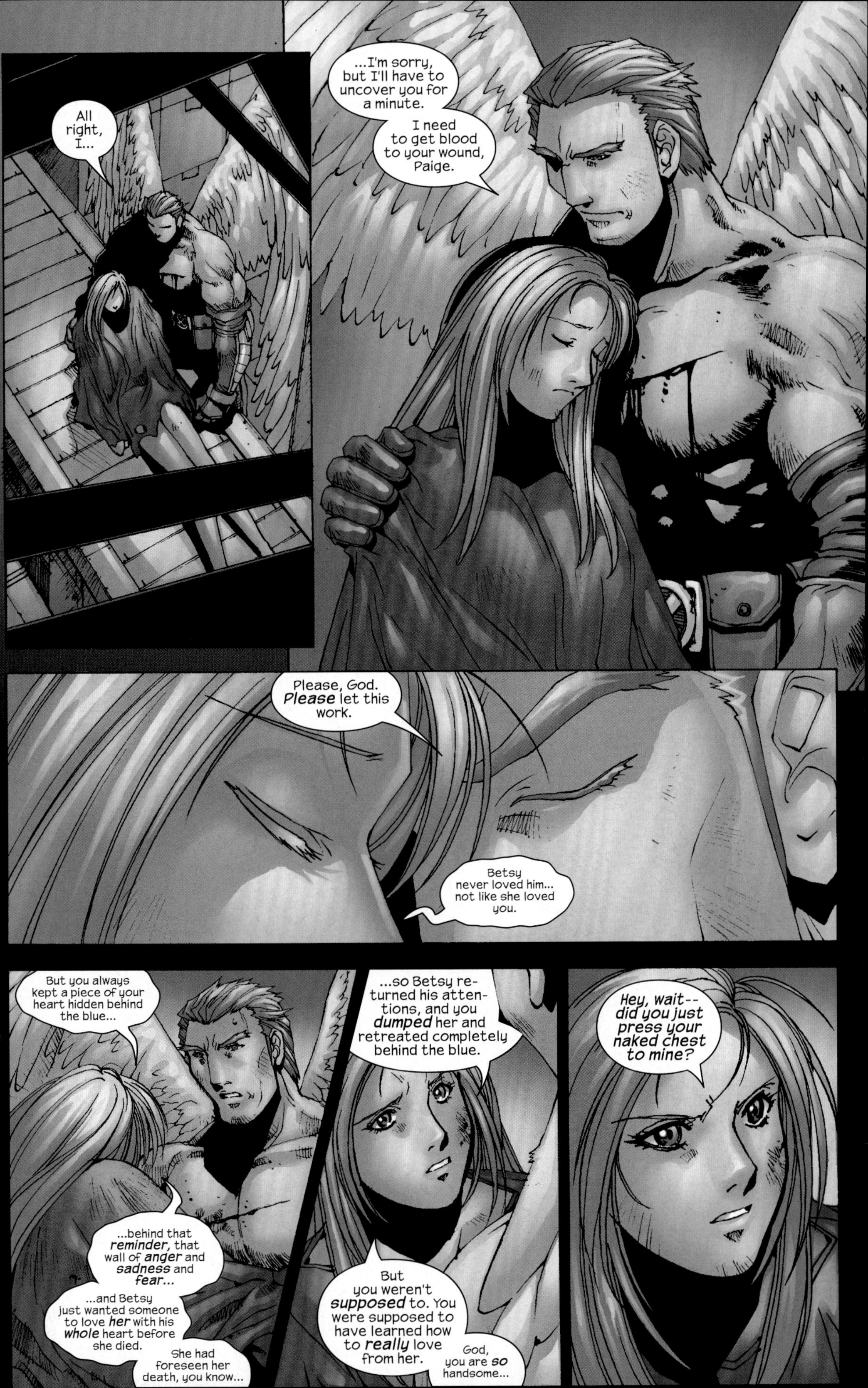
All right, I...
...I'm sorry, but I'll have to uncover you for a minute.
I need to get blood to your wound, Paige.
Please, God. Please let this work.
Betsy never loved him... not like she loved you.
But you always kept a piece of your heart hidden behind the blue...
...behind that reminder, that wall of anger and sadness and fear...
...and Betsy just wanted someone to love her with his whole heart before she died.
She had foreseen her death, you know...
...so Betsy returned his attentions, and you dumped her and retreated completely behind the blue.
But you weren't supposed to. You were supposed to have learned how to really love from her.
God, you are so handsome...
Hey, wait--did you just press your naked chest to mine?

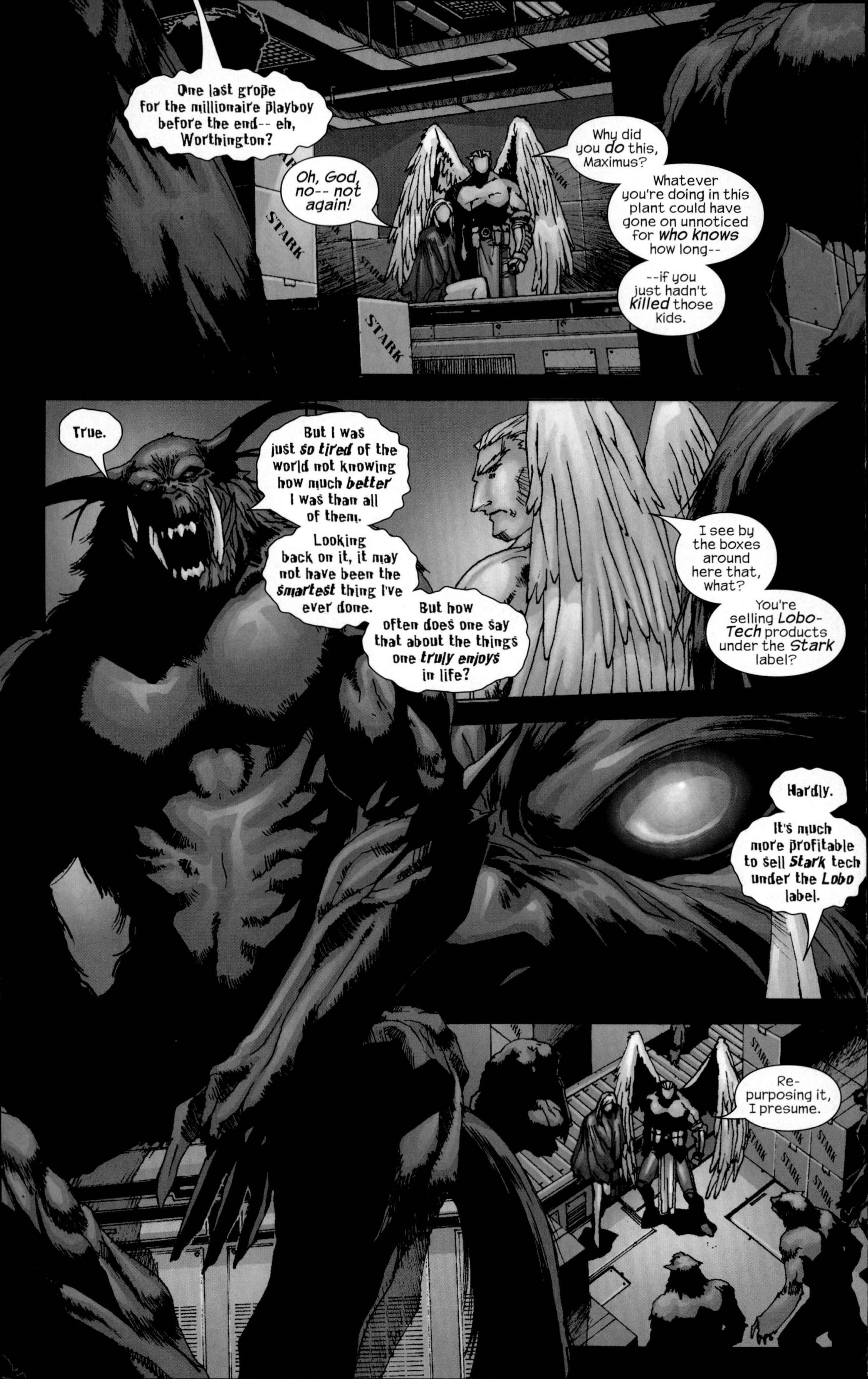

One last grope for the millionaire playboy before the end-- eh, Worthington?
Oh, God, no-- not again!
Why did you do this, Maximus?
Whatever you're doing in this plant could have gone on unnoticed for who knows how long--
--if you just hadn't killed those kids.
True.
But I was just so tired of the world not knowing how much better I was than all of them.
Looking back on it, it may not have been the smartest thing I've ever done.
But how often does one say that about the things one truly enjoys in life?
I see by the boxes around here that, what?
You're selling Lobo-Tech products under the Stark label?
Hardly.
It's much more profitable to sell Stark tech under the Lobo label.
Re-purposing it, I presume.

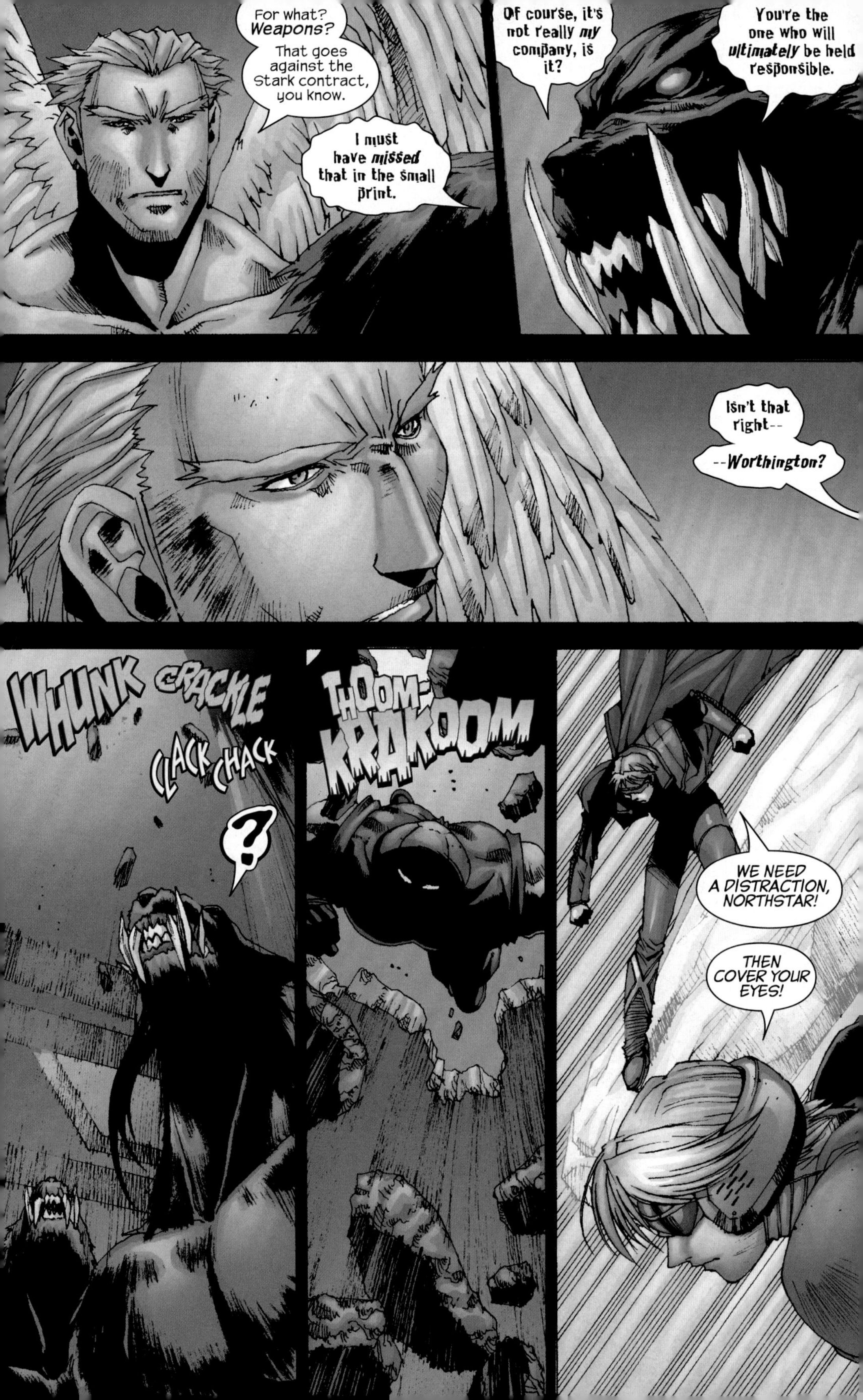

For what? Weapons?
That goes against the Stark contract, you know.
I must have missed that in the small print.
Of course, it's not really my company, is it?
You're the one who will ultimately be held responsible.
Isn't that right--
--Worthington?
WHUNK
CRACKLE
CLACK
CHACK
?
THOOM-
KRAKOOM
WE NEED A DISTRACTION, NORTHSTAR!
THEN COVER YOUR EYES!

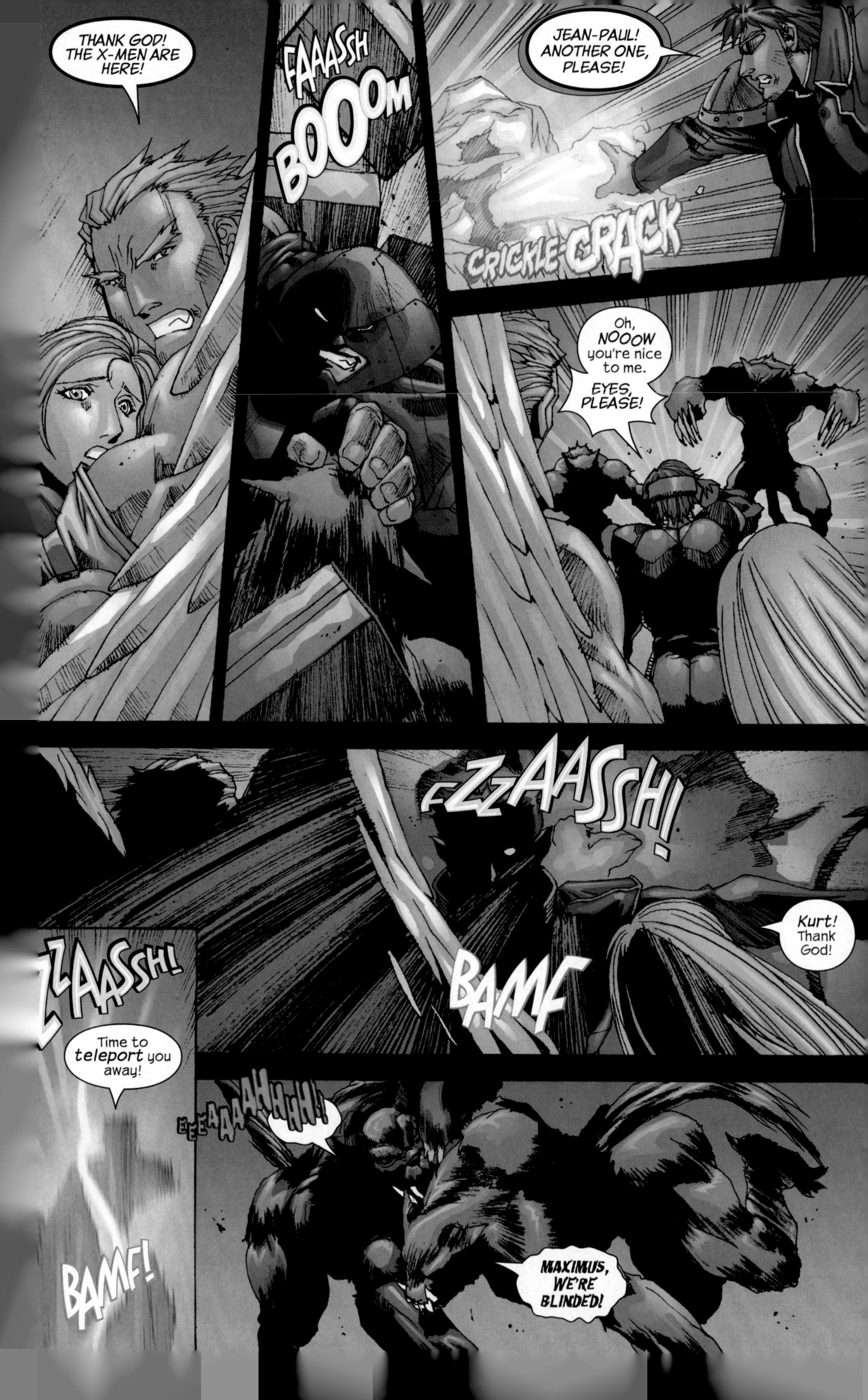
THANK GOD! THE X-MEN ARE HERE!
FAAASSH
BOOOM
JEAN-PAUL! ANOTHER ONE, PLEASE!
CRICKLE-CRACK
Oh, NOOOW you're nice to me.
EYES, PLEASE!
FZZAASSH!
Kurt! Thank God!
BAMF
ZZAASSH!
Time to teleport you away!
EEEAAAAHHHHH!
BAMF!
MAXIMUS, WE'RE BLINDED!

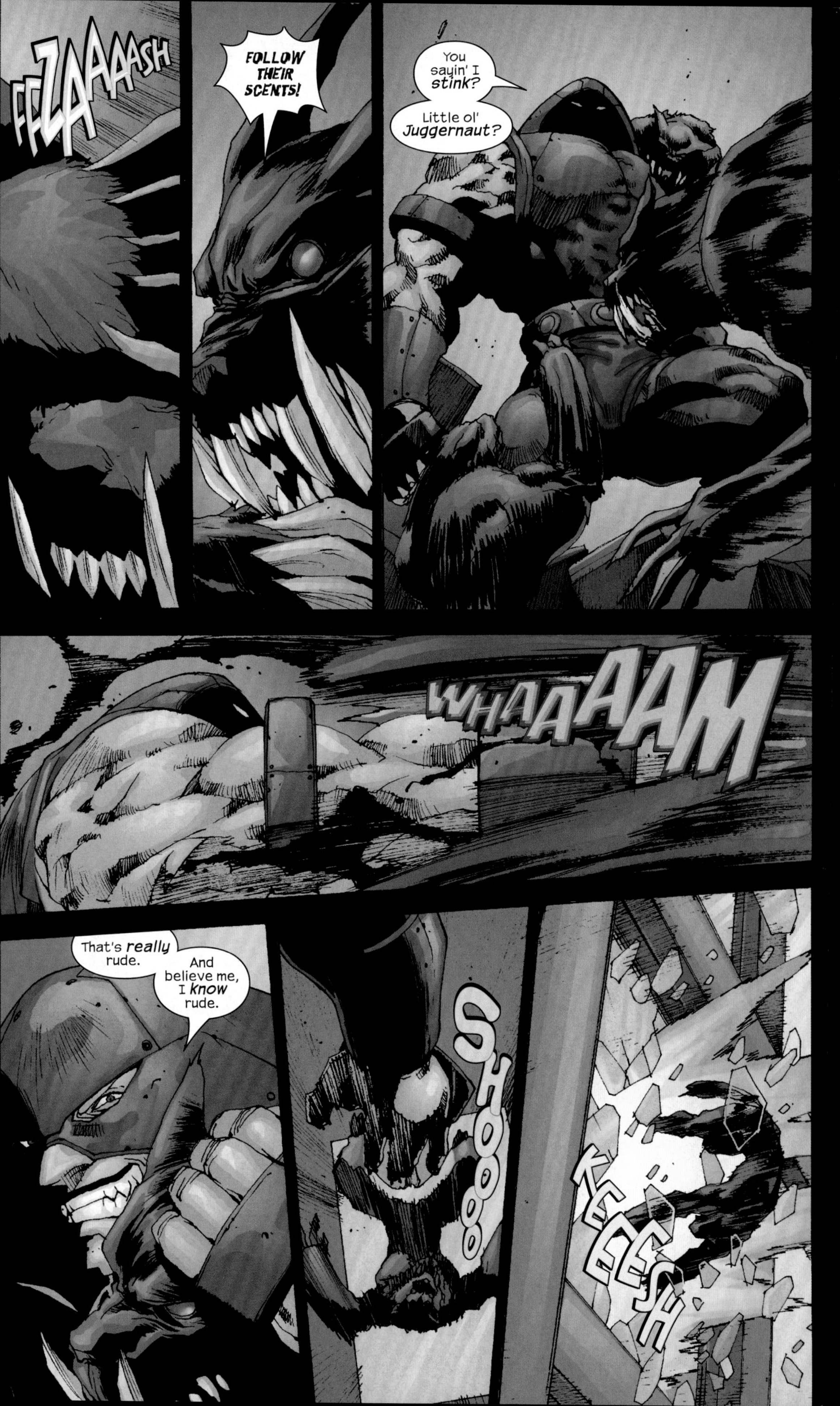
FFZAAAAASH
FOLLOW THEIR SCENTS!
You sayin' I stink?
Little ol' Juggernaut?
WHAAAAAM
That's really rude.
And believe me, I know rude.
SHOOOOO
KEEESH

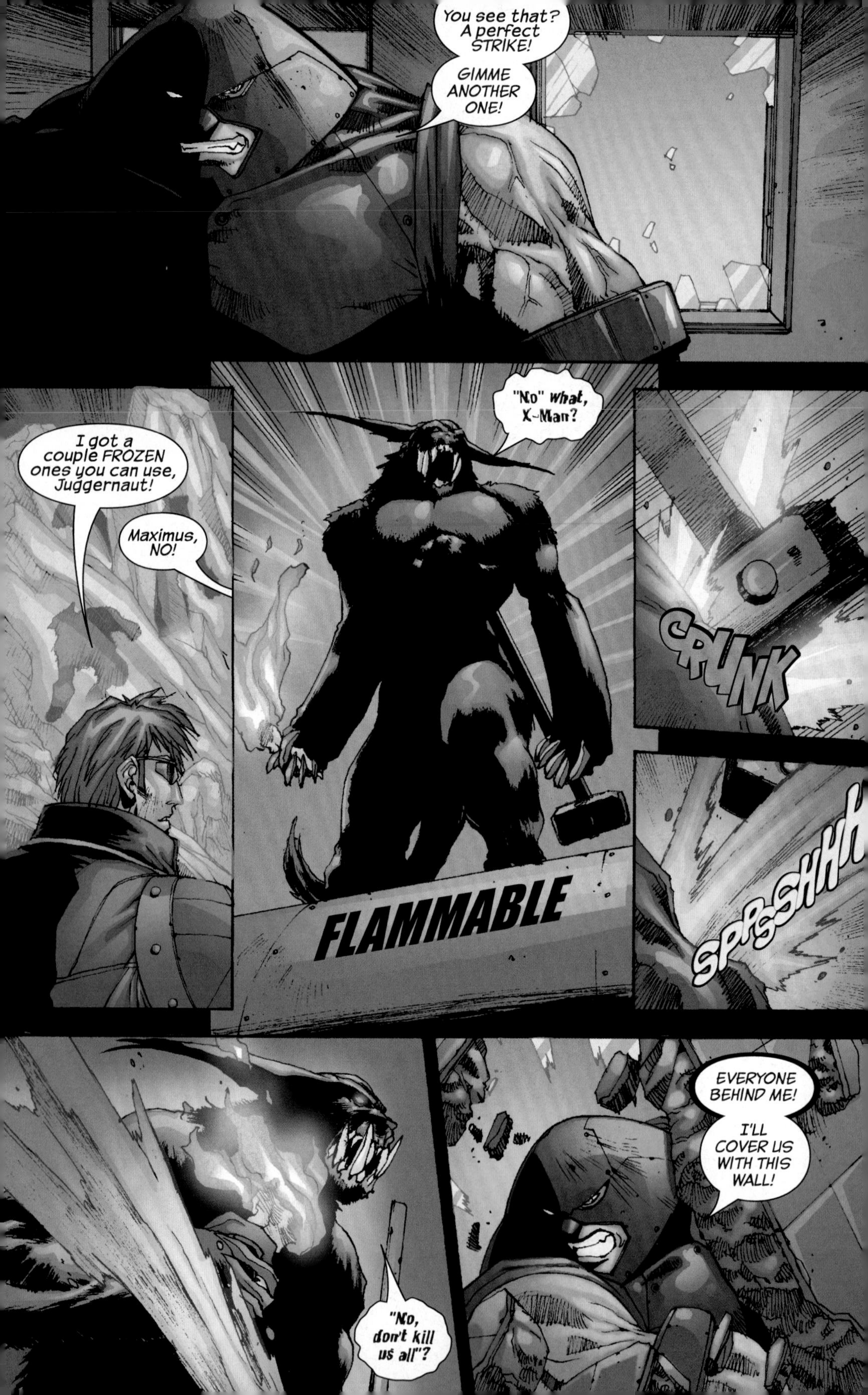

You see that? A perfect STRIKE!
GIMME ANOTHER ONE!
I got a couple FROZEN ones you can use, Juggernaut!
Maximus, NO!
"No" what, X-Man?
FLAMMABLE
CRUNK
SPRSSHHH
"No, don't kill us all"?
EVERYONE BEHIND ME!
I'LL COVER US WITH THIS WALL!

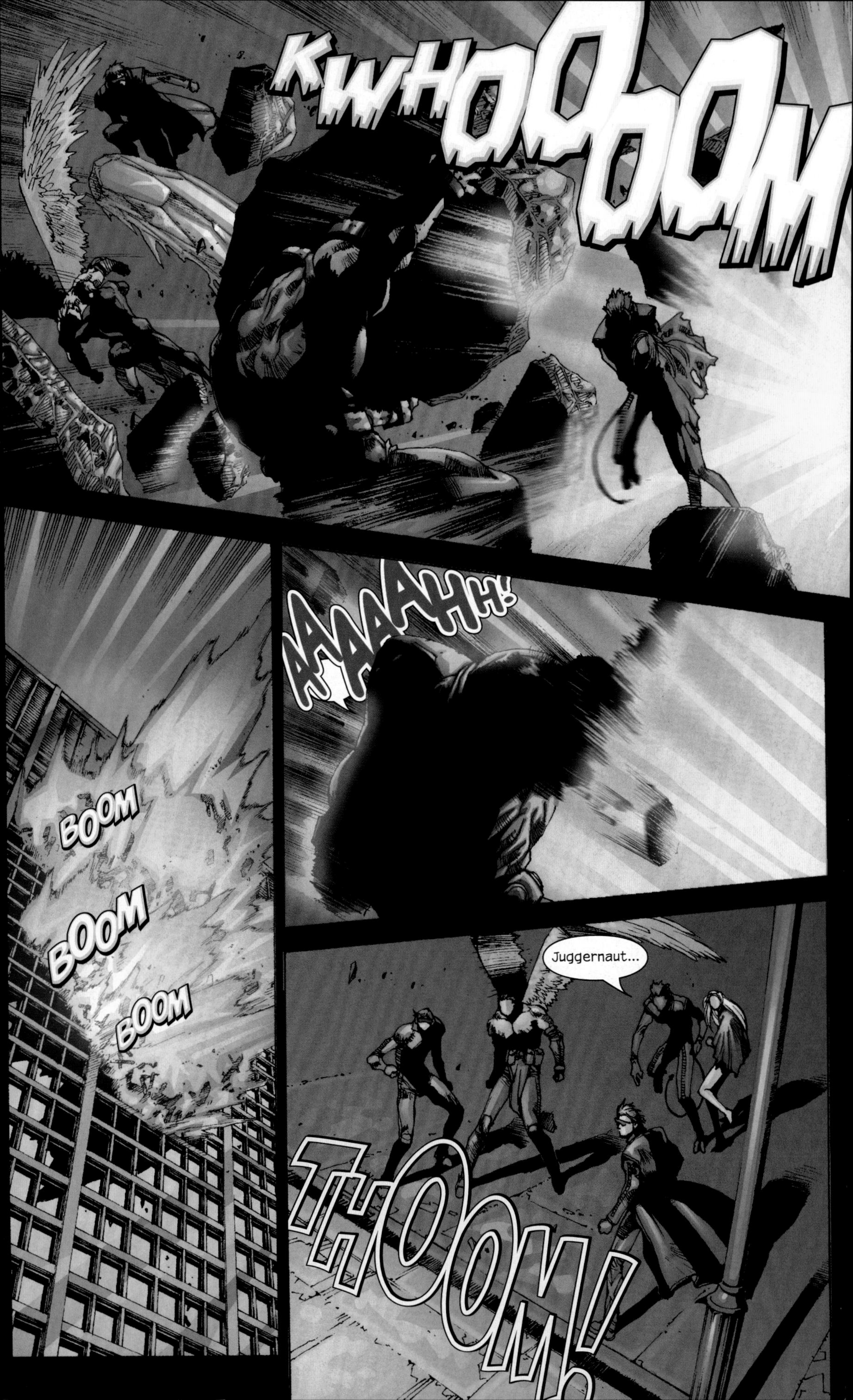
KWHOOOOOOM
AAAAAHH!
BOOM
BOOM
BOOM
Juggernaut...
THOOOM!

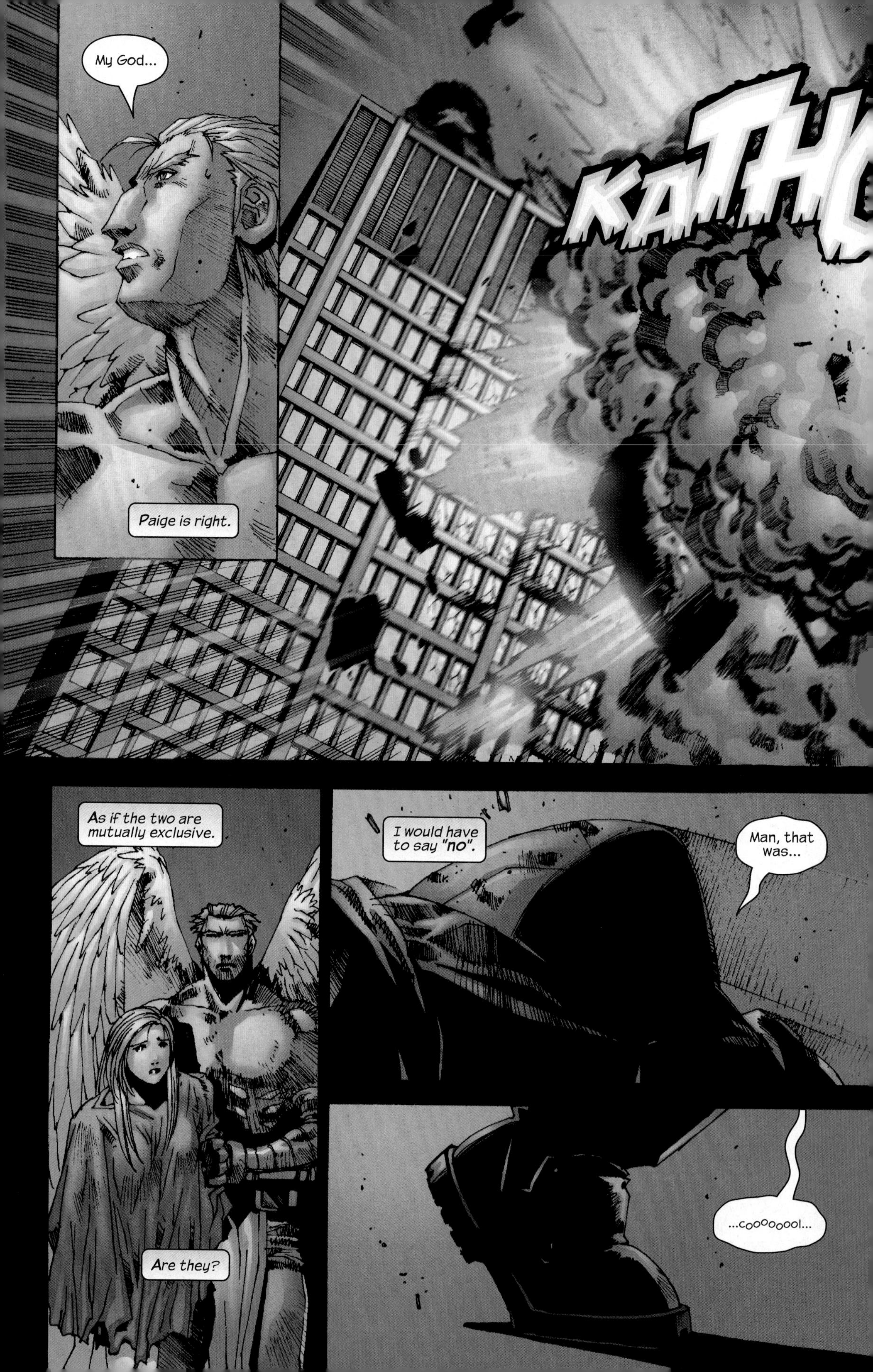
My God...
Paige is right.
KATHO
As if the two are mutually exclusive.
Are they?
I would have to say "no".
Man, that was...
...cooooooool...

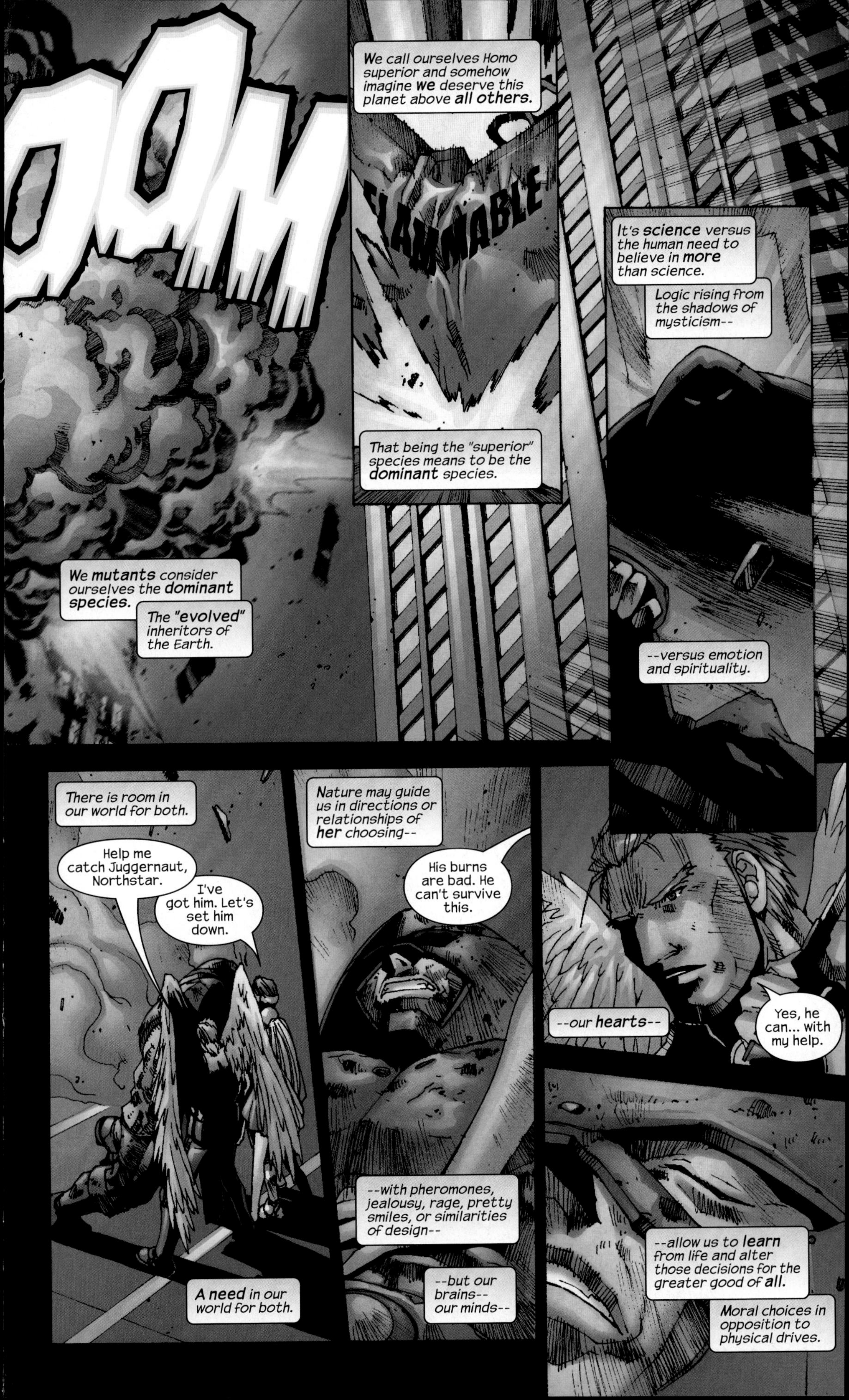
DOOM
We mutants consider ourselves the dominant species.
The "evolved" inheritors of the Earth.
We call ourselves Homo superior and somehow imagine we deserve this planet above all others.
FLAMMABLE
That being the "superior" species means to be the dominant species.
It's science versus the human need to believe in more than science.
Logic rising from the shadows of mysticism--
--versus emotion and spirituality.
There is room in our world for both.
Help me catch Juggernaut, Northstar.
I've got him. Let's set him down.
A need in our world for both.
Nature may guide us in directions or relationships of her choosing--
His burns are bad. He can't survive this.
--with pheromones, jealousy, rage, pretty smiles, or similarities of design--
--but our brains-- our minds--
--our hearts--
Yes, he can... with my help.
--allow us to learn from life and alter those decisions for the greater good of all.
Moral choices in opposition to physical drives.

X LATER...

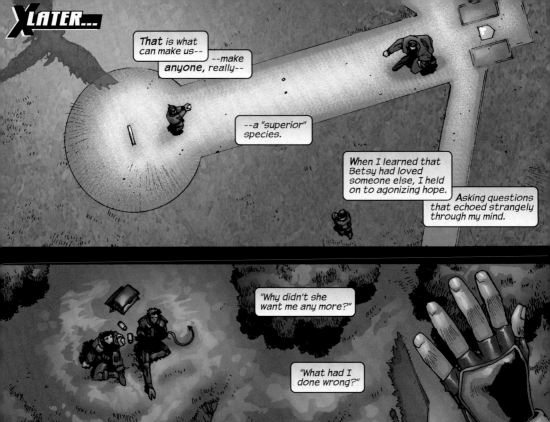

That is what can make us-- --make *anyone*, really-- --a "superior" species.

When I learned that Betsy had loved someone else, I held on to agonizing hope. Asking questions that echoed strangely through my mind.

"Why didn't she want me any more?"

"What had I done wrong?"

"Wouldn't I have been better off never having loved her?"

When I awoke from having died, I realized my words echoed--

--because they were the *same* words spoken to me so many times before-- --by women who had loved me when I couldn't love them.

Words usually spoken through *tears*.

I know you're near me, Betsy. That you can hear me.

Tears I now-- --at *last*-- --understand.

Before Betsy I loved casually--

Thank you, my love.

--or not at all.

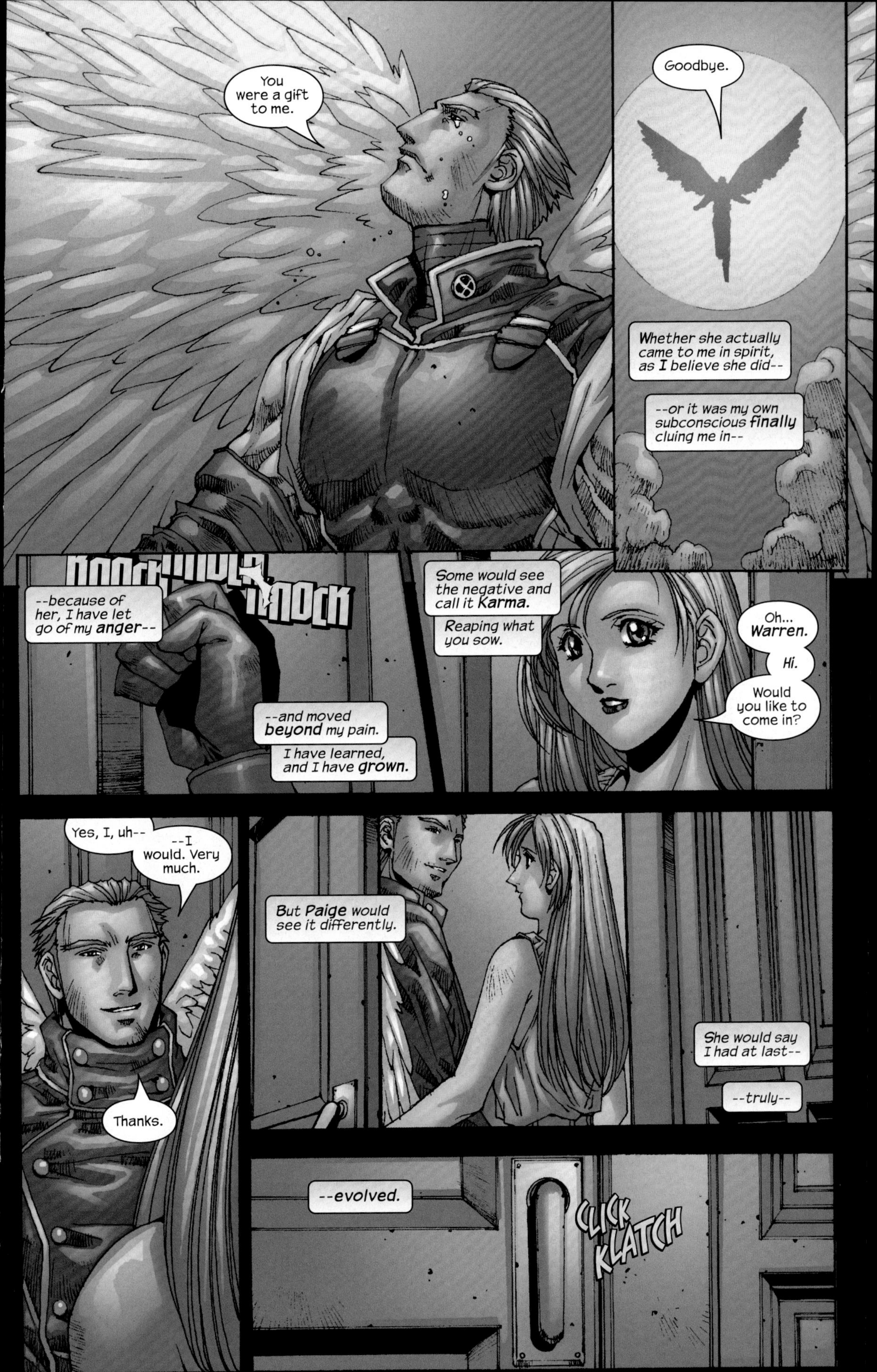
You were a gift to me.
Goodbye.
Whether she actually came to me in spirit, as I believe she did--
--or it was my own subconscious finally cluing me in--
--because of her, I have let go of my anger--
--and moved beyond my pain.
I have learned, and I have grown.
Some would see the negative and call it Karma.
Reaping what you sow.
Oh... Warren.
Hi.
Would you like to come in?
Yes, I, uh--
--I would. Very much.
Thanks.
But Paige would see it differently.
She would say I had at last--
--truly--
--evolved.
CLICK
KLATCH

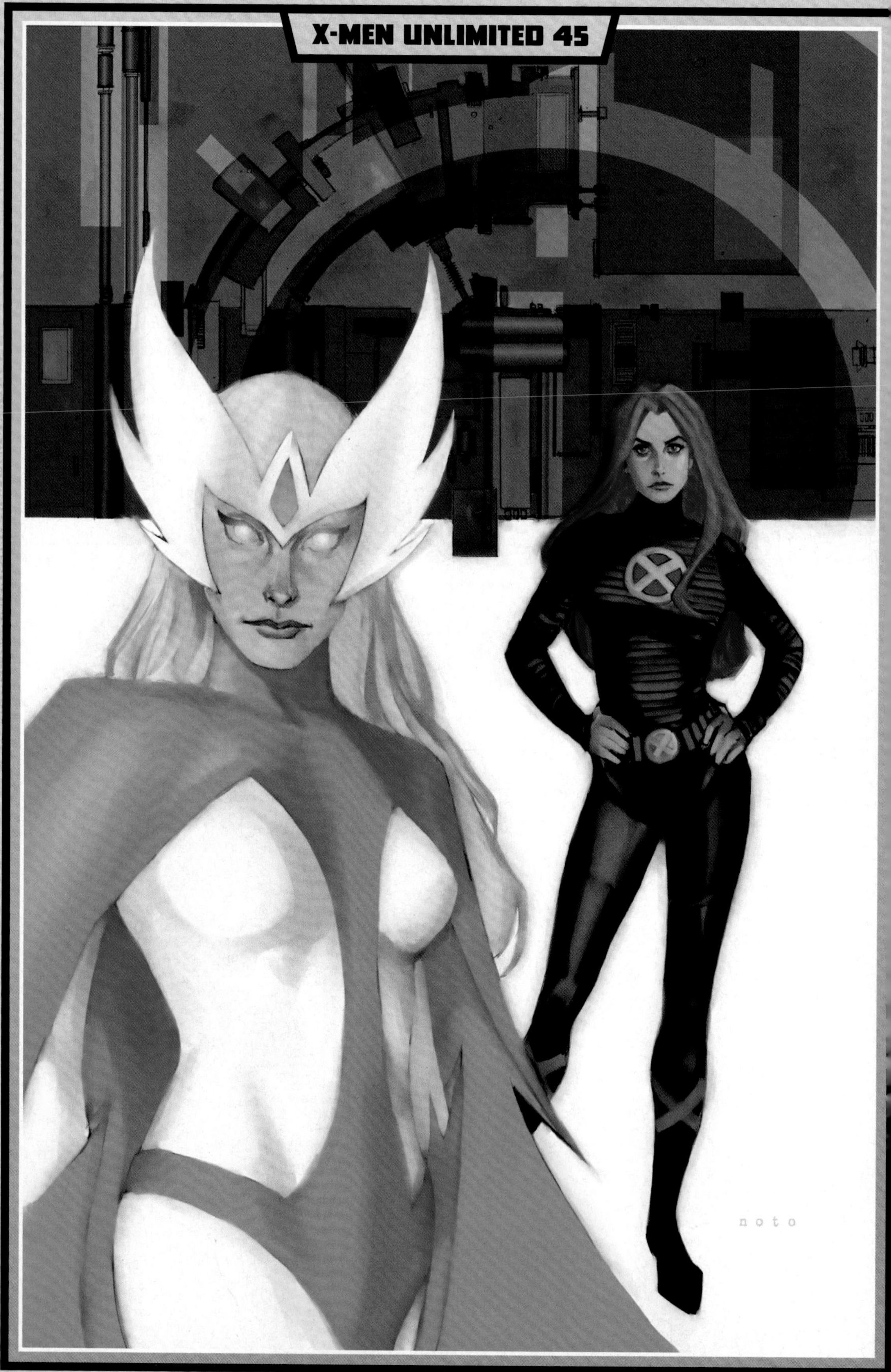
X-MEN UNLIMITED 45
noto

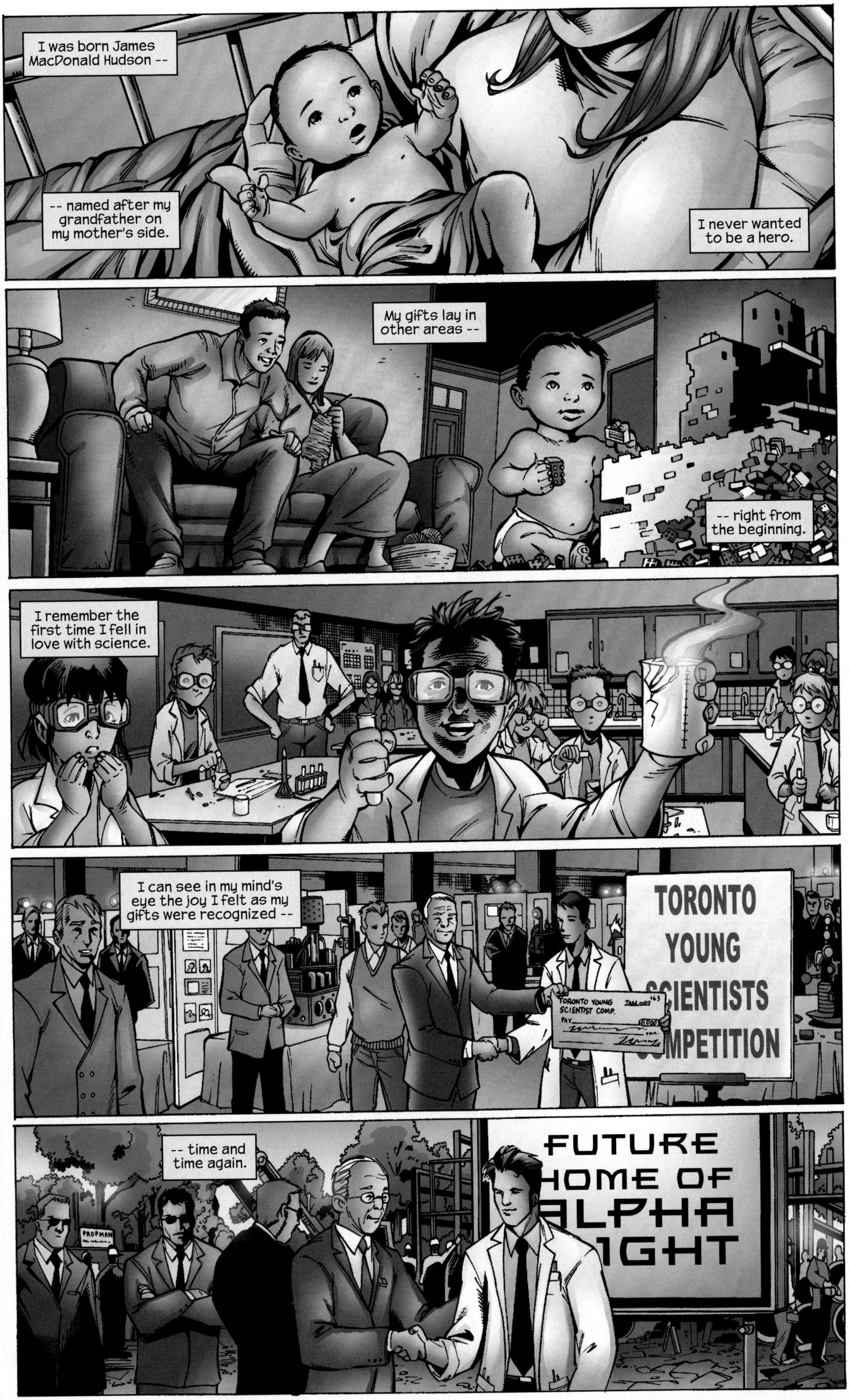
I was born James MacDonald Hudson --
-- named after my grandfather on my mother's side.
I never wanted to be a hero.
My gifts lay in other areas --
-- right from the beginning.
I remember the first time I fell in love with science.
I can see in my mind's eye the joy I felt as my gifts were recognized --
TORONTO YOUNG SCIENTISTS COMPETITION
TORONTO YOUNG SCIENTIST COMP.
-- time and time again.
FUTURE HOME OF ALPHA FLIGHT

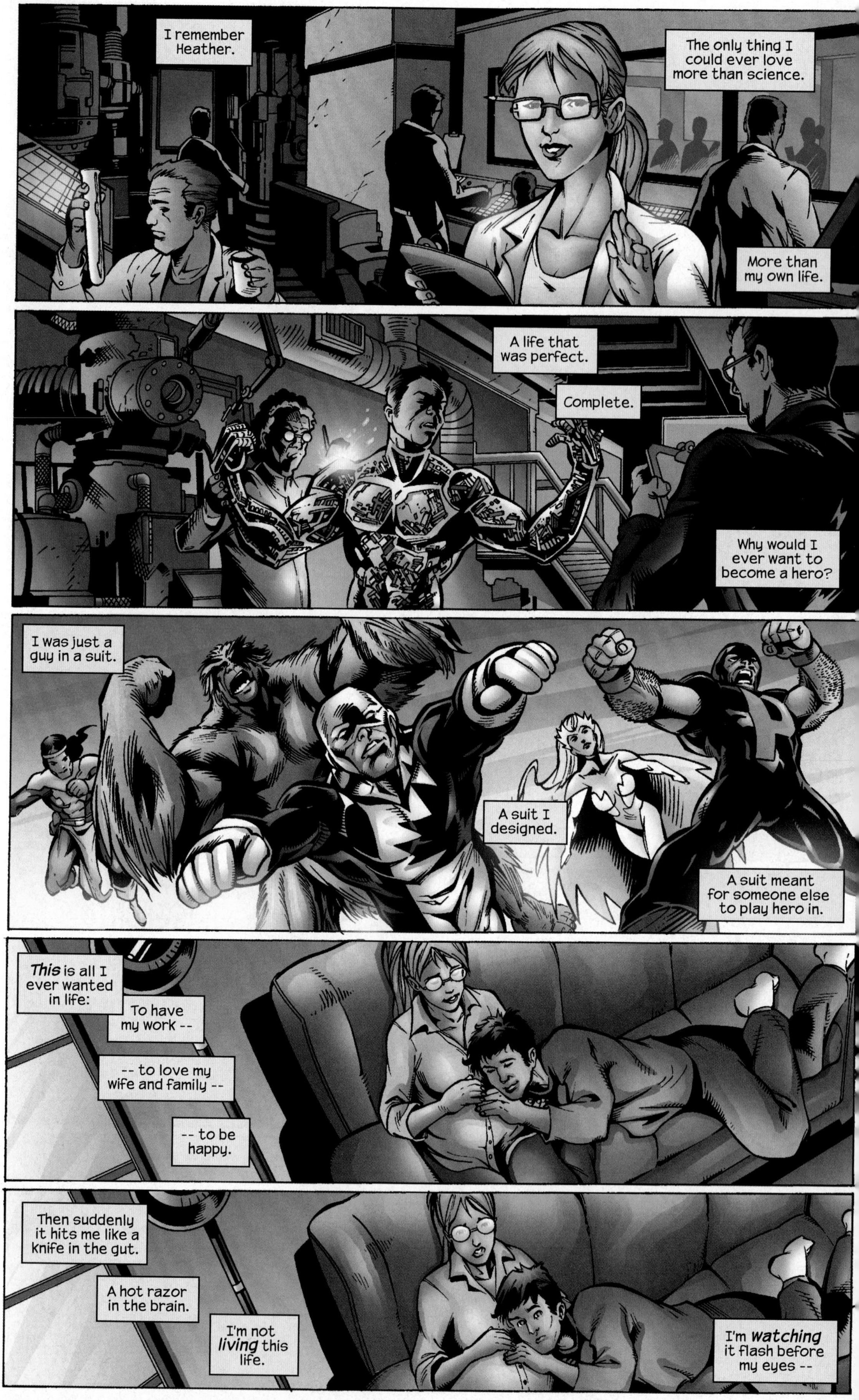
I remember Heather.
The only thing I could ever love more than science.
More than my own life.
A life that was perfect.
Complete.
Why would I ever want to become a hero?
I was just a guy in a suit.
A suit I designed.
A suit meant for someone else to play hero in.
This is all I ever wanted in life:
To have my work --
-- to love my wife and family --
-- to be happy.
Then suddenly it hits me like a knife in the gut.
A hot razor in the brain.
I'm not *living* this life.
I'm *watching* it flash before my eyes --

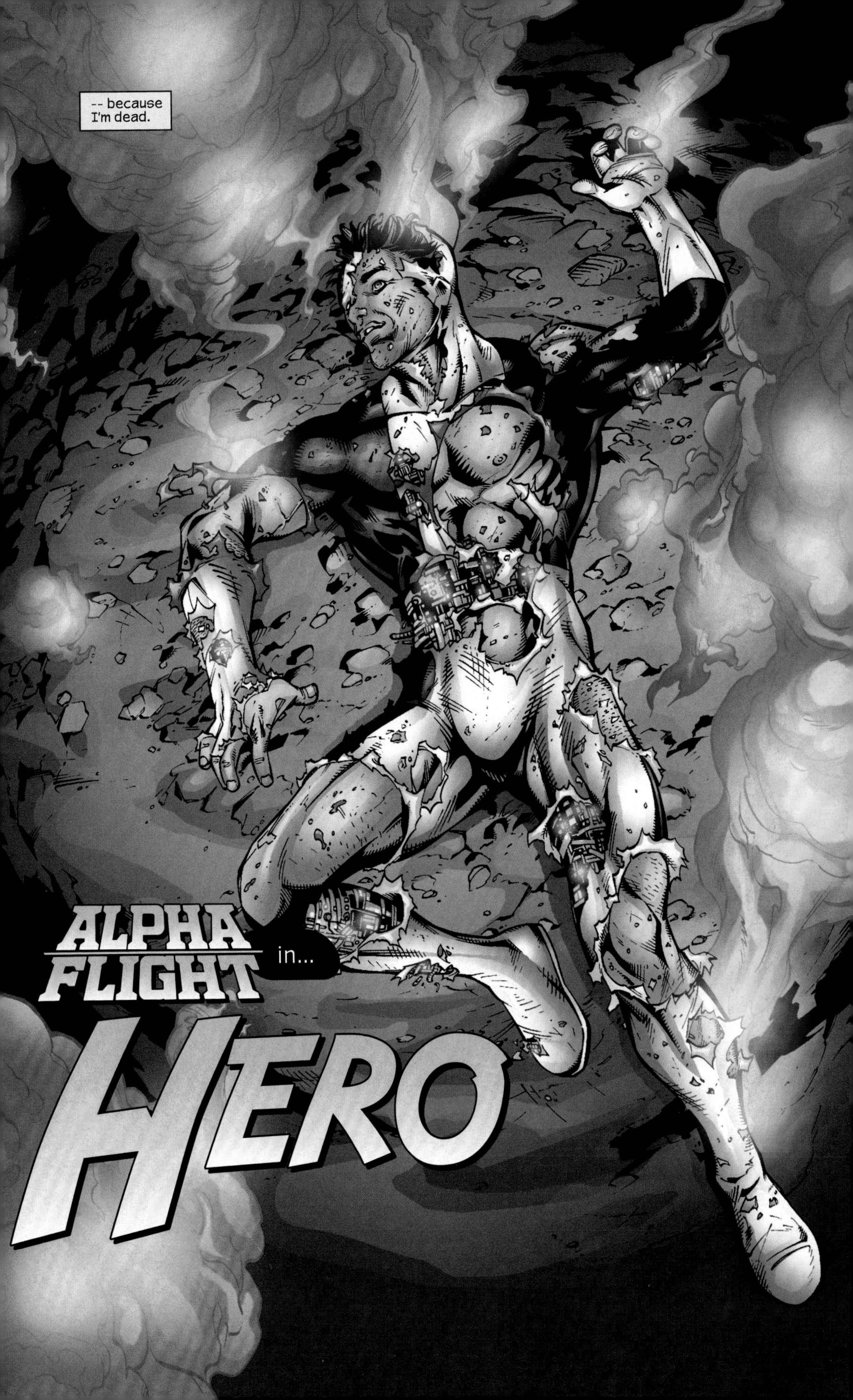

-- because I'm dead.
ALPHA FLIGHT
in...
HERO

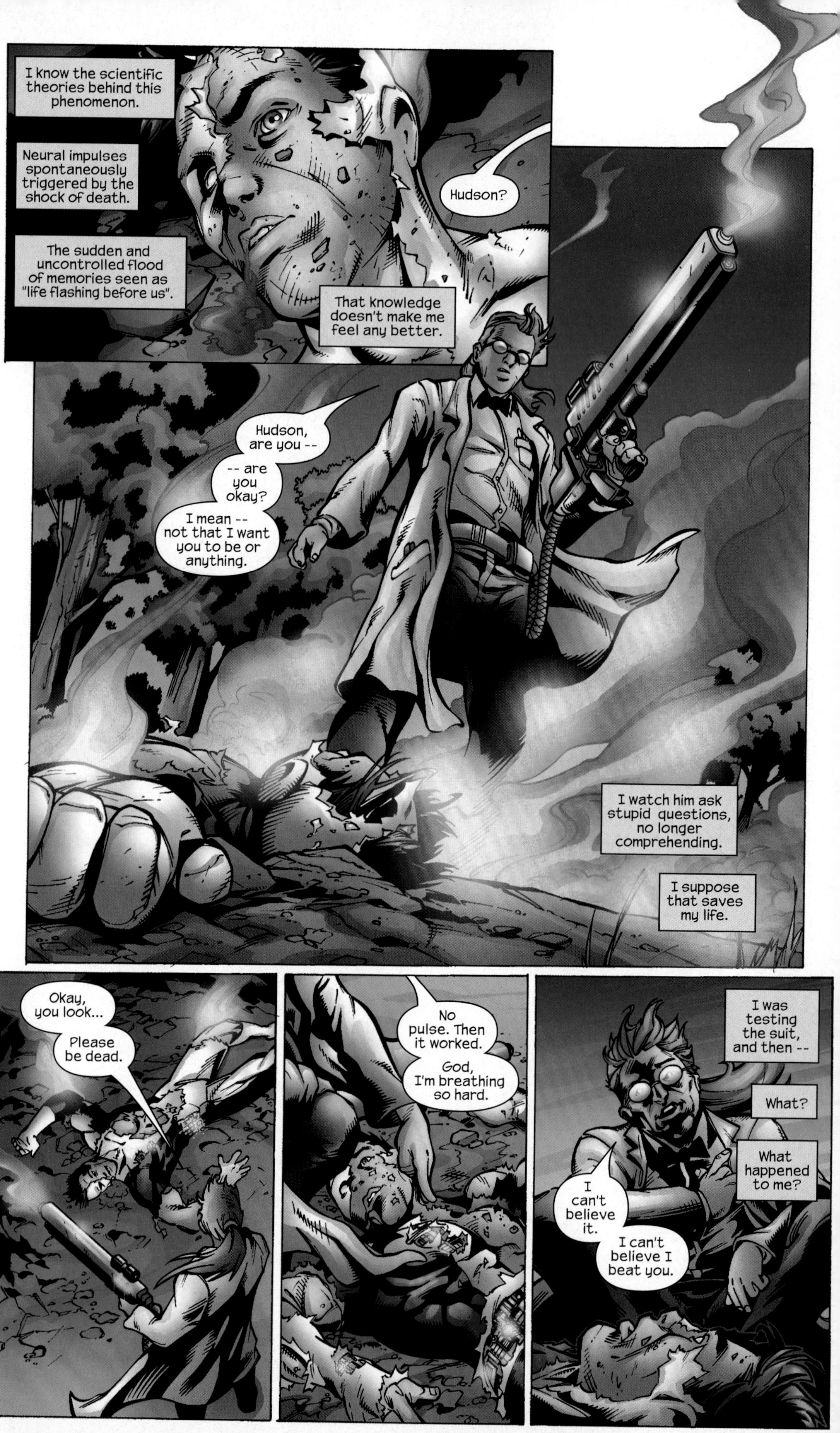
I know the scientific theories behind this phenomenon.
Neural impulses spontaneously triggered by the shock of death.
The sudden and uncontrolled flood of memories seen as "life flashing before us".
Hudson?
That knowledge doesn't make me feel any better.
Hudson, are you --
-- are you okay?
I mean -- not that I want you to be or anything.
I watch him ask stupid questions, no longer comprehending.
I suppose that saves my life.
Okay, you look...
Please be dead.
No pulse. Then it worked.
God, I'm breathing so hard.
I was testing the suit, and then --
What?
What happened to me?
I can't believe it.
I can't believe I beat you.

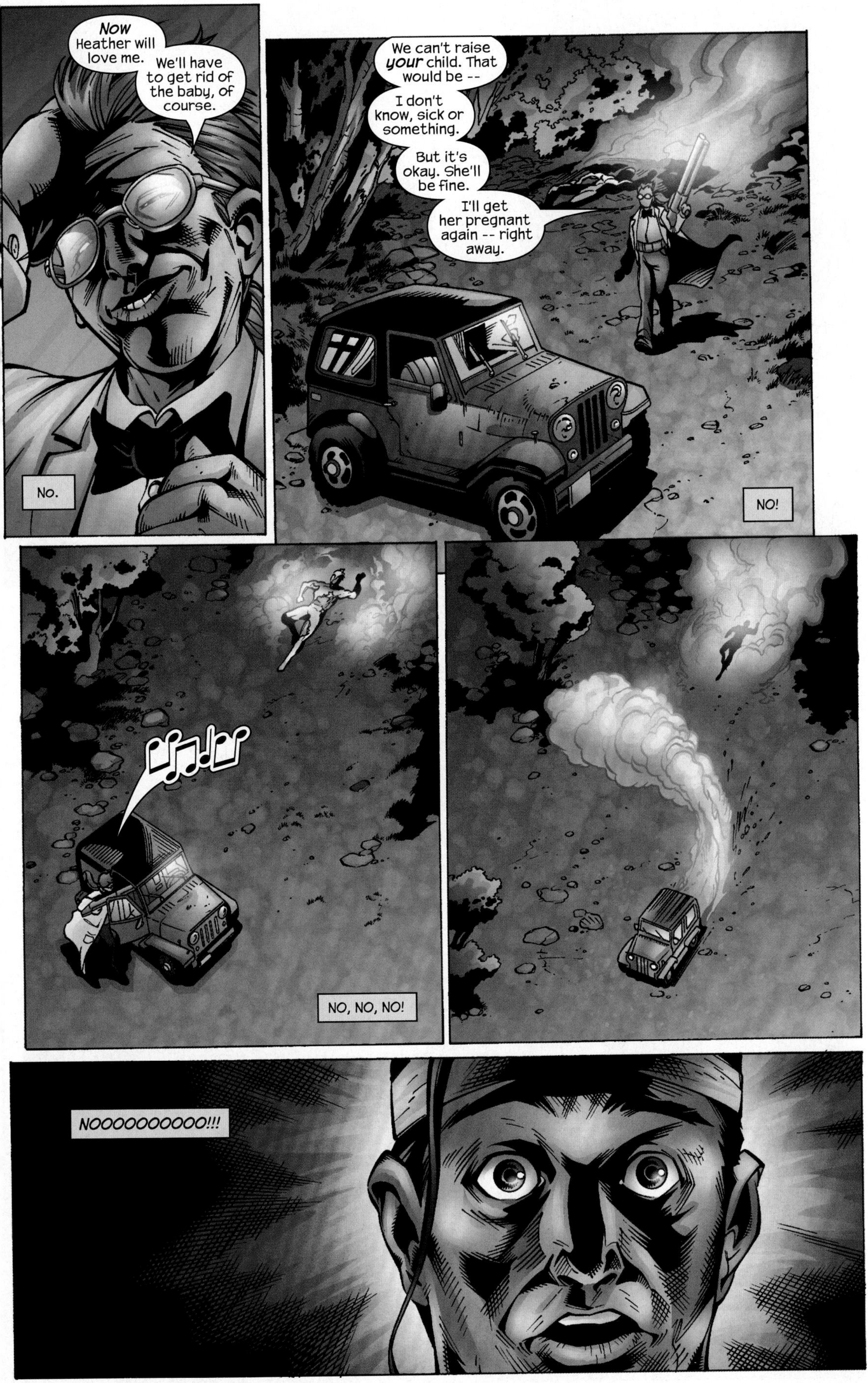

Now Heather will love me.
We'll have to get rid of the baby, of course.
No.
We can't raise your child. That would be --
I don't know, sick or something.
But it's okay. She'll be fine.
I'll get her pregnant again -- right away.
NO!
NO, NO, NO!
NOOOOOOOOOO!!!

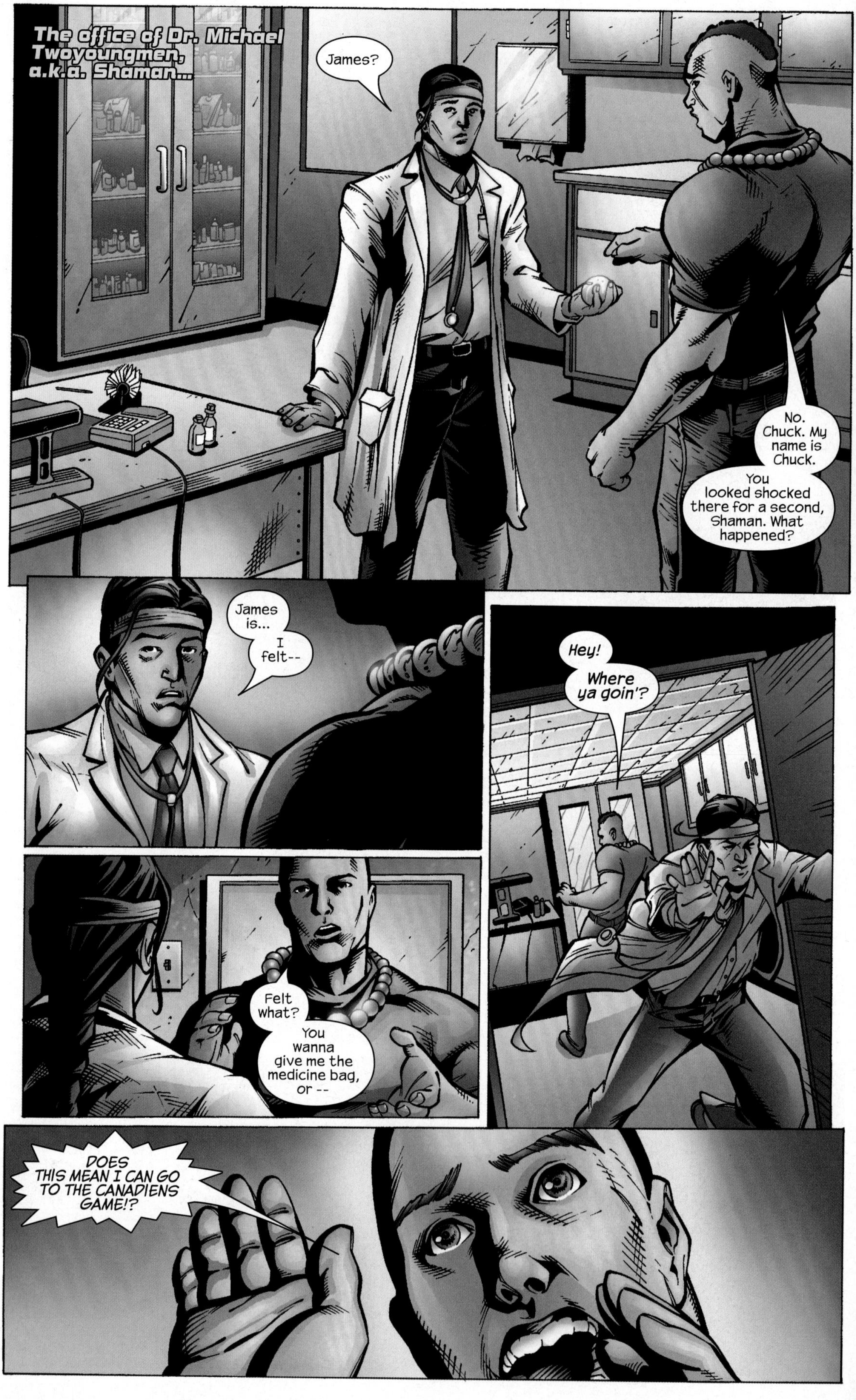
The office of Dr. Michael Twoyoungmen, a.k.a. Shaman...
James?
No. Chuck. My name is Chuck.
You looked shocked there for a second, Shaman. What happened?
James is... I felt--
Hey! Where ya goin'?
Felt what?
You wanna give me the medicine bag, or --
DOES THIS MEAN I CAN GO TO THE CANADIENS GAME!?

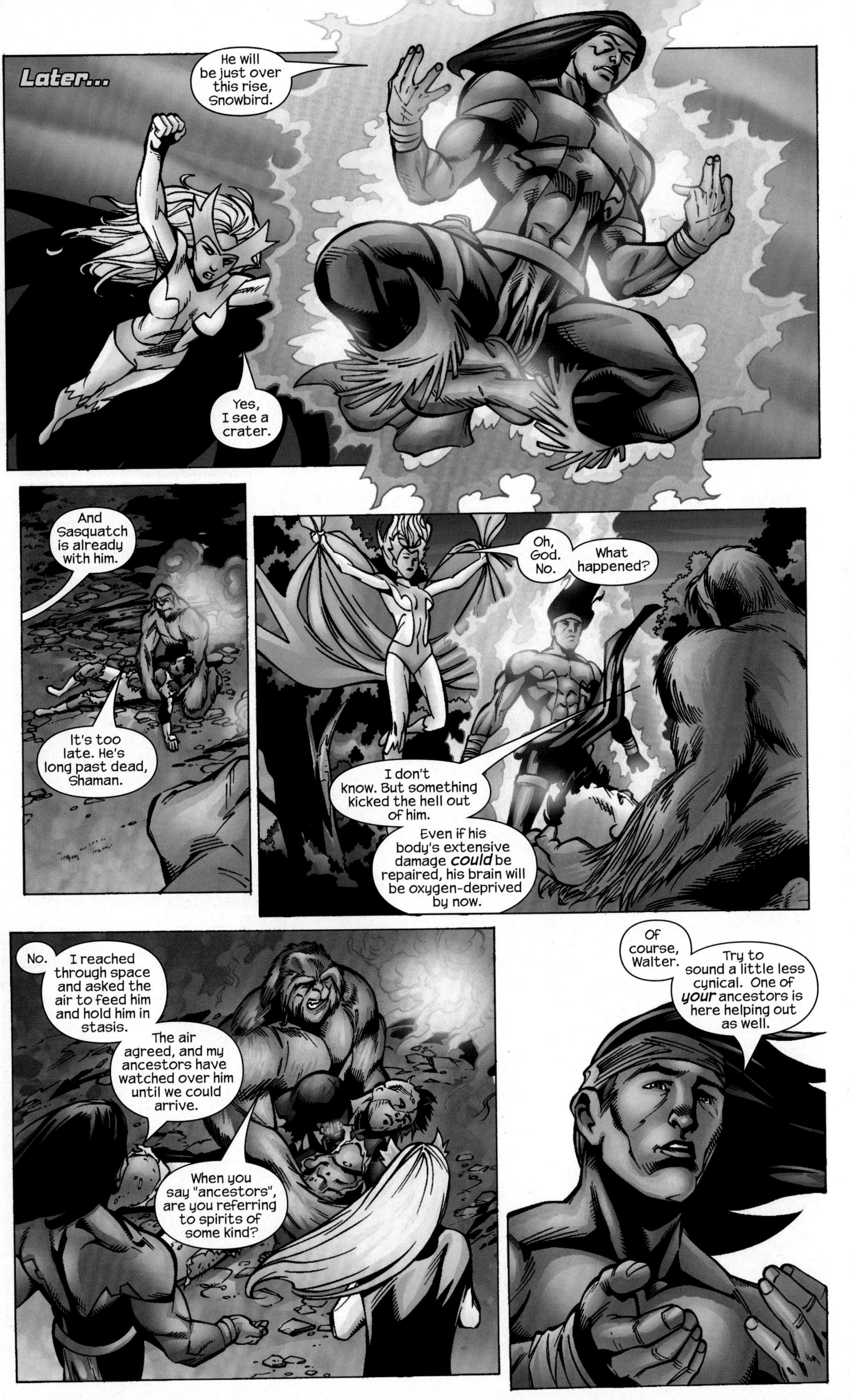
Later...
He will be just over this rise, Snowbird.
Yes, I see a crater.
And Sasquatch is already with him.
It's too late. He's long past dead, Shaman.
Oh, God. No.
What happened?
I don't know. But something kicked the hell out of him.
Even if his body's extensive damage could be repaired, his brain will be oxygen-deprived by now.
No.
I reached through space and asked the air to feed him and hold him in stasis.
The air agreed, and my ancestors have watched over him until we could arrive.
When you say "ancestors", are you referring to spirits of some kind?
Of course, Walter.
Try to sound a little less cynical. One of your ancestors is here helping out as well.

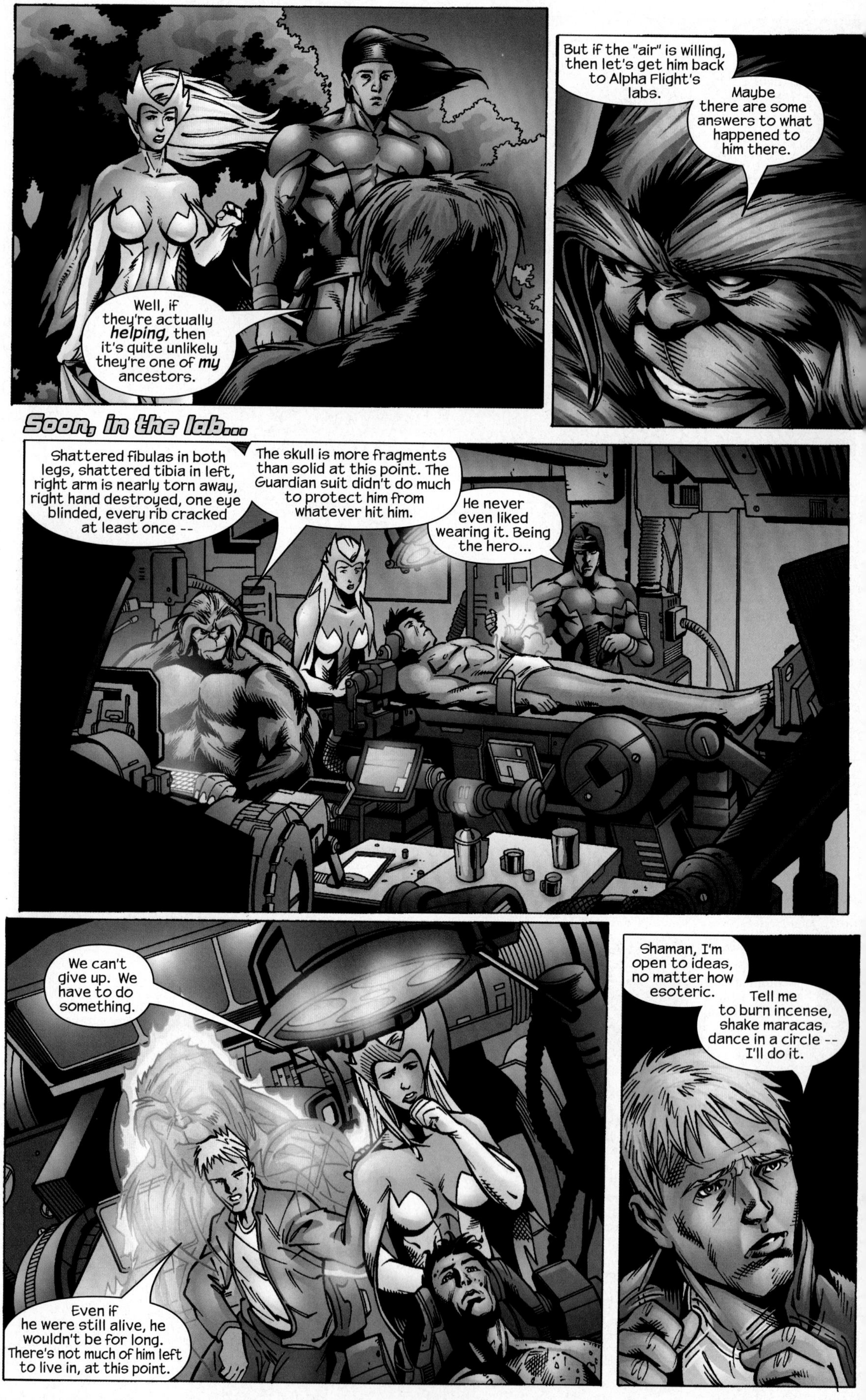
Well, if they're actually *helping,* then it's quite unlikely they're one of *my* ancestors.
But if the "air" is willing, then let's get him back to Alpha Flight's labs.
Maybe there are some answers to what happened to him there.
Soon, in the lab...
Shattered fibulas in both legs, shattered tibia in left, right arm is nearly torn away, right hand destroyed, one eye blinded, every rib cracked at least once --
The skull is more fragments than solid at this point. The Guardian suit didn't do much to protect him from whatever hit him.
He never even liked wearing it. Being the hero...
We can't give up. We have to do something.
Even if he were still alive, he wouldn't be for long. There's not much of him left to live in, at this point.
Shaman, I'm open to ideas, no matter how esoteric.
Tell me to burn incense, shake maracas, dance in a circle -- I'll do it.

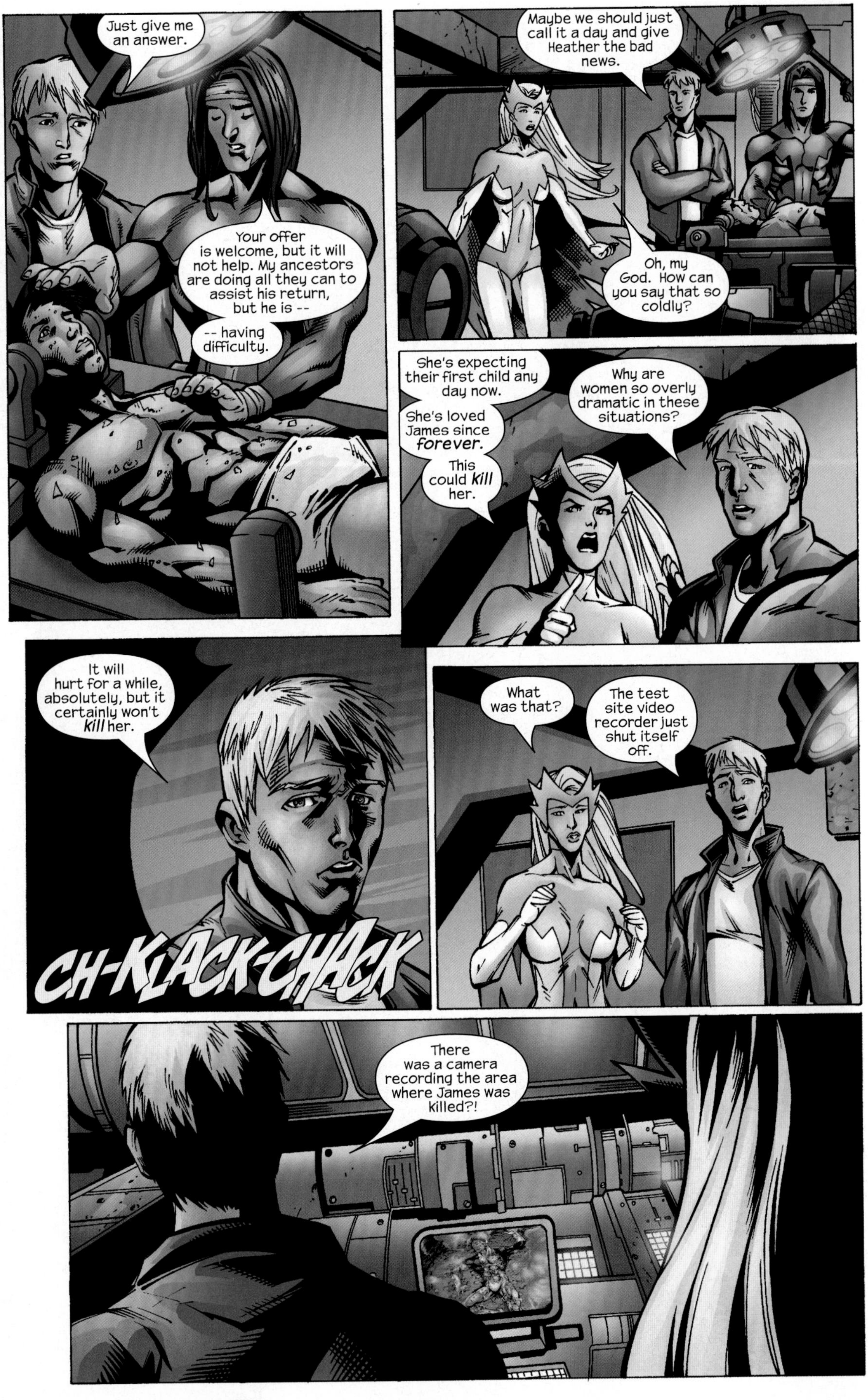
Just give me an answer.
Your offer is welcome, but it will not help. My ancestors are doing all they can to assist his return, but he is --
-- having difficulty.
Maybe we should just call it a day and give Heather the bad news.
Oh, my God. How can you say that so coldly?
She's expecting their first child any day now.
She's loved James since forever.
This could kill her.
Why are women so overly dramatic in these situations?
It will hurt for a while, absolutely, but it certainly won't kill her.
CH-KLACK-CHACK
What was that?
The test site video recorder just shut itself off.
There was a camera recording the area where James was killed?!

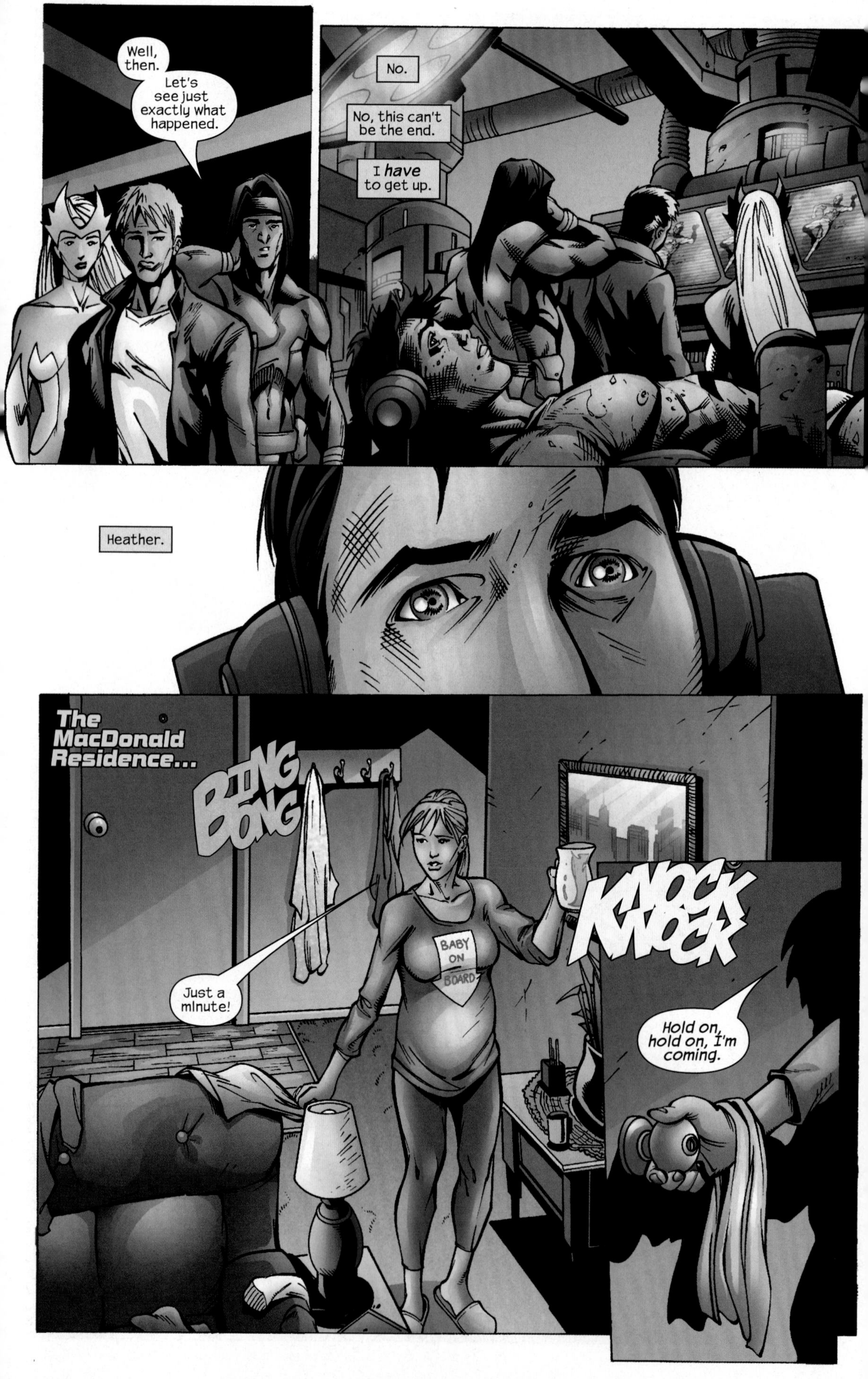

Well, then.
Let's see just exactly what happened.
No.
No, this can't be the end.
I *have* to get up.
Heather.
The MacDonald Residence...
BING BONG
BABY ON BOARD
Just a minute!
KNOCK KNOCK
Hold on, hold on, I'm coming.

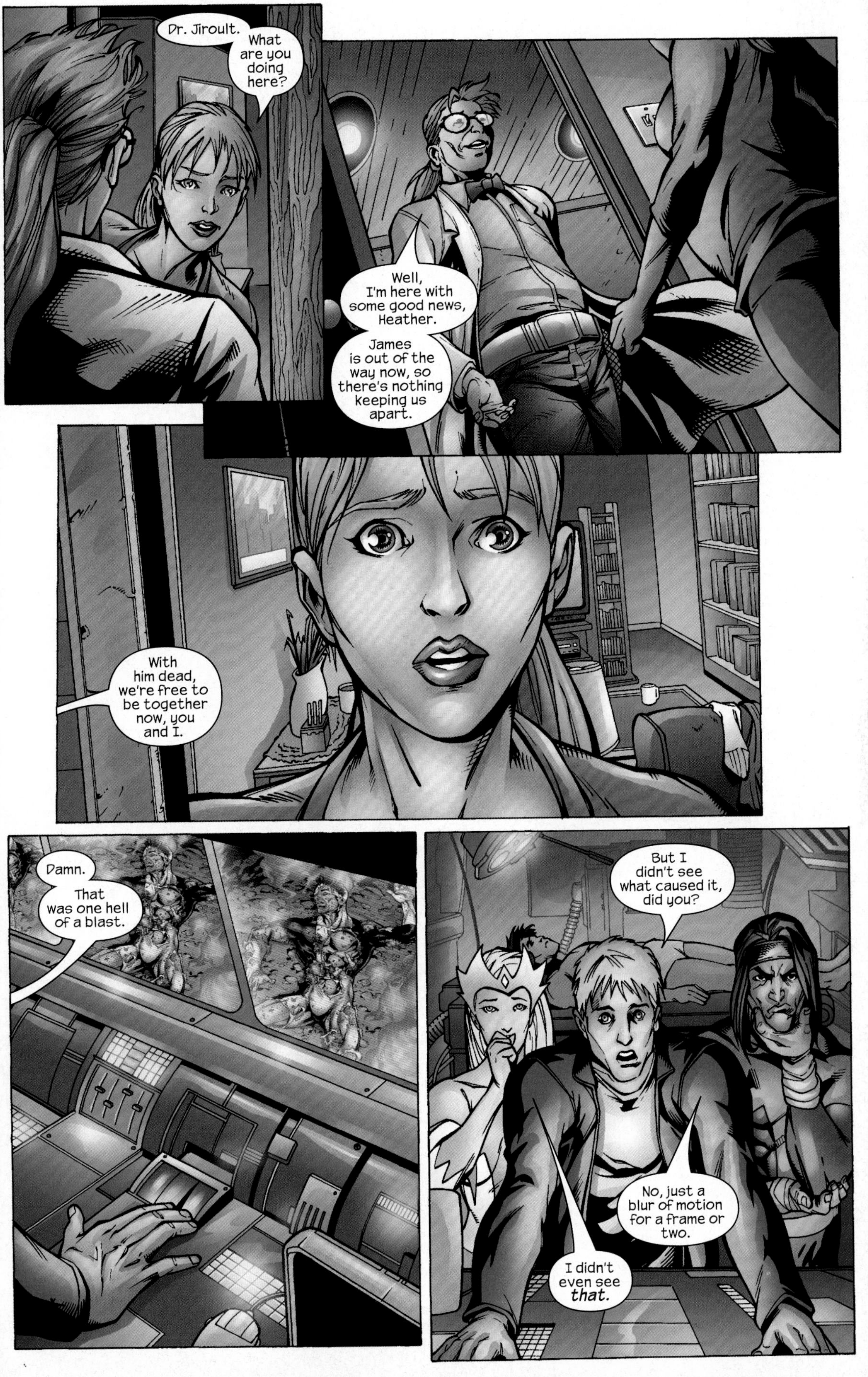
Dr. Jiroult.
What are you doing here?
Well, I'm here with some good news, Heather.
James is out of the way now, so there's nothing keeping us apart.
With him dead, we're free to be together now, you and I.
Damn.
That was one hell of a blast.
But I didn't see what caused it, did you?
No, just a blur of motion for a frame or two.
I didn't even see *that.*

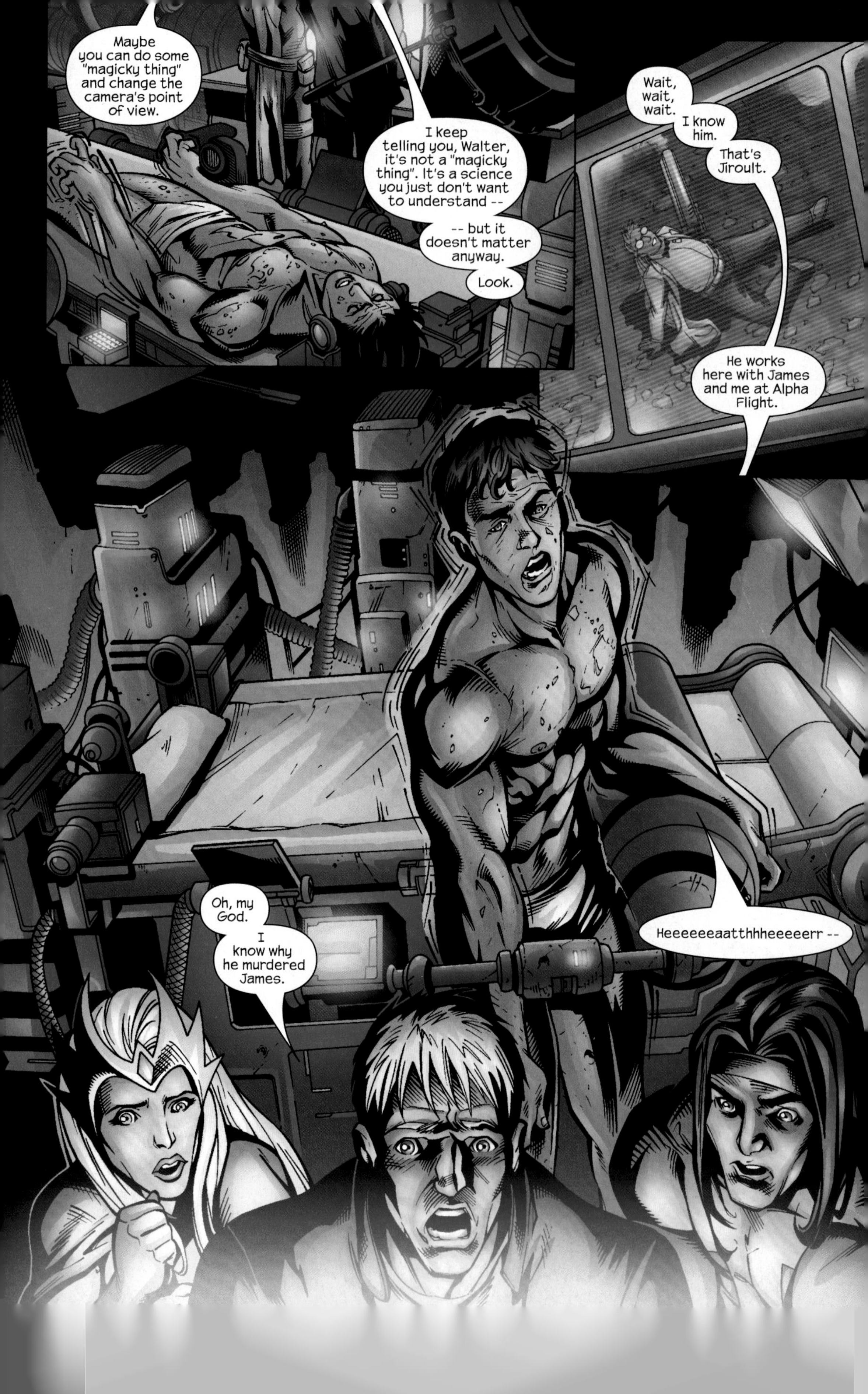
Maybe you can do some "magicky thing" and change the camera's point of view.
I keep telling you, Walter, it's not a "magicky thing". It's a science you just don't want to understand --
-- but it doesn't matter anyway.
Look.
Wait, wait, wait.
I know him.
That's Jiroult.
He works here with James and me at Alpha Flight.
Oh, my God.
I know why he murdered James.
Heeeeeeaatthhheeeeerr --

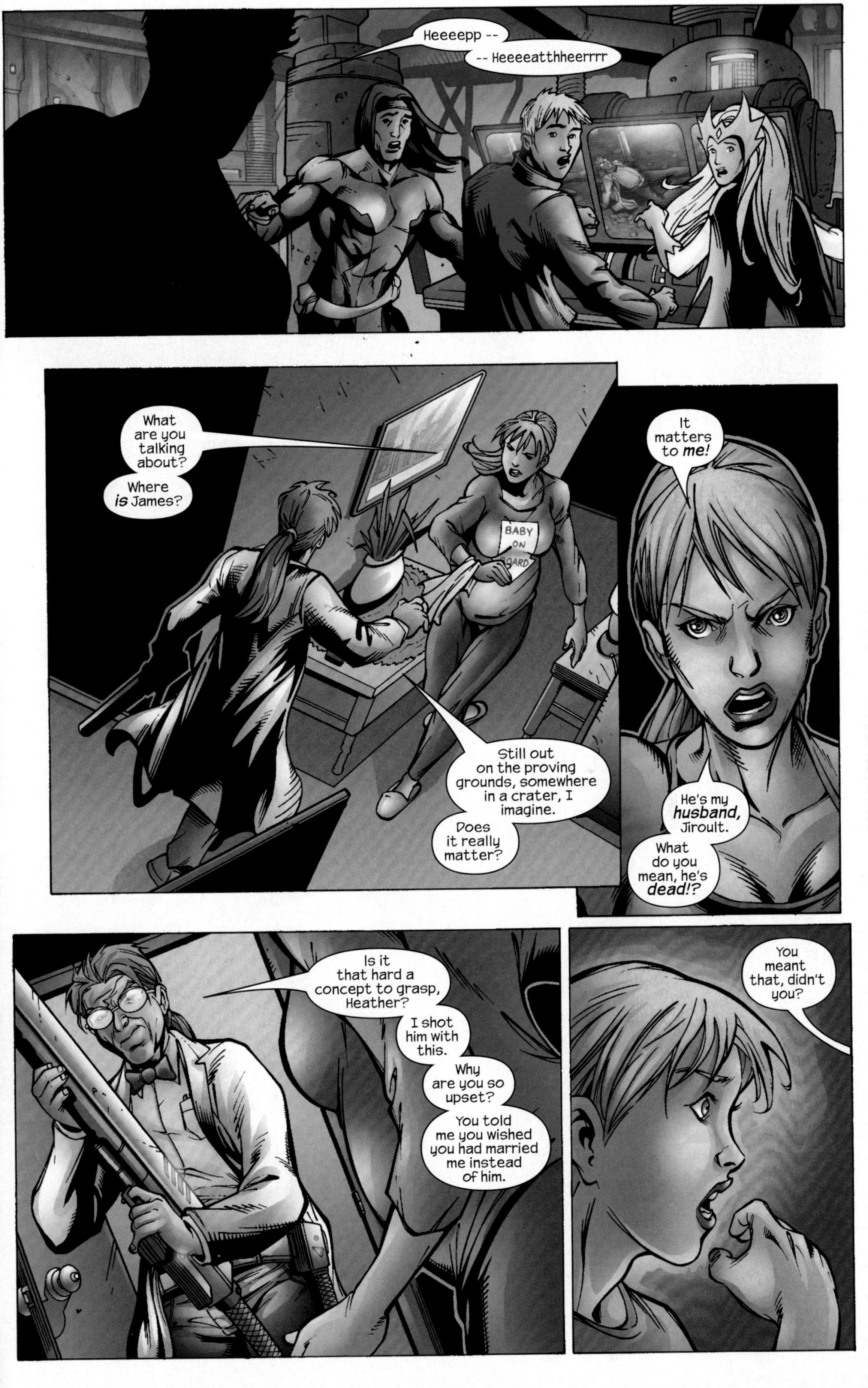
Heeeepp --
-- Heeeeatthheerrrr
What are you talking about?
Where *is* James?
Still out on the proving grounds, somewhere in a crater, I imagine.
Does it really matter?
BABY ON BOARD
It matters to *me!*
He's my *husband,* Jiroult.
What do you mean, he's *dead!?*
Is it that hard a concept to grasp, Heather?
I shot him with this.
Why are you so upset?
You told me you wished you had married me instead of him.
You meant that, didn't you?

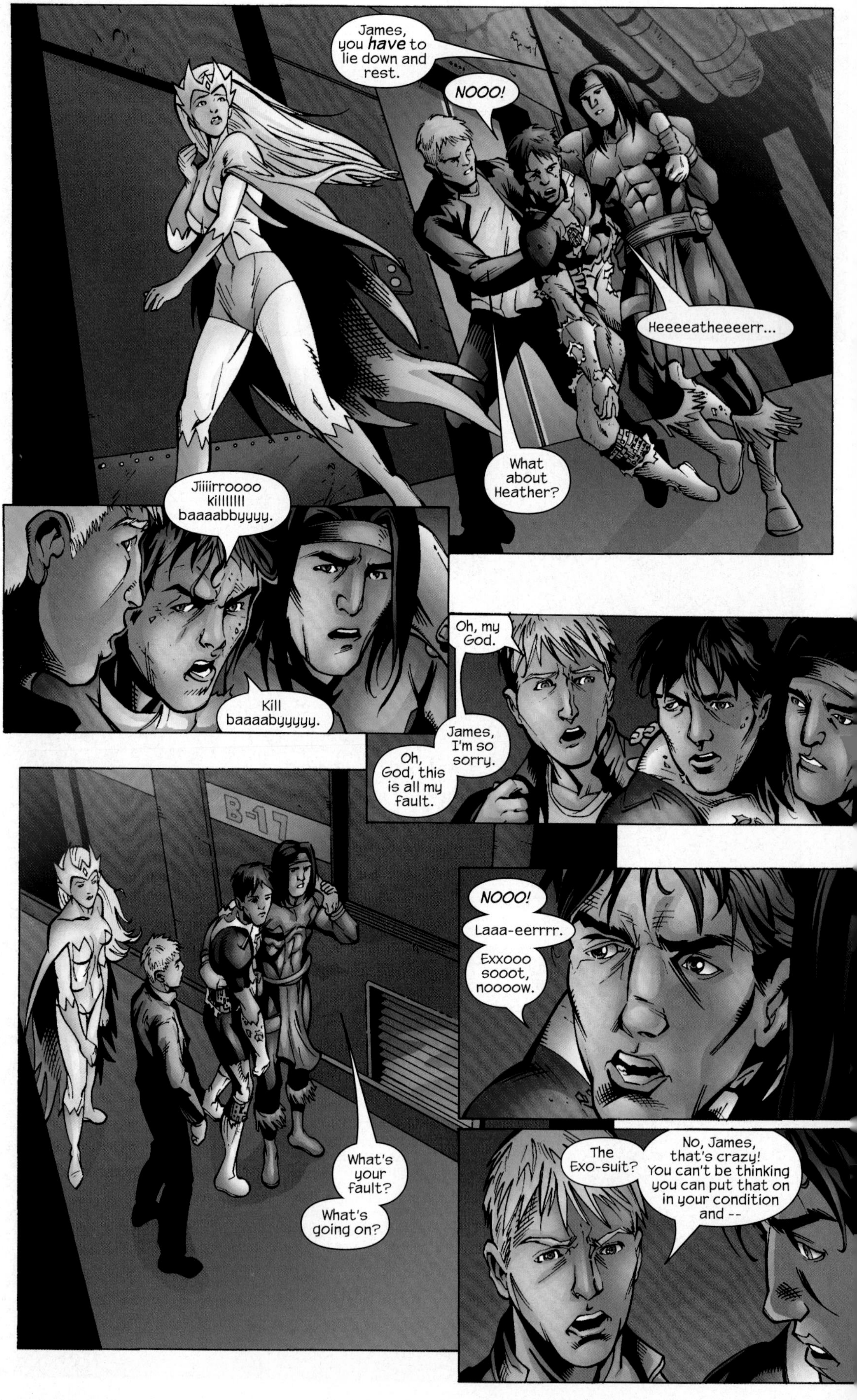

James, you *have* to lie down and rest.
NOOO!
Heeeeatheeeerr...
What about Heather?
Jiiiirroooo killllllll baaaabbyyyy.
Kill baaaabyyyyy.
Oh, my God.
James, I'm so sorry.
Oh, God, this is all my fault.
B-17
What's your fault?
What's going on?
NOOO!
Laaa-eerrrr.
Exxooo sooot, nooooow.
The Exo-suit?
No, James, that's crazy! You can't be thinking you can put that on in your condition and --

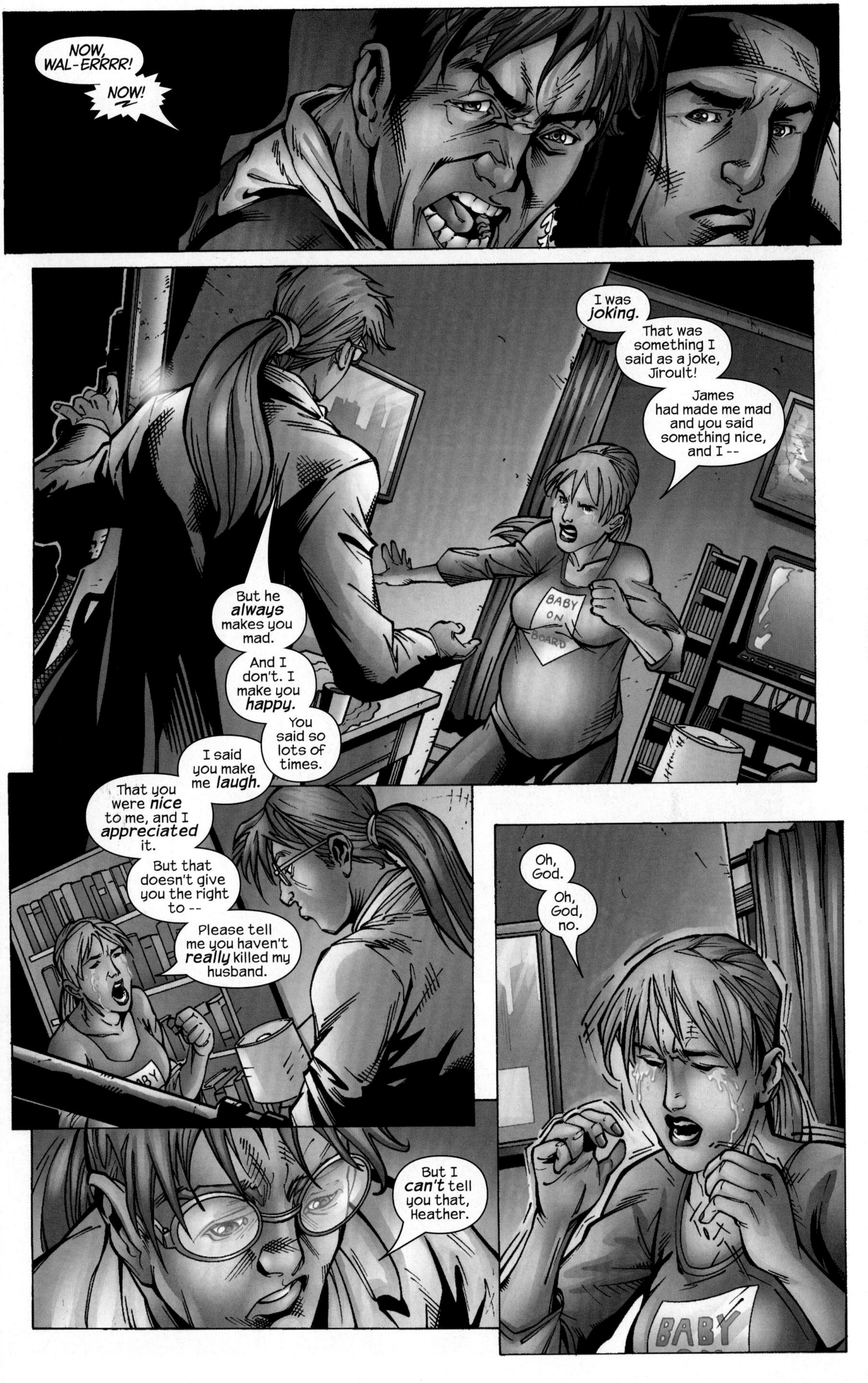
NOW, WAL-ERRRR!
NOW!
I was joking.
That was something I said as a joke, Jiroult!
James had made me mad and you said something nice, and I --
But he always makes you mad.
And I don't. I make you happy.
You said so lots of times.
BABY ON BOARD
I said you make me laugh.
That you were nice to me, and I appreciated it.
But that doesn't give you the right to --
Please tell me you haven't really killed my husband.
Oh, God.
Oh, God, no.
But I can't tell you that, Heather.
BABY

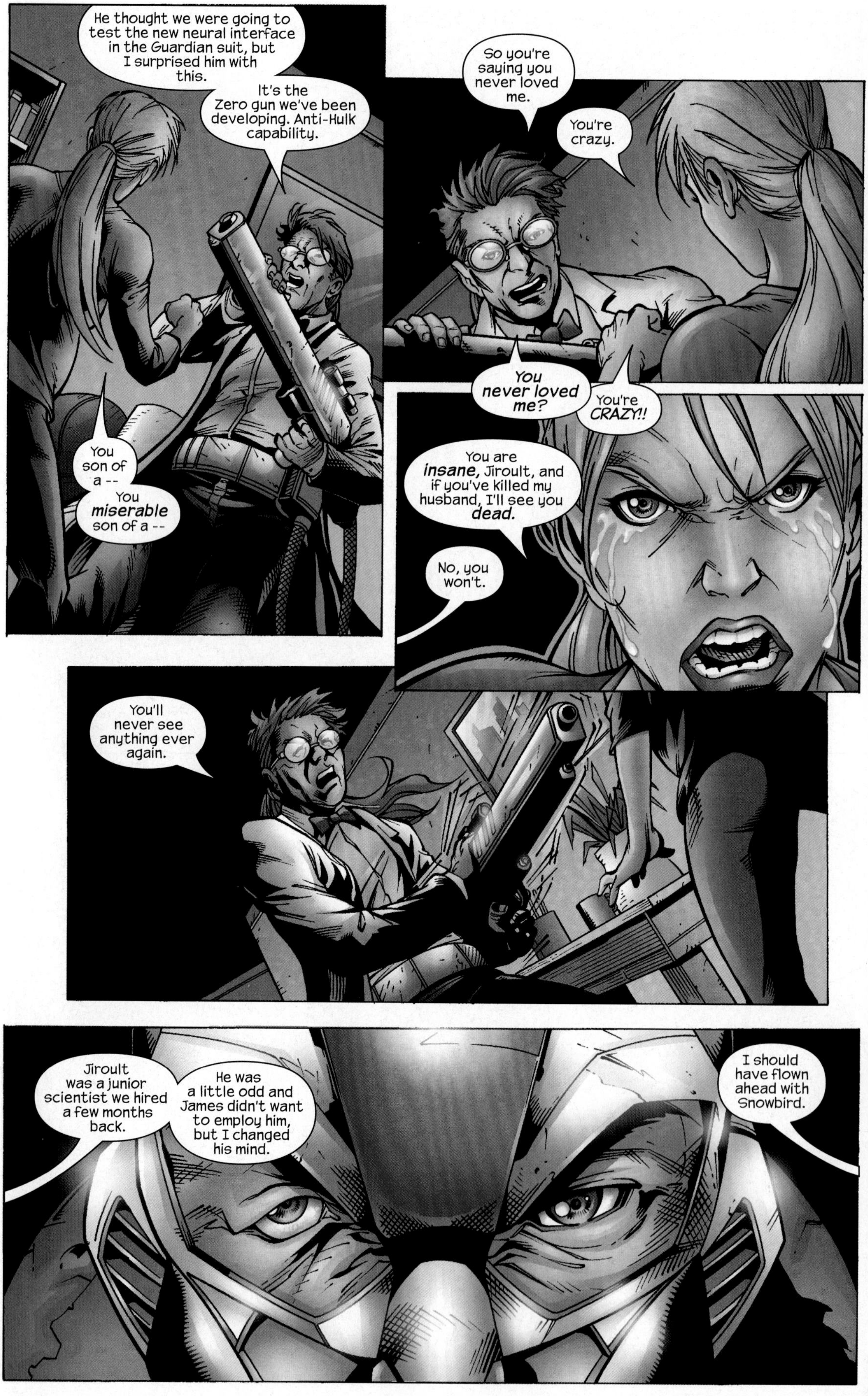

He thought we were going to test the new neural interface in the Guardian suit, but I surprised him with this.
It's the Zero gun we've been developing. Anti-Hulk capability.
You son of a --
You *miserable* son of a --
So you're saying you never loved me.
You're crazy.
You never loved me?
You're *CRAZY!!*
You are *insane,* Jiroult, and if you've killed my husband, I'll see you *dead.*
No, you won't.
You'll never see anything ever again.
Jiroult was a junior scientist we hired a few months back.
He was a little odd and James didn't want to employ him, but I changed his mind.
I should have flown ahead with Snowbird.

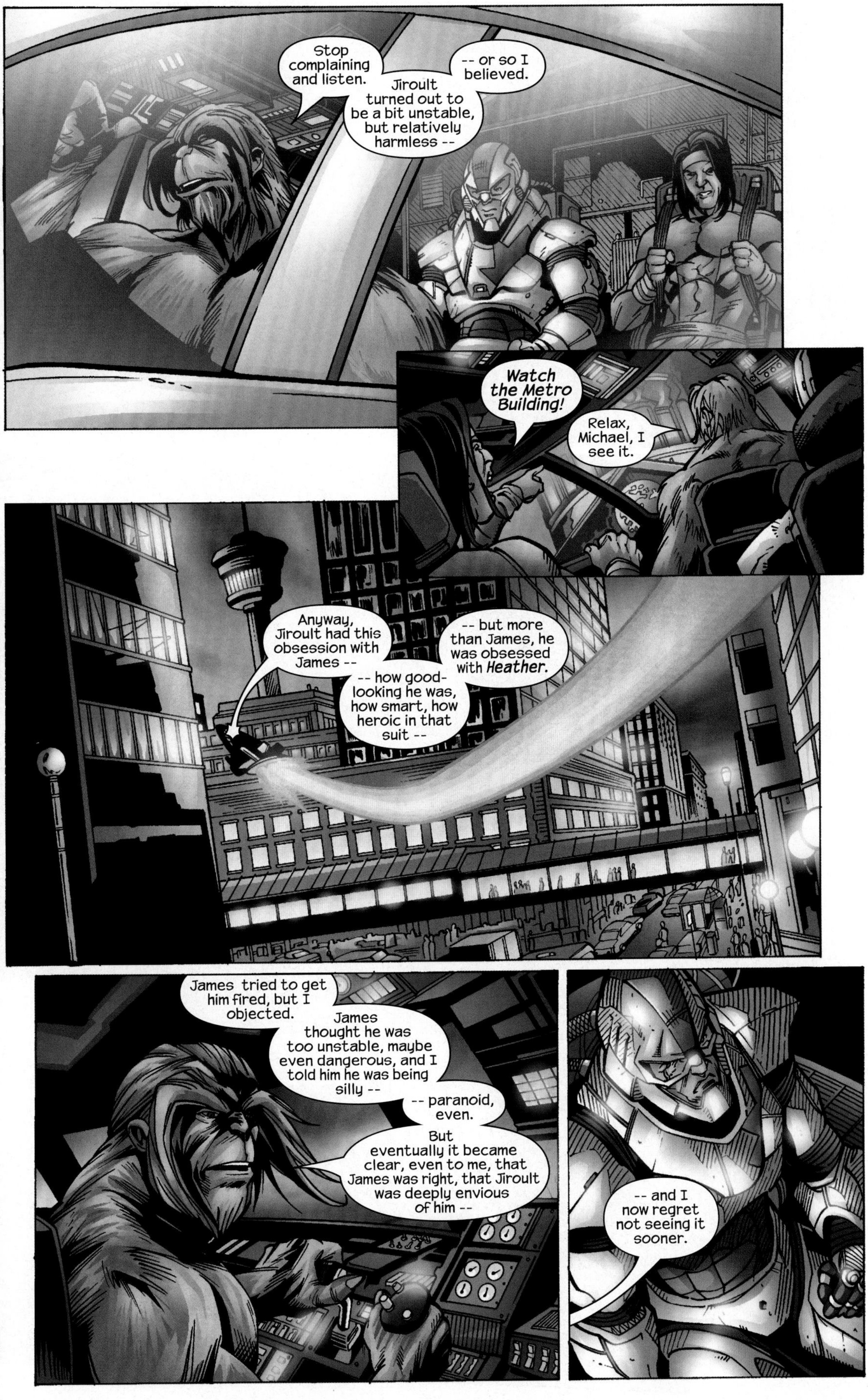
Stop complaining and listen.
-- or so I believed.
Jiroult turned out to be a bit unstable, but relatively harmless --
Watch the Metro Building!
Relax, Michael, I see it.
Anyway, Jiroult had this obsession with James --
-- how good-looking he was, how smart, how heroic in that suit --
-- but more than James, he was obsessed with *Heather.*
James tried to get him fired, but I objected.
James thought he was too unstable, maybe even dangerous, and I told him he was being silly --
-- paranoid, even.
But eventually it became clear, even to me, that James was right, that Jiroult was deeply envious of him --
-- and I now regret not seeing it sooner.

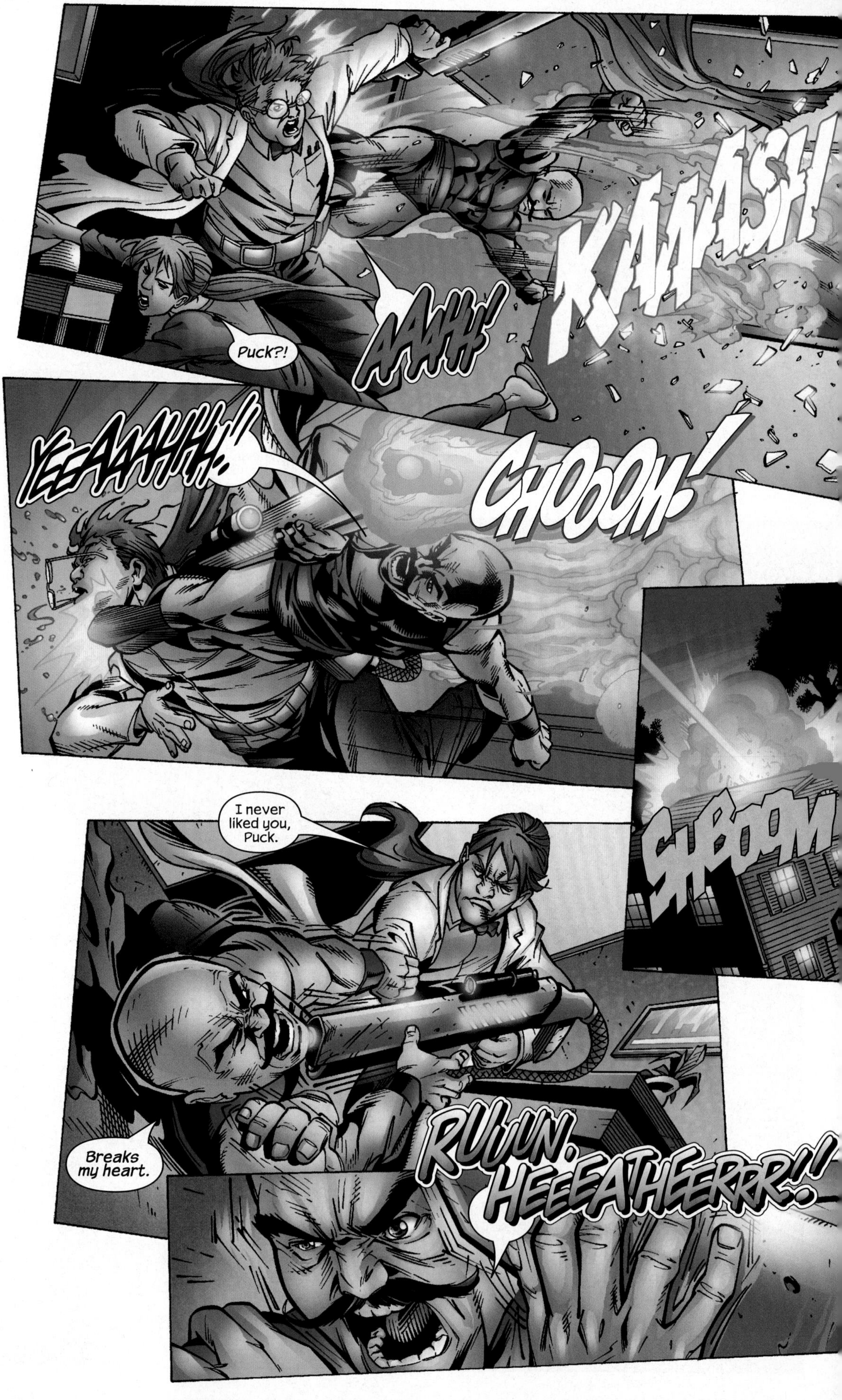
KRAASH
Puck?!
AAAHH!
YEEAAAHH!
CHOOOM!
SHBOOM
I never liked you, Puck.
Breaks my heart.
RUUUN. HEEEATHEERRR!!

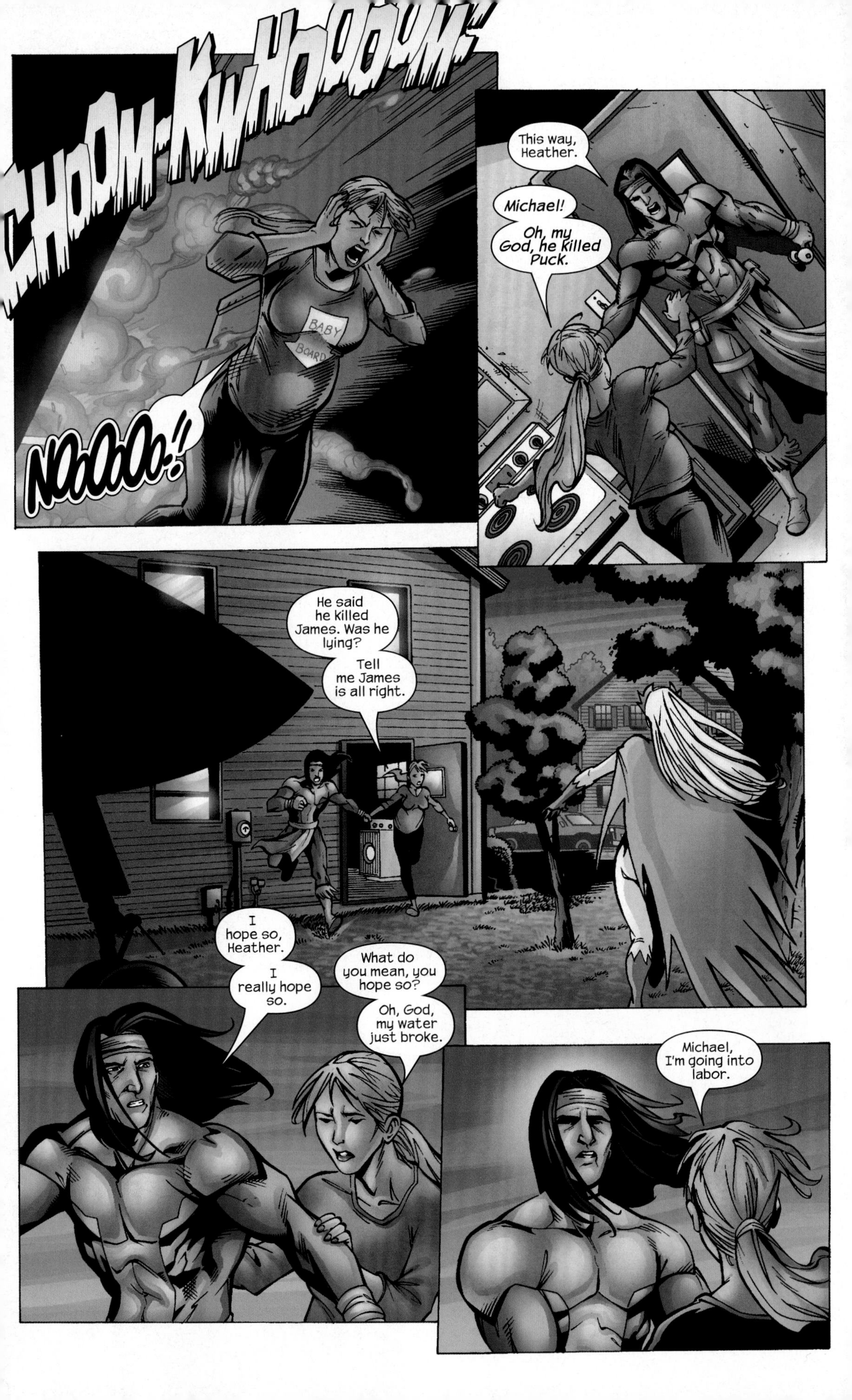
CHOOM-KWHOOOOM!
NOOOOO!!
This way, Heather.
Michael!
Oh, my God, he killed Puck.
He said he killed James. Was he lying?
Tell me James is all right.
I hope so, Heather.
I really hope so.
What do you mean, you hope so?
Oh, God, my water just broke.
Michael, I'm going into labor.

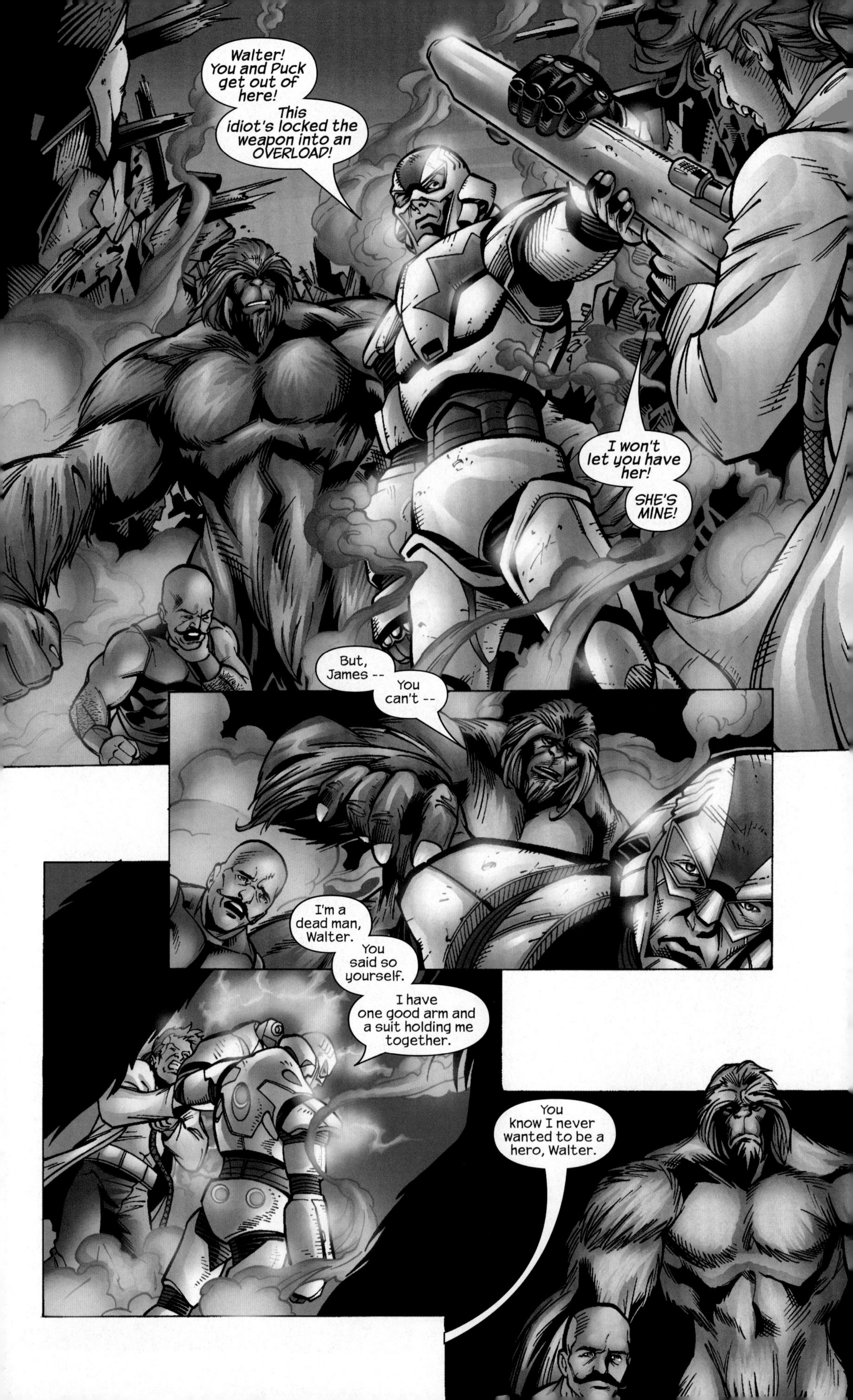
Walter! You and Puck get out of here!
This idiot's locked the weapon into an OVERLOAD!
I won't let you have her!
SHE'S MINE!
But, James --
You can't --
I'm a dead man, Walter.
You said so yourself.
I have one good arm and a suit holding me together.
You know I never wanted to be a hero, Walter.

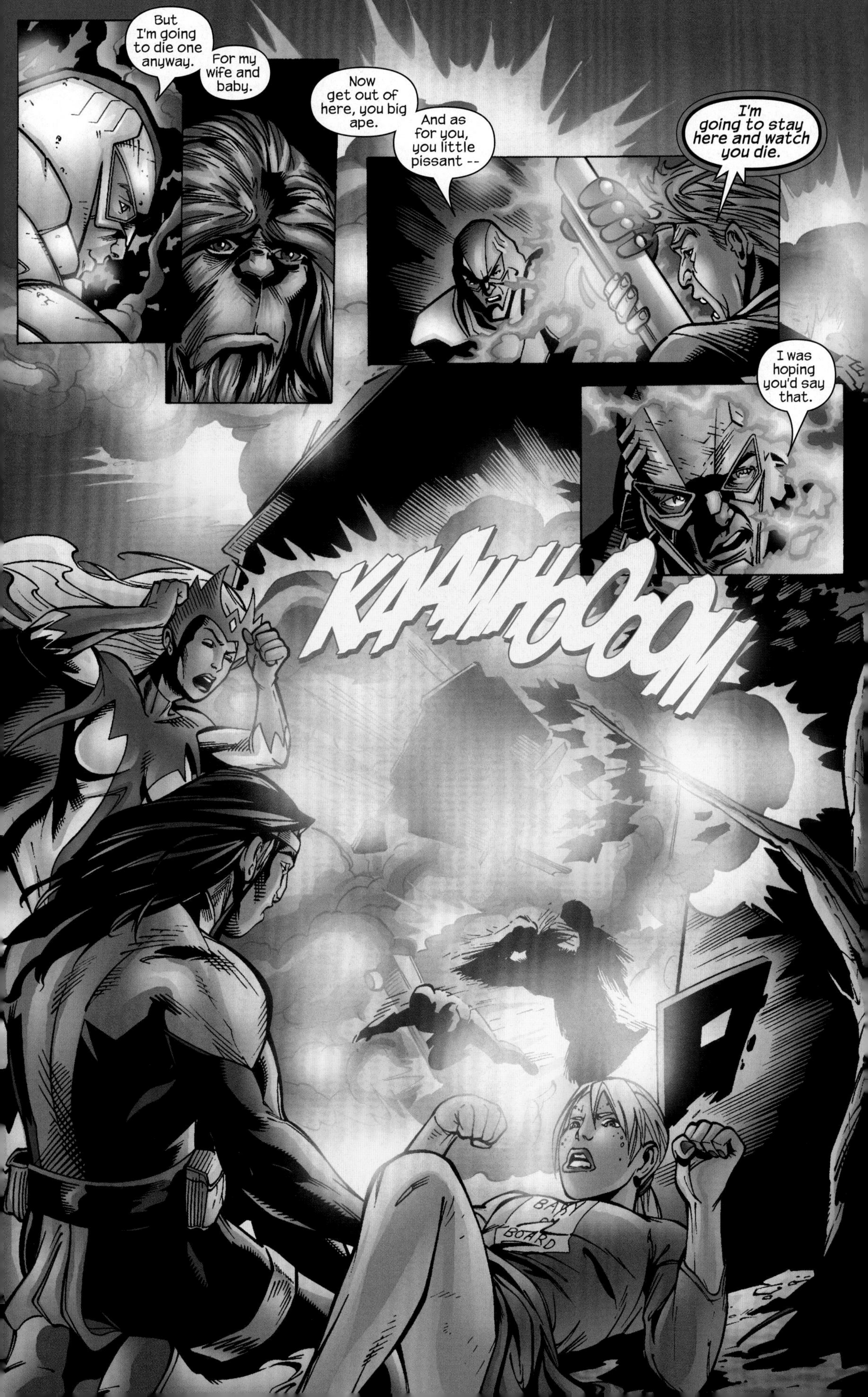
But I'm going to die one anyway.
For my wife and baby.
Now get out of here, you big ape.
And as for you, you little pissant --
I'm going to stay here and watch you die.
I was hoping you'd say that.
KAWHOOOOM
BABY ON BOARD

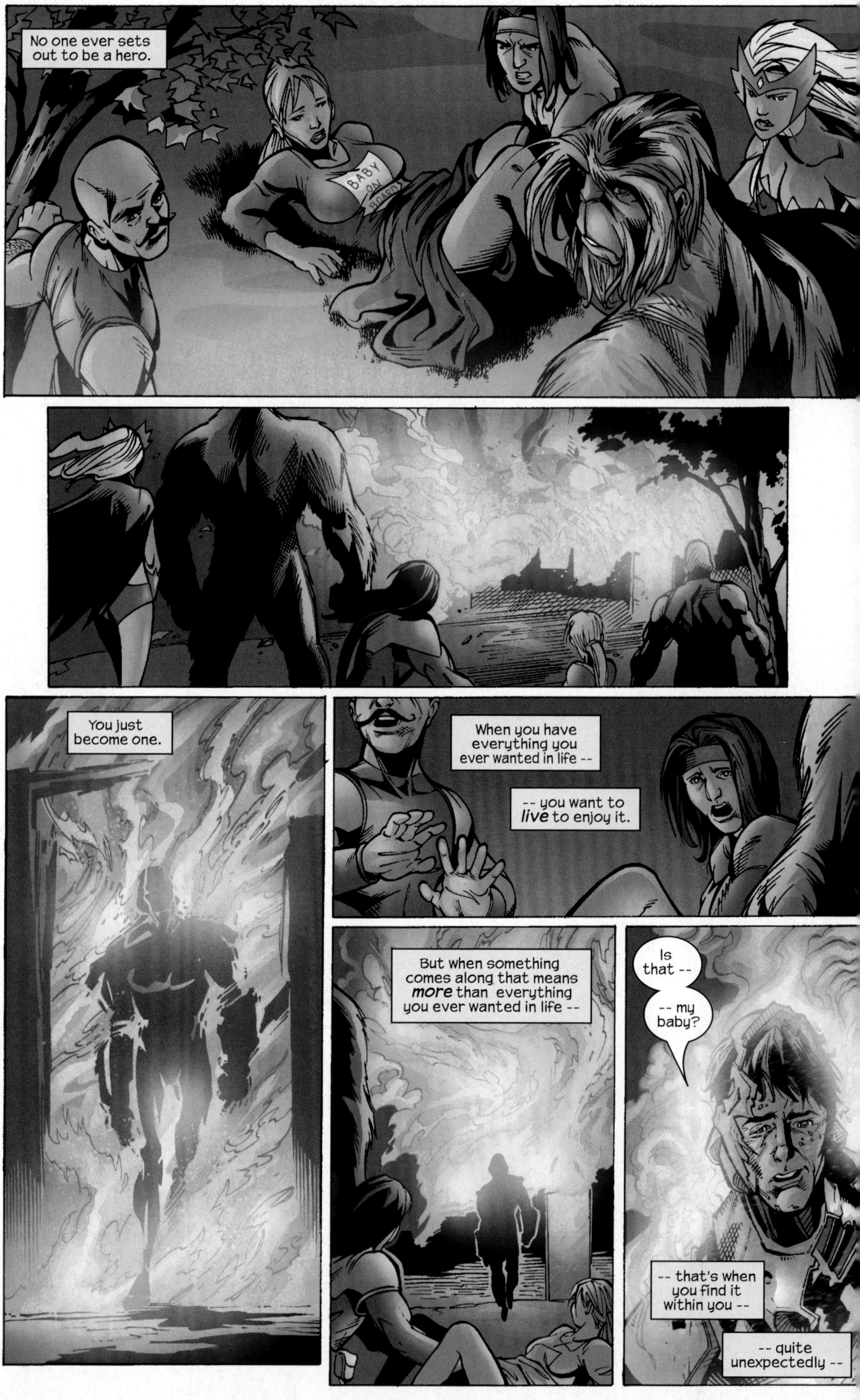

No one ever sets out to be a hero.
BABY ON BOARD
You just become one.
When you have everything you ever wanted in life --
-- you want to live to enjoy it.
But when something comes along that means more than everything you ever wanted in life --
Is that --
-- my baby?
-- that's when you find it within you --
-- quite unexpectedly --

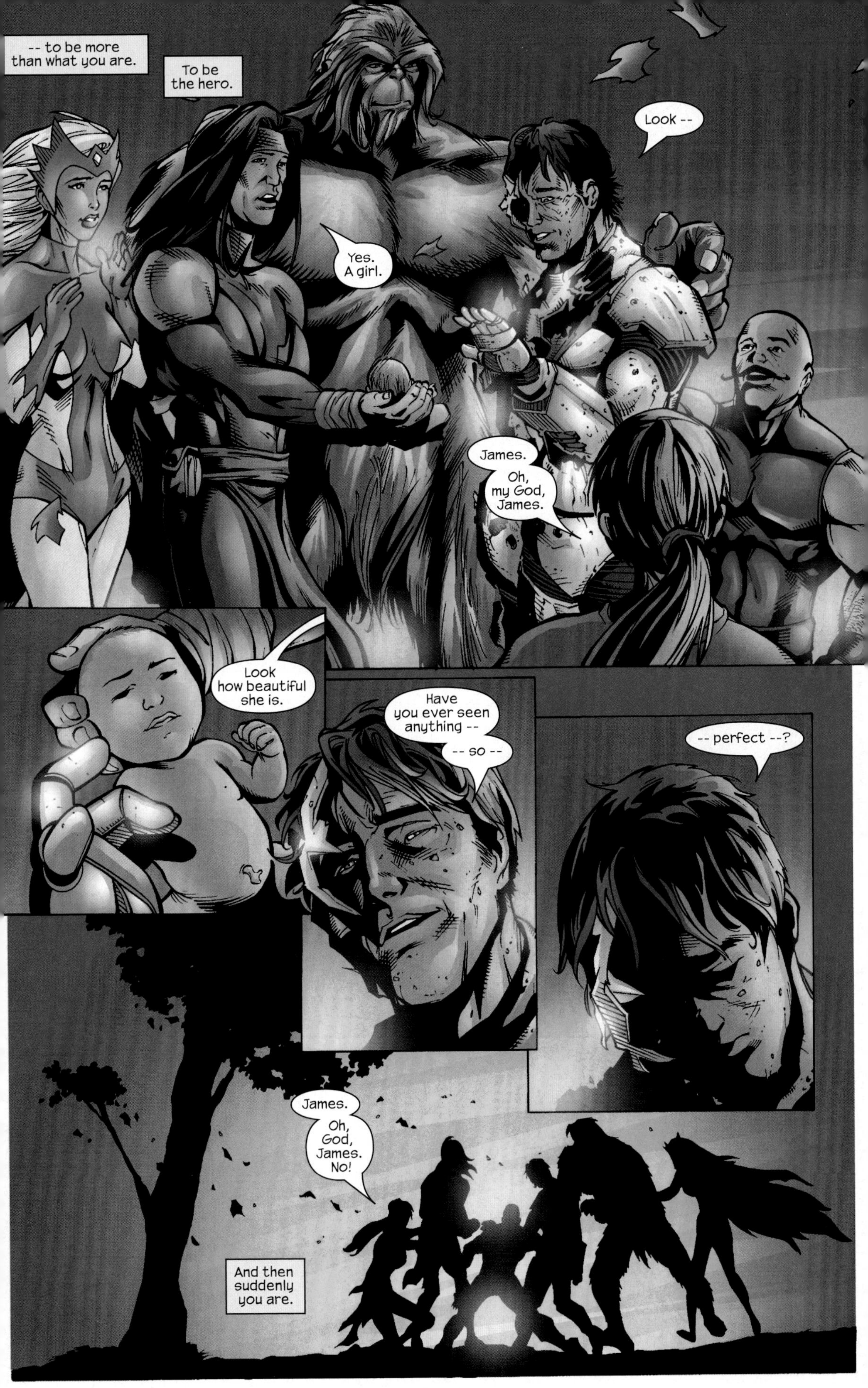
-- to be more than what you are.
To be the hero.
Look --
Yes. A girl.
James.
Oh, my God, James.
Look how beautiful she is.
Have you ever seen anything --
-- so --
-- perfect --?
James.
Oh, God, James. No!
And then suddenly you are.

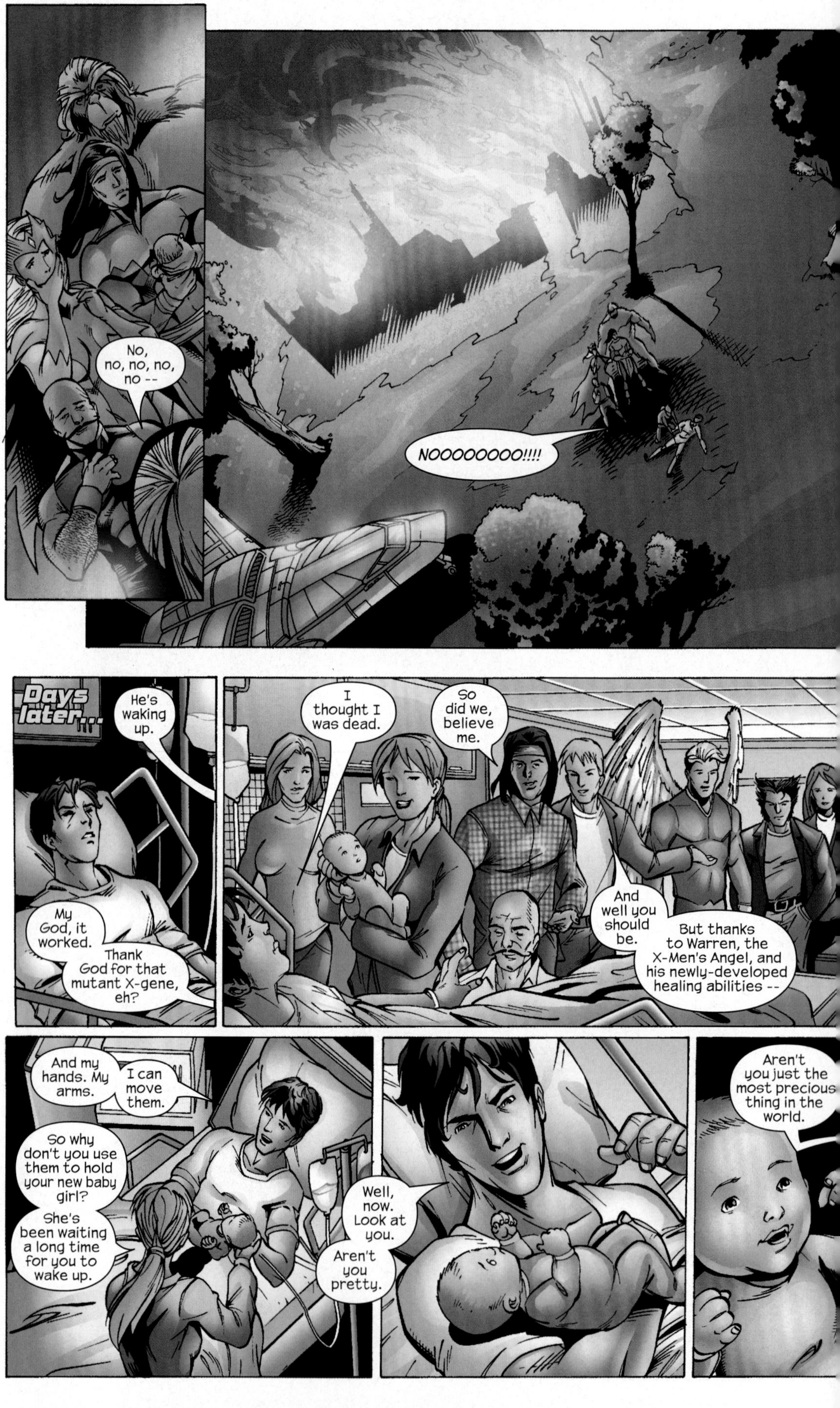
No, no, no, no, no --
NOOOOOOOO!!!!
Days later...
He's waking up.
My God, it worked.
Thank God for that mutant X-gene, eh?
I thought I was dead.
So did we, believe me.
And well you should be.
But thanks to Warren, the X-Men's Angel, and his newly-developed healing abilities --
And my hands. My arms.
I can move them.
So why don't you use them to hold your new baby girl?
She's been waiting a long time for you to wake up.
Well, now. Look at you.
Aren't you pretty.
Aren't you just the most precious thing in the world.

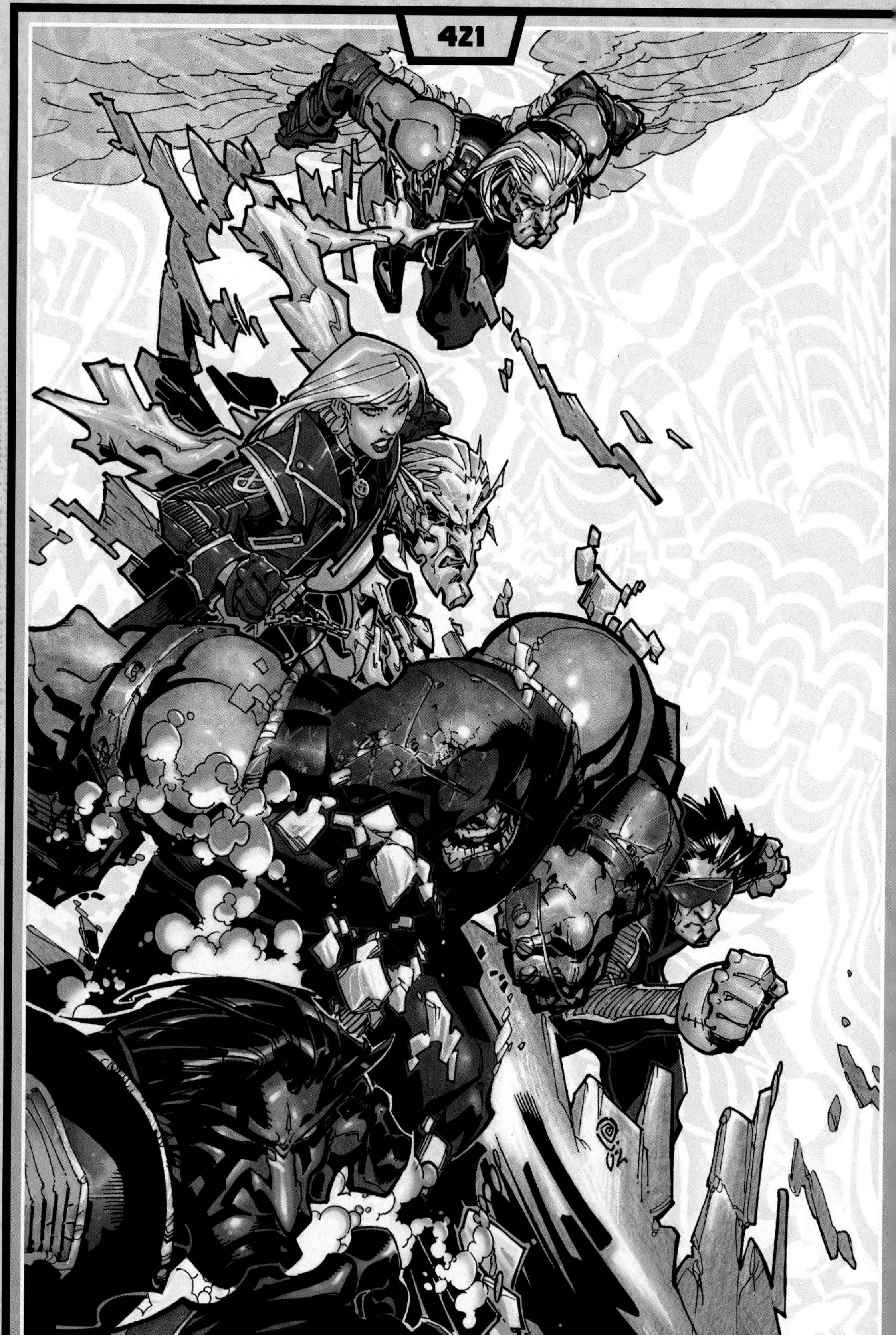
421

RULES OF ENGAGEMENT, PART 1 OF 2

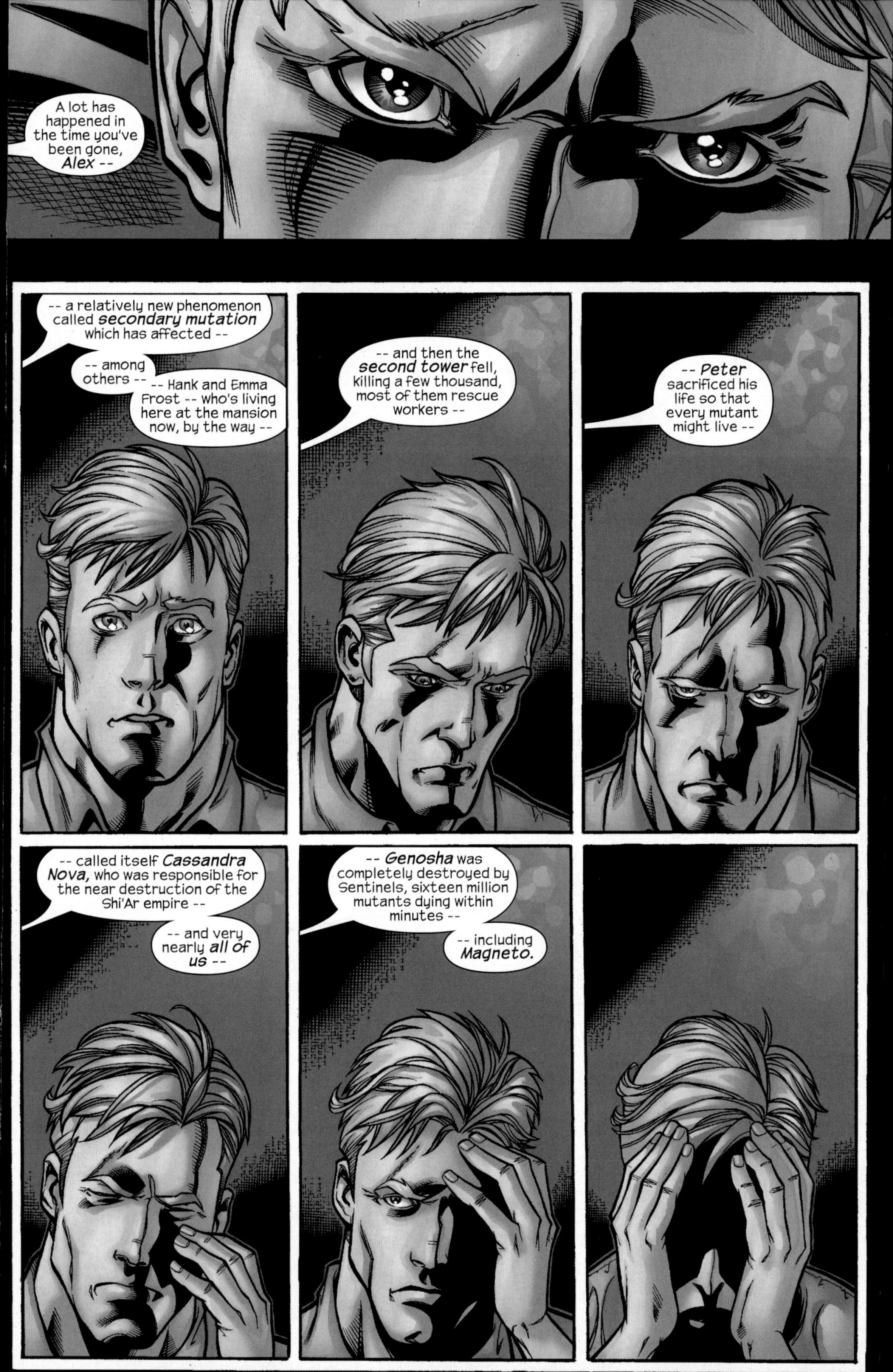

A lot has happened in the time you've been gone, *Alex* --
-- a relatively new phenomenon called *secondary mutation* which has affected --
-- among others --
-- Hank and Emma Frost -- who's living here at the mansion now, by the way --
-- and then the *second tower* fell, killing a few thousand, most of them rescue workers --
-- *Peter* sacrificed his life so that every mutant might live --
-- called itself *Cassandra Nova,* who was responsible for the near destruction of the Shi'Ar empire --
-- and very nearly *all of us* --
-- *Genosha* was completely destroyed by Sentinels, sixteen million mutants dying within minutes --
-- including *Magneto.*

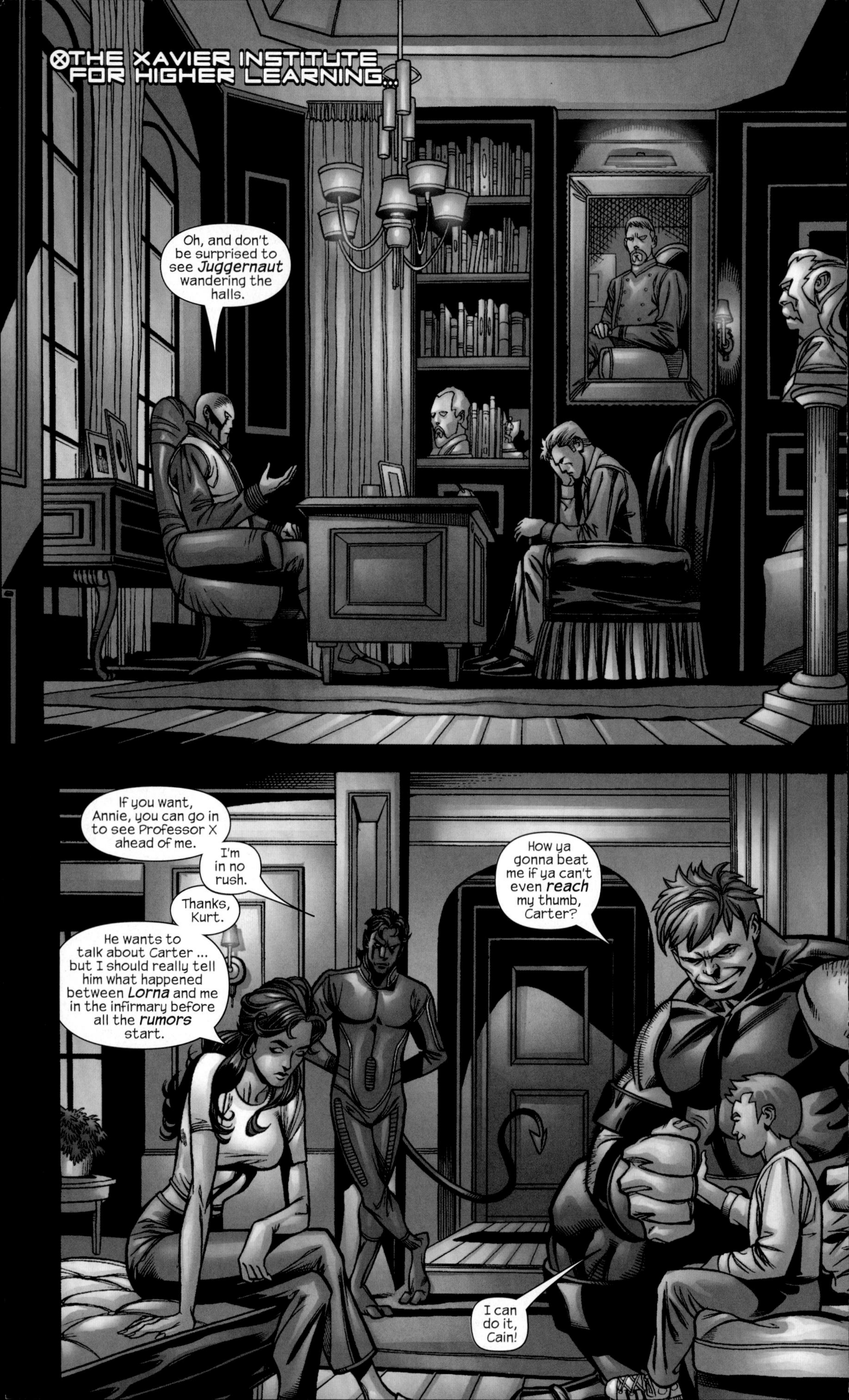

THE XAVIER INSTITUTE FOR HIGHER LEARNING...
Oh, and don't be surprised to see Juggernaut wandering the halls.
If you want, Annie, you can go in to see Professor X ahead of me.
I'm in no rush.
Thanks, Kurt.
He wants to talk about Carter ... but I should really tell him what happened between Lorna and me in the infirmary before all the rumors start.
How ya gonna beat me if ya can't even reach my thumb, Carter?
I can do it, Cain!

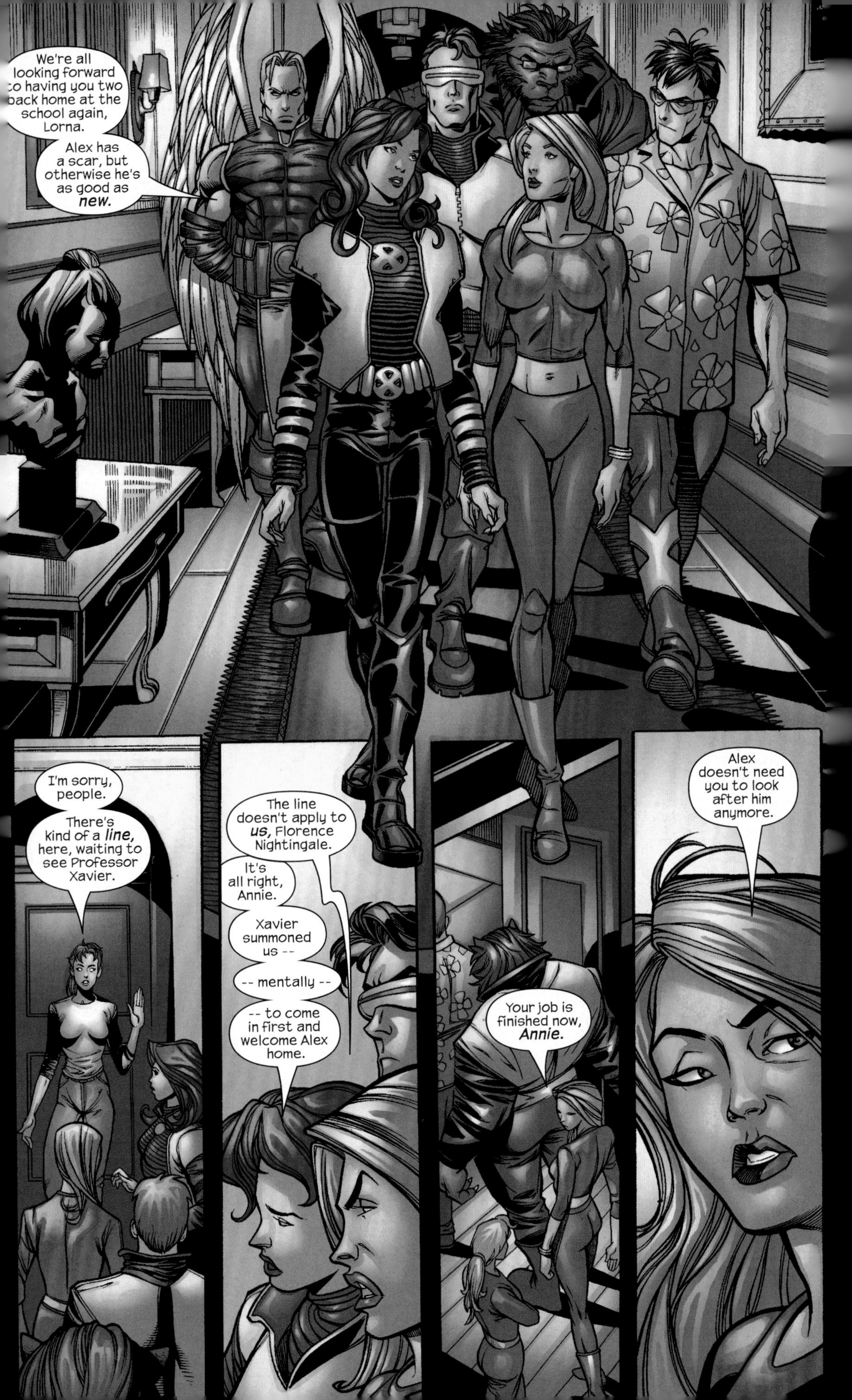
We're all looking forward to having you two back home at the school again, Lorna.
Alex has a scar, but otherwise he's as good as new.
I'm sorry, people.
There's kind of a line, here, waiting to see Professor Xavier.
The line doesn't apply to us, Florence Nightingale.
It's all right, Annie.
Xavier summoned us --
-- mentally --
-- to come in first and welcome Alex home.
Your job is finished now, Annie.
Alex doesn't need you to look after him anymore.

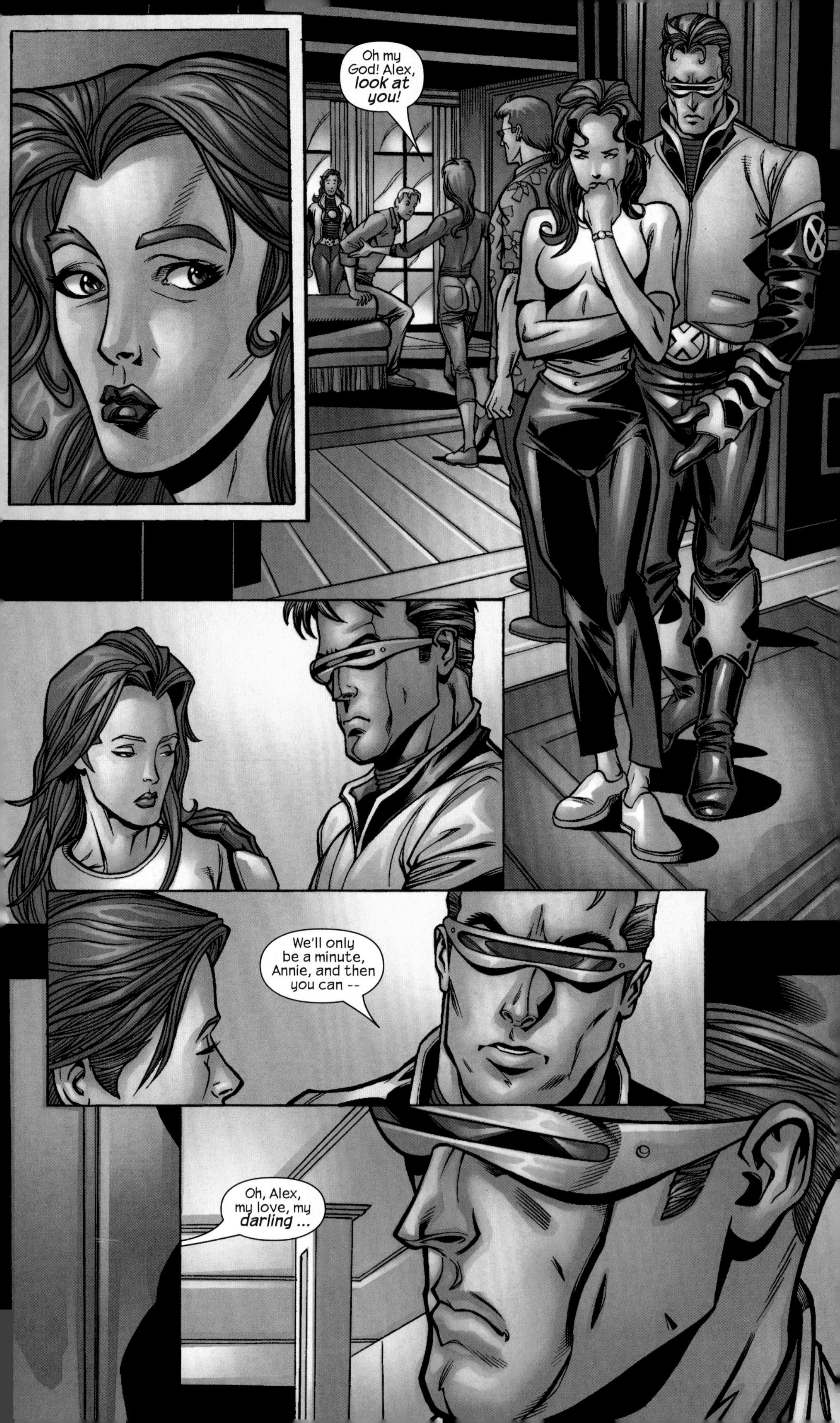
Oh my God! Alex, look at you!
We'll only be a minute, Annie, and then you can --
Oh, Alex, my love, my darling ...

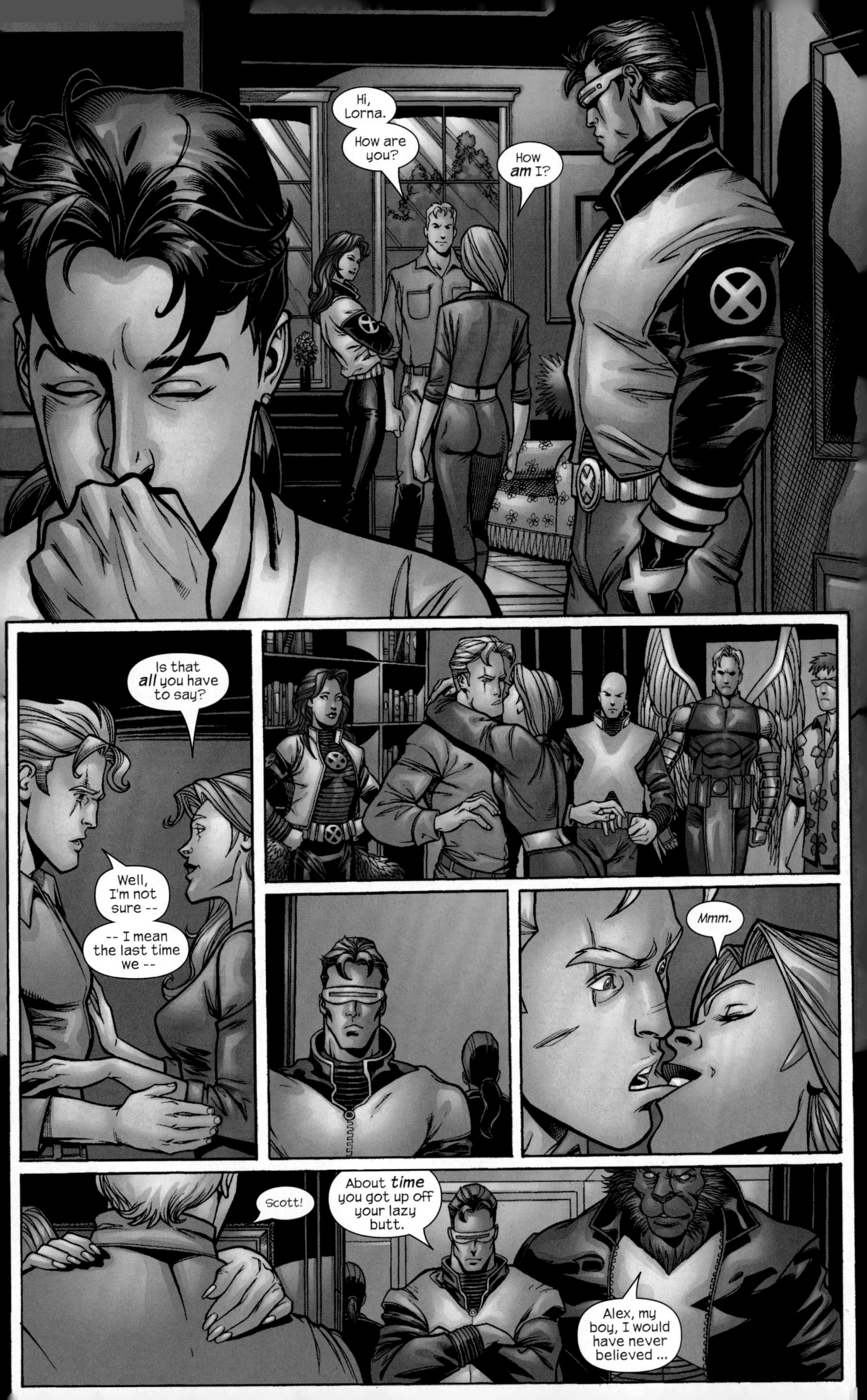
Hi, Lorna.
How are you?
How *am* I?
Is that *all* you have to say?
Well, I'm not sure --
-- I mean the last time we --
Mmm.
Scott!
About *time* you got up off your lazy butt.
Alex, my boy, I would have never believed ...

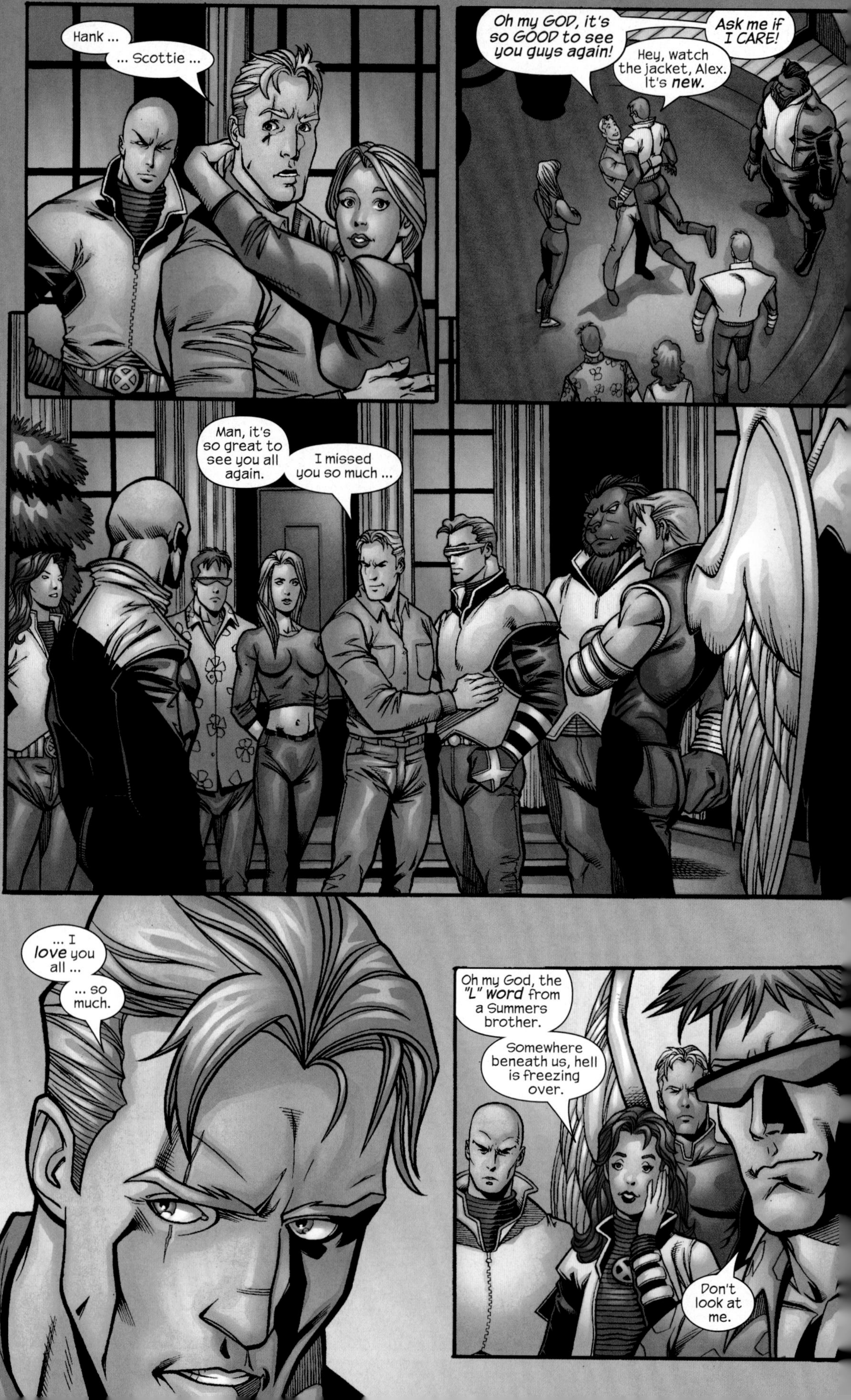

Hank ...
... Scottie ...
Oh my GOD, it's so GOOD to see you guys again!
Ask me if I CARE!
Hey, watch the jacket, Alex. It's new.
Man, it's so great to see you all again.
I missed you so much ...
... I love you all ...
... so much.
Oh my God, the "L" word from a Summers brother.
Somewhere beneath us, hell is freezing over.
Don't look at me.

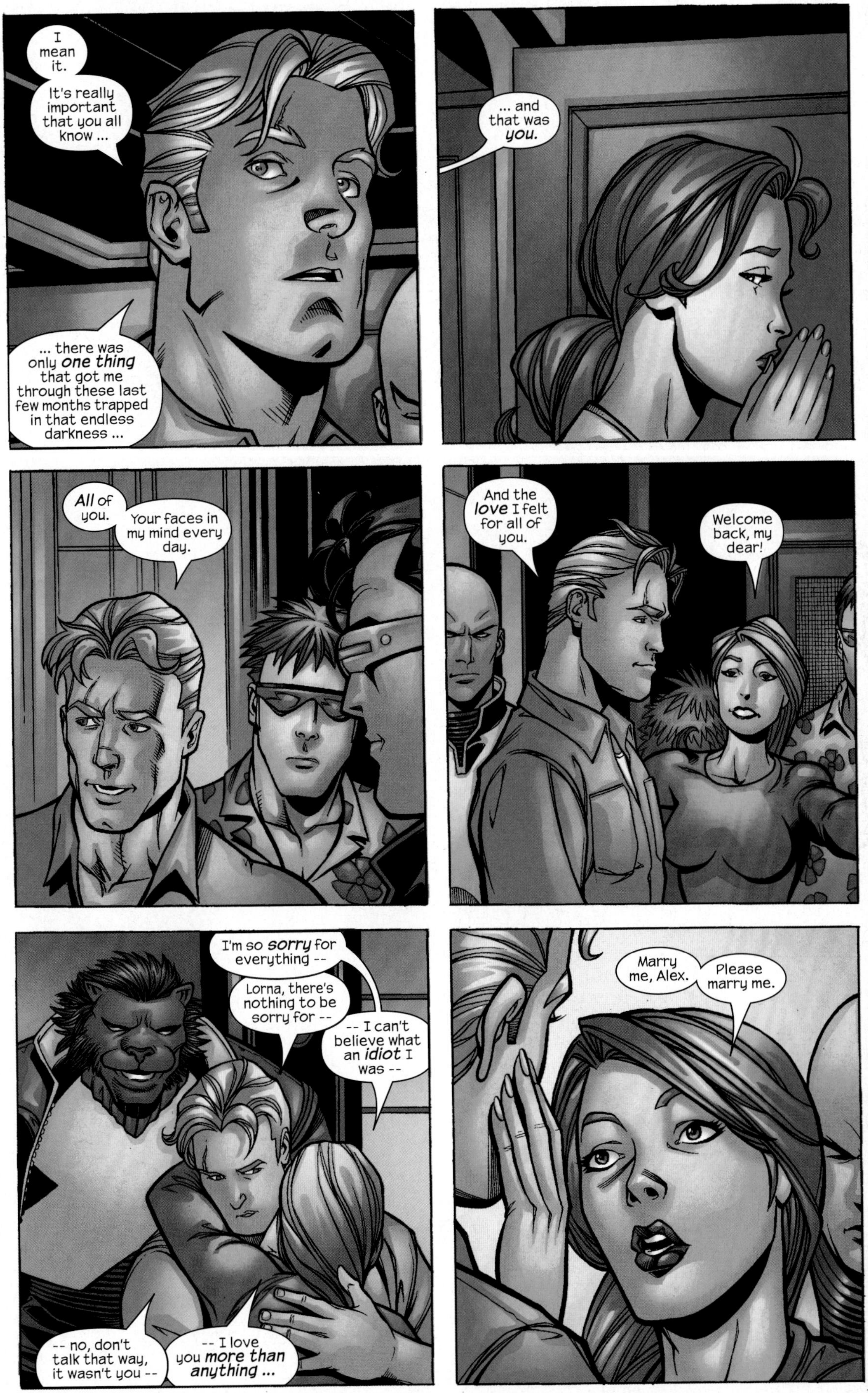

I mean it.
It's really important that you all know ...
... there was only *one thing* that got me through these last few months trapped in that endless darkness ...
... and that was *you.*
All of you.
Your faces in my mind every day.
And the *love* I felt for all of you.
Welcome back, my dear!
I'm so *sorry* for everything --
Lorna, there's nothing to be sorry for --
-- I can't believe what an *idiot* I was --
-- no, don't talk that way, it wasn't you --
-- I love you *more than anything ...*
Marry me, Alex.
Please marry me.

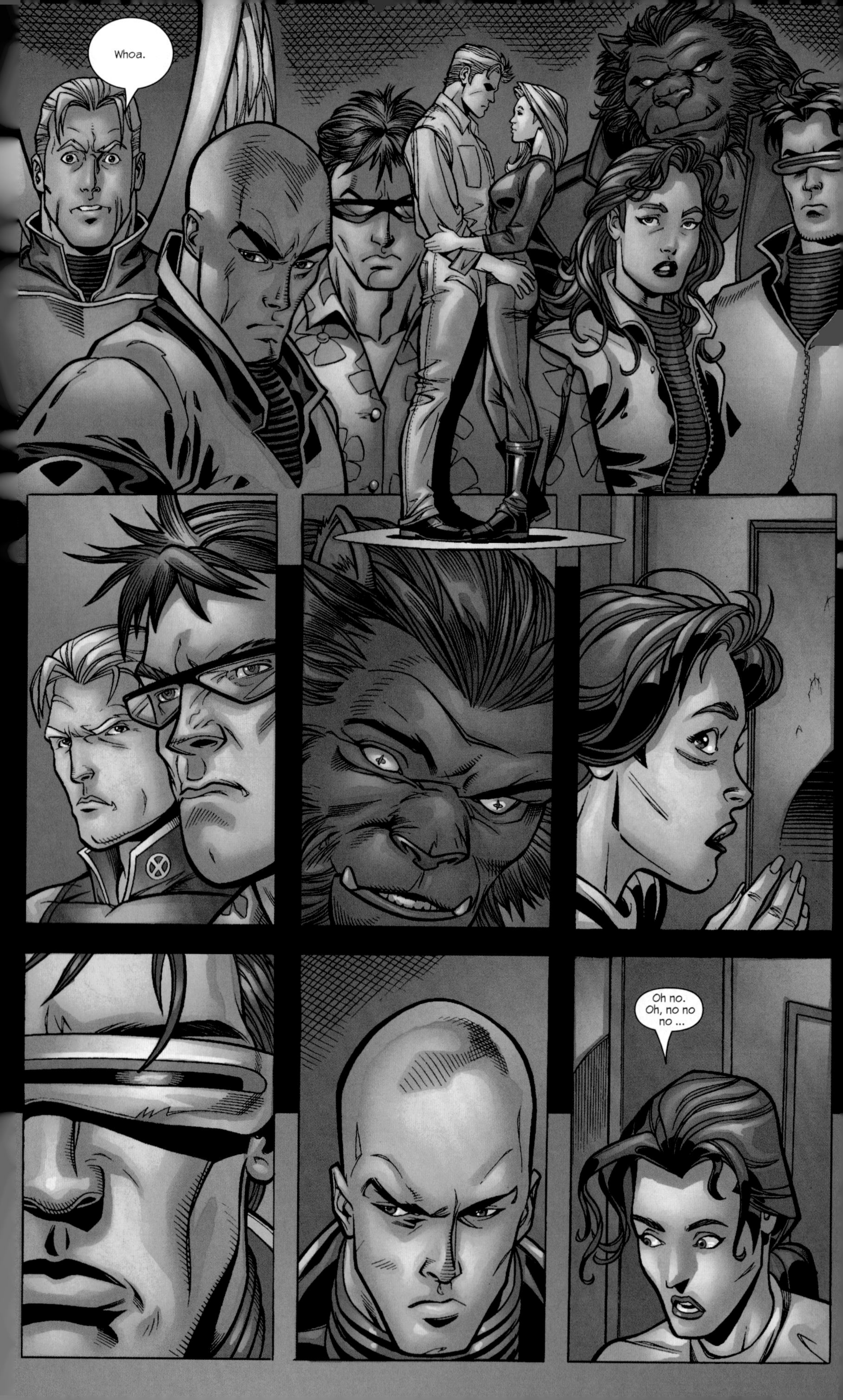
Whoa.
Oh no. Oh, no no no ...

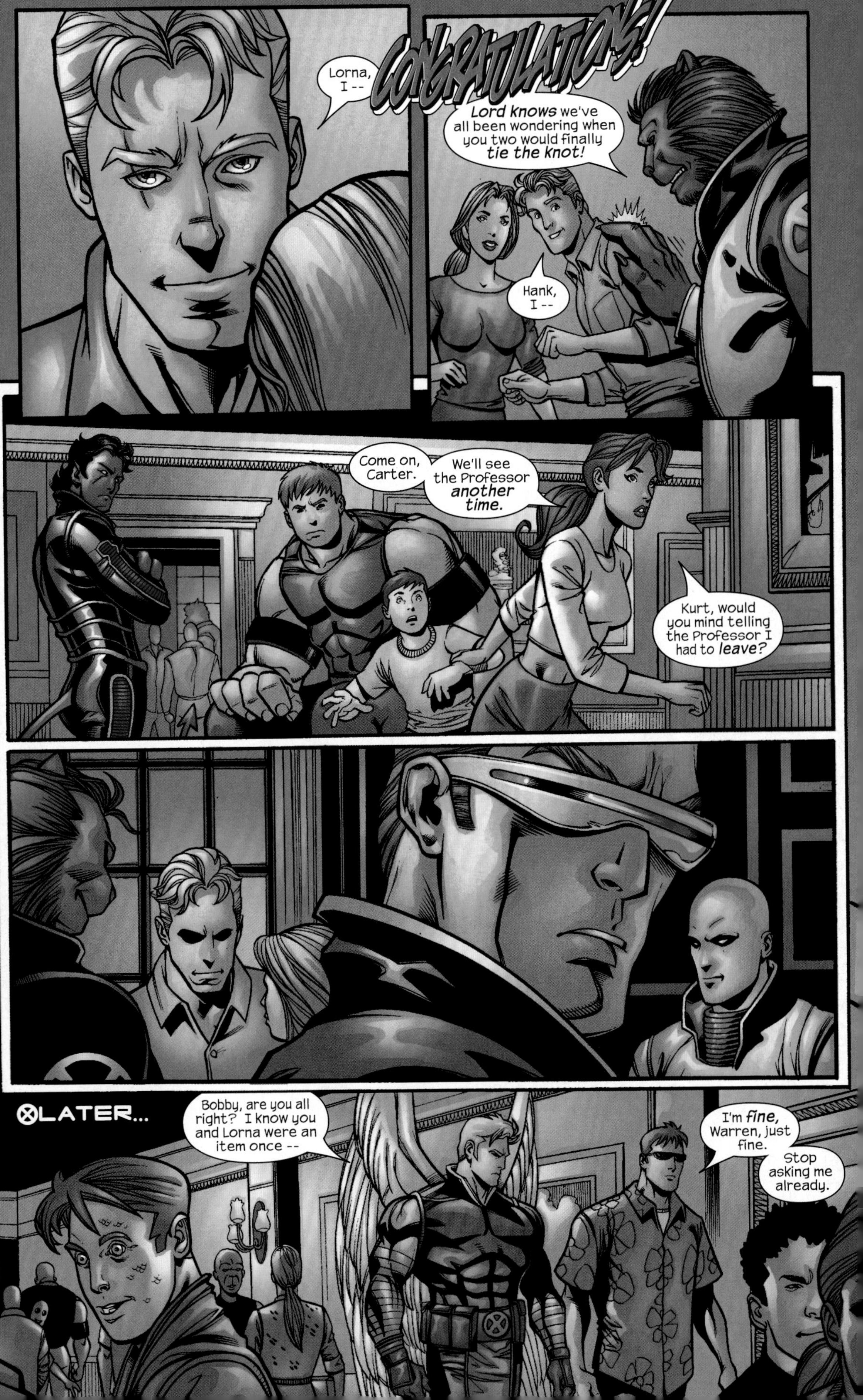
Lorna, I --
CONGRATULATIONS!
Lord knows we've all been wondering when you two would finally tie the knot!
Hank, I --
Come on, Carter.
We'll see the Professor another time.
Kurt, would you mind telling the Professor I had to leave?
LATER...
Bobby, are you all right? I know you and Lorna were an item once --
I'm fine, Warren, just fine.
Stop asking me already.

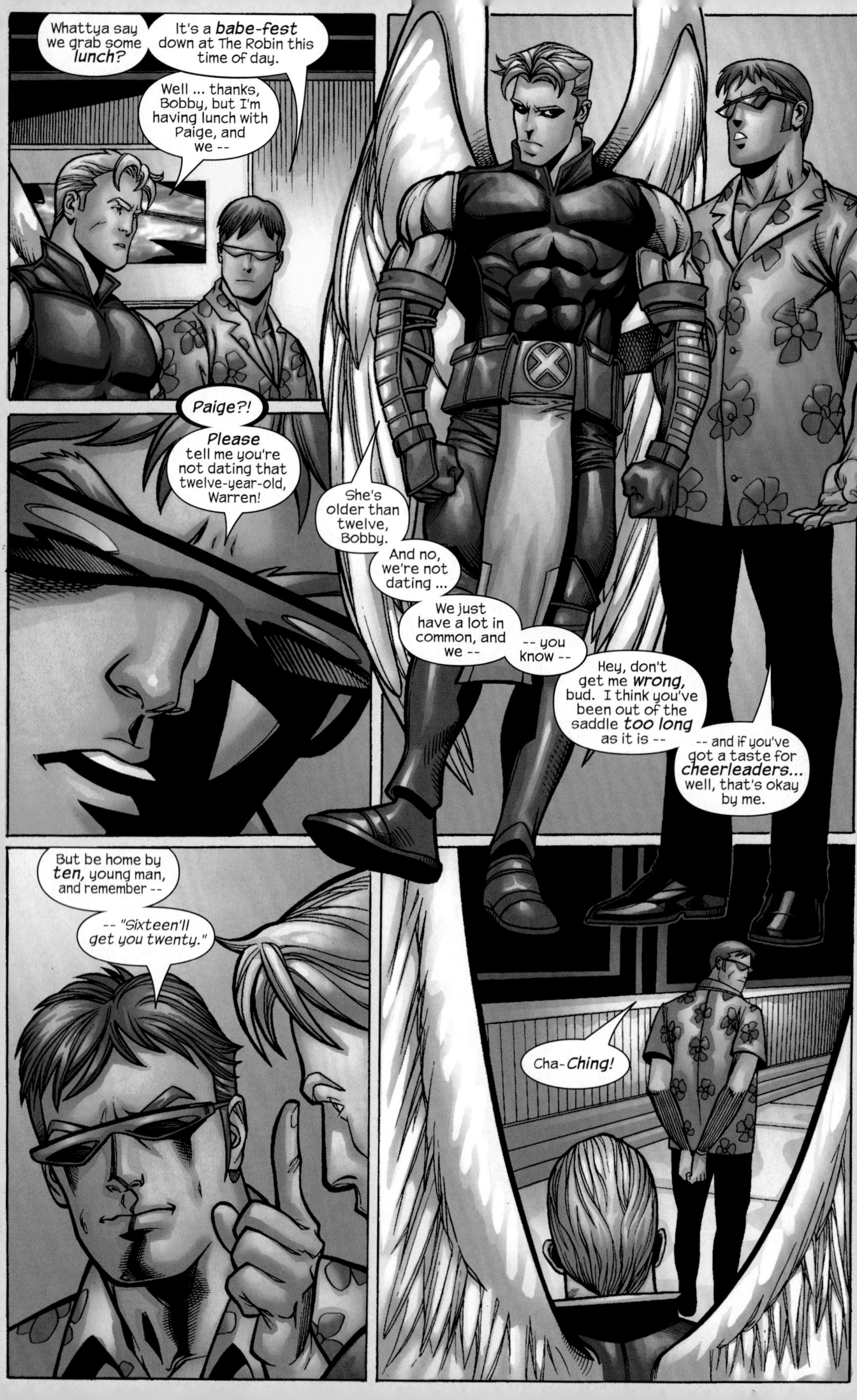
Whattya say we grab some lunch?
It's a babe-fest down at The Robin this time of day.
Well ... thanks, Bobby, but I'm having lunch with Paige, and we --
Paige?!
Please tell me you're not dating that twelve-year-old, Warren!
She's older than twelve, Bobby.
And no, we're not dating ...
We just have a lot in common, and we --
-- you know --
Hey, don't get me wrong, bud. I think you've been out of the saddle too long as it is --
-- and if you've got a taste for cheerleaders... well, that's okay by me.
But be home by ten, young man, and remember --
-- "Sixteen'll get you twenty."
Cha-Ching!

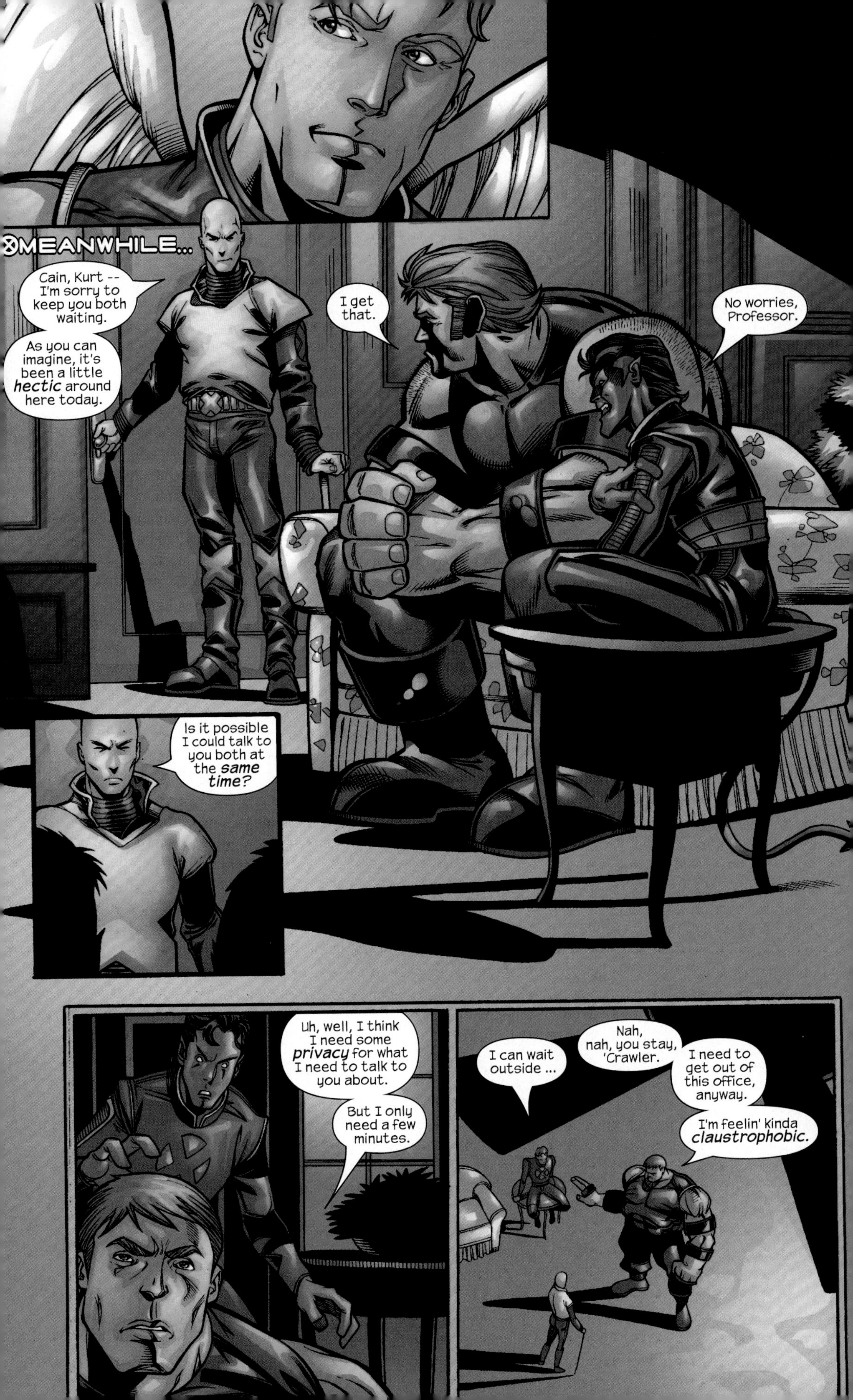
MEANWHILE...
Cain, Kurt -- I'm sorry to keep you both waiting.
As you can imagine, it's been a little *hectic* around here today.
I get that.
No worries, Professor.
Is it possible I could talk to you both at the *same time?*
Uh, well, I think I need some *privacy* for what I need to talk to you about.
But I only need a few minutes.
I can wait outside ...
Nah, nah, you stay, 'Crawler.
I need to get out of this office, anyway.
I'm feelin' kinda *claustrophobic.*

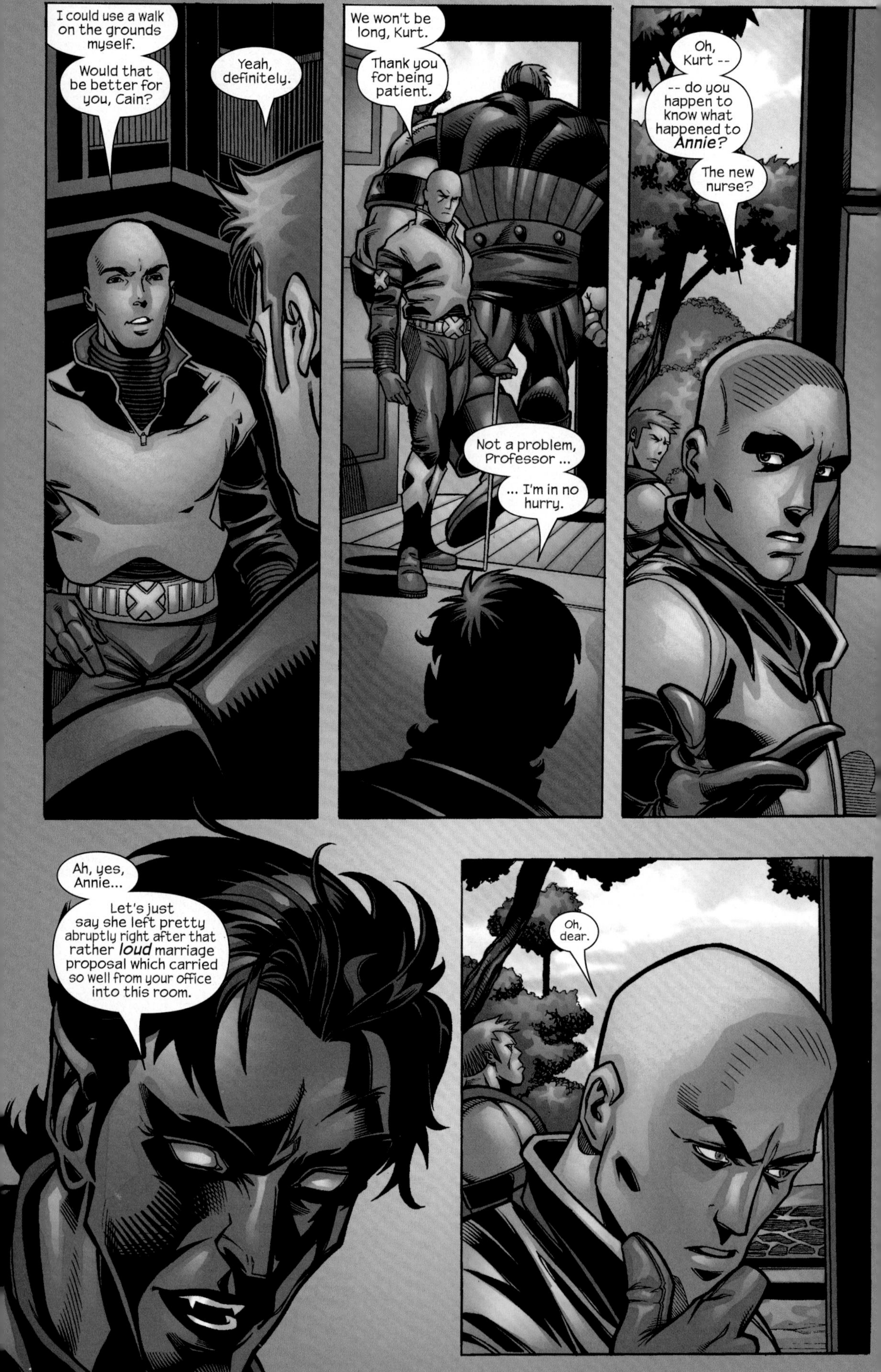
I could use a walk on the grounds myself.
Would that be better for you, Cain?
Yeah, definitely.
We won't be long, Kurt.
Thank you for being patient.
Not a problem, Professor ...
... I'm in no hurry.
Oh, Kurt --
-- do you happen to know what happened to *Annie*?
The new nurse?
Ah, yes, Annie...
Let's just say she left pretty abruptly right after that rather *loud* marriage proposal which carried so well from your office into this room.
Oh, dear.

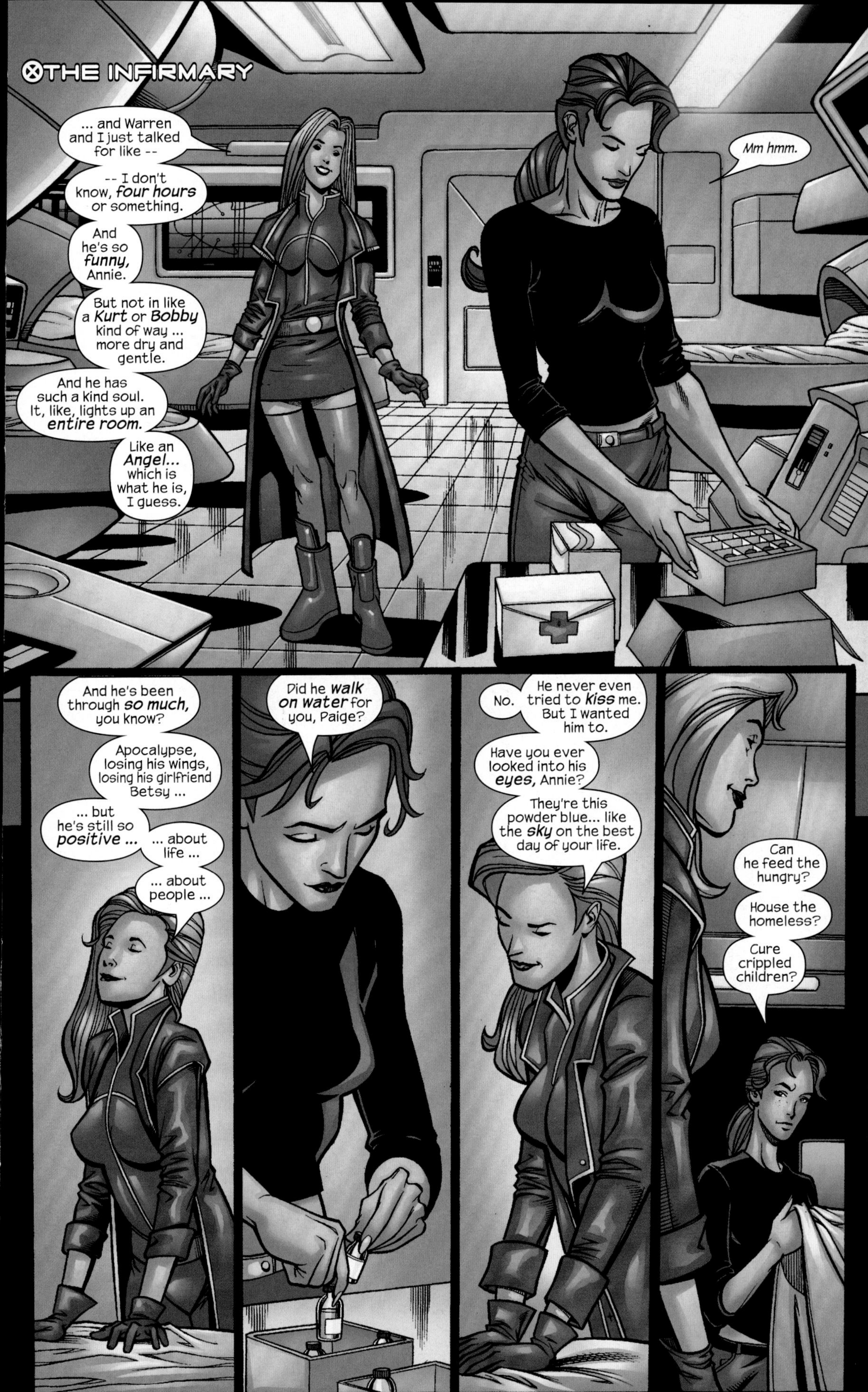
THE INFIRMARY
... and Warren and I just talked for like --
-- I don't know, *four hours* or something.
Mm hmm.
And he's so *funny,* Annie.
But not in like a *Kurt* or *Bobby* kind of way ... more dry and gentle.
And he has such a kind soul. It, like, lights up an *entire room.*
Like an *Angel...* which is what he is, I guess.
And he's been through *so much,* you know?
Apocalypse, losing his wings, losing his girlfriend Betsy ...
... but he's still so *positive ...*
... about life ...
... about people ...
Did he *walk on water* for you, Paige?
No.
He never even tried to *kiss* me. But I wanted him to.
Have you ever looked into his *eyes,* Annie?
They're this powder blue... like the *sky* on the best day of your life.
Can he feed the hungry?
House the homeless?
Cure crippled children?

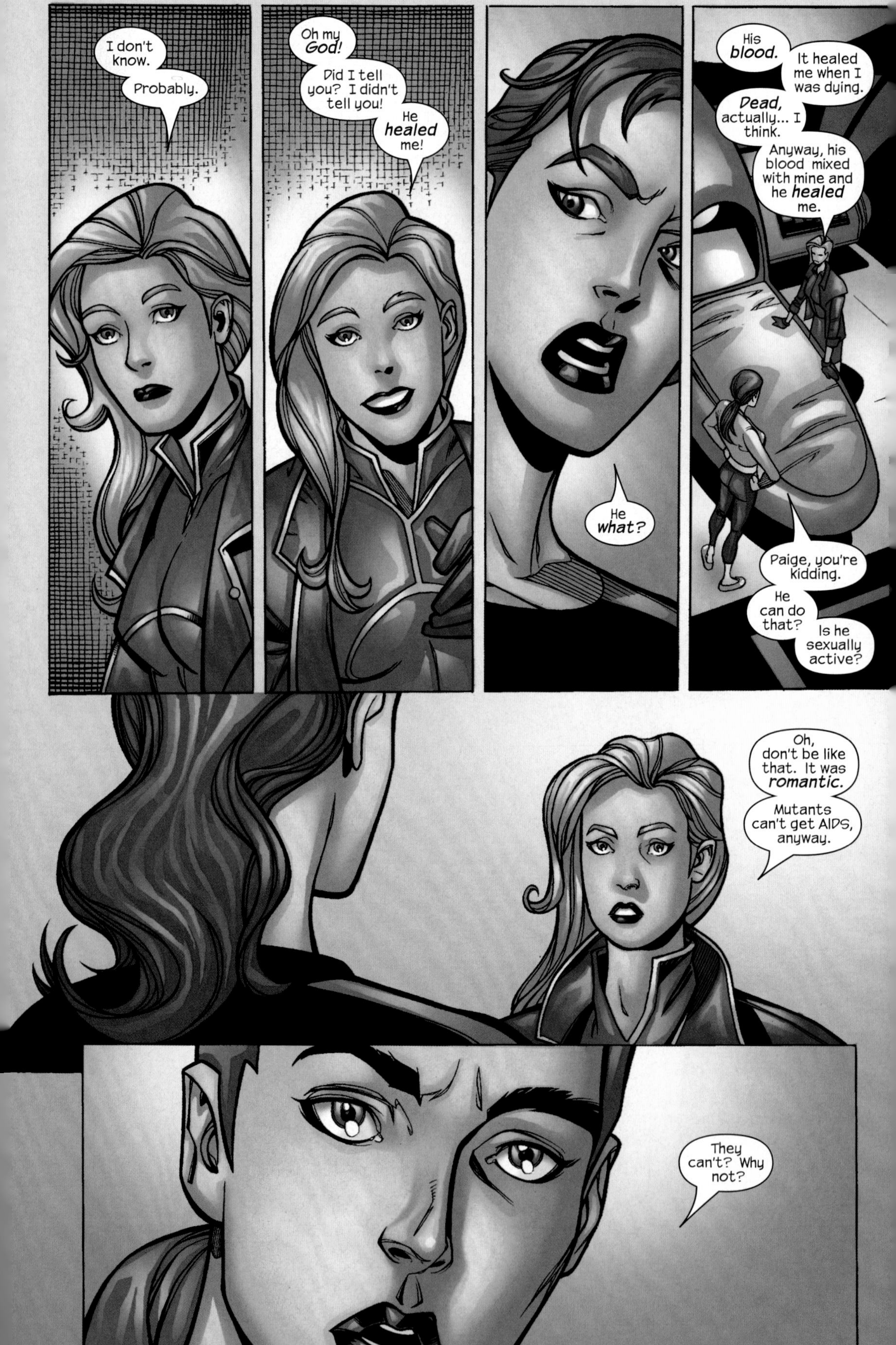
I don't know.
Probably.
Oh my God!
Did I tell you? I didn't tell you!
He healed me!
He what?
His blood.
It healed me when I was dying.
Dead, actually... I think.
Anyway, his blood mixed with mine and he healed me.
Paige, you're kidding.
He can do that?
Is he sexually active?
Oh, don't be like that. It was romantic.
Mutants can't get AIDS, anyway.
They can't? Why not?

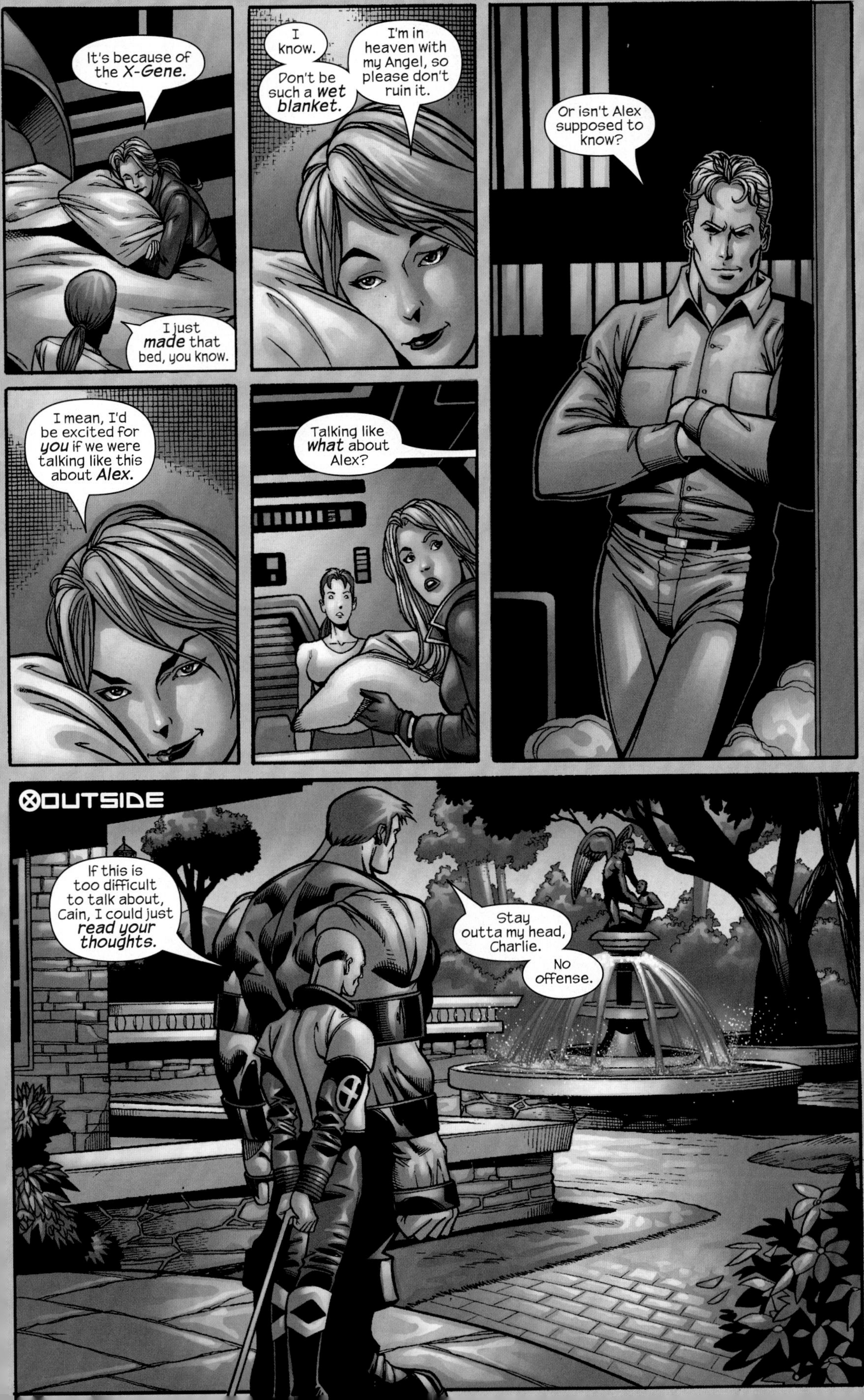

It's because of the *X-Gene.*
I just *made* that bed, you know.
I know.
Don't be such a ***wet blanket.***
I'm in heaven with my Angel, so please don't ruin it.
Or isn't Alex supposed to know?
I mean, I'd be excited for ***you*** if we were talking like this about ***Alex.***
Talking like ***what*** about Alex?
OUTSIDE
If this is too difficult to talk about, Cain, I could just ***read your thoughts.***
Stay outta my head, Charlie.
No offense.

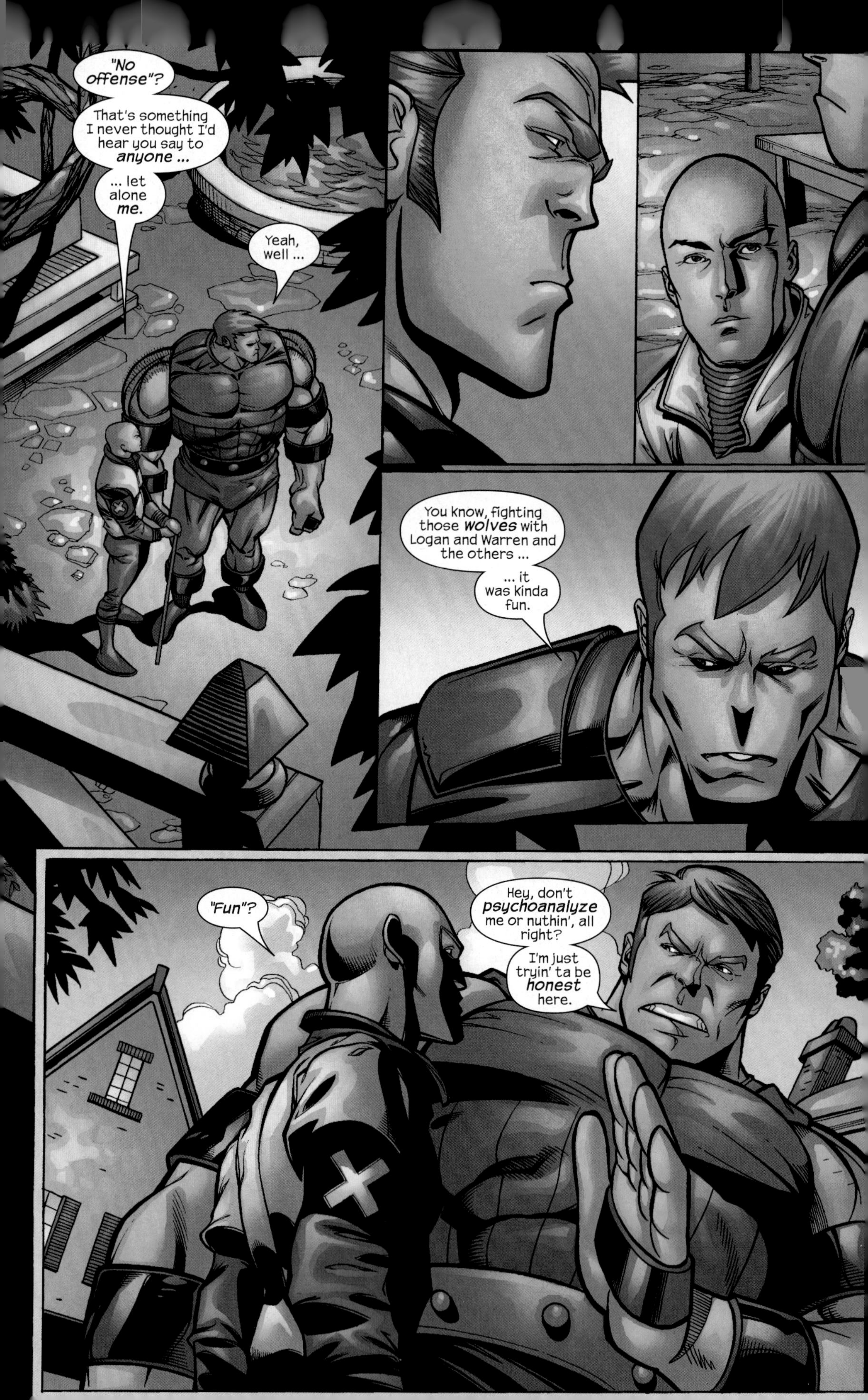
"No offense"?
That's something I never thought I'd hear you say to anyone ...
... let alone me.
Yeah, well ...
You know, fighting those wolves with Logan and Warren and the others ...
... it was kinda fun.
"Fun"?
Hey, don't psychoanalyze me or nuthin', all right?
I'm just tryin' ta be honest here.

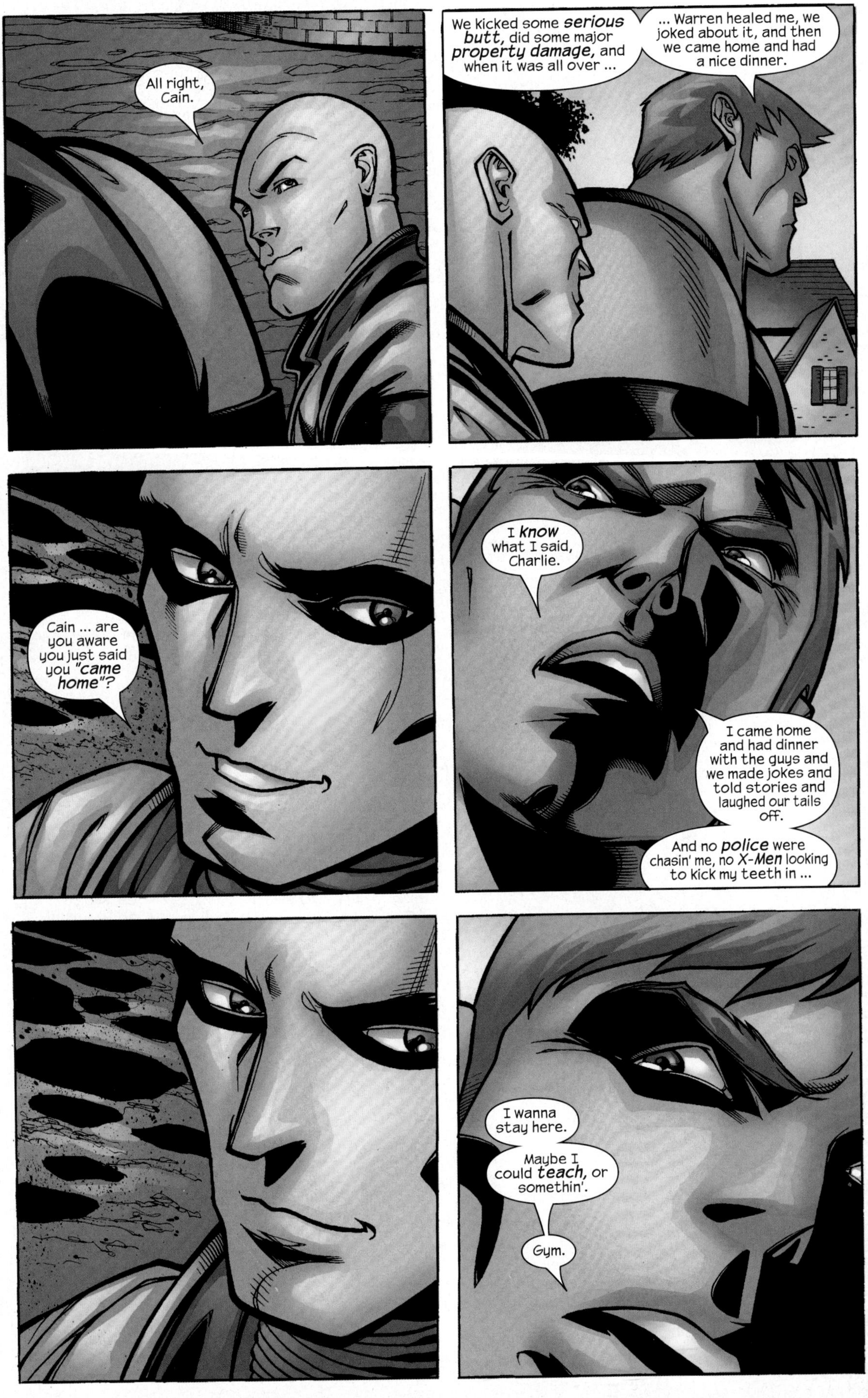

All right, Cain.
We kicked some serious butt, did some major property damage, and when it was all over ...
... Warren healed me, we joked about it, and then we came home and had a nice dinner.
Cain ... are you aware you just said you "came home"?
I know what I said, Charlie.
I came home and had dinner with the guys and we made jokes and told stories and laughed our tails off.
And no police were chasin' me, no X-Men looking to kick my teeth in ...
I wanna stay here.
Maybe I could teach, or somethin'.
Gym.

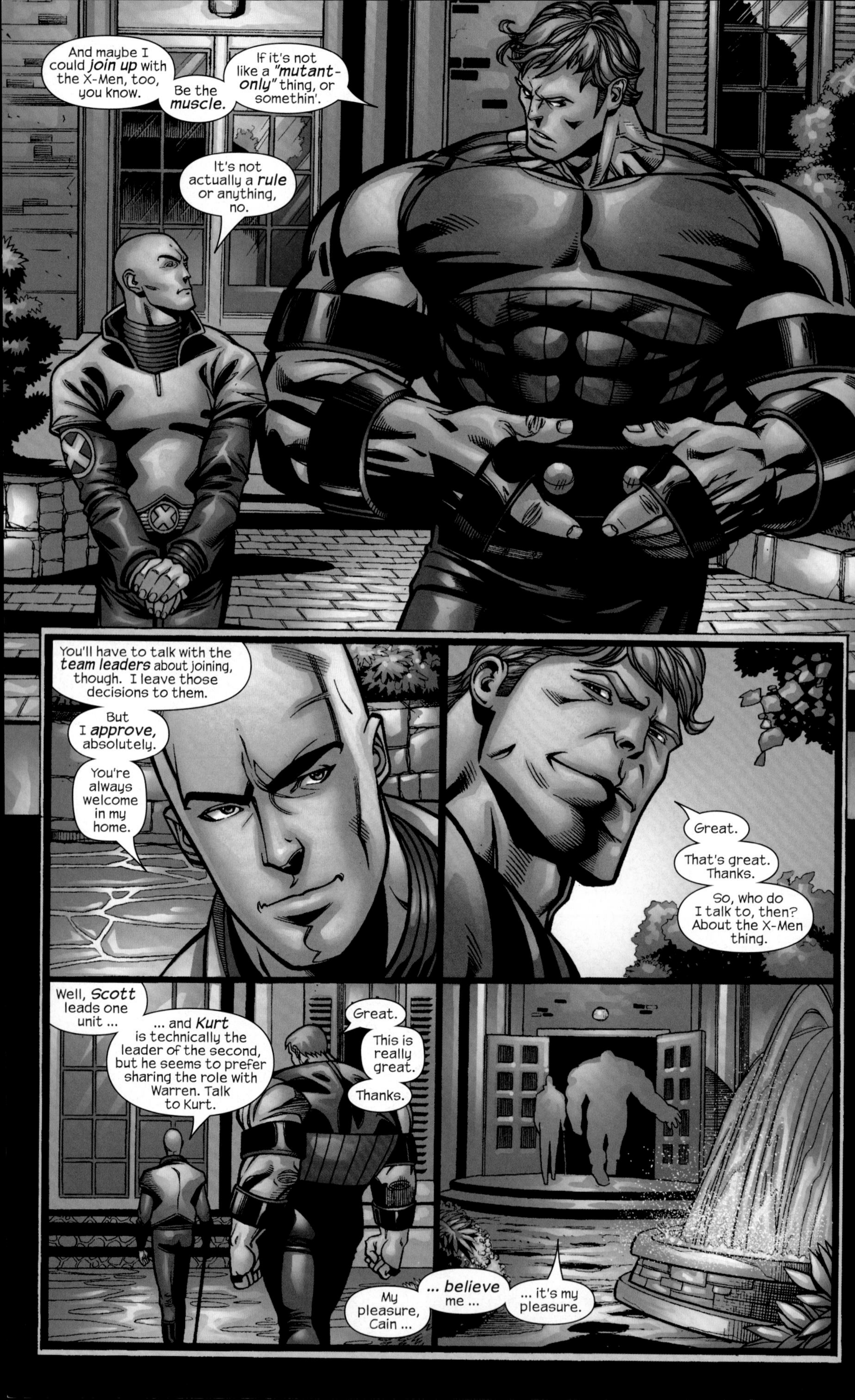
And maybe I could join up with the X-Men, too, you know.
Be the muscle.
If it's not like a "mutant-only" thing, or somethin'.
It's not actually a rule or anything, no.
You'll have to talk with the team leaders about joining, though. I leave those decisions to them.
But I approve, absolutely.
You're always welcome in my home.
Great.
That's great. Thanks.
So, who do I talk to, then? About the X-Men thing.
Well, Scott leads one unit ...
... and Kurt is technically the leader of the second, but he seems to prefer sharing the role with Warren. Talk to Kurt.
Great.
This is really great.
Thanks.
My pleasure, Cain ...
... believe me ...
... it's my pleasure.

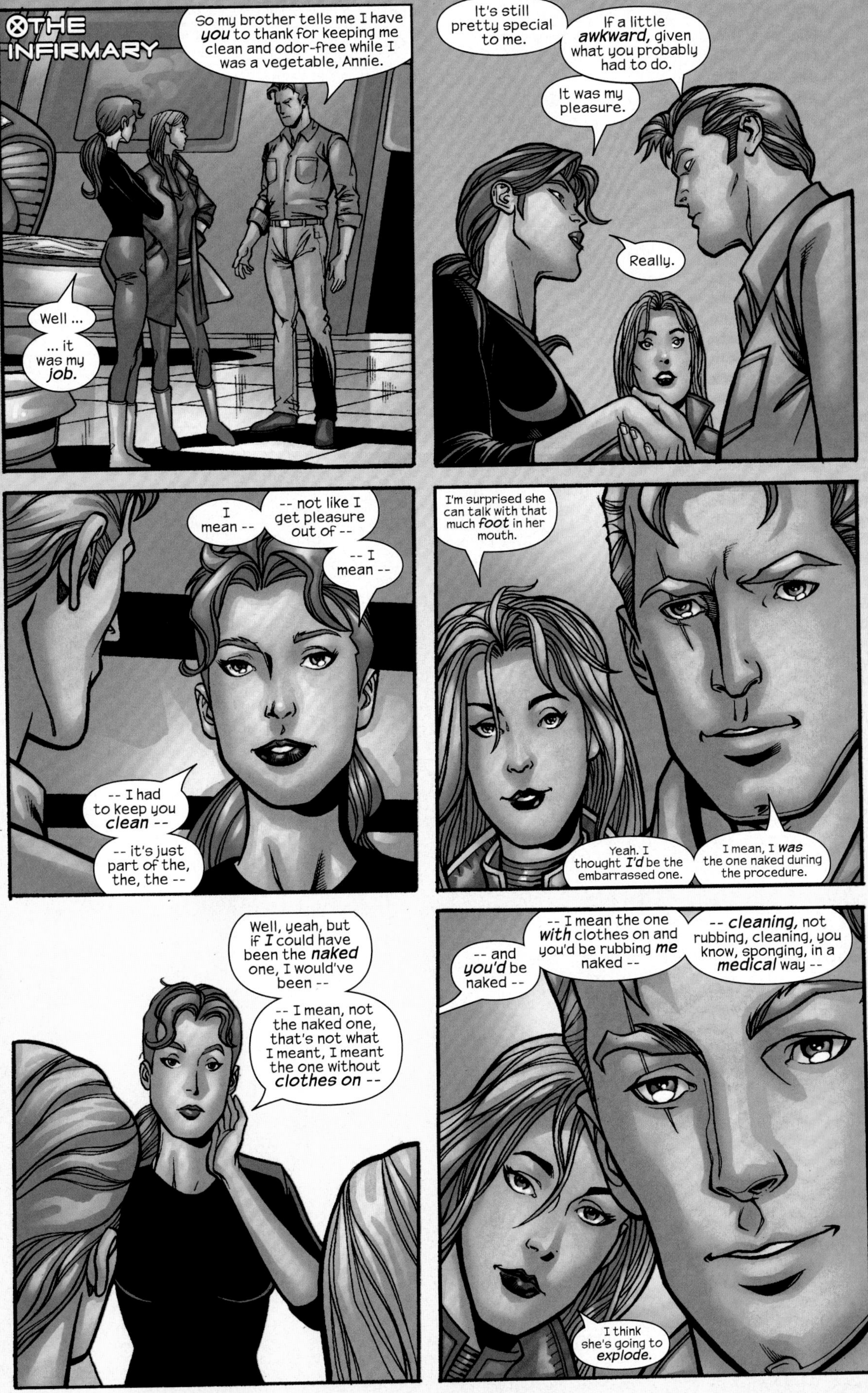
THE INFIRMARY
So my brother tells me I have you to thank for keeping me clean and odor-free while I was a vegetable, Annie.
Well ...
... it was my job.
It's still pretty special to me.
If a little awkward, given what you probably had to do.
It was my pleasure.
Really.
I mean --
-- not like I get pleasure out of --
-- I mean --
-- I had to keep you clean --
-- it's just part of the, the, the --
I'm surprised she can talk with that much foot in her mouth.
Yeah. I thought I'd be the embarrassed one.
I mean, I was the one naked during the procedure.
Well, yeah, but if I could have been the naked one, I would've been --
-- I mean, not the naked one, that's not what I meant, I meant the one without clothes on --
-- and you'd be naked --
-- I mean the one with clothes on and you'd be rubbing me naked --
-- cleaning, not rubbing, cleaning, you know, sponging, in a medical way --
I think she's going to explode.

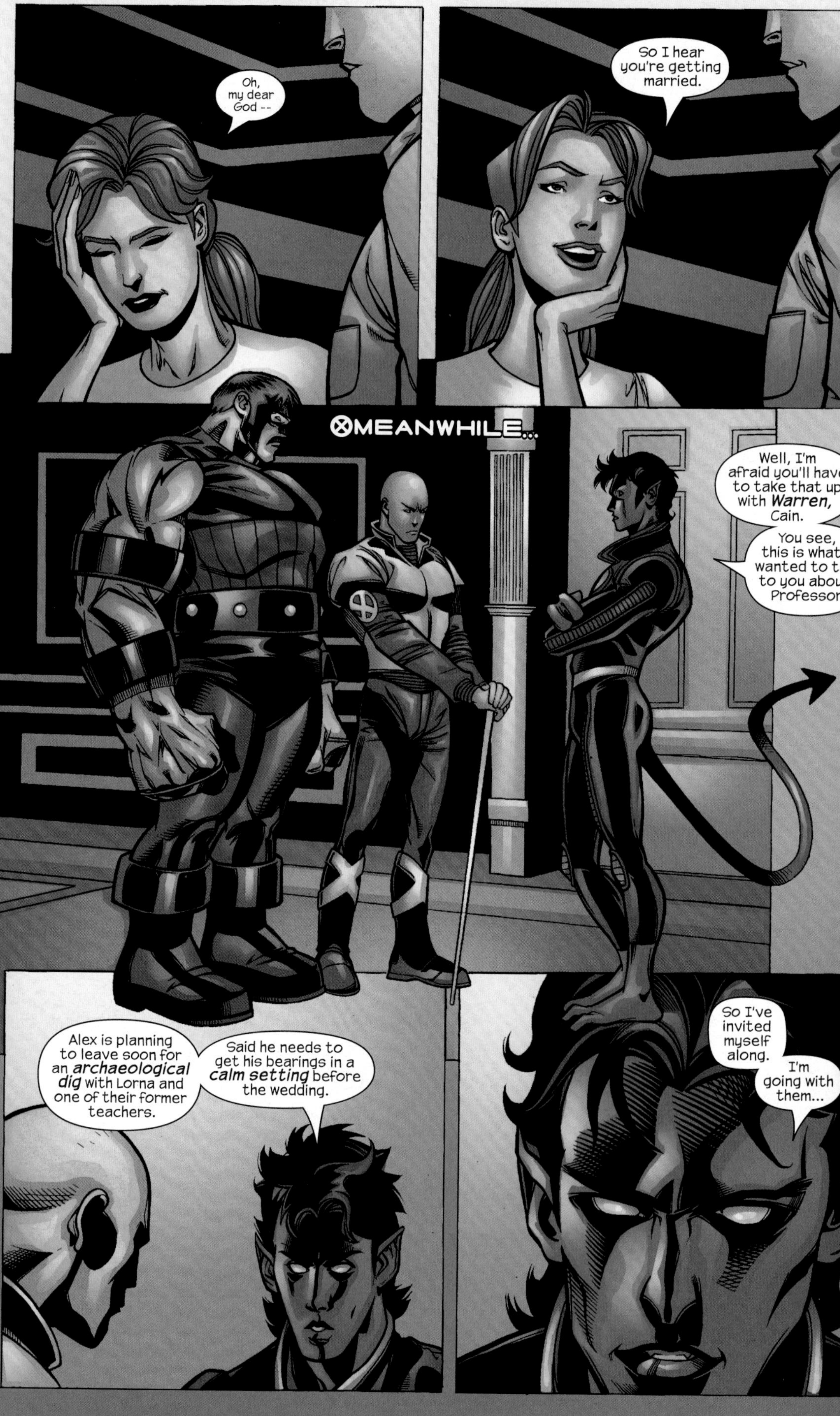
Oh, my dear God --
So I hear you're getting married.
MEANWHILE...
Well, I'm afraid you'll have to take that up with *Warren,* Cain.
You see, this is what I wanted to talk to you about, Professor.
Alex is planning to leave soon for an *archaeological dig* with Lorna and one of their former teachers.
Said he needs to get his bearings in a *calm setting* before the wedding.
So I've invited myself along.
I'm going with them...

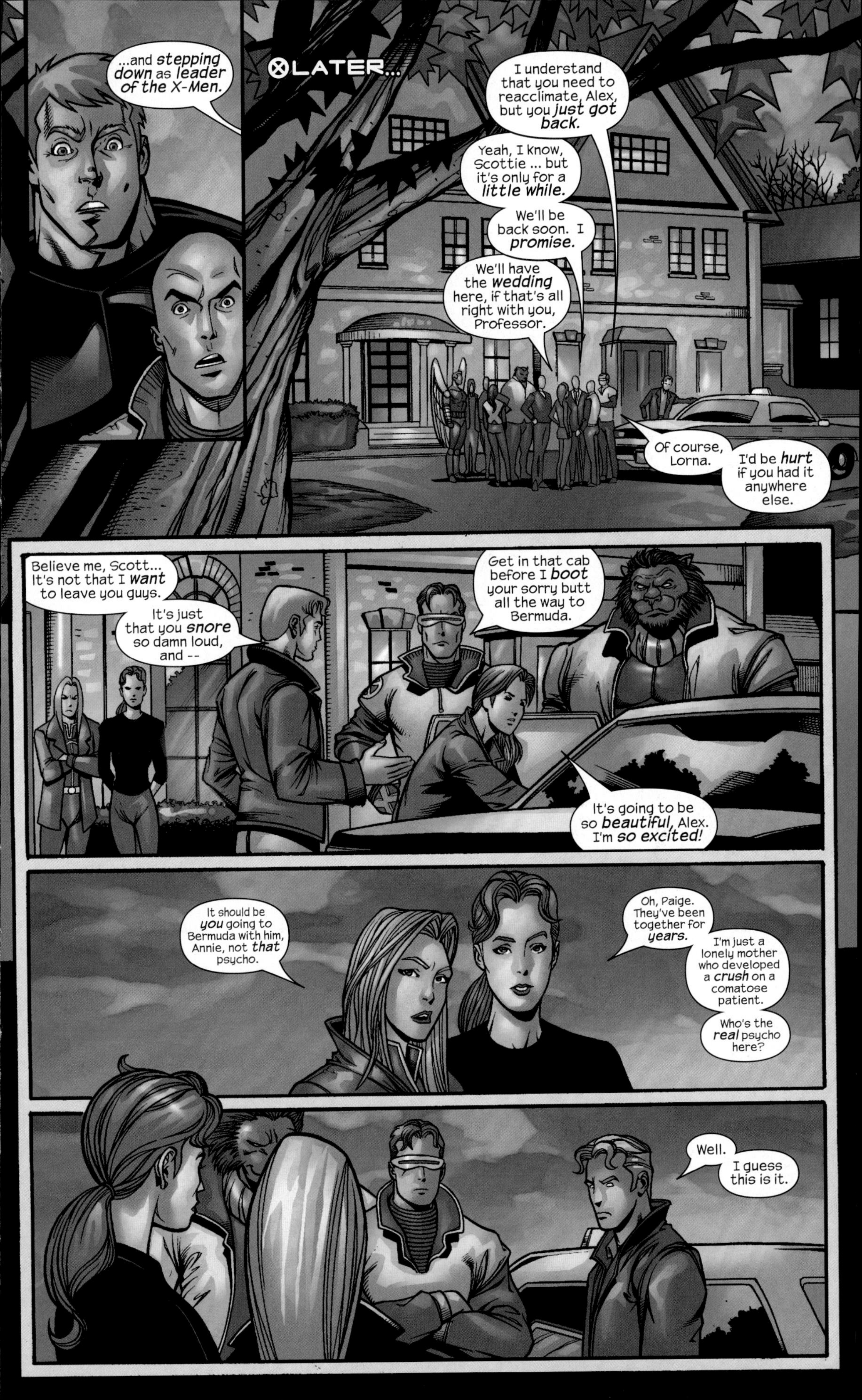

...and stepping down as leader of the X-Men.
LATER...
I understand that you need to reacclimate, Alex, but you just got back.
Yeah, I know, Scottie ... but it's only for a little while.
We'll be back soon. I promise.
We'll have the wedding here, if that's all right with you, Professor.
Of course, Lorna.
I'd be hurt if you had it anywhere else.
Believe me, Scott... It's not that I want to leave you guys.
It's just that you snore so damn loud, and --
Get in that cab before I boot your sorry butt all the way to Bermuda.
It's going to be so beautiful, Alex. I'm so excited!
It should be you going to Bermuda with him, Annie, not that psycho.
Oh, Paige. They've been together for years.
I'm just a lonely mother who developed a crush on a comatose patient.
Who's the real psycho here?
Well. I guess this is it.

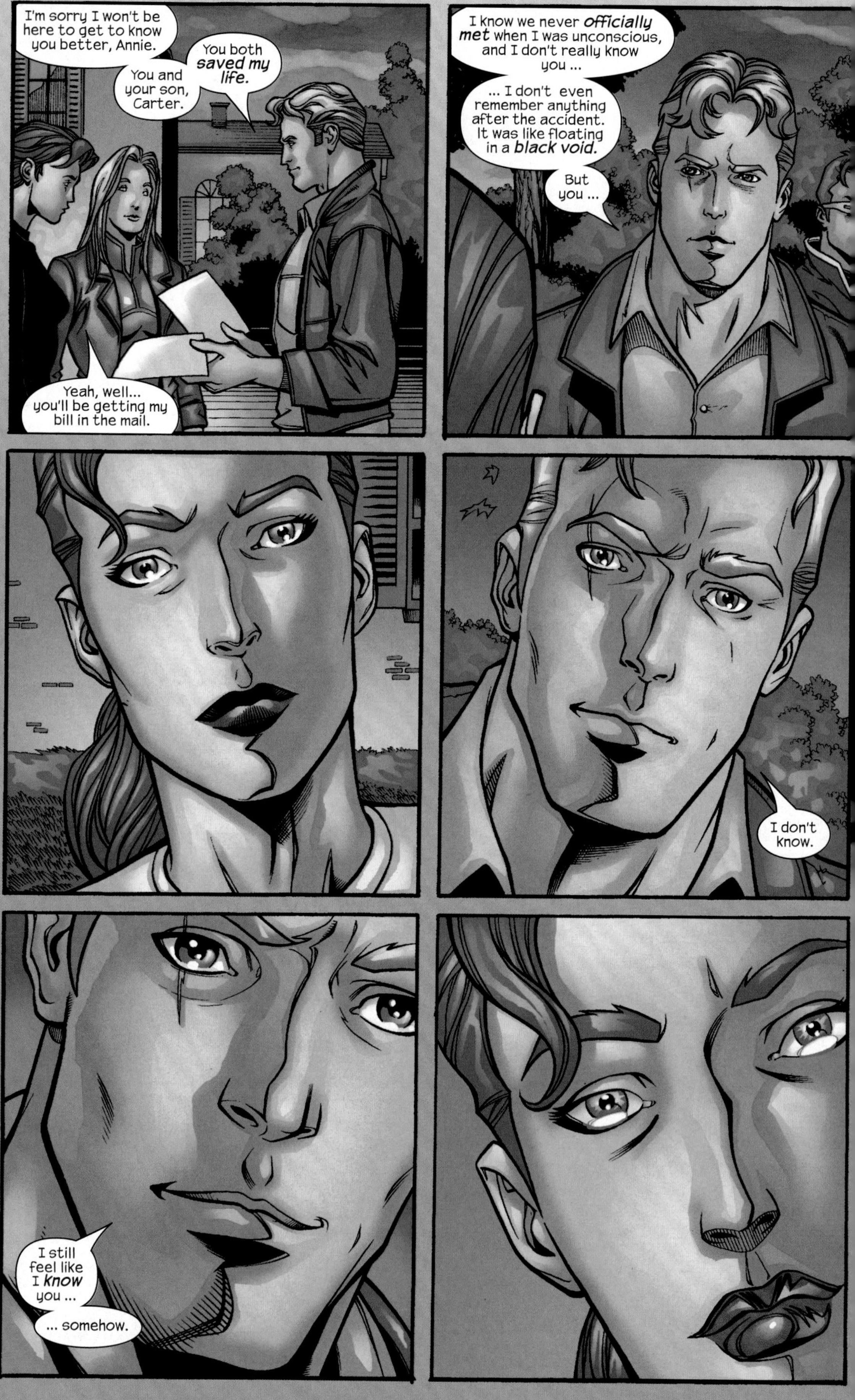

I'm sorry I won't be here to get to know you better, Annie.
You and your son, Carter.
You both *saved my life.*
Yeah, well... you'll be getting my bill in the mail.
I know we never *officially met* when I was unconscious, and I don't really know you ...
... I don't even remember anything after the accident. It was like floating in a *black void.*
But you ...
I don't know.
I still feel like I *know* you ...
... somehow.

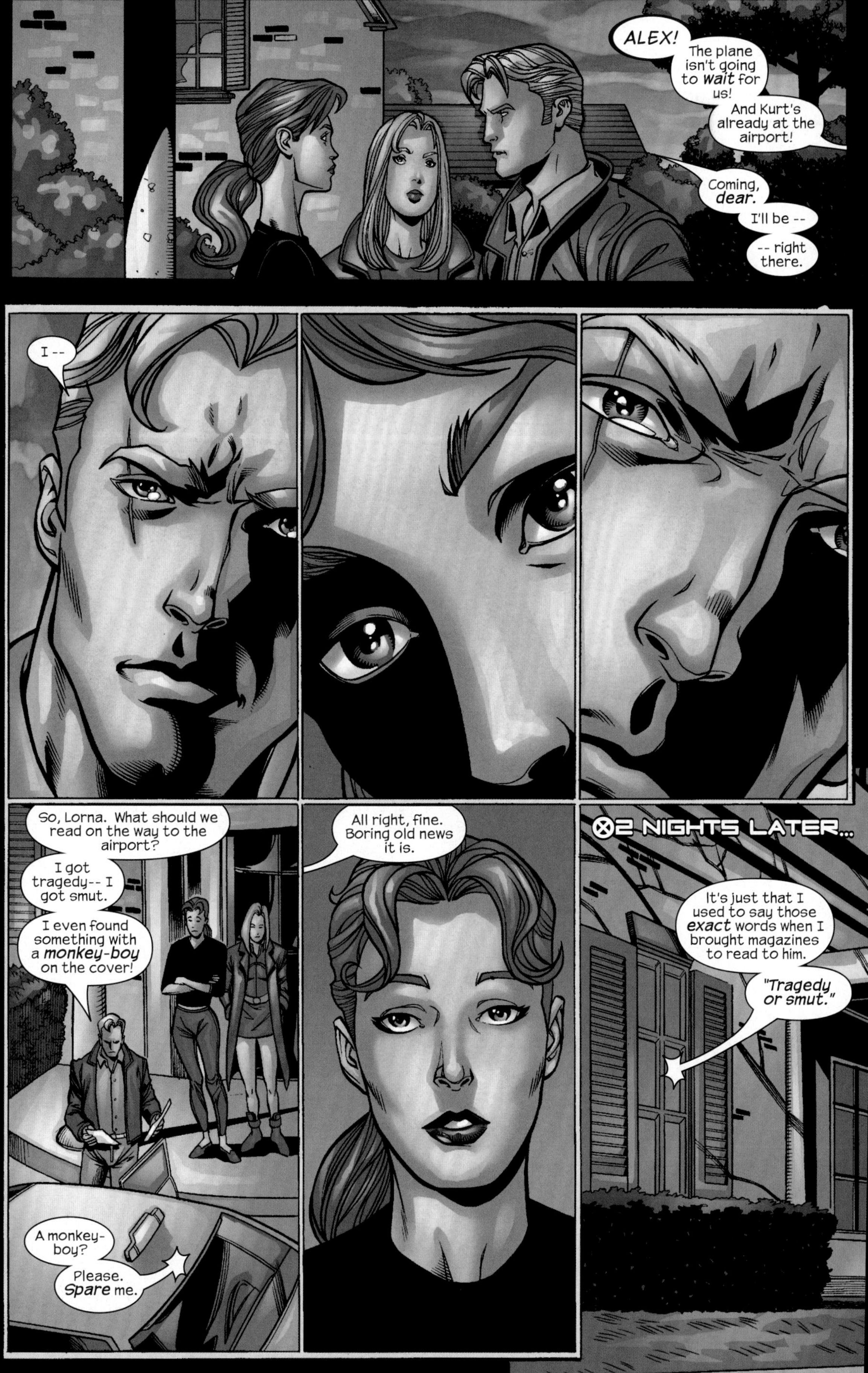
ALEX!
The plane isn't going to *wait* for us!
And Kurt's already at the airport!
Coming, **dear.**
I'll be --
-- right there.
I --
So, Lorna. What should we read on the way to the airport?
I got tragedy-- I got smut.
I even found something with a ***monkey-boy*** on the cover!
A monkey-boy?
Please. ***Spare*** me.
All right, fine. Boring old news it is.
2 NIGHTS LATER...
It's just that I used to say those ***exact*** words when I brought magazines to read to him.
"Tragedy or smut."

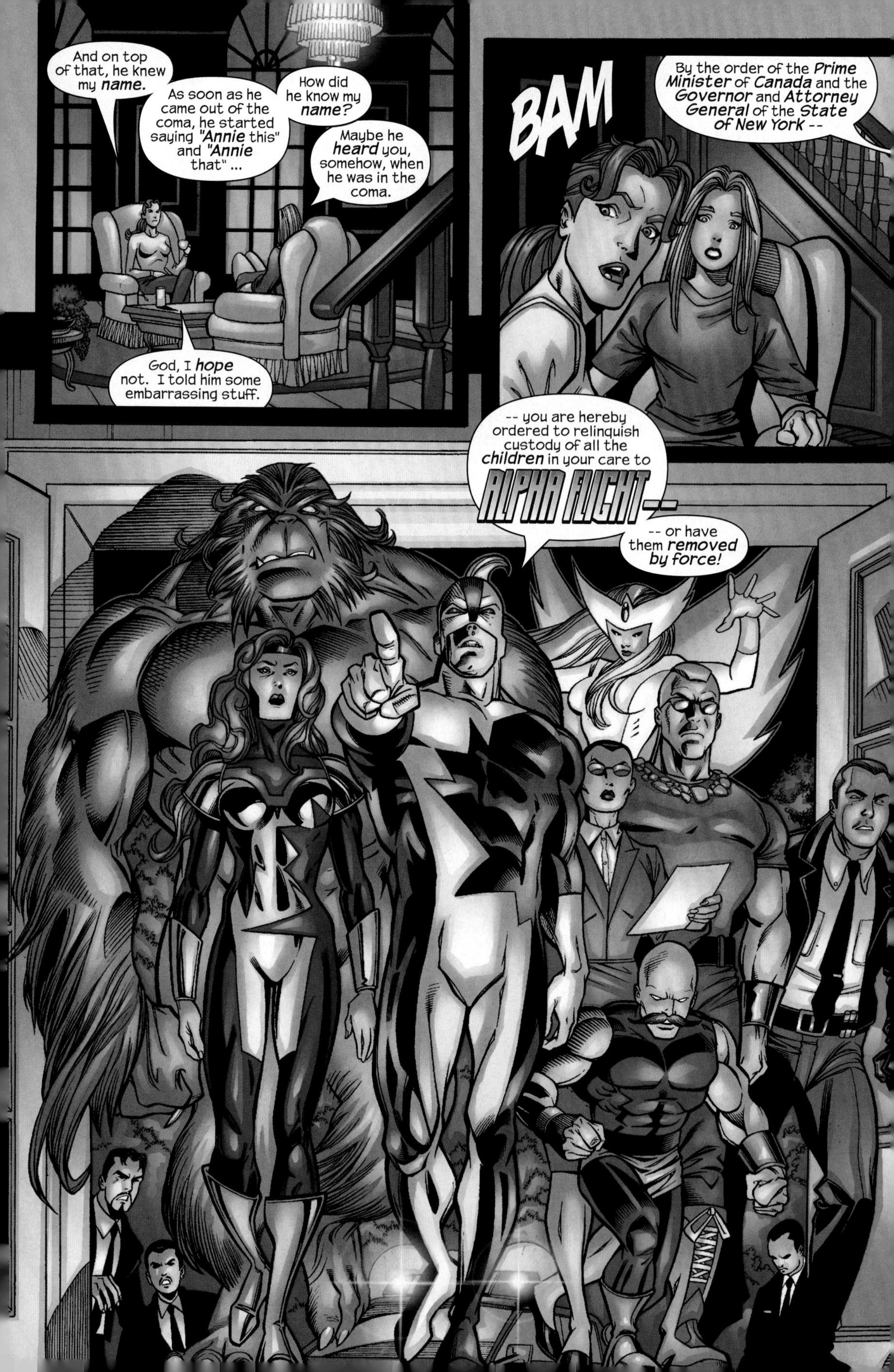
And on top of that, he knew my *name.*
As soon as he came out of the coma, he started saying "*Annie* this" and "*Annie* that" ...
How did he know my *name?*
Maybe he *heard* you, somehow, when he was in the coma.
God, I *hope* not. I told him some embarrassing stuff.
BAM
By the order of the *Prime Minister* of *Canada* and the *Governor* and *Attorney General* of the *State of New York* --
-- you are hereby ordered to relinquish custody of all the *children* in your care to
ALPHA FLIGHT--
-- or have them *removed* by *force!*

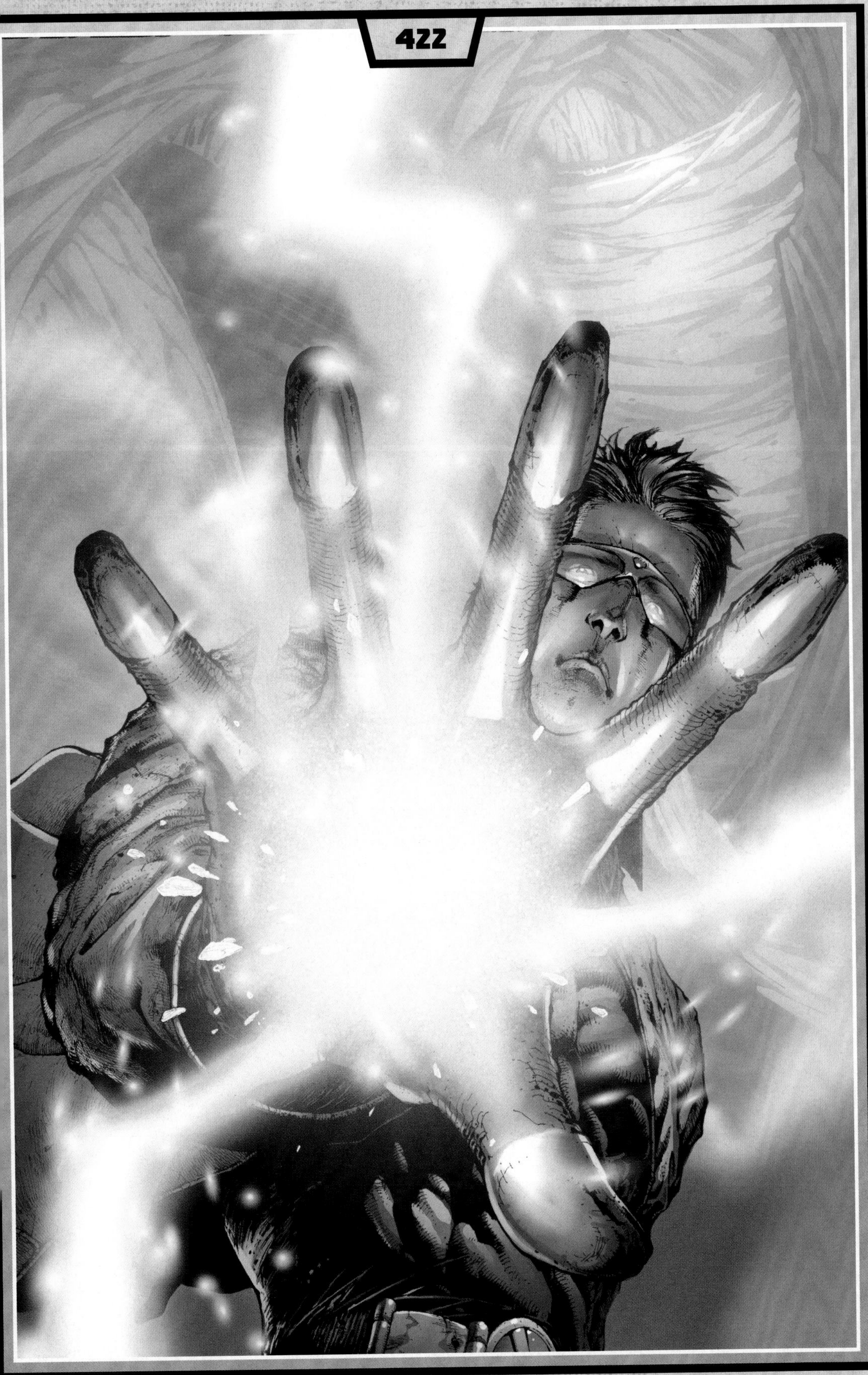
422

RULES OF ENGAGEMENT, PART 2 OF 2

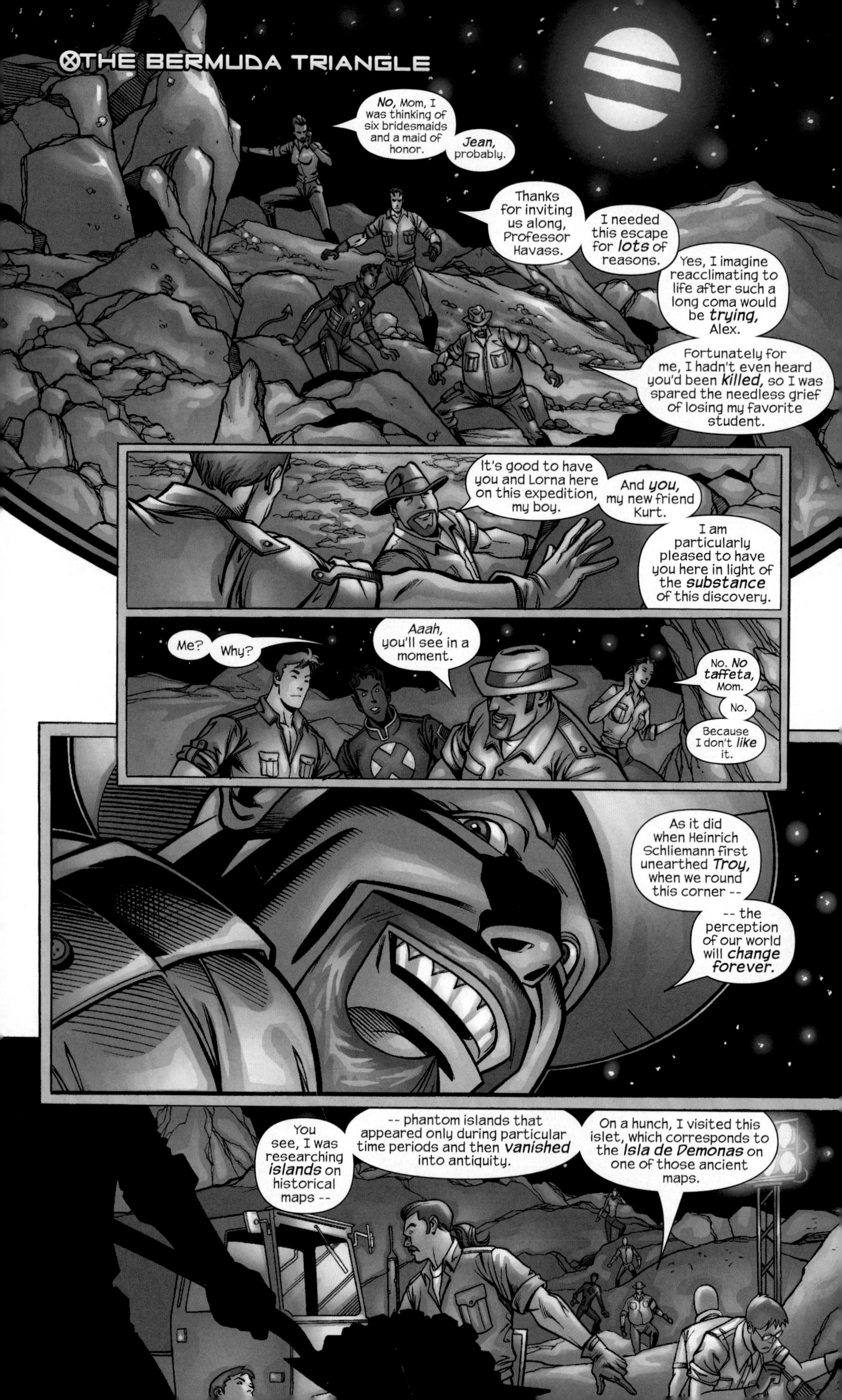
THE BERMUDA TRIANGLE
No, Mom, I was thinking of six bridesmaids and a maid of honor.
Jean, probably.
Thanks for inviting us along, Professor Havass.
I needed this escape for lots of reasons.
Yes, I imagine reacclimating to life after such a long coma would be trying, Alex.
Fortunately for me, I hadn't even heard you'd been killed, so I was spared the needless grief of losing my favorite student.
It's good to have you and Lorna here on this expedition, my boy.
And you, my new friend Kurt.
I am particularly pleased to have you here in light of the substance of this discovery.
Me?
Why?
Aaah, you'll see in a moment.
No. No taffeta, Mom.
No.
Because I don't like it.
As it did when Heinrich Schliemann first unearthed Troy, when we round this corner --
-- the perception of our world will change forever.
You see, I was researching islands on historical maps --
-- phantom islands that appeared only during particular time periods and then vanished into antiquity.
On a hunch, I visited this islet, which corresponds to the Isla de Demonas on one of those ancient maps.

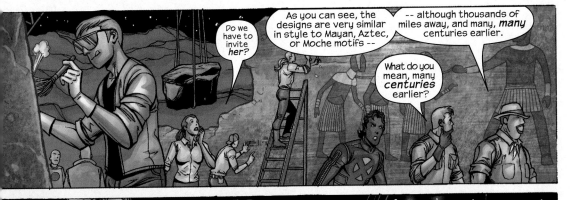

Do we have to invite *her*?

As you can see, the designs are very similar in style to Mayan, Aztec, or Moche motifs --

-- although thousands of miles away, and many, *many* centuries earlier.

What do you mean, many *centuries* earlier?

Are these anthropomorphic features given to the warriors a common artistic practice, Professor?

Aaah, you cut to the *heart*, friend Kurt.

It is common in Egyptian motifs, yes --

Can we get away with inviting her and *not* her parents?

This one looks like *you*, Kurt.

Usually.

Look at the tail.

-- but such depictions usually represent costuming, or ceremonial decorations in Moche and Aztec art.

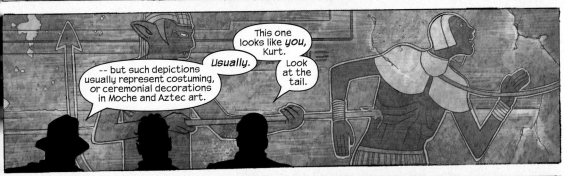

That is your *tail*, right?

What do *you* think?

HA!

No, Mom, Kurt just said something funny.

Yeah, he's the blue furry one.

Professor, you're hinting at something that seems pretty big here, and I'm *dying* to know what it is.

Then come this way, Alex, and let's end the mystery --

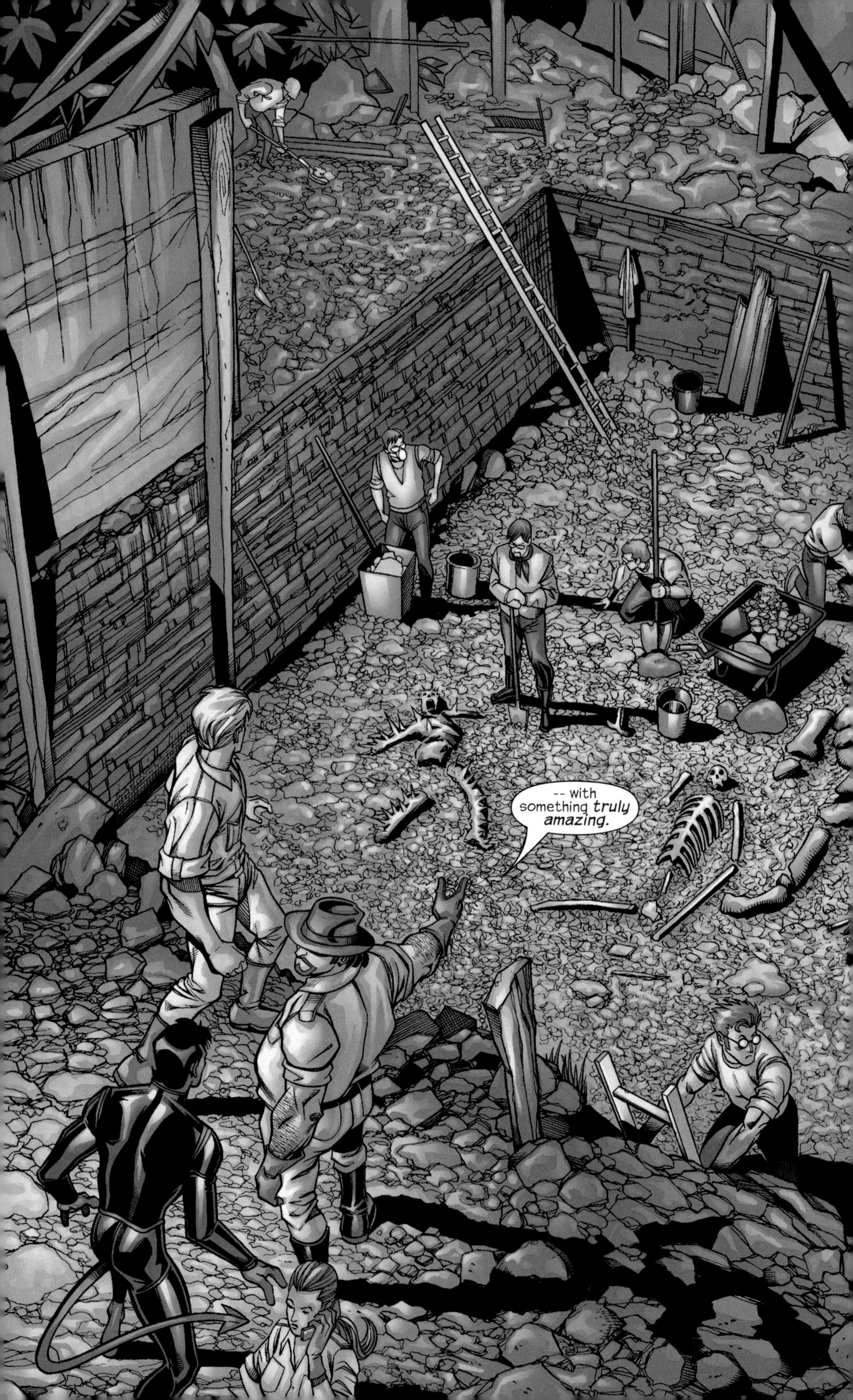
-- with something *truly amazing.*

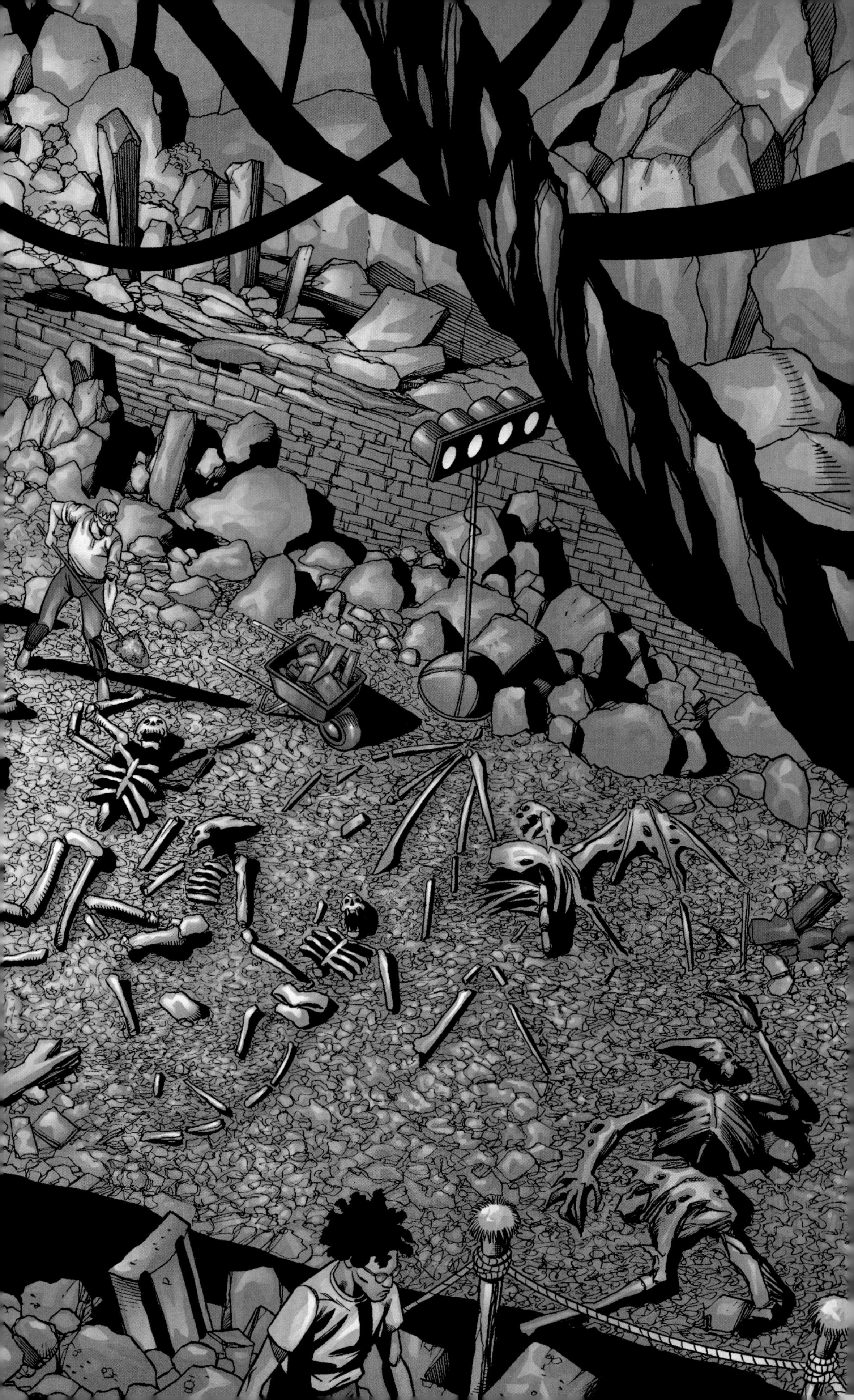

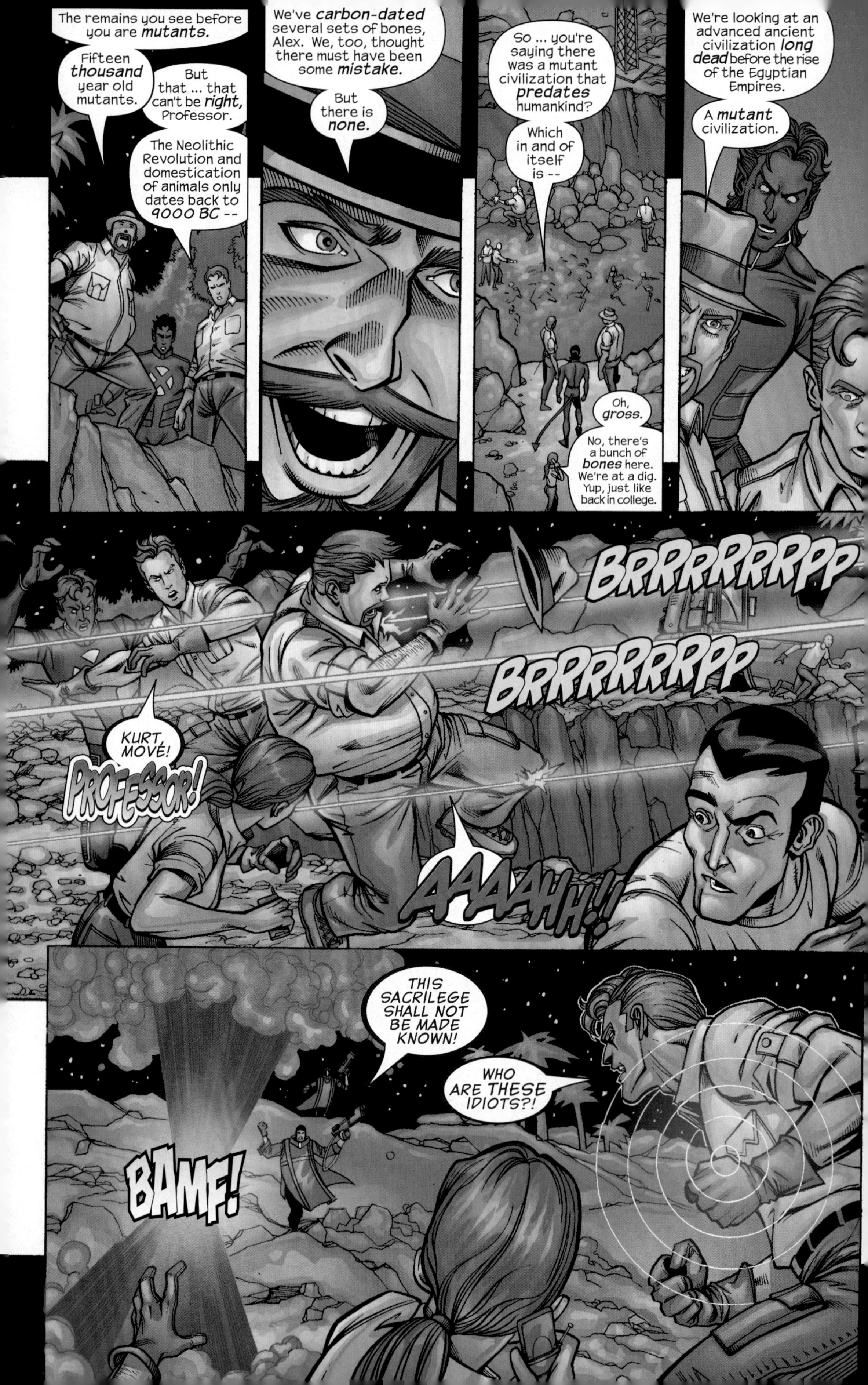
The remains you see before you are mutants.
Fifteen thousand year old mutants.
But that ... that can't be right, Professor.
The Neolithic Revolution and domestication of animals only dates back to 9000 BC --
We've carbon-dated several sets of bones, Alex. We, too, thought there must have been some mistake.
But there is none.
So ... you're saying there was a mutant civilization that predates humankind?
Which in and of itself is --
Oh, gross.
No, there's a bunch of bones here. We're at a dig. Yup, just like back in college.
We're looking at an advanced ancient civilization long dead before the rise of the Egyptian Empires.
A mutant civilization.
BRRRRRRRPP
BRRRRRRRPP
KURT, MOVE!
PROFESSOR!
AAAAHH!!
THIS SACRILEGE SHALL NOT BE MADE KNOWN!
WHO ARE THESE IDIOTS?!
BAMF!

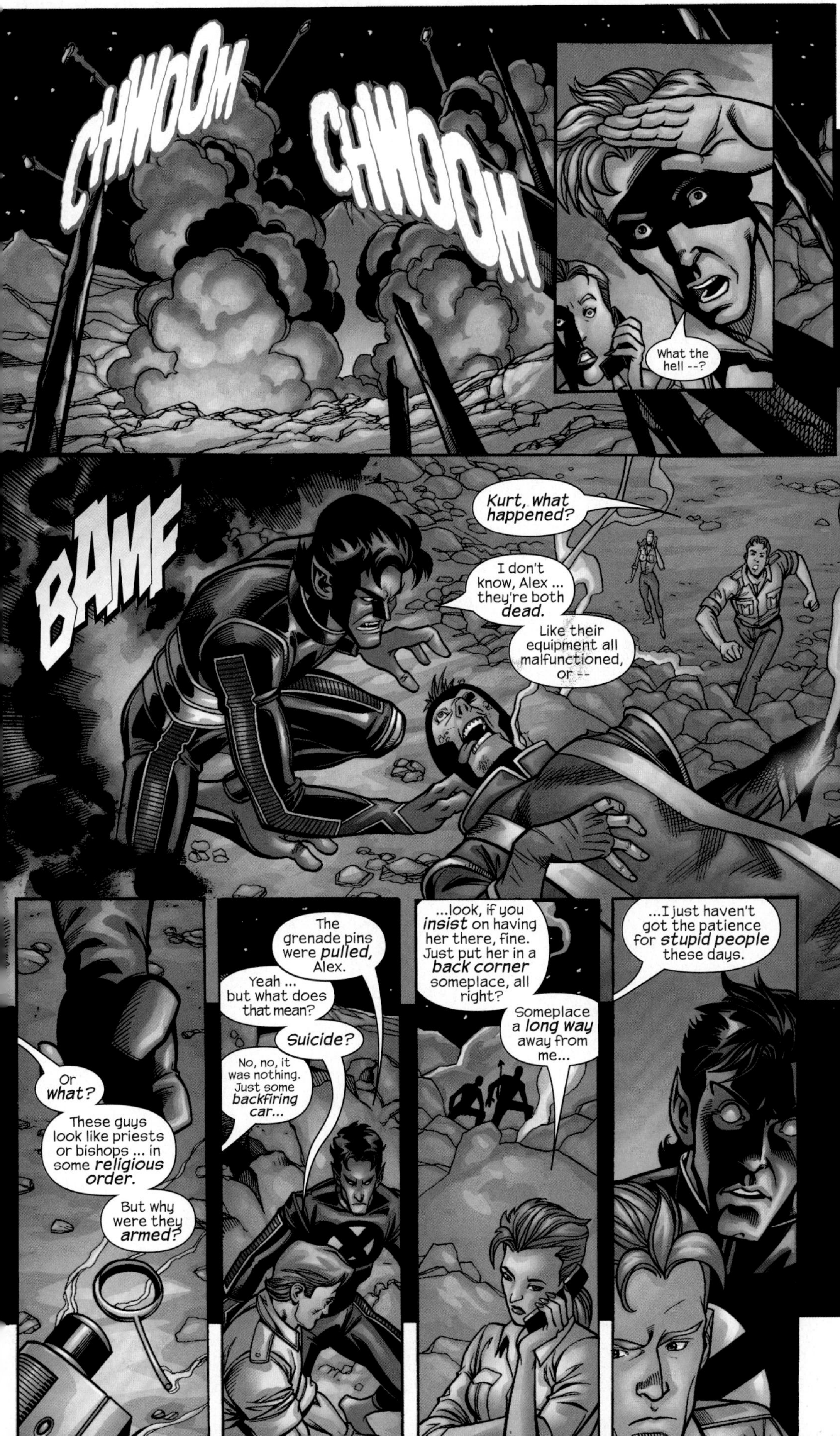
CHWOOM
CHWOOM
What the hell --?
BAMF
Kurt, what happened?
I don't know, Alex ... they're both dead.
Like their equipment all malfunctioned, or --
Or what?
These guys look like priests or bishops ... in some religious order.
But why were they armed?
The grenade pins were pulled, Alex.
Yeah ... but what does that mean?
Suicide?
No, no, it was nothing. Just some backfiring car...
...look, if you insist on having her there, fine. Just put her in a back corner someplace, all right?
Someplace a long way away from me...
...I just haven't got the patience for stupid people these days.

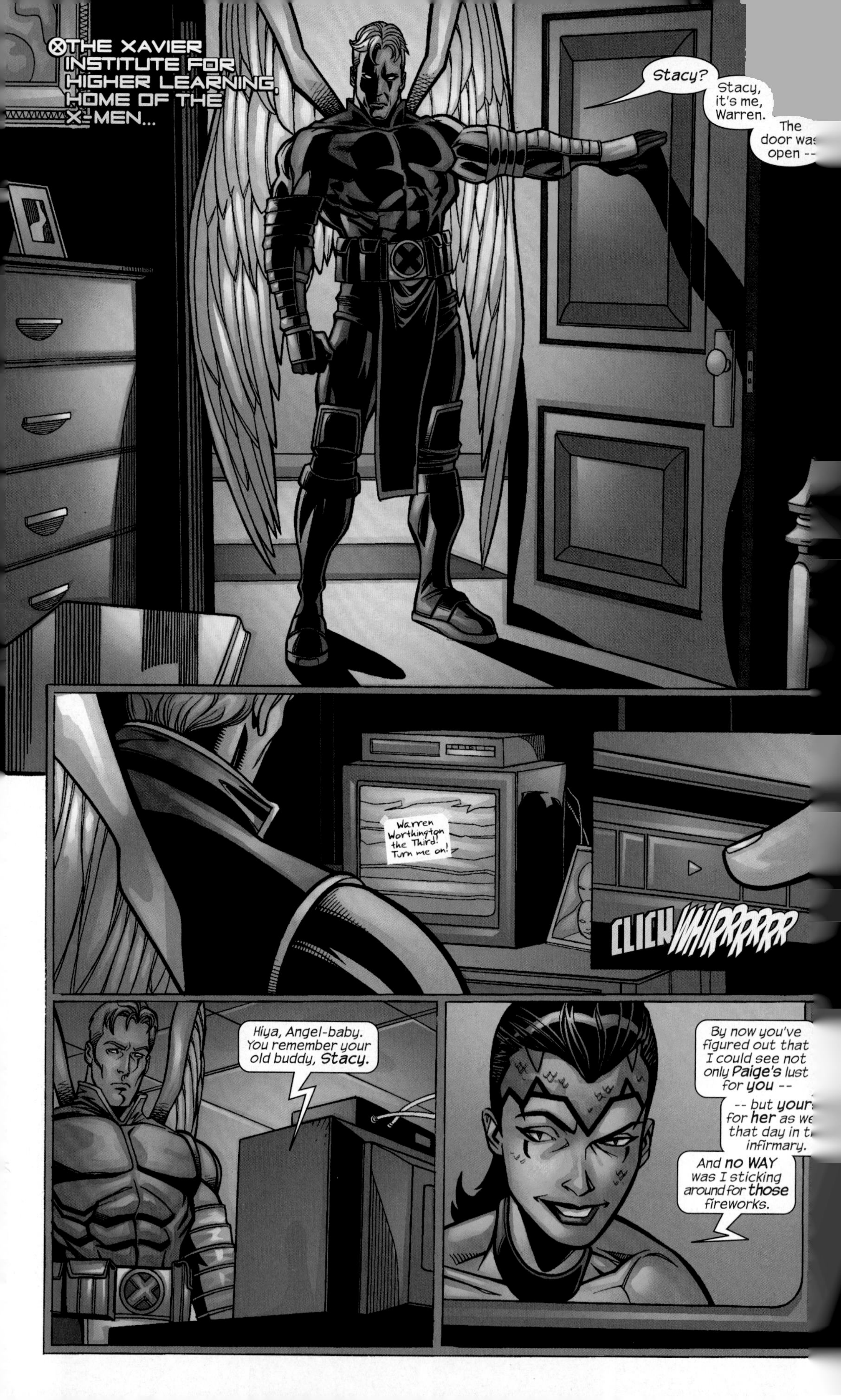
THE XAVIER INSTITUTE FOR HIGHER LEARNING, HOME OF THE X-MEN...
Stacy?
Stacy, it's me, Warren.
The door was open --
Warren Worthington the Third! Turn me on!
CLICK WHIRRRRRR
Hiya, Angel-baby. You remember your old buddy, Stacy.
By now you've figured out that I could see not only Paige's lust for you --
-- but yours for her as well that day in the infirmary.
And no WAY was I sticking around for those fireworks.

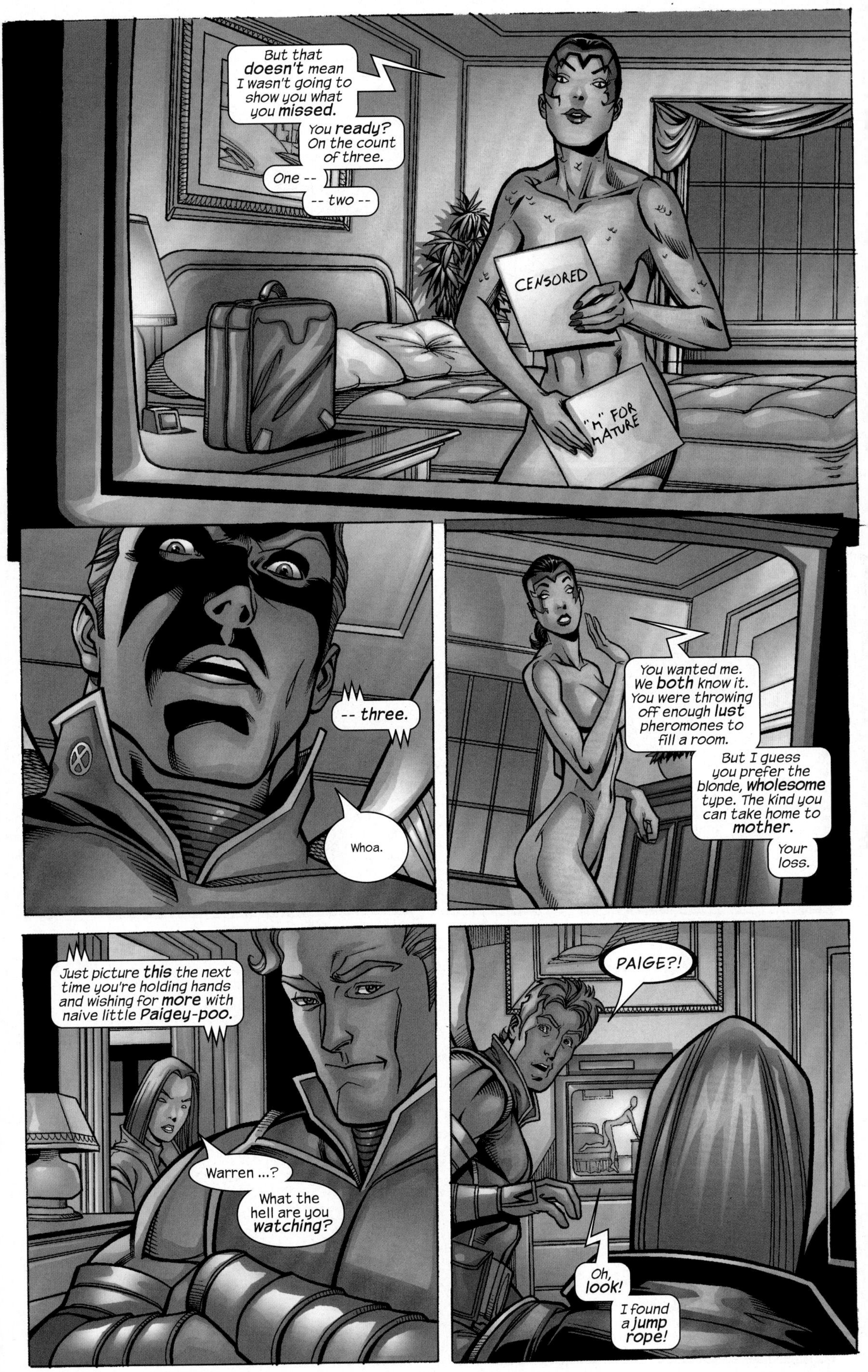
But that doesn't mean I wasn't going to show you what you missed.
You ready? On the count of three.
One --
-- two --
CENSORED
"M" FOR MATURE
-- three.
Whoa.
You wanted me. We both know it. You were throwing off enough lust pheromones to fill a room.
But I guess you prefer the blonde, wholesome type. The kind you can take home to mother.
Your loss.
Just picture this the next time you're holding hands and wishing for more with naive little Paigey-poo.
Warren ...?
What the hell are you watching?
PAIGE?!
Oh, look!
I found a jump rope!

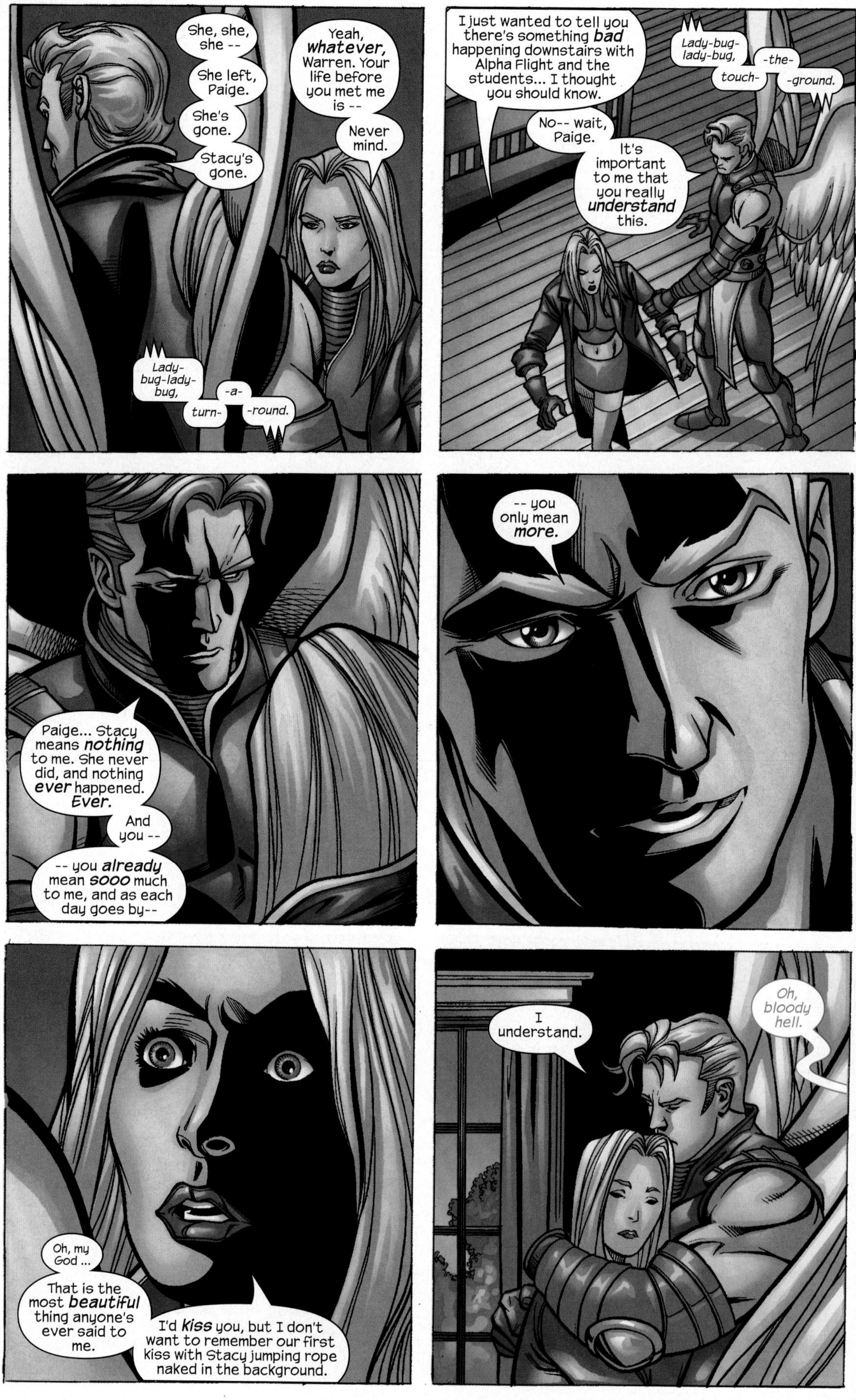
She, she, she --
She left, Paige.
She's gone.
Stacy's gone.
Yeah, whatever, Warren. Your life before you met me is --
Never mind.
Lady-bug-lady-bug,
turn-
-a-
-round.
I just wanted to tell you there's something bad happening downstairs with Alpha Flight and the students... I thought you should know.
Lady-bug-lady-bug,
touch-
-the-
-ground.
No-- wait, Paige.
It's important to me that you really understand this.
Paige... Stacy means nothing to me. She never did, and nothing ever happened. Ever.
And you --
-- you already mean sooo much to me, and as each day goes by--
-- you only mean more.
Oh, my God ...
That is the most beautiful thing anyone's ever said to me.
I'd kiss you, but I don't want to remember our first kiss with Stacy jumping rope naked in the background.
I understand.
Oh, bloody hell.

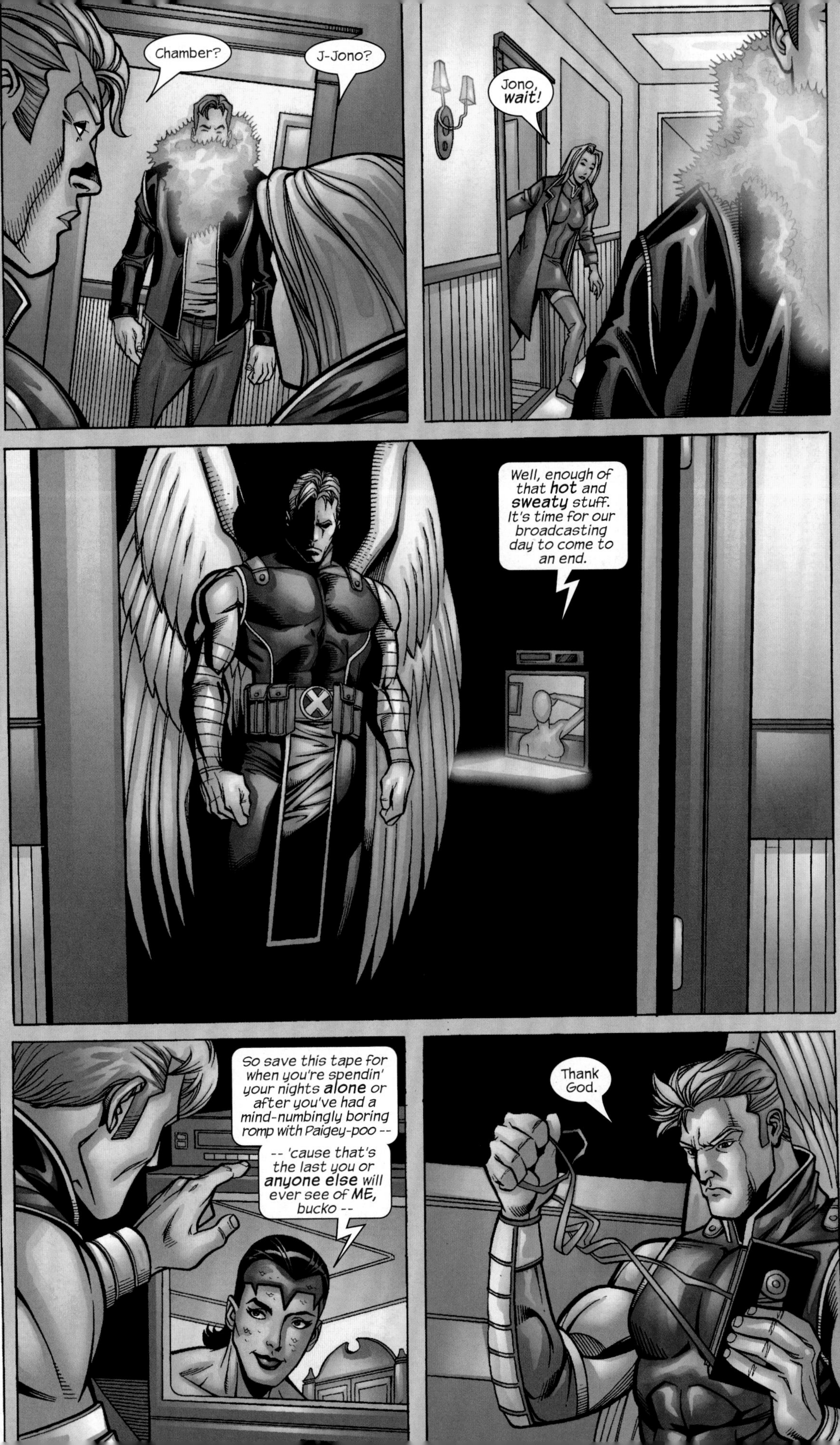
Chamber?
J-Jono?
Jono, wait!
Well, enough of that hot and sweaty stuff. It's time for our broadcasting day to come to an end.
So save this tape for when you're spendin' your nights alone or after you've had a mind-numbingly boring romp with Paigey-poo --
-- 'cause that's the last you or anyone else will ever see of ME, bucko --
Thank God.

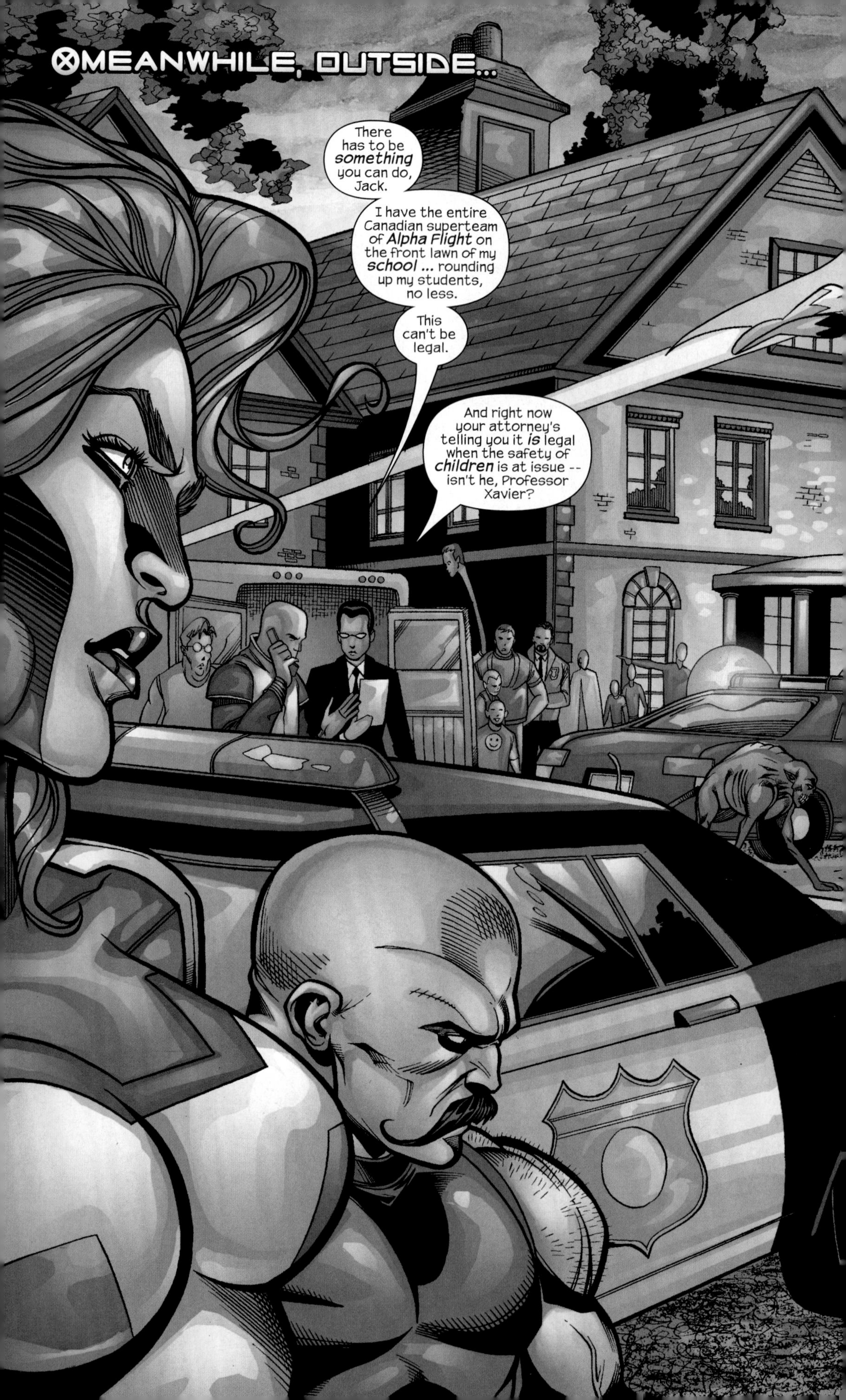
MEANWHILE, OUTSIDE...
There has to be *something* you can do, Jack.
I have the entire Canadian superteam of *Alpha Flight* on the front lawn of my *school ...* rounding up my students, no less.
This can't be legal.
And right now your attorney's telling you it *is* legal when the safety of *children* is at issue -- isn't he, Professor Xavier?

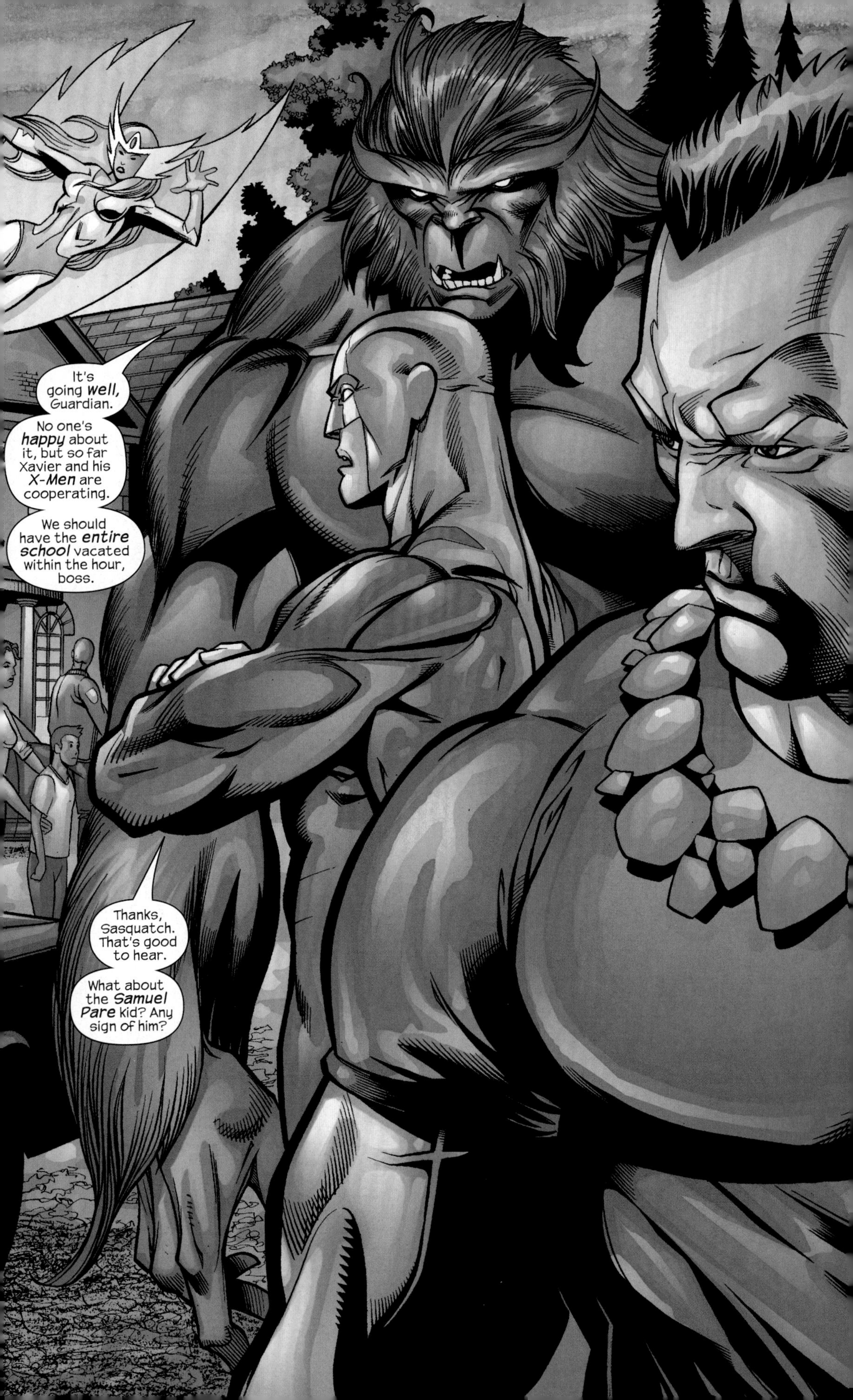

It's going well, Guardian.
No one's happy about it, but so far Xavier and his X-Men are cooperating.
We should have the entire school vacated within the hour, boss.
Thanks, Sasquatch. That's good to hear.
What about the Samuel Pare kid? Any sign of him?

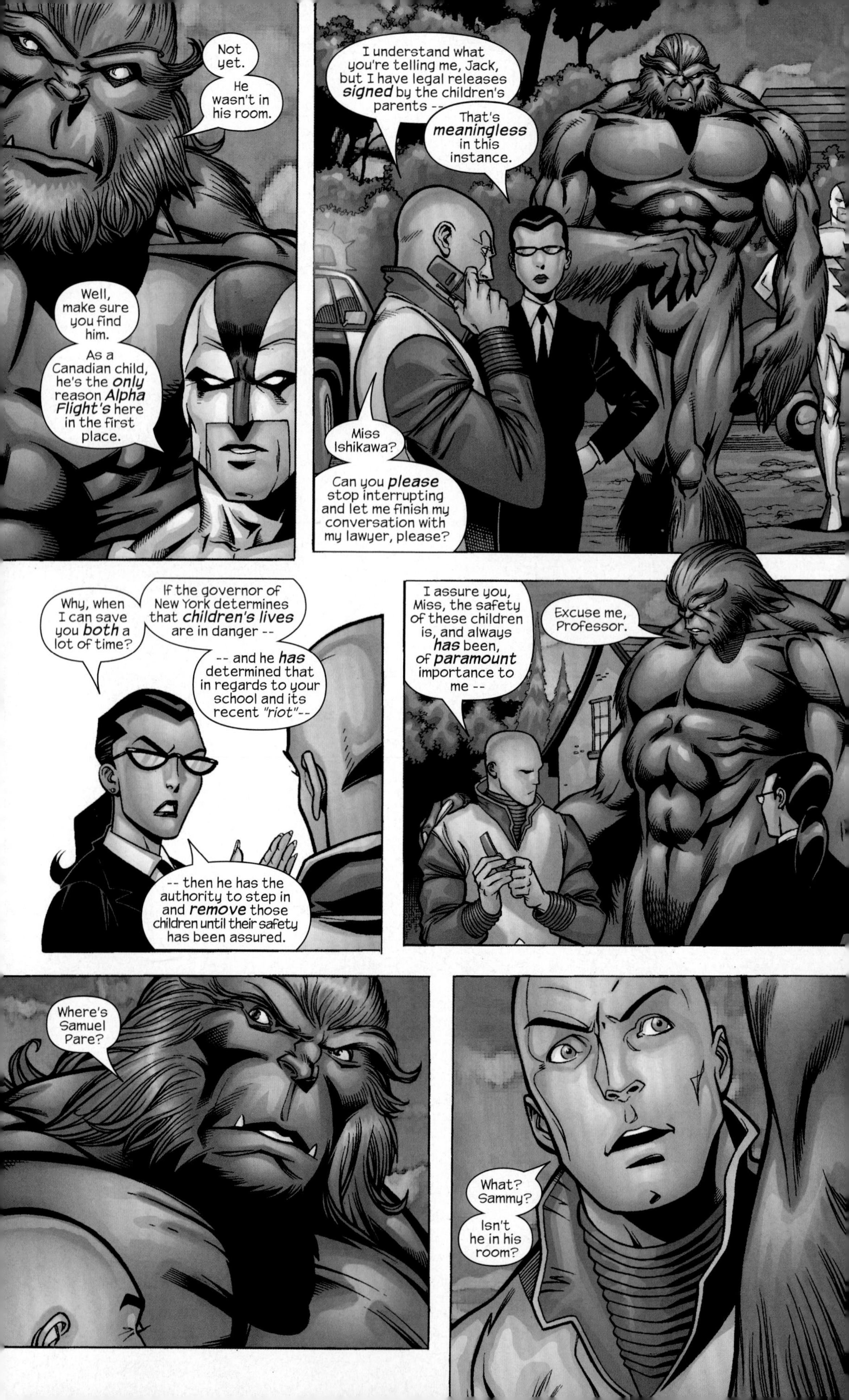
Not yet.
He wasn't in his room.
Well, make sure you find him.
As a Canadian child, he's the only reason Alpha Flight's here in the first place.
I understand what you're telling me, Jack, but I have legal releases signed by the children's parents --
That's meaningless in this instance.
Miss Ishikawa?
Can you please stop interrupting and let me finish my conversation with my lawyer, please?
Why, when I can save you both a lot of time?
If the governor of New York determines that children's lives are in danger --
-- and he has determined that in regards to your school and its recent "riot"--
-- then he has the authority to step in and remove those children until their safety has been assured.
I assure you, Miss, the safety of these children is, and always has been, of paramount importance to me --
Excuse me, Professor.
Where's Samuel Pare?
What? Sammy?
Isn't he in his room?

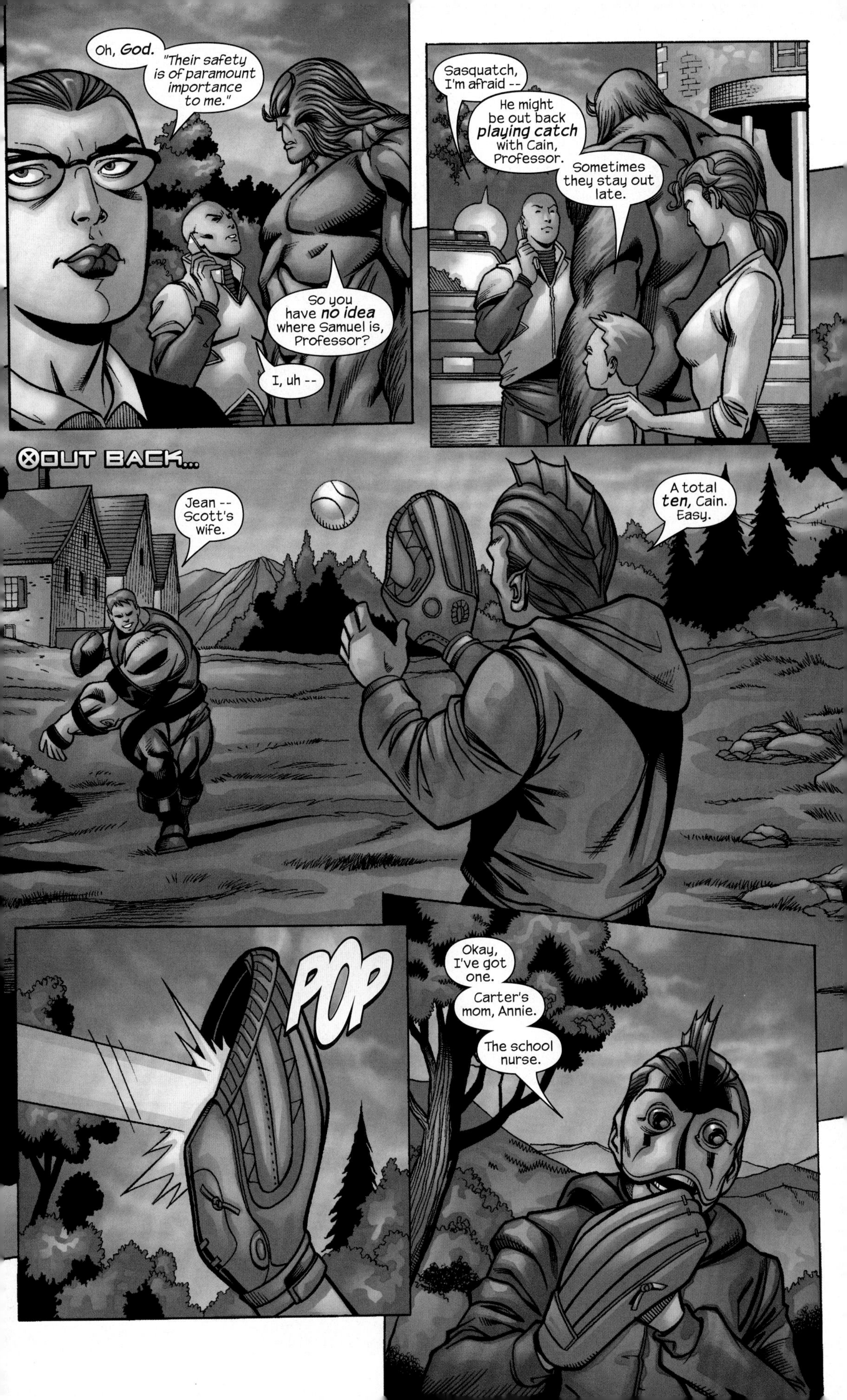

Oh, God.
"Their safety is of paramount importance to me."
So you have no idea where Samuel is, Professor?
I, uh --
Sasquatch, I'm afraid --
He might be out back playing catch with Cain, Professor.
Sometimes they stay out late.
OUT BACK...
Jean -- Scott's wife.
A total ten, Cain. Easy.
POP
Okay, I've got one.
Carter's mom, Annie.
The school nurse.

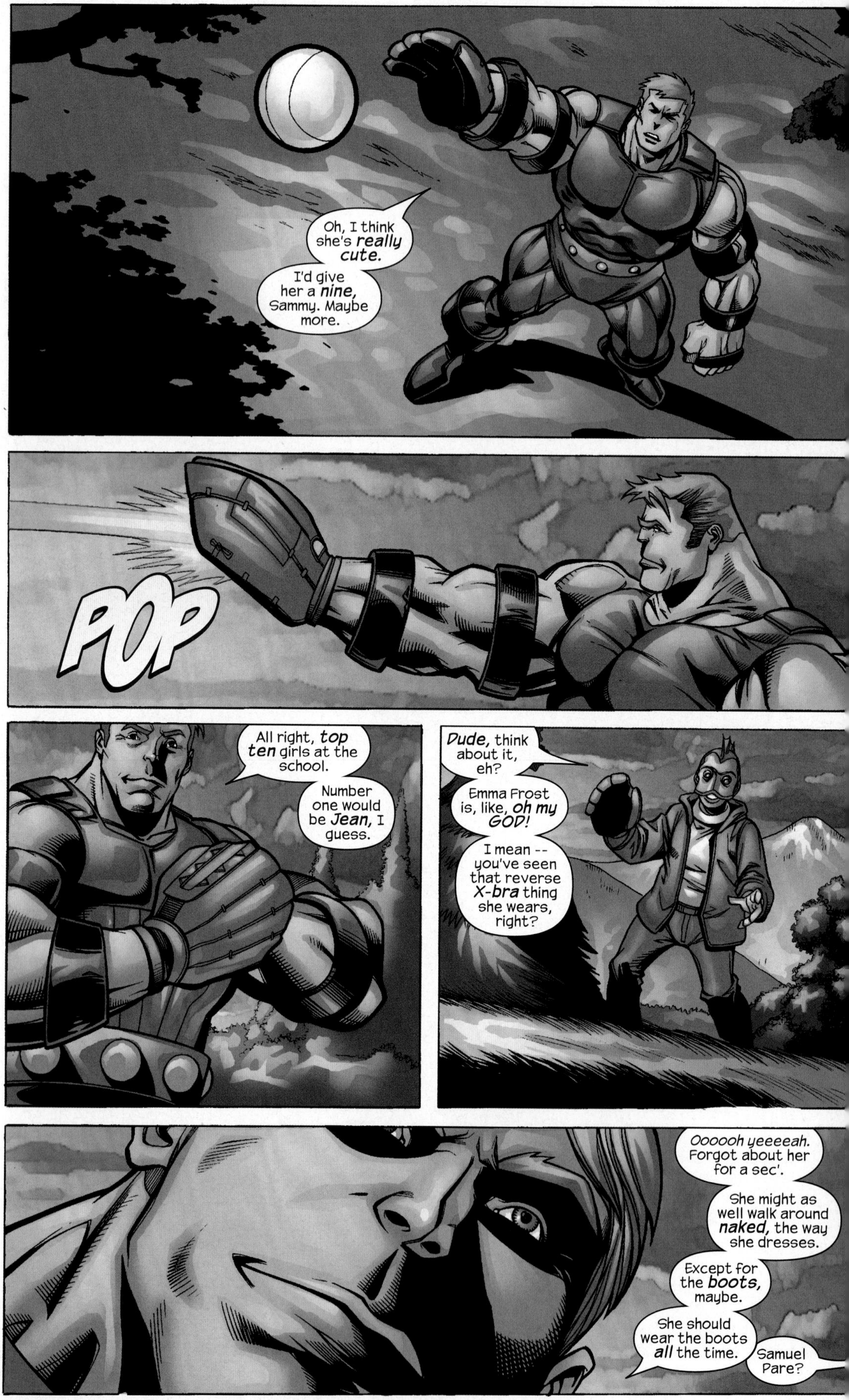
Oh, I think she's *really* *cute.*
I'd give her a *nine,* Sammy. Maybe more.
POP
All right, *top* *ten* girls at the school.
Number one would be *Jean,* I guess.
Dude, think about it, eh?
Emma Frost is, like, *oh my GOD!*
I mean -- you've seen that reverse *X-bra* thing she wears, right?
Oooooh yeeeeah. Forgot about her for a sec'.
She might as well walk around *naked,* the way she dresses.
Except for the *boots,* maybe.
She should wear the boots *all* the time.
Samuel Pare?

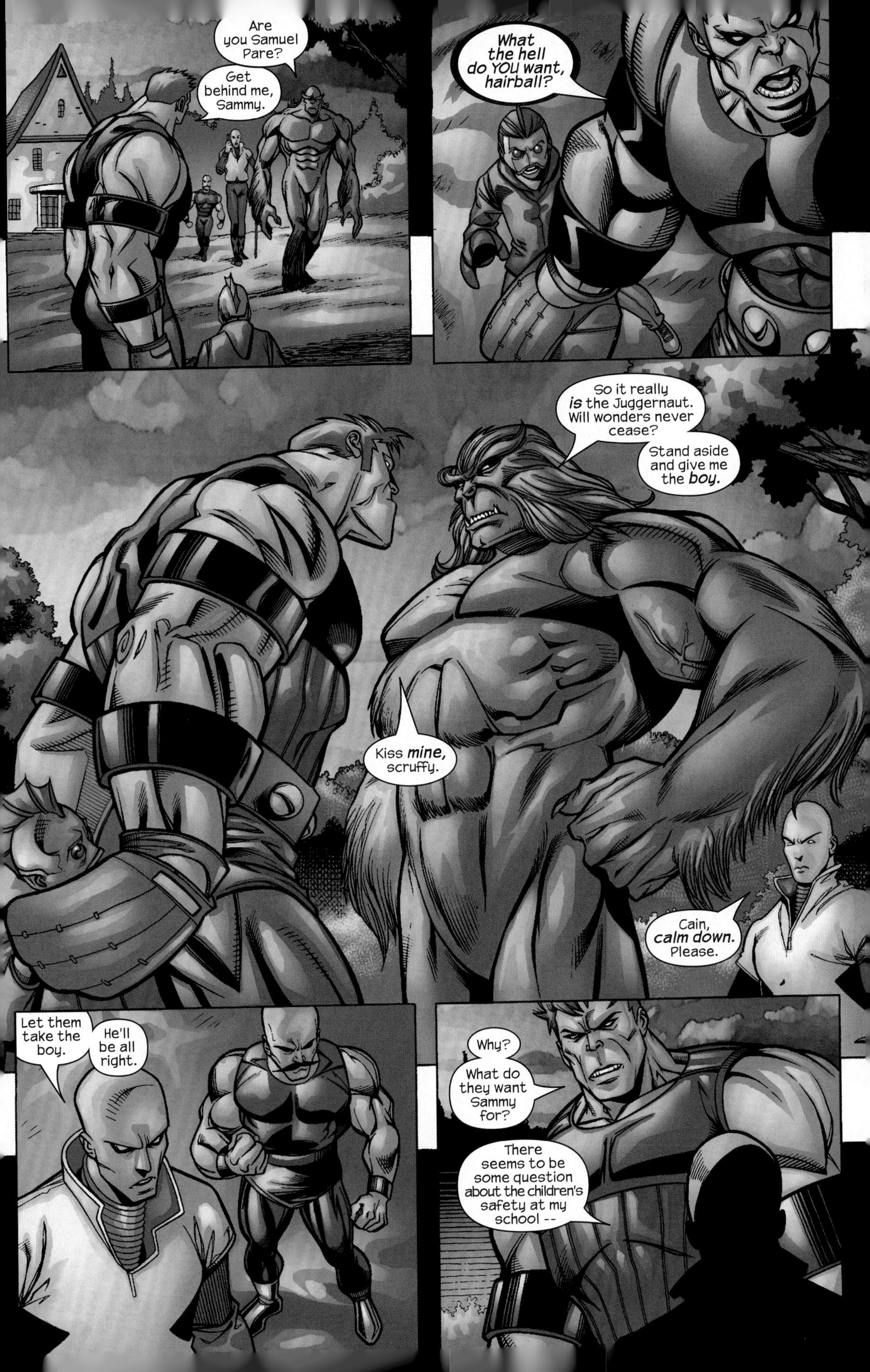

Are you Samuel Pare?
Get behind me, Sammy.
What the hell do YOU want, hairball?
So it really is the Juggernaut. Will wonders never cease?
Stand aside and give me the boy.
Kiss mine, scruffy.
Cain, calm down. Please.
Let them take the boy.
He'll be all right.
Why?
What do they want Sammy for?
There seems to be some question about the children's safety at my school --

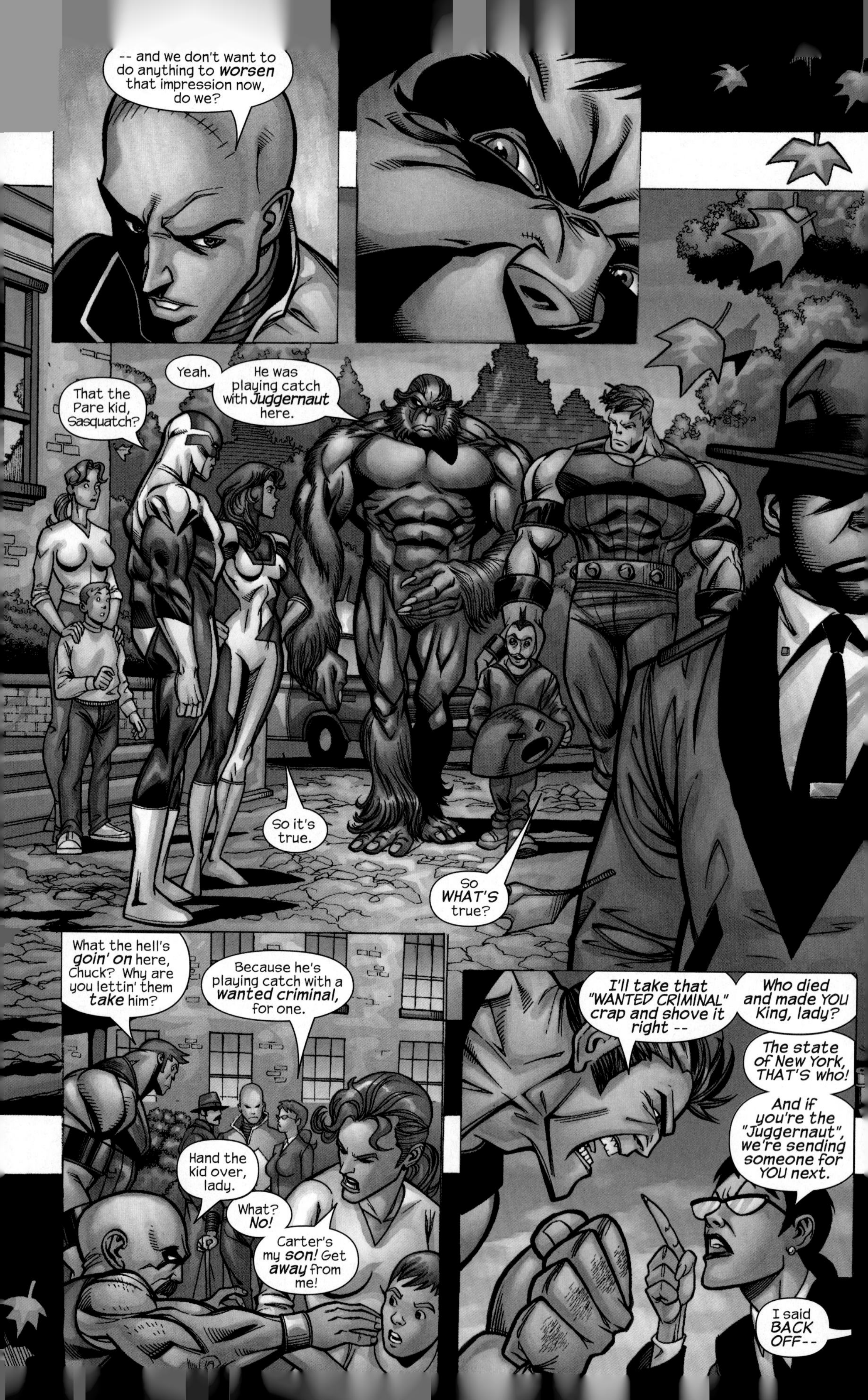
-- and we don't want to do anything to worsen that impression now, do we?
That the Pare kid, Sasquatch?
Yeah.
He was playing catch with Juggernaut here.
So it's true.
So WHAT'S true?
What the hell's goin' on here, Chuck? Why are you lettin' them take him?
Because he's playing catch with a wanted criminal, for one.
Hand the kid over, lady.
What? No!
Carter's my son! Get away from me!
I'll take that "WANTED CRIMINAL" crap and shove it right --
Who died and made YOU King, lady?
The state of New York, THAT'S who!
And if you're the "Juggernaut", we're sending someone for YOU next.
I said BACK OFF--

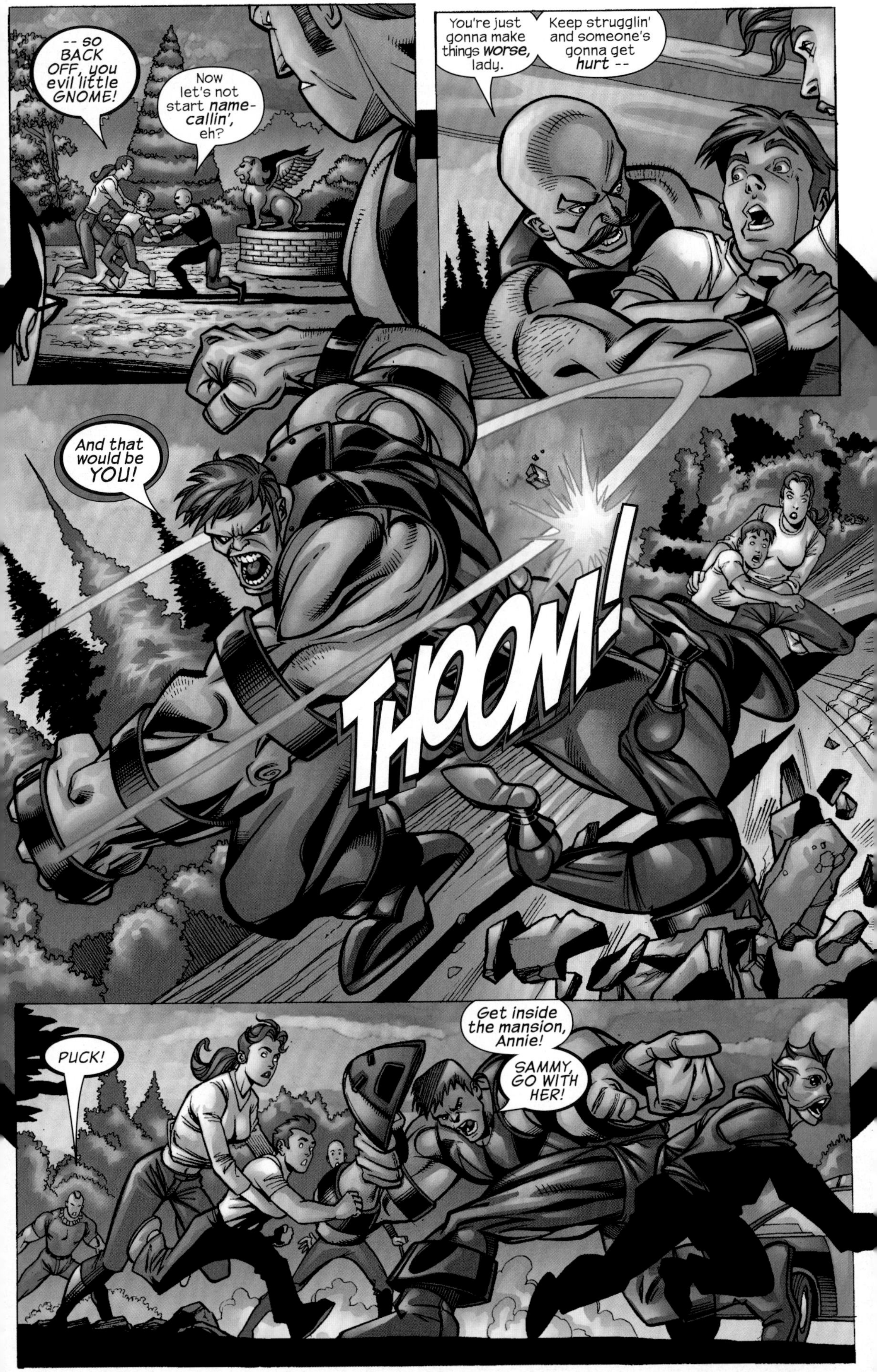
-- SO BACK OFF, you evil little GNOME!
Now let's not start name-callin', eh?
You're just gonna make things worse, lady.
Keep strugglin' and someone's gonna get hurt --
And that would be YOU!
THOOM!
PUCK!
Get inside the mansion, Annie!
SAMMY, GO WITH HER!

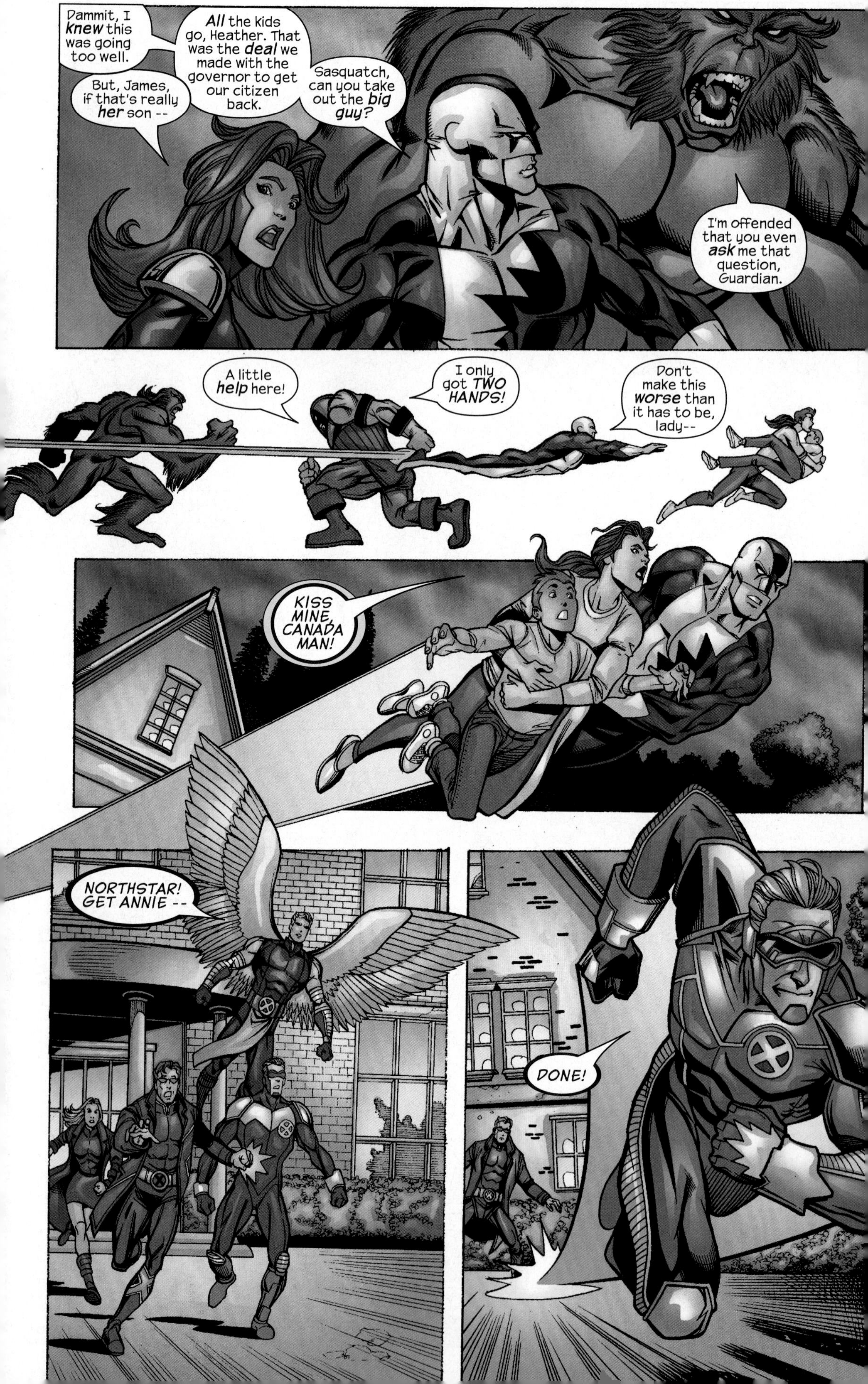
Dammit, I knew this was going too well.
But, James, if that's really her son --
All the kids go, Heather. That was the deal we made with the governor to get our citizen back.
Sasquatch, can you take out the big guy?
I'm offended that you even ask me that question, Guardian.
A little help here!
I only got TWO HANDS!
Don't make this worse than it has to be, lady--
KISS MINE, CANADA MAN!
NORTHSTAR! GET ANNIE --
DONE!

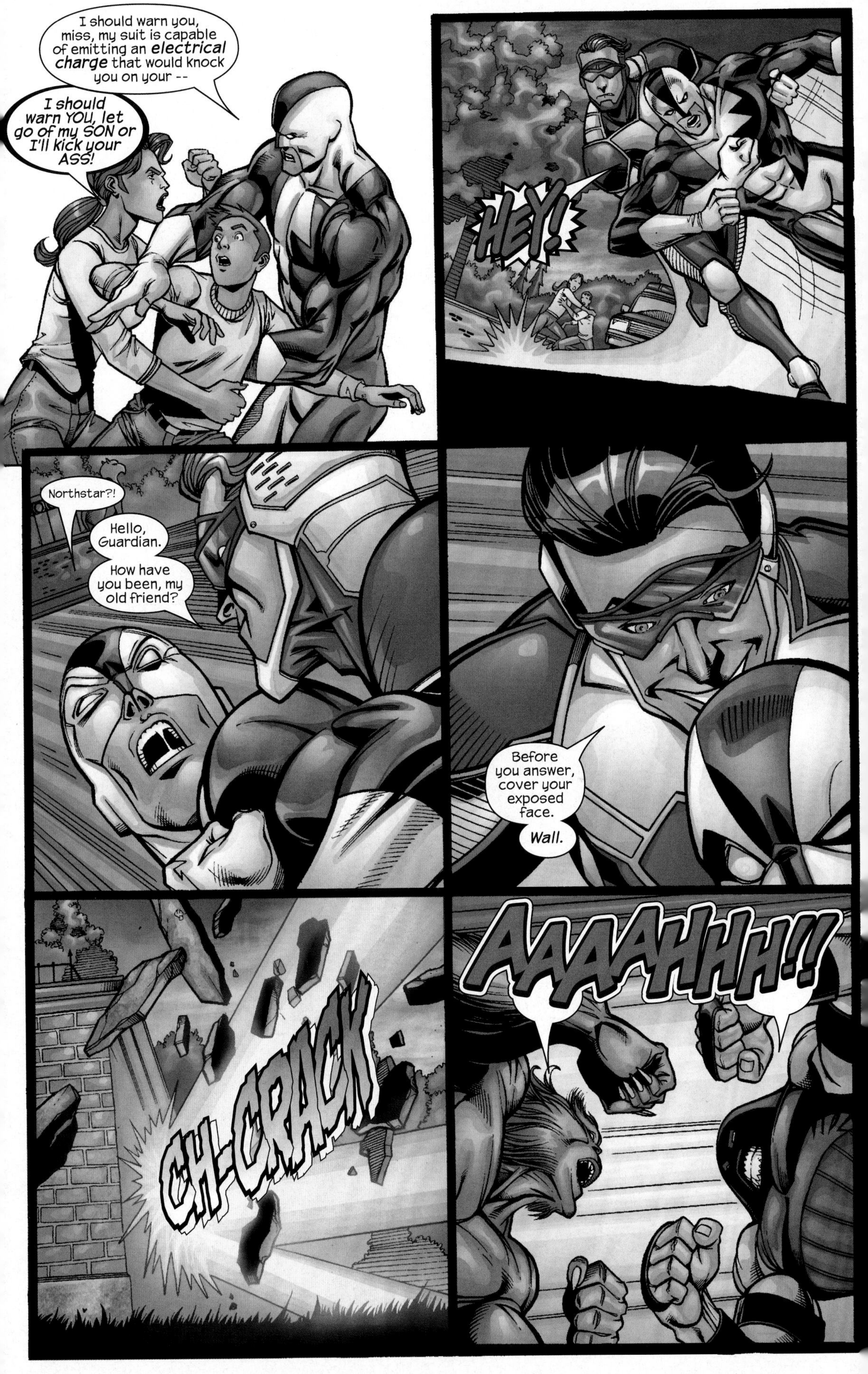
I should warn you, miss, my suit is capable of emitting an *electrical charge* that would knock you on your --
I should warn YOU, let go of my SON or I'll kick your ASS!
HEY!
Northstar?!
Hello, Guardian.
How have you been, my old friend?
Before you answer, cover your exposed face.
Wall.
CH-CRACK
AAAAHHH!!

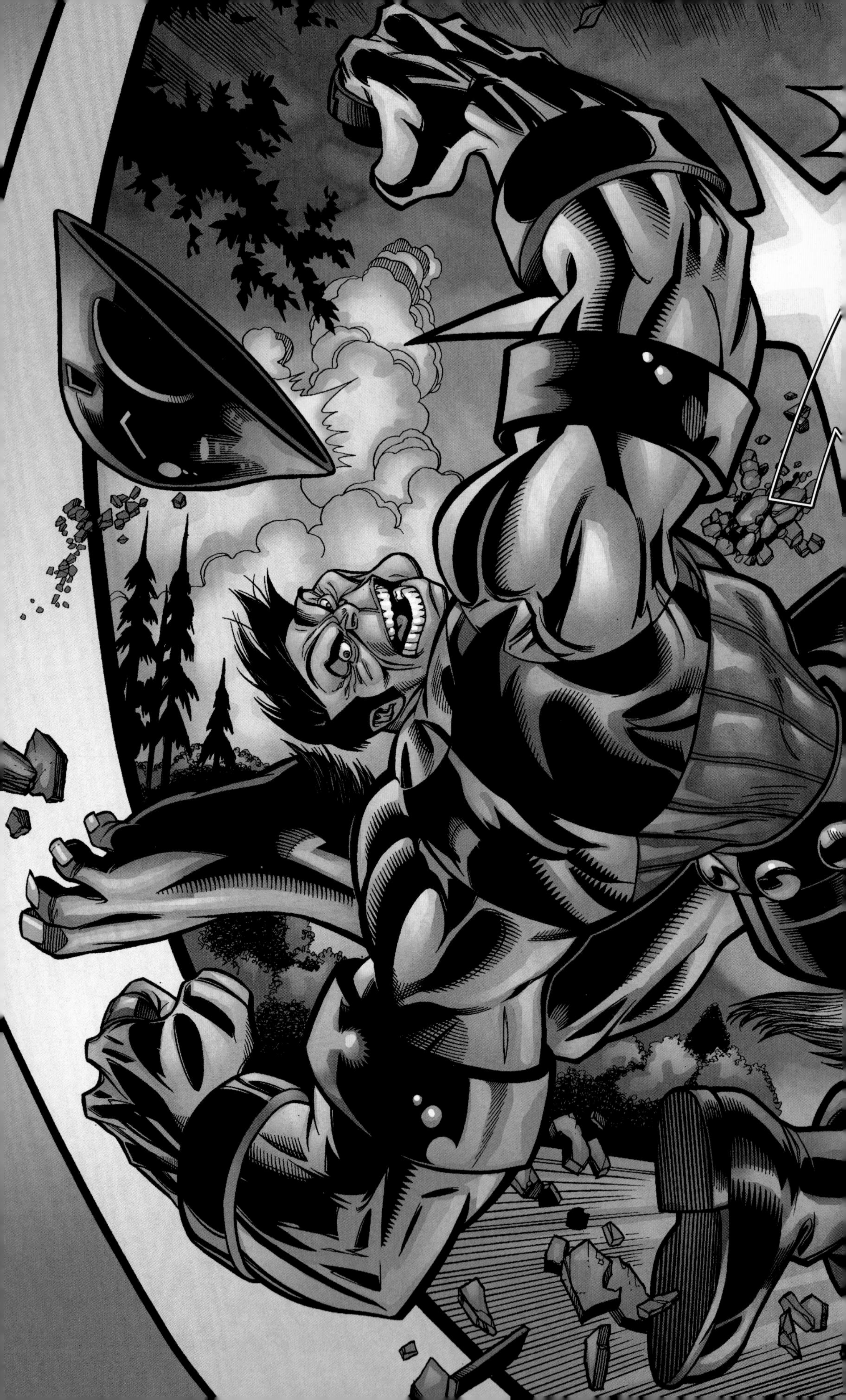

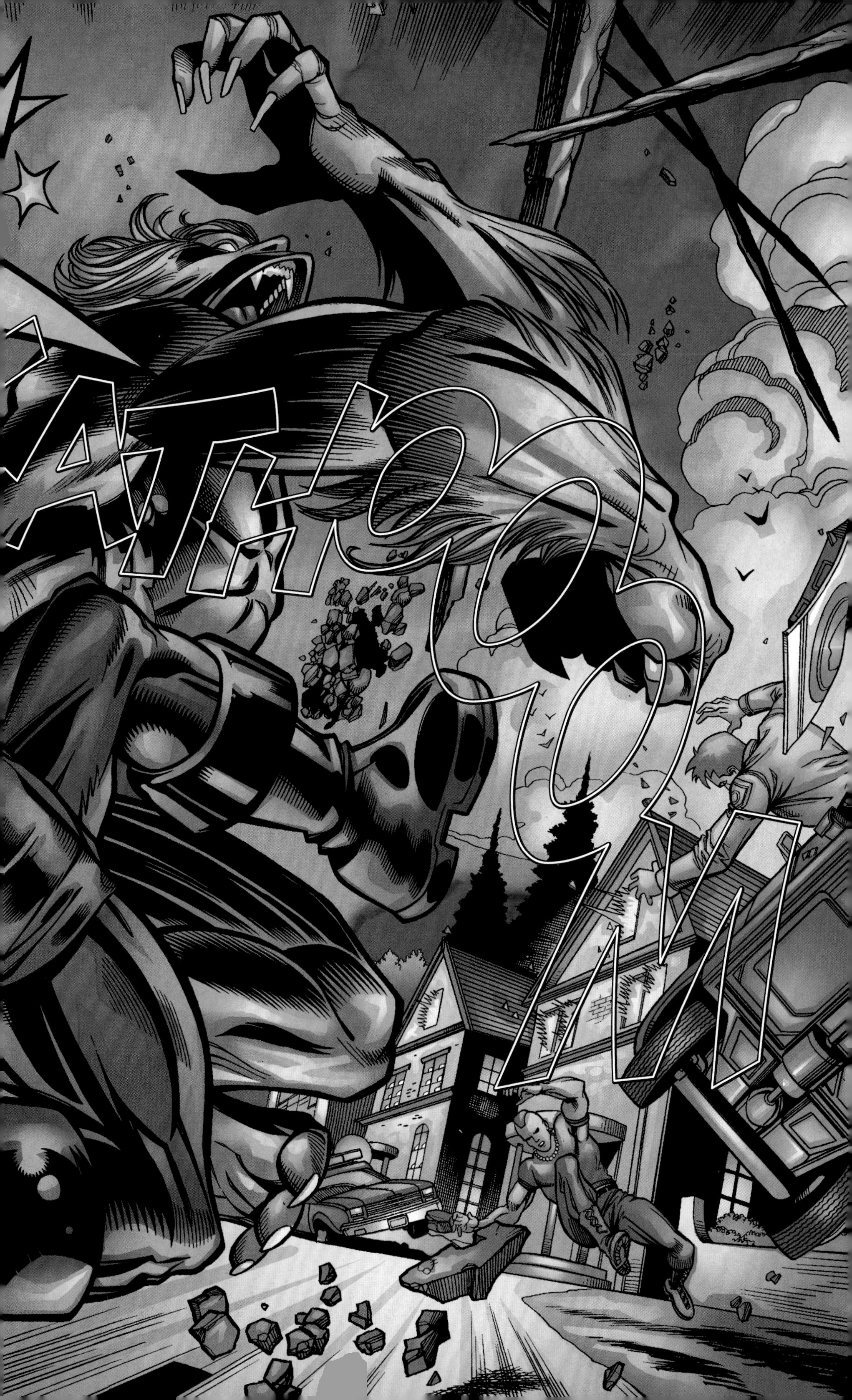
ATHOOOOM

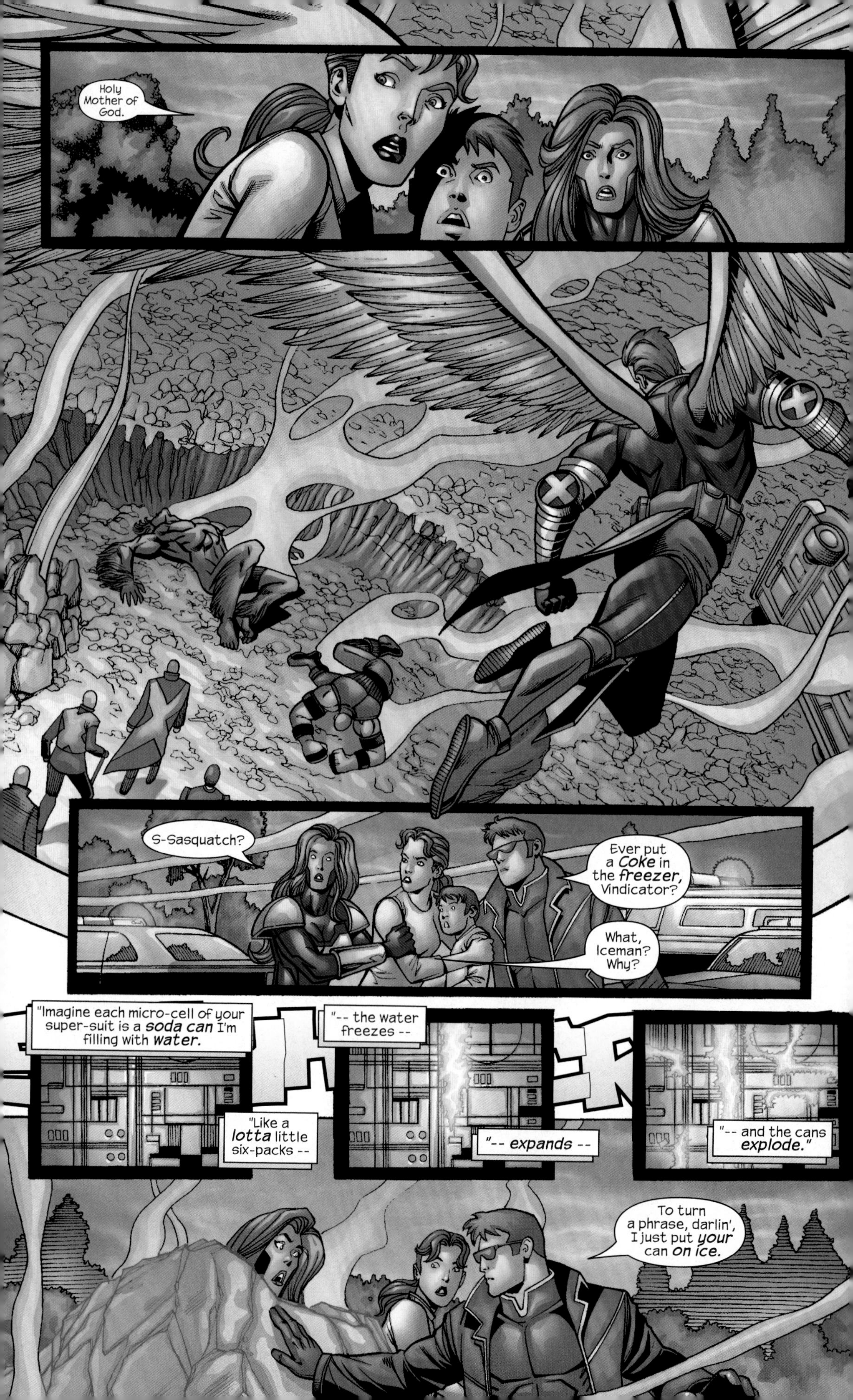
Holy Mother of God.
S-Sasquatch?
Ever put a Coke in the freezer, Vindicator?
What, Iceman? Why?
"Imagine each micro-cell of your super-suit is a soda can I'm filling with water.
"Like a lotta little six-packs --
"-- the water freezes --
"-- expands --
"-- and the cans explode."
To turn a phrase, darlin', I just put your can on ice.

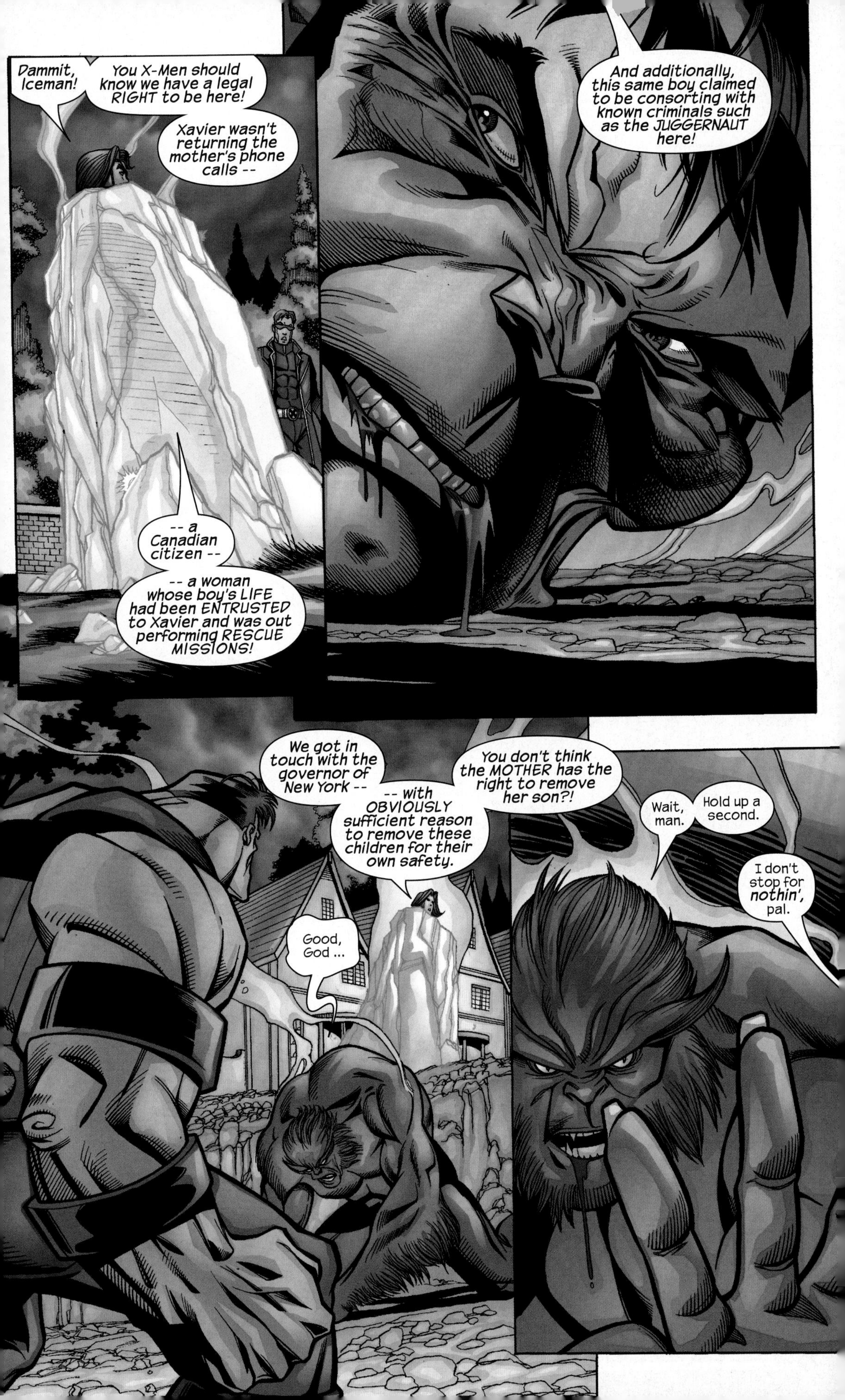

Dammit, Iceman!
You X-Men should know we have a legal RIGHT to be here!
Xavier wasn't returning the mother's phone calls --
-- a Canadian citizen --
-- a woman whose boy's LIFE had been ENTRUSTED to Xavier and was out performing RESCUE MISSIONS!
And additionally, this same boy claimed to be consorting with known criminals such as the JUGGERNAUT here!
We got in touch with the governor of New York --
-- with OBVIOUSLY sufficient reason to remove these children for their own safety.
You don't think the MOTHER has the right to remove her son?!
Good, God ...
Wait, man.
Hold up a second.
I don't stop for nothin', pal.

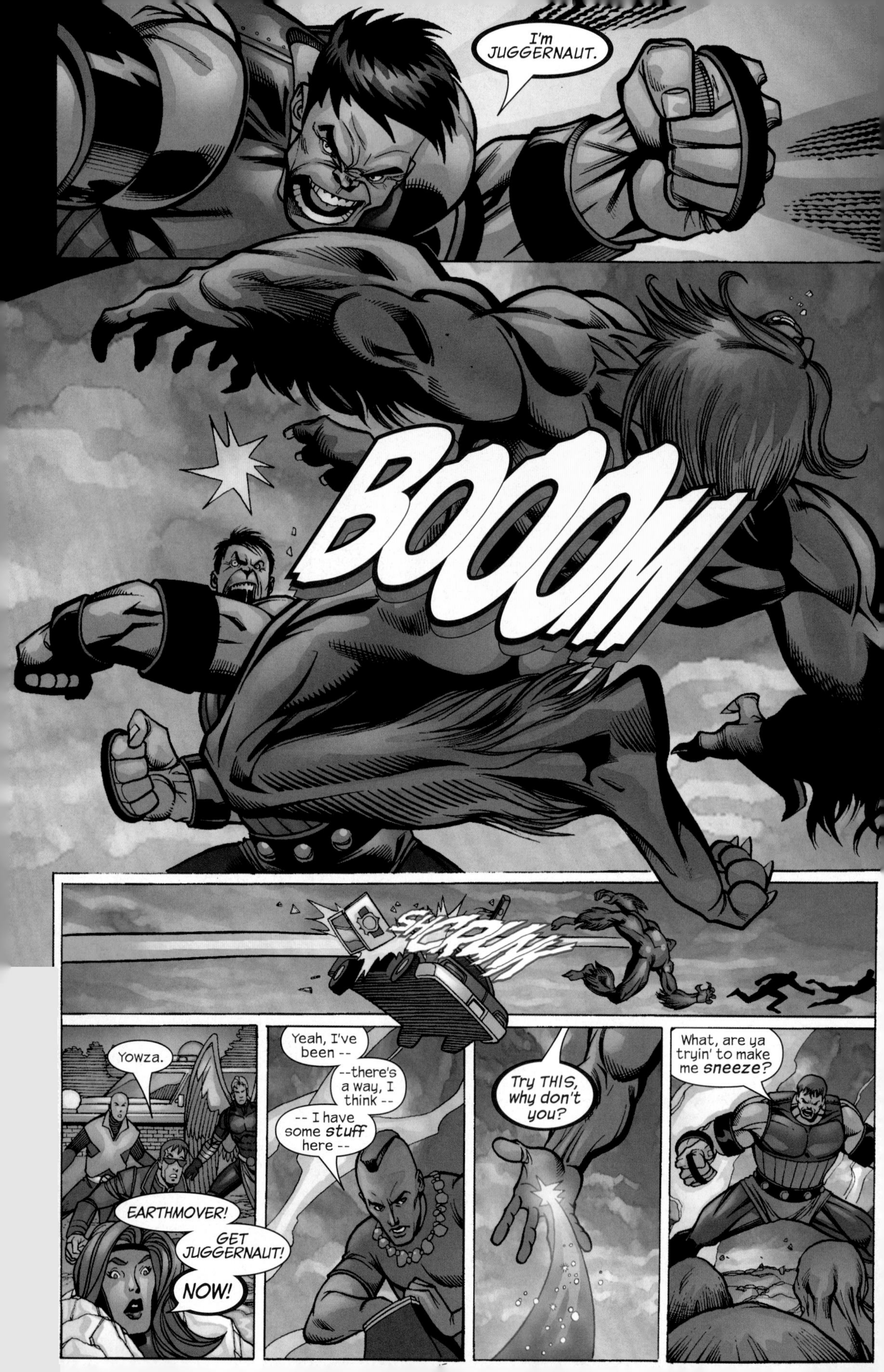
I'm JUGGERNAUT.
BOOOM
SHCRUNK
Yowza.
EARTHMOVER!
GET JUGGERNAUT!
NOW!
Yeah, I've been --
--there's a way, I think --
-- I have some stuff here --
Try THIS, why don't you?
What, are ya tryin' to make me sneeze?

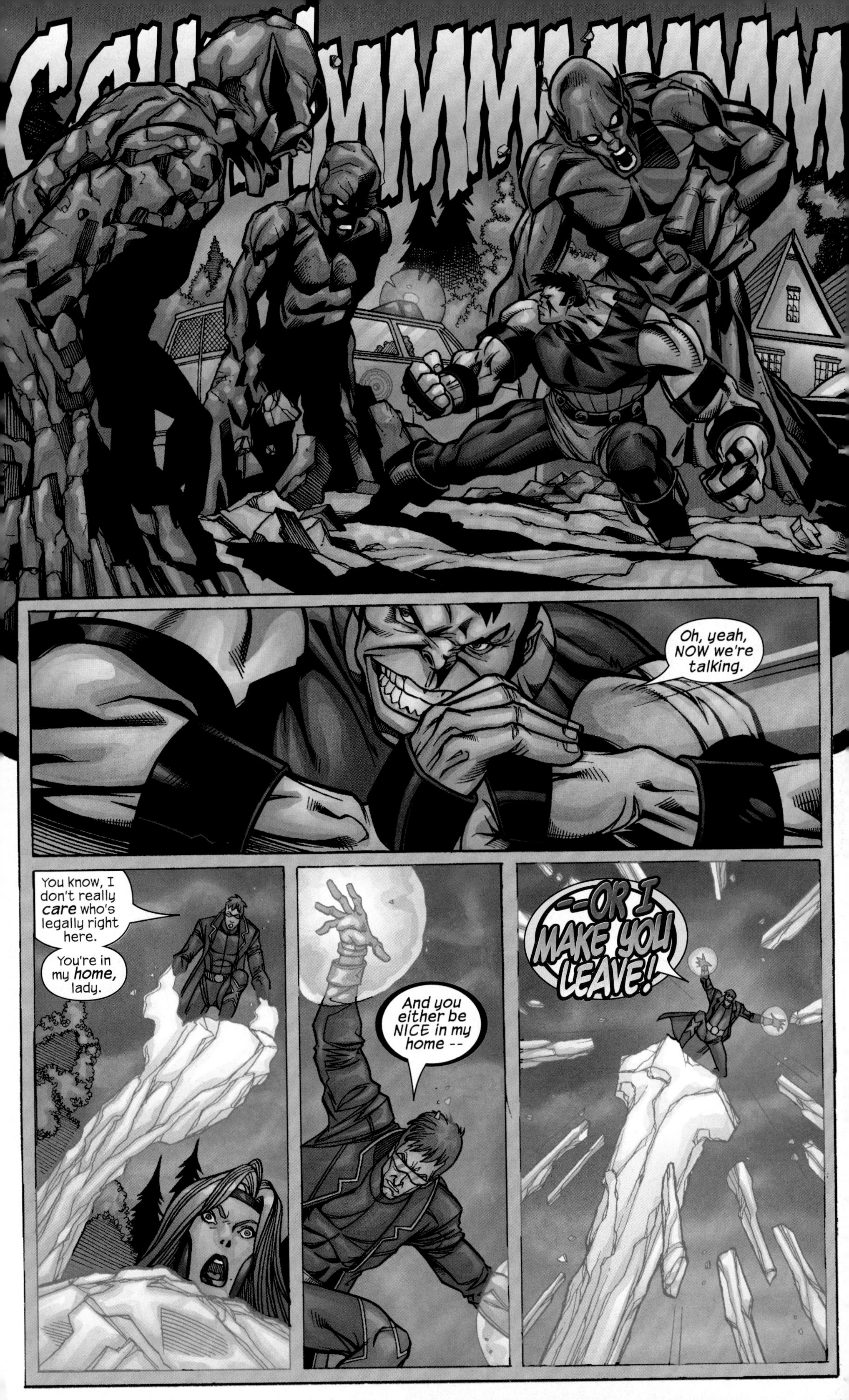

Oh, yeah, NOW we're talking.
You know, I don't really care who's legally right here.
You're in my home, lady.
And you either be NICE in my home --
--OR I MAKE YOU LEAVE!

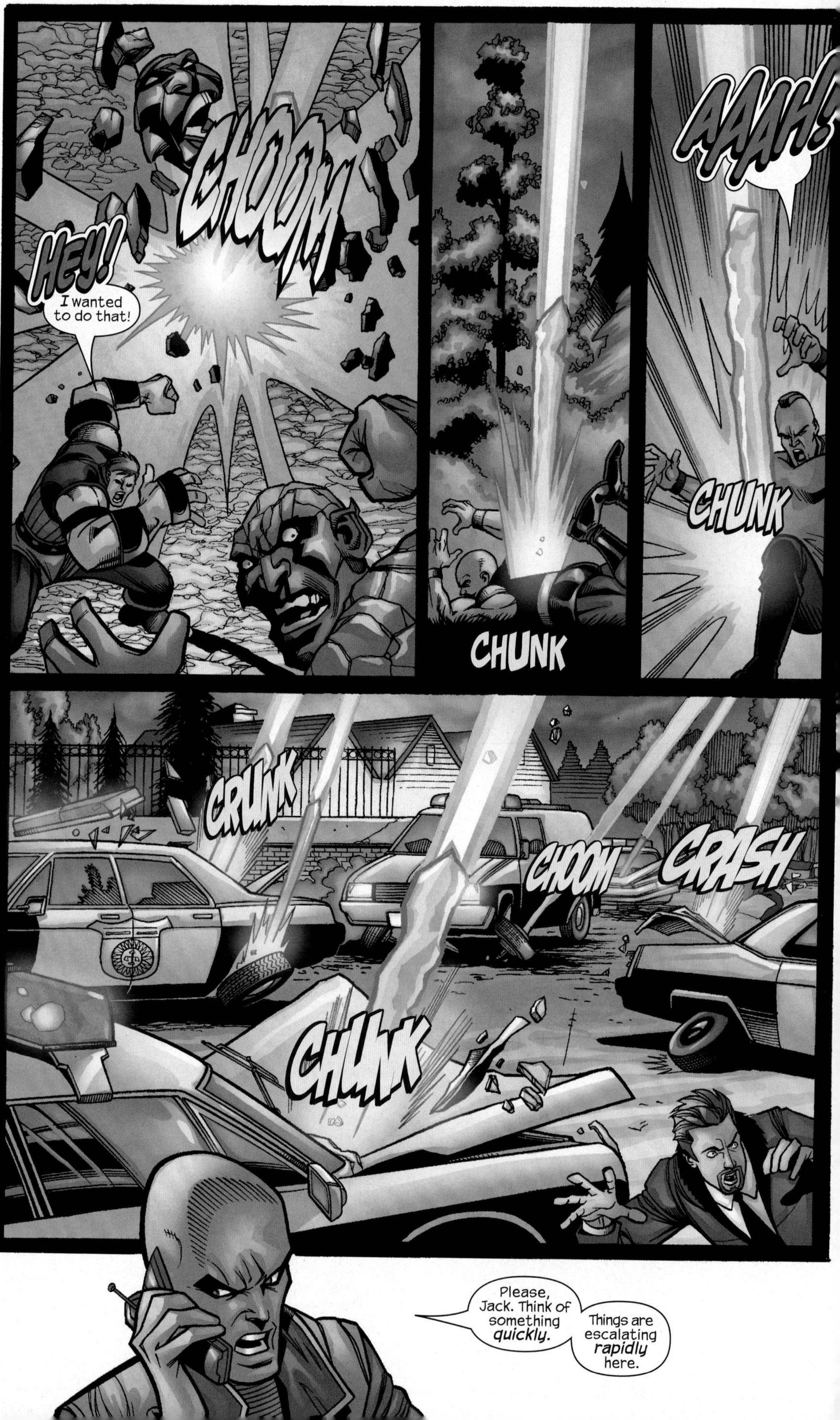
CHOOM
HEY! I wanted to do that!
CHUNK
AAAH!
CHUNK
CRUNK
CHOOM
CRASH
CHUNK
Please, Jack. Think of something quickly.
Things are escalating rapidly here.

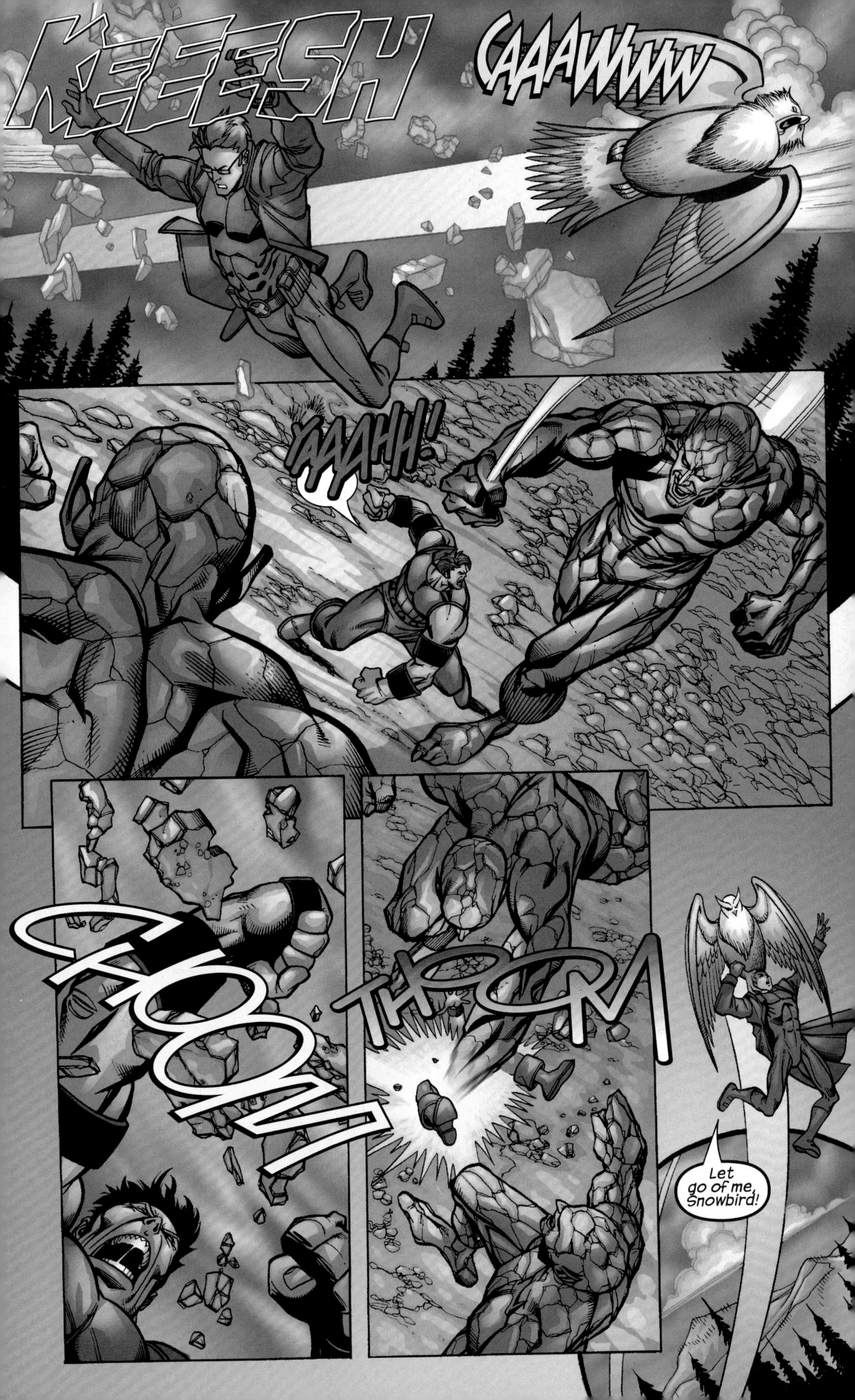

KEEESH
CAAAWWW
YAAAHH!
CHOOM
THOOM
Let go of me, Snowbird!

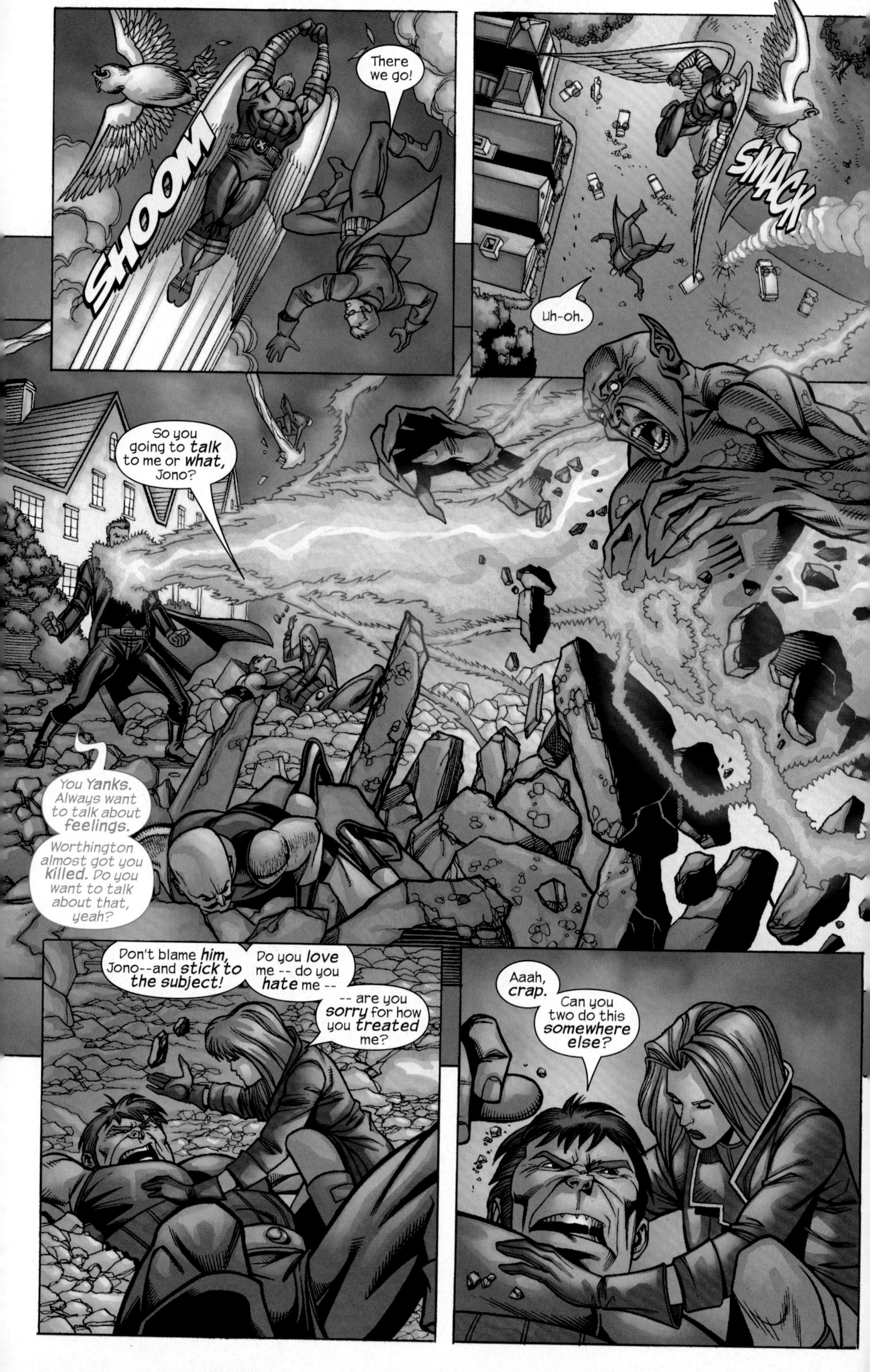
SHOOM
There we go!
SMACK
Uh-oh.
So you going to talk to me or what, Jono?
You Yanks. Always want to talk about feelings.
Worthington almost got you killed. Do you want to talk about that, yeah?
Don't blame him, Jono--and stick to the subject!
Do you love me -- do you hate me --
-- are you sorry for how you treated me?
Aaah, crap.
Can you two do this somewhere else?

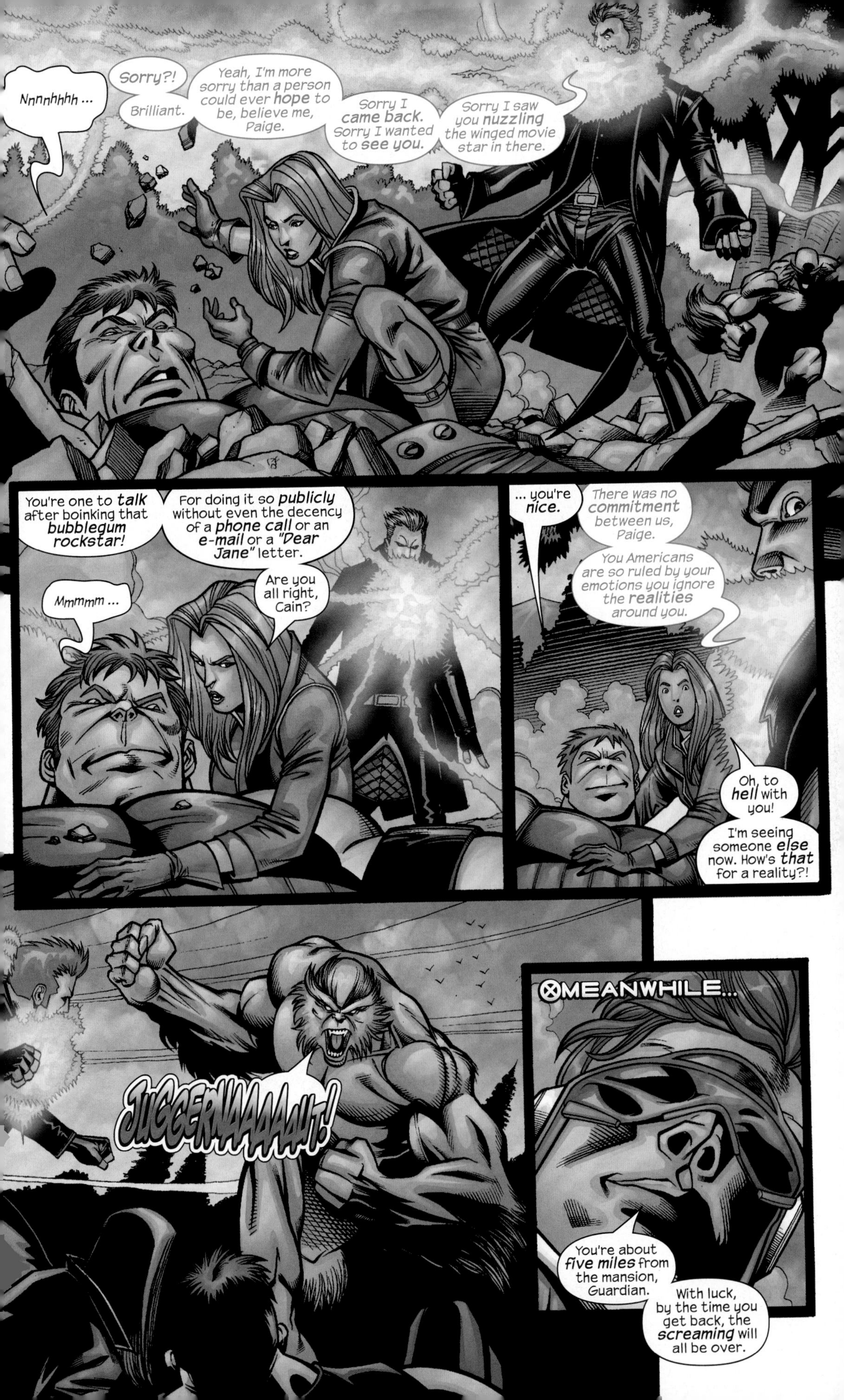
Nnnnhhhh ...
Sorry?!
Brilliant.
Yeah, I'm more sorry than a person could ever hope to be, believe me, Paige.
Sorry I came back. Sorry I wanted to see you.
Sorry I saw you nuzzling the winged movie star in there.
You're one to talk after boinking that bubblegum rockstar!
For doing it so publicly without even the decency of a phone call or an e-mail or a "Dear Jane" letter.
Mmmmm ...
Are you all right, Cain?
... you're nice.
There was no commitment between us, Paige.
You Americans are so ruled by your emotions you ignore the realities around you.
Oh, to hell with you!
I'm seeing someone else now. How's that for a reality?!
JUGGERNAAAAAUT!
MEANWHILE...
You're about five miles from the mansion, Guardian.
With luck, by the time you get back, the screaming will all be over.

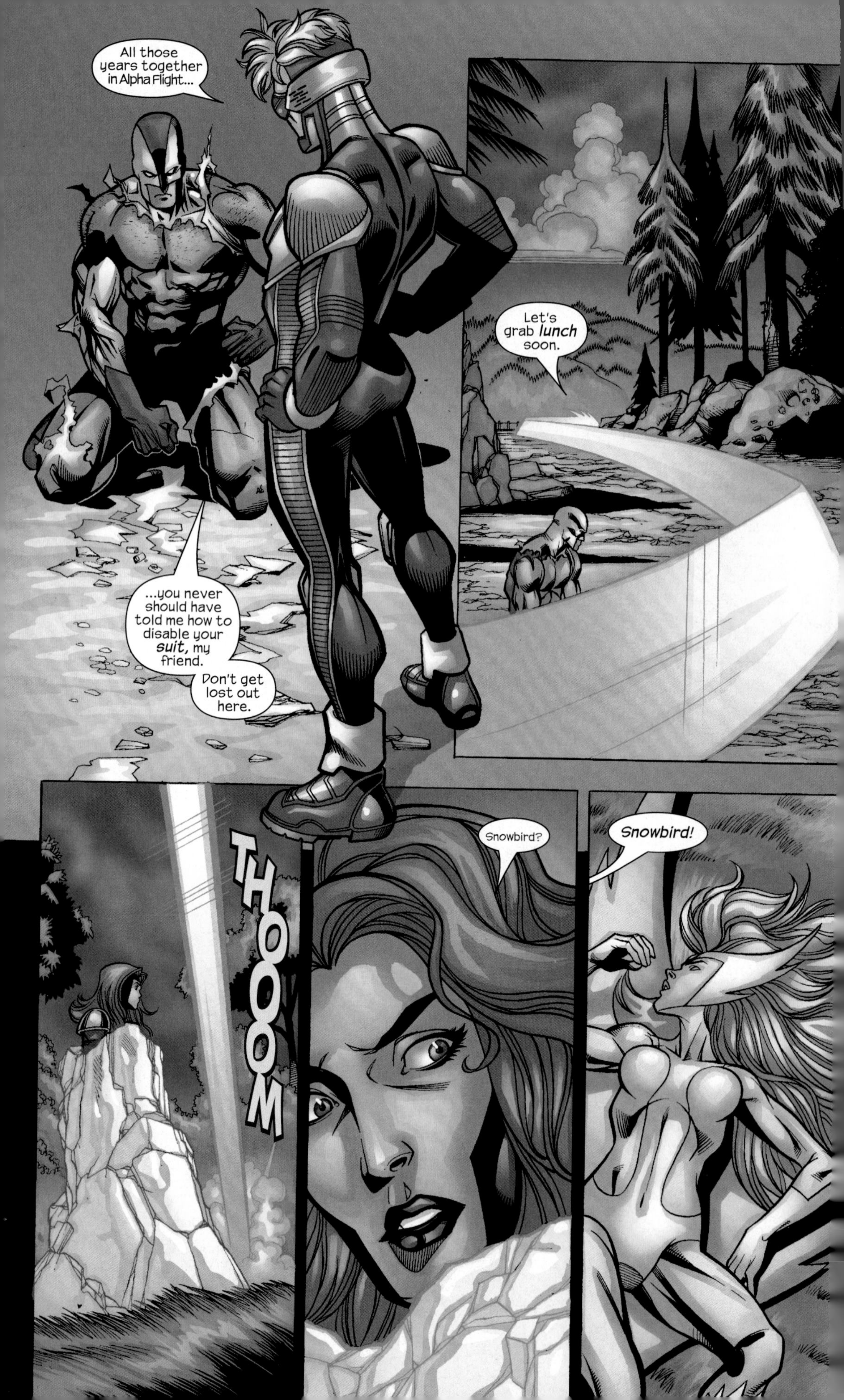
All those years together in Alpha Flight...
...you never should have told me how to disable your suit, my friend.
Don't get lost out here.
Let's grab lunch soon.
THOOOM
Snowbird?
Snowbird!

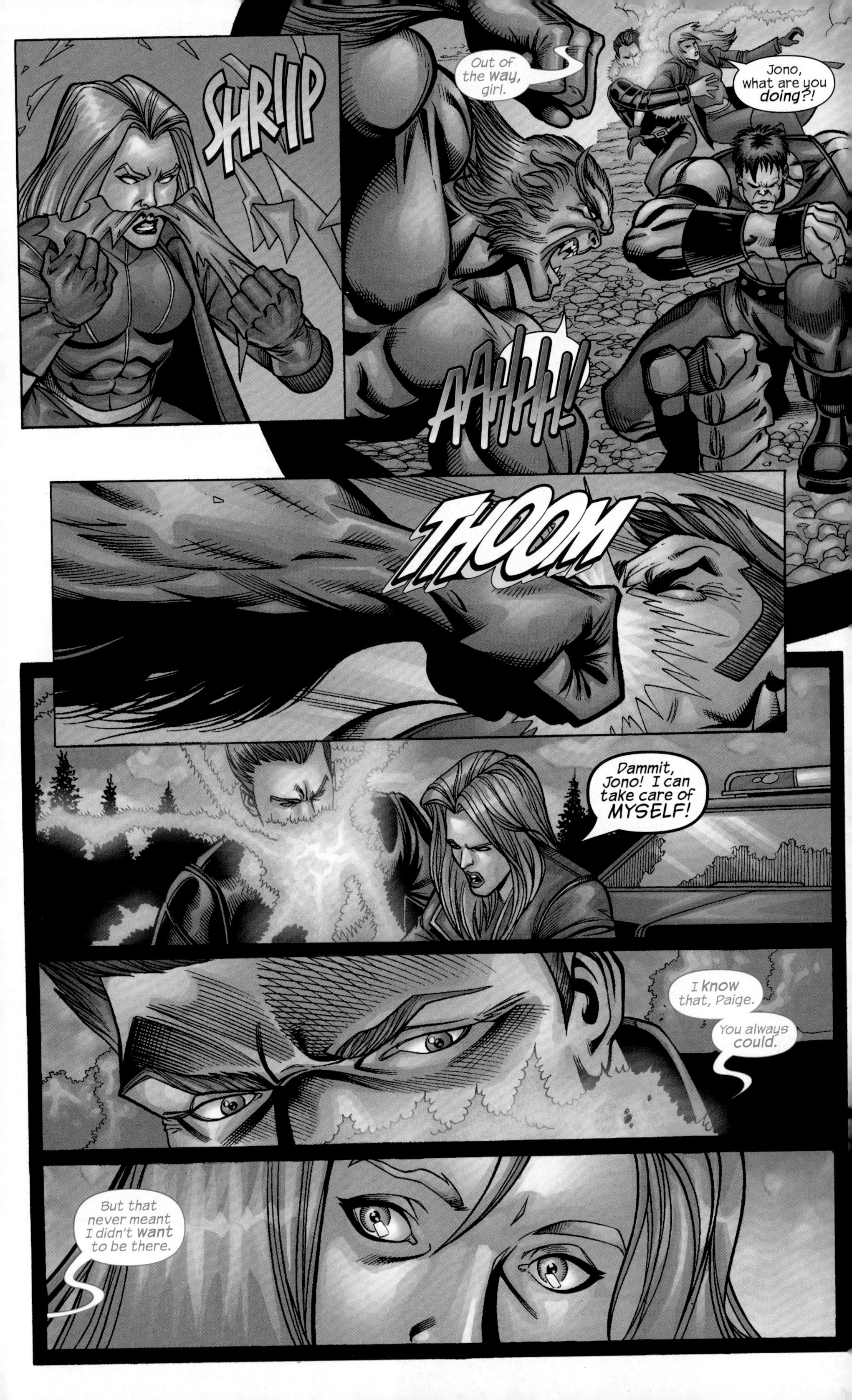
SHRIIP
Out of the way, girl.
Jono, what are you doing?!
AAHHH!
THOOM
Dammit, Jono! I can take care of MYSELF!
I know that, Paige.
You always could.
But that never meant I didn't want to be there.

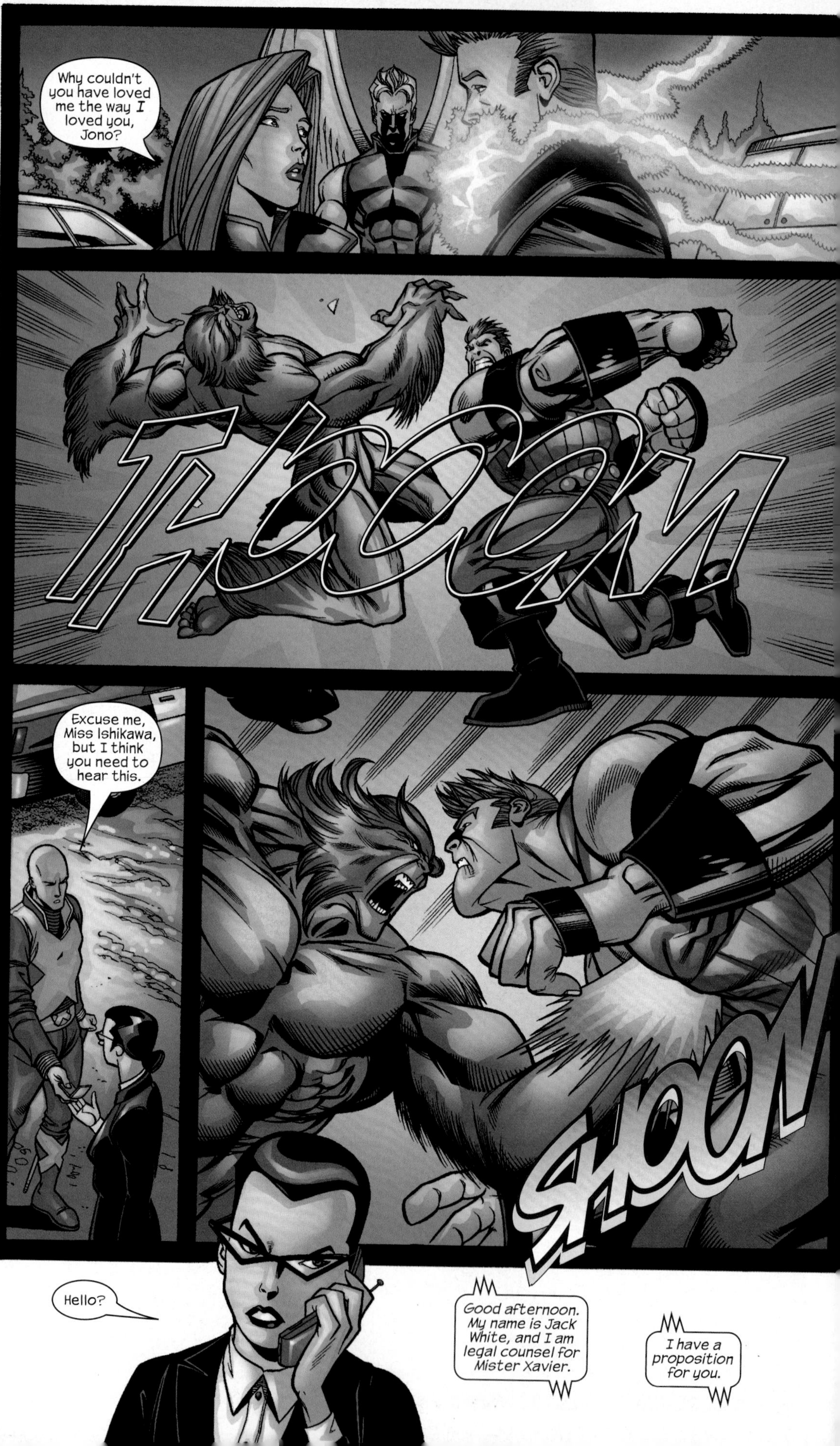
Why couldn't you have loved me the way I loved you, Jono?
THOOM
Excuse me, Miss Ishikawa, but I think you need to hear this.
SHOOM
Hello?
Good afternoon. My name is Jack White, and I am legal counsel for Mister Xavier.
I have a proposition for you.

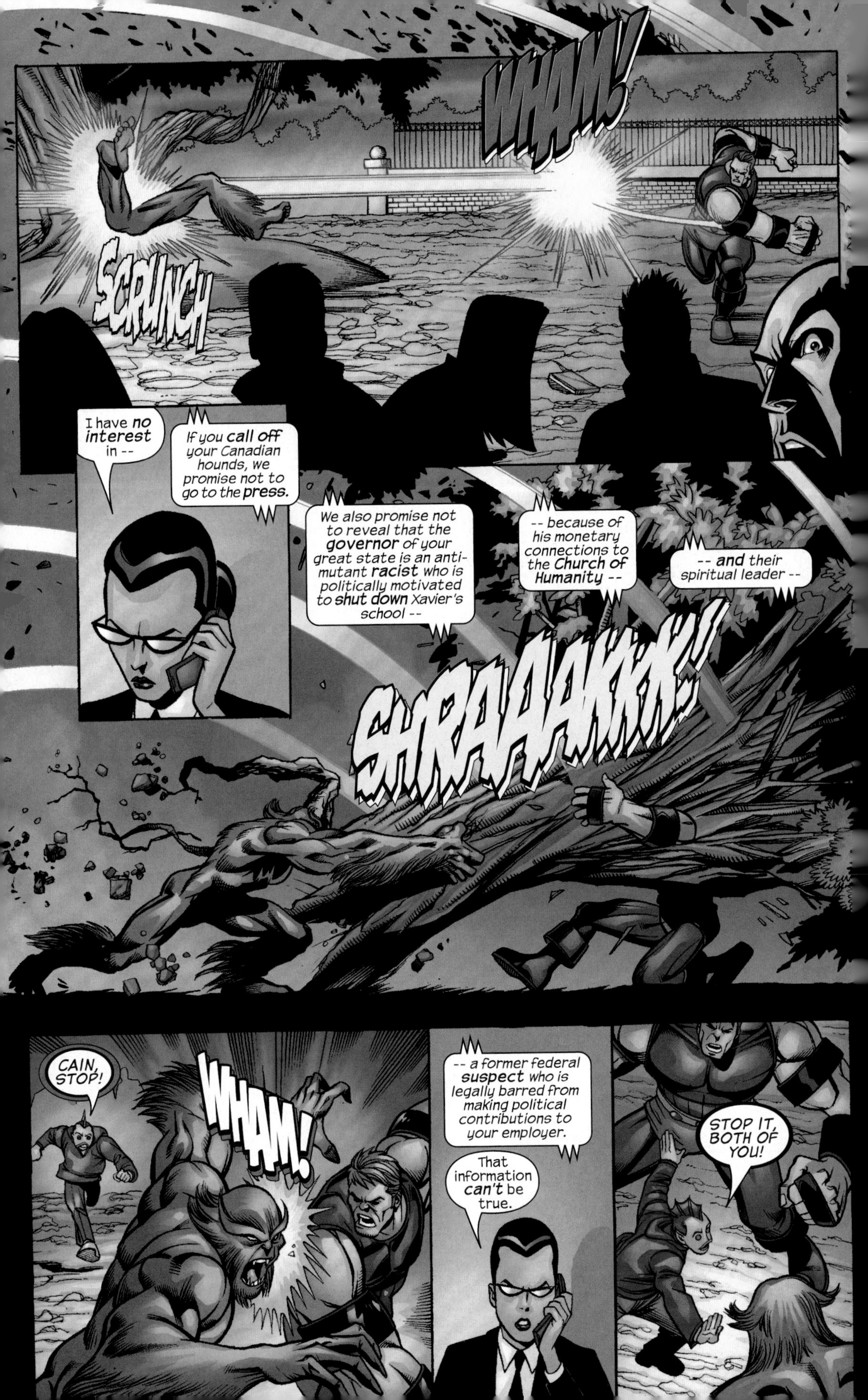
WHAM!
SCRUNCH
I have no interest in --
If you call off your Canadian hounds, we promise not to go to the press.
We also promise not to reveal that the governor of your great state is an anti-mutant racist who is politically motivated to shut down Xavier's school --
-- because of his monetary connections to the Church of Humanity --
-- and their spiritual leader --
SHRAAAKKK!
CAIN, STOP!
WHAM!
-- a former federal suspect who is legally barred from making political contributions to your employer.
That information can't be true.
STOP IT, BOTH OF YOU!

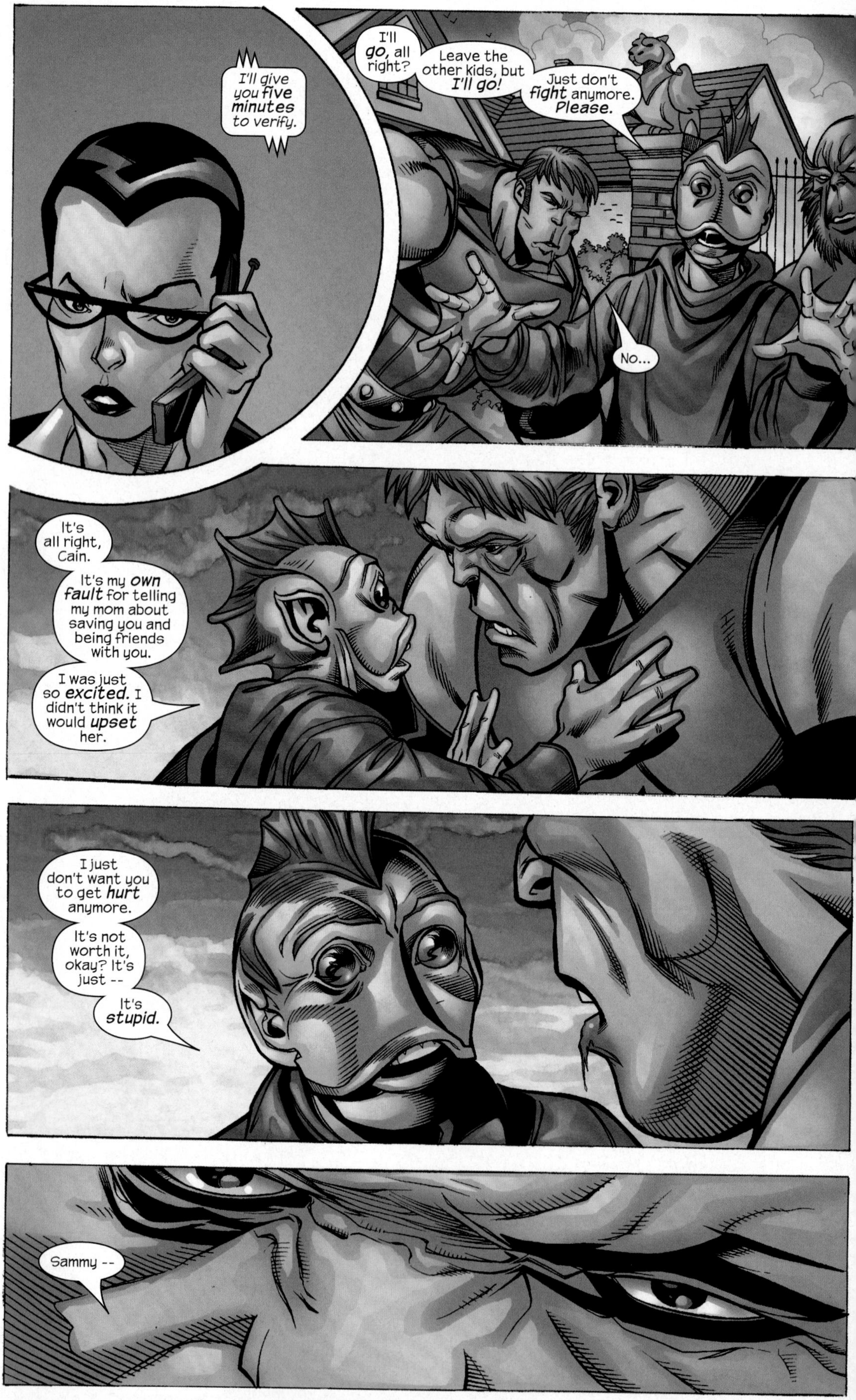
I'll give you *five minutes* to verify.
I'll *go,* all right?
Leave the other kids, but *I'll go!*
Just don't *fight* anymore. *Please.*
No...
It's all right, Cain.
It's my *own fault* for telling my mom about saving you and being friends with you.
I was just so *excited.* I didn't think it would *upset* her.
I just don't want you to get *hurt* anymore.
It's not worth it, okay? It's just --
It's *stupid.*
Sammy --

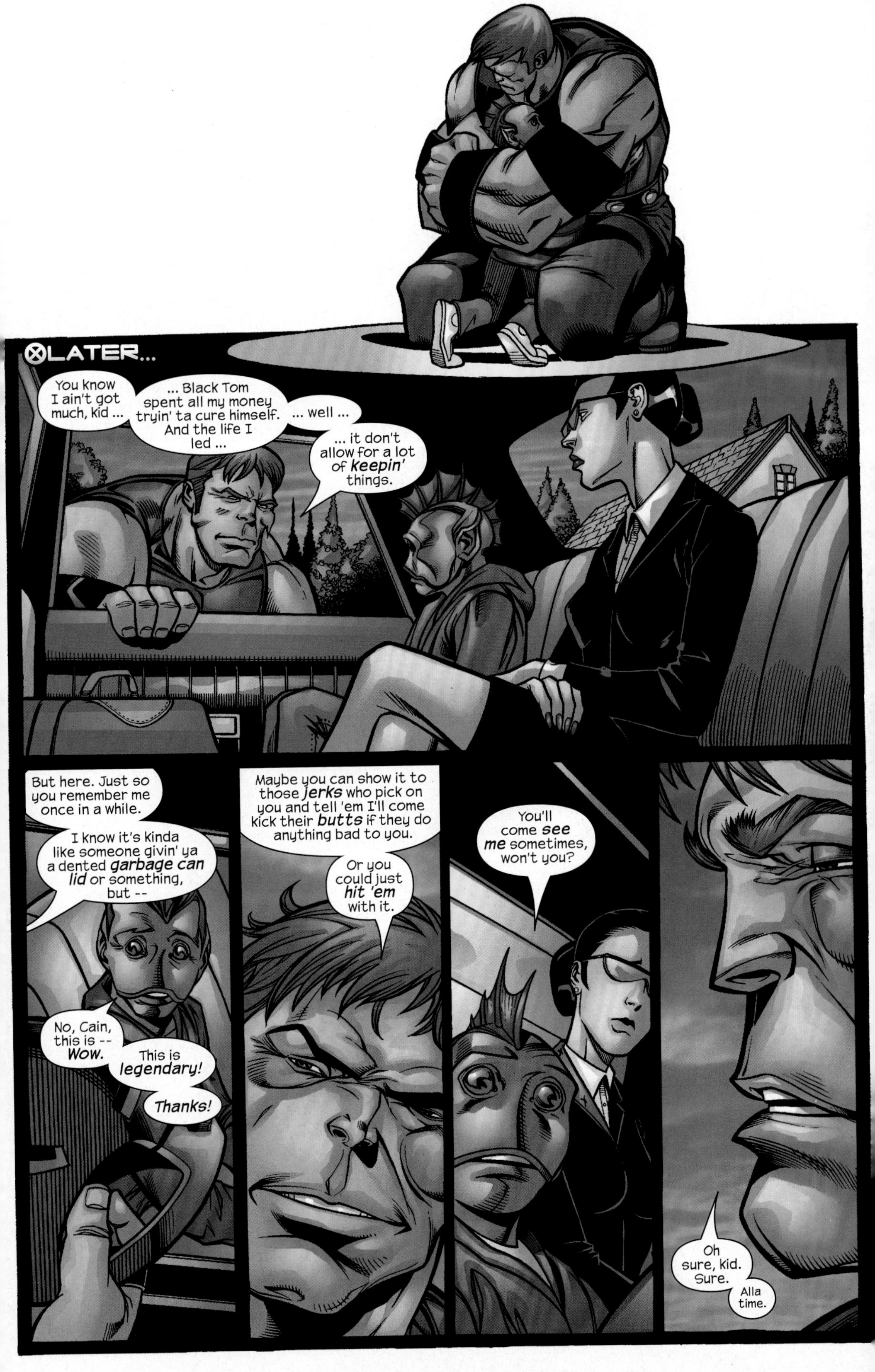
LATER...
You know I ain't got much, kid ...
... Black Tom spent all my money tryin' ta cure himself. And the life I led ...
... well ...
... it don't allow for a lot of keepin' things.
But here. Just so you remember me once in a while.
I know it's kinda like someone givin' ya a dented garbage can lid or something, but --
No, Cain, this is -- Wow.
This is legendary!
Thanks!
Maybe you can show it to those jerks who pick on you and tell 'em I'll come kick their butts if they do anything bad to you.
Or you could just hit 'em with it.
You'll come see me sometimes, won't you?
Oh sure, kid. Sure.
Alla time.

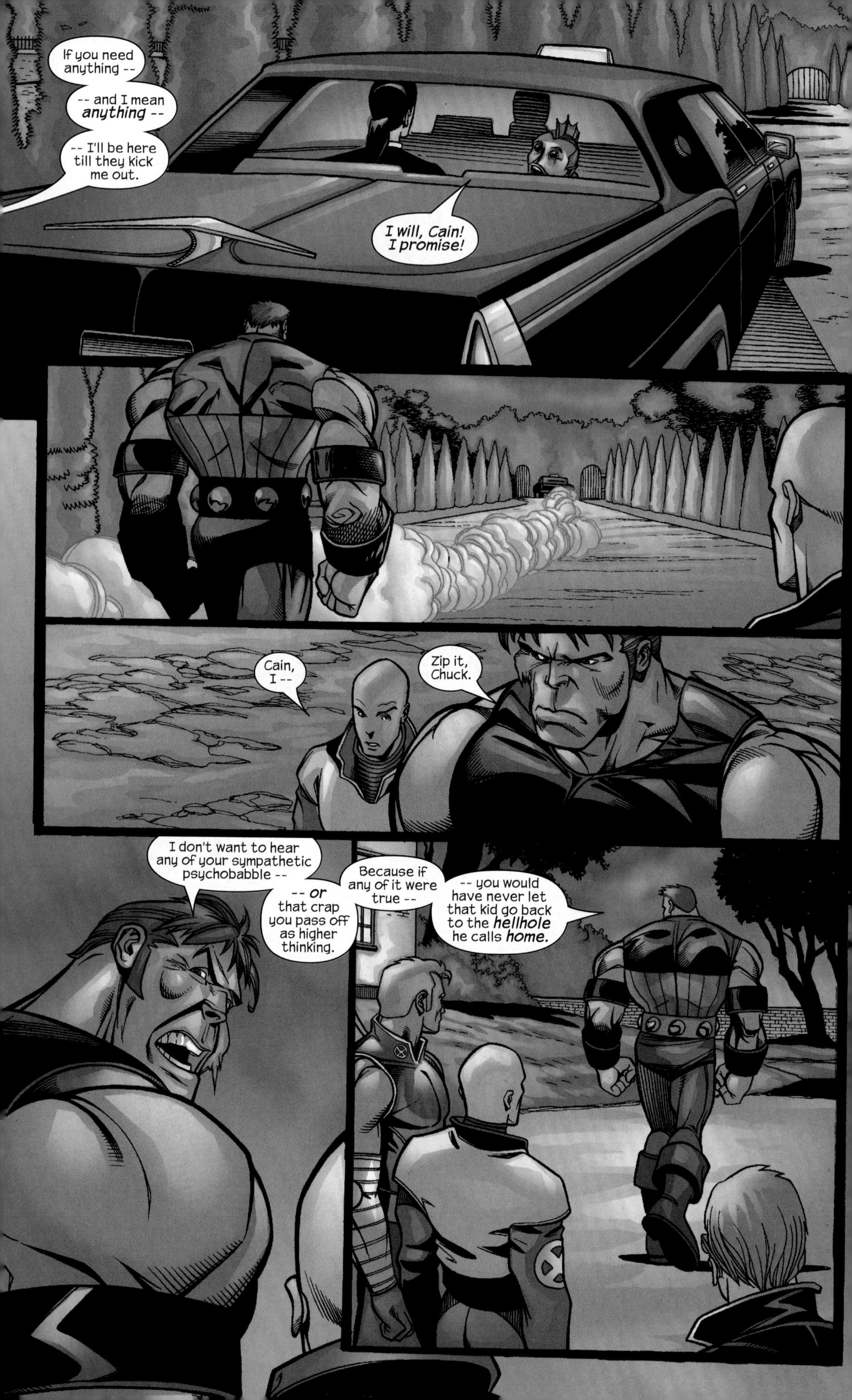
If you need anything --
-- and I mean *anything* --
-- I'll be here till they kick me out.
I will, Cain! I promise!
Cain, I --
Zip it, Chuck.
I don't want to hear any of your sympathetic psychobabble --
-- *or* that crap you pass off as higher thinking.
Because if any of it were true --
-- you would have never let that kid go back to the *hellhole* he calls *home.*

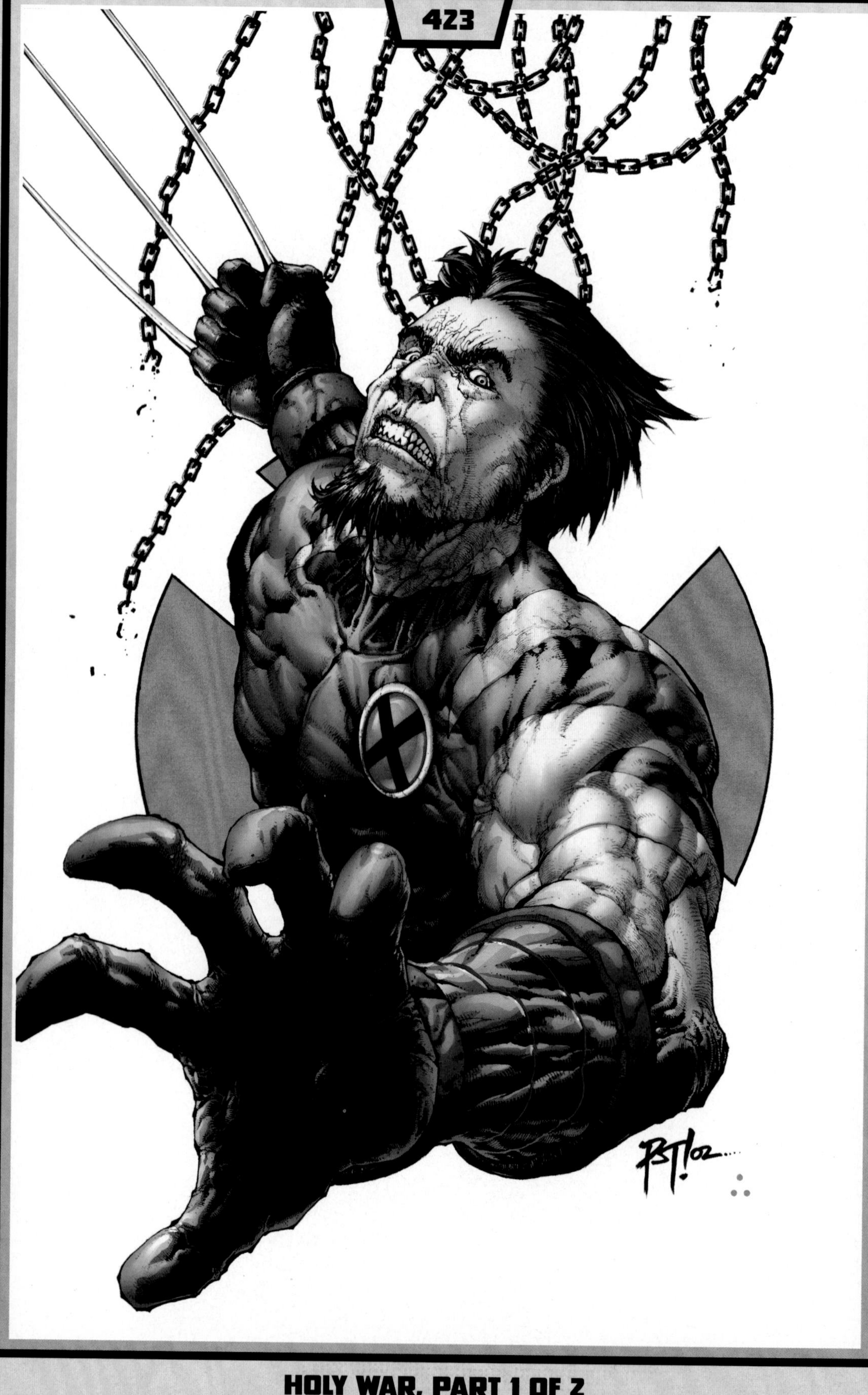
423
BT!02

HOLY WAR, PART 1 OF 2

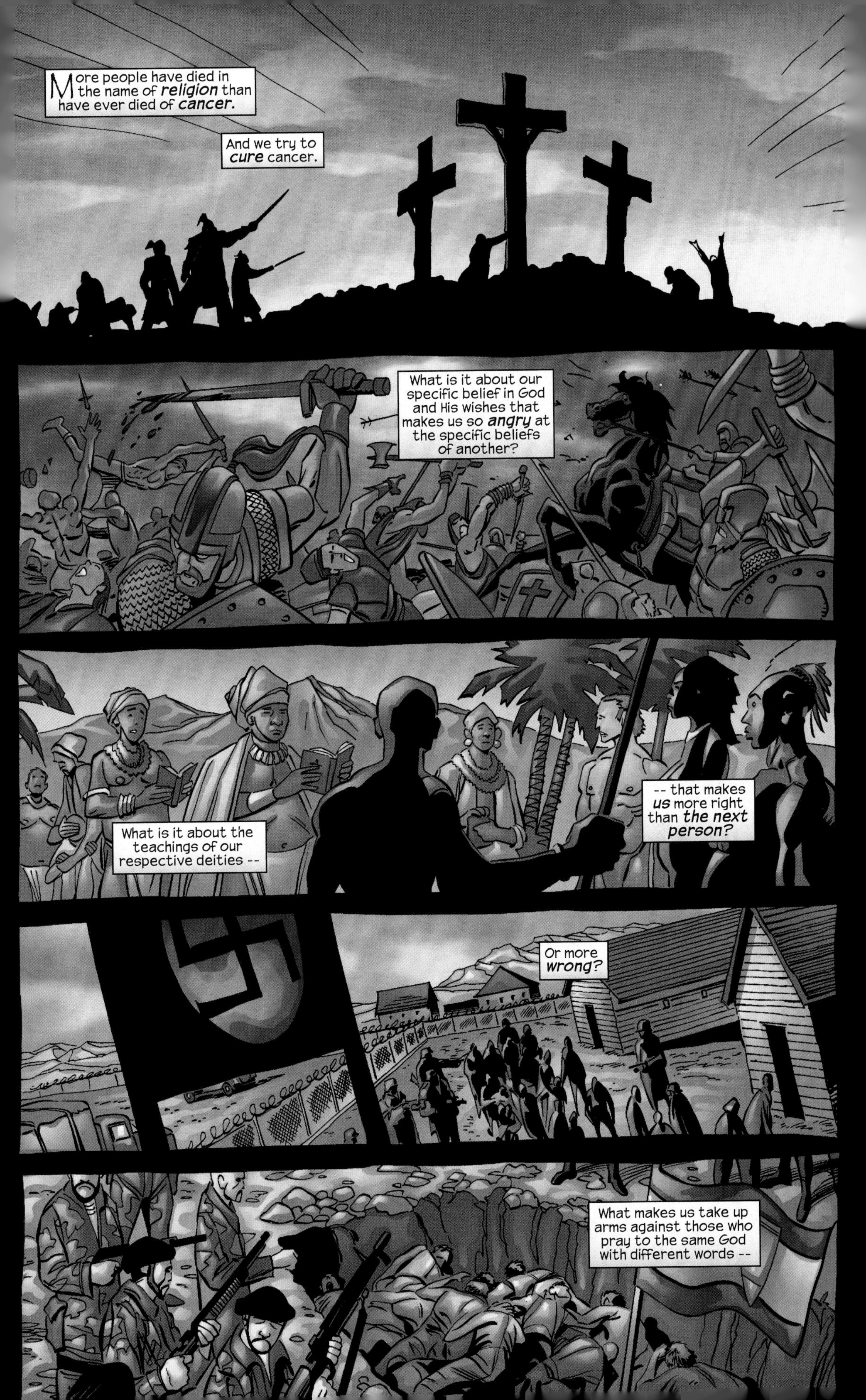

More people have died in the name of *religion* than have ever died of *cancer.*
And we try to *cure* cancer.
What is it about our specific belief in God and His wishes that makes us so *angry* at the specific beliefs of another?
What is it about the teachings of our respective deities --
-- that makes *us* more right than *the next person?*
Or more *wrong?*
What makes us take up arms against those who pray to the same God with different words --

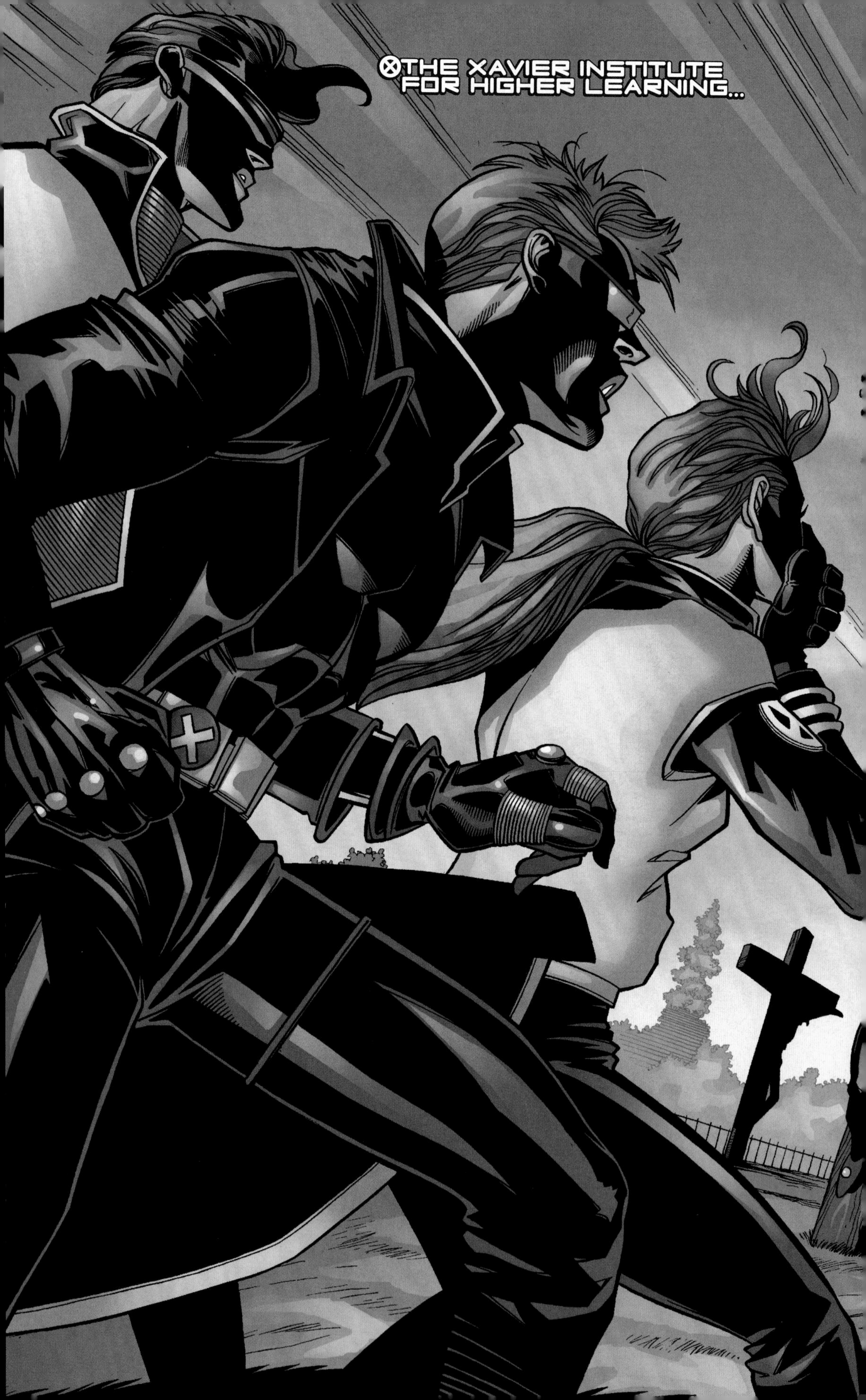
THE XAVIER INSTITUTE FOR HIGHER LEARNING...

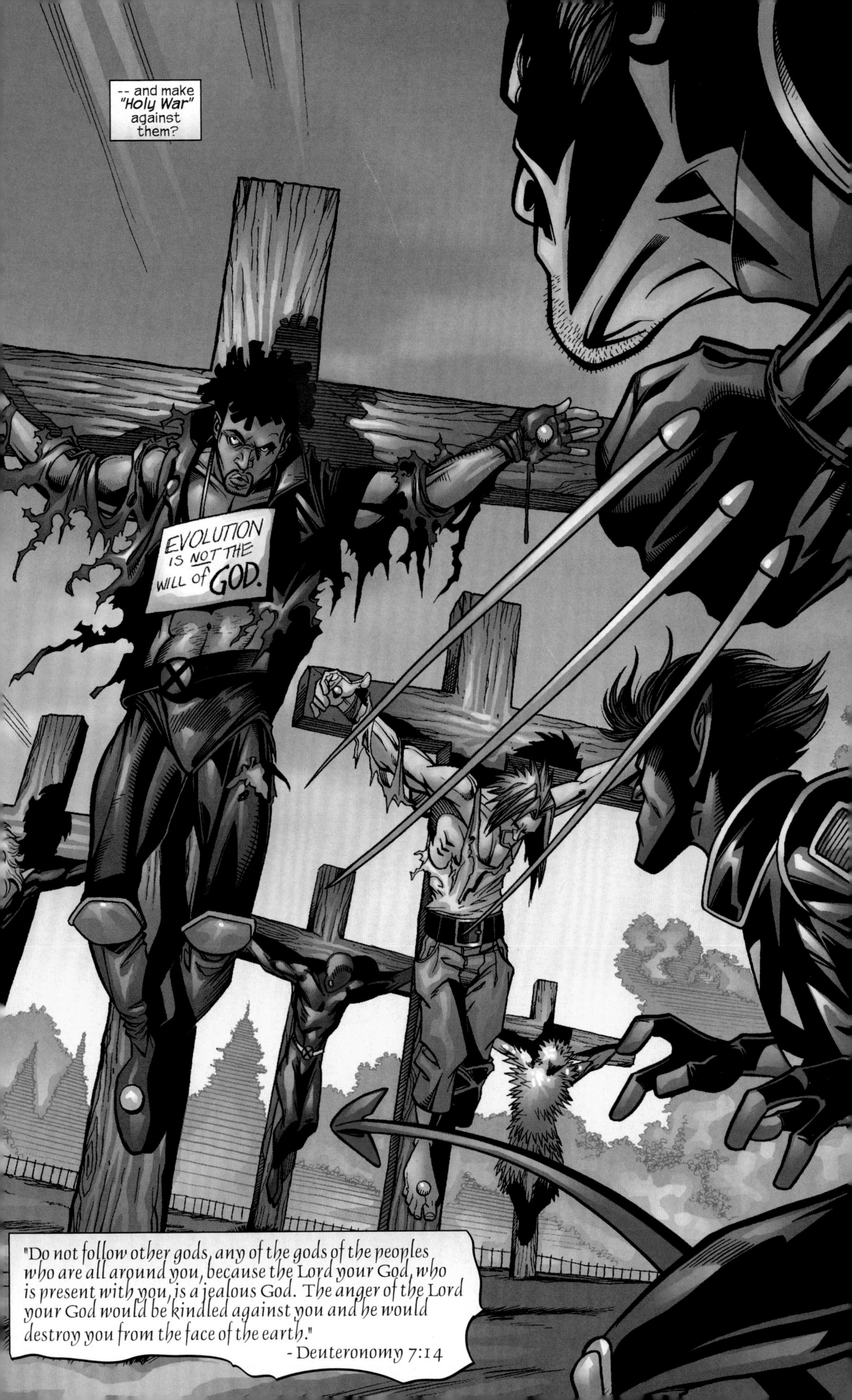
-- and make "Holy War" against them?
EVOLUTION IS NOT THE WILL OF GOD.
"Do not follow other gods, any of the gods of the peoples who are all around you, because the Lord your God, who is present with you, is a jealous God. The anger of the Lord your God would be kindled against you and he would destroy you from the face of the earth."
- Deuteronomy 7:14

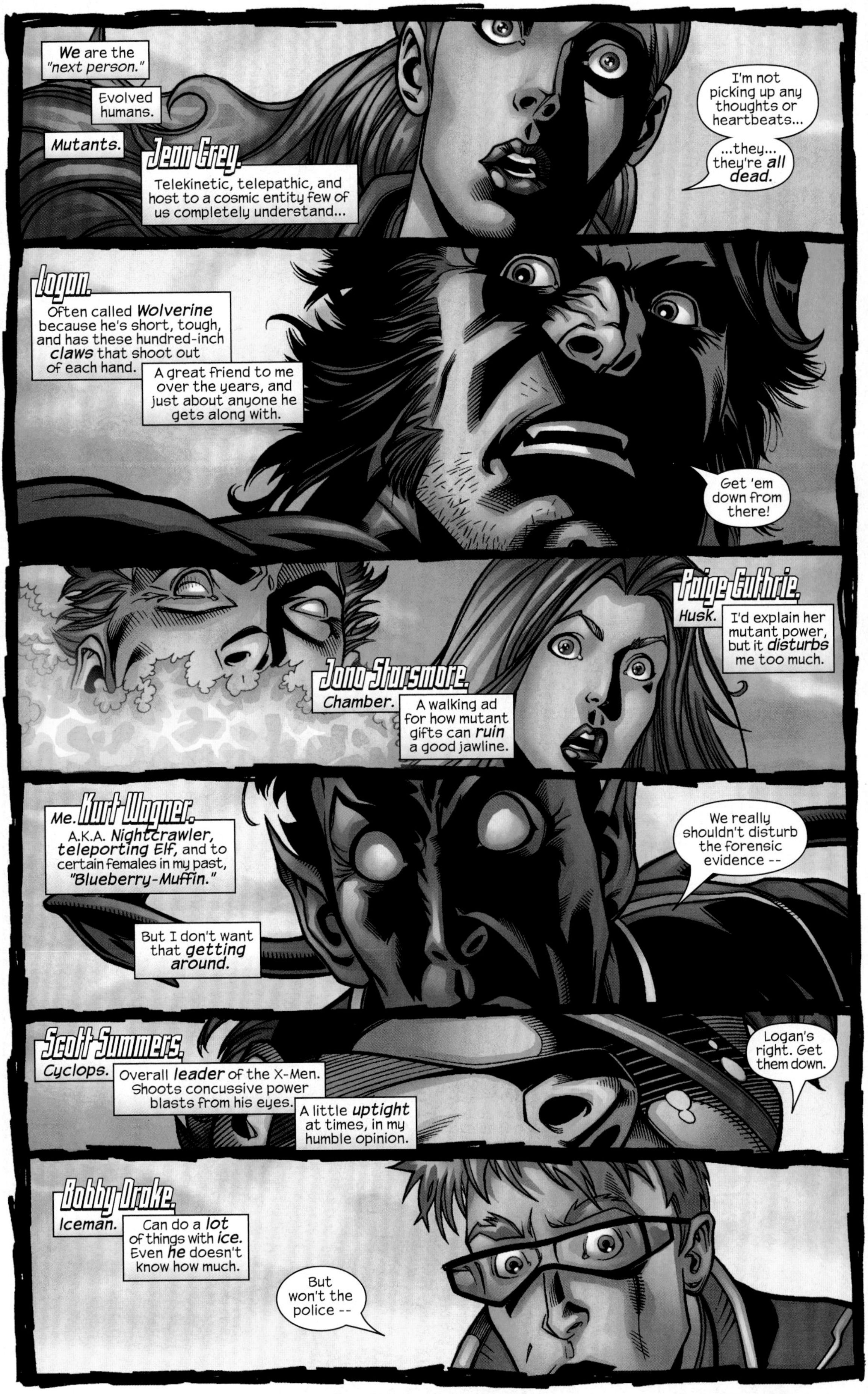
We are the "next person."
Evolved humans.
Mutants.
Jean Grey.
Telekinetic, telepathic, and host to a cosmic entity few of us completely understand...
I'm not picking up any thoughts or heartbeats...
...they... they're all dead.
Logan.
Often called Wolverine because he's short, tough, and has these hundred-inch claws that shoot out of each hand.
A great friend to me over the years, and just about anyone he gets along with.
Get 'em down from there!
Paige Guthrie.
Husk.
I'd explain her mutant power, but it disturbs me too much.
Jono Starsmore.
Chamber.
A walking ad for how mutant gifts can ruin a good jawline.
Me. Kurt Wagner.
A.K.A. Nightcrawler, teleporting Elf, and to certain females in my past, "Blueberry-Muffin."
But I don't want that getting around.
We really shouldn't disturb the forensic evidence --
Scott Summers.
Cyclops.
Overall leader of the X-Men. Shoots concussive power blasts from his eyes.
A little uptight at times, in my humble opinion.
Logan's right. Get them down.
Bobby Drake.
Iceman.
Can do a lot of things with ice. Even he doesn't know how much.
But won't the police --

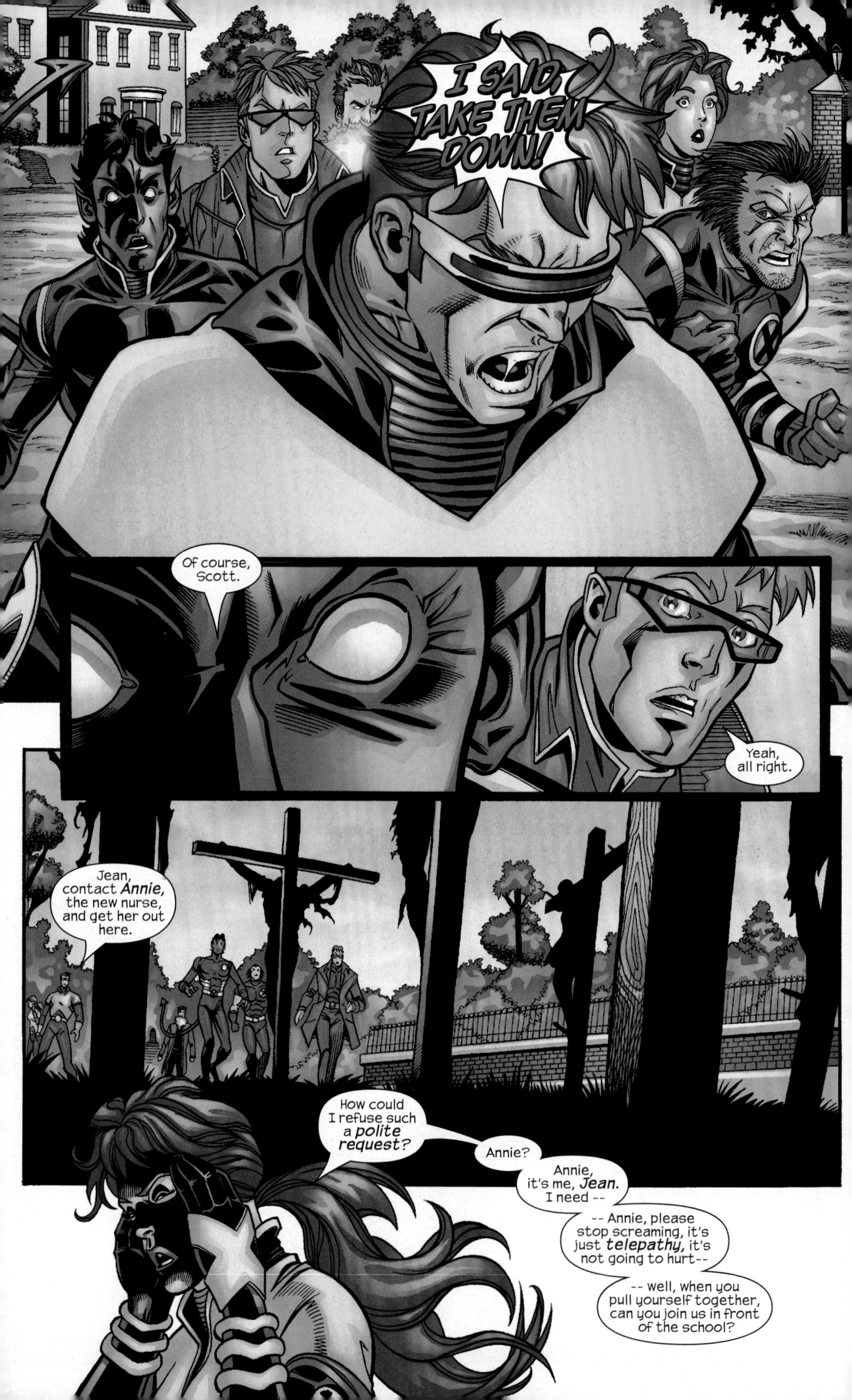
I SAID, TAKE THEM DOWN!
Of course, Scott.
Yeah, all right.
Jean, contact Annie, the new nurse, and get her out here.
How could I refuse such a polite request?
Annie?
Annie, it's me, Jean. I need --
-- Annie, please stop screaming, it's just telepathy, it's not going to hurt--
-- well, when you pull yourself together, can you join us in front of the school?

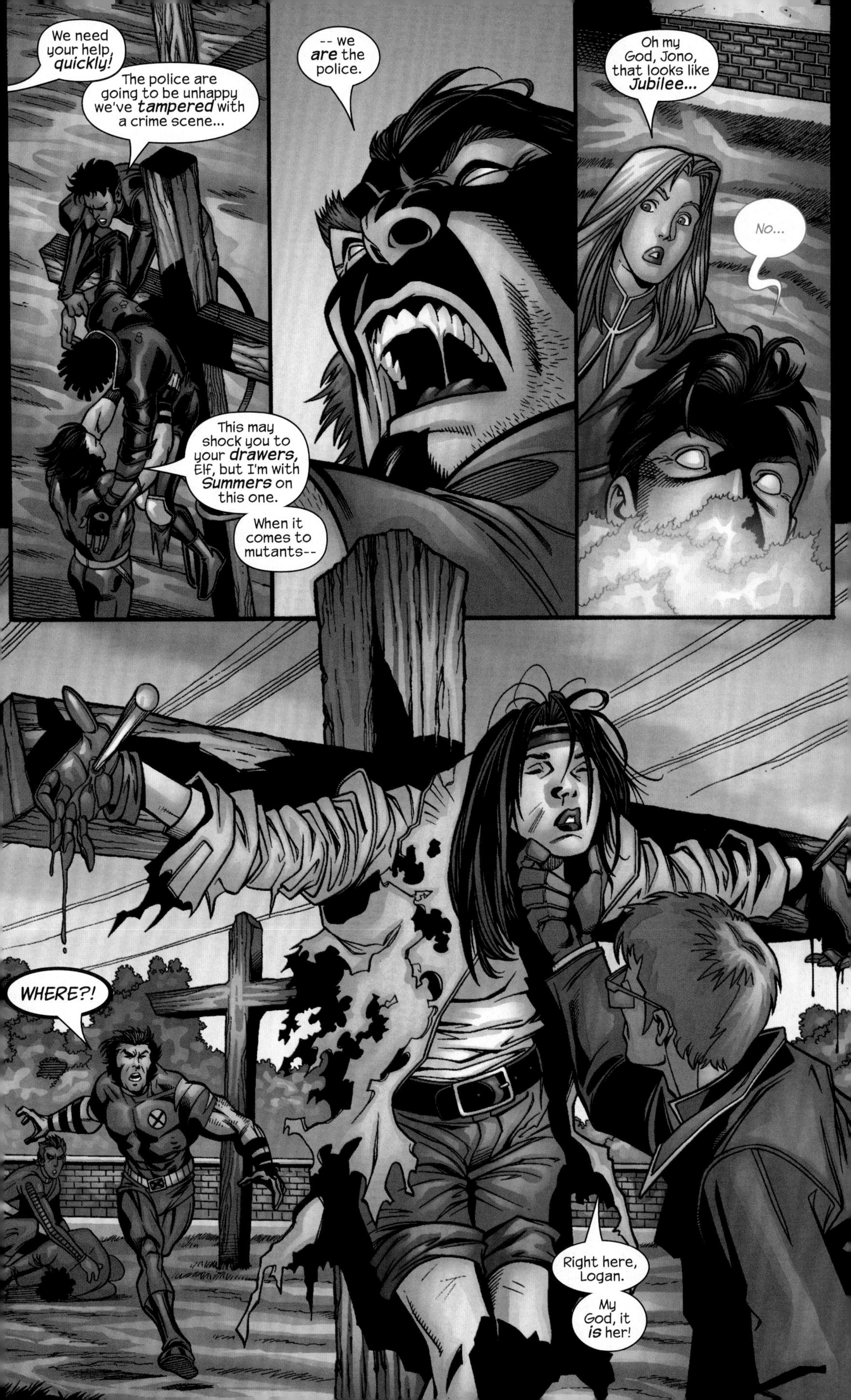
We need your help, *quickly!*
The police are going to be unhappy we've *tampered* with a crime scene...
-- we *are* the police.
Oh my God, Jono, that looks like *Jubilee...*
No...
This may shock you to your *drawers,* Elf, but I'm with *Summers* on this one.
When it comes to mutants--
WHERE?!
Right here, Logan.
My God, it *is* her!

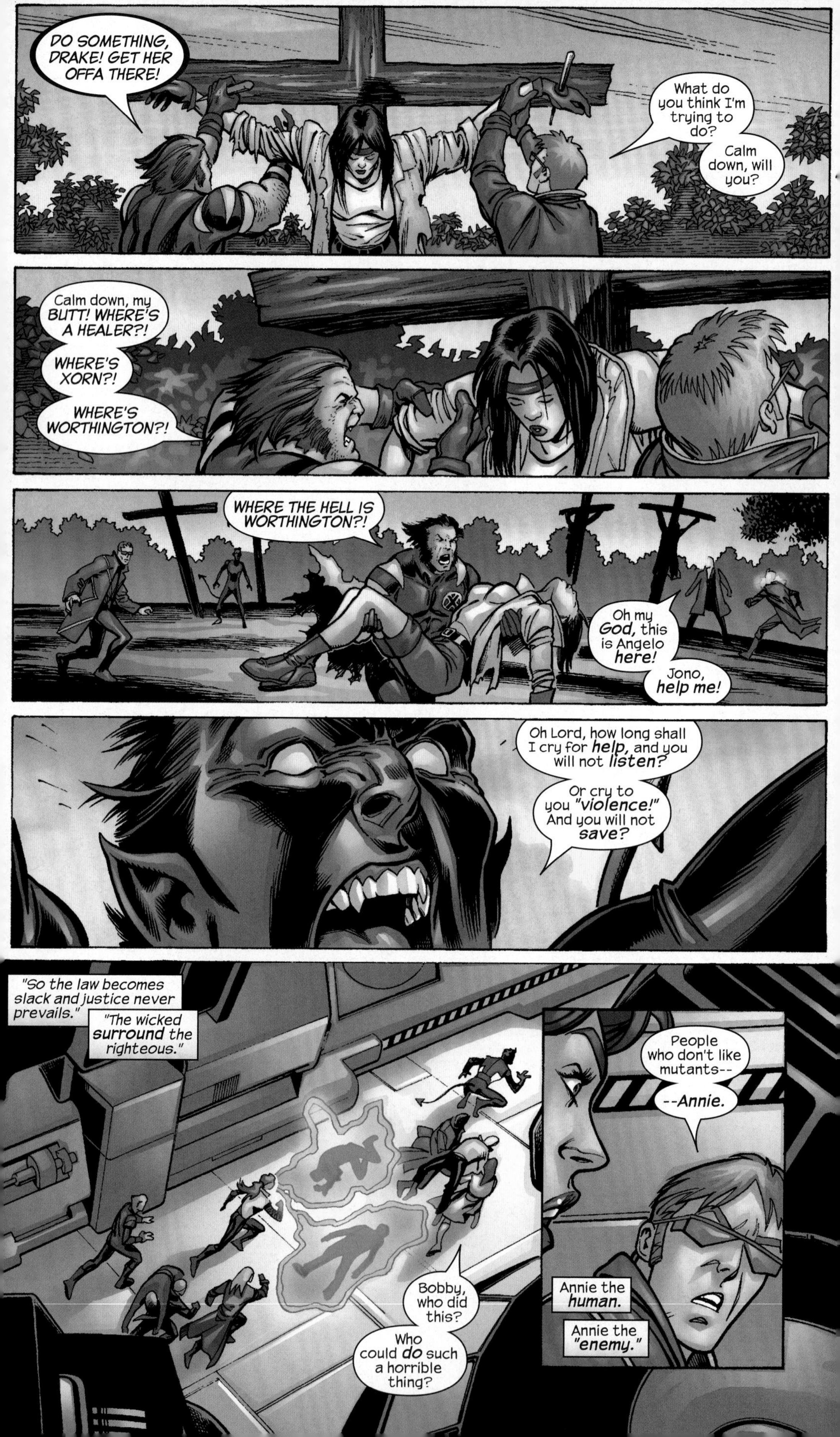
DO SOMETHING, DRAKE! GET HER OFFA THERE!
What do you think I'm trying to do?
Calm down, will you?
Calm down, my BUTT! WHERE'S A HEALER?!
WHERE'S XORN?!
WHERE'S WORTHINGTON?!
WHERE THE HELL IS WORTHINGTON?!
Oh my God, this is Angelo here!
Jono, help me!
Oh Lord, how long shall I cry for help, and you will not listen?
Or cry to you "violence!" And you will not save?
"So the law becomes slack and justice never prevails."
"The wicked surround the righteous."
Bobby, who did this?
Who could do such a horrible thing?
People who don't like mutants--
--Annie.
Annie the human.
Annie the "enemy."

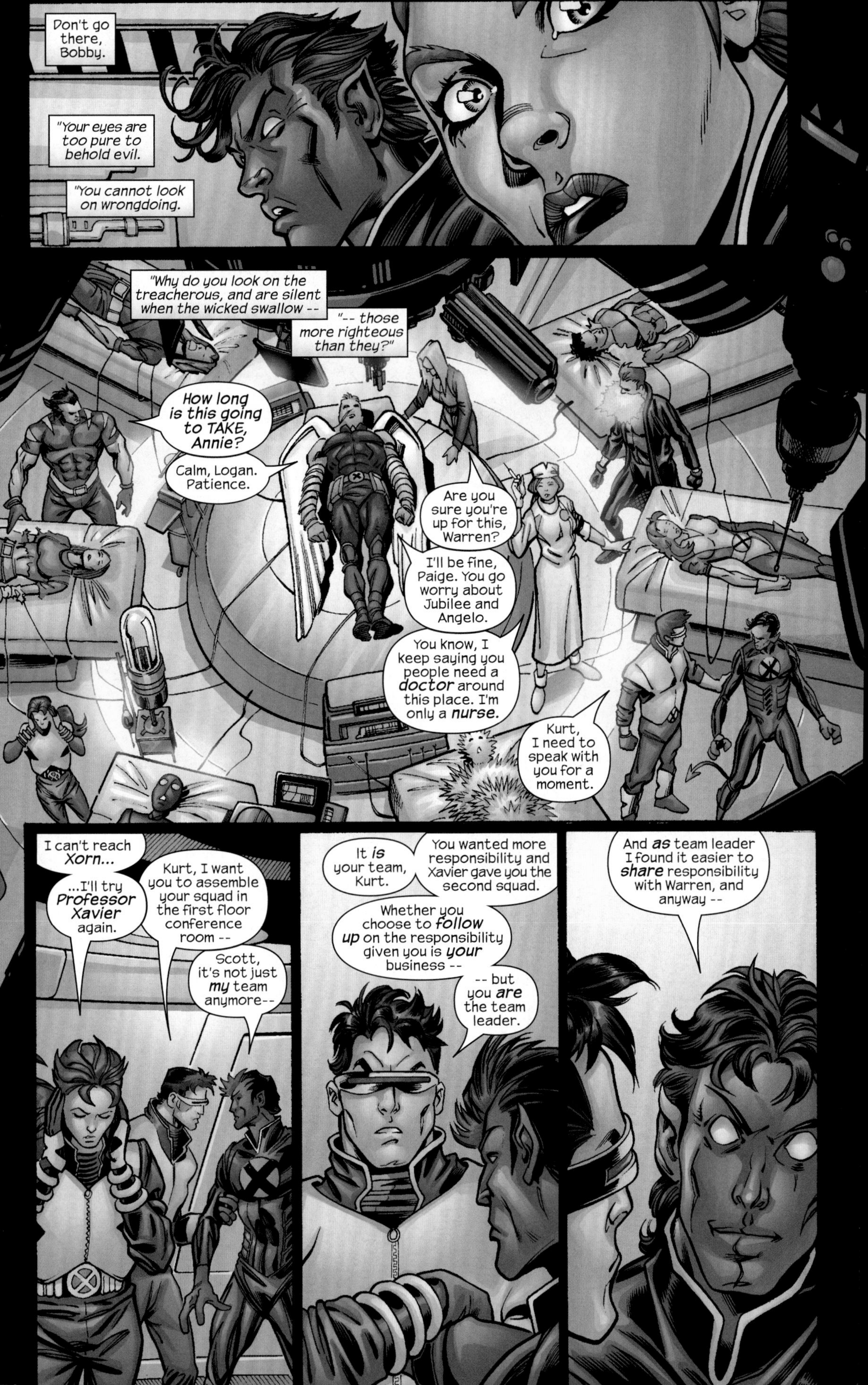

Don't go there, Bobby.
"Your eyes are too pure to behold evil.
"You cannot look on wrongdoing.
"Why do you look on the treacherous, and are silent when the wicked swallow --
"-- those more righteous than they?"
How long is this going to TAKE, Annie?
Calm, Logan. Patience.
Are you sure you're up for this, Warren?
I'll be fine, Paige. You go worry about Jubilee and Angelo.
You know, I keep saying you people need a doctor around this place. I'm only a nurse.
Kurt, I need to speak with you for a moment.
I can't reach Xorn...
...I'll try Professor Xavier again.
Kurt, I want you to assemble your squad in the first floor conference room --
Scott, it's not just my team anymore--
It is your team, Kurt.
You wanted more responsibility and Xavier gave you the second squad.
Whether you choose to follow up on the responsibility given you is your business --
-- but you are the team leader.
And as team leader I found it easier to share responsibility with Warren, and anyway --

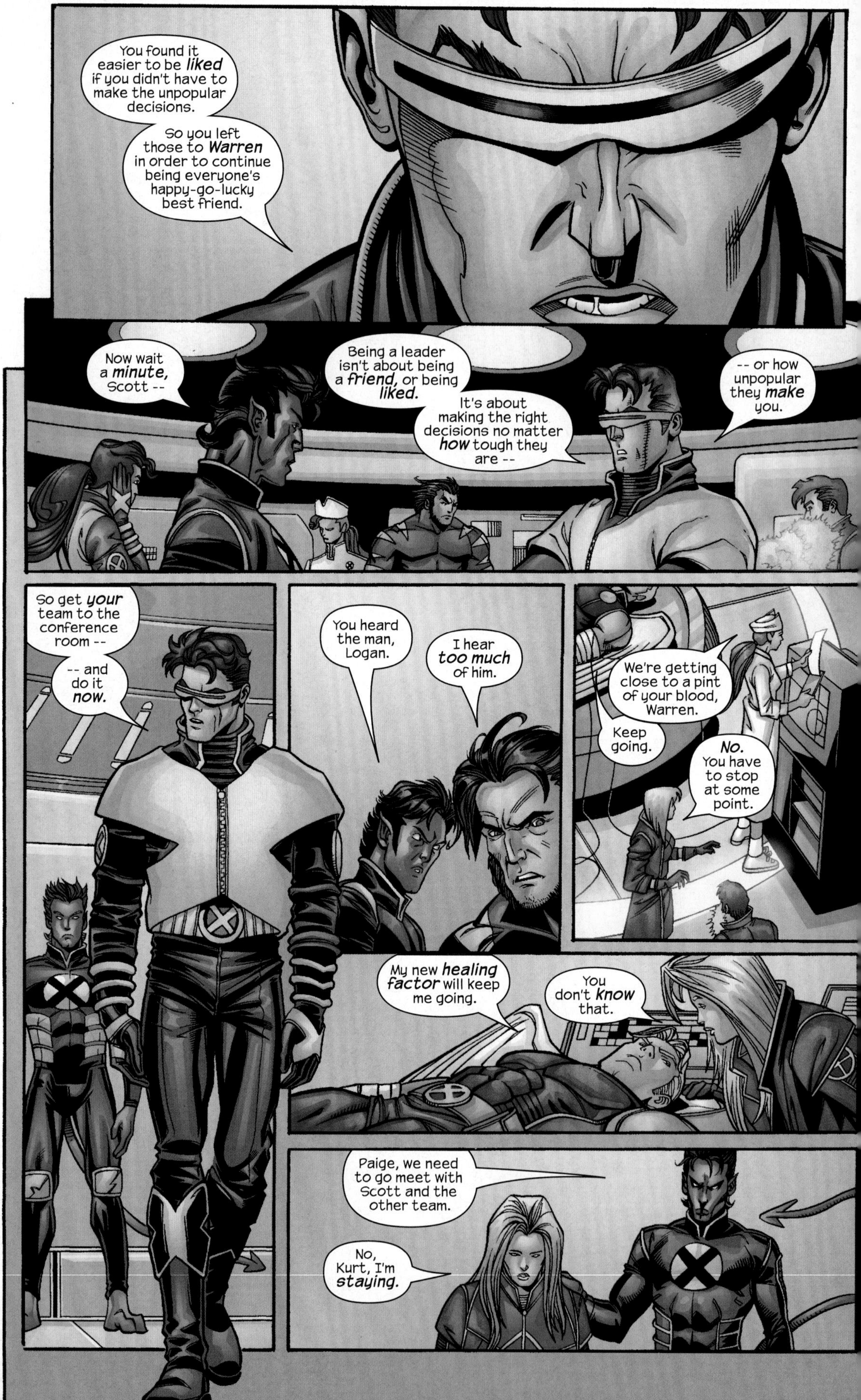
You found it easier to be liked if you didn't have to make the unpopular decisions.
So you left those to Warren in order to continue being everyone's happy-go-lucky best friend.
Now wait a minute, Scott --
Being a leader isn't about being a friend, or being liked.
It's about making the right decisions no matter how tough they are --
-- or how unpopular they make you.
So get your team to the conference room --
-- and do it now.
You heard the man, Logan.
I hear too much of him.
We're getting close to a pint of your blood, Warren.
Keep going.
No. You have to stop at some point.
My new healing factor will keep me going.
You don't know that.
Paige, we need to go meet with Scott and the other team.
No, Kurt, I'm staying.

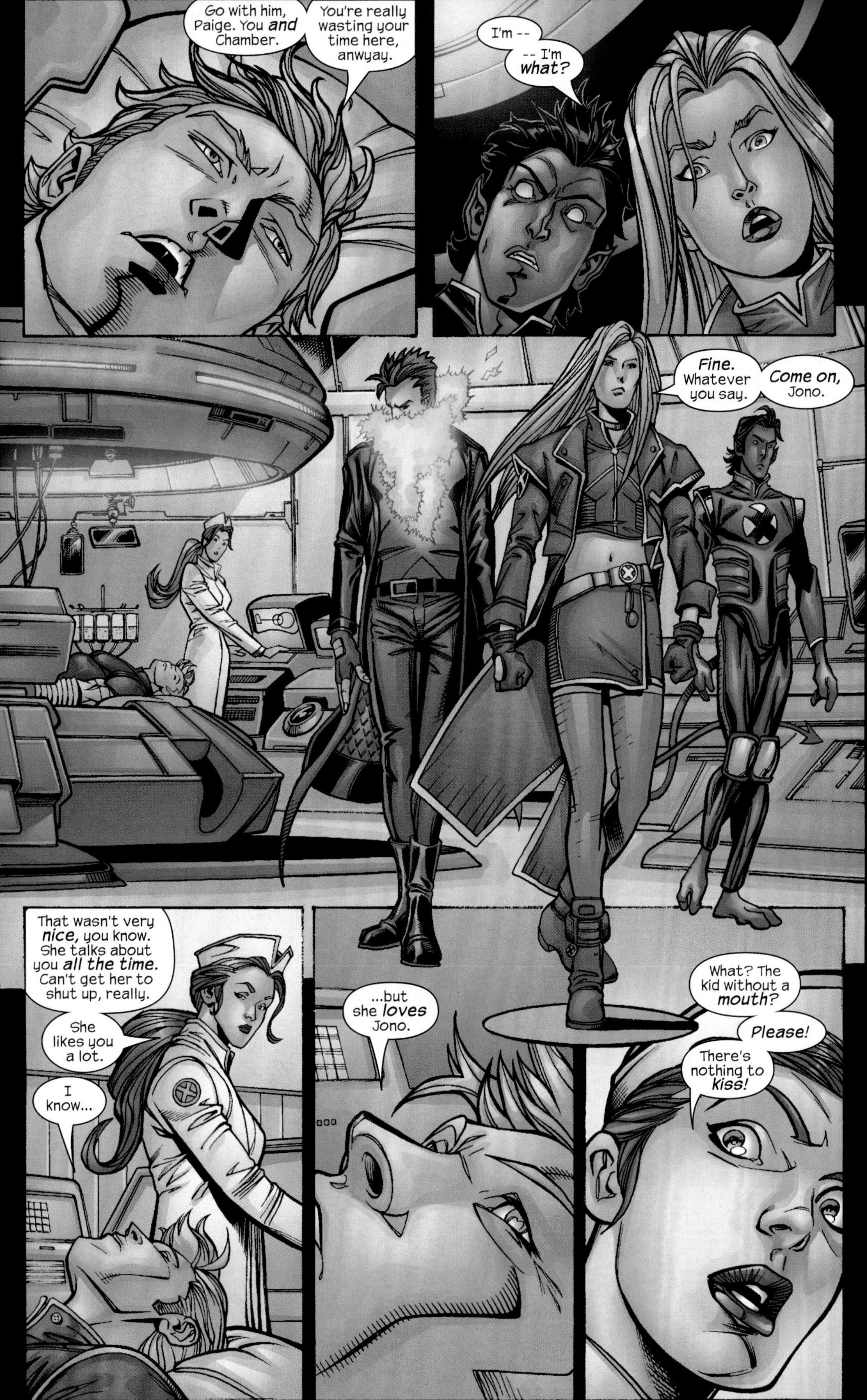

Go with him, Paige. You *and* Chamber.
You're really wasting your time here, anwyay.
I'm --
-- I'm *what?*
Fine. Whatever you say.
Come on, Jono.
That wasn't very *nice,* you know. She talks about you *all the time.* Can't get her to shut up, really.
She likes you a lot.
I know...
...but she *loves* Jono.
What? The kid without a *mouth?*
Please!
There's nothing to *kiss!*

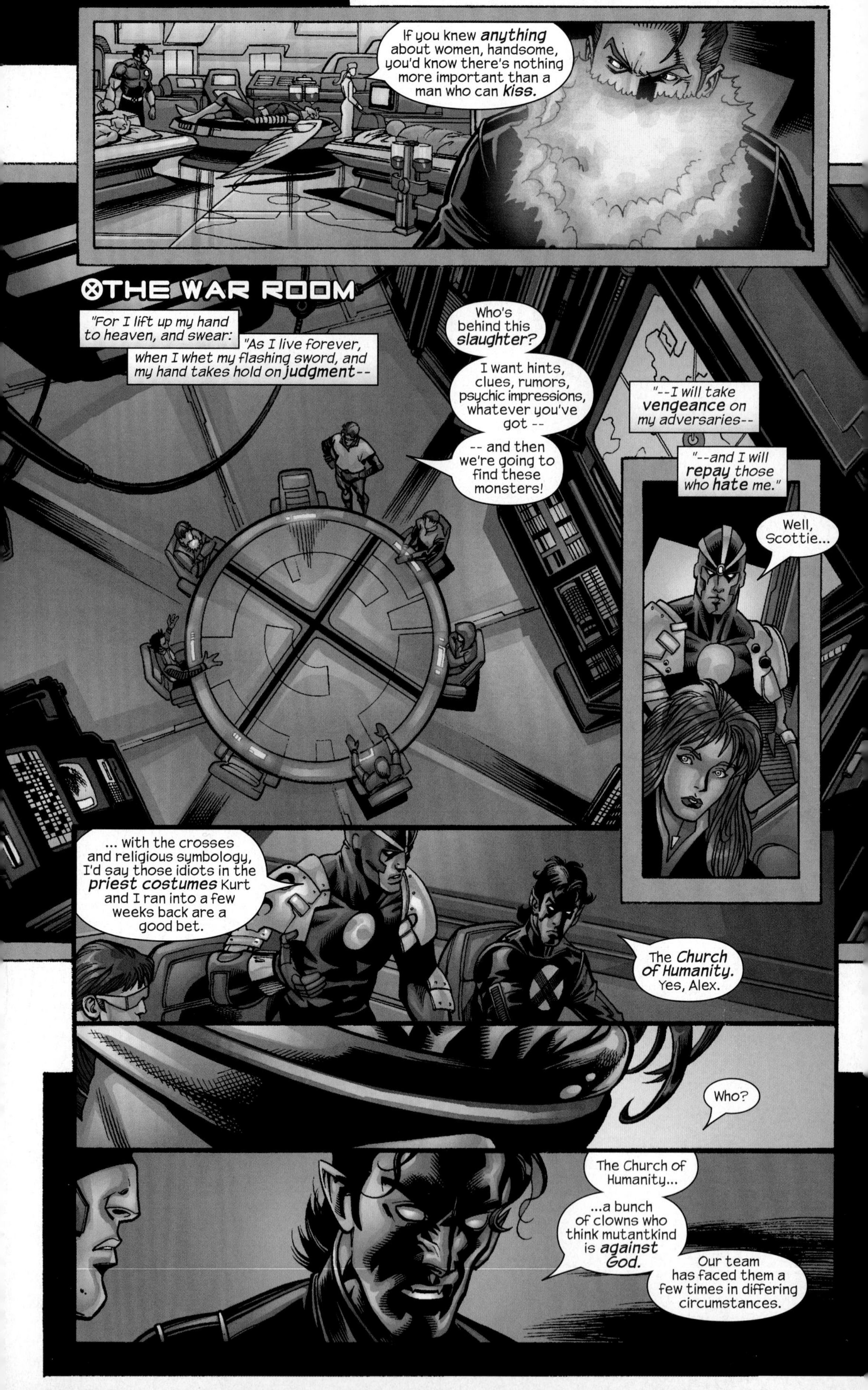
If you knew anything about women, handsome, you'd know there's nothing more important than a man who can kiss.
THE WAR ROOM
"For I lift up my hand to heaven, and swear:
"As I live forever, when I whet my flashing sword, and my hand takes hold on judgment--
Who's behind this slaughter?
I want hints, clues, rumors, psychic impressions, whatever you've got --
-- and then we're going to find these monsters!
"--I will take vengeance on my adversaries--
"--and I will repay those who hate me."
Well, Scottie...
... with the crosses and religious symbology, I'd say those idiots in the priest costumes Kurt and I ran into a few weeks back are a good bet.
The Church of Humanity. Yes, Alex.
Who?
The Church of Humanity...
...a bunch of clowns who think mutantkind is against God.
Our team has faced them a few times in differing circumstances.

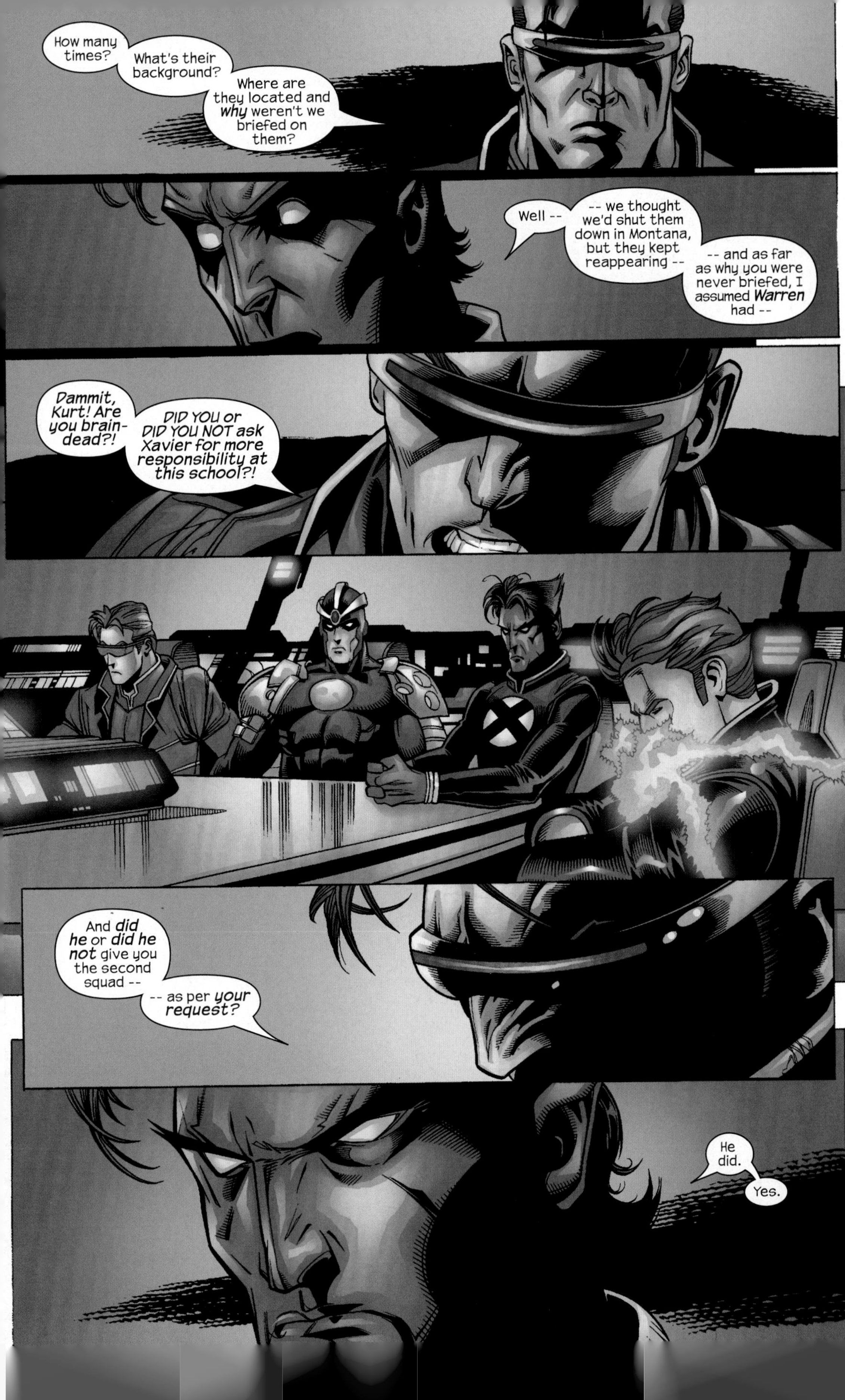
How many times?
What's their background?
Where are they located and *why* weren't we briefed on them?
Well --
-- we thought we'd shut them down in Montana, but they kept reappearing --
-- and as far as why you were never briefed, I assumed *Warren* had --
Dammit, Kurt! Are you brain-dead?!
DID YOU or DID YOU NOT ask Xavier for more responsibility at this school?!
And ***did he*** or ***did he not*** give you the second squad --
-- as per ***your request?***
He did.
Yes.

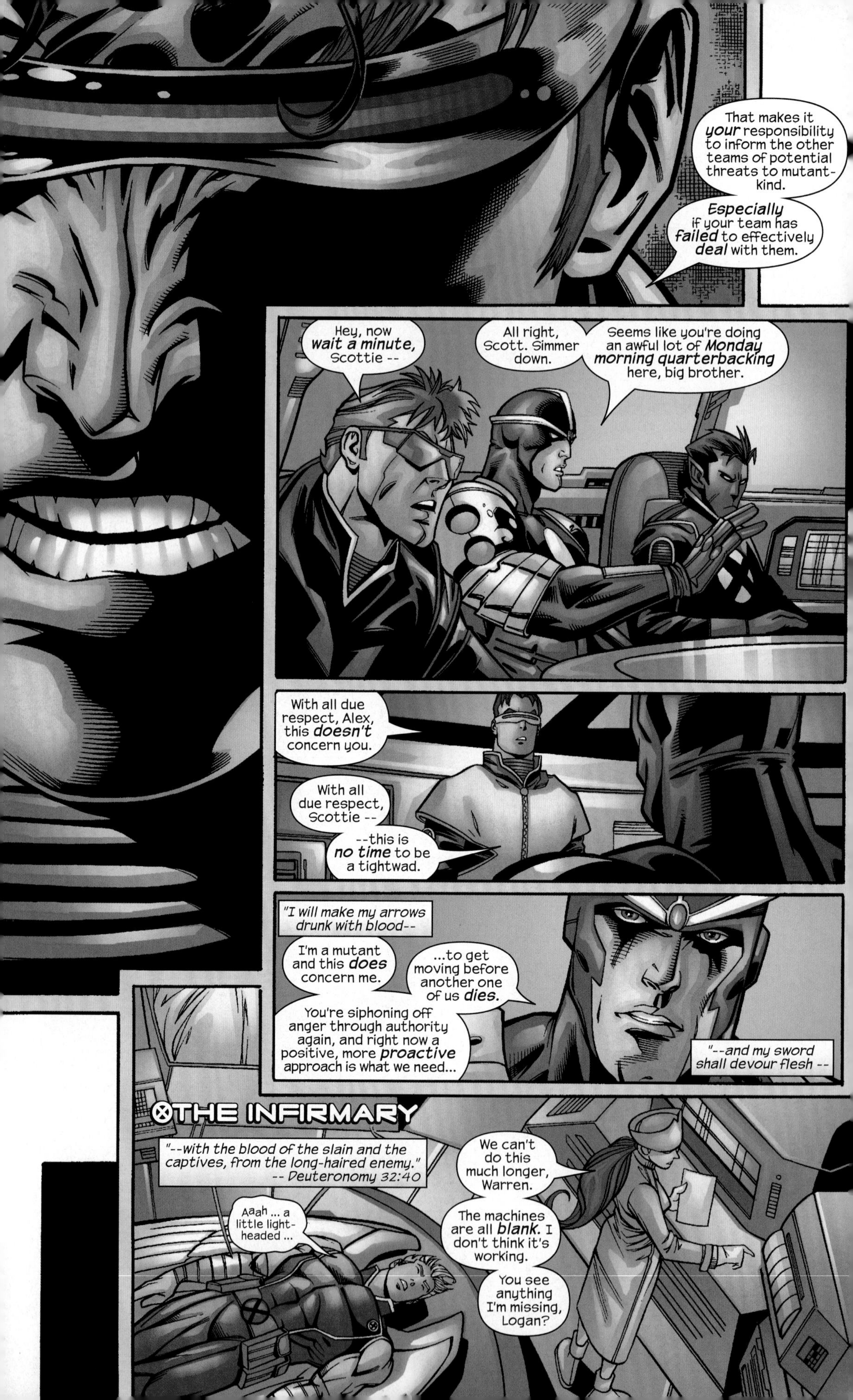

That makes it your responsibility to inform the other teams of potential threats to mutant-kind.
Especially if your team has failed to effectively deal with them.
Hey, now wait a minute, Scottie --
All right, Scott. Simmer down.
Seems like you're doing an awful lot of Monday morning quarterbacking here, big brother.
With all due respect, Alex, this doesn't concern you.
With all due respect, Scottie --
--this is no time to be a tightwad.
"I will make my arrows drunk with blood--
I'm a mutant and this does concern me.
...to get moving before another one of us dies.
You're siphoning off anger through authority again, and right now a positive, more proactive approach is what we need...
"--and my sword shall devour flesh --
THE INFIRMARY
"--with the blood of the slain and the captives, from the long-haired enemy." -- Deuteronomy 32:40
We can't do this much longer, Warren.
Aaah ... a little light-headed ...
The machines are all blank. I don't think it's working.
You see anything I'm missing, Logan?

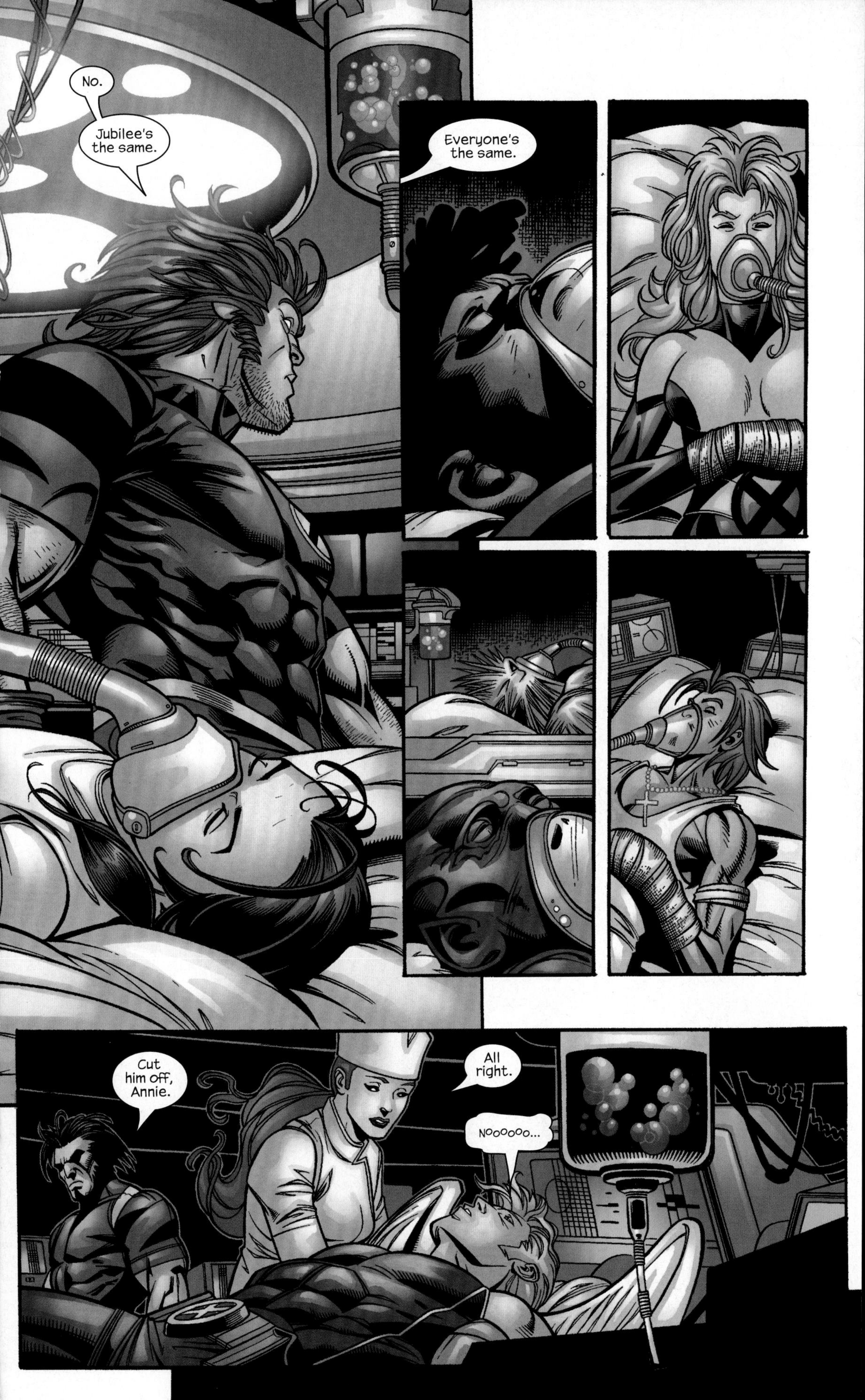
No.
Jubilee's the same.
Everyone's the same.
Cut him off, Annie.
All right.
Nooooooo...

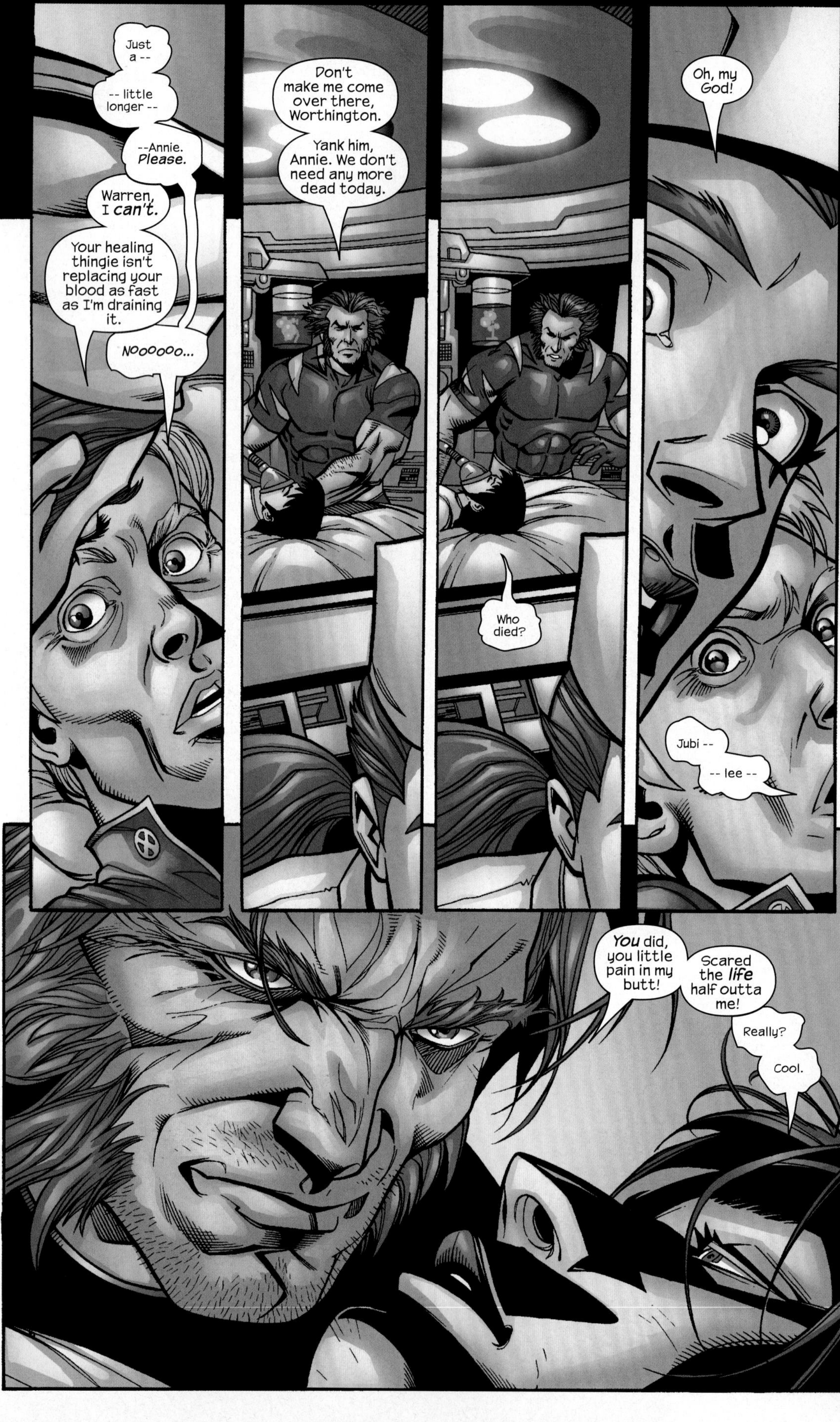
Just a --
-- little longer --
--Annie. Please.
Warren, I can't.
Your healing thingie isn't replacing your blood as fast as I'm draining it.
Noooooo...
Don't make me come over there, Worthington.
Yank him, Annie. We don't need any more dead today.
Who died?
Oh, my God!
Jubi --
-- lee --
You did, you little pain in my butt!
Scared the life half outta me!
Really?
Cool.

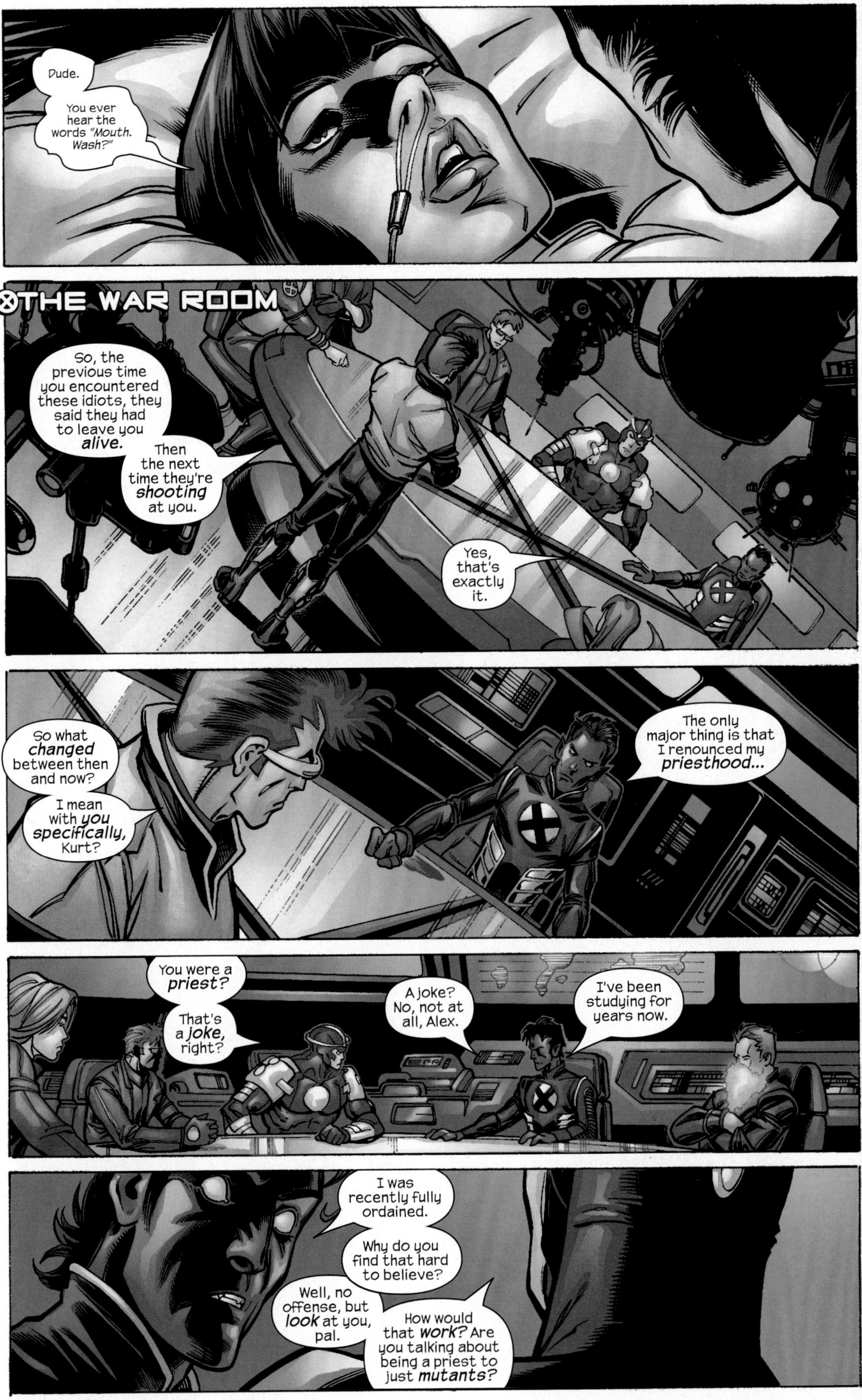
Dude.
You ever hear the words "Mouth. Wash?"
THE WAR ROOM
So, the previous time you encountered these idiots, they said they had to leave you alive.
Then the next time they're shooting at you.
Yes, that's exactly it.
So what changed between then and now?
I mean with you specifically, Kurt?
The only major thing is that I renounced my priesthood...
You were a priest?
That's a joke, right?
A joke? No, not at all, Alex.
I've been studying for years now.
I was recently fully ordained.
Why do you find that hard to believe?
Well, no offense, but look at you, pal.
How would that work? Are you talking about being a priest to just mutants?

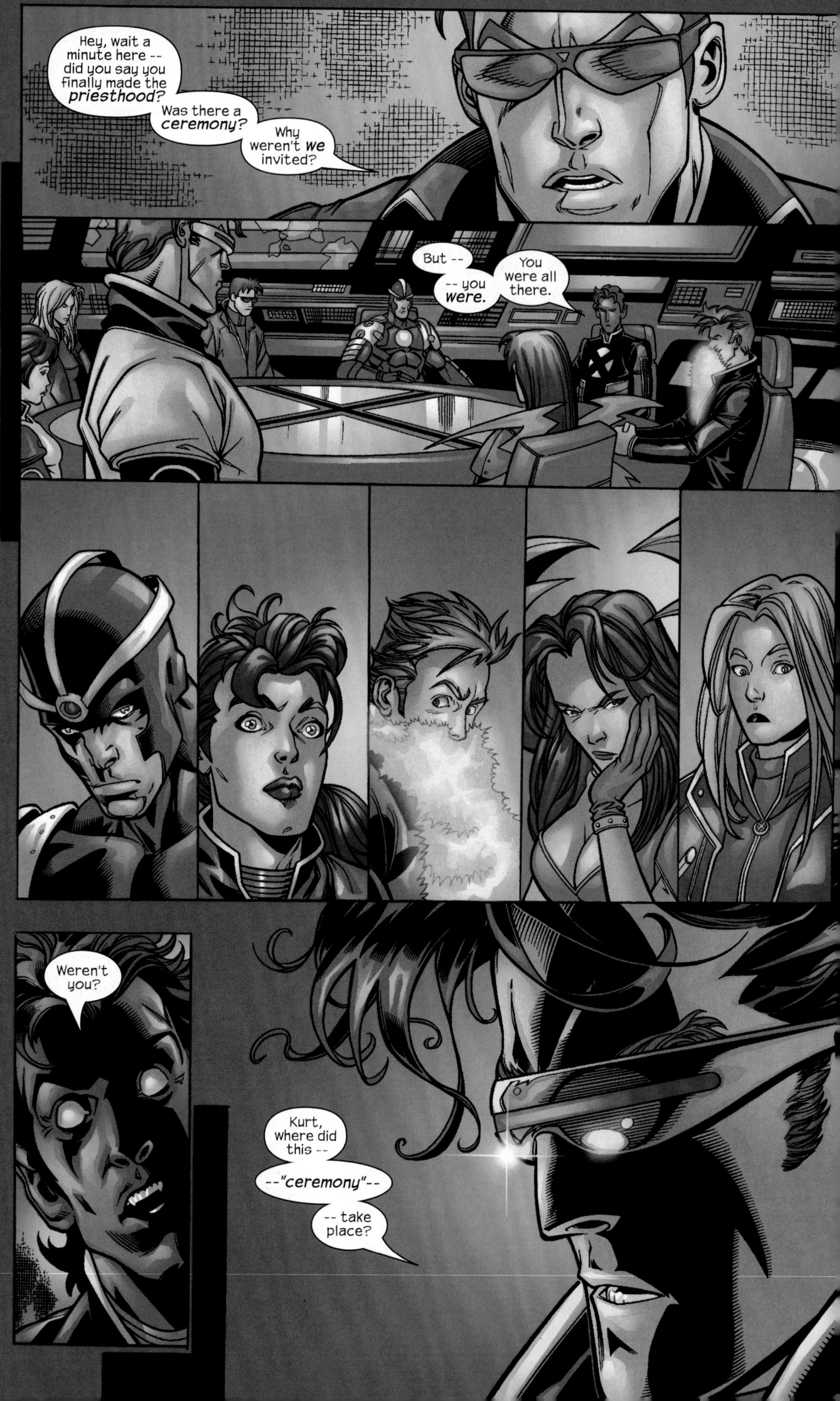
Hey, wait a minute here -- did you say you finally made the priesthood?
Was there a ceremony?
Why weren't we invited?
But --
-- you were.
You were all there.
Weren't you?
Kurt, where did this --
--"ceremony"--
-- take place?

Take it easy, Magma.

Drink this, and don't sit up too fast.

Logan, we need you!

JUBES!

OH MY GOD, YOU'RE ALIVE!

Trust that old Guthrie enthusiasm.

Hey, what's the matter?

Why are you--?

Oh no.

Oh, Angelo...

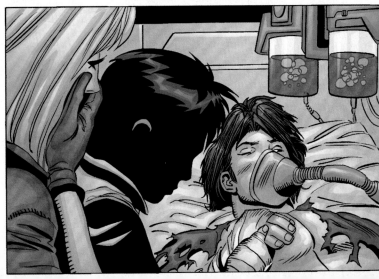

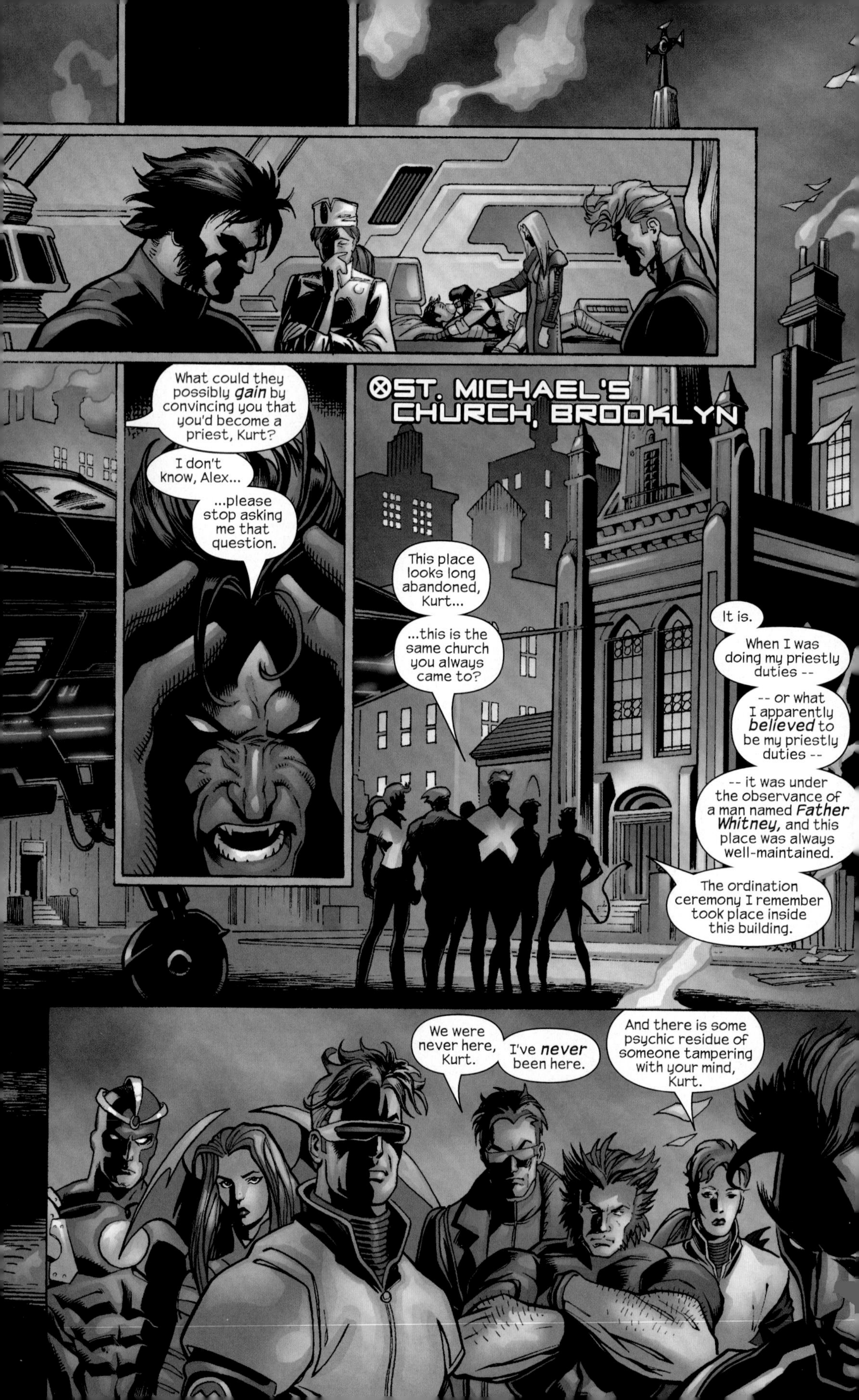
What could they possibly gain by convincing you that you'd become a priest, Kurt?
I don't know, Alex...
...please stop asking me that question.
ST. MICHAEL'S CHURCH, BROOKLYN
This place looks long abandoned, Kurt...
...this is the same church you always came to?
It is.
When I was doing my priestly duties --
-- or what I apparently believed to be my priestly duties --
-- it was under the observance of a man named Father Whitney, and this place was always well-maintained.
The ordination ceremony I remember took place inside this building.
We were never here, Kurt.
I've never been here.
And there is some psychic residue of someone tampering with your mind, Kurt.

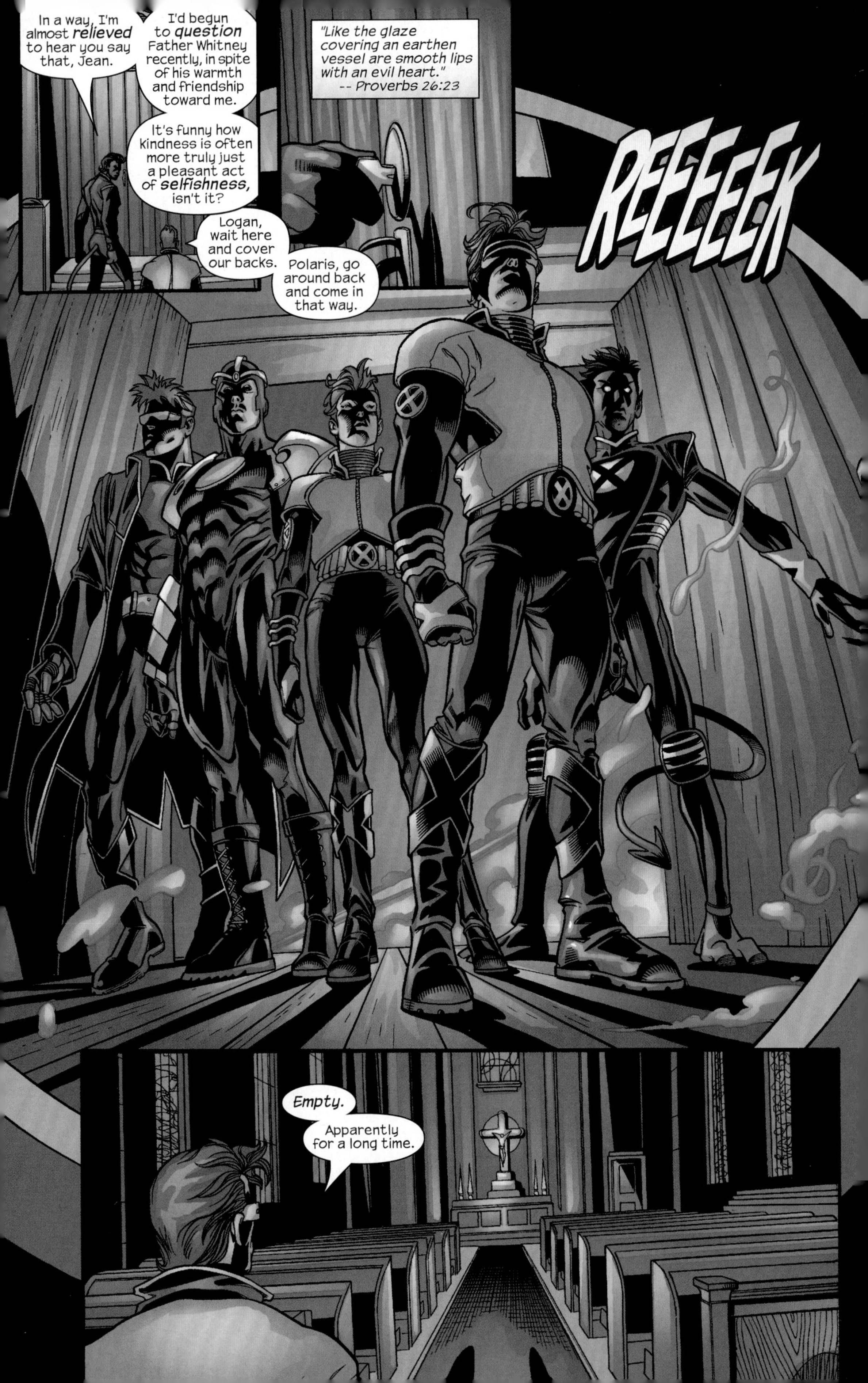
In a way, I'm almost **relieved** to hear you say that, Jean.
I'd begun to **question** Father Whitney recently, in spite of his warmth and friendship toward me.
It's funny how kindness is often more truly just a pleasant act of **selfishness**, isn't it?
"Like the glaze covering an earthen vessel are smooth lips with an evil heart." -- Proverbs 26:23
REEEEEK
Logan, wait here and cover our backs.
Polaris, go around back and come in that way.
Empty.
Apparently for a long time.

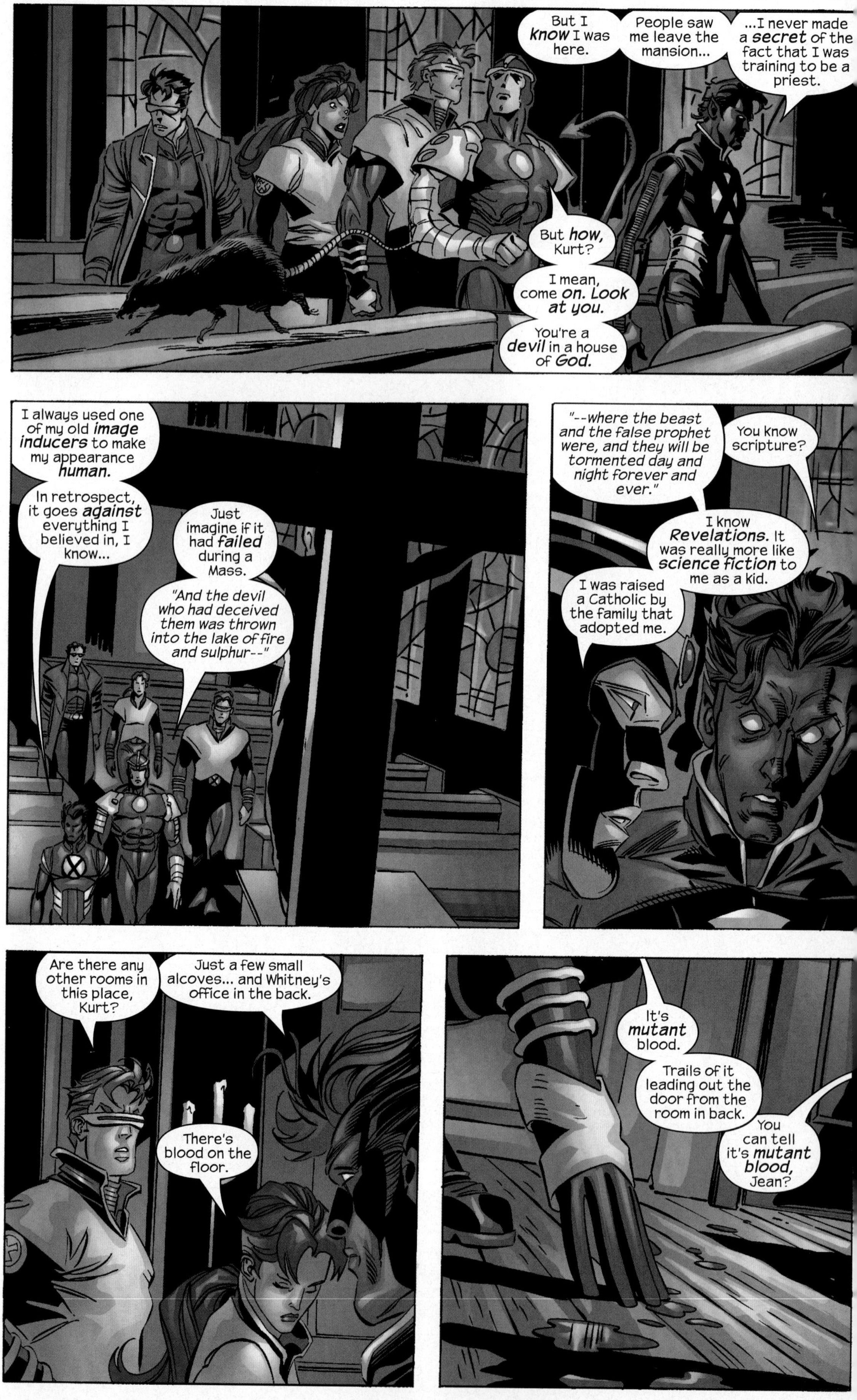

But I know I was here.
People saw me leave the mansion...
...I never made a secret of the fact that I was training to be a priest.
But how, Kurt?
I mean, come on. Look at you.
You're a devil in a house of God.
I always used one of my old image inducers to make my appearance human.
In retrospect, it goes against everything I believed in, I know...
Just imagine if it had failed during a Mass.
"And the devil who had deceived them was thrown into the lake of fire and sulphur--"
"--where the beast and the false prophet were, and they will be tormented day and night forever and ever."
You know scripture?
I know Revelations. It was really more like science fiction to me as a kid.
I was raised a Catholic by the family that adopted me.
Are there any other rooms in this place, Kurt?
Just a few small alcoves... and Whitney's office in the back.
There's blood on the floor.
It's mutant blood.
Trails of it leading out the door from the room in back.
You can tell it's mutant blood, Jean?

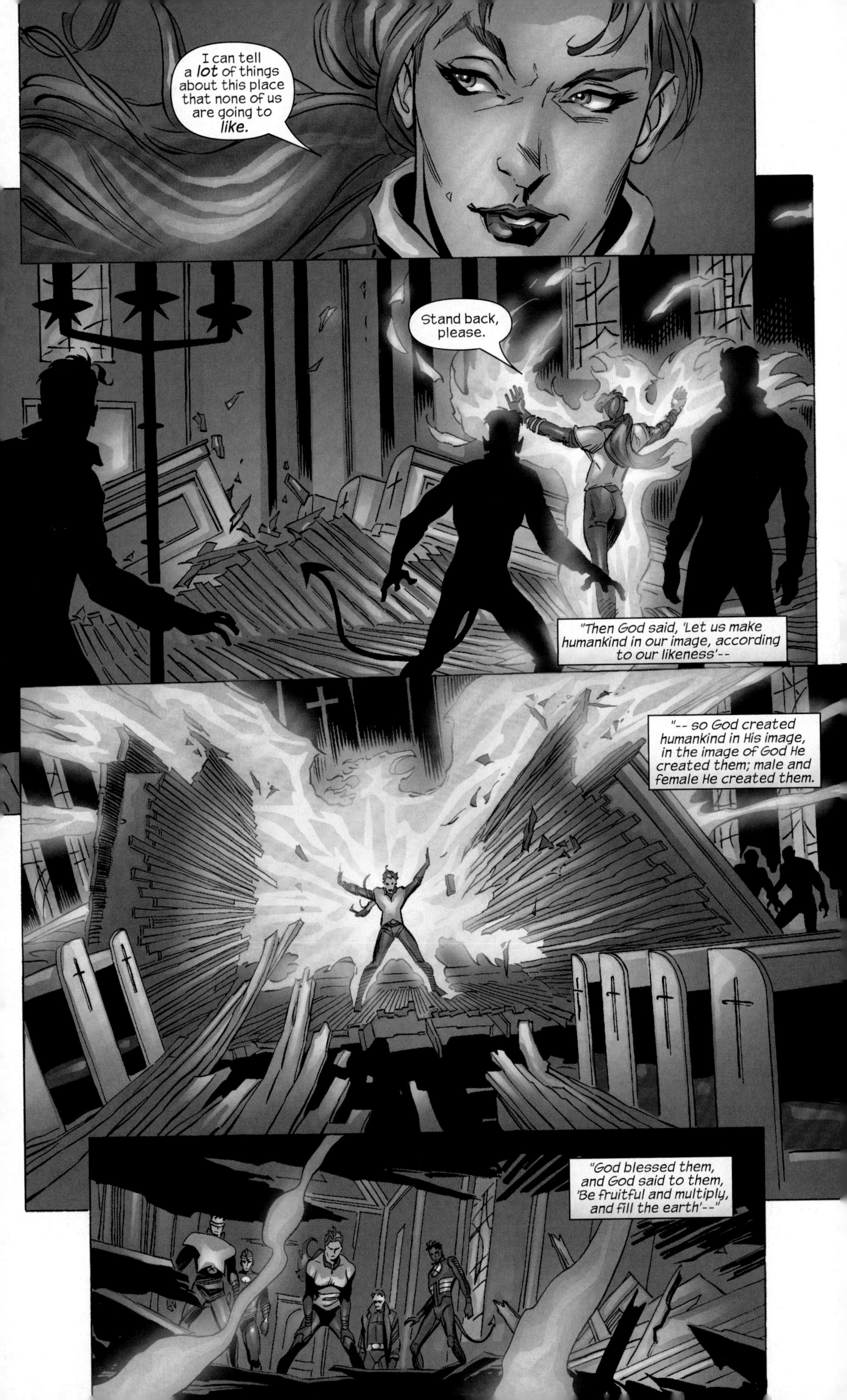

I can tell a *lot* of things about this place that none of us are going to *like.*
Stand back, please.
"Then God said, 'Let us make humankind in our image, according to our likeness'--
"-- so God created humankind in His image, in the image of God He created them; male and female He created them.
"God blessed them, and God said to them, 'Be fruitful and multiply, and fill the earth'--"

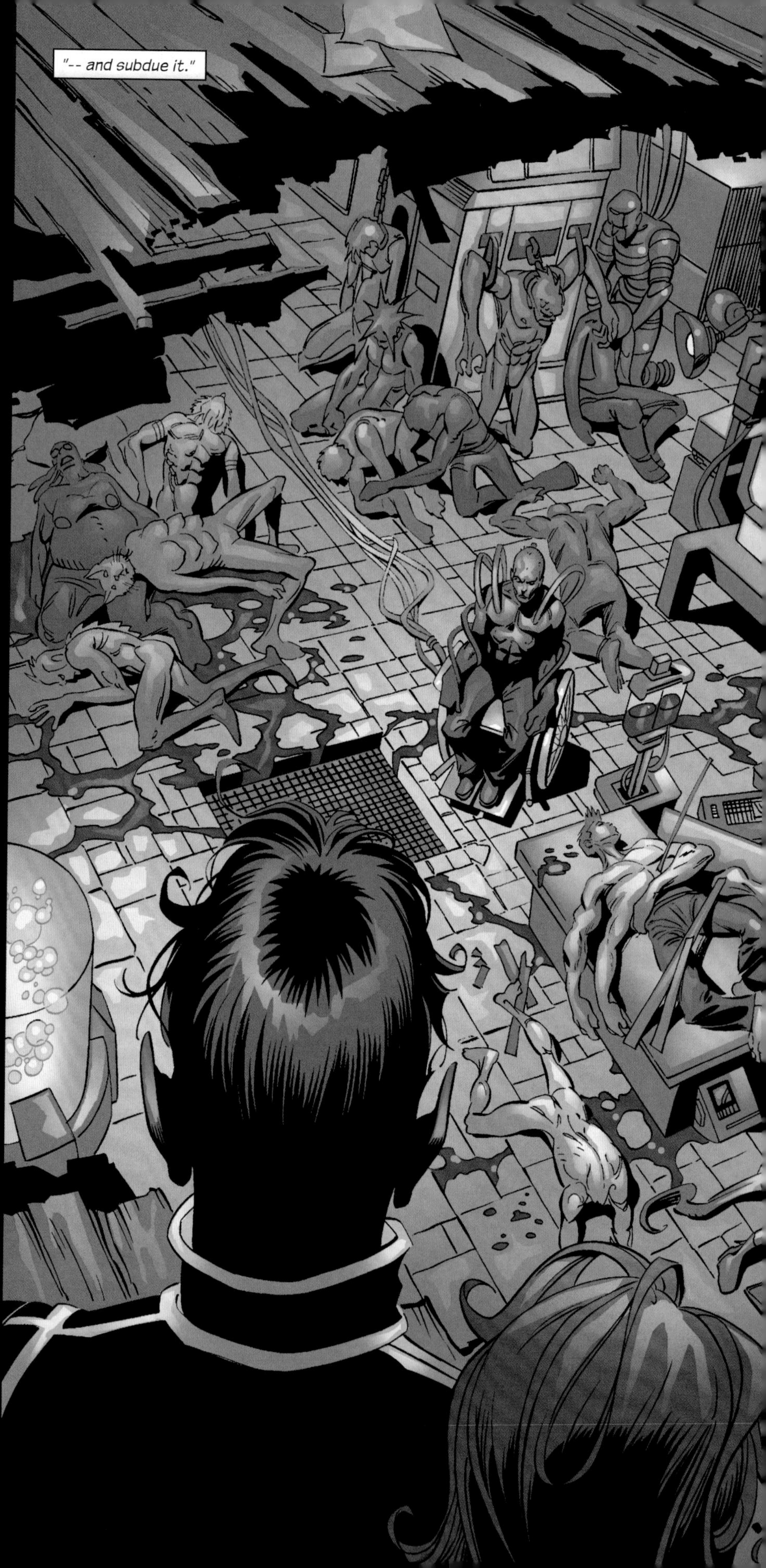
"-- and subdue it."

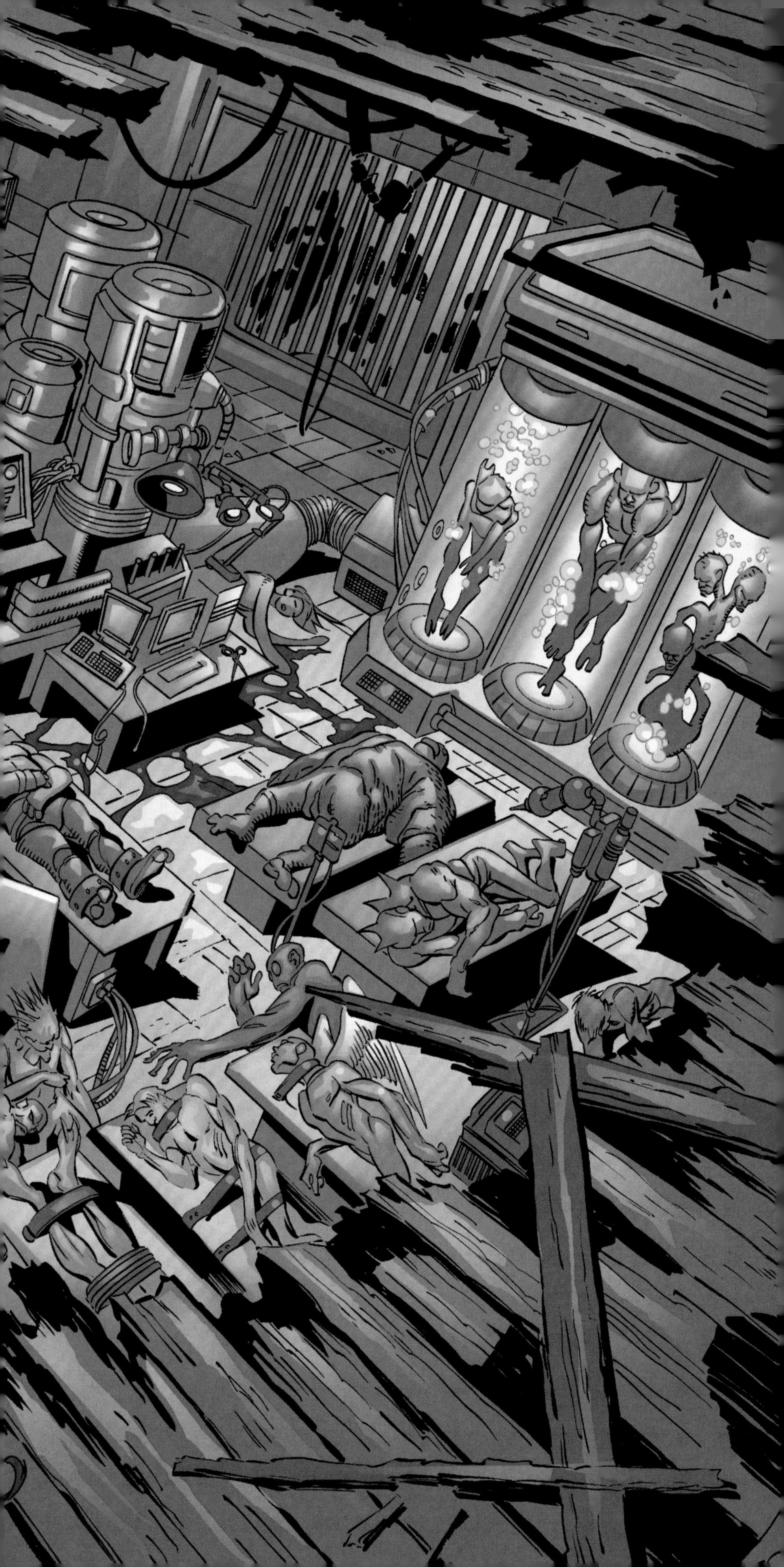

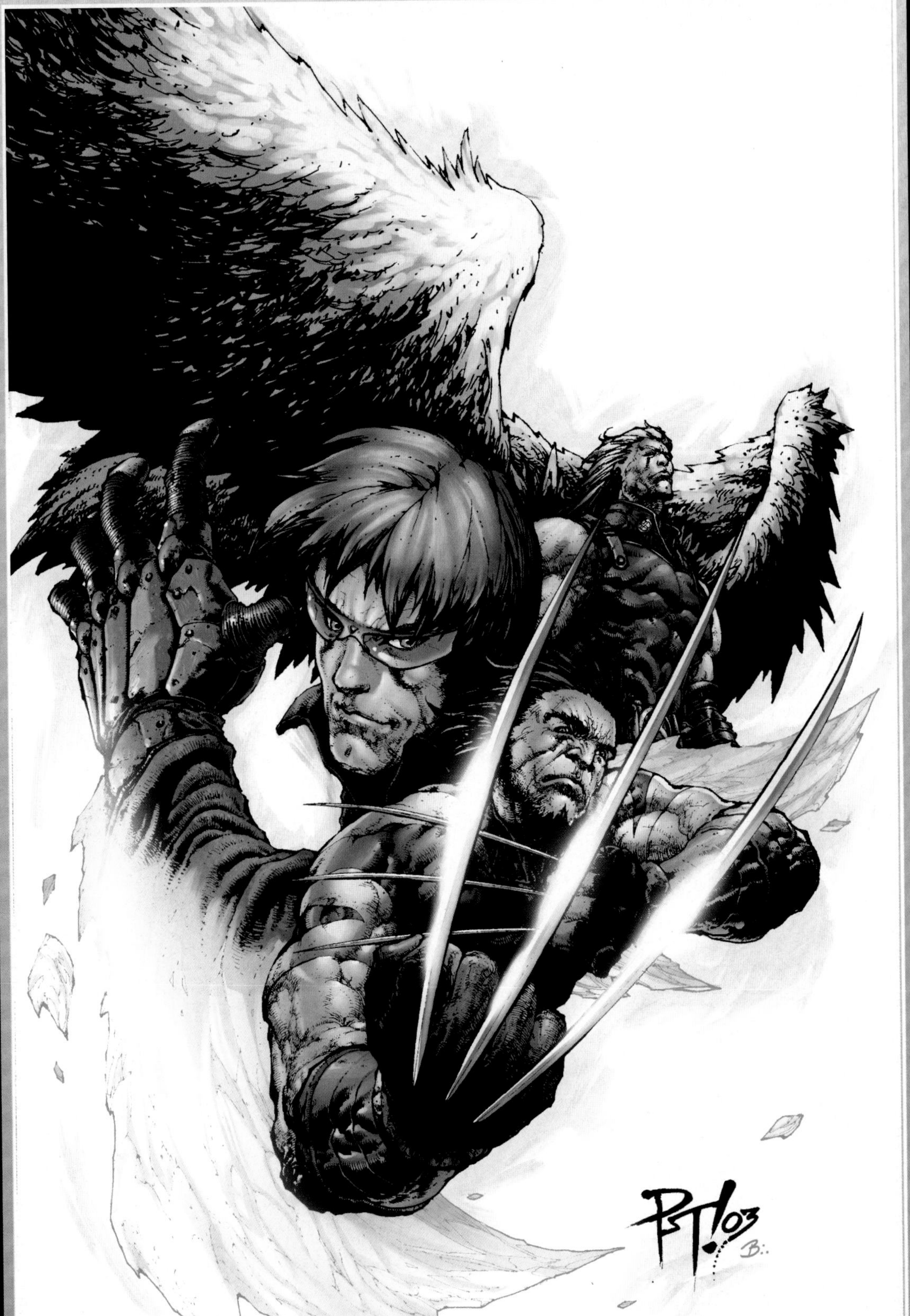
BT!03
B:.

HOLY WAR, PART 2 OF 2

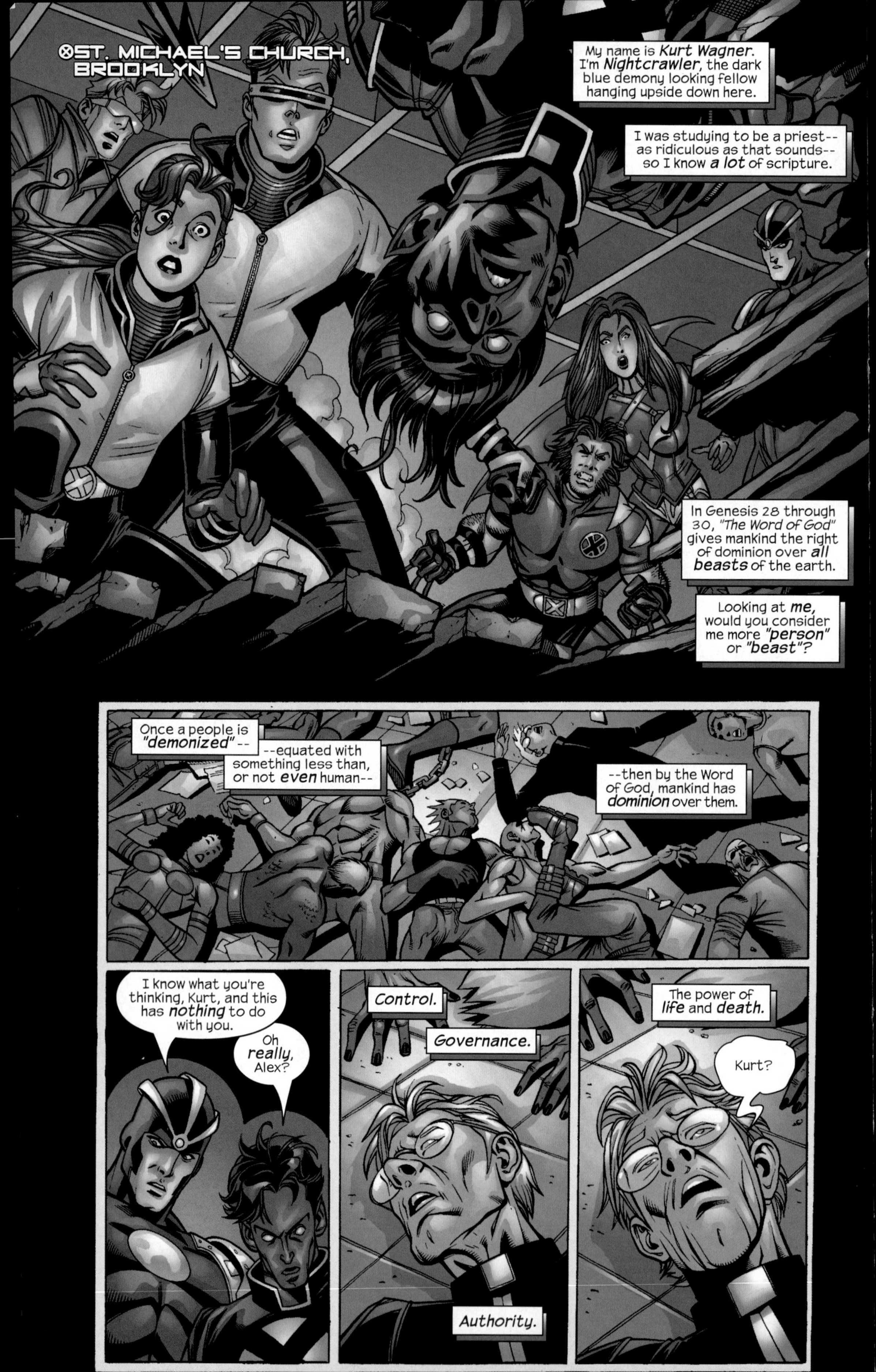

ST. MICHAEL'S CHURCH, BROOKLYN
My name is Kurt Wagner. I'm Nightcrawler, the dark blue demony looking fellow hanging upside down here.
I was studying to be a priest--as ridiculous as that sounds--so I know a lot of scripture.
In Genesis 28 through 30, "The Word of God" gives mankind the right of dominion over all beasts of the earth.
Looking at me, would you consider me more "person" or "beast"?
Once a people is "demonized" --
--equated with something less than, or not even human--
--then by the Word of God, mankind has dominion over them.
I know what you're thinking, Kurt, and this has nothing to do with you.
Oh really, Alex?
Control.
Governance.
Authority.
The power of life and death.
Kurt?

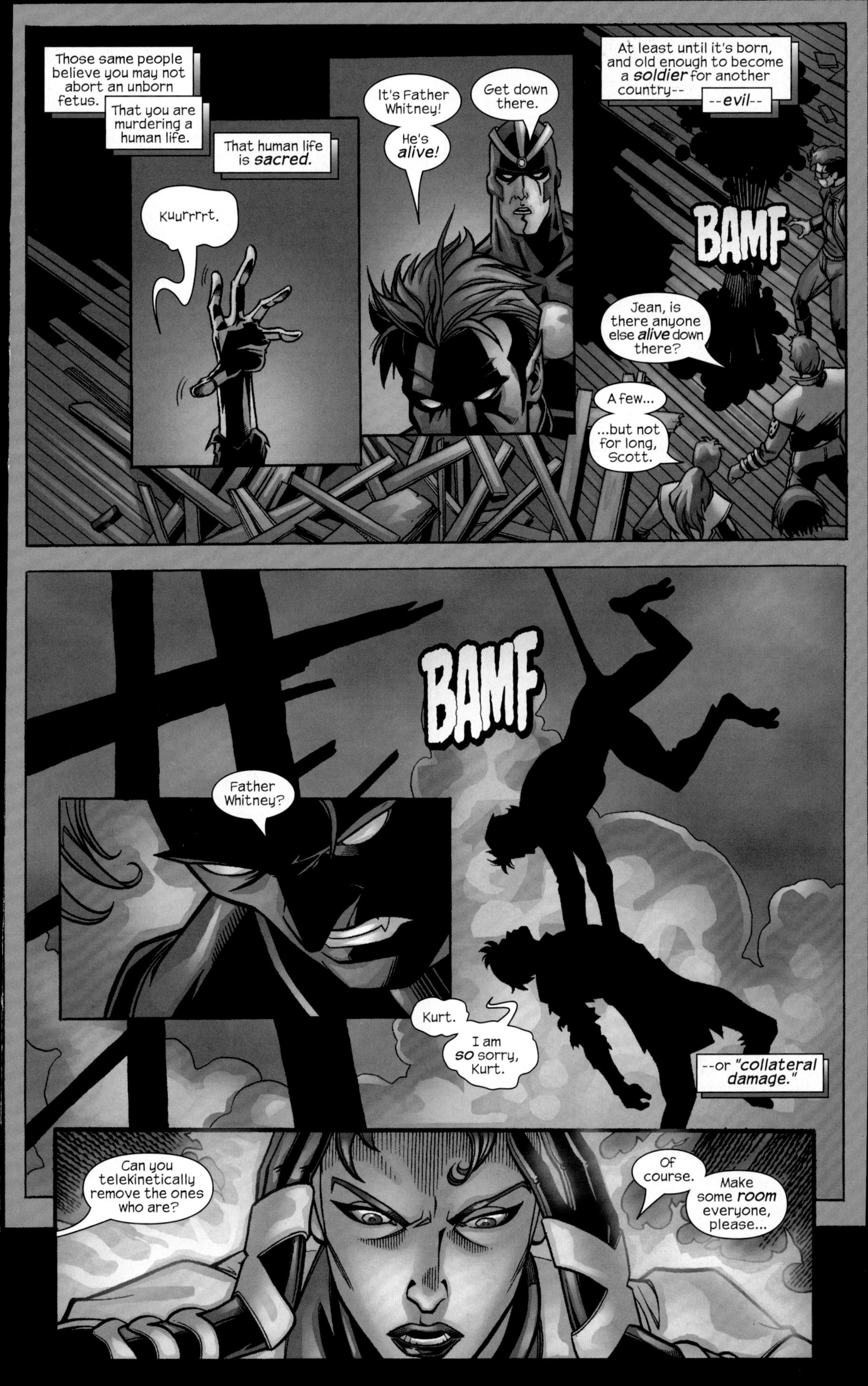
Those same people believe you may not abort an unborn fetus.
That you are murdering a human life.
That human life is *sacred.*
Kuurrrrt.
It's Father Whitney!
He's *alive!*
Get down there.
At least until it's born, and old enough to become a *soldier* for another country--
--*evil*--
BAMF
Jean, is there anyone else *alive* down there?
A few...
...but not for long, Scott.
BAMF
Father Whitney?
Kurt.
I am *so* sorry, Kurt.
--or *"collateral damage."*
Can you telekinetically remove the ones who are?
Of course.
Make some *room* everyone, please...

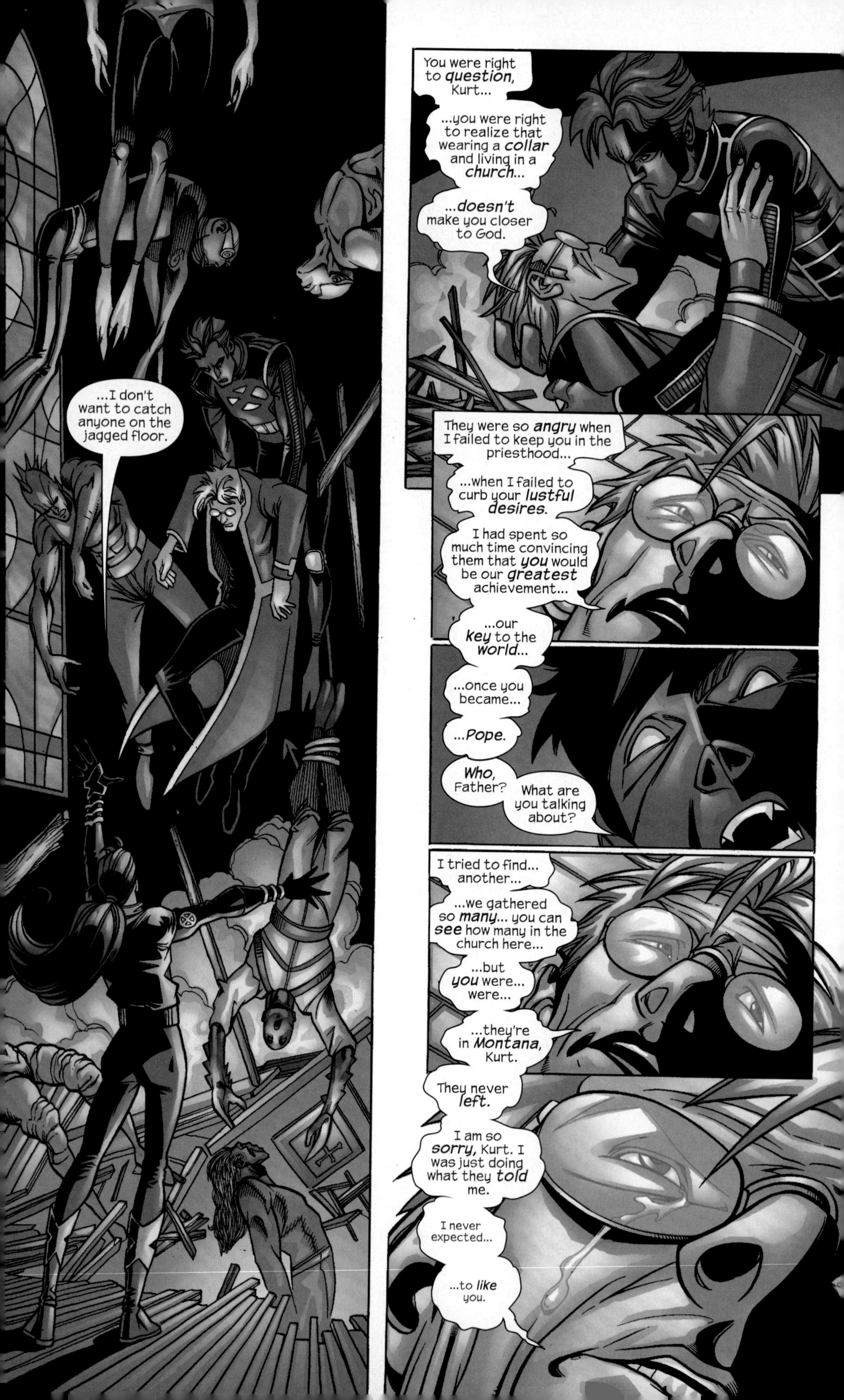

...I don't want to catch anyone on the jagged floor.
You were right to question, Kurt...
...you were right to realize that wearing a collar and living in a church...
...doesn't make you closer to God.
They were so angry when I failed to keep you in the priesthood...
...when I failed to curb your lustful desires.
I had spent so much time convincing them that you would be our greatest achievement...
...our key to the world...
...once you became...
...Pope.
Who, Father?
What are you talking about?
I tried to find... another...
...we gathered so many... you can see how many in the church here...
...but you were... were...
...they're in Montana, Kurt.
They never left.
I am so sorry, Kurt. I was just doing what they told me.
I never expected...
...to like you.

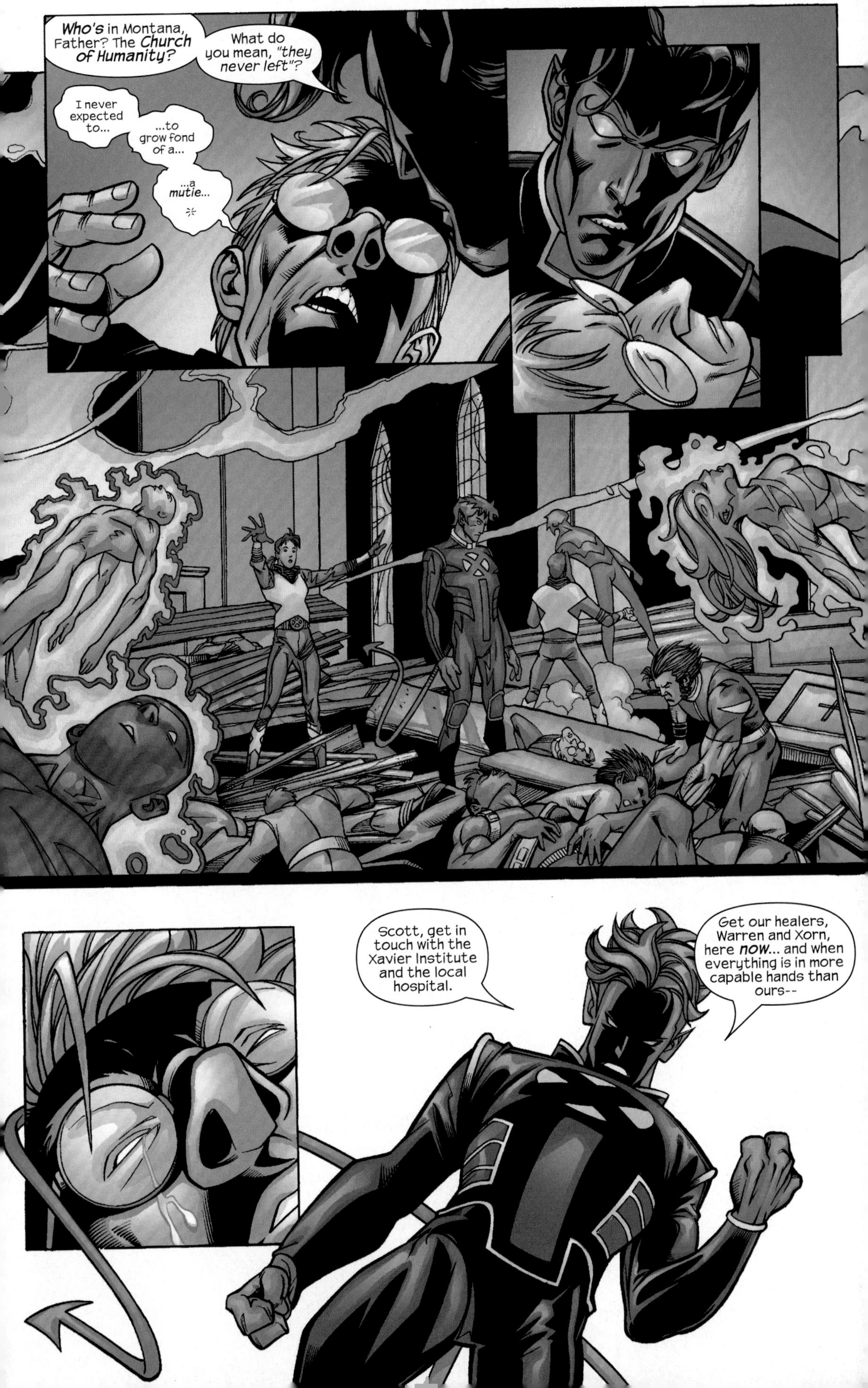

Who's in Montana, Father? The Church of Humanity?
What do you mean, "they never left"?
I never expected to...
...to grow fond of a...
...a mutie...
Scott, get in touch with the Xavier Institute and the local hospital.
Get our healers, Warren and Xorn, here NOW... and when everything is in more capable hands than ours--

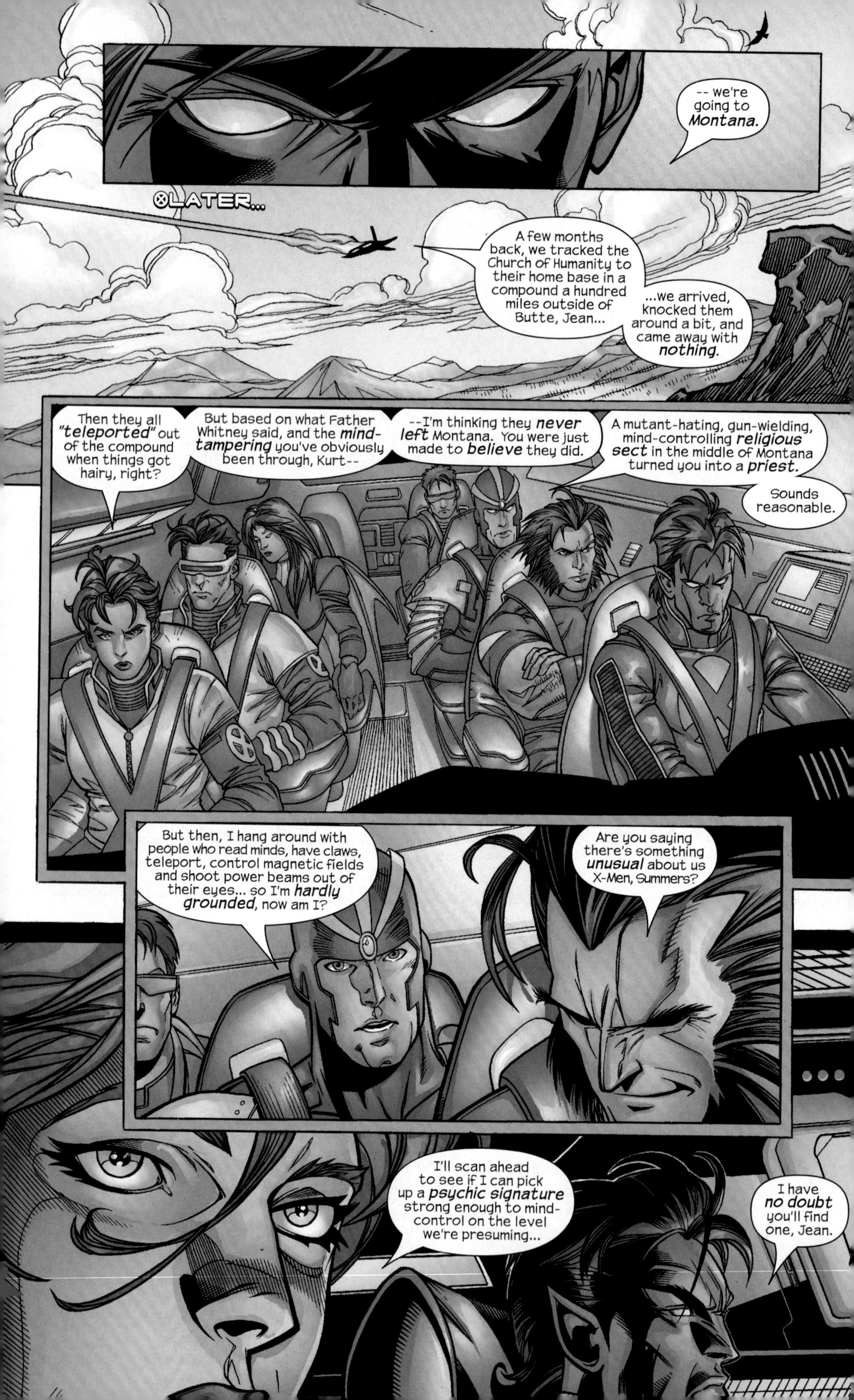
-- we're going to Montana.
LATER...
A few months back, we tracked the Church of Humanity to their home base in a compound a hundred miles outside of Butte, Jean...
...we arrived, knocked them around a bit, and came away with nothing.
Then they all "teleported" out of the compound when things got hairy, right?
But based on what Father Whitney said, and the mind-tampering you've obviously been through, Kurt--
--I'm thinking they never left Montana. You were just made to believe they did.
A mutant-hating, gun-wielding, mind-controlling religious sect in the middle of Montana turned you into a priest.
Sounds reasonable.
But then, I hang around with people who read minds, have claws, teleport, control magnetic fields and shoot power beams out of their eyes... so I'm hardly grounded, now am I?
Are you saying there's something unusual about us X-Men, Summers?
I'll scan ahead to see if I can pick up a psychic signature strong enough to mind-control on the level we're presuming...
I have no doubt you'll find one, Jean.

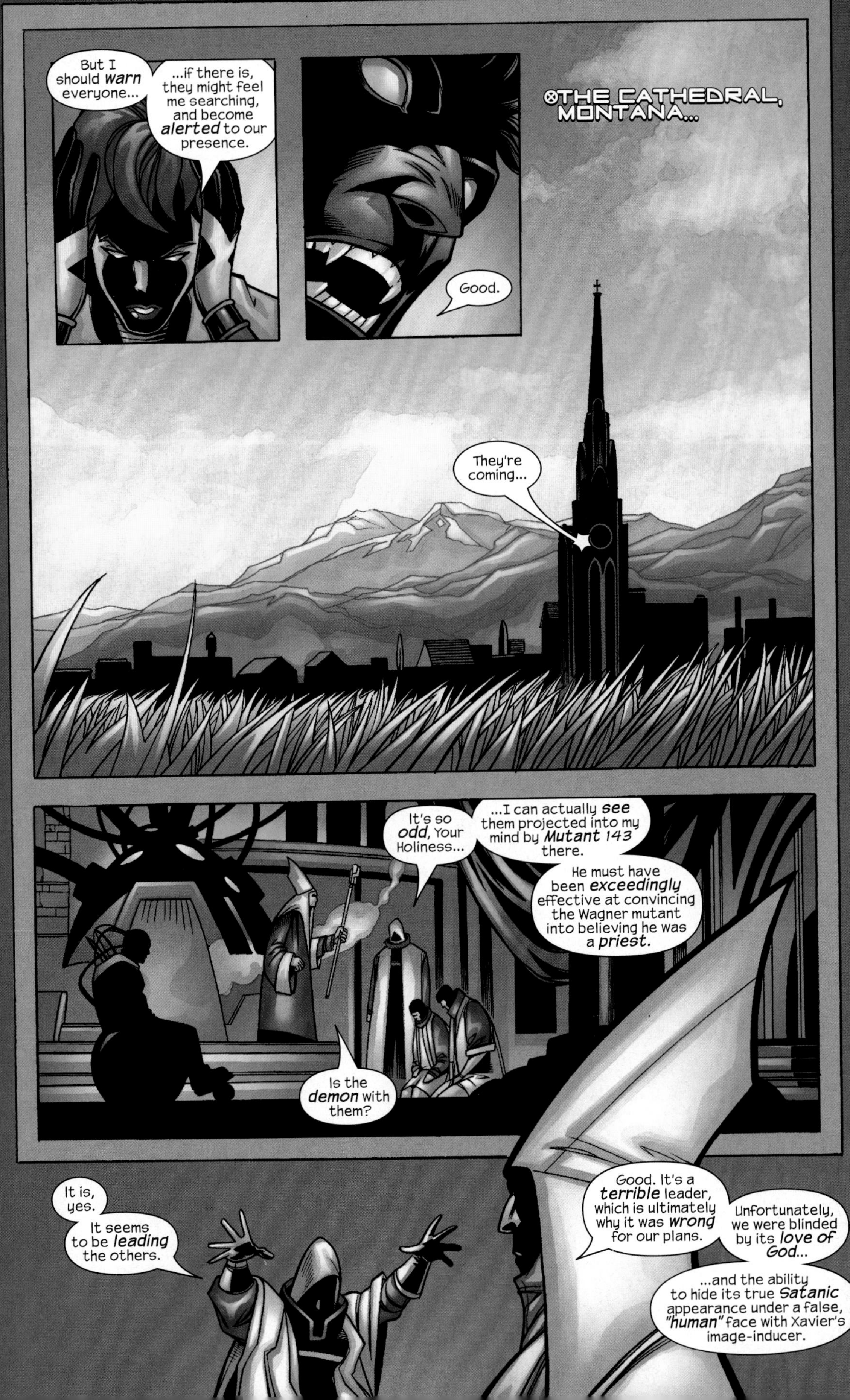

But I should *warn* everyone...
...if there is, they might feel me searching, and become *alerted* to our presence.
Good.
THE CATHEDRAL, MONTANA...
They're coming...
It's so *odd*, Your Holiness...
...I can actually *see* them projected into my mind by *Mutant 143* there.
He must have been *exceedingly* effective at convincing the Wagner mutant into believing he was a *priest.*
Is the *demon* with them?
It is, yes.
It seems to be *leading* the others.
Good. It's a *terrible* leader, which is ultimately why it was *wrong* for our plans.
Unfortunately, we were blinded by its *love of God*...
...and the ability to hide its true *Satanic* appearance under a false, *"human"* face with Xavier's image-inducer.

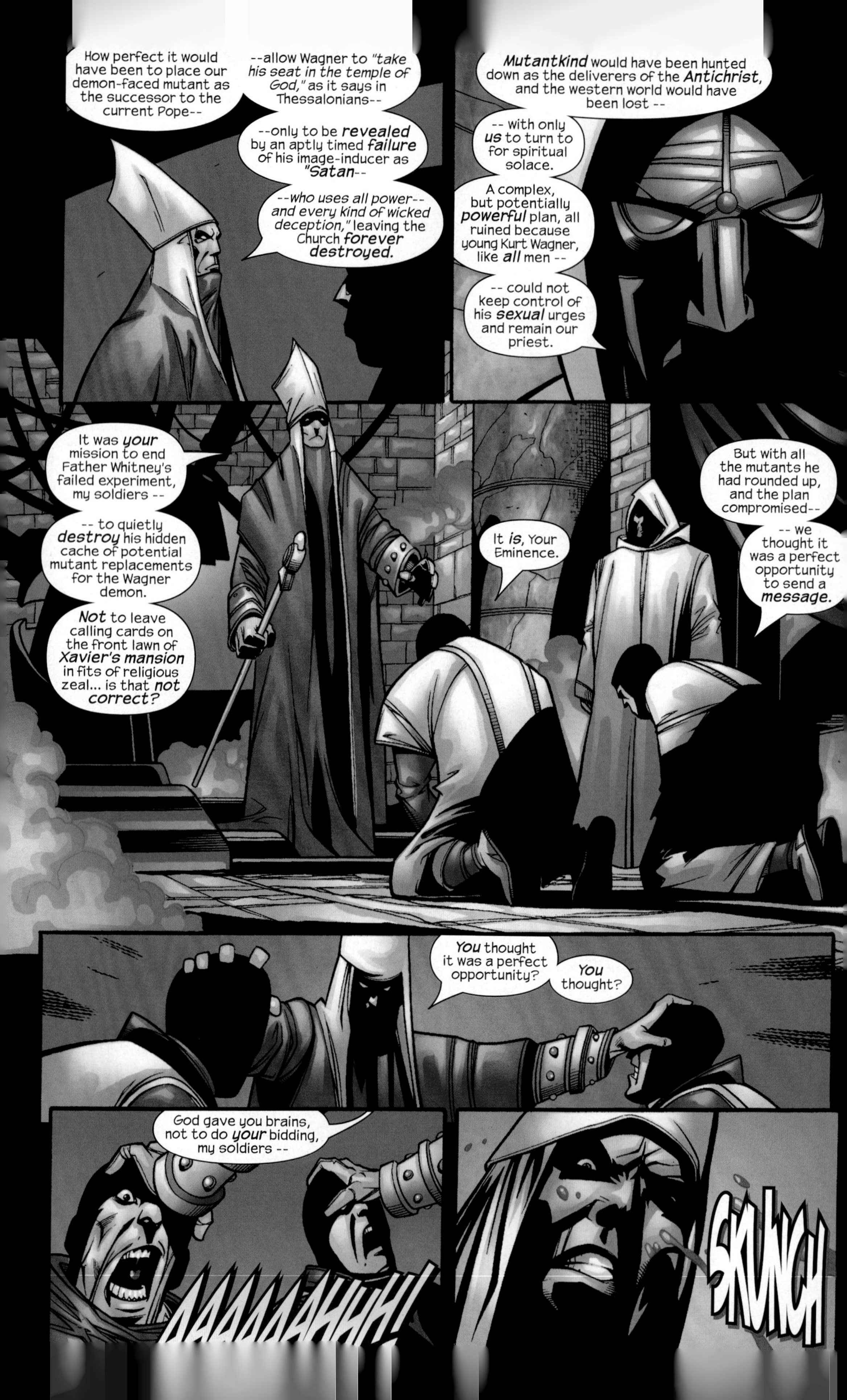
How perfect it would have been to place our demon-faced mutant as the successor to the current Pope--
--allow Wagner to "take his seat in the temple of God," as it says in Thessalonians--
--only to be revealed by an aptly timed failure of his image-inducer as "Satan--
--who uses all power--and every kind of wicked deception," leaving the Church forever destroyed.
Mutantkind would have been hunted down as the deliverers of the Antichrist, and the western world would have been lost --
-- with only us to turn to for spiritual solace.
A complex, but potentially powerful plan, all ruined because young Kurt Wagner, like all men --
-- could not keep control of his sexual urges and remain our priest.
It was your mission to end Father Whitney's failed experiment, my soldiers --
-- to quietly destroy his hidden cache of potential mutant replacements for the Wagner demon.
Not to leave calling cards on the front lawn of Xavier's mansion in fits of religious zeal... is that not correct?
It is, Your Eminence.
But with all the mutants he had rounded up, and the plan compromised--
-- we thought it was a perfect opportunity to send a message.
You thought it was a perfect opportunity?
You thought?
God gave you brains, not to do your bidding, my soldiers --
AAAAAAHHH!
SKUNCH

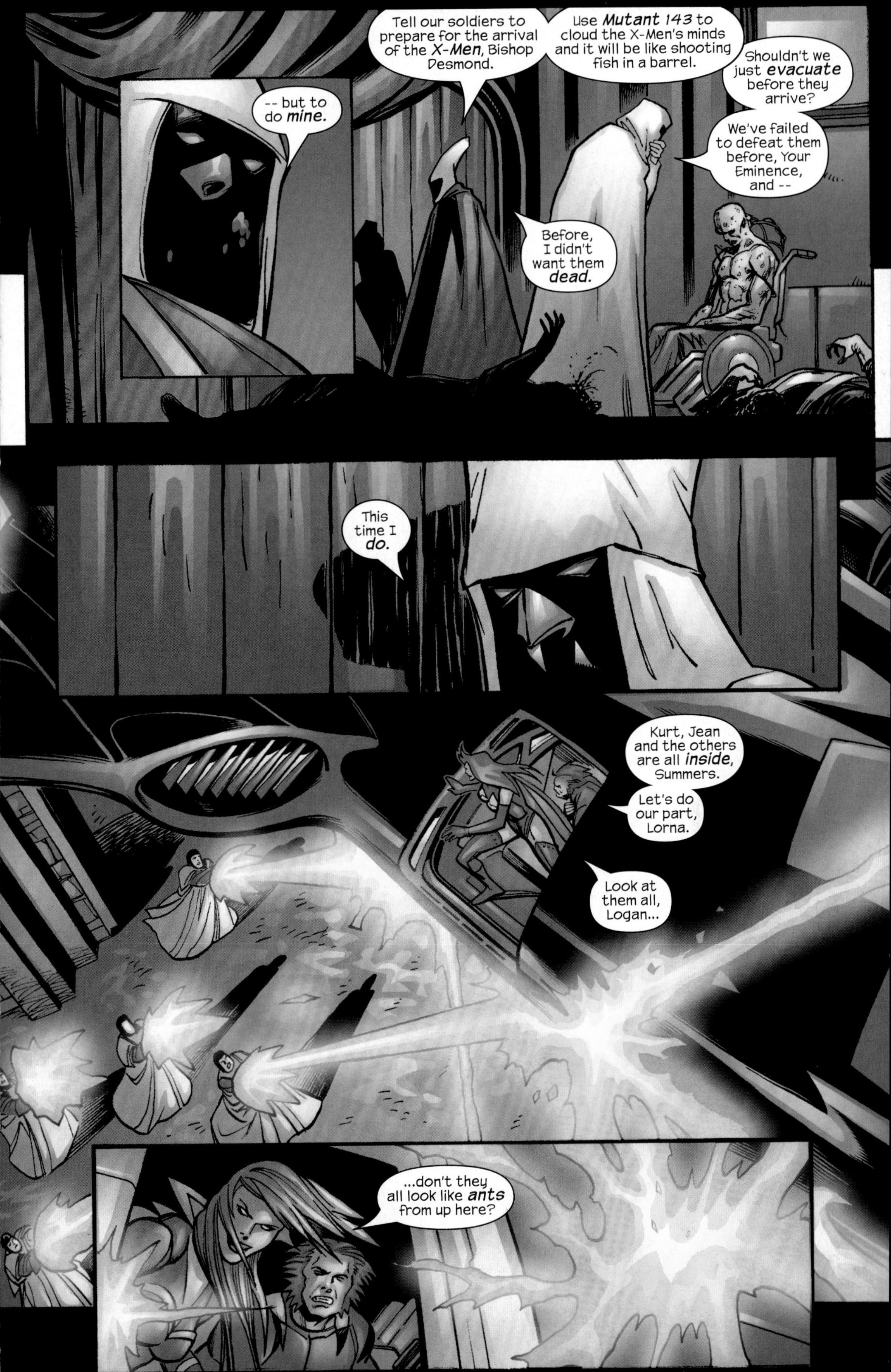

-- but to do *mine.*
Tell our soldiers to prepare for the arrival of the *X-Men*, Bishop Desmond.
Use *Mutant 143* to cloud the X-Men's minds and it will be like shooting fish in a barrel.
Shouldn't we just *evacuate* before they arrive?
We've failed to defeat them before, Your Eminence, and --
Before, I didn't want them *dead.*
This time I *do.*
Kurt, Jean and the others are all *inside*, Summers.
Let's do our part, Lorna.
Look at them all, Logan...
...don't they all look like *ants* from up here?

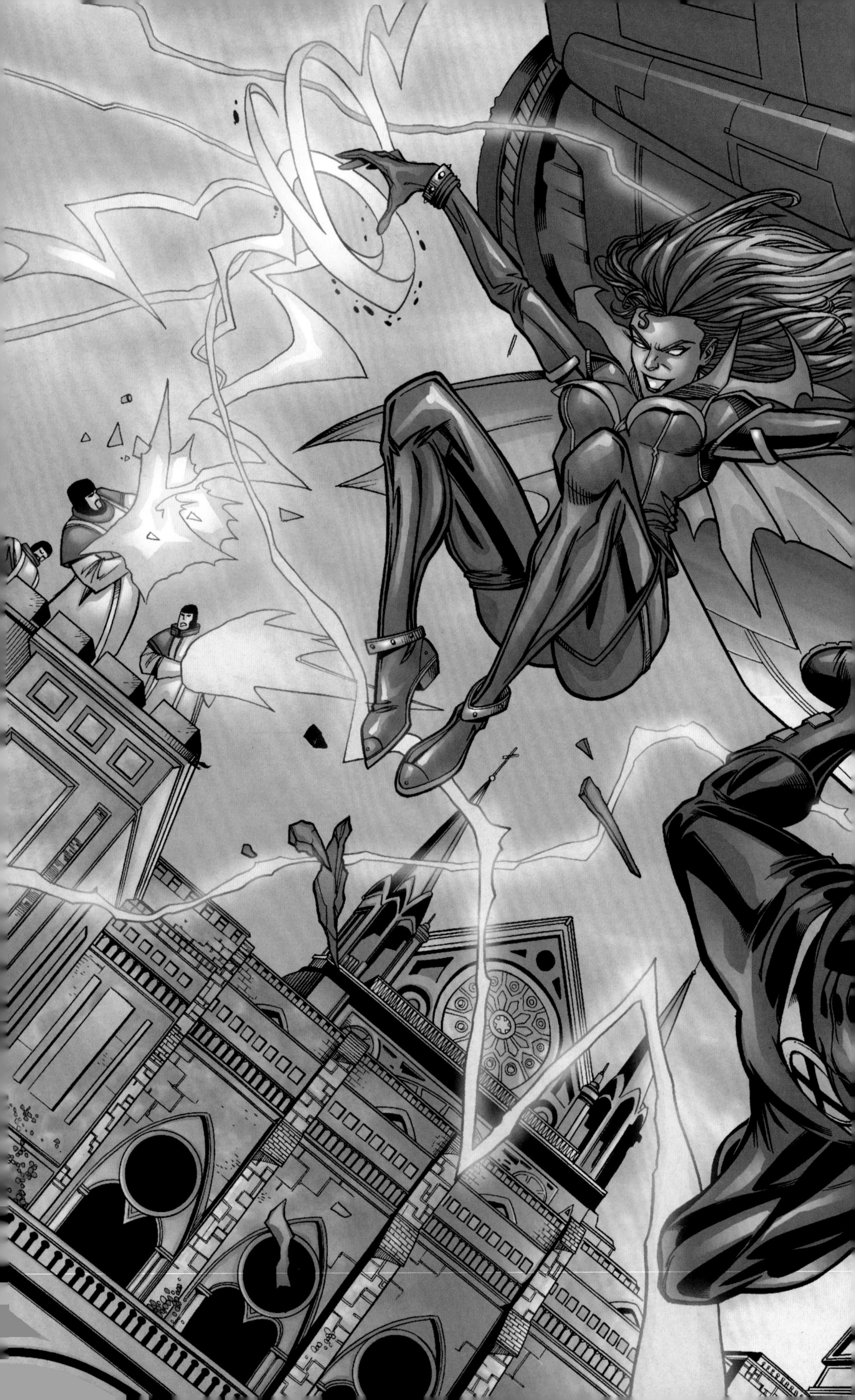

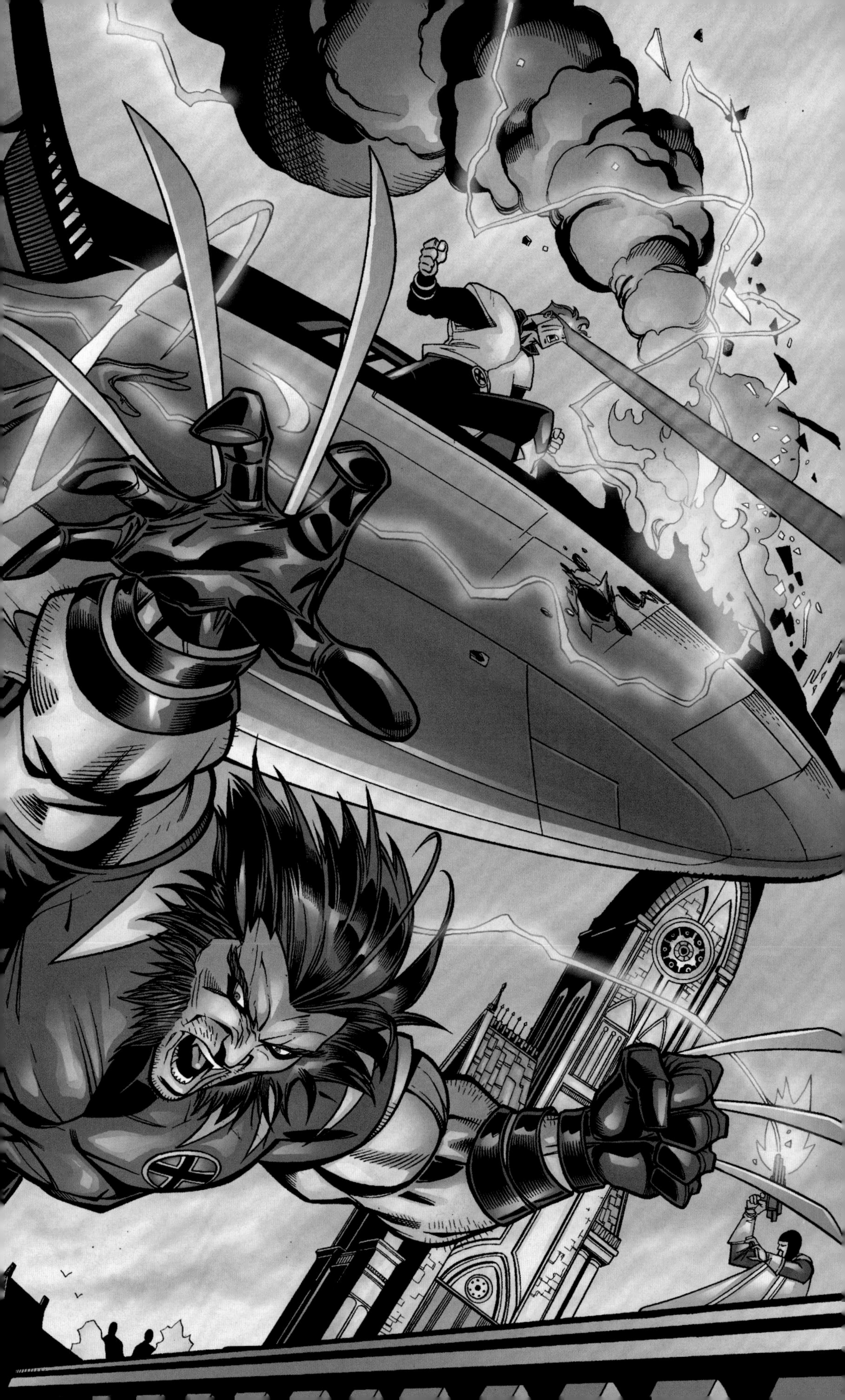

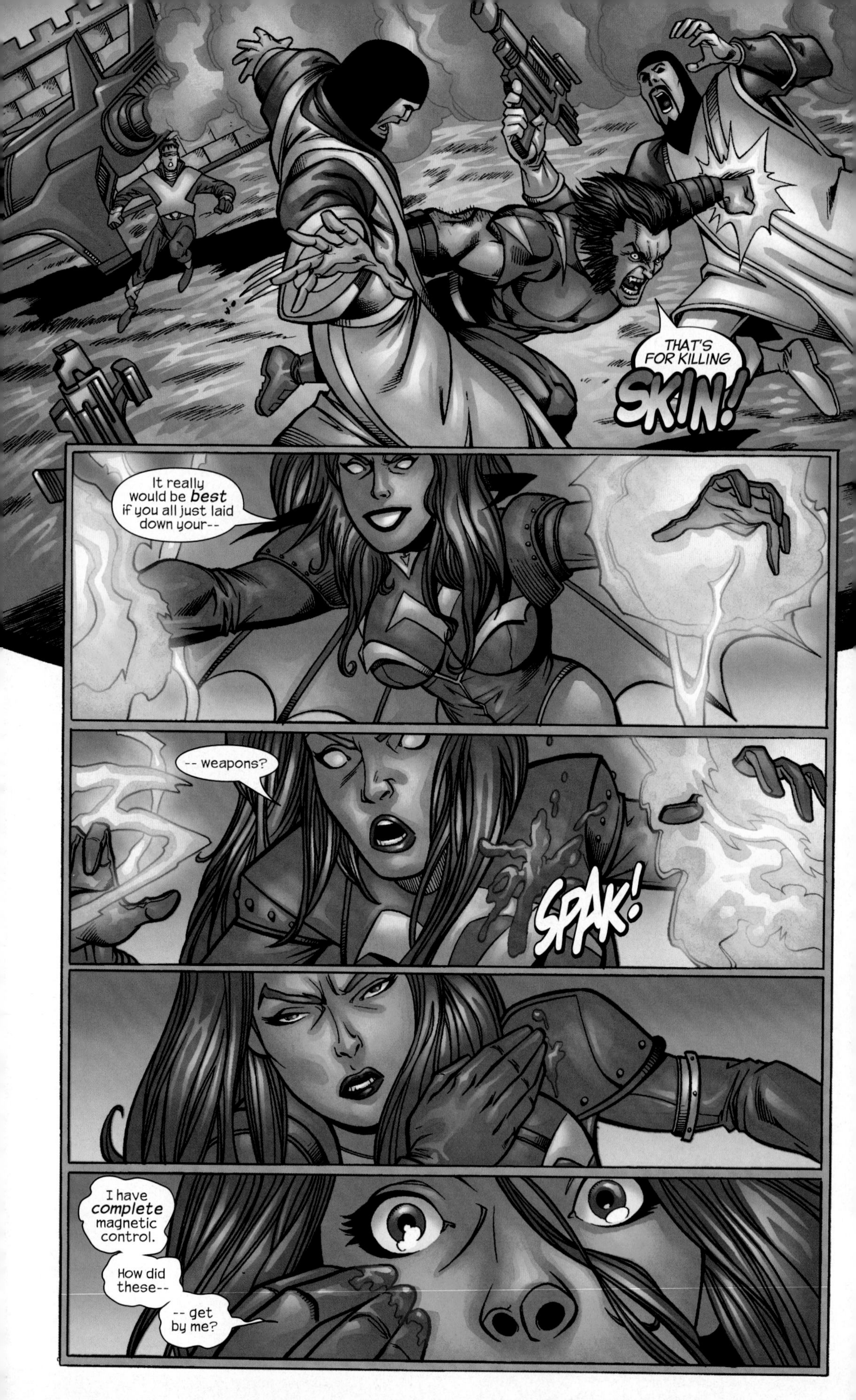

THAT'S FOR KILLING SKIN!
It really would be *best* if you all just laid down your--
-- weapons?
SPAK!
I have *complete* magnetic control.
How did these--
-- get by me?

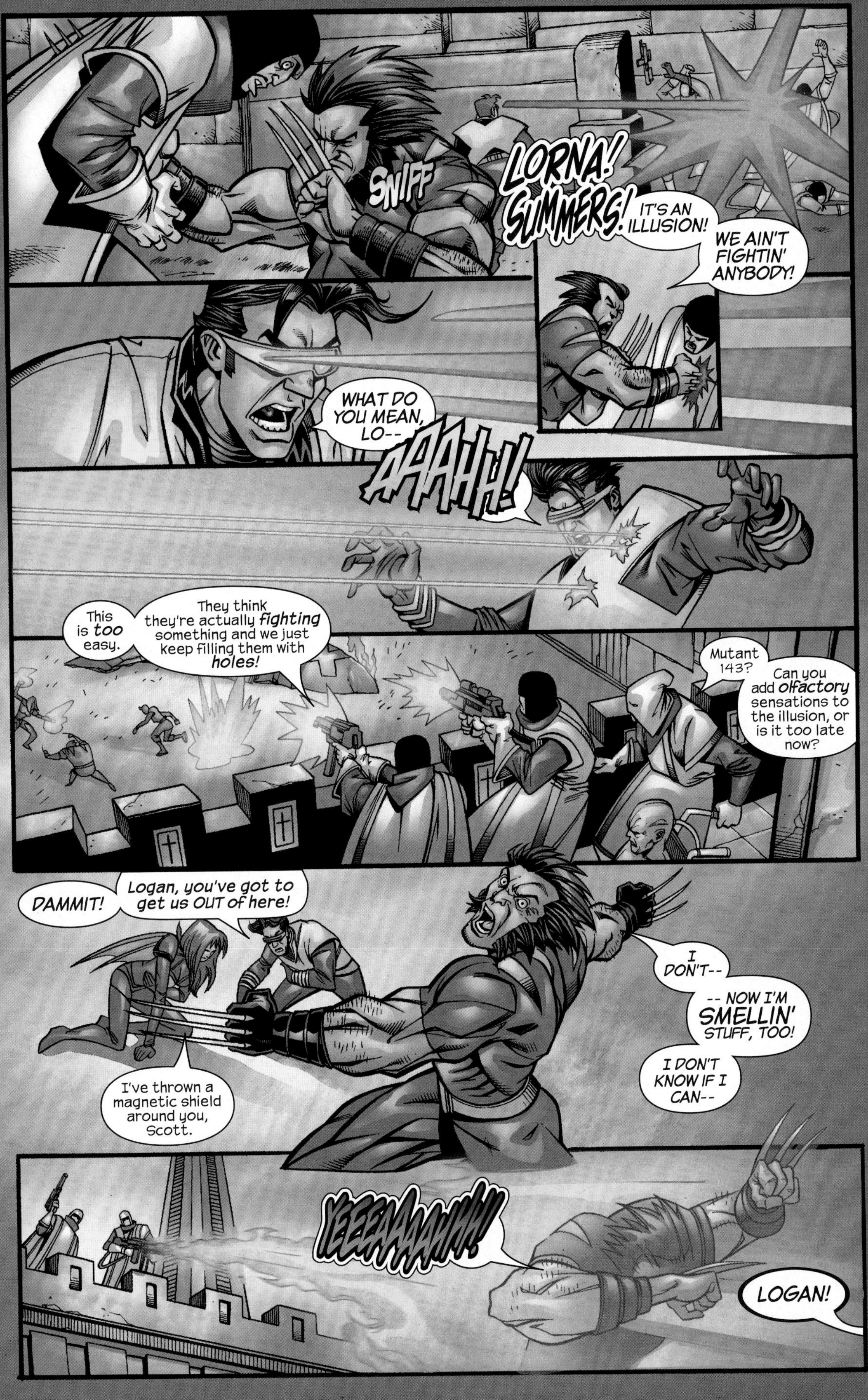
SNIFF
LORNA! SUMMERS!
IT'S AN ILLUSION!
WE AIN'T FIGHTIN' ANYBODY!
WHAT DO YOU MEAN, LO--
AAAHH!
This is too easy.
They think they're actually fighting something and we just keep filling them with holes!
Mutant 143?
Can you add olfactory sensations to the illusion, or is it too late now?
DAMMIT!
Logan, you've got to get us OUT of here!
I DON'T--
-- NOW I'M SMELLIN' STUFF, TOO!
I DON'T KNOW IF I CAN--
I've thrown a magnetic shield around you, Scott.
YEEEAAAAAHHH!
LOGAN!

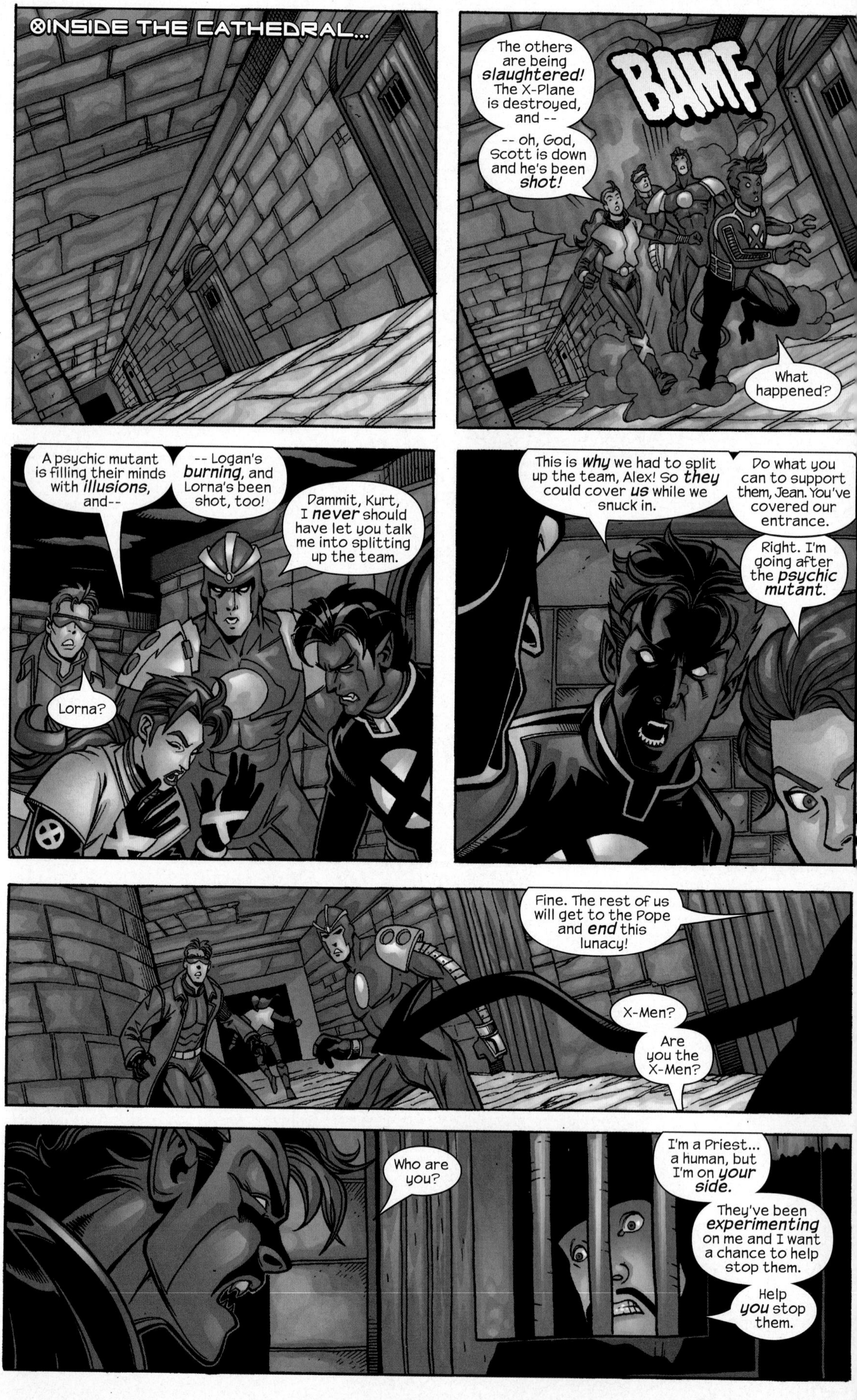
INSIDE THE CATHEDRAL...
BAMF
The others are being slaughtered! The X-Plane is destroyed, and --
-- oh, God, Scott is down and he's been shot!
What happened?
A psychic mutant is filling their minds with illusions, and--
-- Logan's burning, and Lorna's been shot, too!
Dammit, Kurt, I never should have let you talk me into splitting up the team.
Lorna?
This is why we had to split up the team, Alex! So they could cover us while we snuck in.
Do what you can to support them, Jean. You've covered our entrance.
Right. I'm going after the psychic mutant.
Fine. The rest of us will get to the Pope and end this lunacy!
X-Men?
Are you the X-Men?
Who are you?
I'm a Priest... a human, but I'm on your side.
They've been experimenting on me and I want a chance to help stop them.
Help you stop them.

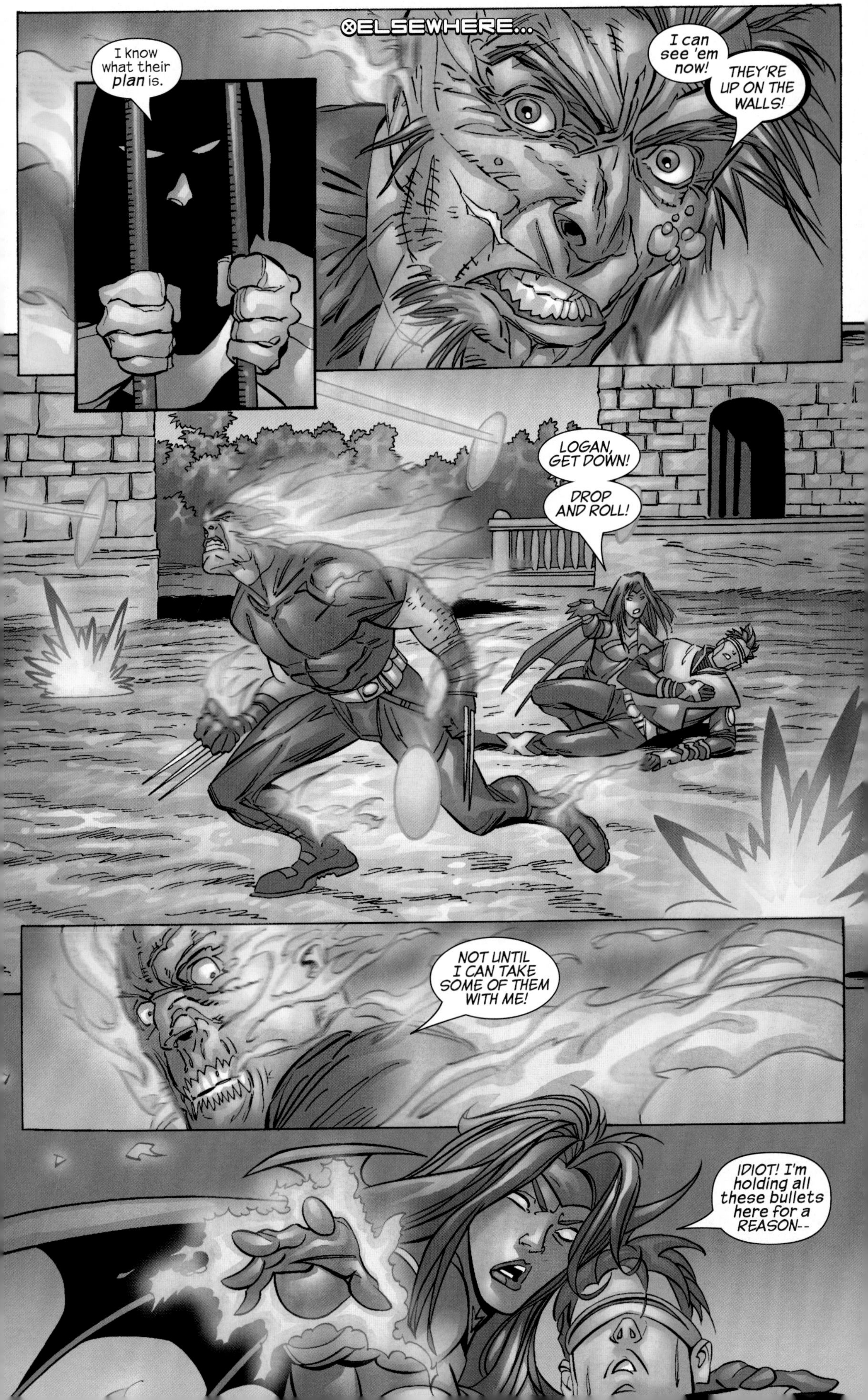
ELSEWHERE...
I know what their plan is.
I can see 'em now!
THEY'RE UP ON THE WALLS!
LOGAN, GET DOWN!
DROP AND ROLL!
NOT UNTIL I CAN TAKE SOME OF THEM WITH ME!
IDIOT! I'm holding all these bullets here for a REASON--

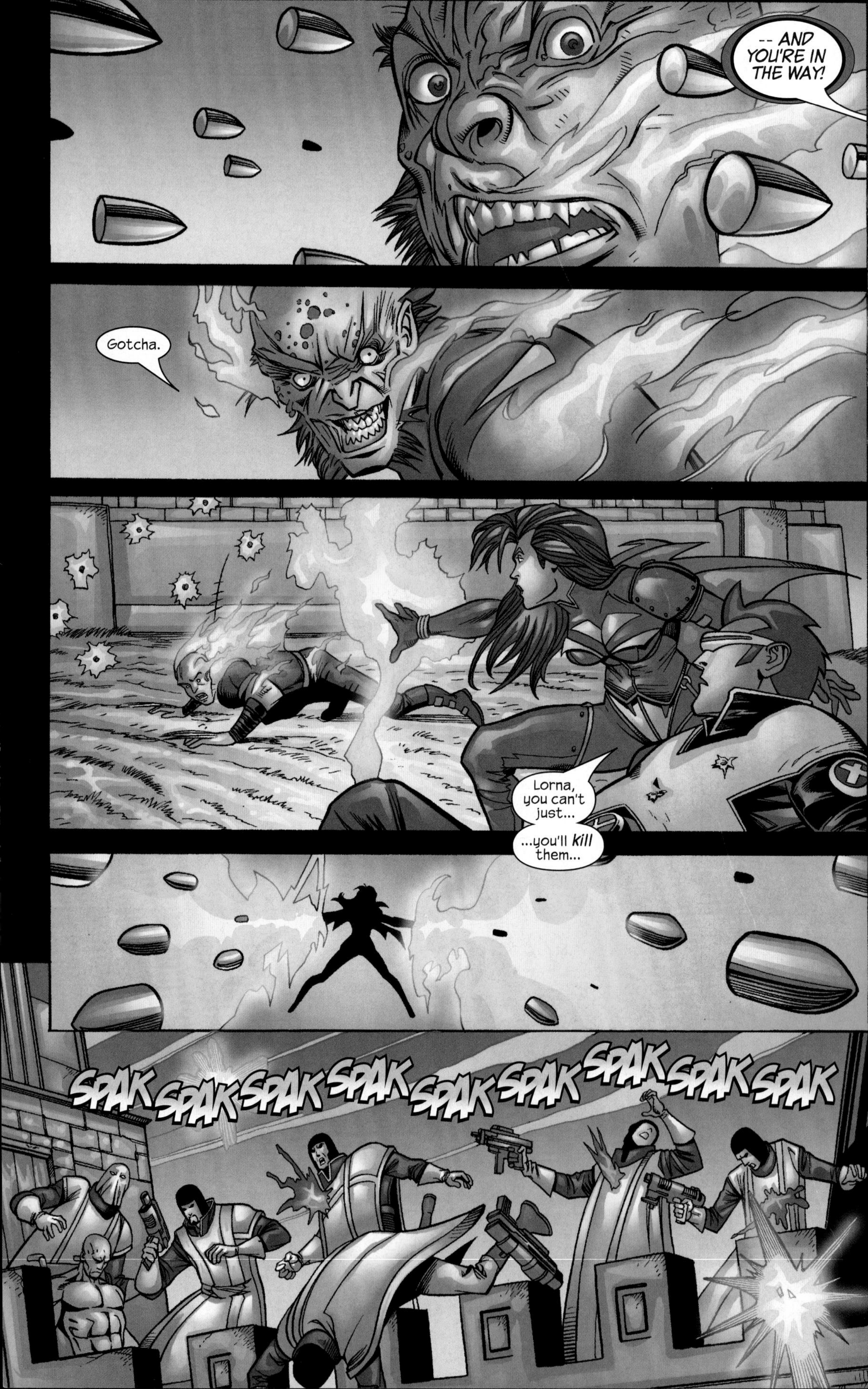
-- AND YOU'RE IN THE WAY!
Gotcha.
Lorna, you can't just...
...you'll kill them...
SPAK SPAK SPAK SPAK SPAK SPAK SPAK SPAK SPAK

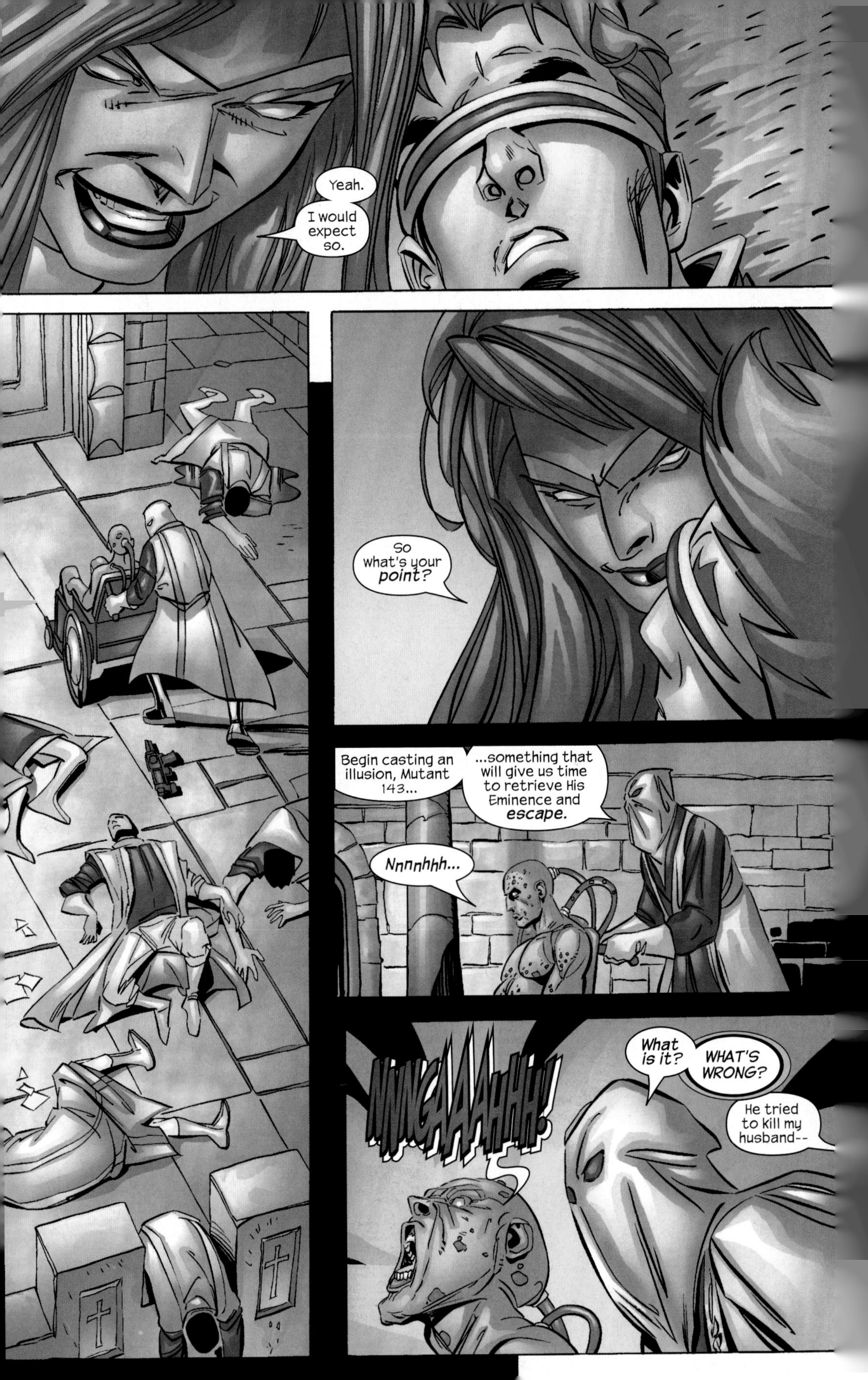
Yeah.
I would expect so.
So what's your point?
Begin casting an illusion, Mutant 143...
...something that will give us time to retrieve His Eminence and escape.
Nnnnhhh...
NNNGAAAHHH!
What is it?
WHAT'S WRONG?
He tried to kill my husband--

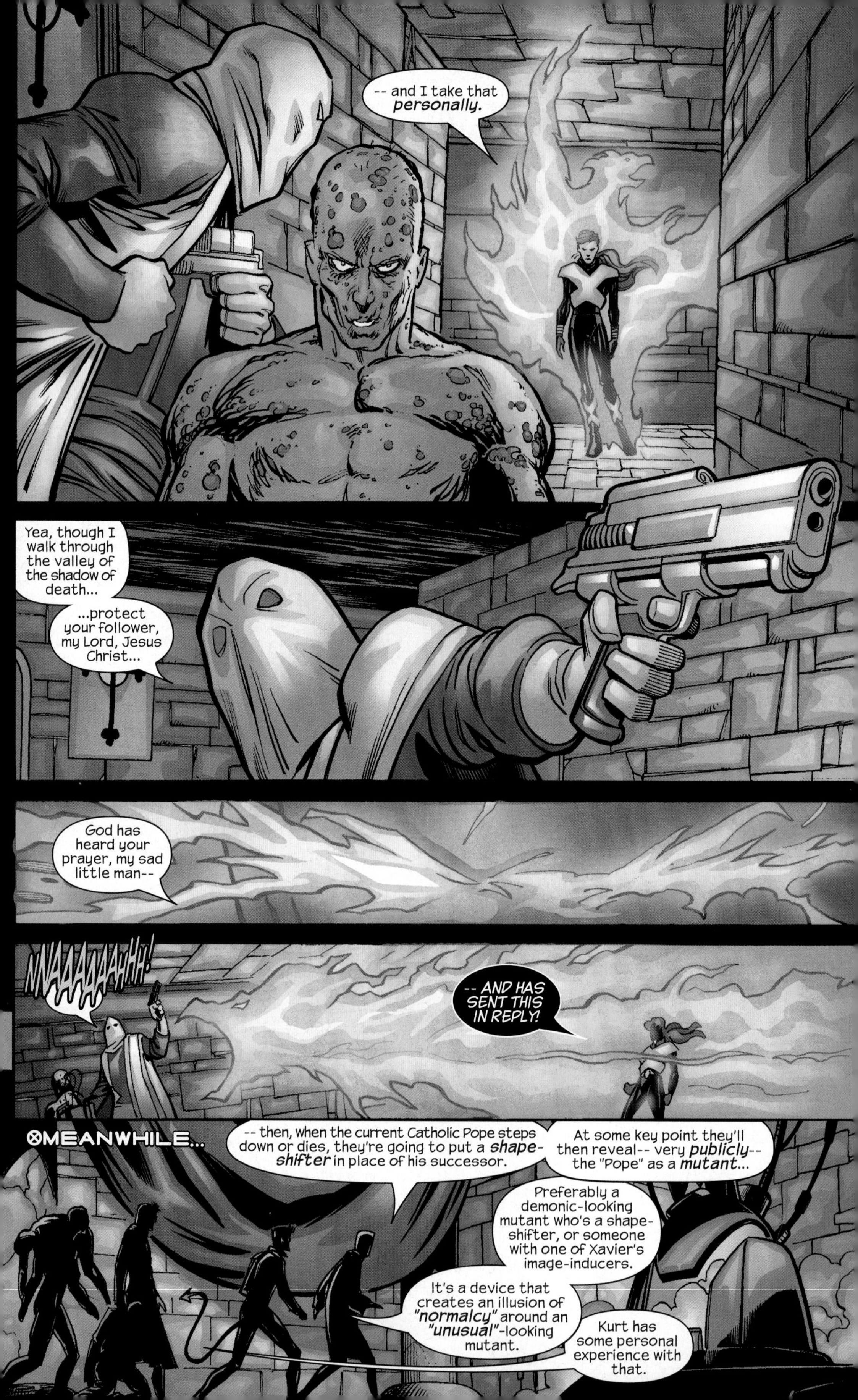

-- and I take that *personally.*
Yea, though I walk through the valley of the shadow of death...
...protect your follower, my Lord, Jesus Christ...
God has heard your prayer, my sad little man--
NNAAAAAAAHHH!
-- AND HAS SENT THIS IN REPLY!
MEANWHILE...
-- then, when the current Catholic Pope steps down or dies, they're going to put a *shape-shifter* in place of his successor.
At some key point they'll then reveal-- very *publicly*-- the "Pope" as a *mutant*...
Preferably a demonic-looking mutant who's a shape-shifter, or someone with one of Xavier's image-inducers.
It's a device that creates an illusion of *"normalcy"* around an *"unusual"*-looking mutant.
Kurt has some personal experience with that.

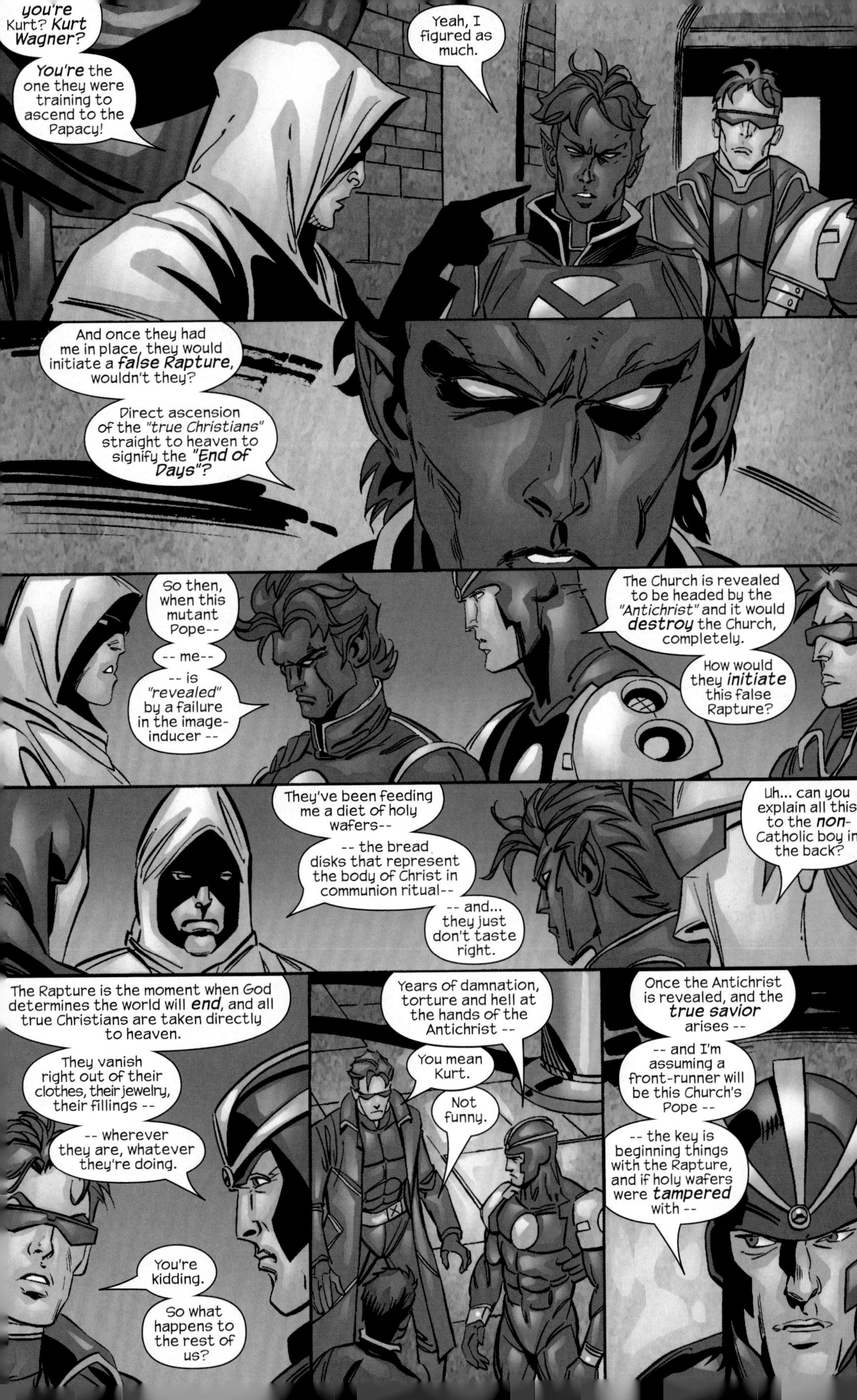

you're Kurt? Kurt Wagner?
You're the one they were training to ascend to the Papacy!
Yeah, I figured as much.
And once they had me in place, they would initiate a false Rapture, wouldn't they?
Direct ascension of the "true Christians" straight to heaven to signify the "End of Days"?
So then, when this mutant Pope--
-- me--
-- is "revealed" by a failure in the image-inducer --
The Church is revealed to be headed by the "Antichrist" and it would destroy the Church, completely.
How would they initiate this false Rapture?
They've been feeding me a diet of holy wafers--
-- the bread disks that represent the body of Christ in communion ritual--
-- and... they just don't taste right.
Uh... can you explain all this to the non-Catholic boy in the back?
The Rapture is the moment when God determines the world will end, and all true Christians are taken directly to heaven.
They vanish right out of their clothes, their jewelry, their fillings --
-- wherever they are, whatever they're doing.
You're kidding.
So what happens to the rest of us?
Years of damnation, torture and hell at the hands of the Antichrist --
You mean Kurt.
Not funny.
Once the Antichrist is revealed, and the true savior arises --
-- and I'm assuming a front-runner will be this Church's Pope --
-- the key is beginning things with the Rapture, and if holy wafers were tampered with --

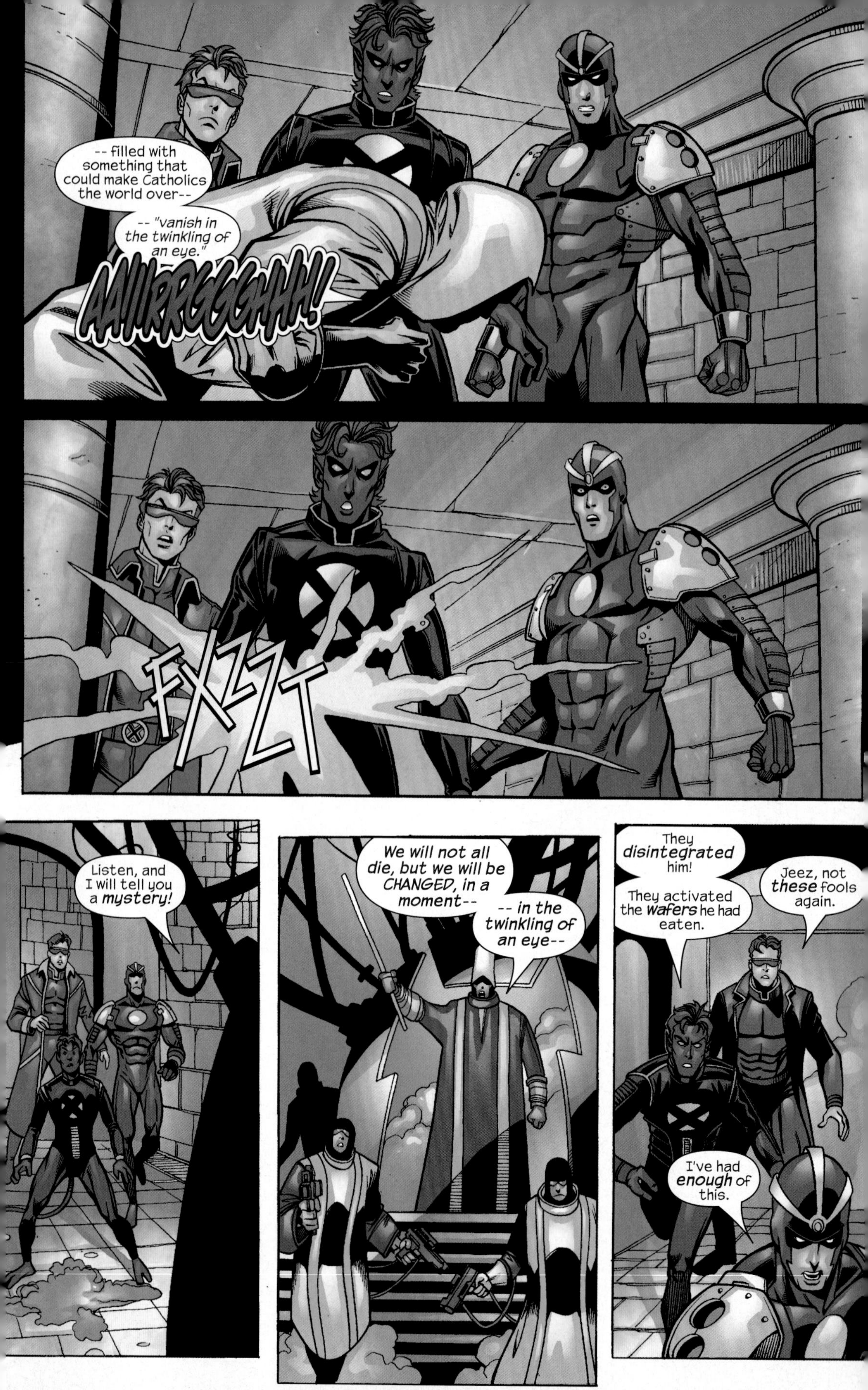

-- filled with something that could make Catholics the world over--
-- "vanish in the twinkling of an eye."
AAIIIRRGGGHHH!
FXZZZT
Listen, and I will tell you a mystery!
We will not all die, but we will be CHANGED, in a moment--
-- in the twinkling of an eye--
They disintegrated him!
They activated the wafers he had eaten.
Jeez, not these fools again.
I've had enough of this.

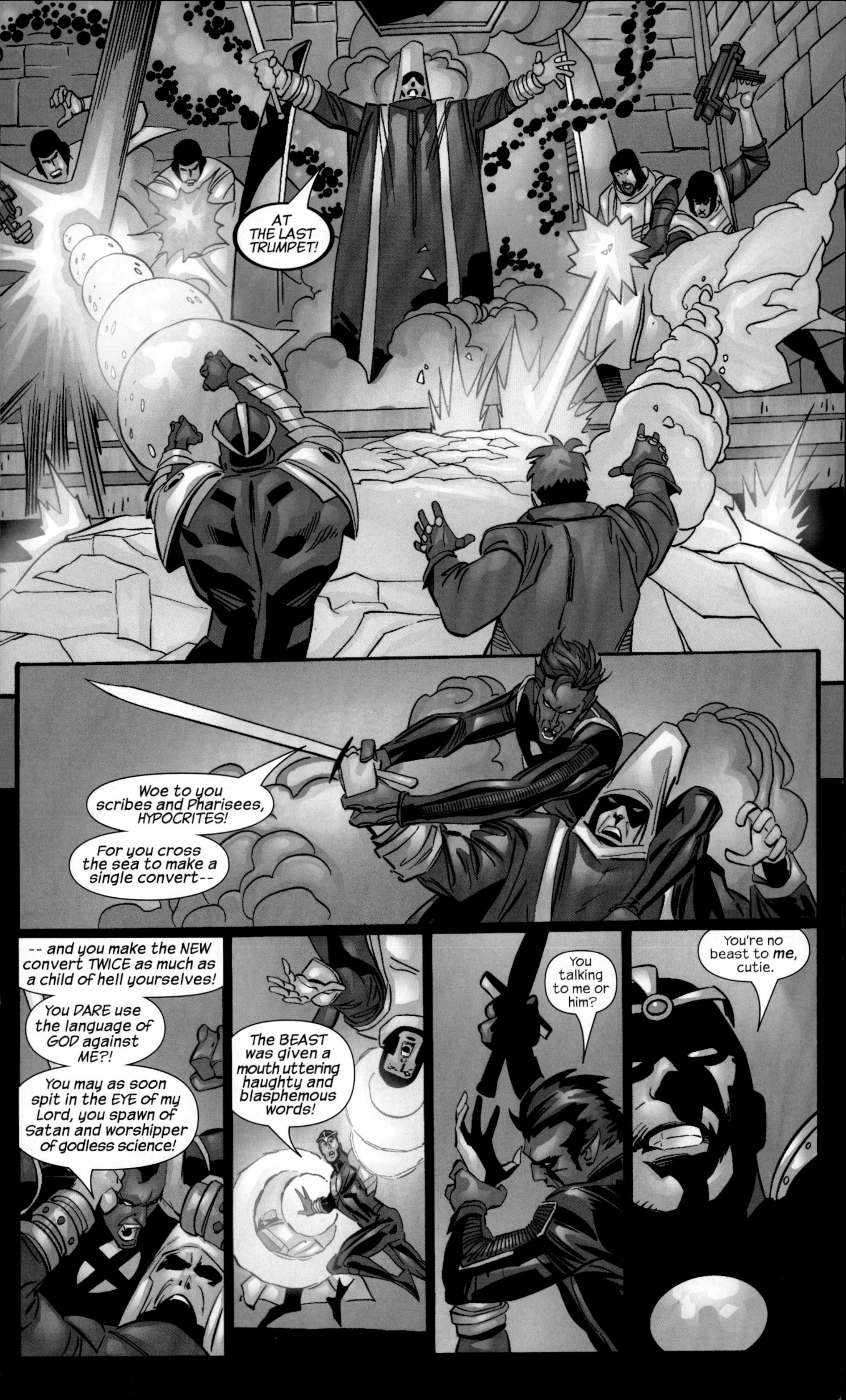
AT THE LAST TRUMPET!
Woe to you scribes and Pharisees, HYPOCRITES!
For you cross the sea to make a single convert--
-- and you make the NEW convert TWICE as much as a child of hell yourselves!
You DARE use the language of GOD against ME?!
You may as soon spit in the EYE of my Lord, you spawn of Satan and worshipper of godless science!
The BEAST was given a mouth uttering haughty and blasphemous words!
You talking to me or him?
You're no beast to me, cutie.

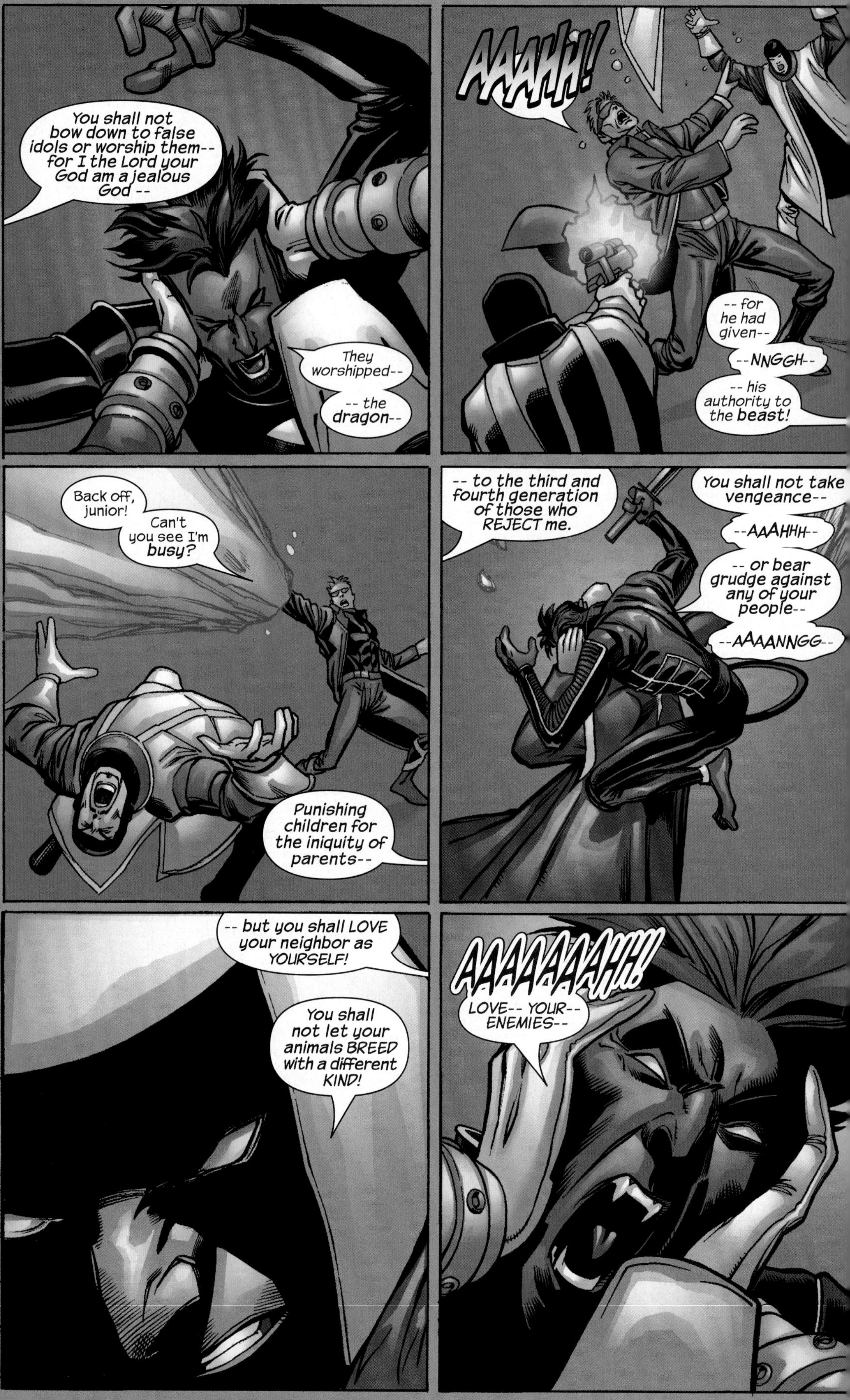
You shall not bow down to false idols or worship them-- for I the Lord your God am a jealous God --
They worshipped--
-- the dragon--
AAAHH!
-- for he had given--
--NNGGH--
-- his authority to the beast!
Back off, junior!
Can't you see I'm busy?
Punishing children for the iniquity of parents--
-- to the third and fourth generation of those who REJECT me.
You shall not take vengeance--
--AAAHHH--
-- or bear grudge against any of your people--
--AAAANNGG--
-- but you shall LOVE your neighbor as YOURSELF!
You shall not let your animals BREED with a different KIND!
AAAAAAAAHH!
LOVE-- YOUR-- ENEMIES--

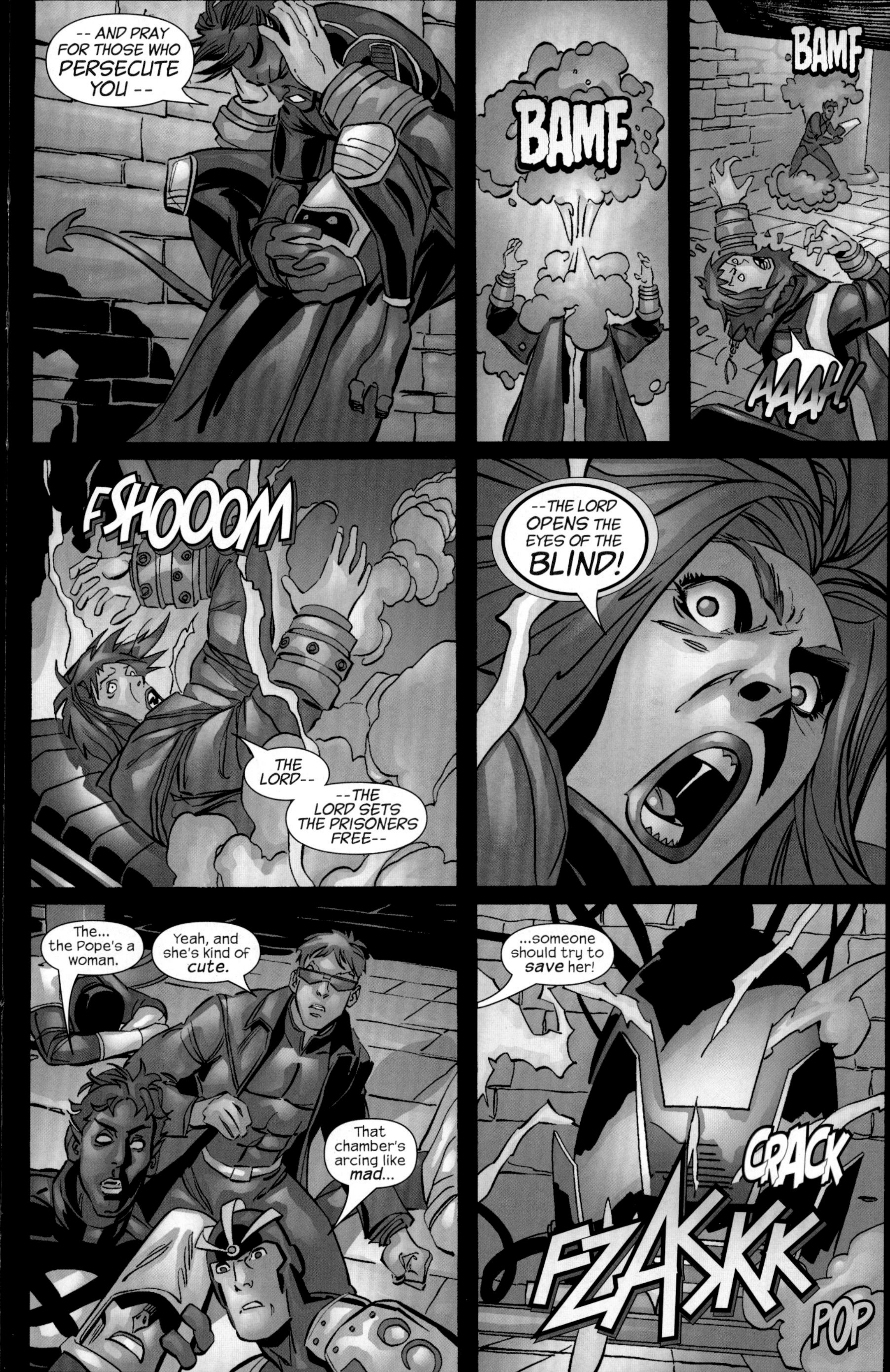

-- AND PRAY FOR THOSE WHO PERSECUTE YOU --
BAMF
BAMF
AAAH!
FSHOOOM
THE LORD--
--THE LORD SETS THE PRISONERS FREE--
--THE LORD OPENS THE EYES OF THE BLIND!
The... the Pope's a woman.
Yeah, and she's kind of cute.
That chamber's arcing like mad...
...someone should try to save her!
CRACK
FZAKKK
POP

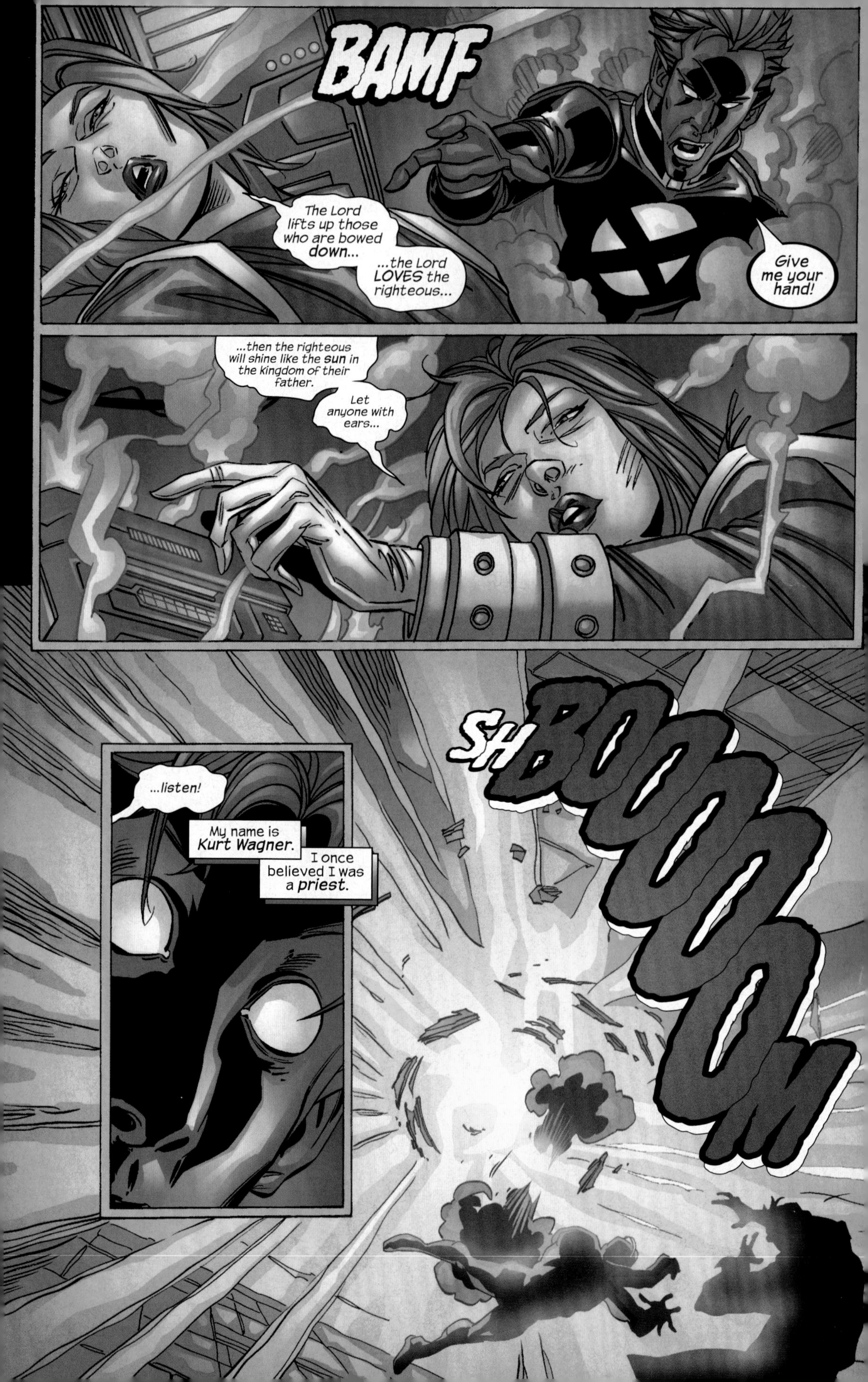
BAMF
The Lord lifts up those who are bowed down...
...the Lord LOVES the righteous...
Give me your hand!
...then the righteous will shine like the sun in the kingdom of their father.
Let anyone with ears...
SHBOOOOOOM
...listen!
My name is Kurt Wagner.
I once believed I was a priest.

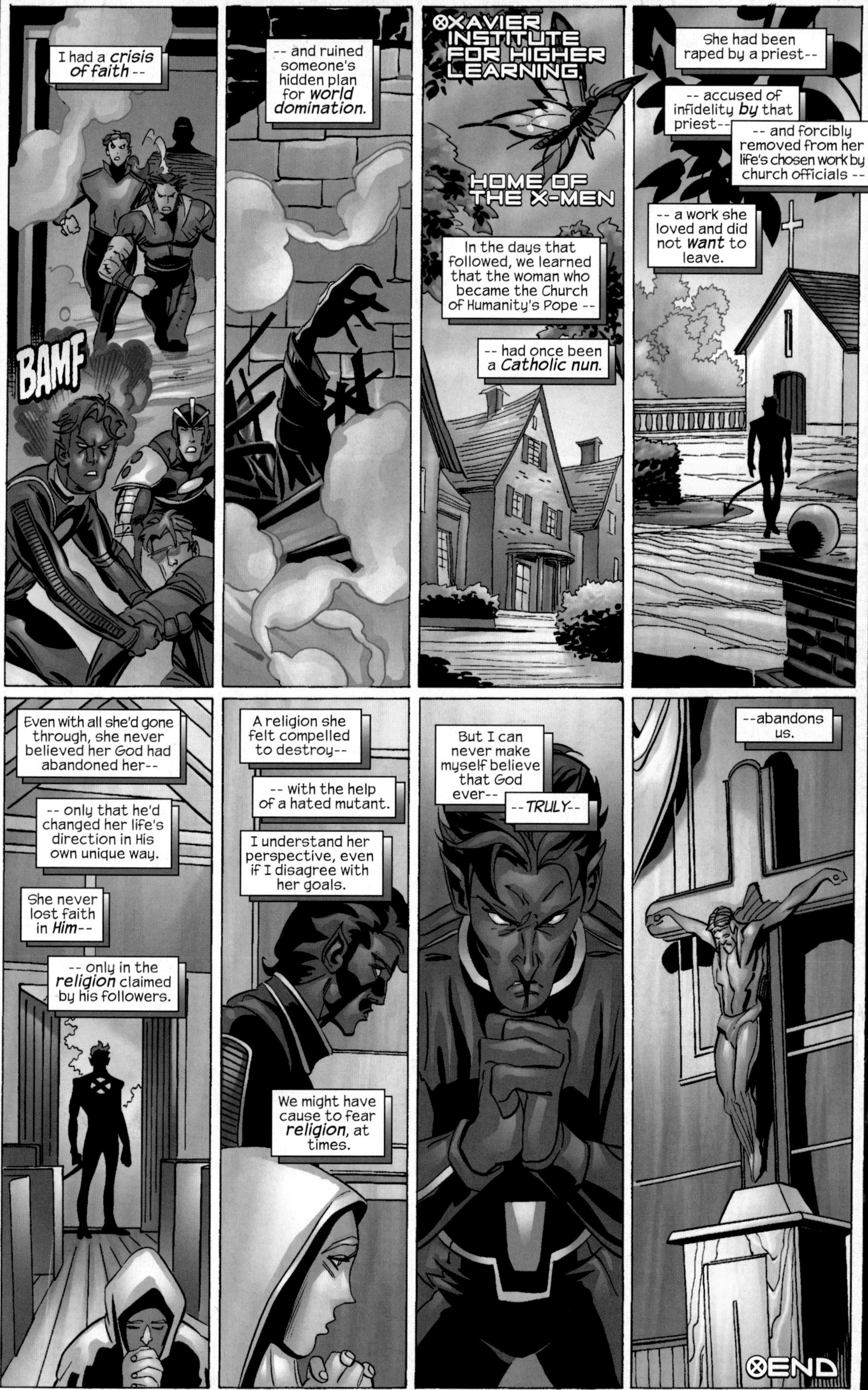
I had a crisis of faith--
BAMF
-- and ruined someone's hidden plan for world domination.
XAVIER INSTITUTE FOR HIGHER LEARNING.
HOME OF THE X-MEN
In the days that followed, we learned that the woman who became the Church of Humanity's Pope --
-- had once been a Catholic nun.
She had been raped by a priest--
-- accused of infidelity by that priest--
-- and forcibly removed from her life's chosen work by church officials --
-- a work she loved and did not want to leave.
Even with all she'd gone through, she never believed her God had abandoned her--
-- only that he'd changed her life's direction in His own unique way.
She never lost faith in Him--
-- only in the religion claimed by his followers.
A religion she felt compelled to destroy--
-- with the help of a hated mutant.
I understand her perspective, even if I disagree with her goals.
We might have cause to fear religion, at times.
But I can never make myself believe that God ever--
--TRULY--
--abandons us.
END

UNCANNY X-MEN #422, PAGE 33 ART BY RON GARNEY & MARK MORALES

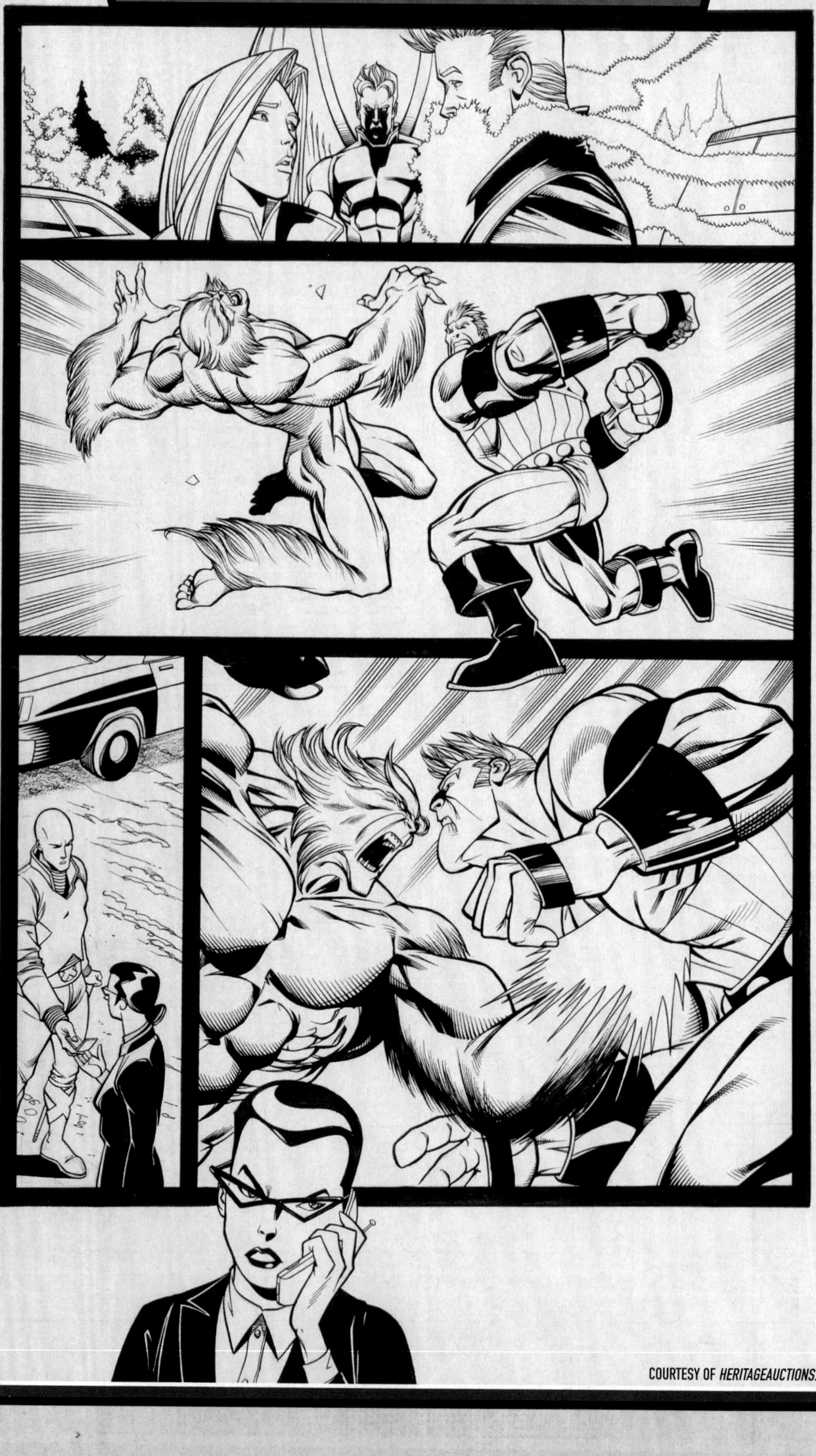

COURTESY OF *HERITAGEAUCTIONS.COM*